Generative AI-Driven Application Development with Java

Leveraging Large Language Models in Modern Java Applications

Satej Kumar Sahu

Apress®

Generative AI-Driven Application Development with Java: Leveraging Large Language Models in Modern Java Applications

Satej Kumar Sahu
Berhampur, Odisha, India

ISBN-13 (pbk): 979-8-8688-1608-6 ISBN-13 (electronic): 979-8-8688-1609-3
https://doi.org/10.1007/979-8-8688-1609-3

Managing Director, Apress Media LLC: Welmoed Spahr
Acquisitions Editor: Melissa Duffy
Desk Editor: Laura Berendson
Editorial Project Manager: Gryffin Winkler

Cover image designed by Gláuber Sampaio on Unsplash

Distributed to the book trade worldwide by Springer Science+Business Media New York, 1 New York Plaza, New York, NY 10004. Phone 1-800-SPRINGER, fax (201) 348-4505, e-mail orders-ny@springer-sbm.com, or visit www.springeronline.com. Apress Media, LLC is a Delaware LLC and the sole member (owner) is Springer Science + Business Media Finance Inc (SSBM Finance Inc). SSBM Finance Inc is a **Delaware** corporation.

For information on translations, please e-mail booktranslations@springernature.com; for reprint, paperback, or audio rights, please e-mail bookpermissions@springernature.com.

Apress titles may be purchased in bulk for academic, corporate, or promotional use. eBook versions and licenses are also available for most titles. For more information, reference our Print and eBook Bulk Sales web page at http://www.apress.com/bulk-sales.

Any source code or other supplementary material referenced by the author in this book is available to readers on https://github.com/Apress/Generative-AI-Driven-Application-Development-with-Java.
For more detailed information, please visit https://www.apress.com/gp/services/source-code.

If disposing of this product, please recycle the paper

To my beloved parents, Kusum and Kiran,

for your unwavering love, your endless encouragement, and the values you've instilled in me.

And to my sister, Lipsa,

for always standing by me with faith and support—

this journey wouldn't have been possible without you.

With all my love and gratitude.

Table of Contents

About the Author

Satej Kumar Sahu is a principal engineer at Zalando SE with 15 years of hands-on experience designing large-scale, data-intensive systems for global brands including Boeing, Adidas, and Honeywell. He is passionate about technology, people, and nature. A specialist in software architecture, big-data pipelines, and applied machine learning, he has shepherded multiple projects from whiteboard sketches to production deployments serving millions of users.

Satej has been working with large language models since their earliest open-source releases, piloting retrieval-augmented generation and agentic patterns long before they became industry buzzwords. He is the author of two previous programming books—*Building Secure PHP Applications* and *PHP 8 Basics*—and is a frequent speaker at developer conferences and meet-ups around the world.

When he isn't translating cutting-edge AI research into practical code, you'll find him mentoring engineering teams, contributing to open-source projects, or tinkering with the newest transformer models in his home lab. He believes that through technology and conscientious decision-making, each of us has the power to make this world a better place.

About the Technical Reviewer

Jerzy Plocha is an accountable, results-driven cloud computing architect and team manager with strong analytical skills, a passion for well-designed code and scalable architectures, and a proven track record in managing teams and developing actionable metrics that drive business success. As a reviewer, he has provided technical guidance on cloud-architecture patterns and security best practices.

Acknowledgments

I would like to thank my parents for always believing in and having patience with me while I pursued my interest in technology and for giving me the freedom to explore and try different things. Also, thanks to my sister Lipsa for always being beside me whenever I needed her. I would like to thank all my teachers for being with me during my journey, Runish for the foundational mentoring support at the start of my career, Mindfire Solutions for my first career opportunity, and all with whom I have had an opportunity to interact and learn from. Last but not least, I would like to thank Melissa for the awesome opportunity to write my second book and the wonderful team at Apress for all their support without whom this book would not have been possible.

Introduction

In recent years, generative AI (Gen AI) and large language models (LLMs) have reshaped the boundaries of what software can do. From chatbots that sound eerily human to code-generation tools that augment developer productivity, the rise of transformer-based architectures has opened up a new paradigm in application design. But while much of this innovation has played out in Python-centric ecosystems, Java developers—especially those working on enterprise-scale systems—have often found themselves on the sidelines, grappling with integration gaps, unclear tooling, or limited examples.

This book aims to change that.

Generative AI-Driven Application Development with Java is a hands-on, code-first guide built explicitly for Java practitioners. Whether you're a backend engineer fluent in Spring Boot or a performance-minded developer building reactive systems in Quarkus, this book provides a clear, structured roadmap for integrating LLMs into modern Java applications.

You'll start from first principles, understanding what makes Gen AI "generative," how LLMs like GPT-4o and Mistral work, and why models are only one part of a much larger ecosystem. From there, you'll dive into building real-world applications such as chat assistants, retrieval-augmented systems, tool-using agents, and even multimodal apps that read and write images. You'll explore hosted APIs from OpenAI and Azure and also self-host your own models using tools like Ollama and Jlama—all without leaving the JVM.

But this book goes beyond the "Hello, World" demos.

With each chapter, you'll learn to wire up production-grade systems: prompt engineering patterns, memory management, evaluation harnesses, API guardrails, and observability pipelines. You'll explore the new breed of Java-native AI tooling—from LangChain4j and Spring AI to DJL and ONNX—while keeping scalability, security, and maintainability front and center.

This book is not just for Java developers looking to "add a chatbot." It's for engineers, architects, and DevOps professionals who need to bring AI into their core platforms—responsibly, reliably, and at scale.

Who Should Read This Book

This book is written for:

- Java developers and architects eager to add LLM capabilities to new or legacy systems
- Backend engineers seeking a code-first approach to integrating GenAI
- DevOps and MLOps professionals looking to operationalize AI features in production
- Educators and data scientists who prefer Java-centric workflows over Python

No prior experience with AI or machine learning is required, but a working knowledge of Java and modern application development frameworks (like Spring Boot or Quarkus) will help you get the most out of the examples and exercises.

By the time you finish this book, you won't just understand how to connect Java to LLMs—you'll know how to **build**, **test**, **observe**, and **ship** real-world AI applications with confidence.

Let's get started.

Note to Readers

As the AI landscape evolves, the models and APIs discussed in this book may change or become unavailable over time. This includes shifts in OpenAI's offerings and the introduction of new platforms like Ollama. You can leverage Ollama as an API layer, along with other available models, to maintain flexibility and avoid being tied to a single provider. These alternatives and strategies for adapting to new technologies are woven throughout the book, ensuring that you focus on the core principles and remain agile in the face of ongoing changes. Be sure to check the latest documentation and explore different options to stay ahead in this rapidly evolving field.

CHAPTER 1

Megabrains 101: Generative AI and LLMs Unboxed

This chapter provides an overview of generative AI (Gen AI), focusing on large language models (LLMs). It familiarizes readers with the fundamentals of LLMs and their significance in modern software development.

Specifically, we will get you acquainted with the world of Gen AI and LLMs so you can understand them. Then, we will present some use-case scenarios around Gen AI. This will help you to understand how as a software developer you can help build interfaces and applications around these systems. Finally, you get some hands-on experience a Gen AI interface. After all, what's the fun without some practice?

Understanding Gen AI

Put simply, Gen AI is like a magical artist or storyteller that can make new creations just for you. We can imagine telling it:

> "Draw me a picture of a dragon!" And it can create a dragon just from your words.
>
> "Tell me a bedtime story!" And it creates a whole new story that no one has ever heard before.
>
> "Sing me a song!" It can write a song from scratch.

S. K. Sahu, *Generative AI-Driven Application Development with Java*,
https://doi.org/10.1007/979-8-8688-1609-3_1

It learns by looking at lots and lots of pictures, stories, and songs, so it gets really good at imagining new ones. It's like having a super-smart imaginary friend who can create cool things whenever you ask! As a developer, it is important to have this base understanding of Gen AI before you build applications in the Gen AI ecosystem. Next, let's slowly ramp up the technical level to help you understand Gen AI.

Gen AI is a revolutionary field that has been transforming the way we create, interact with, and understand digital content. At its core, Gen AI refers to a class of machine learning models that can generate new, previously unseen data, such as images, videos, music, text, or even entire worlds. Figure 1-1 shows the presence of Gen AI in the overall hierarchy of AI and machine learning.

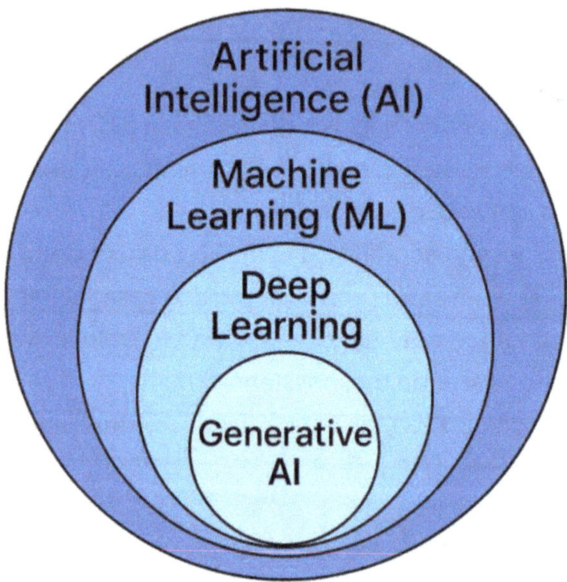

Figure 1-1. *Gen AI hierarchy in machine learning*

These models use complex algorithms and vast amounts of training data to learn patterns and relationships within the input data, enabling them to produce novel outputs that are often surprisingly realistic. From the eerie landscapes generated by AI artists to the witty conversations sparked by chatbots, Gen AI is increasingly being used in a wide range of applications, from entertainment and education to marketing and product design.

But what exactly does it mean for an AI model to be "generative"? In essence, it means the model has learned to synthesize new data from existing patterns, rather than simply processing or analyzing them. This allows Gen AI models to generate not just predictions or answers but entire datasets of original content, with their own unique characteristics and nuances.

Understanding LLMs

An LLM is a type of neural network designed to predict the next token in a sequence of text. This can be as simple as predicting the next word in a sentence or as complex as generating entire articles or even books. LLMs are trained on massive datasets, often comprising billions of words, and use self-supervised learning techniques to learn patterns and relationships within language. Figure 1-2 shows a general representation of this.

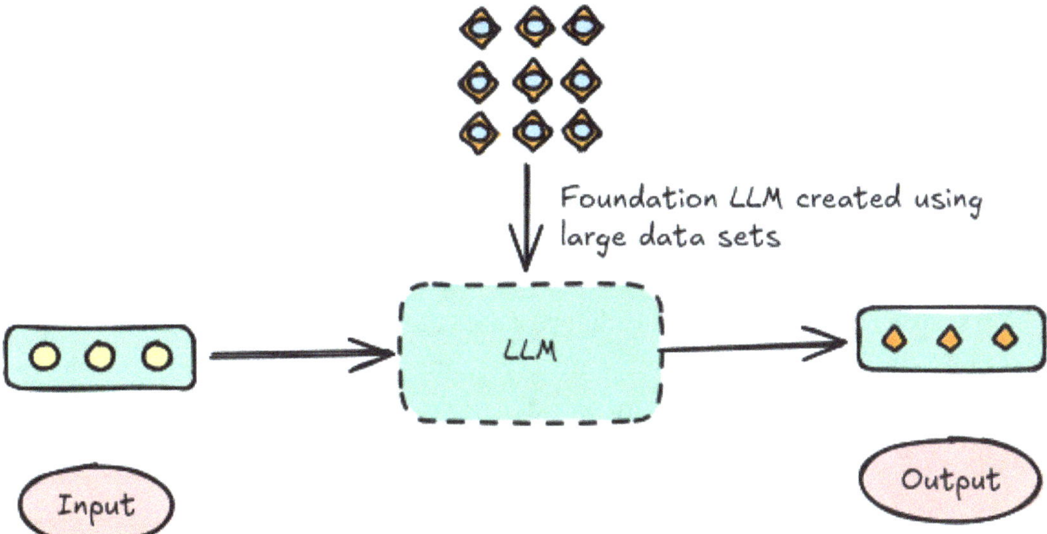

Figure 1-2. *General working representation of an LLM*

LLMs have revolutionized the field of natural language processing (NLP), enabling machines to understand, generate, and interact with human-like text. At their core, LLMs are deep learning models that use complex algorithms to process and analyze vast amounts of linguistic data. The term *LLM* is generally used for foundation language models.

Foundational language models are LLMs that have been trained using lots of datasets using the transformer architecture, for example, on hundreds to thousands of graphical processing unit (GPU) machines from days to months and sometimes for a period of a year. Nowadays, there are many small language models (SLMs) that either have been trained using a small dataset or have been distilled or subsetted from an LLM. (If this is confusing, do not worry as we will be discussing more on this later in this chapter.)

Foundation LLMs have been trained to achieve some generalized tasks like text summarization, prediction or completion of text, generation of text, sentiment analysis, etc. As shown in Figure 1-3, the LLM helps in language translation by taking in input in the English language with the text "I love programming" and outputting the Spanish version of it with "Me encanta programar." Based on the foundation dataset on which the LLM was trained, the LLM can help with not only a dual language translation but with multiple language support.

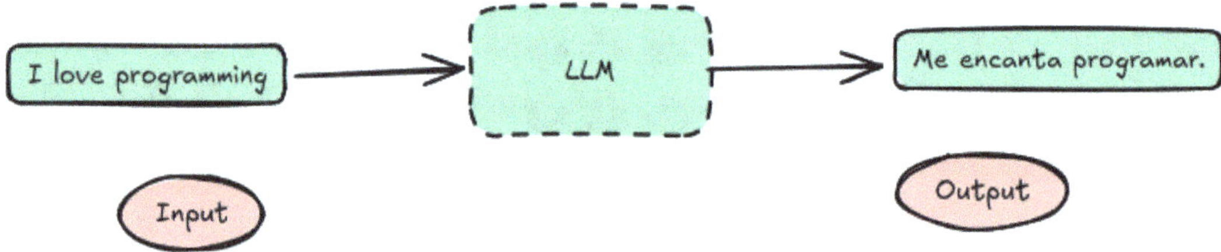

Figure 1-3. *An LLM performing language translation*

Let's talk a bit about the inner workings of the LLM. We will just dive into the high-level stuff in this chapter. (There are plenty of resources that do a dive deep into it if you are interested in going further into the world of transformers and machine learning.) At their simplest, LLM models are based on a transformer architecture (see Figure 1-4).

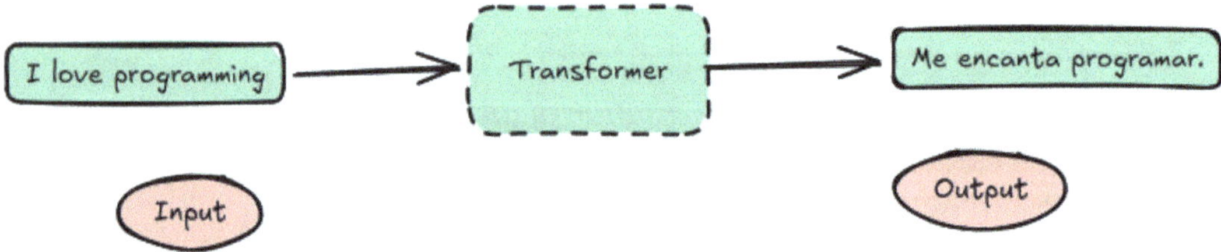

Figure 1-4. *Input and output from an encoder-decoder Transformer layer*

The transformer architecture consists of the encoder and the decoder layers (see Figure 1-5). The encoder takes in our input and outputs a matrix representation of that input. For instance, the English sentence "I love programming" is the input. The decoder takes that encoded representation and iteratively generates the output, which in our example is the translated sentence "Me encanta programar."

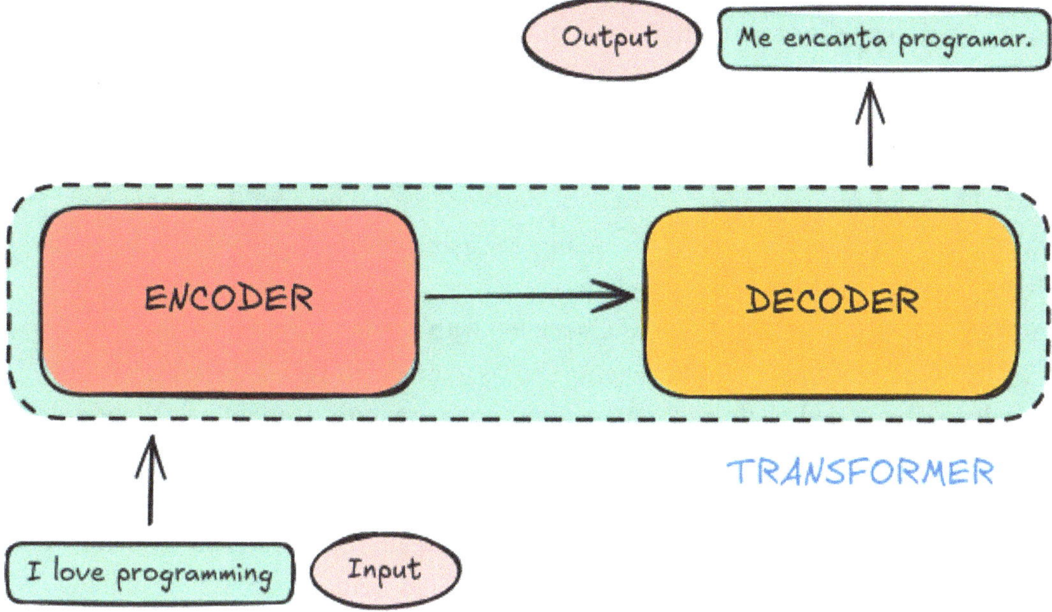

Figure 1-5. *Internal representation of encoder-decoder layer in a transformer*

Understanding the Role of Hugging Face in the LLM World

Hugging Face is a leading platform and ecosystem that provides tools, libraries, and repositories for working with machine learning models, particularly in the field of NLP. Founded with the mission to democratize AI, Hugging Face offers resources for building, training, and deploying models with ease. At its core, Hugging Face is known for its Transformers library, which simplifies access to state-of-the-art LLMs like GPT, BERT, and T5. It also includes a Model Hub, a centralized repository for pretrained models across various tasks, and datasets, which streamline the process of preparing training data for machine learning projects. Hugging Face is not just a technical toolset; it is also a vibrant community where developers and researchers collaborate to advance the field of AI.

The platform has made a name for itself by making complex AI technology accessible to both experts and beginners. Hugging Face's libraries and tools abstract away much of the complexity of working with transformers and LLMs, allowing developers to focus on application development rather than model training. The open-source nature of Hugging Face and its commitment to transparency and ethical AI practices have further cemented its role as a leader in the AI landscape.

Hugging Face plays a transformative role in advancing the adoption and evolution of LLMs. It is a one-stop shop for researchers, developers, and enterprises to access cutting-edge AI models, fine-tune them for specific use cases, and deploy them seamlessly. This platform has become indispensable in modern AI workflows, enabling faster innovation and reducing the technical overhead associated with LLM adoption.

Much like GitHub is to code, Hugging Face is to models and datasets. GitHub provides a centralized platform for managing code repositories, enabling collaboration, version control, and sharing. Similarly, Hugging Face centralizes machine learning resources, hosting thousands of pretrained models and datasets that developers can freely access, adapt, and contribute to. Just as GitHub revolutionized software development by democratizing code, Hugging Face has democratized AI by making state-of-the-art models accessible to the global community.

Hugging Face provides the Transformers library, which acts as a bridge between developers and the complex architectures of LLMs. It supports a wide range of tasks such as text classification, summarization, and question answering, making it easy for developers to integrate powerful language models into their applications. Beyond the library, the Model Hub hosts thousands of pretrained models, complete with versioning and metadata that detail their capabilities and limitations. This allows developers to quickly find and implement the best model for their needs without starting from scratch.

The community-driven nature of Hugging Face is another key feature, making it a hub for collaboration and innovation. Much like GitHub enables open-source contributions to software, Hugging Face fosters a culture of sharing and learning, with developers contributing models, datasets, and tutorials. This community engagement accelerates progress and ensures that even small teams or independent developers can leverage world-class AI tools.

In addition to technical resources, Hugging Face emphasizes responsible AI usage. Features like model cards provide transparency about the training data, intended uses, and ethical considerations of each model. This focus on accountability aligns with the growing demand for ethical AI development and ensures that users are aware of potential risks and biases in the models they employ.

Ecosystem Around LLMs

We will now discuss some of the LLMs that are in use and also the ecosystem around them. As programmers, we know that we can build applications with simple language constructs in languages like Java, Python, PHP, etc., although it would be quite a complex and arduous task with the absence of standardized interfaces when collaborating on a global scale. This was one of the main reasons for the creation of frameworks like Spring Boot and Quarkus in Java. Similarly, one can access an LLM and pass it input and outputs, but frameworks in this ecosystem make it easier to develop applications based on LLM and help with many of the complementary aspects such as standardization, security, modularization, etc. We will touch on many of these aspects in the next chapters while exploring them.

Table 1-1 summarizes the popular LLMs, their parameter sizes, and their licensing terms.

Table 1-1. Popular LLMs

Model Name	Parameter Sizes	License Type	Usage Permissions
GPT-4	Not publicly disclosed	Closed source	Accessible via API; commercial use permitted
Llama 3	8B, 70B, 405B	Source available (Meta Llama 3.2 Community License)	Research and commercial use with restrictions
Mistral 7B	7.3B	Open source (Apache 2.0)	Free for research and commercial use
BLOOM	176B	Open access (bigscience-bloom-rail-1.0)	Research use; commercial use with restrictions
Falcon 2	11B	Open source (Apache 2.0 with acceptable use policy)	Free for research and commercial use with acceptable use policy
DeepSeek-V2	236B	Custom license	Free with usage restrictions; models trained on DeepSeek outputs become DeepSeek derivatives
Fugaku-LLM	13B	Custom license	Free with usage restrictions
Yi-1.5	6B, 9B, 34B	Open source (Apache 2.0)	Free for research and commercial use
DeepSeek-V2-Lite	16B	Custom license	Free with usage restrictions; models trained on DeepSeek outputs become DeepSeek derivatives
Phi-3	4B, 128B	Custom license	Usage rights vary; refer to specific license terms

Table 1-1 is just a sampling of the popular LLMs. The parameter size helps us to understand the size of the LLM, which could be helpful when selecting one based on a specific use case. Suppose we have restricted memory limits, for example. In that case, we can limit our LLM search to low parameter sizes. LLMs with huge parameter sizes take a lot of memory to load into the memory ,and the latency is high to respond with output. SLMs and LLMs with low parameter sizes take a small memory, and the latency is low to respond with output since their base dataset with which they were trained was small.

Frameworks make things easier for development. They play a critical role in shaping the ecosystem around LLMs and their development. They address the challenges developers face when building robust, scalable, and context-aware applications that leverage LLMs. One of their most significant contributions is simplifying complex workflows. Developing applications with LLMs involves intricate processes such as preprocessing data, crafting effective prompts, orchestrating retrieval pipelines, and evaluating outputs. These frameworks streamline these tasks, providing modular tools that allow developers to build and experiment quickly without reinventing the wheel.

A particularly important area they enhance is the integration of LLMs with external knowledge sources. LLMs, while powerful, have a fixed knowledge cutoff and often hallucinate or provide inaccurate information. Frameworks are invaluable here because they enable seamless connections between LLMs and external databases or document repositories. This capability facilitates the development of retrieval-augmented generation (RAG) pipelines, where the LLM queries a database or vector store to provide factually grounded, contextually relevant responses.

Additionally, these frameworks optimize the handling of unstructured data. For instance, Haystack is designed for efficient search and question-answering workflows, while LlamaIndex focuses on transforming raw, unstructured data into structured indices tailored for LLM querying. This makes it easier to deploy LLMs for real-world tasks involving large datasets, such as customer support systems or legal document analysis.

LangChain, on the other hand, brings unique value to multistep workflows and logical task orchestration. It allows developers to construct chains of prompts and integrate advanced reasoning, memory management, and tool usage within LLM-based applications. This makes LangChain particularly effective for building conversational agents or applications that require structured decision-making and multimodal integration.

Another vital aspect is their support for integration with various LLMs and APIs. These frameworks often provide compatibility with leading LLM providers like OpenAI, Hugging Face, and Cohere, while also supporting tools like Pinecone and Weaviate for vector search. This flexibility ensures that developers can choose the best combination of tools and models for their specific use. In terms of scalability, these frameworks are production-ready and include features like caching, parallel processing, and asynchronous execution. This makes them suitable for applications with high traffic or demanding data processing needs. For instance, Haystack and LlamaIndex can handle large-scale document retrieval tasks, while LangChain enables dynamic interaction with external APIs and tools to enhance application functionality.

Another notable benefit is the open-source nature of many of these frameworks. This openness fosters a collaborative environment where developers and researchers can contribute, share innovations, and leverage a growing library of plugins and integrations. This collaborative ecosystem accelerates progress and democratizes access to cutting-edge AI capabilities.

Challenges and Considerations in Using LLMs

Using LLMs brings immense possibilities, but it also presents challenges that require careful consideration and strategic management. One of the foremost issues is the accuracy of LLM outputs. While these models generate coherent and contextually relevant responses, they are prone to hallucinations, where the information presented is plausible but incorrect. This becomes particularly critical in high-stakes domains such as healthcare, legal, or financial services, where incorrect outputs can lead to serious consequences. Developers often mitigate this by integrating RAG pipelines or implementing human oversight mechanisms to enhance accuracy.

Another pressing concern is bias/fairness. LLMs are trained on large datasets sourced from the Internet, which inevitably include biases reflective of societal inequalities. Consequently, these biases can appear in model outputs, leading to harmful stereotypes or discriminatory responses. Addressing this issue requires thoughtful dataset curation, fine-tuning for inclusivity, and the implementation of bias detection tools to ensure fairness across diverse user bases.

Ethical considerations also play a significant role in LLM deployment. The potential for misuse is substantial, whether it's generating convincing fake news, phishing content, or malicious code. This raises the importance of embedding ethical guidelines into development processes and incorporating guardrails to detect and prevent misuse. Responsible usage policies and monitoring systems are essential for mitigating these risks.

From a technical perspective, the resource intensity of LLMs is a notable challenge. Training and deploying these models demands vast computational resources and energy, which not only creates barriers for smaller organizations but also raises concerns about environmental sustainability. Techniques such as model compression, efficient architecture design, and leveraging pretrained models can help reduce resource demands, but these often require additional expertise.

Data privacy and security are equally important considerations. Since LLMs process user data to generate responses, there's a risk of data leakage or misuse, especially when integrated into applications handling sensitive information. Ensuring compliance with regulations like GDPR or HIPAA and adopting privacy-preserving techniques such as encryption or federated learning can address these concerns.

Another challenge lies in the explainability of LLMs. These models operate as black-box systems, making it difficult to understand how they arrive at specific outputs. This lack of transparency can be problematic in critical applications where accountability is essential, such as in healthcare or legal settings. Researchers and developers are exploring ways to make AI systems more interpretable, but progress in this area is still ongoing.

Additionally, practical limitations like context and memory constraints can hinder LLM effectiveness. Many models have token limits that restrict the amount of information they can process at once, making it difficult to handle long documents or maintain memory across interactions. Workarounds like summarization or chunking help address this but add complexity to implementation.

Cost is another factor that cannot be overlooked. Real-time applications of LLMs, especially at scale, can be expensive due to the computational requirements of model inference and the infrastructure needed to support them. Developers must balance these costs against the benefits, often using optimizations like caching and batch processing to improve efficiency.

On a broader level, regulatory and compliance concerns are growing as governments and organizations scrutinize AI applications for ethical and societal impacts. Ensuring compliance with emerging AI regulations and standards is an evolving challenge, requiring proactive adaptation and monitoring.

Cultural and global sensitivities also need attention. LLMs often lack awareness of nuanced cultural contexts, which can lead to inappropriate or insensitive outputs. Developers must strive for localization and ensure their models respect cultural diversity and linguistic differences.

In addressing these challenges, strategies like incorporating human-in-the-loop systems, fine-tuning for specific domains, and conducting robust monitoring and auditing become crucial. Transparency in model capabilities and limitations, combined with adherence to ethical AI guidelines, further ensures responsible and effective LLM deployment.

Setting the Stage: LLMs in Java Development

LLMs are reshaping the software development landscape, and Java, as one of the most widely used programming languages, is finding its unique role in this transformation. Traditionally, LLM integration has been more accessible in the Python and JavaScript ecosystems, leaving Java developers with fewer tools and frameworks. However, the emergence of dedicated libraries like LangChain4j and Spring AI, as well as extensions such as Quarkus LangChain4j, is bridging this gap, empowering Java developers to harness the capabilities of LLMs effectively.

One of the key challenges in working with LLMs is managing the diversity of APIs provided by various model vendors, such as OpenAI, Anthropic, and Google Vertex AI. Each provider has its proprietary API, which can make switching between LLMs cumbersome. Frameworks like LangChain4j address this by offering unified APIs, enabling developers to switch between LLM providers or embedding stores (e.g., Pinecone, Milvus) with minimal code changes. This abstraction simplifies experimentation and integration, ensuring that developers focus on business logic rather than API-specific intricacies.

The Java ecosystem now benefits from frameworks that encapsulate common patterns and techniques for LLM-powered applications. LangChain4j, for instance, supports everything from prompt templating and chat memory management to function calling and RAG pipelines. This comprehensive toolbox allows developers to build diverse applications, whether it's creating conversational agents, implementing Q&A systems over large datasets, or integrating LLMs with existing workflows.

Integrating LLMs into Java applications has become increasingly accessible with the advent of specialized frameworks and tools. These solutions streamline the development process, allowing Java developers to leverage advanced AI capabilities effectively.

LangChain4j addresses the challenge of diverse APIs from various LLM providers by offering a unified interface. This abstraction enables developers to switch between different LLMs or embedding stores without extensive code modifications, facilitating experimentation and integration. LangChain4j supports more than 15 popular LLM providers and embedding stores, providing a comprehensive toolkit that includes prompt templating, chat memory management, and function calling. This versatility allows developers to build a wide range of applications, from chatbots to RAG systems.

Spring AI applies the modular and portable design principles of the Spring ecosystem to AI integration. It offers structured APIs for interacting with major AI providers and vector databases, enabling seamless connection between enterprise data and AI models.

Features such as structured outputs, observability, and document injection frameworks make Spring AI particularly appealing for enterprises aiming to adopt LLMs within complex environments. Its support for Spring Boot auto-configuration ensures that developers can get started quickly, leveraging familiar tools and patterns.

Quarkus LangChain4j caters to developers building cloud-native applications by integrating LLMs into Quarkus applications using a declarative approach. Interactions with LLMs are modeled through interfaces, with annotations like @SystemMessage and @UserMessage simplifying the definition of AI behavior. The integration of tools and document stores extends the LLM's knowledge base with real-time and domain-specific data, highlighting how Java frameworks can adopt and tailor LLM capabilities to enterprise-grade applications.

Amazon Bedrock SDK for Java provides a robust platform for building and deploying generative AI applications. It offers access to a variety of foundation models from Amazon and leading AI startups, enabling developers to create applications that generate text, images, and more. The SDK includes comprehensive code examples and documentation, facilitating the integration of Amazon Bedrock into Java applications. For instance, the AWS SDK for Java 2.x provides examples demonstrating how to perform actions and implement common scenarios using Amazon Bedrock. Additionally, the AWS SDK for Java API Reference offers detailed information on classes and interfaces, such as the BedrockClient, which is essential for accessing Amazon Bedrock services.

These frameworks and tools collectively enhance the Java ecosystem's ability to integrate LLMs, providing developers with the necessary resources to build sophisticated AI-powered applications. By offering unified APIs, comprehensive toolsets, and robust SDKs, they simplify the complexities associated with LLM integration, enabling developers to focus on innovation and application development.

Conclusion

This chapter introduced you to the fascinating world of Gen AI and LLMs, emphasizing their transformative potential in modern software development. Starting with a simplified understanding of Gen AI, the chapter guided you through its ability to create novel, contextually relevant outputs, whether in text, images, or other modalities. This sets the stage for comprehending the significance of LLMs, which have revolutionized natural language processing through their ability to analyze and generate human-like text based on the transformer architecture.

The chapter also highlights the rapidly evolving ecosystem around LLMs. Frameworks like LangChain4j, Spring AI, and Quarkus LangChain4j demonstrate how Java developers can leverage these advancements effectively, bridging gaps that previously existed in Java's AI integration capabilities. These tools simplify interactions with LLMs, enabling seamless connections to external knowledge sources, efficient handling of unstructured data, and integration with diverse APIs.

Moreover, the challenges and considerations of LLMs, such as biases, hallucinations, and resource intensity, are addressed, along with strategies to mitigate them. The chapter sets the stage for Java developers by showcasing frameworks and SDKs like Amazon Bedrock that provide robust, enterprise-grade solutions for integrating LLMs into applications.

This chapter served as a foundational guide, equipping you with the knowledge and tools to confidently embark on your journey into Gen AI and LLM-driven development. It sets the tone for deeper exploration in subsequent chapters, where theoretical insights will transform into practical, hands-on applications.

CHAPTER 2

First Contact: "Hello, LLM" with Spring Boot

In this chapter, you will learn the basic concepts associated with LLMs from a practical viewpoint using Java.

Introduction

In this chapter, you will get your hands dirty with some coding. What fun is there without writing code? You will learn as you go throughout this chapter many interesting facts about large language modesl (LLMs) and their ecosystem. First, you will learn about OpenAI and its importance in LLM development. Then you will start exploring some of its application programming interfaces (APIs) through a Spring Boot application. We will not limit the discussion to just OpenAI but try out different LLMs. This is similar to how you would try different databases to see which one best suits you. Just remember one thing that will help you in the world of generative AI (Gen AI): there is change happening every day, so you need to keep exploring and learning.

What Is OpenAI?

OpenAI was founded in December 2015 by visionaries including Sam Altman, Greg Brockman, Ilya Sutskever, and Elon Musk with an ambitious goal of ensuring that artificial general intelligence (AGI) benefits all of humanity. Originally founded as a charity, OpenAI sought to progress artificial intelligence in a manner consistent with human ideals and needs.

S. K. Sahu, *Generative AI-Driven Application Development with Java*,
https://doi.org/10.1007/979-8-8688-1609-3_2

Particularly in the field of generative artificial intelligence, OpenAI's path has been distinguished by innovative artificial intelligence developments. One pieceof evidence of OpenAI's creative energy is the Generative Pre-trained Transformer (GPT) series' growth. Beginning with GPT-1 and working through GPT-4, every iteration has shown amazing gains in knowledge and creation of human-like prose. These models have created new benchmarks in natural language processing (NLP), allowing uses ranging from content production to conversational agents.

OpenAI debuted GPT-4o, a multimodal model able of analyzing and creating text, pictures, and audio, in May 2024. In many benchmarks, GPT-4o produced state-of-the-art performance, setting new benchmarks in audio speech recognition and translating. On the Mass Multitask Language Understanding (MMLU) test, it achieved 88.7%, higher than its predecessor, GPT-4.

OpenAI's impact transcends language models. The company has created DALL-E, an artificial intelligence system that generates graphics from textual descriptions, therefore highlighting the possibilities of generative artificial intelligence in visual creativity. OpenAI also unveiled Codex, a technology meant to convert natural language into code that drives GitHub Copilot to help programmers with coding chores.

OpenAI's progress has been much aided by cooperation. Particularly important is the cooperation with Microsoft, which incorporates OpenAI's ideas into Microsoft's goods and services including the Azure OpenAI Service. This cooperation has helped several sectors implement AI technologies, hence improving production and creativity.

OpenAI's programs to guarantee safety and democratize AI access clearly show its dedication to ethical AI development. The company has supported studies on artificial intelligence morality and participated in debates on the responsible application of AI technologies.

By means of its pioneering research, creative products, and strategic alliances, Open AI keeps a major influence on the direction of artificial intelligence, ensuring that its developments are safe, ethical, and good for all.

Creating Your First Spring Boot LLM Application

OpenAI has created many small and large language models that are proprietary in nature. These models are hosted by OpenAI internally and exposed to the world through software development kits (SDKs) and APIs. In the current context, OpenAI does not provide an SDK in the Java Language, although it supports in Python. Python is the predominant SDK that is supported across the ecosystem. This should not be a reason for us to be disheartened, though, as we will see in later chapters the increasing plethora of ecosystems in development and use in the Java environment.

There are two ways to use LLMs. You can use an API for an LLM hosted by another system or host your own LLM in a server and expose it through an API. We will cover both of these uses in this book. In this chapter, you will try the first method, which uses the API exposed by OpenAI to interact with the LLM.

Figure 2-1 shows the different components that you will learn to build and leverage to integrate the OpenAI API with a Spring Boot application.

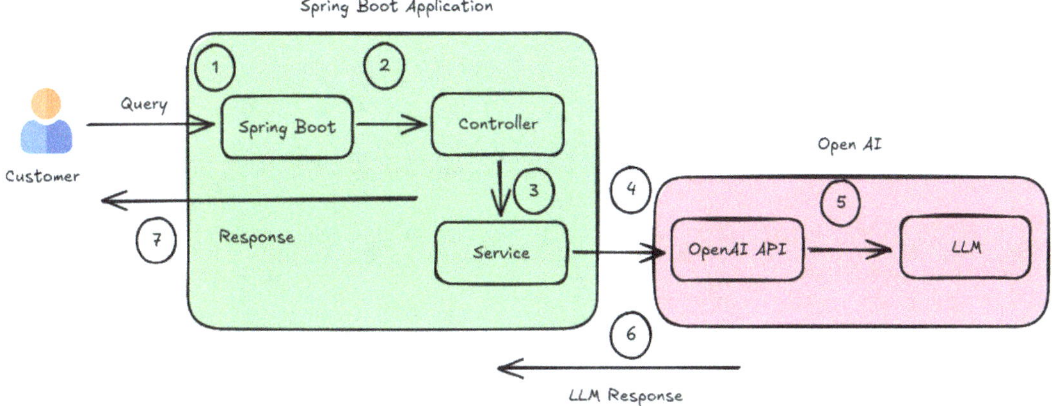

Figure 2-1. *Request flow through Spring Boot application to Open AI API*

First head to the Spring Initializr site at `https://start.spring.io/` and create a starter template for the project with a Spring Web dependency, as shown in Figure 2-2.

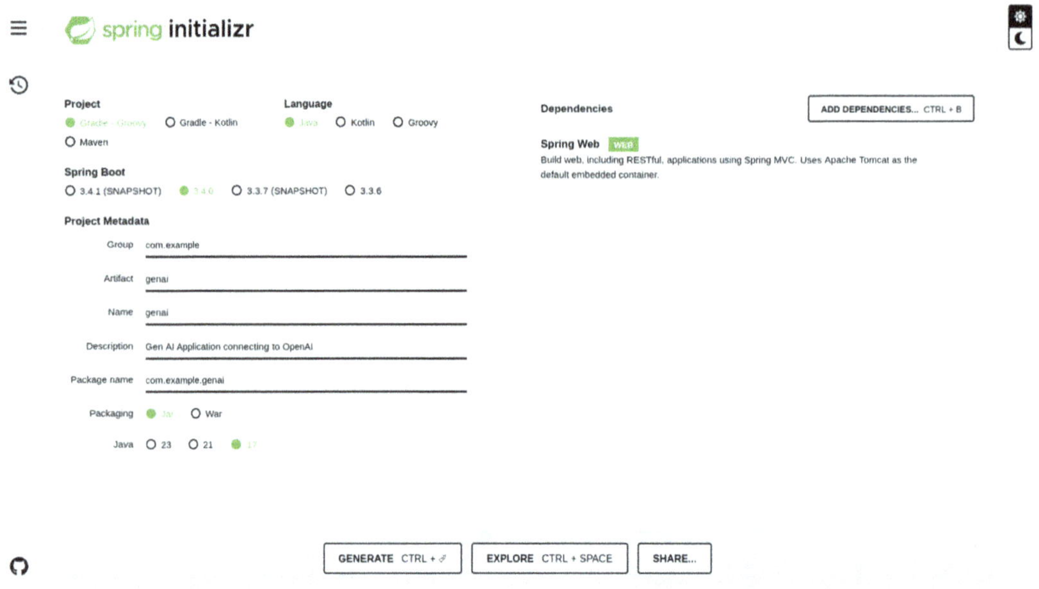

Figure 2-2. Spring Initializr website with Spring Web dependency for basic application setup

These are the prerequisites:

- Java 17+
- Open AI API Key
- IntelliJ or VSCode IDE
- Spring Boot Knowledge

Let's unzip the downloaded template, open it in our IDE of choice, and run it, as shown in Figure 2-3.

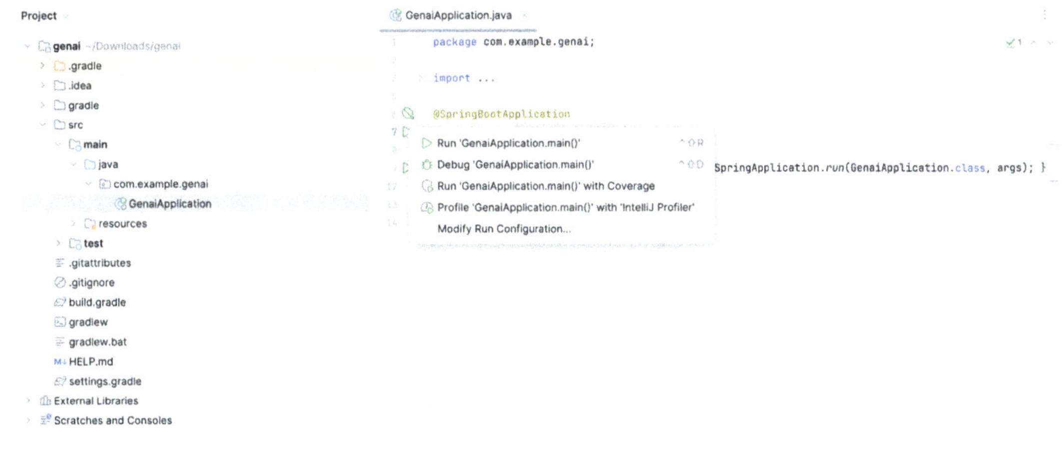

Figure 2-3. *Starting the Spring Boot application from the IntelliJ IDE*

Let's head over to http://localhost:8080 to see our application running and also verify it in the console. Figure 2-4 shows the Spring boot application running, and Figure 2-5 shows the response when accessing the application at http://localhost:8080. This means your application has started correctly.

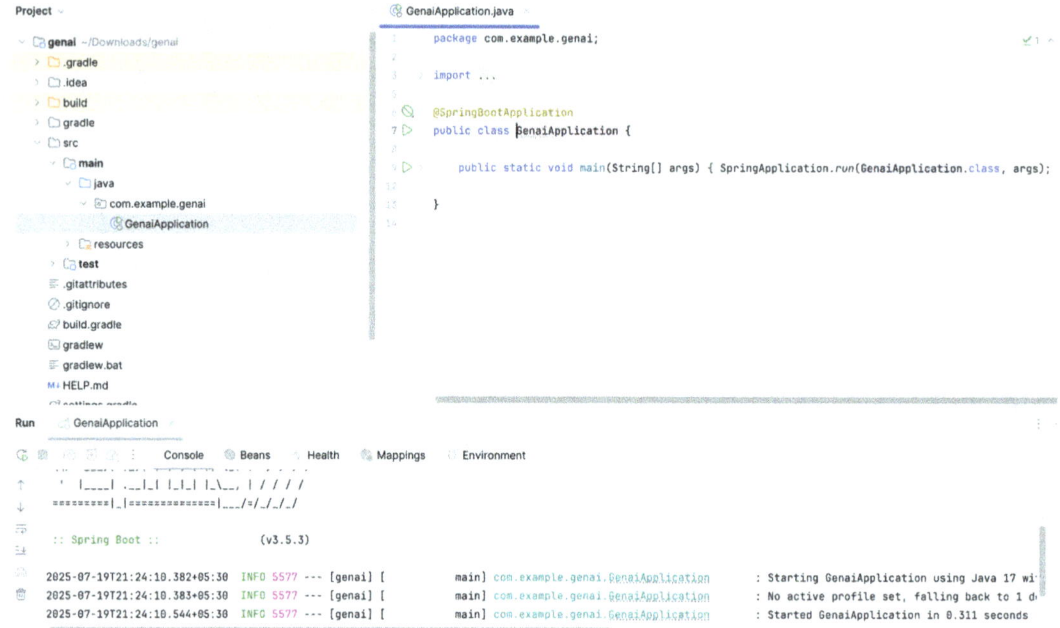

***Figure 2-4.** Spring Boot startup success*

Whitelabel Error Page

This application has no explicit mapping for /error, so you are seeing this as a fallback.

Sun Dec 01 10:38:27 UTC 2024
There was an unexpected error (type=Not Found, status=404).

***Figure 2-5.** Spring Boot API response at http://localhost:8080*

Exploring the OpenAI Chat API

This verifies your application is bootstrapped, so you are good to start from here. OpenAI provides a RESTful API to interact with its hosted LLMs. The API documentation and list can be referenced by visiting the page at `https://platform.openai.com/docs/api-reference/introduction` (Figure 2-6).

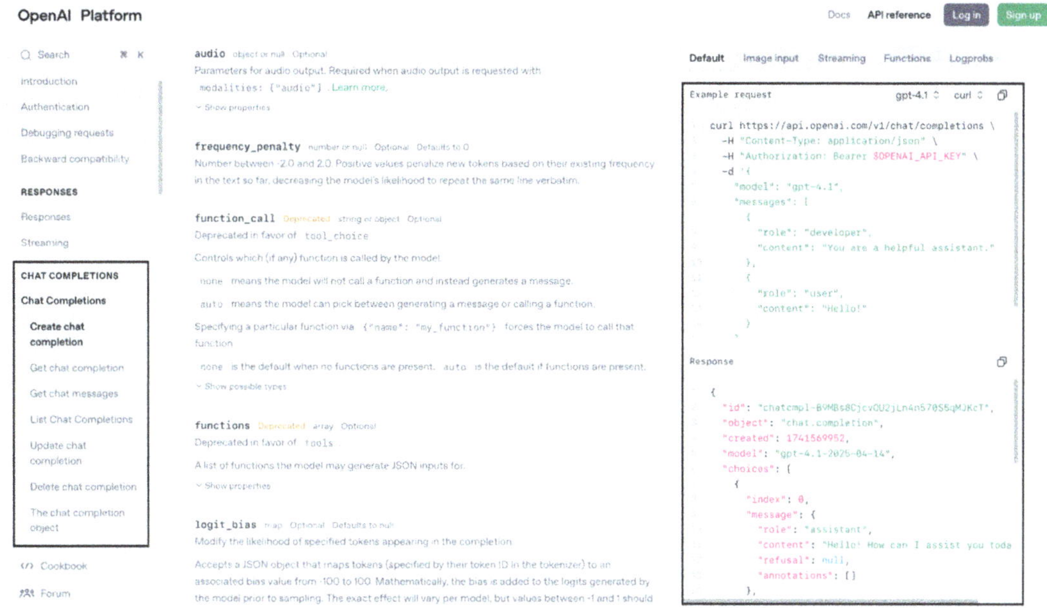

Figure 2-6. OpenAI API reference

You can leverage the APIs available in the sidebar panel displayed as endpoints, particularly starting with Chat (see Figure 2-7).

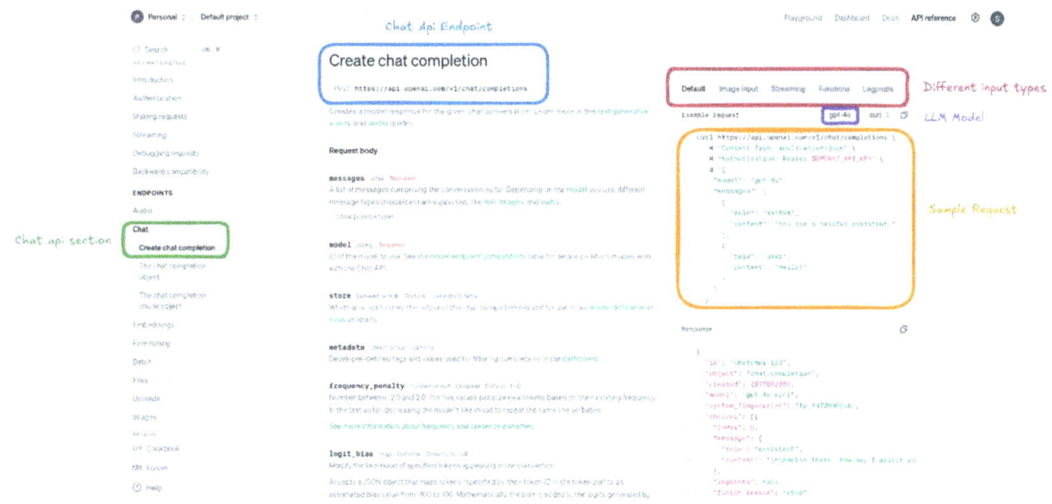

Figure 2-7. OpenAI API reference for Chat

Go to the Chat API section, as highlighted in Figure 2-7. Once in this section, you can see the documentation related to the endpoint and request body parameters in the central section. Also, it has a handy interface to choose the different input format types such as text, image, and corresponding `curl` request. In the same interface, you can choose from the different LLM models supported by OpenAI.

If you observe the `curl` request carefully, you can see it needs an OPENAI_API_KEY that can be created from the dashboard page at `https://platform.openai.com/api-keys`, as shown in Figure 2-8.

```
curl https://api.openai.com/v1/chat/completions \
 -H "Content-Type: application/json" \
 -H "Authorization: Bearer $OPENAI_API_KEY" \
 -d '{
"model": "gpt-4o-mini",
"messages": [
   {
     "role": "system",
     "content": "You are a helpful assistant."
   },
   {
     "role": "user",
     "content": "Hello!"
   }
]
 }'
```

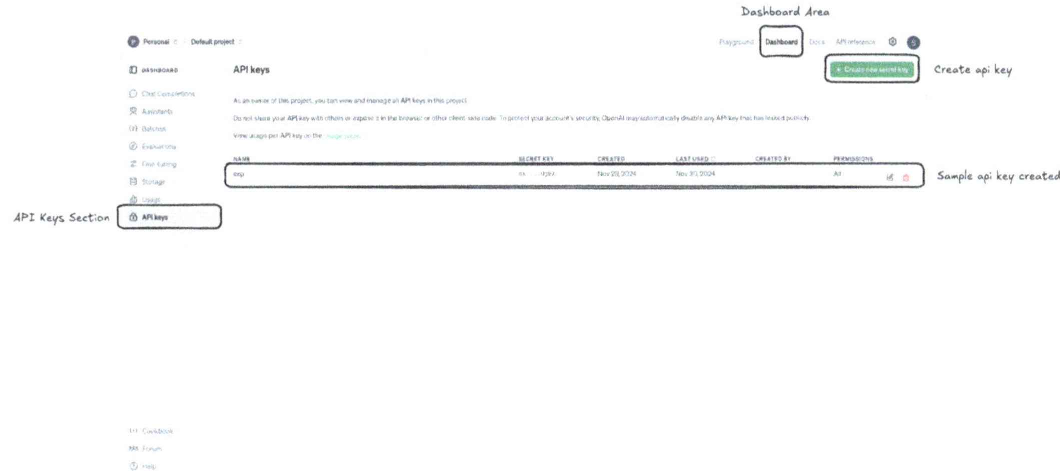

Figure 2-8. OpenAI API secret key creation

Visit the dashboard page by clicking at the top, visiting the API keys section, and clicking the "Create new secret key" button, as highlighted in Figure 2-8. To create an OPENAI_API_KEY, you will need a paid account. It costs a few bucks but is worth the cost in terms of the future applications that you are going to create that leverage LLMs.

Now that you have an OpenAI API key, let's execute a sample `curl` request to get a "Hello!" message from it. First export your key into the environment so that you don't have to write it directly into your `curl` command for the best safety. Using the following `curl` request, you are suggesting to the LLM that it should act as a helpful assistant. This tells it the context of the interaction it is supposed to be in. The following message "Hello!" is our first message to it in this context, and we want to know how it will respond to us.

```
$ export OPENAI_API_KEY=YOUR_API_KEY
$ curl https://api.openai.com/v1/chat/completions \
 -H "Content-Type: application/json" \
 -H "Authorization: Bearer $OPENAI_API_KEY" \
 -d '{
"model": "gpt-4o-mini",
"messages": [
   {
     "role": "system",
     "content": "You are a helpful assistant."
   },
```

```
    {
      "role": "user",
      "content": "Hello!"
    }
]
 }'
```

Output:

```
{
  "id": "chatcmpl-AZcBXXqaydyddov2mtXXBXtVOb9fK",
  "object": "chat.completion",
  "created": 1733051627,
  "model": "gpt-4o-mini-2024-07-18",
  "choices": [
    {
      "index": 0,
      "message": {
        "role": "assistant",
        "content": "Hello! How can I assist you today?",
        "refusal": null
      },
      "logprobs": null,
      "finish_reason": "stop"
    }
  ],
  "usage": {
    "prompt_tokens": 19,
    "completion_tokens": 9,
    "total_tokens": 28,
    "prompt_tokens_details": {
      "cached_tokens": 0,
      "audio_tokens": 0
    },
    "completion_tokens_details": {
      "reasoning_tokens": 0,
```

```
      "audio_tokens": 0,
      "accepted_prediction_tokens": 0,
      "rejected_prediction_tokens": 0
    }
  },
  "system_fingerprint": "fp_0705bf87c0"
}
```


Congratulations on your first interaction with an LLM! You can see in the output section in the JSON structure a field called *choices* that is a list of outputs. The first output is the message from the LLM in the subfield called *content*. If you look carefully, the output is also a field called *usage*, which displays a few fields called `prompt_tokens`, `completion_tokens`, and `total_tokens`. To understand this, you can compare it to the CPU limit for software applications.

Specifically, every software application has an optimal CPU requirement to perform and will not work if the CPU processing power is less than that. And if you are in a cloud environment, you are charged on the CPU type usage based on hours.

Similarly, tokens are the basic unit of messaging in the LLM world. Each LLM has a maximum token limit it can handle per request, and OpenAI charges based on the total number of tokens used. `prompt_tokens` is the number of tokens in our input message called the *prompt message*, and `completion_tokens` is the output message from the LLM. Both together are the total tokens used by the LLM to respond. You will learn more about this terminology later in the chapter, so do not worry. For now, you will learn as you go.

Integrating OpenAI API with Spring Boot

Now that you have your API working, the next task is to integrate it with a Spring Boot application. You will first create a controller with a GET request type route so that you have an API that can be exposed to your end users. Then you will create a service that will connect and request to OpenAI API and finally connect the controller to use the service.

The following is the final code structure, and Figure 2-9 shows the component use and interaction.

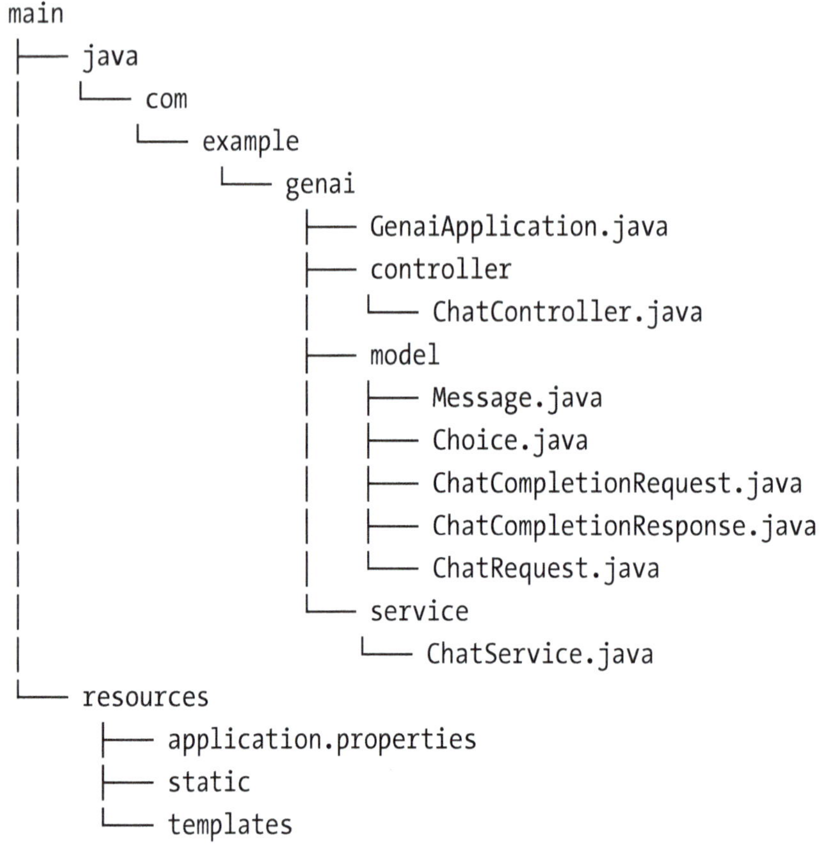

```
main
├── java
│   └── com
│       └── example
│           └── genai
│               ├── GenaiApplication.java
│               ├── controller
│               │   └── ChatController.java
│               ├── model
│               │   ├── Message.java
│               │   ├── Choice.java
│               │   ├── ChatCompletionRequest.java
│               │   ├── ChatCompletionResponse.java
│               │   └── ChatRequest.java
│               └── service
│                   └── ChatService.java
└── resources
    ├── application.properties
    ├── static
    └── templates
```

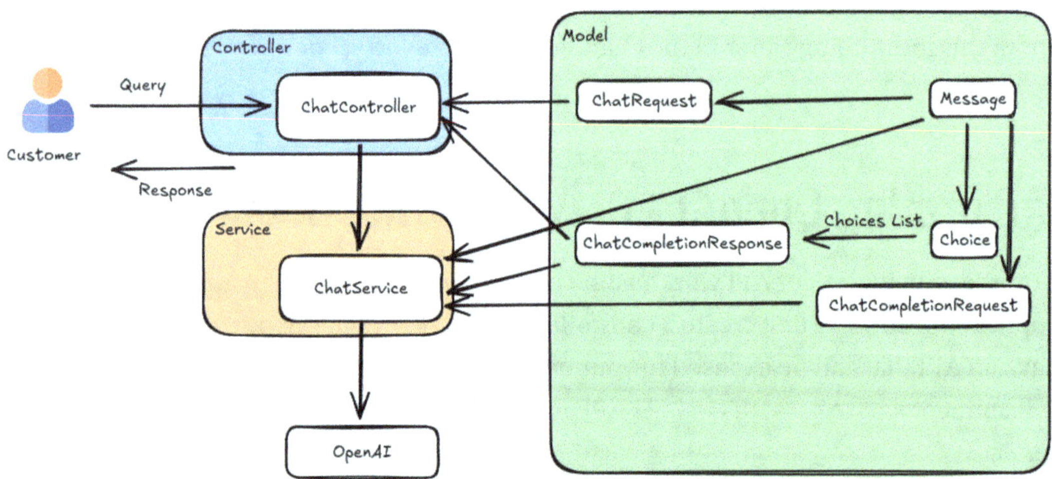

Figure 2-9. *Spring Boot basic components for OpenAI API integration*

Let's start by focusing on the model POJO entities first. From the curl request and response, you see a particular structure around which you can create four POJO objects: Message, Choice, ChatCompletionRequest, and ChatCompletionResponse. These will be used by the ChatService class to map the message format, request, and response.

So first, create a directory called model and create three files with the following content:

File: model/Message.java

```
package com.example.genai.model;

public class Message {

    private String role;
    private String content;

   public String getRole() {
        return role;
    }

    public void setRole(String role) {
        this.role = role;
    }

    public String getContent() {
        return content;
    }

    public void setContent(String content) {
        this.content = content;
    }
}
```

In the previous file, you are creating getter and setter attributes and methods for the Message entity for the role and content of the message, as shown in the following response element:

```
$ curl https://api.openai.com/v1/chat/completions \
 -H "Content-Type: application/json" \
 -H "Authorization: Bearer $OPENAI_API_KEY" \
```

```
 -d '{
"model": "gpt-4o-mini",
"messages": [
   {
     "role": "system",
     "content": "You are a helpful assistant." <-- Message POJO Object
   },
   {
     "role": "user",
     "content": "Hello!"
   }
]
 }'
```

File: model/ChatCompletionRequest.java

```
package com.example.genai.model;

import java.util.List;

public class ChatCompletionRequest {
    private String model;
    private List<Message> messages;

    public String getModel() {
        return model;
    }

    public void setModel(String model) {
        this.model = model;
    }

    public List<Message> getMessages() {
        return messages;
    }

    public void setMessages(List<Message> messages) {
        this.messages = messages;
    }
}
```

The `Message` entity acts as the unit message object, which then needs to be collected and sent in the messages field along with the model parameter. This is contextualized in the `ChatCompletionRequest.java` file through getters and setters for the `model` and `messages` parameters. The relevant sections for these in the `curl` request are shown here:

```
$ curl https://api.openai.com/v1/chat/completions \
 -H "Content-Type: application/json" \
 -H "Authorization: Bearer $OPENAI_API_KEY" \
 -d '{
"model": "gpt-4o-mini", <-- ChatCompletionRequest POJO Object
"messages": [                                        ^
   {                                                 |
      "role": "system",                              |
      "content": "You are a helpful assistant." <-- Message POJO Object
   },
   {
      "role": "user",
      "content": "Hello!"
   }
]
 }'
```

Now that we have our request-related POJO objects, let's focus on the response POJO object structure. Reviewing the following `curl` response, you will need two POJO objects, one for the inner choice and one for an outer response POJO. The other fields are not relevant for our use case at this moment, so you do not need to parse them.

```
{
  "id": "chatcmpl-AZcBXXqayd...",      <--- ChatCompletionResponse POJO
  "object": "chat.completion",                              ^
  "created": 1733051627,                                    |
  "model": "gpt-4o-mini-2024-07-18",                        |
  "choices": [                                              |
    {                                            <--- Choice POJO
      "index": 0,                                           ^
      "message": {                                <--- Message POJO
      "role": "assistant",
```

```
        "content": "Hello! How can I assist you today?",
        "refusal": null
        },
        "logprobs": null,
        "finish_reason": "stop"
      }
    ],
    "usage": {
      ...
    },
    "system_fingerprint": "fp_0705bf87c0"
}
```

Now you will create getter and setter objects for the previous POJO objects. The Message POJO is already available, so you do need not to create it again.

File: model/choice.java

```
package com.example.genai.model;

public class Choice {
    private int index;
    private Message message;

   public int getIndex() {
        return index;
    }

   public void setIndex(int index) {
        this.index = index;
    }

   public Message getMessage() {
        return message;
    }

   public void setMessage(Message message) {
        this.message = message;
    }
}
```

File: model/ChatCompletionResponse.java

```
package com.example.genai.model;

import java.util.List;

public class ChatCompletionResponse {

    private String id;
    private String object;
    private long created;
    private String model;
    private List<Choice> choices;

    public String getId() {
        return id;
    }

    public void setId(String id) {
        this.id = id;
    }

    public String getObject() {
        return object;
    }

    public void setObject(String object) {
        this.object = object;
    }

    public long getCreated() {
        return created;
    }

    public void setCreated(long created) {
        this.created = created;
    }

    public String getModel() {
        return model;
    }
```

```
    public void setModel(String model) {
        this.model = model;
    }

    public List<Choice> getChoices() {
        return choices;
    }

    public void setChoices(List<Choice> choices) {
        this.choices = choices;
    }
}
```

The base model POJO objects are all set up. They need to be composed inside the Service class next to make requests to OpenAI and fetch the response. Create a file named `ChatService.java` inside the service directory.

File: src/main/resources/application.properties

```
spring.application.name=genai
openai.api.key=YOUR_API_KEY  <--- Replace with your own openai api key. In
production setup, use environment variables instead
```

File: service/ChatService.java

```
package com.example.genai.service;

// POJO Object References
import com.example.genai.model.ChatCompletionRequest;
import com.example.genai.model.ChatCompletionResponse;
import com.example.genai.model.Message;

import org.springframework.beans.factory.annotation.Value;
import org.springframework.stereotype.Service;
import org.springframework.web.client.RestTemplate;
import org.springframework.http.*;
import java.util.Arrays;
```

```
@Service
public class ChatService {

    @Value("${openai.api.key}")
    private String openAiApiKey;

    private final RestTemplate restTemplate;

    // Constructor injection
   public ChatService(RestTemplate restTemplate) {
        this.restTemplate = restTemplate;
    }

    private static final String OPENAI_API_URL = "https://api.openai.com/
    v1/chat/completions";

    public ChatCompletionResponse getChatResponse(String userMessage) {
        // Build the request body
       ChatCompletionRequest request = new ChatCompletionRequest();
        request.setModel("gpt-4o-mini");
        Message systemMessage = new Message();
        systemMessage.setRole("system");
        systemMessage.setContent("You are a helpful assistant.");

        Message userChatMessage = new Message();
        userChatMessage.setRole("user");
        userChatMessage.setContent(userMessage);

       request.setMessages(Arrays.asList(systemMessage, userChatMessage));

        // Set up headers
       HttpHeaders headers = new HttpHeaders();
        headers.setContentType(MediaType.APPLICATION_JSON);
        headers.setBearerAuth(openAiApiKey);

       HttpEntity<ChatCompletionRequest> entity = new HttpEntity<>(request,
       headers);
```

```
        // Make the POST request
         ResponseEntity<ChatCompletionResponse> response = this.
         restTemplate.postForEntity(
                OPENAI_API_URL,
                entity,
                ChatCompletionResponse.class
         );

        return response.getBody();
    }
}
```

This completes the setup of the service layer. The controller needs to leverage the service layer to make API requests to OpenAI. For this you will need a POJO object to store the structure of the incoming JSON request from the UI side and then a controller to use this POJO object and make a request to the Service layer.

File: model/ChatRequest.java

```
package com.example.genai.model;

public class ChatRequest {

    private String userMessage;

    public String getUserMessage() {
        return userMessage;
    }

    public void setUserMessage(String userMessage) {
        this.userMessage = userMessage;
    }
}
```

File: controller/ChatController.java

```
package com.example.genai.controller;

// POJO object reference
import com.example.genai.model.ChatCompletionResponse;
import com.example.genai.model.ChatRequest;
```

```
import com.example.genai.service.ChatService;
import org.springframework.beans.factory.annotation.Autowired;
import org.springframework.web.bind.annotation.*;

import java.util.HashMap;
import java.util.Map;

@RestController
@RequestMapping("/api/chat")
public class ChatController {

   @Autowired
    private ChatService chatService;

   @PostMapping
    public Map<String, String> chat(@RequestBody ChatRequest chatRequest) {
        ChatCompletionResponse response = chatService.
        getChatResponse(chatRequest.getUserMessage());

        // Extracting the content from the response
        String content = response.getChoices().get(0).getMessage().
        getContent();

       // Creating a response map
        Map<String, String> responseMap = new HashMap<>();
        responseMap.put("content", content);

       return responseMap;
    }
}
```

Wow! That was a whole lot of code to write. Now, to see the fruits of your hard work, let's start the application and make a `curl` request to see it working.

```
curl -X POST "http://localhost:8080/api/chat" -H "Content-Type:
application/json" -d '{"userMessage": "Hello!"}'

{"content":"Hello! How can I assist you today?"}
```

Conclusion

In this chapter, you grasped the fundamental principles of dealing with large language models by using Java and Spring Boot. You started by exploring the relevance of OpenAI, its contributions to the evolution of innovative LLMs, and the transformative potential of tools such as GPT-4 and GPT-4o. Knowing OpenAI's development helps us to frame your practical investigation of creating an LLM-based application.

Then you created your first Spring Boot application to interact with the potent models of OpenAI. You investigated the OpenAI Chat API and discovered how to properly create API requests and manage responses. You developed several components step-by-step, starting from defining POJOs to building a service class that connects with the OpenAI API. Lastly, you combined it all in a RESTful controller to make the interaction available via a basic endpoint. The code structure lets you easily ask and get answers from the LLM, thus offering a versatile and extendable solution for next development.

You also explored several important facets of interacting with LLMs—such as tokens, usage, and how timely engineering shapes the results you obtain. This knowledge helped you to acquire a useful sense of how LLMs ingest inputs and generate outputs as well as how those map to API calls. Like CPU or bandwidth use in cloud architecture, you found that the main indicators to control LLM use are token limits and consumption.

This chapter was essentially about learning by doing—using theoretical knowledge in hands-on projects. You can now extend your abilities to work with other LLMs and have the basis required to engage properly with OpenAI's API. The next chapters will be a stepping stone derived from this pragmatic experience.

Remember that working with LLMs is always changing, much like software ecosystems are—they evolve, adapt, and grow often. As you advance, stay inquisitive, keep experimenting, and keep learning. Having these foundations in place helps you to tackle more complex ideas, hence increasing your capacity to create intelligent applications driven by LLMs. Let's keep traveling into the realm of Gen AI!

CHAPTER 3

The Transformer Saga—From Attention to Fine-Tuning

The goal of this chapter is for you to understand the fundamental structure behind large language models (LLMs), which are transformers.

Introduction

Large language models have brought about a new paradigm shift in today's world. They have abilities to generate new content based on their foundational training on huge amounts of data. This data is multimodal, meaning in different formats like text, image, audio, videos, etc. This enables the LLMs to respond in different formats too. They are generally deep neural networks that have trained on massive amounts of data. Internally through this training the networks are able to understand the different patterns of the underlying data used for their training.

With this training, they are able to perform multiple tasks like content generation, question answering, summarization, and multiple other tasks. In this chapter, we will delve into the transformer architecture, which is the fundamental building block for LLMs and the history that led to it. It delves a bit into the theory part of LLMs and their technical history. If you choose to skip this chapter, this won't affect the skills needed to build generative AI applications using Java.

S. K. Sahu, *Generative AI-Driven Application Development with Java*,
https://doi.org/10.1007/979-8-8688-1609-3_3

Importance of LLMs

If you have any knowledge of state-of-the-art natural language processing (NLP) techniques, you know they are focused on solving a particular problem like entity extraction or language translation, but not both. This is where LLMs are the current state-of-the-art content-trained models that are able to process content in multiple formats and achieve multiple tasks like content generation, question answering, summarization, and language translation, all through the same single LLM. This is truly a revolution. LLMs are a general foundation model but capable of performing multiple kinds of tasks.

These models can be trained on domain-specific data to make them more oriented toward a particular task. They can also be trained or asked to reply in a certain style or perform activities in which they were not previously trained to by leveraging the art of prompt engineering, tuning the creativity level through temperature variation. As LLMs are evolving, their maximum token process capability has been improving, making them suitable for more content processing.

There are also techniques that you will learn about that create a fine-grained smaller model that can perform on a similar if a bit reduced level as compared to the larger models. It is still fast when loading, processing, and running on cheaper commodity central processing units (CPUs), if not graphical processing units (GPUs), thus bringing about the era of small language models. You will learn more about some of these in the coming sections.

It's interesting to use LLMs to build applications and see them performing these tasks with such ease for that previously you might have needed an expert team of specialized machine learning engineers. You might wonder how they work, though. The white paper "Attention is all you need" by Google is the foundation of all LLMs (`https://arxiv.org/abs/1706.03762`). It's an interesting read and recommended for everyone who wants to learn how LLMs work.

How Large Language Models Work

Think of a giant friendly teddy bear who has spent years listening to every bedtime story, song, and joke it could find. All those words and sentences are now squished inside its fluffy head like millions of colorful story blocks. When you ask the bear a question or start telling it a half-finished tale, it reaches into that big pile of blocks, remembers all the patterns it heard (like how "happily" often comes after "ever"), and quickly snaps together the next words that make the most sense. It isn't magic or real thinking; it's more like a super-fast guessing game based on everything it has heard before. Because the teddy bear has listened to *so* many stories, its guesses usually come out sounding just like something a person would say, whether you want a joke, an answer, or a brand-new bedtime adventure.

In essence, this is how a large language model functions. It predicts the probabilities of a sequence of words in its vocabulary. Typically, when a fragment of text is supplied, a language model estimates the likelihood of each possible next word.

Let's review step-by-step how an LLM strings a sentence together, shown as a numbered sequence of mini decisions. We'll use the starter phrase **"The tallest animal on Earth is..."** to keep things concrete.

Here are the steps:

1. **Read the starter words.**

   The model turns each word—"The," "tallest," "animal," "on," "Earth," "is"—into numbers it can process (called *tokens*).

2. **Look back at everything so far.**

   Inside the model, an "attention" mechanism lets every word peek at every other word in the prefix, so it fully understands the topic (size ➤ animal ➤ Earth).

3. **Guess the next word.**

   Based on patterns it learned during training, the model produces a probability list for the very next token.

   Example distribution:

   - "giraffe" → **0.65**
   - "elephant" → 0.10
   - "building" → 0.02
   - "pizza" → 0.01

4. **Pick (or sample) the winner.**

   Most decoding methods choose the word with the highest probability ("giraffe") or sample from the top few choices to keep things varied.

5. **Attach the chosen word.**

   The sentence now reads: "The tallest animal on Earth is **giraffe**..."

6. **Loop with the new context.**

   The model feeds the updated sentence back into itself, recalculates attention, and guesses the *next* token.

   New distribution for token after "giraffe":

   - "." (period) → **0.50**
   - "the" → 0.25
   - "and" → 0.05

7. **Decide whether to finish.**

   Selecting the period ends the sentence:

   "The tallest animal on Earth is giraffe."

8. **If not finished, keep going.**

   Had the model picked "the," it would continue the cycle—re-evaluating context, producing another probability list, selecting a word, and so on—until it reaches a natural stopping point or a preset length limit.

In short, an LLM forms a sentence by **repeatedly** glancing at all the words it has so far, computing probabilities for what comes next, and committing to one token at a time until it decides the thought is complete.

Transformer

Imagine a big box of story blocks where each block is a word and, hovering over it, is a super-helpful robot called a transformer that builds sentences and stories. It spreads all the blocks out and looks at everything at once so it can spot which words belong together—just like noticing that "ice" usually sits near "cream." Then its magic sparkles of **attention** light up the words that matter most—so when it sees "dog," it points to "fluffy," "barks," and "tail," never confusing the pup with a "hot dog.". Next, the robot stacks layer upon layer of thinking caps, each one re-examining the sentence and adding a dose of extra cleverness, like building a taller and smarter LEGO tower. After all that thinking, it picks the next best word block and lines up the story so it sounds exactly right, whether it's finishing your sentence, answering a question, or inventing a bedtime tale. In short, the transformer is a super-fast story-building robot that sees all the words together, decides which ones matter most, and piles up many tiny thoughts to say something new and helpful.

The original transformer had two components: an encoder and a decoder, as shown in Figure 3-1. Imagine the transformer is asked to turn the Italian sentence **"Il gatto dorme sul divano"** ("The cat is sleeping on the couch") into English.

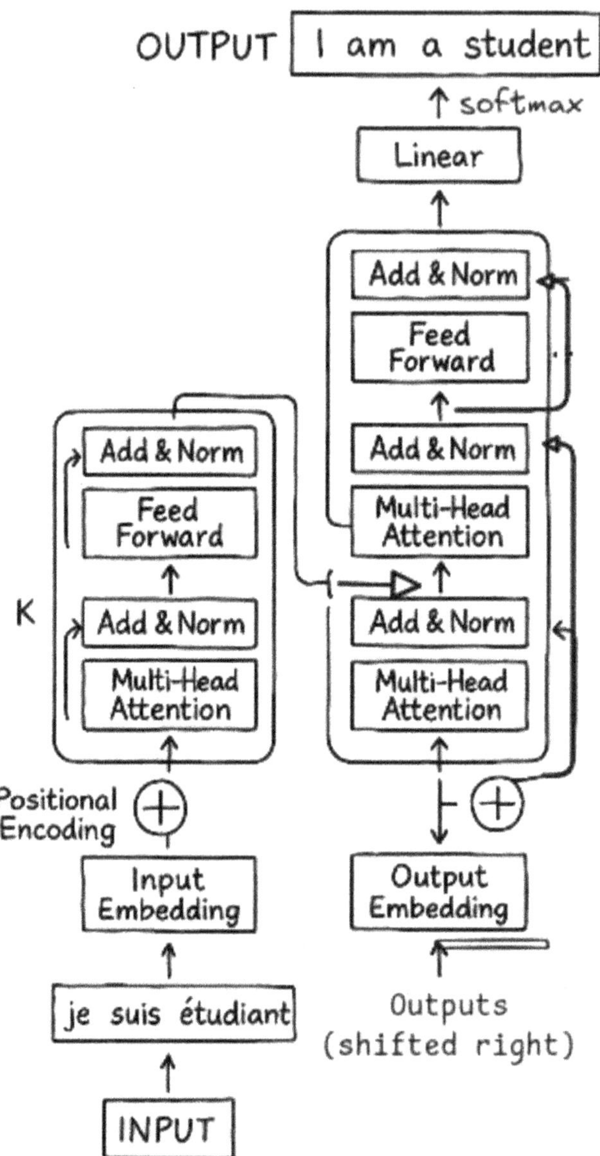

***Figure 3-1.** Original transformer architecture*

Let's decode how it does the job step-by-step to understand the process:

1. **Encoder, the super listener:**

   First, the model "hears" the Italian words *Il gatto dorme sul divano* and changes each one into tiny number blocks it understands. All the encoder layers peek at the whole sentence at once and notice the important links—like that **"gatto"** (cat) is the thing doing **"dorme"** (sleeping). When it finishes listening, it isn't holding Italian words anymore—just a neat bundle that captures the meaning of "cat…sleeping…couch."

2. **Decoder, the careful talker:**

   Next, the decoder grabs that bundle of meaning and starts speaking English, one word at a time. It thinks, "Given what I know, which English word should come first?" It picks **"The."** Then it looks again at the meaning plus the word it just said and chooses the next one, **"cat,"** and then **"is," "sleeping," "on," "the,"** and **"couch."** After every new word, its little attention sparkles double-check that the sentence still matches the original idea.

3. **Layers, stacks of thinking caps:**

   Both the encoder and decoder consist of many identical layers—like stacking lots of thinking caps. Each cap adds a sprinkle of extra smarts, catching details such as the order of "on the couch" so the English comes out naturally.

4. **Why it works for any language:**

   Because the encoder stores only pure meaning and the decoder worries only about saying that meaning in the target language, you can swap Italian for Spanish, Japanese, or even emoji sentences—as long as the model has seen enough example pairs to learn from.

So, in simple words, the transformer **listens** to the whole Italian sentence, **packs** its meaning into a tidy bundle, and then **speaks** the English sentence one word at a time—always checking itself—until it proudly says: **"The cat is sleeping on the couch."**

Evolution of Transformers

Since the release of the 2017 paper *"Attention Is All You Need"*, transformers have undergone a rapid evolution, centered around three main trends: scaling up, becoming more efficient, and specializing for different use cases (see Figure 3-2). Much of this innovation has been fueled by the rise of open-source models and the continued contributions from leading research labs like OpenAI.

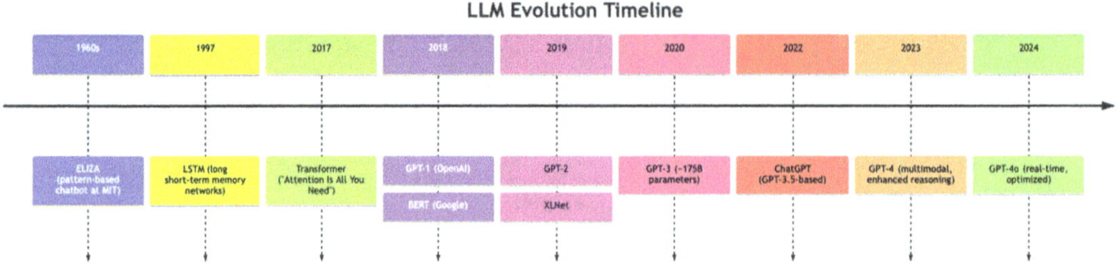

Figure 3-2. *LLM evolution timeline*

Among open-source models, Meta's LLaMA series has been a key driver. LLaMA 1 surprised the community by delivering near-GPT-3 performance with just 7 billion parameters. LLaMA 2 extended the context window to 4,096 tokens, improved quality with more training data, and introduced commercially usable models. With LLaMA 3, Meta scaled even further—offering up to 128,000-token context, better safety alignment, and quantized builds that can run on edge devices, making powerful language models more accessible and efficient.

Another standout is Mistral's Mixtral 8×7B, which uses a *Mixture of Experts* architecture. Instead of running the full 47 billion parameters, the model routes each token through only two expert networks, activating just 13 billion parameters per inference. This gives it top-tier performance—comparable to much larger models—while keeping latency low and making local deployment practical.

OpenAI has pushed the frontier in a different direction: explicit reasoning and planning. Its o1 model family is designed not just to generate fluent language, but to plan answers step-by-step using reinforcement learning. This approach has led to state-of-the-art results in math, science, and programming, where thoughtful, multistep reasoning matters more than surface-level fluency.

Another major contributor is DeepSeek, which takes a novel approach to self-improvement. Its DeepSeek-R1 model achieves competitive performance without relying heavily on large, labeled datasets. Instead, it uses a training technique called *group relative policy optimization*—allowing the model to evaluate and refine its own outputs iteratively. This self-training approach improves both quality and efficiency, pushing boundaries in reasoning and generalization with minimal human supervision.

Beyond these leaders, many organizations are contributing to a fast-growing open ecosystem. Releases like Alibaba's Qwen 1.5, 01. ai's Yi, xAI's Grok 3, NVIDIA's NVLM, and Databricks' DBRX are extending context windows to hundreds of thousands—or even a million—tokens, adding support for multimodal inputs, and experimenting with compressed formats like 4-bit quantization to make models lighter and faster.

Together, these developments show a clear shift in direction. It's no longer just about building massive models; it's about building smarter, more efficient, and more accessible ones. Whether through better reasoning, smaller deployment footprints, or open licensing, the Transformer architecture continues to adapt and lead. With innovation now thriving not just in closed labs but across the open-source community, the future of transformers looks more collaborative, capable, and inclusive than ever.

Fine-Tuning LLMs

After an LLM is trained on massive amounts of general text during pretraining, it gains a solid grasp of language and can perform a variety of tasks through prompting. However, to make it truly useful, safe, or specialized for certain applications, it often needs fine-tuning—a second stage of training that adapts the base model to behave in more specific, controlled, or helpful ways. This section introduces the most common fine-tuning techniques and how they work.

Supervised Fine-Tuning

Supervised fine-tuning (SFT) is the most direct approach. In this method, the model is trained on carefully curated, labeled examples that demonstrate how it should behave. Each training example typically consists of a prompt and the correct response—such as a question and its answer, a document and its summary, or an instruction and the desired output. This teaches the model to follow specific tasks more accurately. SFT is especially useful for making the model follow instructions, generate consistent outputs, or understand domain-specific data. While it's less costly than pretraining, it still requires significant computing if applied across the entire model.

Dialogue and Instruction Tuning

Two common SFT use cases are instruction tuning, where the model learns to follow complex tasks like summarizing, writing, or coding from instructions, and dialogue tuning, where it's trained on conversational question-answer pairs. Dialogue tuning is essential for building chatbots or virtual assistants that can carry on multiturn conversations naturally and coherently.

Safety Tuning

To reduce harmful, biased, or toxic outputs, models can be fine-tuned using safety-focused datasets. This includes filtering harmful data, using human reviews, and incorporating explicit rules during training. Safety tuning ensures that the model avoids offensive or unethical content and behaves more responsibly in sensitive scenarios.

Reinforcement Learning from Human Feedback

Reinforcement Learning from Human Feedback (RLHF) is a powerful method used after SFT to make the model's responses align more closely with human preferences. Instead of only learning from good examples (like in SFT), RLHF also teaches the model what *not* to do by penalizing undesired responses. The process involves training a reward model using human feedback—where humans compare two model responses and indicate which one is better. The LLM is then further trained using this reward model and reinforcement learning techniques, improving qualities like helpfulness, truthfulness, and safety.

Parameter-Efficient Fine-Tuning

Full model fine-tuning (PEFT) is often computationally expensive. PEFT techniques reduce the cost by training only a small set of additional parameters while keeping the original model mostly frozen. These methods make it easier to adapt models to new tasks without retraining everything from scratch.

- **Adapter-based fine-tuning**: Small trainable modules (adapters) are added between layers of the model. Only these adapters are trained, significantly reducing memory and compute usage.
- **Low-rank adaptation (LoRA)**: Instead of updating the entire weight matrix, LoRA uses two small matrices to adjust the model. It's efficient, is easy to swap in and out, and can be combined with quantization for even more savings (e.g., QLoRA).
- **Soft prompting**: Instead of changing the model, this technique learns a few artificial prompt tokens (vectors) that steer the model's behavior. It's extremely light-weight—sometimes using just a handful of tokens—while enabling flexible task conditioning.

While full fine-tuning still offers the highest performance, PEFT techniques strike a strong balance between quality, speed, and cost, making them ideal for many real-world applications. Together, these methods allow developers to refine large models into more focused, friendly, and functional tools.

Inference Optimization Techniques

Once an LLM is trained and fine-tuned, optimizing its inference—how it generates outputs in real time—is crucial for making it efficient, fast, and cost-effective. This section summarizes key inference optimization methods, categorized by their approach and impact, and explains how they help reduce latency and resource consumption while maintaining or improving model quality.

Quantization

What it is: Reduces the precision of model weights and activations (e.g., from 32-bit to 8-bit), making computations lighter and faster.

Variants:

- **Post-training quantization**: Applied after training, mainly for inference.
- **Quantization-aware training (QAT)**: Incorporates quantization during training, allowing the model to adapt to the lower precision and recover quality.

  Why it helps: Speeds up inference and lowers memory usage, especially useful when balancing cost and quality.

Distillation

What it is: Trains a smaller model (student) to mimic a larger model (teacher), improving the student's performance without full-scale training.

Types of distillation:

- **Data distillation**: Uses a large model to generate synthetic data to train the smaller model.
- **Knowledge distillation**: Aligns the output distributions (e.g., token probabilities) of the student with those of the teacher for better efficiency.
- **On-policy distillation**: In reinforcement learning setups, the student learns from the teacher's evaluations of its own outputs.

  Why it helps: Allows deployment of smaller, faster models while retaining most of the accuracy of larger models.

Output-Preserving Optimizations

What it is: Techniques that reduce inference time without altering the model's output in any way.

Key methods:

- **FlashAttention**: Rewrites attention computation to reduce memory traffic between slower and faster memory in GPUs/TPUs. Achieves 2–4× speedups without changing the result.
- **Prefix Caching**: Stores intermediate computation (KV cache) from previous inputs so they don't have to be recalculated in multiturn conversations or repeated prompts.

  Why it helps: These methods are risk-free optimizations—perfect for reducing latency without any trade-off in output quality.

Speculative Decoding

What it is: Uses a smaller model (drafter) to predict several tokens ahead and then has the main model verify them in parallel.

How it works: The main model doesn't blindly trust the drafter—it checks the predictions token by token and accepts only the verified outputs.

Why it helps: Significantly speeds up the slow, step-by-step decoding phase of LLMs without sacrificing output correctness.

Batching and Parallelization

What it is: Classic software optimization strategies adapted for LLMs to boost throughput.

- **Batching**: Combines multiple requests so they can be processed simultaneously on the same hardware. Particularly effective during the decode phase.
- **Parallelization**: Distributes the model across multiple machines or hardware cores using techniques like tensor parallelism, pipeline parallelism, or sequence parallelism.

  Why it helps: Maximizes hardware usage and accelerates response time, though careful design is needed to manage communication overhead between devices.

Category	Key Benefit	Typical Use Case
Quantization	Smaller, faster models	Edge deployment, memory-constrained environments
Distillation	Compresses model size with minimal quality loss	Lightweight chatbots, mobile apps
Output-Preserving	Fast, safe latency reduction	Enterprise LLMs, chat apps, document Q&A
Speculative Decoding	Parallelizes sequential steps	Real-time assistants, search
Batching & Parallelization	Throughput and latency improvements	High-volume API servers, model serving platforms

Together, these techniques allow LLMs to respond faster, run more efficiently, and scale across different hardware and user needs—all without compromising the integrity of the model's outputs.

Conclusion

In this chapter, you journeyed through the foundation of today's most advanced AI systems—transformers, the architecture at the heart of all large language models . You explored their structure, the groundbreaking innovation of self-attention, and how they evolved into the scalable, multimodal giants used today. From understanding how transformers predict and generate language to tracing the rapid evolution of models like GPT, LLaMA, Gemini, and Mixtral, we saw how the field has shifted from building just large models to making them *efficient*, *safe*, and *adaptable*.

You also examined the vital role of fine-tuning, where pretrained models are tailored to follow instructions, engage in dialogue, or behave more safely—often using advanced techniques like RLHF or lightweight methods like LoRA and soft prompting. Finally, you looked at how inference optimization ensures these powerful models can run affordably and in real time, whether on cloud servers or mobile devices.

In essence, transformers aren't just a technical marvel—they are the engine powering the current AI revolution. Understanding their mechanics, history, and practical adaptations equips you with the context to better design, optimize, or simply appreciate the intelligence behind today's generative AI. While you don't need to master these details to build applications using Java, having this foundational knowledge makes you a more informed and capable developer in this rapidly evolving landscape.

The next chapter covers self-hosting LLMs using Ollama.

CHAPTER 4

Bring Your Own Model: Self-Hosting with Ollama

This chapter guides you through the process of setting up a locally hosted large language models (LLMs)/small language models (SLMs), which you can use to test your applications.

Introduction

In Chapter 2, you learned how to integrate your applications with OpenAI APIs to drive results using prompt engineering. When using OpenAI APIs, there is always a case of vendor lock-in. In the world of software engineering, we have all been exposed to open-source alternatives that are best of breed. The more choice, the better in terms of developer friendliness, flexibility, and ability to choose what works best for you. There is also the cost aspect of it where you are charged on a per-usage basis for your requests. In this case, self-hosting in a cloud environment may make better sense in your context. Finally, there is the aspect of privacy. We all have concerns as to how our application data and user/customer data is being used by OpenAI. There are containerized versions of OpenAI plans that allow different customers to leverage the same APIs without them being used to train their internal models, so you always have to be cognizant of this. This is where applications like Ollama come into use to democratize Generative AI (Gen AI) hosting without being locked in or being dependent on a particular vendor.

In this chapter, you will learn about Ollama and what self-hosting an LLM means. You will install Ollama and use it to run an LLM on your local computer. All this does not make sense if you have to change your APIs and their request format since you have

S. K. Sahu, *Generative AI-Driven Application Development with Java*,
https://doi.org/10.1007/979-8-8688-1609-3_4

already integrated OpenAI APIs into your integration. Worry not, this is where the APIs exposed by Ollama come into picture. They are compliant with OpenAI APIs, meaning your application works as it is now with no change.

Self-Hosting LLMs

Running LLM models locally on your own hardware under self-hosting LLMs offers advantages including increased control over the models, more privacy, and less dependency on cloud services. Choosing the appropriate model comes first in order to get going.

Popular options for self-hosting are BERT or T5 in addition to GPT-based versions like GPT-2 or GPT-Neo. Given that larger models—such as GPT-3—demand far more powerful technology than smaller variants like GPT-2, the model size is a major consideration. Another important consideration is meeting the hardware needs. Usually, running LLMs efficiently calls for a high-performance GPU—especially for bigger models. For simple chores or smaller models, a good CPU could be enough. Regarding memory and storage, big models can call for significant resources; some models need tens or even hundreds of gigabytes of random access memory (RAM). For really big models, cloud services or specialized hardware—such as servers with many GPUs—may be required.

Locally running the model will require machine learning frameworks including TensorFlow, PyTorch, or Hugging Face Transformers, which provide the required infrastructure for model deployment. The model can be contained using Docker, therefore streamlining the installation and administration process. Furthermore, helping to lower memory use and raise the general model efficiency are optimization methods including mixed precision (FP16) and model quantization.

Quantization involves converting model weights from high-precision formats like 32-bit floats to lower-precision types such as 8-bit integers. For example, a weight of 0.865 in float32 might be approximated as 111 on the int8 scale, using a simple mapping function. While this introduces minor accuracy trade-offs, it significantly reduces the model's memory footprint and computational cost. We'll explore quantization in more detail with hands-on examples in a subsequent chapter.

Once the model is operational, you can expose its features by means of an API, therefore facilitating a simple interface with other programs or users. For inference jobs, a REST or gRPC API can be configured using well-known frameworks such as Spring or FastAPI or Flask. Creating a web app using tools like Streamlit or Gradio is a terrific way if you're seeking a more user-friendly interface.

Still, self-hosting has some expenses. Particularly if you use high-performance GPUs, initial hardware expenditures can be really large. Particularly in systems running continually, operational expenses like electricity for running the hardware and cooling systems can also mount up. Another continuous responsibility is maintaining the infrastructure supporting hardware and software. Having said that, the main benefit of self-hosting is data privacy. By executing the model locally, you have complete control over the data and therefore lower the dangers connected with using outside cloud solutions. Strong security measures, like encryption and API key authentication, will be necessary, though, should you expose the model to the Internet via an API to guarantee the system is protected from harmful usage.

Self-hosting LLMs can be aided using several tools and frameworks. One such solution that streamlines the local operation of LLMs and provides an easy-to-use interface for model deployment and management is Ollama. Pretrained models and an inference API also come from Hugging Face, which would be helpful for local or cloud server deployment. Excellent substitutes for more costly models like GPT-3 and fit for self-hosting are open-source models including GPT-Neo, GPT-J, and GPT-2. Appropriate for implementation in resource-limited contexts, Meta's LLaMA models are another open-source solution that strikes performance and resource balance. That said, self-hosting big models presents difficulties including hardware restrictions, maintaining current software, and infrastructure scaling for several users or high-demand programs. Effectively running LLMs at scale depends on balancing these difficulties.

Ollama

Ollama is a platform and tool for running small and large language models locally on your own machine. It allows users to implement LLMs for tasks like text generation, summarization, and other AI-driven language tasks, without needing to rely on cloud-based services. This can offer benefits like increased privacy, faster response times, and the ability to work offline.

Ollama typically provides an easy interface to interact with models like GPT-style models, enabling you to integrate and experiment with these models in a more localized, controlled environment. It's designed to be simple to set up and use, and it supports various models that can be downloaded and run directly on our computer.

Privacy is one of the most compelling reasons to run models locally. When data never leaves your device or controlled infrastructure, the risk of it being intercepted, logged, or used for model training by third-party vendors is significantly reduced. This is especially critical for sensitive domains like healthcare, finance, and legal services. However, privacy is only as strong as the security mechanisms in place, and local deployments must be secured to ensure data protection.

To help safeguard against unauthorized access, Ollama can be configured with several best-practice security measures:

- Bind APIs to localhost by default, preventing remote access unless explicitly configured otherwise.
- If remote access is needed (e.g., across a local network or for team collaboration), network-level protections such as firewalls or VPNs should be used.
- Reverse proxies (e.g., NGINX or Traefik) can be deployed with HTTPS and basic auth or token-based authentication to protect public-facing endpoints.
- Ollama itself can integrate with authentication layers, and additional middleware can enforce rate-limiting and access control policies.

These mechanisms give developers confidence that their private data stays private, even when models are accessed via local APIs.

Alternatives to Ollama

While Ollama offers a streamlined and developer-friendly experience, it's not the only option available for self-hosting LLMs. Table 4-1 compares the different platforms.

***Table 4-1.** Ollama Alternatives*

Platform	Highlights
LM Studio	Best GUI-based desktop app. Great for nondevelopers, with model discovery and a chat interface; model interaction remains local and private.
Text-generation-webui	A full-featured web interface supporting multiple backend engines (transformers, llama.cpp, etc.) and extensive customization options.
GPT4All	A beginner-friendly app focused on local chat experiences; highly polished desktop application.
LocalAI	A drop-in OpenAI API replacement enabling flexible local model serving for developers.
vLLM	High-throughput inference engine optimized for handling concurrent requests at scale.
OpenLLM	Provides OpenAI-compatible APIs, Docker/Kubernetes integrations, optimized inference backends, and enterprise deployment tooling.
Llama.cpp	Low-level C/C++ inference engine with fine-grained control, advanced quantization (2-bit to 8-bit), multi-hardware support, and OpenAI-compatible server via llama-server.
Llamafile	Combines llama.cpp + model into a single portable executable; significantly faster prompt handling—30% to 500% speed gain over llama.cpp in many cases.

Why choose Ollama?

- It's exceptionally easy to set up with command-line simplicity.
- Great cross-platform support, especially on macOS.
- Active model support and default privacy-first behavior.

Why consider others?

- For a rich graphical interface, LM Studio or GPT4All may be better suited (especially for nontechnical users).

- For production-grade serving or high concurrency, OpenLLM or vLLM offer enhanced scalability and integrations.
- Developers needing deep backend flexibility or OpenAI API emulation might prefer LocalAI or text-generation-webui.

Installing Ollama

Ollama can be installed on macOS, Linux, and Windows. This section goes through the steps for each of them. Always make sure to check the Ollama downloads documentation page at `https://ollama.com/download` to refer to the latest information.

Installing Ollama on macOS:

Ollama provides DMG packages that can be downloaded and then installed. The steps are self-explanatory to follow through. The package can be downloaded by visiting `https://ollama.com/download/Ollama-darwin.zip`. It requires macOS 11 Big Sur or later. The package size is approximately around 180MB to download. Unzip it once downloaded.

As shown in Figure 4-1, Ollama starts up, and the system instructs you if you should move it to the `Applications` folder first and then start the installation process. In our case, you can choose Do Not Move and proceed. See Figure 4-2.

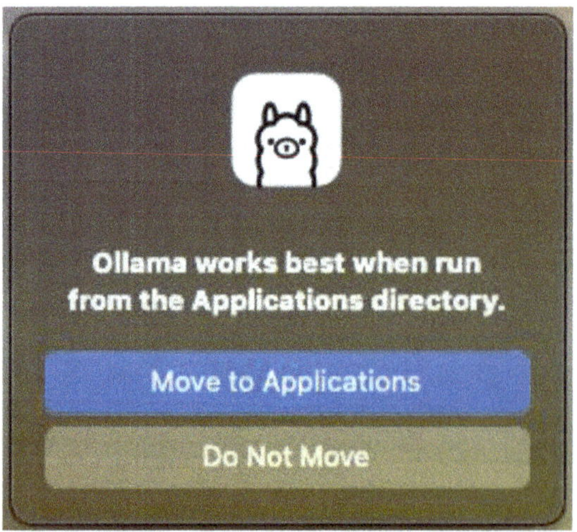

Figure 4-1. *Starting Ollama for the first time after downloading*

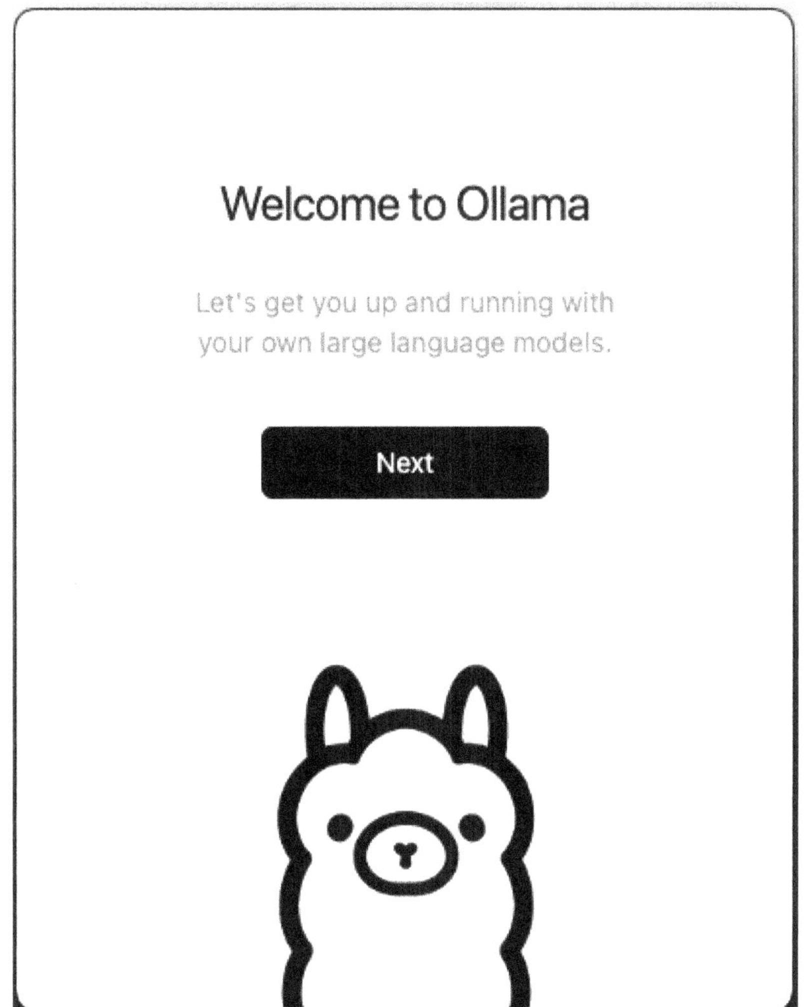

Figure 4-2. *Starting Ollama*

Ollama now starts up, and you can click Next to proceed to installing the command line, as shown in Figure 4-3. Once this is installed, you can open a terminal and run the `ollama` command to see output similar to what you saw in the "Installing Ollama in Linux" section.

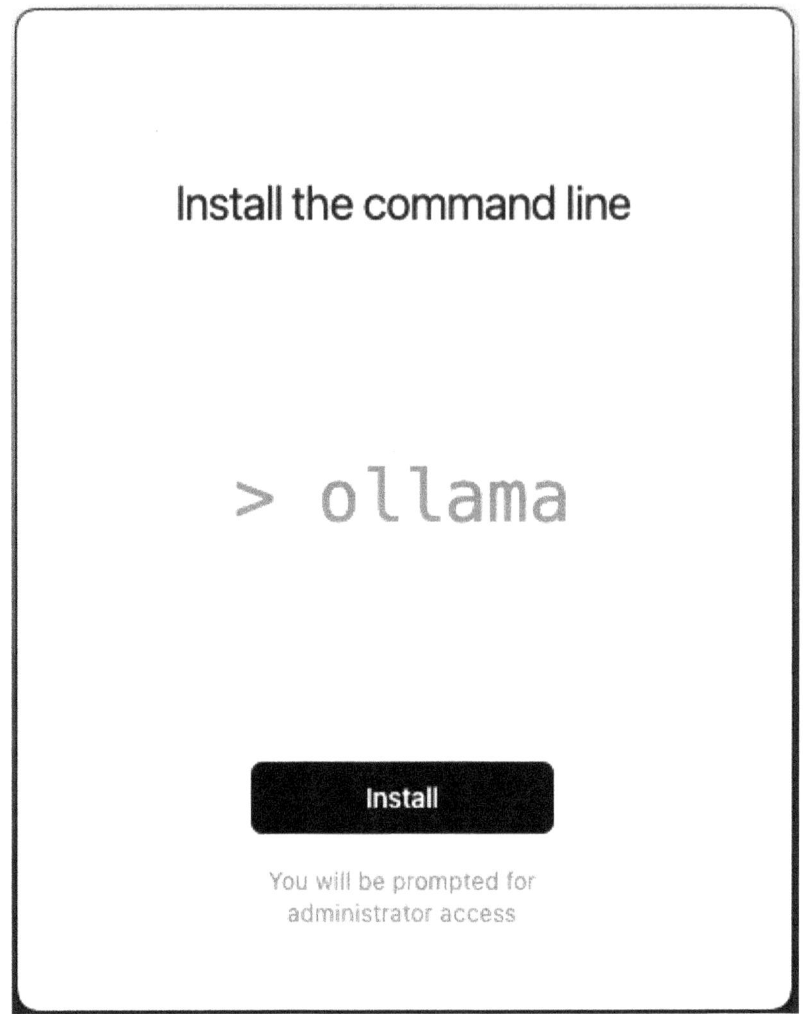

Figure 4-3. *Installing Ollama*

Installing Ollama in Windows:

Ollama provides Windows executable that can be downloaded and then installed. The steps are self-explanatory to follow through. The executable can be downloaded by visiting `https://ollama.com/download/OllamaSetup.exe`. The download size is approximately 745 MB, and the version downloaded is 0.5.7. Once it is downloaded, run the executable, which should guide you to Figure 4-4 to install Ollama.

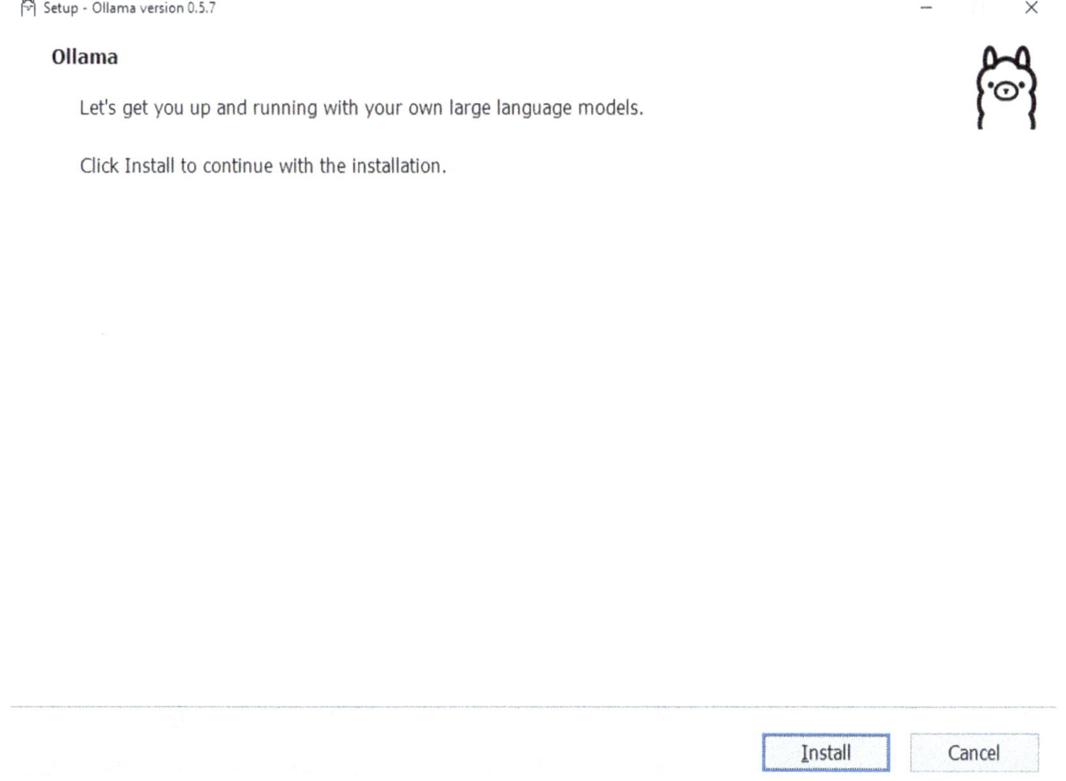

Figure 4-4. *Ollama installation window*

Proceed by clicking the Install button to start the installation, as shown in Figure 4-5.

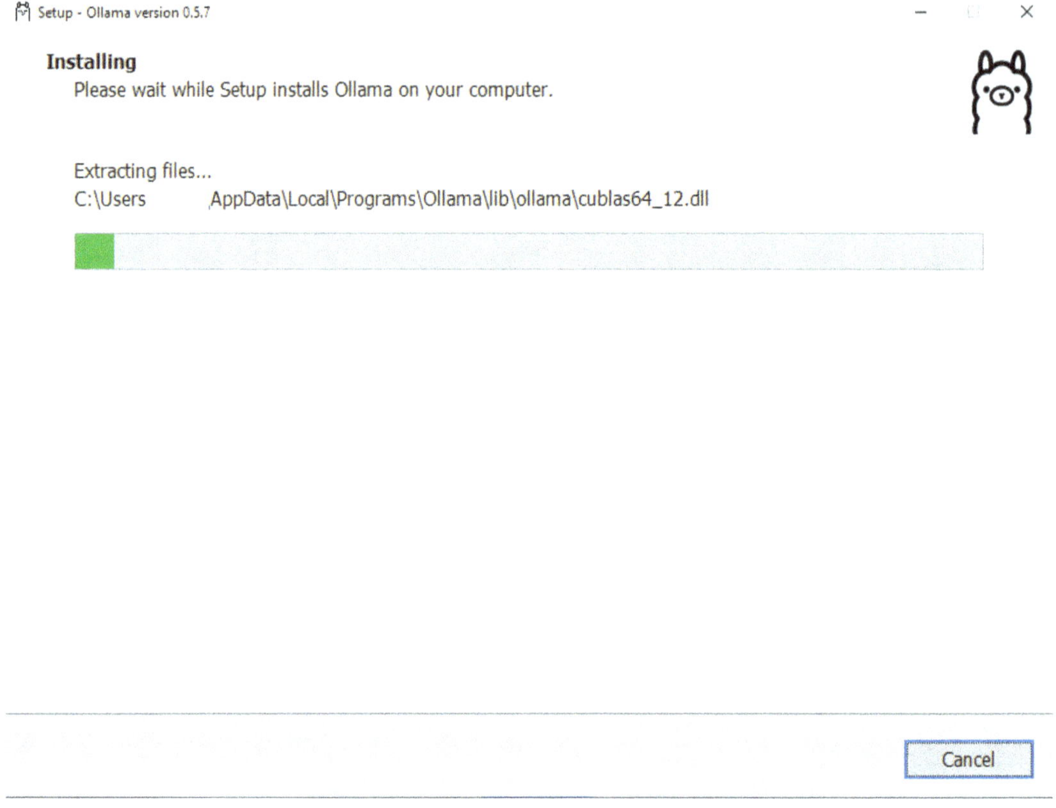

Figure 4-5. *Installing Ollama*

Once the installation is complete, an Ollama icon will pop up in the bottom-right task bar. Right-click it to see logs or exit Ollama. Open a command prompt or PowerShell and run the `ollama` command to see it in effect.

```
ollama
```

Output:

```
C:\Users\username>ollama

Usage:
 ollama [flags]
 ollama [command]

Available Commands:
 serve      Start ollama
 create     Create a model from a Modelfile
```

```
 show       Show information for a model
 run        Run a model
 stop       Stop a running model
 pull       Pull a model from a registry
 push       Push a model to a registry
 list       List models
 ps         List running models
 cp         Copy a model
 rm         Remove a model
 help       Help about any command

Flags:
 -h, --help     help for ollama
 -v, --version   Show version information

Use "ollama [command] --help" for more information about a command.
```

Installing Ollama in Linux:

Ollama can be installed in Linux by running the following `curl` command in a terminal. Make sure you have sudo permissions on the system since it will prompt for your password to install it to the `/usr/local` directory. It will then start downloading the Linux bundle specific to your system architecture, which in my case was amd64. It will try to detect the GPU to see if it can leverage it. If not, it works in CPU-only mode, which is good in this case.

```
curl -fsSL https://ollama.com/install.sh | sh
```

Output:

```
>>> Installing ollama to /usr/local

[sudo] password for <PLACEHOLDER_FOR_YOUR_SYSTEM_USERNAME>:

###################################################################### 100.0%

>>> Creating ollama user...
>>> Adding ollama user to render group...
>>> Adding ollama user to video group...
>>> Adding current user to ollama group...
>>> Creating ollama systemd service...
>>> Enabling and starting ollama service...
```

```
Created symlink /etc/systemd/system/default.target.wants/ollama.service →
/etc/systemd/system/ollama.service.
>>> The Ollama API is now available at 127.0.0.1:11434.
>>> Install complete. Run "ollama" from the command line.
WARNING: No NVIDIA/AMD GPU detected. Ollama will run in CPU-only mode.
```

As you can see in the output toward the end, it shares some information about the Ollama API being exposed at 127.0.0.1:11434. We will come back to this part in the "Exploring the APIs exposed by Ollama" section. This marks the completion of installing Ollama.

You can now type `ollama` in the terminal to see its usage and commands available.

```
ollama
```

Output:

```
Usage:
 ollama [flags]
  ollama [command]

Available Commands:
  serve       Start ollama
  create      Create a model from a Modelfile
  show        Show information for a model
  run         Run a model
  stop        Stop a running model
  pull        Pull a model from a registry
  push        Push a model to a registry
  list        List models
  ps          List running models
  cp          Copy a model
  rm          Remove a model
  help        Help about any command

Flags:
  -h, --help     help for ollama
  -v, --version   Show version information

Use "ollama [command] --help" for more information about a command.
```

Running a Locally Hosted LLM

Ollama provides hosting and running different open-source SLM/LLM models. The list keeps changing based on the recent developments, and it's quite fast. At this moment, visiting the models page at `https://ollama.com/search` shows the models in Figure 4-6 at first glance ordered by popularity.

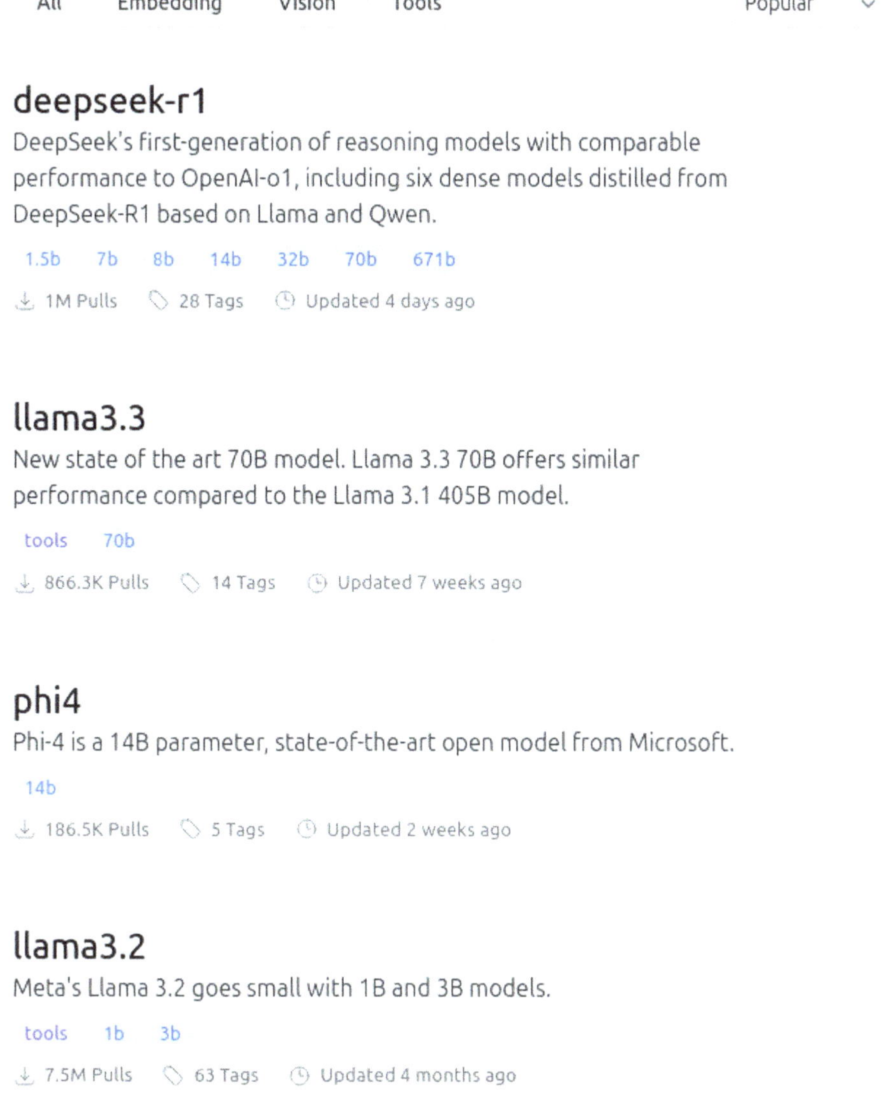

Figure 4-6. *SLM/LLM models ordered by popularity*

Let's explore the information shared here for a moment (see Figure 4-7).

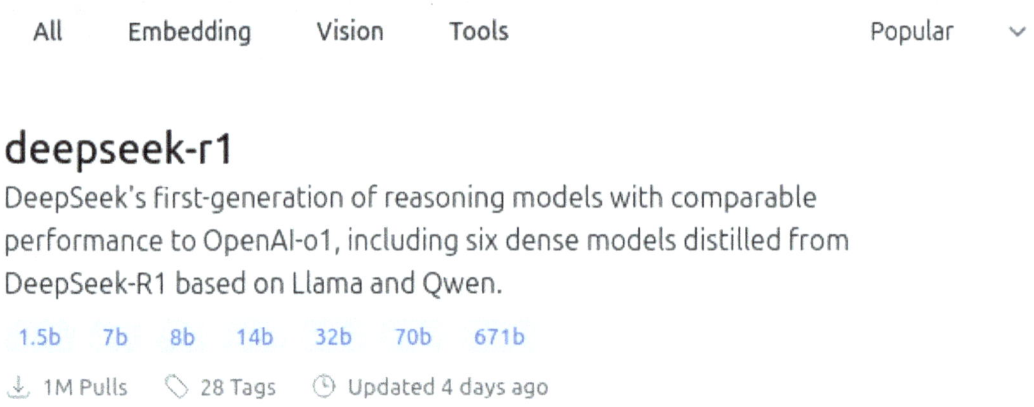

All Embedding Vision Tools Popular

deepseek-r1

DeepSeek's first-generation of reasoning models with comparable performance to OpenAI-o1, including six dense models distilled from DeepSeek-R1 based on Llama and Qwen.

1.5b 7b 8b 14b 32b 70b 671b

1M Pulls 28 Tags Updated 4 days ago

Figure 4-7. *deepseek-r1 model information*

As shown, the interface shares information about the category of models available, namely, All, Embedding, Vision, and Tools. You will learn more about these in future chapters. For the moment, you will work in the All category. On the right, you can order by either Popular or Newest models. For a particular model, it shares the name, which in this case is deepseek-r1, followed by a description of it, and then the different model sizes available for download and experimentation. At this moment, this has been pulled for installation approximately 1 million times and was updated last four days ago.

We will try the deepseek-r1 model of 1.5b size since it's small, fast, and quick to download and run on a local machine. On top of it, it is open-source, very efficient compared to OpenAI's `o1` model, which is available only through a paid subscription and proprietary. Click the model you want to run, in this case deepseek-r1. It takes us to the library page of the model at `https://ollama.com/library/deepseek-r1` (see Figure 4-8).

deepseek-r1

DeepSeek's first-generation of reasoning models with comparable performance to OpenAI-o1, including six dense models distilled from DeepSeek-R1 based on Llama and Qwen.

1.5b 7b 8b 14b 32b 70b 671b

1M Pulls Updated 4 days ago

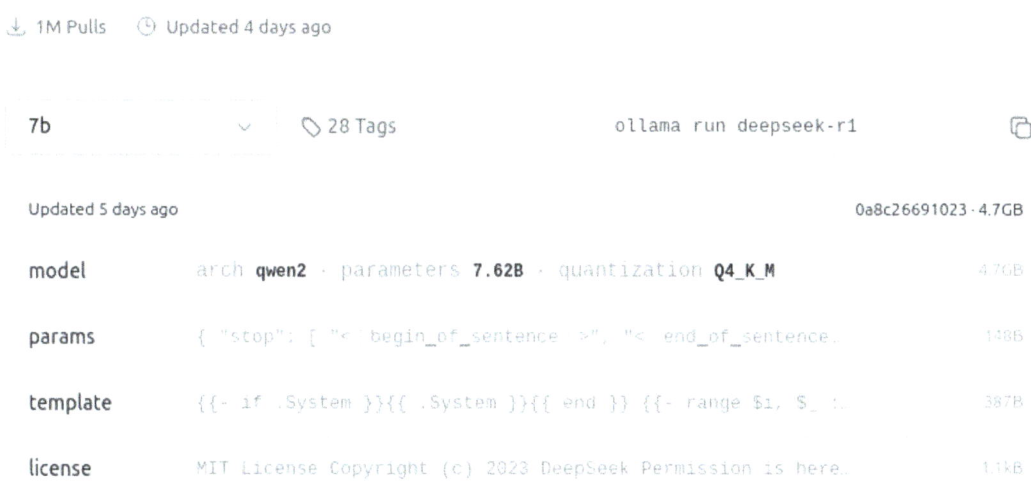

Figure 4-8. Model-specific information along with default model size and installation run command

Figure 4-9 shows some general information like the model and what architecture is based upon and the parameter size. You can click the drop-down to choose the specific model you want to run and see the command specific to it (see Figure 4-10).

1.5b

28 Tags

ollama run deepseek-r1:1.5b

Updated 5 days ago

a42b25d8c10a · 1.1GB

model arch qwen2 · parameters 1.78B · quantization Q4_K_M

params

template

license

Figure 4-9. deepseek-r1 1.5b size model information

Readme

DeepSeek's first-generation reasoning models, achieving performance comparable to OpenAI-o1 across math, code, and reasoning tasks.

Models

DeepSeek-R1

```
ollama run deepseek-r1:671b
```

Distilled models

DeepSeek team has demonstrated that the reasoning patterns of larger models can be distilled into smaller models, resulting in better performance compared to the reasoning patterns discovered through RL on small models.

Below are the models created via fine-tuning against several dense models widely used in the research community using reasoning data generated by DeepSeek-R1. The evaluation results demonstrate that the distilled smaller dense models perform exceptionally well on benchmarks.

Figure 4-10. *Model-specific information*

Figure 4-11 shows what different models are available and more documentation, which is always helpful to understand, along with license information. The license information lets you know if it can be used commercially, which is important when building applications.

License

The model weights are licensed under the MIT License. DeepSeek-R1 series support commercial use, allow for any modifications and derivative works, including, but not limited to, distillation for training other LLMs. Please note that:

The Qwen distilled models are derived from Qwen-2.5 series, which are originally licensed under Apache 2.0 License, and now finetuned with 800k samples curated with DeepSeek-R1.

The Llama 8B distilled model is derived from Llama3.1-8B-Base and is originally licensed under llama3.1 license.

The Llama 70B distilled model is derived from Llama3.3-70B-Instruct and is originally licensed under llama3.3 license.

***Figure 4-11.** License information*

Let's copy the command to run 1.5b size model.

```
ollama run deepseek-r1:1.5b
```

Output

```
pulling manifest
pulling aabd4debf0c8... 100%
|████████████████████████████████████| 1.1 GB
pulling 369ca498f347... 100%
|████████████████████████████████████|  387 B
pulling 6e4c38e1172f... 100%
████████████████████████████████████| 1.1 KB
pulling f4d24e9138dd... 100%
|████████████████████████████████████|  148 B
pulling a85fe2a2e58e... 100%
|████████████████████████████████████|  487 B

verifying sha256 digest
writing manifest
success
```

```
>>> Send a message (/? for help)
```

```
Type a prompt / query to start interacting with the deepseek model through
Ollama by saying a Hello.
```

```
>>> Hello
<think>
</think>

Hello! How can I assist you today? 😊

>>> Send a message (/? for help)
```

This specific model is meant for reasoning-based questions. Let's try one.

```
>>> solve u^2−5u−14=0

<think>
Okay, so I have this equation here: \( u^2 - 5u - 14 = 0 \). It's a
quadratic equation in terms of 'u'. Quadratic equations are pretty common
in algebra, and they usually have two solutions. Let me see how to find
those solutions.

First, I remember that for any quadratic equation in the form \( ax^2 + bx
+ c = 0 \), there is a formula called the quadratic formula that can be
used to find the roots:
\[
u = \frac{-b \pm \sqrt{b^2 - 4ac}}{2a}
\]
In this equation, 'a' is 1 (the coefficient of \( u^2 \)), 'b' is -5 (the
coefficient of 'u'), and 'c' is -14.

Let me plug these values into the quadratic formula:
\[
u = \frac{-(-5) \pm \sqrt{(-5)^2 - 4(1)(-14)}}{2(1)}
\]
Simplifying step by step:
1. Compute \( -b \): \( -(-5) = 5 \)
2. Compute \( b^2 \): \( (-5)^2 = 25 \)
3. Compute \( 4ac \): \( 4 * 1 * (-14) = -56 \)
```

```
4. Compute the discriminant (\( b^2 - 4ac \)): \( 25 - (-56) = 81 \)

Now, plug these back into the formula:
\[
u = \frac{5 \pm \sqrt{81}}{2}
\]
Since \( \sqrt{81} = 9 \), we have:
\[
u = \frac{5 \pm 9}{2}
\]

This gives us two solutions:
1. \( u = \frac{5 + 9}{2} = \frac{14}{2} = 7 \)
2. \( u = \frac{5 - 9}{2} = \frac{-4}{2} = -2 \)

So, the solutions to the equation \( u^2 - 5u - 14 = 0 \) are \( u = 7 \)
and \( u = -2 \).

To verify, let's plug these values back into the original equation:
1. For \( u = 7 \):
\[
(7)^2 - 5(7) - 14 = 49 - 35 - 14 = 0
\]
2. For \( u = -2 \):
\[
(-2)^2 - 5(-2) - 14 = 4 + 10 - 14 = 0
\]

Both values satisfy the equation, so they are indeed the correct
solutions.

In summary, by using the quadratic formula and carefully following each
step, I was able to find that the solutions to \( u^2 - 5u - 14 = 0 \) are
\( u = 7 \) and \( u = -2 \).
</think>

To solve the quadratic equation \( u^2 - 5u - 14 = 0 \), we can use the
quadratic formula:
```

```
\[
u = \frac{-b \pm \sqrt{b^2 - 4ac}}{2a}
\]

Here, \( a = 1 \), \( b = -5 \), and \( c = -14 \).

Plugging in these values:

\[
u = \frac{-(-5) \pm \sqrt{(-5)^2 - 4(1)(-14)}}{2(1)}
\]
\[
u = \frac{5 \pm \sqrt{25 + 56}}{2}
\]
\[
u = \frac{5 \pm \sqrt{81}}{2}
\]
\[
u = \frac{5 \pm 9}{2}
\]

This gives two solutions:

1. \( u = \frac{5 + 9}{2} = 7 \)
2. \( u = \frac{5 - 9}{2} = -2 \)

**Verification:**

- For \( u = 7 \):
\[
(7)^2 - 5(7) - 14 = 0
\]
\[
49 - 35 - 14 = 0
\]

- For \( u = -2 \):
\[
(-2)^2 - 5(-2) - 14 = 0
```

```
\]
\[
4 + 10 - 14 = 0
\]

Both values satisfy the equation, confirming they are correct.

**Final Answer:**

The solutions to \( u^2 - 5u - 14 = 0 \) are:
\[
u = 7 \quad \text{and} \quad u = -2
\]
```

Wow, pretty interesting stuff!

This is so easy to set up and start prompting the other models available for vision and other use cases. You can test with a model and different sizes to see which gives you satisfactory responses specific to your use case. This enables you to experiment in an open-source, efficient, and cost-effective way. Please always keep in mind that Ollama is not recommended to be used to host LLMs in production context but instead is for prototyping and experimenting.

Exploring the APIs Exposed by Ollama

As noted previously, Ollama has exposed an API at `http://127.0.0.1:11434`. In this section, you will first run a `curl` command against it to confirm it's available, up, and running.

```
curl http://127.0.0.1:11434
```

```
Ollama is running
```

You can find the Ollama documentation at `https://github.com/ollama/ollama/tree/main/docs`, as shown in Figure 4-12.

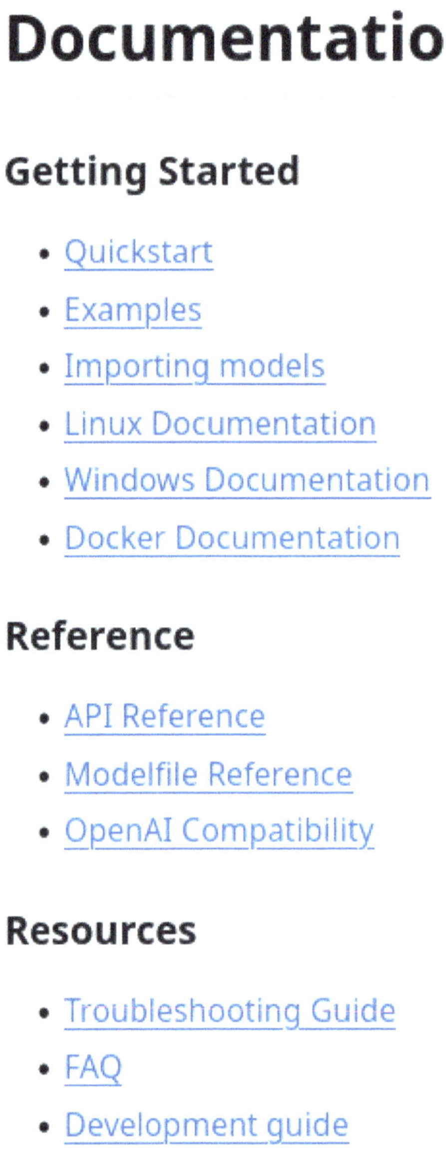

Documentation

Getting Started

- Quickstart
- Examples
- Importing models
- Linux Documentation
- Windows Documentation
- Docker Documentation

Reference

- API Reference
- Modelfile Reference
- OpenAI Compatibility

Resources

- Troubleshooting Guide
- FAQ
- Development guide

Figure 4-12. *Ollama documentation*

You can explore the documentation relevant to what you're learning in this section at `https://github.com/ollama/ollama/blob/main/docs/api.md` (see Figure 4-13).

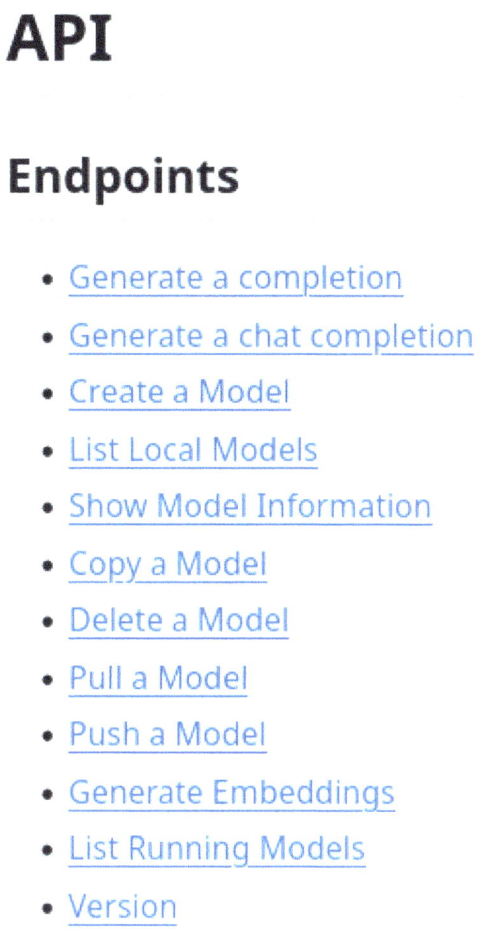

API

Endpoints

- Generate a completion
- Generate a chat completion
- Create a Model
- List Local Models
- Show Model Information
- Copy a Model
- Delete a Model
- Pull a Model
- Push a Model
- Generate Embeddings
- List Running Models
- Version

Figure 4-13. *Documentation: Ollama API endpoints*

Let's generate a completion using the API documentation shown in Figure 4-14. It takes three arguments, namely, the model, which in this case is deepseek-r1:1.5b, and the prompt, which is a query with an option to enable streaming. In this case, you can keep it as false. The output has a response field for the output answer to our query and other fields for duration, count, etc.

Request (No streaming)

Request

A response can be received in one reply when streaming is off.

```
curl http://localhost:11434/api/generate -d '{
  "model": "llama3.2",
  "prompt": "Why is the sky blue?",
  "stream": false
}'
```

Response

If `stream` is set to `false`, the response will be a single JSON object:

```
{
  "model": "llama3.2",
  "created_at": "2023-08-04T19:22:45.499127Z",
  "response": "The sky is blue because it is the color of the sky.",
  "done": true,
  "context": [1, 2, 3],
  "total_duration": 5043500667,
  "load_duration": 5025959,
  "prompt_eval_count": 26,
  "prompt_eval_duration": 325953000,
  "eval_count": 290,
  "eval_duration": 4709213000
}
```

Figure 4-14. *Completion API for text*

The response of the query/prompt from DeepSeek can be seen in the following request:

```
curl http://localhost:11434/api/generate -d '{
 "model": "deepseek-r1:1.5b",
 "prompt": "Why is the sky blue?",
 "stream": false
}'
```

Output:

```
{"model":"deepseek-r1:1.5b","created_at":"2025-01-26T15:46:02.88934847
8Z","response":"\u003cthink\u003e\n\n\u003c/think\u003e\n\nThe sky
appearing blue is known as the \"blue sky effect.\" This optical
phenomenon occurs due to a combination of factors, primarily the Earth's
atmosphere acting as an absorbent medium. Here's how it works:\n\n1.
**Rainbow Formation**: When sunlight enters the Earth's atmosphere,
it consists of a spectrum of colors. The sunlight passes through tiny
particles in the air, which act like tiny prongs or fibers that bend and
```

```
refract the light.\n\n2. **Scattering and Dispersion**: As the rainbow-
colored light travels from the sun to Earth, some of it is scattered
away at larger angles (scattering) due to the atmosphere's density.
The remaining colors are then refracted through smaller angles as they
exit the Earth, appearing in a more visible order-this is known as
dispersion.\n\n3. **Layered Appearance**: Due to the refraction and
reflection within the atmosphere, we perceive the sky as a layered effect,
with multiple layers of light overlapping and creating the illusion of
color variation across the sky.\n\nThis combination of scattering and
dispersion results in the blue color that dominates over other colors
when observed from Earth.","done":true,"done_reason":"stop","conte
xt":[151644,10234,374,279,12884,6303,30,151645,151648,271,151649,271,
785,12884,25377,6303,374,3881,438,279,330,12203,12884,2456,1189,1096,2829
3,24844,13666,4152,311,264,10601,315,9363,11,15503,279,9237,594,16566,1535
8,438,458,34306,306,11051,13,5692,594,1246,432,4278,1447,16,13,3070,5903
9,15439,71366,95518,3197,39020,28833,279,9237,594,16566,11,432,17167,31
5,264,19745,315,7987,13,576,39020,16211,1526,13673,18730,304,279,3720,1
1,892,1160,1075,13673,548,13181,476,48674,429,36820,323,19353,531,279,310
0,382,17,13,3070,3326,30336,323,69730,1325,95518,1634,279,47613,57722,310
0,34192,504,279,7015,311,9237,11,1045,315,432,374,36967,3123,518,8131,2594
1,320,2388,30336,8,4152,311,279,16566,594,17457,13,576,9664,7987,525,122
1,19353,22167,1526,9155,25941,438,807,4869,279,9237,11,25377,304,264,80
3,9434,1973,2293,574,374,3881,438,85612,382,18,13,3070,9188,291,60616,9551
8,23662,311,279,2053,16199,323,21844,2878,279,16566,11,582,44393,279,1288
4,438,264,63141,2456,11,448,5248,13617,315,3100,49817,323,6825,279,4081
9,315,1894,22990,3941,279,12884,382,1986,10601,315,71816,323,85612,3059,30
4,279,6303,1894,429,82878,916,1008,7987,979,13166,504,9237,13],"total_
duration":20513640704,"load_duration":4621213098,"prompt_eval_
count":9,"prompt_eval_duration":425000000,"eval_count":232,"eval_
duration":15464000000}
```


This is very helpful. You have already built your application centered around the OpenAI APIs. The following is the `curl` commands, and it does not match the format for the `curl` for the Ollama APIs.

```
curl https://api.openai.com/v1/chat/completions \
 -H "Content-Type: application/json" \
 -H "Authorization: Bearer $OPENAI_API_KEY" \
 -d '{
 "model": "gpt-4o-mini",
 "messages": [{"role": "user", "content": "Say this is a test!"}],
 "temperature": 0.7
  }'
```

Not to worry, since OpenAI APIs are quite popular, many LLM hosting vendors similar to Ollama have created abstractions on their API so that your existing APIs to OpenAI still work with a minor adjustment to the URL of the OpenAI you are using. As shown in Figure 4-15 at `https://ollama.com/blog/openai-compatibility`, Ollama has built-in compatibility with OpenAI APIs. You can review more documentation specific to it at `https://github.com/ollama/ollama/blob/main/docs/openai.md`.

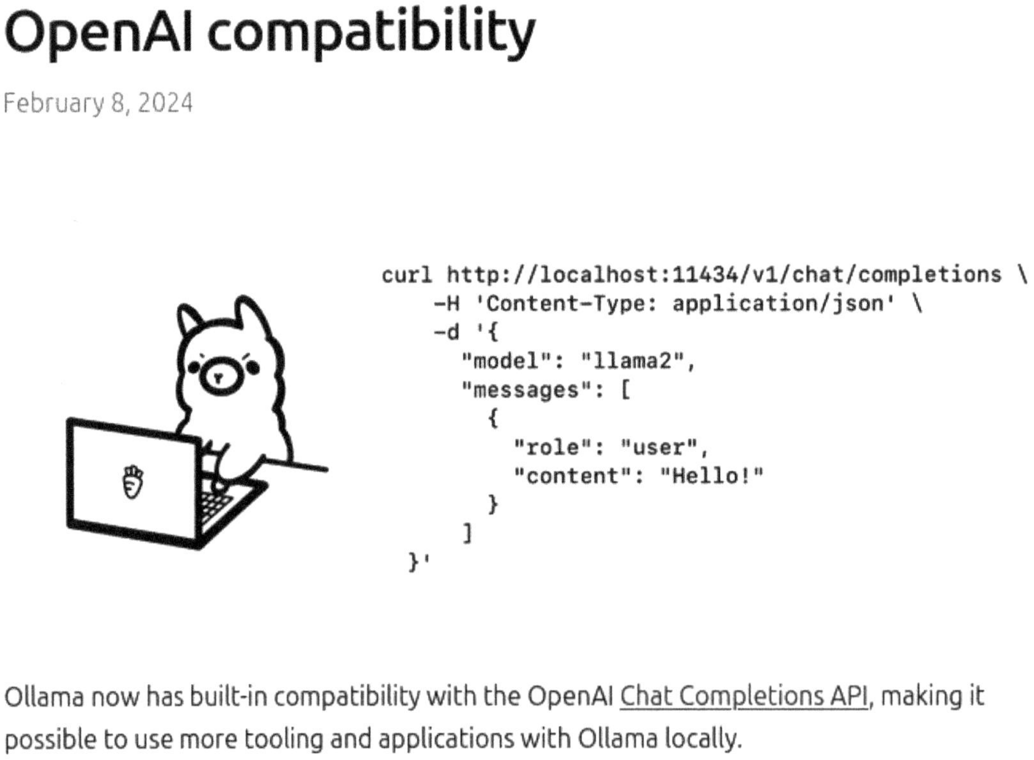

***Figure 4-15.** Ollama OpenAI API compatibility*

So let's try this in steps. Our OpenAI API format is as follows:

```
curl https://api.openai.com/v1/chat/completions \
 -H "Content-Type: application/json" \
 -H "Authorization: Bearer $OPENAI_API_KEY" \
 -d '{
 "model": "gpt-4o-mini",
 "messages": [{"role": "user", "content": "Say this is a test!"}],
 "temperature": 0.7
  }'
```

Let's convert it to use our Ollama API. As per the documentation, we just need to change the API base URL endpoint, which in our case would be http://localhost:11434. That is all you need to do. You do not need to change anything else in your code. In this case, let's also change the model, since we are using deepseek. gpt-40-mini is not available to it since it is available internally to OpenAI and is proprietary.

```
curl http://localhost:11434/v1/chat/completions \
 -H "Content-Type: application/json" \
 -H "Authorization: Bearer $OPENAI_API_KEY" \
 -d '{
 "model": "deepseek-r1:1.5b",
 "messages": [{"role": "user", "content": "Say this is a test!"}],
 "temperature": 0.7
  }'
```

Output:


```
{
  "id":"chatcmpl-290",
  "object":"chat.completion",
  "created":1737907542,
  "model":"deepseek-r1:1.5b",
  "system_fingerprint":"fp_ollama",
  "choices":[{
    "index":0,
```

```
    "message":{
      "role":"assistant",
      "content":"\u003cthink\u003e\n\n\u003c/think\u003e\n\nYes, it's a test!"
    },
    "finish_reason":"stop"
  }],
  "usage": {
    "prompt_tokens":9,
    "completion_tokens":12,
    "total_tokens":21
  }
}
```

As you can see in Figure 4-16, the JSON response is pretty similar to the output of the OpenAI response.

```
{
    "id": "chatcmpl-abc123",
    "object": "chat.completion",
    "created": 1677858242,
    "model": "gpt-4o-mini",
    "usage": {
        "prompt_tokens": 13,
        "completion_tokens": 7,
        "total_tokens": 20,
        "completion_tokens_details": {
            "reasoning_tokens": 0,
            "accepted_prediction_tokens": 0,
            "rejected_prediction_tokens": 0
        }
    },
    "choices": [
        {
            "message": {
                "role": "assistant",
                "content": "\n\nThis is a test!"
            },
            "logprobs": null,
            "finish_reason": "stop",
            "index": 0
        }
    ]
}
```

Figure 4-16. *OpenAI API* `curl` *response*

Integrating Ollama with Your Existing Application

Let's revisit your Spring Boot application and see what and where you need to make changes to integrate Ollama API so as to have it still be functional and running. First, let's make sure Ollama is installed in the system where you are running your Spring Boot application. Then you need to update the OpenAI API base URL to point to Ollama instead and update from gpt-4o-mini to the deepseek-r1:1.5b model, which can be done in the `ChatService.java` file.

File: src/main/java/com/example/genai/service/ChatService.java

```
private static final String OPENAI_API_URL = "http://localhost:11434/v1/
chat/completions";

public ChatCompletionResponse getChatResponse(String userMessage) {
    RestTemplate restTemplate = new RestTemplate();

   // Build the request body
    ChatCompletionRequest request = new ChatCompletionRequest();
    request.setModel("deepseek-r1:1.5b");
}
```

That should be it. It looks easy enough. Let's run the application and see the output for the same `curl` command you tried in Chapter 2 with the OpenAI API enabled:

```
curl -X POST "http://localhost:8080/api/chat" -H "Content-Type:
application/json" -d '{"userMessage": "Hello!"}'

{"content":"<think>\nAlright, the user just said \"Hello!\" I need to
respond in a friendly and welcoming manner. I should let them know I'm here
to help with whatever they need. Maybe I can ask how I can assist them
today to keep the conversation open.\n</think>\n\nHello! How can I assist
you today?"}
```

Conclusion

This chapter provided a comprehensive guide to self-hosting LLMs using Ollama, offering readers the knowledge and steps required to set up and run these models locally. By exploring the advantages of local hosting—such as enhanced privacy, reduced dependency on external cloud services, and cost-efficiency—we've seen how Ollama simplifies the deployment of language models on local systems. Additionally, the chapter covered the installation process for macOS, Windows, and Linux, along with how to interact with models through Ollama's intuitive API.

When venturing into self-hosting large language models using tools like Ollama, adhering to a set of best practices ensures a smoother, more secure, and more efficient experience. First and foremost, choose the right model for your hardware—balance performance and memory usage with your system's capabilities. Always test smaller models first before scaling to larger ones to assess feasibility. Regularly monitor system resources (CPU, GPU, memory) to prevent unexpected crashes or slowdowns, especially when hosting development machines. Keep Ollama and any related dependencies updated to the latest stable version to benefit from security patches and performance enhancements. If you're exposing APIs, secure them with authentication mechanisms such as API keys or OAuth, and use HTTPS in production environments. For integration, mirror your API contracts with OpenAI's as closely as possible to maintain compatibility and minimize refactoring. While Ollama is ideal for experimentation and prototyping, always evaluate production-readiness by stress-testing the system and planning for scalability, uptime, and long-term support before deploying self-hosted LLMs into live environments.

You also explored how Ollama's API is compatible with OpenAI's, ensuring a smooth transition for developers already working with OpenAI models in their applications. With minimal changes to the API request format, users can switch from OpenAI's cloud service to their own local setup, preserving functionality while cutting down on external dependencies. Finally, the chapter demonstrated the integration process into an existing application, reinforcing how seamless this transition can be with Ollama.

This chapter has set a strong foundation for those looking to experiment with LLMs locally, whether for prototyping or developing applications. While Ollama offers a robust environment for development, it is important to remember that for production-level use, other considerations such as scalability, support, and infrastructure will need to be evaluated. Nonetheless, for anyone looking to explore the world of self-hosting LLMs, Ollama provides an accessible and powerful tool to begin this journey. Let us move on to LangChain.

CHAPTER 5

Power Tools: LangChain4j Quick-Start

This chapter introduces LangChain4j, the Java framework designed to simplify the integration of LLMs into Java applications. It covers the installation, setup, and use of key features and capabilities.

Introduction

In this chapter, you will start our journey by beginning to work hands-on with LLM frameworks, particularly LangChain4j. While doing so, you will keep learning about many of the concepts and processes in building LLM applications. Let's start with a simple application that just invokes an LLM by passing it some input and receiving some output. Then you improve the output and architecture of the application by using prompt engineering and then retrieval-augmented generation (RAG). The application you will be building will help users get customer support, book tickets, and various other actions that would be applicable in an airline management system, but through a chat interface. You will not be concerned with the user interface and will be limiting yourself to the application programming interface (API) interfaces.

What Is LangChain4j?

LangChain is a popular LLM orchestration framework. It contains modularized components that can be connected through different steps, from processing your inputs to fetching data from vector databases to invoking tools. You will learn about all these aspects as you follow along in the chapter. LangChain is written in Python, and

S. K. Sahu, *Generative AI-Driven Application Development with Java*,
https://doi.org/10.1007/979-8-8688-1609-3_5

LangChain4j means LangChain for Java. LangChain4j is the Java language counterpart for LangChain. I will be using the term LangChain4j going ahead. Where explicitly needed, I will refer to LangChain when particular differences or features need to be pointed out.

LangChain4j provides a unified framework and API interface to help you build chatbots, assistants, and other aspects around LLMs. It integrates smoothly into frameworks like Spring Boot and Quarkus. It provides a wide range of features applicable to LLM frameworks like prompt templating, chat memory management, output parsing, and other such functionalities. You will learn about all of these later in the chapter. You can find more information at `https://docs.langchain4j.dev/`.

Installation and Setup of LangChain4j

These are the prerequisites:

- Java 17+
- Gradle/Maven
- IntelliJ/VS Code/any relevant integration development environment (IDE)

Start the setup by initializing a basic simple Spring Boot application using the Spring Initializer at `https://start.spring.io/`, as shown in Figure 5-1. For the following instructions, I will use Gradle. The steps could be easily replaced with Maven-based instructions.

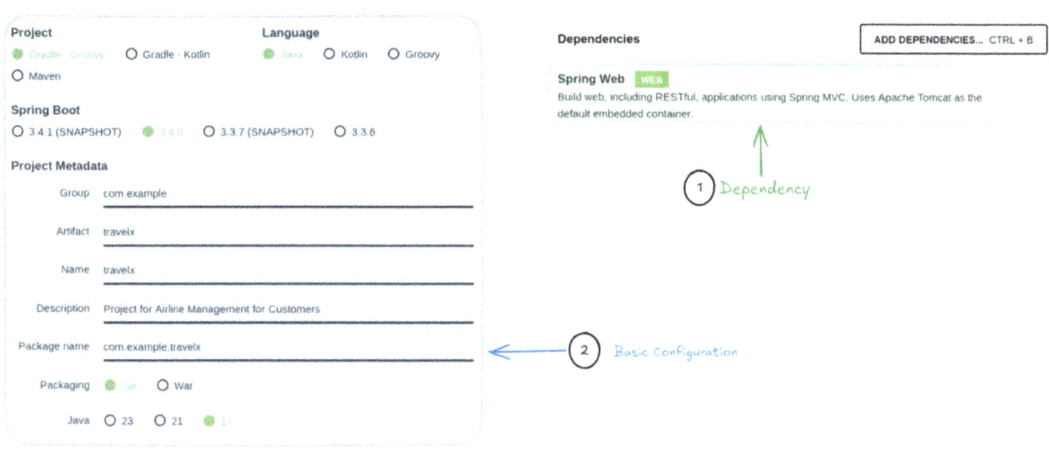

Figure 5-1. *Spring Initializr dependencies*

We will be working for a hypothetical company named TravelX. In the very first iteration, you will build an API endpoint that can be used by front-end teams. This API takes input in the form of text and gives back a response from LLM. In this iteration, you want to expose an interface to customers where they can chat with your bot.

As the first step, you will unzip the sample Spring Boot zip downloaded.

```
unzip travelx.zip
cd travelx
./gradlew build
```

Let's now add the LangChain4j dependency to the project. If you are using Maven, please add the following dependency to the `pom.xml` file:

```
<dependency>
    <groupId>dev.langchain4j</groupId>
    <artifactId>langchain4j-open-ai</artifactId>
    <version>0.36.2</version>
</dependency>
<dependency>
    <groupId>dev.langchain4j</groupId>
    <artifactId>langchain4j</artifactId>
    <version>0.36.2</version>
</dependency>
```

For Gradle, please add the following to the build.gradle file:

```
implementation 'dev.langchain4j:langchain4j-open-ai:0.36.2'
implementation 'dev.langchain4j:langchain4j:0.36.2'
```

File: build.gradle

```
plugins {
    id 'java'
    id 'org.springframework.boot' version '3.4.0'
    id 'io.spring.dependency-management' version '1.1.6'
}

group = 'com.example'
version = '0.0.1-SNAPSHOT'

java {
    toolchain {
       languageVersion = JavaLanguageVersion.of(17)
    }
}

repositories {
    mavenCentral()
}

dependencies {
    implementation 'org.springframework.boot:spring-boot-starter-web'
    implementation 'dev.langchain4j:langchain4j-open-ai:0.36.2'
    implementation 'dev.langchain4j:langchain4j:0.36.2'
    testImplementation 'org.springframework.boot:spring-boot-starter-test'
    testRuntimeOnly 'org.junit.platform:junit-platform-launcher'
}

tasks.named('test') {
    useJUnitPlatform()
}
```

Initial Project Setup: Creating Your First LangChain4j Application

You will integrate with OpenAI API, which is an API interface for LLM models created by OpenAI. Figure 5-2 shows the project architecture.

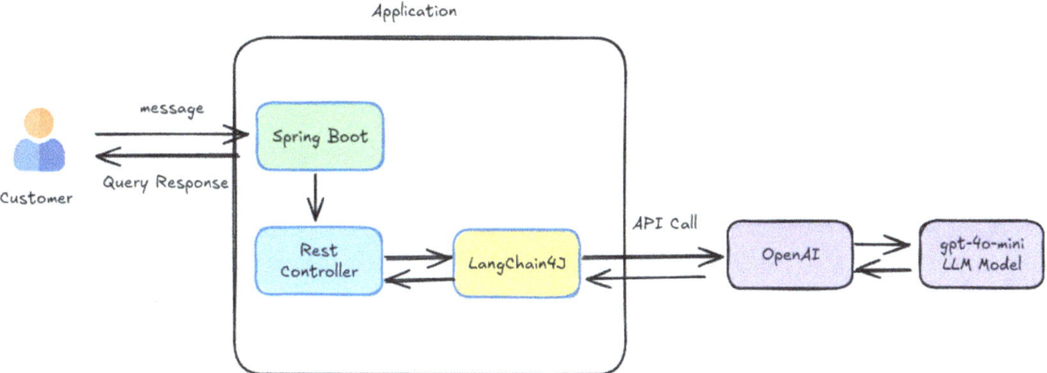

Figure 5-2. *Initial project architecture*

For this, you will need an OpenAI API key. LangChain4j provides an OpenAI key called *demo* for testing purposes that you can use. Let's set the key in `application.properties`, although the best practice would be to set it in your environment variables.

File: application.properties

```
openai.api-key=demo
```

Next, you will create a bean configuration for connecting to OpenAI and choosing a language model. You can choose gpt-4o-mini, which is a small language model and gives faster response. Let's create a file called `LangchainConfig.java` with the following code. It imports the OpenAiChatModel from LangChain4j and builds a connection config to OpenAI by passing in the API key and the language model you want to invoke for the requests to OpenAI.

```
package com.example.travelx;

import org.springframework.beans.factory.annotation.Value;
import org.springframework.context.annotation.Bean;
import org.springframework.context.annotation.Configuration;
import dev.langchain4j.model.openai.OpenAiChatModel;
```

```
@Configuration
public class LangchainConfig {

    @Value("${openai.api-key}")
    private String apiKey;

    @Bean
    public OpenAiChatModel openAiChatModel() {
        return OpenAiChatModel.builder()
                .apiKey(apiKey)
                .modelName("gpt-4o-mini")
                .build();
    }
}
```

To handle chat requests from the UI, let's create a simple POJO to define the structure of the request in a file called ChatRequest.java.

```
package com.example.travelx;

class ChatRequest {
    private String message;

    public String getMessage() {
        return message;
    }

    public void setMessage(String message) {
        this.message = message;
    }
}
```

Once you have the previous two files set up, the final goal is to create a REST controller that leverages these two files. Name the file ChatController.java and add the following content in it:

```
package com.example.travelx;

import org.springframework.beans.factory.annotation.Autowired;
import org.springframework.web.bind.annotation.*;
```

```
import dev.langchain4j.model.openai.OpenAiChatModel;

@RestController
@RequestMapping("/api/chat")
public class ChatController {

   private final OpenAiChatModel chatModel;

   @Autowired
    public ChatController(OpenAiChatModel chatModel) {
        this.chatModel = chatModel;
    }

   @PostMapping
    public String chat (@RequestBody ChatRequest chatRequest) {
        return chatModel.generate(chatRequest.getMessage());
    }
}
```

Let's restart the Spring Boot Application and issue a POST request against it at `/api/chat`. You should receive a response from the API saying "Hello, World!" Hurray, you have your first interaction with the world of LLMs and your first requirement.

```
curl -X POST http://localhost:8080/api/chat -H "Content-Type: application/
json" -d '{
 "message": "Say Hello World"
}'

Hello, World!
```

Conclusion

In this chapter, you explored the foundational aspects of integrating LangChain4j into a Java application, focusing on its use within the context of a Spring Boot project. LangChain4j, the Java counterpart to LangChain, provides a seamless way to integrate LLMs into Java-based applications with features such as prompt engineering, chat memory, and output parsing.

We began by understanding LangChain4j's purpose and capabilities, emphasizing its utility in developing modular and scalable applications. The chapter provided step-by-step instructions for setting up a basic Spring Boot project and integrating LangChain4j dependencies. You configured the OpenAI API connection, chose a lightweight language model (`gpt-4o-mini`), and built a simple chatbot endpoint.

Through a practical example, you implemented a REST controller that processes user inputs, invokes the LLM, and returns generated responses. By running the application and issuing a test request, you successfully saw a chatbot's interaction, completing your first integration with LangChain4j.

This chapter has equipped you with the knowledge to get started with LangChain4j, laying a strong foundation for developing advanced applications involving LLMs. The next steps involve exploring more advanced features like RAG, enhanced prompt engineering, and integrating tools for richer interactions.

CHAPTER 6

Integrating LLMs with Java Applications

This chapter guides you through the process of integrating large language models (LLMs) into Java applications using LangChain4j. It covers connecting to various LLM providers and using a unified API to simplify interactions.

Introduction

In this chapter, you will continue your work started in the previous chapter and delve a bit deeper into some of the other features of LangChain4j and generative AI (Gen AI). Now that you are able to connect to an LLM through the OpenAI API, you will learn about prompt engineering. You will then focus on the concept of retrieval-augmented generation (RAG), which is helpful to get more context into your application.

Prompt Engineering

Now, your application from the previous chapter is a good start, but you may question how valuable it is to your business. A simple, general-purpose chatbot could perform these tasks. If the customer requests some information related to your company, it would not be able to answer it. What do you think?

```
curl -X POST http://localhost:8080/api/chat -H "Content-Type: application/
json" -d '{
 "message": "What are the different features of TravelX Airlines?"
}'
```


S. K. Sahu, *Generative AI-Driven Application Development with Java*,
https://doi.org/10.1007/979-8-8688-1609-3_6

Output:

```
As of my last update in October 2023, I don't have specific information
about an airline named TravelX Airlines. However, if you are referring to
a fictional airline or a new airline that has emerged after that date, I
can provide you with a general overview of common features that airlines
typically offer.

Here are some features that airlines often provide:

1. **Flight Options**: A variety of domestic and international routes,
including direct and connecting flights.

2. **Cabin Classes**: Different classes of service, such as Economy,
Premium Economy, Business, and First Class, each offering varying levels of
comfort and amenities.

3. **Frequent Flyer Program**: Loyalty programs that reward frequent
travelers with points or miles that can be redeemed for free flights,
upgrades, and other benefits.

4. **In-flight Entertainment**: Options such as movies, TV shows, music,
and games available on personal screens or via app streaming.

5. **Wi-Fi Connectivity**: Onboard internet access for passengers to stay
connected during their flights.

6. **In-flight Dining**: A range of meal options, including special dietary
meals, snacks, and beverages, with some airlines offering complimentary
meals while others use a buy-on-board model.

7. **Baggage Allowance**: Policies regarding free checked baggage, carry-on
limits, and fees for excess baggage.

8. **Customer Service**: Support through various channels, including phone,
email, chat, and social media, for booking assistance and resolving issues.

9. **Online Check-in**: The ability for passengers to check in online and
select seats before arriving at the airport.
```

```
10. **Lounge Access**: Airport lounges for premium passengers or frequent
flyers, offering a comfortable space to relax before flights.

11. **Flexible Booking Options**: Policies that allow for changes or
cancellations, often with options for insurance.

12. **Sustainability Initiatives**: Efforts to reduce environmental impact,
such as using fuel-efficient aircraft and carbon offset programs.

If you have a specific focus or details about TravelX Airlines or any other
airline, please provide more context, and I'd be glad to assist further!
```

As you can see, the LLM is able to answer the question since one of the challenges with LLMs is that they hallucinate. Hallucination results from the fact that these LLMs have been trained on massive amounts of datasets and they try their best to answer your question even if they might not have any information relevant to the question. This can be a problem and result in providing incorrect information to users. Although it is not entirely avoidable, you can mitigate hallucination by providing context to the LLM that it should not share information if it does not have any contextual knowledge of it. This helps the LLM limit its response to knowable facts. Let's give this a shot.

Returning to the previous experiment, you passed a message called Say Hello World to the Open API LLM. To simply change the context, you can prepend the message with your mitigating message to limit it to known facts. This practice of changing the message to be more contextual is called *prompt engineering*, and the whole message being sent results in a prompt. Let's modify the prompt in the file `ChatRequest.java`.

File: ChatRequest.java

```java
package com.example.travelx;

class ChatRequest {
    private String message;
    private String prompt = "Please limit the responses to known facts. If
    you do not know about the context, simply say 'Sorry, I am not aware
    of this context. Please let me know if I can help you with any other
    requests.'";

    public String getMessage() {
        return prompt + " " + message;
    }
```

```
    public void setMessage(String message) {
         this.message = prompt + " " + message;
     }
}
```

Now, when requesting the API again, you receive following response:

```
curl -X POST http://localhost:8080/api/chat -H "Content-Type: application/
json" -d '{
 "message": "What are the different features of TravelX Airlines?"
}'
Sorry, I am not aware of this context. Please let me know if I can help you
with any other requests.
```

This is super helpful. Just a small change in the prompt gives this more contextual output. That's how powerful prompt engineering is. With the emergence of Gen AI and LLMs, there have been job postings with the requirement of prompt engineering skills. The project manager is pleased with your first iteration and plans to reward the team.

Context into Conversation Memory

If you use your API to make two requests to OpenAI LLM as follows, what do you think the response should be?

1. How is the climate in Europe in May?
2. What are the things I should pack for a trip to Europe in such a climate?

Example 1:

```
curl -X POST http://localhost:8080/api/chat -H "Content-Type: application/
json" -d '{
 "message": "How is the climate in Europe in May?"
}'
In May, the climate in Europe generally varies by region. In Southern
Europe, such as Spain and Italy, temperatures can be warm, often ranging
from 15°C to 25°C (59°F to 77°F). In Central Europe, like Germany and
```

```
France, temperatures are typically mild, ranging from 10°C to 20°C (50°F to
68°F). Northern Europe, including countries like Sweden and Norway, tends
to be cooler, with temperatures ranging from 5°C to 15°C (41°F to 59°F).
May is often characterized by increasing daylight hours and the blooming of
spring flowers across the continent. Rainfall can also be common in many
regions.
```

Example 2: The following conversation is depicted in Figure 6-1:

```
curl -X POST http://localhost:8080/api/chat -H "Content-Type: application/
json" -d '{
 "message": "What are the things I should pack for a trip to Europe in such
 a climate?"
}'
Sorry, I am not aware of this context. Please let me know if I can help you
with any other requests.
```

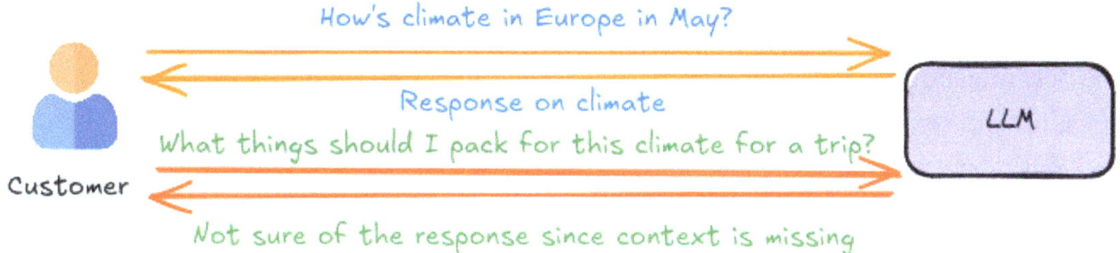

***Figure 6-1.** Example conversation showing the absence of context*

For the first question, the LLM shares the climate details in Europe in the month of May; however, for the next question, it may not be able to answer or might hallucinate. This is because it does not have the context of your first question and answer since although this might be an expectation from the user interface where customers are seeing the questions and answers one after another in a single context, in the API these are sent as independent requests. To solve this, it is important to share this previous conversation with the LLM while asking new questions; that way the LLM has an idea of what the previous context has been and if there is any information from it that it can use to answer related questions.

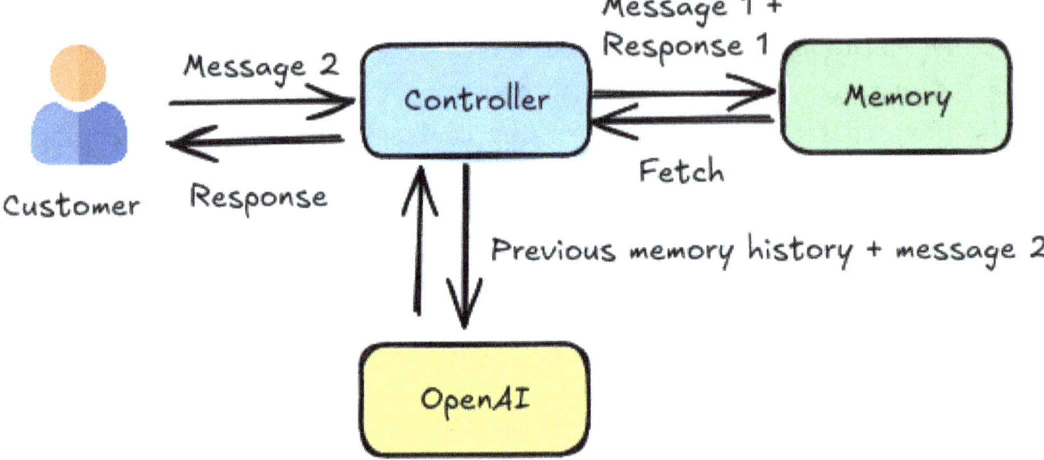

Figure 6-2. *Control flow of request response between Spring Boot and Open AI with memory interaction*

One way to approach this is to have a memory component that collects all previous questions asked by the customer and the response for those questions from the LLM in the sequence of order of their occurrence. This is illustrated in Figure 6-2 above. For any new question, the previous memory history is retrieved and prefixed to the current question and sent to the LLM. This way the LLM has the context of the previous history and may answer any related question. This structure is shown in Figure 6-3.

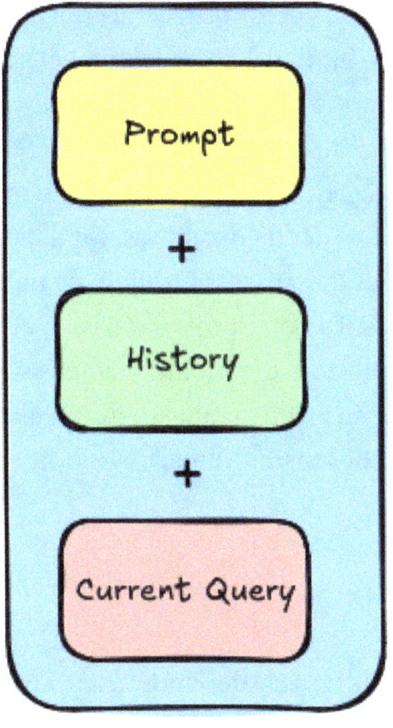

Figure 6-3. *Different components of the message sent to LLM*

When building conversational systems, maintaining context across interactions is critical. A conversation often involves follow-up questions, and users expect the system to "remember" previous interactions. Implementing this manually could involve using variables, memory stores, or concatenation, but LangChain4j simplifies this process with its chat memory feature. This enables your application to retain conversation context seamlessly and improve the quality of interactions.

The persistent chat memory feature allows the application to store and retrieve previous user interactions. For instance:

- When a user asks about the climate in Europe in May and then follows up with "What should I pack?" the system uses stored context to provide a relevant response.
- Without this feature, each question would be treated as an independent query, and the system might fail to provide coherent answers.

By adding persistent memory, you improve the conversational flow and ensure the system behaves more like a human-like assistant. Let's explore how you integrated persistent chat memory into your application step-by-step, examining the changes made to the code and understanding their purpose.

To achieve this, we'll start by enabling persistent chat memory. Instead of managing memory manually with variables or custom stores, we'll use LangChain4j's Chat Memory feature. This simplifies the process by allowing us to define a memory window that stores the last 10 messages. To persist this data, we'll add MapDB, a lightweight embedded database, which will store the memory across sessions. Let's also add `chat-memory.db` to `.gitignore` to ensure the database isn't tracked by version control, keeping your repository clean and free of sensitive data.

File: .gitignore

```
chat-memory.db
chat-memory.db.wal.0
```

Next, you need to add the necessary dependencies. Let's include LangChain4j and MapDB in the `build.gradle` file. LangChain4j provides the tools to handle chat memory and integrate with LLMs, while MapDB will handle persistent storage. Once the dependencies are in place, we'll define the Assistant interface. This interface will define the essential method chat (String message) for handling user queries, making it easy to switch implementations if needed, such as toggling between memory-enabled and memory-less modes.

File: build.gradle

```
dependencies {
    implementation 'org.springframework.boot:spring-boot-starter-web'
    implementation 'dev.langchain4j:langchain4j-open-ai:0.36.2'
    implementation 'dev.langchain4j:langchain4j:0.36.2'
    implementation group: 'org.mapdb', name: 'mapdb', version: '3.1.0'
    testImplementation 'org.springframework.boot:spring-boot-starter-test'
    testRuntimeOnly 'org.junit.platform:junit-platform-launcher'
}
```

Now, we'll move to the configuration. In LangChainConfig, let's set up the OpenAI GPT-4 model with LangChain4j. We'll integrate it with a `PersistentChatMemoryStore` to handle storing, retrieving, and managing chat history in MapDB. This memory store will manage the messages, and by limiting the memory to ten messages, we'll ensure that the system is efficient while still maintaining enough context for meaningful interactions.

File: Assistant.java interface

```
package com.example.travelx;

public interface Assistant {
    String chat(String message);
}
```

Here is a service that is used by the chat controller to keep the controller thin and drive the communication through this service to keep it neat and modular.

File: ServiceWithPersistentMemory.java

```
package com.example.travelx;

import org.springframework.context.annotation.Bean;
import org.springframework.context.annotation.Configuration;

@Configuration
public class ServiceWithPersistentMemory {
    private Assistant assistant;

   @Bean
    public Assistant chatAssistant(Assistant assistant) {
        this.assistant = assistant;
        return this.assistant;
    }

   public String chat(String message) {
        return this.assistant.chat(message);
    }
}
```

File: LangChainConfig.java

```
package com.example.travelx;

import static dev.langchain4j.data.message.ChatMessageDeserializer.
messagesFromJson;
import static dev.langchain4j.data.message.ChatMessageSerializer.
messagesToJson;

import java.util.List;
import java.util.Map;

import org.mapdb.DB;
import org.mapdb.DBMaker;
import static org.mapdb.Serializer.STRING;
import org.springframework.beans.factory.annotation.Value;
import org.springframework.context.annotation.Bean;
import org.springframework.context.annotation.Configuration;

import dev.langchain4j.data.message.ChatMessage;
import static dev.langchain4j.model.openai.OpenAiChatModelName.
GPT_4_O_MINI;
import dev.langchain4j.memory.chat.MessageWindowChatMemory;
import dev.langchain4j.model.openai.OpenAiChatModel;
import dev.langchain4j.service.AiServices;
import dev.langchain4j.store.memory.chat.ChatMemoryStore;

@Configuration
public class LangchainConfig {

   @Value("${openai.api-key}")
    private String apiKey;
    private OpenAiChatModel model;
    private Assistant assistant;
    private MessageWindowChatMemory chatMemory;

    @Bean
    public OpenAiChatModel openAiChatModel() {
        this.model = OpenAiChatModel.builder()
```

```
            .apiKey(apiKey)
            .modelName(GPT_4_O_MINI) // Replace with desired model
            .build();
        return this.model;
    }

    @Bean
    public MessageWindowChatMemory messageWindowChatMemory() {
        this.chatMemory = MessageWindowChatMemory.builder()
                .maxMessages(10)
                .chatMemoryStore(new PersistentChatMemoryStore())
                .build();
        return this.chatMemory;
    }

    @Bean
    public Assistant openAiAssistant() {
        this.chatMemory = this.messageWindowChatMemory();
        this.model = this.openAiChatModel();
        this.assistant = AiServices.builder(Assistant.class)
                .chatLanguageModel(this.model)
                .chatMemory(this.chatMemory)
                .build();
        return this.assistant;
    }

    static class PersistentChatMemoryStore implements ChatMemoryStore {
        private final DB db = DBMaker.fileDB("chat-memory.db").
        transactionEnable().make();
        private final Map<String, String> map = db.hashMap("messages",
        STRING, STRING).createOrOpen();

        @Override
        public List<ChatMessage> getMessages(Object memoryId) {
            String json = map.get((String) memoryId);
            return messagesFromJson(json);
        }
```

```
        @Override
         public void updateMessages(Object memoryId, List<ChatMessage>
         messages) {
             String json = messagesToJson(messages);
             map.put((String) memoryId, json);
             db.commit();
         }

        @Override
         public void deleteMessages(Object memoryId) {
             map.remove((String) memoryId);
             db.commit();
         }
    }
}
```

For the API layer, we'll update the ChatController to connect the back end to the user-facing interface. Let's ensure the ServiceWithPersistentMemory class processes all chat interactions by linking the chat assistant to your memory configuration. The ChatRequest class will format incoming messages with a prompt that instructs the LLM to stick to known facts and provide context-aware responses. This helps avoid hallucinations and ensures the LLM gives accurate information or gracefully admits when it doesn't have the answer.

File: ChatController.java

```
package com.example.travelx;

import org.springframework.web.bind.annotation.*;

@RestController
@RequestMapping("/api/chat")
public class ChatController {
    private ServiceWithPersistentMemory chatService;

   public ChatController(ServiceWithPersistentMemory chatService) {
        this.chatService = chatService;
    }
```

```
    @PostMapping
    public String chat(@RequestBody ChatRequest chatRequest) {
        return this.chatService.chat(chatRequest.getMessage());
    }
}
```

Once everything is configured, let's test the system. You can send a query like, "How is the climate in Europe in May?" The response should describe the mild and variable weather accurately. Now, if you send a follow-up query like "What should I pack for such a climate?" the system should remember the previous context and suggest items like lightweight layers, a compact umbrella, and comfortable shoes. This demonstrates how the memory transforms interactions into cohesive conversations.

Example 1:

```
curl -X POST http://localhost:8080/api/chat -H "Content-Type: application/
json" -d '{
 "message": "How is the climate in Europe in May?"
}'
In May, the climate in Europe generally varies by region but tends to
be mild and increasingly warm as it transitions from spring to summer.
Northern Europe may still experience cool temperatures, while southern
Europe often enjoys warmer weather. Average temperatures can range from
about 10°C (50°F) in the north to around 25°C (77°F) in the south. Rainfall
can also vary, with some areas experiencing more precipitation while others
may be quite dry. Overall, May is often characterized by blooming flowers
and longer daylight hours across the continent.
```

Example 2:

```
curl -X POST http://localhost:8080/api/chat -H "Content-Type: application/
json" -d '{
 "message": "What are the things I should pack for a trip to Europe in such
 a climate?"
}'
```

```
For a trip to Europe in May, consider packing the following items based on
the mild and variable climate:
1. **Clothing Layers:** Lightweight layers such as t-shirts, long-sleeve
shirts, and a light sweater or jacket for cooler days.
2. **Comfortable Shoes:** Good walking shoes or sneakers for exploring.
3. **Rain Gear:** A compact umbrella or a waterproof jacket, as May can
have unpredictable rain showers.
4. **Accessories:** Sunglasses and a hat for sunny days.
5. **Travel Essentials:** Adapter for electronics, toiletries, and any
necessary medications.
6. **Light Scarf:** Useful for cooler evenings or as an extra layer.
Adjust your packing based on specific destinations and personal
preferences.
```

By making these changes now, we're enhancing the system in several ways. Persistent memory ensures context-aware responses, improving the overall user experience. Using MapDB provides scalable and efficient memory management. Leveraging LangChain4j's tools makes the integration straightforward, letting us focus on building functionality rather than managing technical complexities. These updates ensure the application is well-prepared to handle real-world conversational scenarios dynamically and effectively. Your project manager is very happy with your effort.

Switching Between LLM Providers

Now that you have a basic setup of your application, it's important that you are able to try other LLMs to verify which gives you the best results in terms of the output you are expecting. Figure 6-4 shows the options.

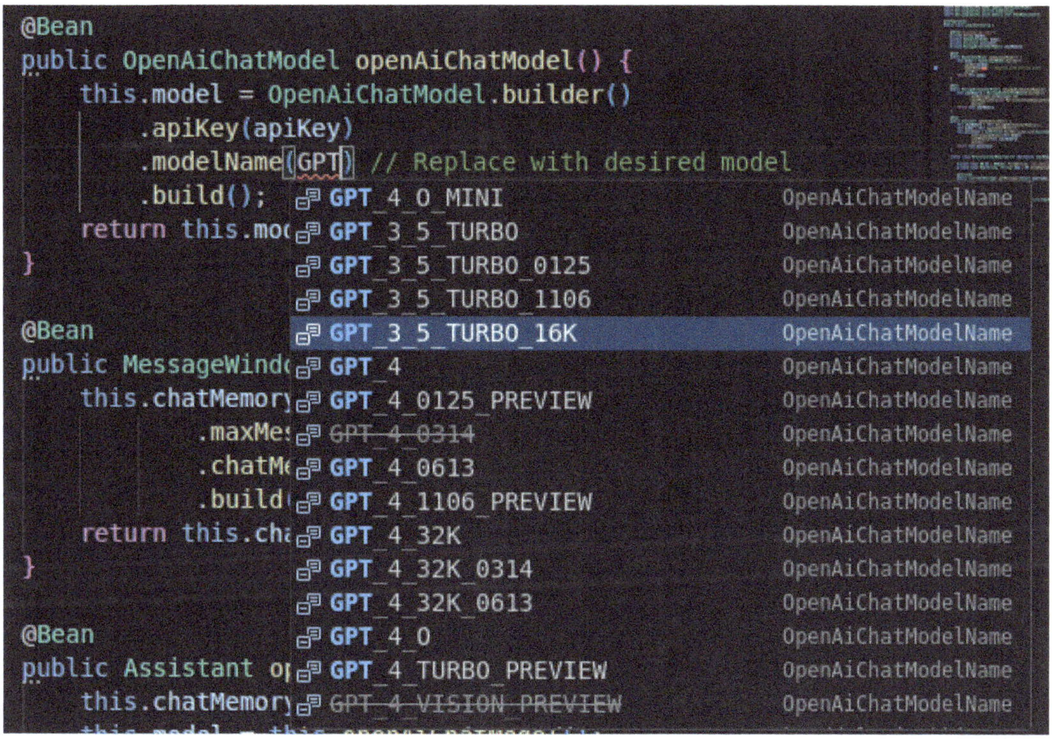

Figure 6-4. Different available model versions of OpenAI

File: LangChainConfig.java

Let's try with GPT-4-O

```
curl -X POST http://localhost:8080/api/chat -H "Content-Type: application/
json" -d '{
 "message": "How is the climate in Europe in May?"
}'
In May, the climate in Europe generally features mild to warm temperatures
as spring progresses towards summer. Average temperatures typically range
from about 10°C (50°F) in northern regions to around 25°C (77°F) in
southern areas. Rainfall can vary widely; some locations may experience
frequent showers, while others remain relatively dry. Days are longer with
more daylight, and many places see blooming flowers and greenery during
this time.
```

```
curl -X POST http://localhost:8080/api/chat -H "Content-Type: application/
json" -d '{
 "message": "What are the things I should pack for a trip to Europe in such
 a climate?"
}'
For a trip to Europe in May, you should consider packing the
following items:
1. **Clothing Layers:** T-shirts, long-sleeve shirts, and a light sweater
or jacket.
2. **Comfortable Shoes:** Walking shoes or sneakers.
3. **Rain Gear:** A waterproof jacket or a compact umbrella.
4. **Accessories:** Sunglasses and a hat.
5. **Travel Essentials:** Power adapter, toiletries, and medications.
6. **Light Scarf:** Useful for cooler evenings.
Adjust based on specific destinations and personal preferences.
```

Handling LLM Outputs

When integrating LLMs into applications, handling outputs effectively is crucial for extracting and processing data in a structured and reliable manner. While LLMs excel at generating natural language text, real-world applications often require structured outputs, such as JSON, to integrate seamlessly with downstream systems. In this section, you will focus on leveraging LangChain4j to extract and handle flight-related information in a structured format that aligns with your application's needs. So as your next requirement, you had a meeting with your manager, and it seems that a lot of your customers need info on their plane related to the manufacturer, the model, how much distance it can cover, etc.

Handling LLM outputs is about ensuring that the data returned is:

- **Accurate**: Captures all relevant details based on the input query.
- **Structured**: Organized into a predefined format, such as JSON, for seamless processing.
- **Reliable**: Adheres to a schema, minimizing errors and reducing post-processing efforts.

Let's continue with the requirement scenario where a customer queries your system for flight information:

Customer Query: *"Tell me about Boeing 777X. I need to know its manufacturer, model, distance it can cover."*

```
curl -X POST http://localhost:8080/api/chat -H "Content-Type: application/
json" -d '{
 "message": "Tell me about Boeing 777X. I need to know its manufacturer,
 model, distance it can cover."
}'
```

Response from LLM:

```
The Boeing 777X is manufactured by **Boeing Commercial Airplanes**. It is a
modern variant of the Boeing 777 family, designed for long-haul operations
with advanced technology and improved efficiency.

### Model Variants:
The Boeing 777X family consists of two main models:
1. **Boeing 777-8**:
   - **Maximum Range**: Approximately **8,000 nautical miles** (about
   **14,800 kilometers**).
   - This variant is designed for ultra-long-haul routes and can
   accommodate around 384 passengers in a two-class configuration.

2. **Boeing 777-9**:
   - **Maximum Range**: Approximately **7,000 nautical miles** (about
     **12,964 kilometers**).
   - The 777-9 is the larger version, typically seating about 426
     passengers in a two-class configuration.

### Key Features:
- **Advanced Wing Design**: The 777X features new, larger wings with
folding wingtips to enhance aerodynamics while allowing for compatibility
at airport gates.
- **GE9X Engines**: It is powered by the GE9X engines, which are the
largest commercial jet engines in operation, designed for improved fuel
efficiency and reduced emissions.
```

```
The 777X aims to set new standards in fuel efficiency, passenger comfort,
and operational performance in the long-haul airline market. For the latest
updates regarding the aircraft, including certification and delivery
status, checking Boeing's official communications would be beneficial.
```

This response is helpful, but your system cannot necessarily know where the contextual elements like the model and manufacturer are located if you send this JSON-formatted output to your UI/UX or to some other downstream application API that expects the output to be in some predefined format.

The system, powered by LangChain4j and with an LLM configured for structured outputs, processes the input and should generate a structured response like this:

```
{
  "manufacturer": "Boeing Commercial Airplanes",
  "model": "Boeing 777X",
  "maxDistance": {
    "Boeing 777-8": "8000 nautical miles (14800 kilometers)",
    "Boeing 777-9": "7000 nautical miles (12964 kilometers)"
  }
}
```

This structured output not only meets the customer's needs but also integrates seamlessly into the application's workflows, allowing for actions like displaying flight details, booking tickets, or combining data with itinerary planning tools.

Structured outputs ensure the reliability and usability of data. They enable:

- **Consistency**: Outputs adhere to a predefined schema, reducing ambiguity.
- **Automation**: JSON responses map directly to Java objects, streamlining integration.
- **Scalability**: Organized outputs support larger systems that rely on consistent data formats.

Structured outputs are a feature offered by some LLM providers (e.g., OpenAI and Google Gemini) that allow responses to conform to a JSON schema. By specifying the schema in the API request, the LLM generates responses that fit this structure, eliminating the need for additional prompt engineering.

For aircraft-related data, a schema might include fields like the `manufacturer`, `model`, and `maxDistance`. This ensures that all essential information is extracted and structured systematically.

Let's explore how to handle aircraft-related information using structured outputs.

```
return
{"manufacturer":"Boeing Commercial Airplanes","model":"777X",
"maxDistance":8730.0}
```

Let's will first create a POJO object representing the `Aircraft` entity. Let's represent this in a file named `Aircraft.java`.

File: Aircraft.java

```
package com.example.travelx;

public class Aircraft {
    private String manufacturer;
    private String model;
    private double maxDistance;

    public String getManufacturer() {
        return manufacturer;
    }

    public void setManufacturer(String manufacturer) {
        this.manufacturer = manufacturer;
    }

    public String getModel() {
        return model;
    }

    public void setModel(String model) {
        this.model = model;
    }

    public double getMaxDistance() {
        return maxDistance;
    }
```

```
    public void setMaxDistance(double maxDistance) {
        this.maxDistance = maxDistance;
    }

    @Override
    public String toString() {
        return "Aircraft {" +
                " manufacturer = \"" + manufacturer + "\"" +
                ", model = \"" + model + "\"" +
                ", maxDistance = " + maxDistance +
                " }";
    }
}
```

Let's then modify the LangchainConfig.java file to use the aircraft structure so that the chat model is aware of your expectations.

File: LangchainConfig.java

```
package com.example.travelx;

import static dev.langchain4j.data.message.ChatMessageDeserializer.
messagesFromJson;
import static dev.langchain4j.data.message.ChatMessageSerializer.
messagesToJson;

import java.util.List;
import java.util.Map;

import org.mapdb.DB;
import org.mapdb.DBMaker;
import static org.mapdb.Serializer.STRING;
import org.springframework.beans.factory.annotation.Value;
import org.springframework.context.annotation.Bean;
import org.springframework.context.annotation.Configuration;

import dev.langchain4j.data.message.ChatMessage;

import static dev.langchain4j.model.openai.OpenAiChatModelName.
GPT_4_O_MINI;
```

```
import dev.langchain4j.memory.chat.MessageWindowChatMemory;
import dev.langchain4j.model.openai.OpenAiChatModel;
import dev.langchain4j.service.AiServices;
import dev.langchain4j.store.memory.chat.ChatMemoryStore;
```

Then you modify the `openAiChatModel` method to create a response format object based on the `Aircraft` model structure. This response format is then passed to your model builder so that this expectation can be set and communicated to your LLM model, which in this case is the OpenAI LLM.

```
private OpenAiChatModel openAiChatModel() {
    this.model = OpenAiChatModel.builder()
            .apiKey(apiKey)
            .modelName(GPT_4_O_MINI)
            .responseFormat("json_schema")
            .strictJsonSchema(true)
            .logRequests(true)
            .logResponses(true)
            .build();

    return this.model;
}
```

Once this is set up, you then need to extract the `Aircraft` JSON response from the LLM output response. This can be accomplished through the use of the extractor method as shared in the following code. You can leverage the `AiServices` package to create an extractor object based on the `AircraftExtractor` interface and `chatModel`, which have information about your Aircraft POJO entity. The extractor service is used to extract the JSON-specific field and data from your output response.

File: ServiceWithPersistentMemory.java

```
package com.example.travelx;

import org.springframework.context.annotation.Bean;
import org.springframework.context.annotation.Configuration;

import dev.langchain4j.model.openai.OpenAiChatModel;
import dev.langchain4j.service.AiServices;
```

```
@Configuration
public class ServiceWithPersistentMemory {

    private Assistant assistant;
     private OpenAiChatModel chatModel;

    @Bean
     public Assistant chatAssistant(Assistant assistant, OpenAiChatModel
     chatModel) {
         this.assistant = assistant;
         this.chatModel = chatModel;
         return this.assistant;
     }

     public Aircraft chat(String message) {
         String response = this.assistant.chat(message);
         AircraftExtractor aircraftExtractor = AiServices.
         create(AircraftExtractor.class, chatModel);
         Aircraft aircraft = aircraftExtractor.
         extractAircraftFrom(response);
         return aircraft;
     }
}
```

File: AircraftExtractor.java

```
package com.example.travelx;

public interface AircraftExtractor {
    Aircraft extractAircraftFrom(String text);
}
```

This allows the application to process and display the flight details efficiently, eliminating manual data transformation.

Handling LLM outputs through structured formats ensures data reliability, minimizes errors, and improves integration with downstream systems. By leveraging features like structured outputs in LangChain4j, you can efficiently extract and process flight information, meeting both customer and application requirements. This approach simplifies the development process while ensuring the accuracy and usability of the data, making it a vital tool in building robust applications.

Security Considerations

When integrating LLMs into Java applications, security becomes a crucial aspect that you can't afford to overlook. While these models are incredibly powerful, they also come with inherent risks, like exposing sensitive data and generating potentially harmful outputs. Let's dive into some key security considerations and how you can implement guardrails to ensure safe and effective operation while you continue building your project.

Initially, let's address sensitive data protection. Since LLMs process whatever input you provide, it's essential to ensure that no confidential or sensitive information is passed along inadvertently. Imagine if a user were to input personally identifiable information (PII) or proprietary business data. Without safeguards, you'd risk data exposure. To prevent this, you can anonymize inputs, replacing sensitive details with placeholders, and ensure that all communication with the LLM happens over secure protocols like HTTPS. This not only keeps data safe but also aligns with best practices in secure API integration. It's worth asking ourselves: does your application already handle sensitive inputs, and if so, how are you managing this risk? If not, this is a good time to add that layer of protection.

Now, API key management is a critical component that can have big consequences if not handled properly. Your API keys act as the gateway to LLMs, and if they fall into the wrong hands, they could lead to unauthorized access and skyrocketing usage costs. Instead of hard-coding these keys into the application, you can store them securely using environment variables or encrypted configuration files. Plus, periodically rotating these keys adds an extra layer of safety. You should also monitor usage to detect any anomalies, like unexpected spikes. Let's make sure your project is covering this aspect; are you already managing keys securely, or do you need to revisit this?

Another area you can't ignore is guardrails for managing outputs. LLMs, as smart as they are, sometimes "hallucinate" by providing incorrect or nonsensical information. Worse, they could generate biased or inappropriate responses if left unchecked. By using prompt engineering, you can limit the model's scope—like you saw earlier when you asked it to stick to known facts. On top of that, you can add a validation layer to review outputs, perhaps using a post-processing step to cross-check facts or filter out undesirable content. This ensures you deliver clean, accurate responses to users. For your application, does this feel like a necessary next step? If so, you can brainstorm what checks would work best for your use case.

Then there's context management, especially in scenarios where users expect the system to remember their previous queries. While context makes interactions feel more seamless, it also raises questions about data retention and access control. You need to set clear policies, like how long you store chat histories and who gets access to them. LangChain4j's chat memory is a great tool here, as it lets you handle context without compromising security. For your project, have you decided how long you'll store user interactions, or is that something to figure out as you go?

Let's also touch on rate limiting and abuse prevention. Without proper limits, your API could be overwhelmed, either accidentally by heavy users or maliciously by bad actors. By setting rate limits per user or IP address and validating inputs to filter out harmful content, you can protect the system from overuse or abuse. This step might sound technical, but it's crucial for maintaining a stable and secure application. Are you already thinking about usage limits, or should you add this to your to-do list?

Finally, you need to think about monitoring and auditing. Logging all requests and responses helps us track how the application is being used and detect unusual activity. Regular audits also keep us aligned with best practices and organizational policies. Let's make sure your logs are thorough yet secure. Have you thought about what level of monitoring you'll need as the project scales?

The great thing is, LangChain4j provides tools that can simplify a lot of this work. Many of these are covered in subsequent chapters in greater detail. Its chat memory lets us handle context without manually managing histories, and its flexibility allows us to experiment with different LLM providers to find the best fit for your needs. Plus, it supports post-processing and filtering for outputs, which helps enforce guardrails seamlessly. With these features in hand, you're well-equipped to address these security challenges.

As you move forward, security is something you'll need to keep iterating on—it's not a one-time setup but an ongoing effort. For now, though, we've got a solid foundation to build on. Let's ensure your system is not only powerful and user-friendly but also safe and secure for everyone involved. Sound like a plan?

Conclusion

In this chapter, you explored how to effectively integrate LLM into Java applications using LangChain4j, a library designed to simplify interactions with LLM providers. You gained a thorough understanding of how to connect with multiple LLM providers through a unified API, enabling us to experiment and optimize applications with various LLMs.

The chapter emphasized the importance of prompt engineering, showcasing how crafting effective prompts can ensure accurate and contextual LLM responses. Through practical examples, you saw how small adjustments in prompts could mitigate hallucinations by enforcing strict contextual boundaries, thus enhancing the reliability of the outputs. You also addressed the challenge of maintaining context across API calls by use chat memory. By retaining previous interactions and building persistent memory, you improved the coherence of responses to related queries, leveraging LangChain4j's features to implement this seamlessly.

You explored the flexibility of switching between LLM providers, comparing outputs and selecting the most suitable model for your specific needs. Additionally, you delved into techniques for handling LLM outputs, emphasizing methods to validate and refine responses to ensure accuracy and reliability. Throughout the chapter, you also considered security aspects, discussing the importance of safeguarding sensitive data, securely managing API keys, and mitigating potential risks such as data leakage.

By working through practical examples and reusable code snippets, you built a strong foundation for integrating LLMs into Java applications. This chapter has equipped you to leverage LangChain4j for developing dynamic, context-aware, and secure applications while optimizing performance and adaptability to various use cases. Now, you will move on to integrating contextual information.

CHAPTER 7

From Chatty to Clever: Retrieval-Augmented Generation

The goal of this chapter is to use contextual information that is more specific to organizations in order to provide context-specific answers to customer questions. This will be introduced by using LangChain4J with retrieval-augmented generation (RAG).

Introduction

In the previous chapter, you learned about using LangChain4j to integrate your Java application with OpenAI to get information related to different aircrafts. This scenario is useful in many cases when you want generalized information. However, customer problems and queries are more often contextual than not to the organization they are interacting with. For example, our imaginary travel company TravelX uses a specific set of aircrafts for travel. In the subsequent sections, you will learn how to leverage contextual information that might be present in PDFs, files, and other systems internal to the organization to give contextual answers to customer queries. Along the way, you will learn about the RAG pattern which helps to find contextual information. There are many components of the RAG paradigm like embeddings and vector stores that we will touch upon while integrating them into your example TravelX application.

S. K. Sahu, *Generative AI-Driven Application Development with Java*,
https://doi.org/10.1007/979-8-8688-1609-3_7

Contextuality in the LLM Ecosystem

If we refer to Figure 7-1, the customer query reaches our Spring Boot application and then is redirected to OpenAI. The response from the LLM is shared with our customers. This simple pattern is helpful in many cases but may not always be up-to-date with the latest information given the model might have been trained only up to a certain point in the past. In the information age of today, current and factual information always helps to serve our customers better. In addition, a company's edge over its competitors is its contextual in-house proprietary data along with any customer-specific data that it has. So, if we ask the application anything particular to our application, without any prompt hinting, it may try to hallucinate. One way to reduce hallucination is to use prompt engineering. You will start with this and incrementally learn and see the usage of the RAG paradigm.

To set the context for your use case, you now want to provide information to your customers about the flights that are operational through our airline TravelX. As per the previous chapter, you were able to get some information related to Aircraft and share the JSON of the information as a response. Since this is a new requirement for your team and you need to share the flight information, you will start with creating foundational entities for the flight details.

Similar to the `Aircraft` class, you will create a POJO for the `Flight` entity. The flight details that you will be sharing with our customers will have a few details like aircraft model, date of departure, from city, to city, departure airport, arrival airport, flight number, departure time, arrival time, and status of the flight. Figure 7-1 depicts the UML diagram for all the classes and relationships you will using throughout this chapter.

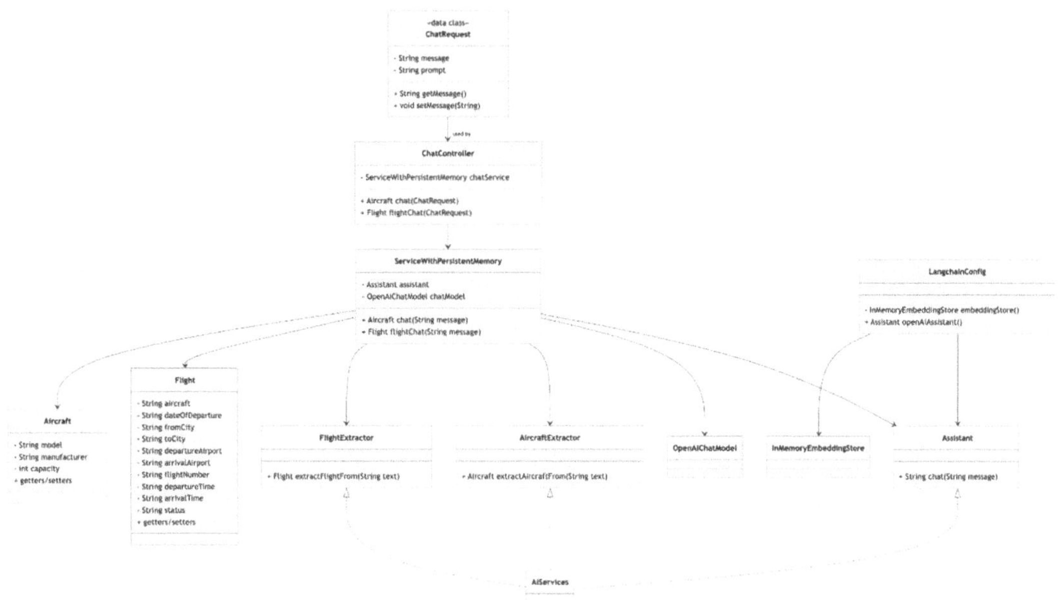

Figure 7-1. *UML diagram of the classes and relationships of project*

File: ./src/main/java/com/example/travelx/Flight.java

```
package com.example.travelx;

public class Flight {
    private String aircraft;
    private String dateOfDeparture;
    private String fromCity;
    private String toCity;
    private String departureAirport;
    private String arrivalAirport;
    private String flightNumber;
    private String departureTime;
    private String arrivalTime;
    private String status;

    // Getters and Setters
   public String getAircraft() {
        return aircraft;
    }
```

```
    public void setAircraft(String aircraft) {
        this.aircraft = aircraft;
    }

    public String getDateOfDeparture() {
        return dateOfDeparture;
    }

    public void setDateOfDeparture(String dateOfDeparture) {
        this.dateOfDeparture = dateOfDeparture;
    }

    public String getFromCity() {
        return fromCity;
    }

    public void setFromCity(String fromCity) {
        this.fromCity = fromCity;
    }

    public String getToCity() {
        return toCity;
    }

    public void setToCity(String toCity) {
        this.toCity = toCity;
    }

    public String getDepartureAirport() {
        return departureAirport;
    }

    public void setDepartureAirport(String departureAirport) {
        this.departureAirport = departureAirport;
    }

    public String getArrivalAirport() {
        return arrivalAirport;
    }
```

```
public void setArrivalAirport(String arrivalAirport) {
    this.arrivalAirport = arrivalAirport;
}

public String getFlightNumber() {
    return flightNumber;
}

public void setFlightNumber(String flightNumber) {
    this.flightNumber = flightNumber;
}

public String getDepartureTime() {
    return departureTime;
}

public void setDepartureTime(String departureTime) {
    this.departureTime = departureTime;
}

public String getArrivalTime() {
    return arrivalTime;
}

public void setArrivalTime(String arrivalTime) {
    this.arrivalTime = arrivalTime;
}

public String getStatus() {
    return status;
}

public void setStatus(String status) {
    this.status = status;
}

@Override
public String toString() {
    return "Flight {" +
            " aircraft = \"" + aircraft + "\"" +
```

```
                ", dateOfDeparture = \"" + dateOfDeparture + "\"" +
                ", fromCity = \"" + fromCity + "\"" +
                ", toCity = \"" + toCity + "\"" +
                ", departureAirport = \"" + departureAirport + "\"" +
                ", arrivalAirport = \"" + arrivalAirport + "\"" +
                ", flightNumber = \"" + flightNumber + "\"" +
                ", departureTime = \"" + departureTime + "\"" +
                ", arrivalTime = \"" + arrivalTime + "\"" +
                ", status = \"" + status + "\"" +
                " }";
    }
}
```

The goal of setting up the previous entity class is to set the structure to extract the LLM response into a JSON format that you can share as response with the customer. The next step is to create the interface similar to `AircraftExtractor` that you created that LangChain4j uses to extract the structure from the LLM response.

File: ./src/main/java/com/example/travelx/FlightExtractor.java

```
package com.example.travelx;

public interface FlightExtractor {
    Flight extractFlightFrom(String text);
}
```

Now, you will create a new method called `flightChat` in the service file to get the flight details.

File: ./src/main/java/com/example/travelx/ServiceWithPersistentMemory.java

```
package com.example.travelx;

import org.springframework.context.annotation.Bean;
import org.springframework.context.annotation.Configuration;

import dev.langchain4j.model.openai.OpenAiChatModel;
import dev.langchain4j.service.AiServices;
```

```
@Configuration
public class ServiceWithPersistentMemory {
    private Assistant assistant;
    private OpenAiChatModel chatModel;

    @Bean
    public Assistant chatAssistant(Assistant assistant, OpenAiChatModel
    chatModel) {
        this.assistant = assistant;
        this.chatModel = chatModel;
        return this.assistant;
    }

    public Aircraft chat(String message) {
        String response = this.assistant.chat(message);
        AircraftExtractor aircraftExtractor = AiServices.
        create(AircraftExtractor.class, chatModel);
        Aircraft aircraft = aircraftExtractor.
        extractAircraftFrom(response);
        return aircraft;
    }

    public Flight flightChat(String message) {
        String response = this.assistant.chat(message);
        FlightExtractor flightExtractor = AiServices.
        create(FlightExtractor.class, chatModel);
        Flight flight = flightExtractor.extractFlightFrom(response);
        return flight;
    }
}
```

The final step to invoke this service method is through the controller where you will create a new route for the path `/api/flight-chat`.

File: ./src/main/java/com/example/travelx/ChatController.java

```
package com.example.travelx;

import org.springframework.web.bind.annotation.*;

@RestController
public class ChatController {

    private ServiceWithPersistentMemory chatService;

    public ChatController(ServiceWithPersistentMemory chatService) {
        this.chatService = chatService;
    }

    @PostMapping("/api/chat")
    public Aircraft chat(@RequestBody ChatRequest chatRequest) {
        return this.chatService.chat(chatRequest.getMessage());
    }

    @PostMapping("/api/flight-chat")
    public Flight flightChat(@RequestBody ChatRequest chatRequest) {
        return this.chatService.flightChat(chatRequest.getMessage());
    }
}
```

Let's power up the application and see the response from this API for a flight that is not available from any airlines in the world at this moment apart from your airline.

```
curl -X POST http://localhost:8080/api/flight-chat -H "Content-Type:
application/json" -d '{
 "message": "Tell me about flight details for AABB101."
}'
```

Output:


```
{"aircraft":"Boeing 737","dateOfDeparture":"2023-10-15","fromCity":
"New York","toCity":"Los Angeles","departureAirport":"JFK","arrivalAirport":
"LAX","flightNumber":"AA1234","departureTime":"14:30","arrivalTime":"17:00",
"status":"On Time"}
```

Note Please make sure to delete the `chat-memory.db` file to remove any historical chat from previous chapters.

The previous is a clear case of hallucination since this flight does not exist in the knowledge base of the trained LLM nor in any real-world scenario. Also, if you observe the output response, the `flightNumber` is different than requested. Essentially the LLM was not able to find the requested flight and instead shared info for some other flight data.

Previously, you had a component to add some prompt engineering in the file `ChatRequest.java` to check for factual responses. Considering its presence, you should not be receiving this response. Let's modify the code slightly to take this into consideration.

File: ./src/main/java/com/example/travelx/ChatRequest.java

```
package com.example.travelx;

class ChatRequest {

    private String message;
    public static String defaultMessage = "Sorry, I am not aware of
    this context. Please let me know if I can help you with any other
    requests.";
    private String prompt = "Please limit the responses to known facts.
    If you do not know about the context or the answer, simply say '" +
    ChatRequest.defaultMessage + "'";

   public String getMessage() {
        return prompt + " " + message;
    }

   public void setMessage(String message) {
        this.message = prompt + " " + message;
    }
}
```

You have created a placeholder for the defaultMessage and used it inside the prompt. This variable will later be reused in the service to check the response from the LLM, and if it has this default message instead of calling extractor, you will send a default class instance with null values to keep it simple for now. Let's see this change in action.

File: ./src/main/java/com/example/travelx/ServiceWithPersistentMemory.java

```
package com.example.travelx;

import org.springframework.context.annotation.Bean;
import org.springframework.context.annotation.Configuration;

import dev.langchain4j.model.openai.OpenAiChatModel;
import dev.langchain4j.service.AiServices;

@Configuration
public class ServiceWithPersistentMemory {

    private Assistant assistant;
    private OpenAiChatModel chatModel;

    @Bean
    public Assistant chatAssistant(Assistant assistant, OpenAiChatModel
    chatModel) {
        this.assistant = assistant;
        this.chatModel = chatModel;
        return this.assistant;
    }

    public Aircraft chat(String message) {
        String response = this.assistant.chat(message);
        Aircraft aircraft = new Aircraft();

        if (!response.equals(ChatRequest.defaultMessage)) {
            AircraftExtractor aircraftExtractor = AiServices.
            create(AircraftExtractor.class, chatModel);
            aircraft = aircraftExtractor.extractAircraftFrom(response);
        }
```

```
        return aircraft;
    }

    public Flight flightChat(String message) {
        String response = this.assistant.chat(message);
        Flight flight = new Flight();

        if (!response.equals(ChatRequest.defaultMessage)) {
            FlightExtractor flightExtractor = AiServices.
            create(FlightExtractor.class, chatModel);
            flight = flightExtractor.extractFlightFrom(response);
        }

        return flight;
    }
}
```

So now you have created a placeholder variable for the aircraft and flight to store the default instance object and check if the response from the LLM is equal to our previously created `defaultMessage`. If it is, you return it; otherwise, you extract the respective object entity from the response.

Let's reboot the application and test this.

```
curl -X POST http://localhost:8080/api/flight-chat -H "Content-Type:
application/json" -d '{
 "message": "Tell me about flight details for AABB101."
}'
```

Output:

{"aircraft":null,"dateOfDeparture":null,"fromCity":null,"toCity":null,"depa
rtureAirport":null,"arrivalAirport":null,"flightNumber":null,"departureTime
":null,"arrivalTime":null,"status":null}

RAG Paradigm

Until this point, you have been using a simple query pattern, as depicted in Figure 7-2 where you are relying on the information of the LLM to answer the user's query.

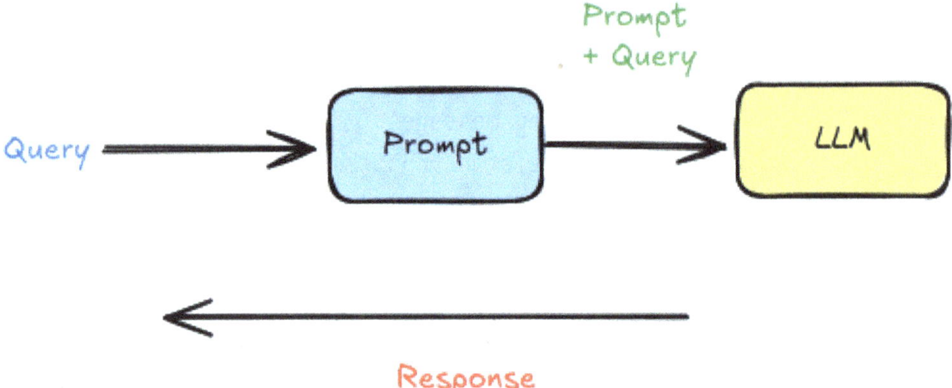

Figure 7-2. *Simple query pattern*

In addition, you have been able to suggest/advise the LLM to consider any rules, facts, or style in which you want it to reply in. Through prompt engineering, you can ask the LLM not to hallucinate through keeping its replies limited to its knowledge base. If you want the LLM to have more knowledge, you have to either rely on creating another foundation model or fine-tune an existing foundational model.

Training a foundational model means creating an LLM from scratch by feeding it large amounts of data. This takes a lot of time, resources in terms of effort, and GPUs costing a lot of money over several days. This method is sometimes out of reach for many organizations and startups that want to leverage LLM. There is another way to supplement the knowledge of existing foundational models, which is training them with additional data specific to your organization, which is effective in terms of cost and training resources and time. This requires some specialized knowledge in terms of building machine learning models using transformers and other architectures, which is out of scope of this book.

There is another cost-effective method in terms of achieving similar results without creating a foundational model from scratch or fine-tuning it. This methodology uses prompt engineering and the token size of the LLM into consideration to solve this problem statement. It's called the RAG paradigm.

RAG stands for retrieval-augmented generation. Let's try to understand it in simple incremental terms. Every LLM/SLM has a token space as the maximum number of tokens it can facilitate in its request-response cycle referred to as its *context length*. The concept of a token is a bit more complex than just considering it as a character, but for this discussion let's assume a token is a character.

Tokens are the fundamental units of text that LLMs use to understand and generate language. A token might be a single character, part of a word, a whole word, or even punctuation—depending on how the model's tokenizer breaks down the input. For example, the word "airplane" might be one token in some models but split into two or more tokens in others. LLMs do not process raw text directly; instead, they convert it into a sequence of tokens before performing any operation. Each model has a fixed *context length*, which is the maximum number of tokens it can handle in a single request, including both the input (prompt and context) and the output (response). If the total number of tokens exceeds this limit, part of the input or output may be truncated, leading to incomplete results. Efficient token management helps ensure that important context is retained and meaningful responses are generated. This is particularly important in tasks like RAG, where additional context is appended to prompts. Understanding how tokens work enables better prompt design and improves the reliability of responses from the LLM.

Let's take the example of the Deepseek-R1 model, which we used in previous chapters. As shown in Figure 7-3, the context length for the R1 model is 128K tokens. This includes the request tokens plus the response tokens.

DeepSeek-R1 Models

Model	#Total Params	#Activated Params	Context Length	Download
DeepSeek-R1-Zero	671B	37B	128K	🤗 HuggingFace
DeepSeek-R1	671B	37B	128K	🤗 HuggingFace

Figure 7-3. *Context length of DeepSeek R1 models(Reference:* `https://github.com/deepseek-ai/DeepSeek-R1`*)*

The request token could be the sum of your customer query plus the conversation history memory tokens plus the prompt message you include to keep the context limited to facts, while the response token is the response from the LLM to answer the prompt request, as shown in Figure 7-4. This context length is specific to the LLM in use. Small foundational models have a smaller context length, while LLMs might have a bigger context length. Context length is helpful in two ways.

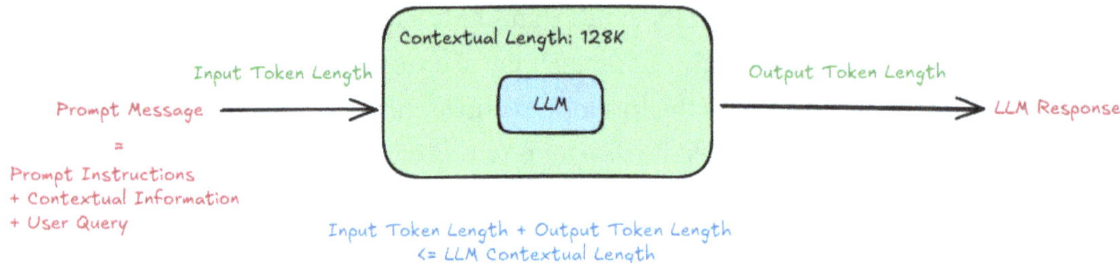

Figure 7-4. *Contextual length and token summary for Deepseek-R1 context length*

First, it is helpful when you are expecting a larger token response from the LLM and it can do so only if it has a larger contextual length by default and you do not take too much of this space through the use of the input tokens, which would reduce the output token length. Second, it is helpful when you are expecting to provide a huge context in the input token you provide it through prompt engineering, which could contain information related to your organization so that the LLM can use this context then to answer your query. Using more token space than the context length will truncate the extending tokens from the output response of the LLM. This will happen in two cases, all of which finally result in overflowing the contextual length.

The first case is when the input prompt message is greater than the contextual length. This results in two side effects. Since the input is greater in size, it is truncated in terms of how many tokens reach the LLM, and since the input is truncated, you are not sure if the LLM received the right question and which part of the prompt was truncated. It depends how you organized your prompt in terms of concatenating the instructions, context, and user query. And since there is no space left for any response in the context length, you will not receive any response in this case.

The second case is when the output that the LLM comes up with is larger than the remaining space of the Context Length - Prompt context length. So, the response might be 60K tokens, but the remaining contextual space might be 40K in which case you will receive only the 40K token length of the previously determined output from the LLM. This will give you an incomplete response.

So eventually token planning and management are crucial aspects of LLM engineering. Now that you understand the concept of contextual length, you can use this to understand how you can share contextual knowledge with the LLM. Let's say you have a document that has all of your organizational information that might be relevant to your customers and it results in a 50K token size. If the context length of the LLM facilitates the input prompt including this 50K token from the organizational contextual knowledge and the response you are expecting, you are good to provide the LLM with more information that it can use to answer the query of the users since it has this information to answer from in the prompt message. So with each prompt message to the LLM, you will always be sending the organization contextual information, as shown in Figure 7-5.

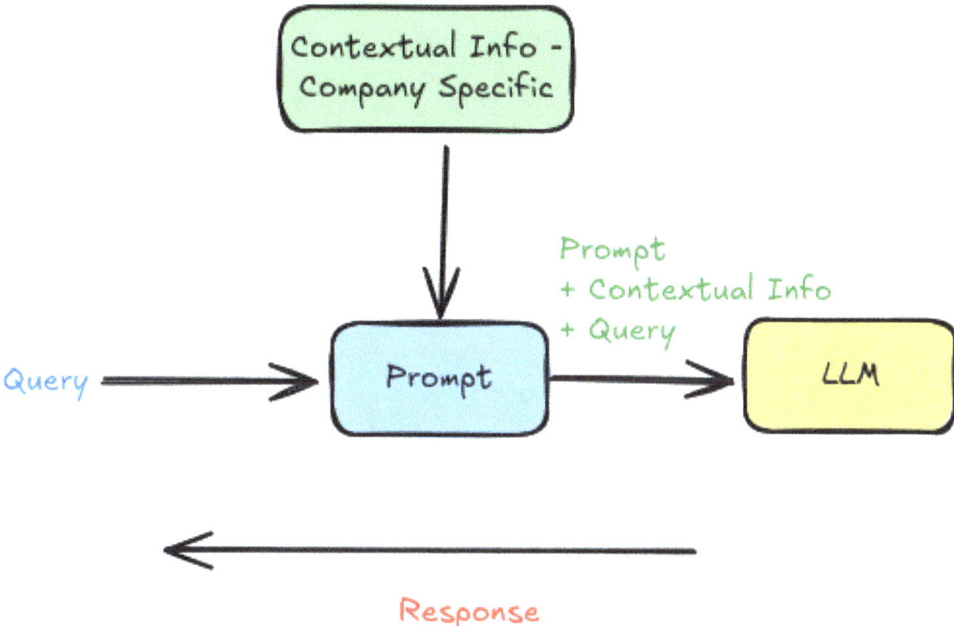

Figure 7-5. *Contextual info in prompt*

This may be fine as your organization is just starting but may not be feasible as you grow. For larger organizations, this data may be in several sources like SharePoint, PDFs, and databases and you cannot bring all of this information and always pass it to the prompt since it will in most cases be more than the context length. Also, not all of the information is helpful in answering the user's query. The whole organization might have information for different contexts like human resources, customers, and operations, while the user query might be relevant only to the operational aspect of the company. So, fetching all the info and feeding it to the LLM might be inefficient and will add to the input-output request-response time while you want to serve requests and solve their queries faster.

What if you could filter out the contextual information that is relevant only to your customer query before passing this information to the LLM? This not only results in less information but saves you contextual token length while being more specific in your response. So, you need a way to do a fast contextual search of your information/documents/resources and then use this information to answer the query of the customer in a natural language friendly manner using an LLM. This is what the RAG methodology does: retrieve (R) contextual information, (A) augment the knowledge of the foundational model, and (G) generate a natural language response to the query of the user using LLMs, as shown in Figure 7-6.

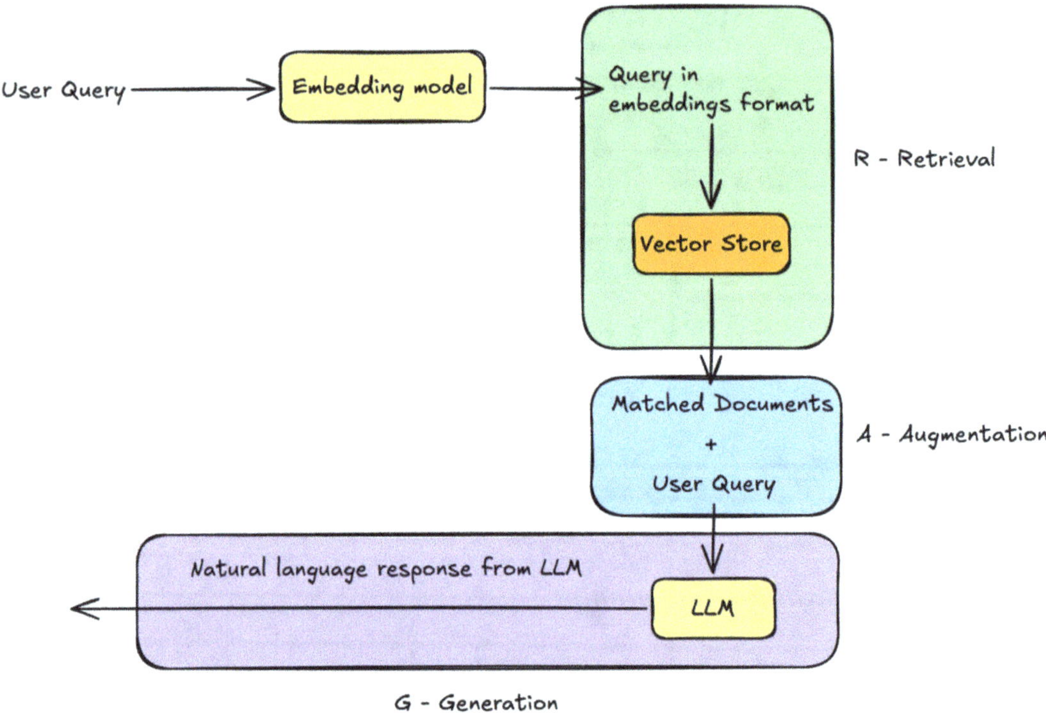

Figure 7-6. *RAG paradigm*

Embeddings

Embeddings are like magic stickers you put on words and pictures. Each sticker has a special number that tells you how similar things are. Imagine you have stickers for animals—dogs get stickers with numbers close to cats, because they're both pets and furry. But a fish would have a sticker with a number far away, because it's different. These magic stickers help computers quickly find things that go together, like matching questions with the best answers!

In the RAG paradigm, *embeddings* are numerical representations of data such as text, speech, images, or videos. Embeddings transform high-dimensional, heterogeneous real-world data into low-dimensional numerical vectors, capturing semantic meaning in a compact form. The geometric distance between these vectors reflects semantic similarity, allowing quick identification of contextually relevant information. For example, words or phrases with similar meanings have embeddings close to each other, enabling efficient retrieval of related documents or data chunks from a large dataset. By embedding both queries and data into the same vector space, RAG leverages vector databases to rapidly retrieve the most relevant contextual information, significantly reducing hallucinations and improving the accuracy of language model responses.

In RAG, embeddings are numerical representations of textual information used to efficiently retrieve relevant context for answering user queries. Embeddings convert words, sentences, or entire documents into vector representations within a high-dimensional space, such that texts with similar meanings or contexts placed closer together, while dissimilar texts are spaced farther apart. Within RAG, embeddings play a critical role by encoding organizational documents, knowledge bases, or databases into these numeric vectors. When a user submits a query, it is also converted into an embedding vector and compared against stored embeddings to swiftly retrieve the most relevant contextual information. This retrieved context is then appended to the query and provided to the language model, significantly reducing hallucinations and improving the accuracy and specificity of the generated response. For example, if a user asks about "flight AA101," their query embedding will closely match stored embeddings of actual flight details, allowing the model to provide precise, context-specific information. Overall, embeddings enable faster retrieval, minimize incorrect information, and enhance the scalability and reliability of answers provided by large language models within the RAG framework.

Vector Store

Imagine you have a special toy box that helps you find your toys really fast. Each toy has a magic sticker with numbers, and toys that are alike, like cars or dolls, have stickers with numbers close to each other. This special toy box is called a *vector store,* and it keeps all your toys organized by their magic stickers.

When you want a certain toy, you show the box another magic sticker that looks like the toy you want. The box quickly searches and finds the toys with stickers closest to the one you showed it—that's called *vector search*. So, instead of searching everywhere, the magic box finds your favorite toys quickly because it knows exactly where similar toys are.

Traditional search methods, such as keyword search and full-text search, rely on matching exact words or phrases within documents. While useful, they fall short when the language used in a query doesn't exactly match the content in the database. For instance, searching for "morning coffee drink" might miss documents that mention only "cappuccino," even though they're semantically related. These traditional systems struggle with synonyms, misspellings, and varied phrasing.

To address this, we've moved toward vector search, which is based on semantic understanding rather than exact text matching. In vector search, both the data (documents, images, etc.) and the user's query are converted into embeddings—numerical vectors that capture the meaning of the content. Once both are in the same vector space, similarity between them can be calculated using mathematical metrics like cosine similarity, Euclidean distance, or dot product. This allows the system to return relevant results even if they use different words than the query.

A *vector store* (or *vector database*) is a specialized database designed to store and manage these embeddings efficiently. It enables high-speed, scalable similarity search across millions of data points. When a query is made, its embedding is compared to those in the vector store, and the closest (i.e., most semantically similar) vectors are retrieved—enabling much more relevant and intelligent results than keyword search.

Some popular open-source vector stores include:

- FAISS (Facebook AI Similarity Search)
- Weaviate
- ChromaDB
- Annoy
- Milvus

There are also managed and enterprise-ready vector search solutions like:

- Google Vertex AI Vector Search
- Pinecone

- ElasticSearch with vector search plugins
- AlloyDB (with pgvector and ScaNN)

These vector stores often support hybrid search, combining both vector (semantic) and keyword (literal) search capabilities for best-of-both-worlds retrieval.

The evolution from keyword to vector search reflects a broader shift toward meaning-based search, where understanding the user's intent and context is more important than exact word matches. This shift is especially critical in AI-driven applications like recommendation systems, fraud detection, question answering, and RAG.

RAG in Action

You will start by using a feature of LangChain4j called easy RAG to get started with the RAG pattern without using any subcomponents involved.

Let's update a dependency in our `build.gradle` file.

File: ./build.gradle

```
dependencies {
      ...
      implementation 'dev.langchain4j:langchain4j-easy-rag:1.0.0-alpha1'
      ...
}
```

Being an airline company, the example company has proprietary flight data. This could be present in any data store and format like CSV, JSON, or relational databases. To keep it simple, you will store all the flight data in a text file in CSV format. The first row will have field names like Aircraft, Date of Departure, From/To, etc., and the subsequent rows will have different flight details. This file can be stored in the `resources` folder.

File: ./src/main/resources/static/flight-details.txt

```
Aircraft,Date of Departure,From (US City),To (US City),Departure
Airport,Arrival Airport,Flight Number,Departure Time,Arrival Time,Status
Boeing 737,2023-11-01,New York,Los Angeles,JFK,LAX,AA101,08:00,1
1:00,On Time
Airbus A320,2023-11-01,Chicago,Miami,ORD,MIA,DL202,09:30,13:00,On Time
```

```
Boeing 787,2023-11-01,San Francisco,Seattle,SFO,SEA,UA303,10:15,1
2:00,Delayed
Airbus A321,2023-11-01,Houston,Dallas,IAH,DFW,SW404,11:45,13:15,On Time
Boeing 737,2023-11-01,Atlanta,Denver,ATL,DEN,AA505,12:30,15:00,On Time
Airbus A320,2023-11-01,Boston,Las Vegas,BOS,LAS,DL606,14:00,17:30,Cancelled
Boeing 787,2023-11-01,Philadelphia,Phoenix,PHL,PHX,UA707,15:45,18:
30,On Time
Airbus A321,2023-11-01,Orlando,San Diego,MCO,SAN,SW808,16:30,19:00,On Time
Boeing 737,2023-11-02,New York,Chicago,JFK,ORD,AA909,07:00,09:00,On Time
Airbus A320,2023-11-02,Los Angeles,Houston,LAX,IAH,DL101,08:30,1
2:00,On Time
Boeing 787,2023-11-02,Miami,Atlanta,MIA,ATL,UA202,10:00,12:00,Delayed
Airbus A321,2023-11-02,Seattle,Dallas,SEA,DFW,SW303,11:15,14:30,On Time
Boeing 737,2023-11-02,Denver,Boston,DEN,BOS,AA4041,13:00,17:00,On Time
Airbus A320,2023-11-02,Las Vegas,Philadelphia,LAS,PHL,DL505,14:30,18:00,
Cancelled Boeing 787,2023-11-02,Phoenix,Orlando,PHX,MCO,UA606,16:00,20:
00,On Time
Airbus A321,2023-11-02,San Diego,New York,SAN,JFK,SW707,17:45,21:30,On Time
Boeing 737,2023-11-03,Chicago,Los Angeles,ORD,LAX,AA808,08:00,10:30,On Time
Airbus A320,2023-11-03,Houston,San Francisco,IAH,SFO,DL909,09:30,1
2:00,On Time
Boeing 787,2023-11-03,Atlanta,Seattle,ATL,SEA,UA101,11:00,14:00,Delayed
Airbus A321,2023-11-03,Dallas,Miami,DFW,MIA,SW202,12:15,15:30,On Time
Boeing 737,2023-11-03,Boston,Denver,BOS,DEN,AA303,13:30,16:30,On Time
Airbus A320,2023-11-03,Philadelphia,Las Vegas,PHL,LAS,DL404,15:00,18:30,
Cancelled Boeing 787,2023-11-03,Orlando,Phoenix,MCO,PHX,UA505,16:45,20:
00,On Time
Airbus A321,2023-11-03,New York,San Diego,JFK,SAN,SW606,18:00,21:30,On Time
Boeing 737,2023-11-04,Los Angeles,Chicago,LAX,ORD,AA707,07:30,10:00,On Time
Airbus A320,2023-11-04,San Francisco,Houston,SFO,IAH,DL808,09:00,1
2:30,On Time
Boeing 787,2023-11-04,Seattle,Atlanta,SEA,ATL,UA909,10:30,13:30,Delayed
Airbus A321,2023-11-04,Miami,Dallas,MIA,DFW,SW101,11:45,14:45,On Time
Boeing 737,2023-11-04,Denver,Boston,DEN,BOS,AA202,13:00,17:00,On Time
```

```
Airbus A320,2023-11-04,Las Vegas,Philadelphia,LAS,PHL,DL303,14:30,18:00,
Cancelled Boeing 787,2023-11-04,Phoenix,Orlando,PHX,MCO,UA404,16:00,20:
00,On Time
Airbus A321,2023-11-04,San Diego,New York,SAN,JFK,SW505,17:45,21:30,On Time
Boeing 737,2023-11-05,Chicago,Los Angeles,ORD,LAX,AA606,08:00,10:30,On Time
Airbus A320,2023-11-05,Houston,San Francisco,IAH,SFO,DL707,09:30,1
2:00,On Time
Boeing 787,2023-11-05,Atlanta,Seattle,ATL,SEA,UA808,11:00,14:00,Delayed
Airbus A321,2023-11-05,Dallas,Miami,DFW,MIA,SW909,12:15,15:30,On Time
Boeing 737,2023-11-07,Chicago,Los Angeles,ORD,LAX,AA404,08:00,10:30,On Time
Airbus A320,2023-11-07,Houston,San Francisco,IAH,SFO,DL505,09:30,1
2:00,On Time
Boeing 787,2023-11-07,Atlanta,Seattle,ATL,SEA,UA606,11:00,14:00,Delayed
Airbus A321,2023-11-07,Dallas,Miami,DFW,MIA,SW707,12:15,15:30,On Time
Boeing 737,2023-11-08,Los Angeles,Chicago,LAX,ORD,AA303,07:30,10:00,On Time
Airbus A320,2023-11-08,San Francisco,Houston,SFO,IAH,DL404,09:00,1
2:30,On Time
Boeing 787,2023-11-08,Seattle,Atlanta,SEA,ATL,UA505,10:30,13:30,Delayed
Airbus A321,2023-11-08,Miami,Dallas,MIA,DFW,SW606,11:45,14:45,On Time
```

You will then extend the `LangchainConfig.java` file from earlier to create an in-memory embedding store that will store the document content for later use. Let's define a private method that parses the text content from the `resources` folder and then loads the documents into the document store.

```
private InMemoryEmbeddingStore<TextSegment> embeddingStore() {
    List<Document> documents = FileSystemDocumentLoader.loadDocuments(
    "/path/to/your/travelx/src/main/resources/static", new
    TextDocumentParser());
    InMemoryEmbeddingStore<TextSegment> embeddingStore = new
    InMemoryEmbeddingStore<>();
    EmbeddingStoreIngestor.ingest(documents, embeddingStore);
    return embeddingStore;
}
```

You will now use the embeddingStore in the search logic by using the contentRetriever method, which references the embedding store.

```
@Bean
public Assistant openAiAssistant() {
    this.chatMemory = this.messageWindowChatMemory();
    this.model = this.openAiChatModel();
    this.assistant = AiServices.builder(Assistant.class)
            .chatLanguageModel(this.model)
            .chatMemory(this.chatMemory)
            .contentRetriever(EmbeddingStoreContentRetriever.from(this.
            embeddingStore()))
            .build();
    return this.assistant;
}
```

The complete code changes necessary have been shared below.

File: ./src/main/java/com/example/travelx/LangchainConfig.java

```
import dev.langchain4j.data.document.Document;
import dev.langchain4j.data.document.loader.FileSystemDocumentLoader;
import dev.langchain4j.data.document.parser.TextDocumentParser;
import dev.langchain4j.data.segment.TextSegment;
import dev.langchain4j.rag.content.retriever.
EmbeddingStoreContentRetriever;
import dev.langchain4j.store.embedding.EmbeddingStoreIngestor;
import dev.langchain4j.store.embedding.inmemory.InMemoryEmbeddingStore;

private InMemoryEmbeddingStore<TextSegment> embeddingStore() {
    List<Document> documents = FileSystemDocumentLoader.loadDocuments("/
    path/to/your/travelx/src/main/resources/static", new
    TextDocumentParser());
    InMemoryEmbeddingStore<TextSegment> embeddingStore = new
    InMemoryEmbeddingStore<>();
    EmbeddingStoreIngestor.ingest(documents, embeddingStore);
    return embeddingStore;
}
```

```
@Bean
public Assistant openAiAssistant() {
    this.chatMemory = this.messageWindowChatMemory();
    this.model = this.openAiChatModel();

    this.assistant = AiServices.builder(Assistant.class)
            .chatLanguageModel(this.model)
            .chatMemory(this.chatMemory)
            .contentRetriever(EmbeddingStoreContentRetriever.from(this.
            embeddingStore()))
            .build();
    return this.assistant;
}
```

With this simple change, you are able to set up a contextual RAG pipeline. Let's start the application and test this.

```
curl -X POST http://localhost:8080/api/flight-chat -H "Content-Type:
application/json" -d '{
 "message": "Tell me about flight details for AA4041."
 Boeing 737,2023-11-02,Denver,Boston,DEN,BOS,AA4041,13:00,17:00,On Time
}'
```

Output:

```
{"aircraft":"Boeing 737","dateOfDeparture":"2023-11-02","fromCity":"Denver",
"toCity":"Boston","departureAirport":"DEN","arrivalAirport":"BOS",
"flightNumber":"AA4041","departureTime":"13:00","arrivalTime":"17:00",
"status":"On Time"}
```

Now, you are able to see your flight details being fetched from your internal data source.

Conclusion

In this chapter, you explored how to integrate contextual information into your LLM ecosystem using the LangChain4j framework and the RAG paradigm. Initially, the application suffered from hallucinations due to the limitations of generalized LLM responses. To address this, you implemented prompt engineering and context-awareness checks within the Spring Boot application, significantly reducing the incorrect outputs. You then used the RAG approach to leverage embeddings and vector stores to retrieve specific organizational data and augment the LLM's knowledge base. By integrating the easy RAG module of LangChain4j, our application could efficiently provide accurate and context-specific answers based on internal documents and proprietary data sources. This enhancement not only improved response accuracy but also enabled the provision of more reliable and organization-specific information to our customers.

For readers interested in exploring these concepts further, consider referring to the official documentation for LangChainjJ, foundational materials on RAG, introductory guides on vector databases like FAISS or Weaviate, and technical overviews of embeddings and tokenization strategies provided by major LLM platforms such as OpenAI or Hugging Face. These resources offer valuable insights into building scalable and context-aware AI applications using modern LLM tooling.

And now, you will move on to integrating the Spring AI library.

CHAPTER 8

Spring AI Ninja Moves

The goal of this chapter is to build an LLM-powered application using the Spring AI ecosystem of Spring Boot.

Introduction

So far we have explored the LangChain4j package and the various features and utilities it provides. Although it's useful and is modularized, we always want to be familiar with other open-source community developer libraries that could also help us with building applications. This is how application developers can build a healthy ecosystem. If you have built Spring Boot applications before using the handy packages of Spring like Spring Web and Spring Data JPA, you know how easy and seamless the developer experience is. Fortunately, there is something similar for the LLM ecosystem too. The Spring AI ecosystem can help with different integrations similar to the ones we built with LangChain4j. In the following sections, you will learn more about Spring AI, including the features and integrations it brings to the ecosystem, and build an application using it.

What Is Spring AI?

Spring AI is an application framework for AI engineering. Its goal is to apply Spring ecosystem design principles such as portability and modular design to the AI domain and promote using Plain Old Java Objects (POJOs) as the building blocks of an application. Figure 8-1 shows the interaction model between Spring Boot and the Gen AI interface through the Spring AI ecosystem.

S. K. Sahu, *Generative AI-Driven Application Development with Java*,
https://doi.org/10.1007/979-8-8688-1609-3_8

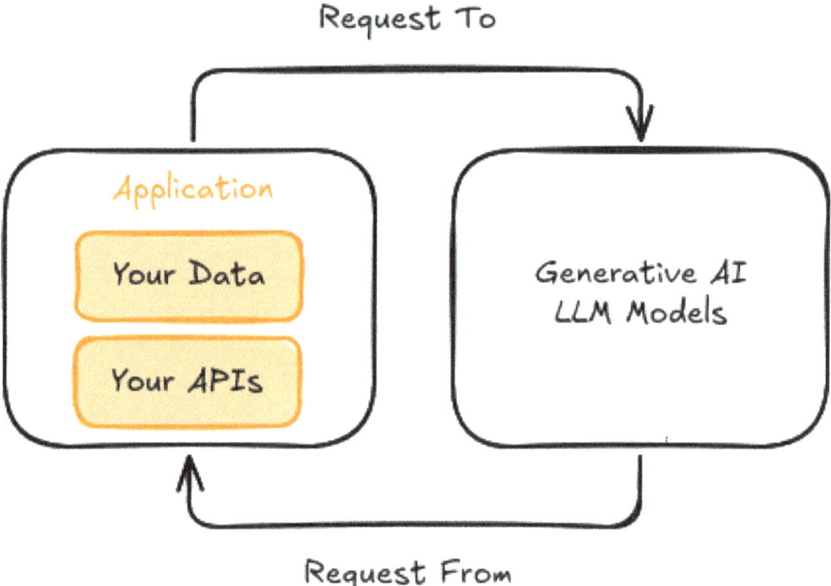

Figure 8-1. *Request-response flow between Spring Boot (Spring AI) and Gen AI Interface*

At its core, Spring AI addresses the fundamental challenge of AI integration: connecting your enterprise data and APIs with the AI models.

Features of Spring AI

Spring AI offers extensive support for major AI model providers, including Anthropic, OpenAI, Microsoft, Amazon, Google, and Ollama. It accommodates various model types such as chat completion, embeddings, text-to-image, audio transcription, text-to-speech, and moderation. The framework provides a portable, unified API that works seamlessly across different AI providers, supporting both synchronous and streaming interactions and allowing access to provider-specific features. Additionally, Spring AI simplifies integration through structured outputs, mapping model responses directly to POJOs.

In terms of vector databases, Spring AI supports prominent providers like Apache Cassandra, Azure Vector Search, Chroma, Milvus, MongoDB Atlas, Neo4j, Oracle, PostgreSQL/PGVector, Pinecone, Qdrant, Redis, and Weaviate. It includes a portable API that spans these vector store providers, featuring an innovative SQL-like metadata filtering capability.

The toolkit also includes advanced capabilities such as tools/function calling, enabling AI models to invoke client-side tools or functions for real-time information retrieval. It promotes observability by providing detailed insights into AI operations. A built-in document injection ETL framework facilitates data engineering processes, while AI model evaluation utilities help ensure generated content's reliability and prevent hallucinated responses. For a complete discussion of choosing metrics, traces, and logs, please refer to Chapter 18.

For developers, Spring AI delivers the ChatClient API, a fluent, intuitive interface similar to WebClient and RestClient APIs, simplifying communication with AI chat models. The Advisors API further encapsulates common generative AI patterns, manages data transformation, and enhances portability across various models and use cases. Additionally, Spring AI supports conversation memory and retrieval-augmented generation (RAG) capabilities.

Spring Boot Auto Configuration and starters are available for effortless setup and integration of AI models and vector stores, accessible via the Spring Initializr (start.spring.io).

Boot Up an Application Using Spring AI

Create a Spring Boot web application with a Spring AI OpenAI boot starter dependency. This Spring Initializr link can help you bootstrap the application:

https://start.spring.io/#!type=maven-project&language=java&platformVersion=3.3.4&packaging=jar&jvmVersion=17&groupId=spring.ai.example&artifactId=spring-ai-demo&name=spring-ai-demo&description=Spring%20AI%20%2C%20getting%20started%20example%2C%20using%20Open%20AI&packageName=spri

Note: With start.spring.io you can select any AI models or vector stores that you want to use in your new applications.

Start by typing **spring ai** in the search box, which will show you many packages supported through the Spring AI ecosystem. Figure 8-2 shows the list of packages/libraries which are supported at this moment. As in the Gen AI world, nothing is fixed, and this list may change.

spring ai
Press Ctrl for multiple adds
Azure AI Search AI
Spring AI vector database support for Azure AI Search. It is an AI-powered information retrieval platform and part of Microsoft's larger AI platform. Among other features, it allows users to query information using vector-based storage and retrieval.
Mistral AI AI
Spring AI support for Mistral AI, the open and portable generative AI for devs and businesses.
Stability AI AI
Spring AI support for Stability AI's text to image generation model.
Markdown Document Reader AI
Spring AI Markdown document reader. It allows to load Markdown documents, converting them into a list of Spring AI Document objects.
Tika Document Reader AI
Spring AI Tika document reader. It uses Apache Tika to extract text from a variety of document formats, such as PDF, DOC/DOCX, PPT/PPTX, and HTML. The documents are converted into a list of Spring AI Document objects.
PDF Document Reader AI
Spring AI PDF document reader. It uses Apache PdfBox to extract text from PDF documents and converting them into a list of Spring AI Document objects.
Anthropic Claude AI
Spring AI support for Anthropic Claude AI models.
Azure OpenAI AI
Spring AI support for Azure's OpenAI offering, powered by ChatGPT. It extends beyond traditional OpenAI capabilities, delivering AI-driven text generation with enhanced functionality.
Amazon Bedrock Converse AI

Figure 8-2. *Spring AI–supported packages*

You will start by selecting a few packages that will be essential to your project, as depicted in Figure 8-3.

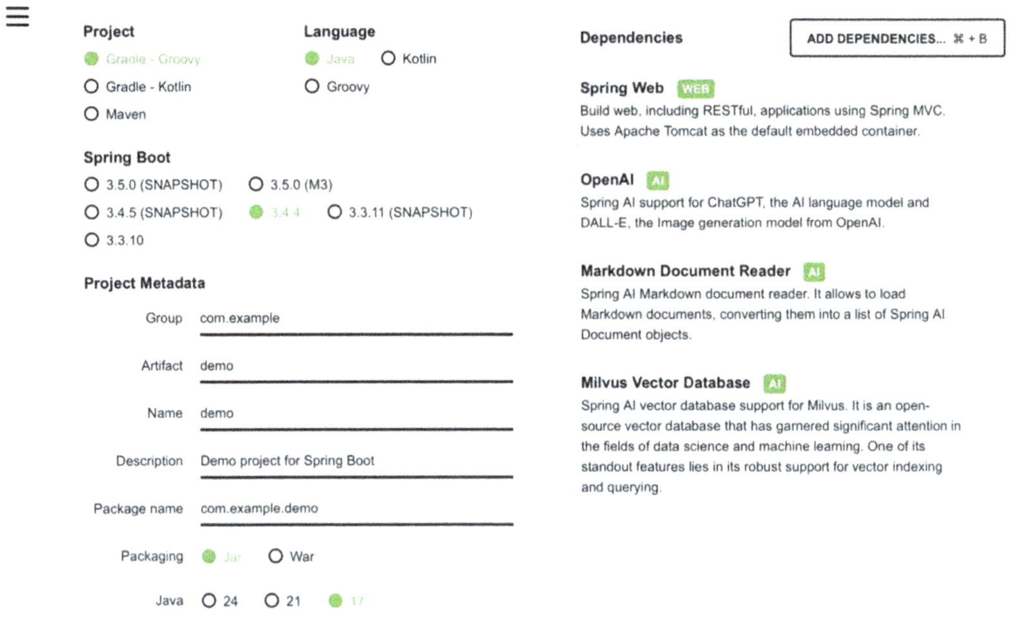

Figure 8-3. *Spring Boot package dependencies in Spring Initializr UI*

The following are the necessary packages:

- Spring Web: This is needed for building a REST endpoint for your chat interface.
- OpenAI: This package is necessary to connect to OpenAI and interact with their LLMs.
- Markdown Document Reader: This package helps to read contents of a Markdown file and generate document objects from it, which is a common format readable by all vector databases in the Spring AI ecosystem.
- Milvus Vector Database: As you have learned earlier, you need an embedded vector database to store your embeddings. Milvus is an open-source vector database, and this package will help to connect and interact with it.

Once the dependencies have been selected, download the archive. Unzip the demo zip archive that was downloaded to your system and open it in your IDE of choice. Let your IDE import the project-specific libraries.

For the next step, you will need an API key from OpenAI, which you can create at `https://platform.openai.com/api-keys`, as depicted in Figure 8-4. Please note that this is the web page at this moment in time. It could change in the future based on OpenAI's direction. Make sure to search in Google or the site map of OpenAI to create an API for your use case.

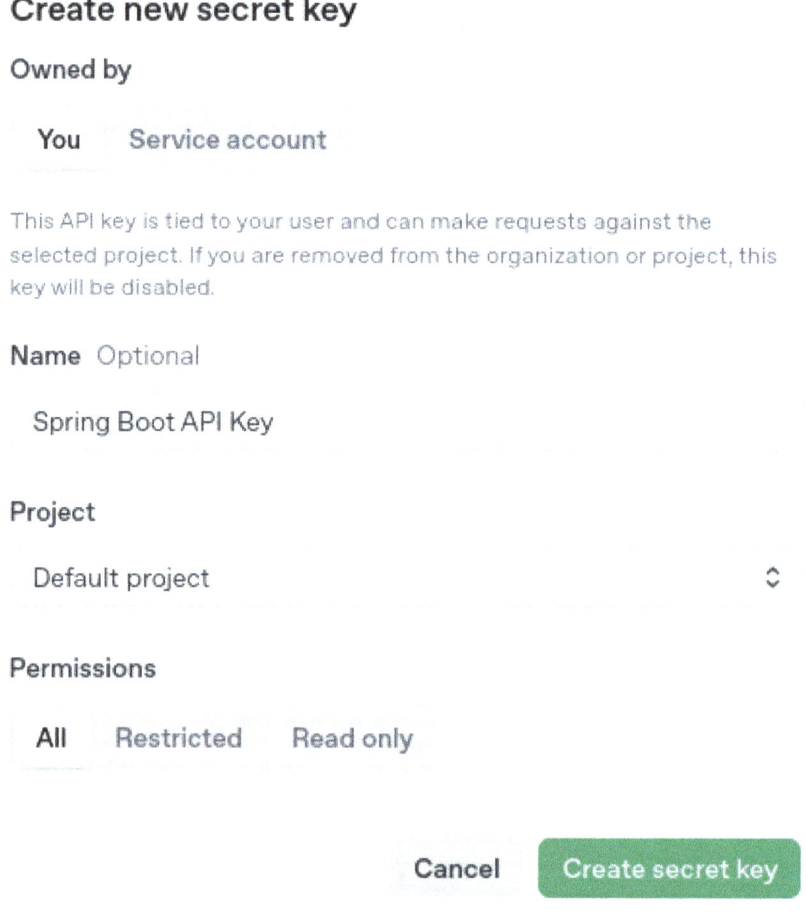

Figure 8-4. *Create an API secret key token from the Open AI platform page*

Once a secret key is created, copy it to safe place from the UI interface, as shown in Figure 8-5, since once this interface is closed, you won't have further access to it.

Save your key

Please save your secret key in a safe place since **you won't be able to view it again**. Keep it secure, as anyone with your API key can make requests on your behalf. If you do lose it, you'll need to generate a new one.

Learn more about API key best practices

sk-proj-83_YlvTW9TZDG0jucXODjYKbuD(

Permissions

Read and write API resources

Done

Figure 8-5. *Copy the secret key in the Open AI interface*

Add your OpenAI key to the `application.properties` file:

File: ./src/main/resources/application.properties

```
spring.application.name=demo
spring.ai.openai.api-key=<YOUR OPENAI KEY>
```

At this point, you want to get something very quickly set up to get started talking to the OpenAI LLMs. For this example, you will use the ChatClient API. The ChatClient provides a fluent API for communicating with AI models. It supports both synchronous and streaming programming models.

Using ChatClient, you can build prompts, which as you know are essentially sets of messages guiding the AI's responses. These messages can be either user inputs or system-generated instructions, and they can include placeholders that dynamically adapt responses based on user-provided information. Additionally, the API also lets you configure specific options, like selecting the AI mode you prefer or adjusting the "temperature," which determines how creative or random the AI-generated responses will be.

ChatClient is created using the ChatClient.Builder object. You can use an autoconfigured ChatClient.Builder instance for any ChatModel Spring Boot autoconfiguration or create one programmatically. For this example, you will use an autoconfigured ChatClient.Builder. In the simplest case, Spring AI provides Spring Boot autoconfiguration, creating a prototype ChatClient.Builder bean for you to inject in your class.

You will create a bean with the CommandLineRunner type to enable running this method when Spring Boot is started and see the output at the command line. The builder instance is injected for you by Spring Boot, and you use this to build an instance of ChatClient. Using the chatClient object, you then create a prompt to tell a joke, call the request, and collect the response in the response variable. The response is then printed out.

Add the following snippet to your SpringAiDemoApplication class:

File: ./src/main/java/com/example/demo/DemoApplication.java

```
package com.example.demo;

import org.springframework.ai.chat.client.ChatClient;
import org.springframework.boot.CommandLineRunner;
import org.springframework.boot.SpringApplication;
import org.springframework.boot.autoconfigure.SpringBootApplication;
import org.springframework.context.annotation.Bean;

@SpringBootApplication
public class DemoApplication {

   public static void main(String[] args) {
        SpringApplication.run(DemoApplication.class, args);
    }

   @Bean
    public CommandLineRunner runner(ChatClient.Builder builder) {
        return args -> {
            ChatClient chatClient = builder.build();
            String response = chatClient.prompt("Tell me a joke").call().
            content();
            System.out.println(response);
        };
    }
}
```

Run the application and you should see output similar to the following in the terminal run space:

```
com.example.demo.DemoApplication              : Started DemoApplication in
4.576 seconds (process running for 5.886)
Why did the scarecrow win an award?

Because he was outstanding in his field!
```

This example shows how easy, quick, and intuitive it is to get started building Gen AI applications using Spring Boot and Spring AI.

Using OpenAI API Through Ollama API in Spring AI

In this section, you will learn about using the familiar OpenAI APIs in Spring AI but without the need to create an account or a payment license for it. You will proxy all the OpenAI API-specific requests through the Ollama API for OpenAI (see Figure 8-6).

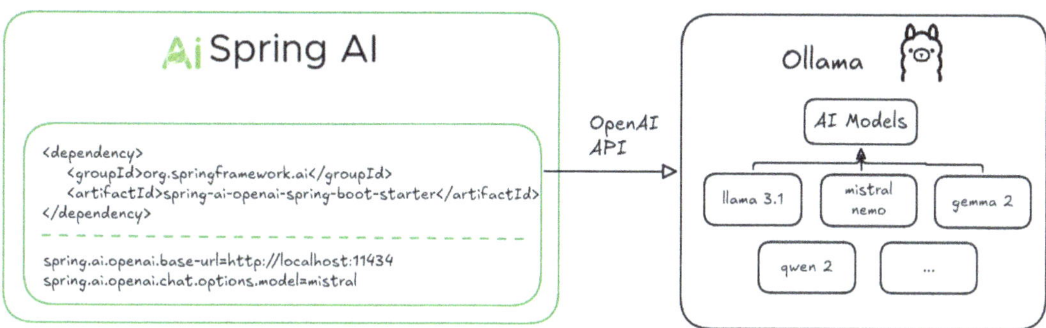

Figure 8-6. *Spring AI Open AI to Ollama connection*

To start, go to the Spring initializr website and choose the following dependencies: Spring Web, OpenAI, and Ollama, as shown in Figure 8-7.

Figure 8-7. *Dependency selection in Spring Initializr*

Once the zip is downloaded, unzip it and open it in your favorite IDE to make sure everything works fine at this stage. Also as a prerequisite, make sure you have Ollama enabled and have the gemma3 model pulled on to your local machine using the following command. This is the 1 billion parameter version of the gemma3 model. You can also choose any other model of your choice as long as it fits the memory requirements of your system.

```
ollama pull gemma3:1b
```

Now, you will set a few config parameters in your `application.properties` file to enable OpenAI and Ollama to work. For Ollama, you need to let Spring AI know the base API URL for Ollama and which model and temperature of the creativity value you want to use for the LLM model.

```
spring.ai.ollama.base-url=http://localhost:11434
spring.ai.ollama.chat.options.temperature=0.7
spring.ai.ollama.chat.model=gemma3:1b
```

Once Ollama is set up for Spring AI, you will need to set the API key for OpenAI, which would be empty in this case; proxy the OpenAI API requests through the Ollama API URI; and set the model to be used with OpenAI in Spring AI.

```
spring.ai.openai.api-key=""
spring.ai.openai.chat.base-url=http://localhost:11434
spring.ai.openai.chat.options.model=gemma3:1b
```

The following are all the code changes for configuration in the `application.properties` file:

File: ./src/main/resources/application.properties

```
spring.application.name=demo
spring.ai.openai.api-key=""
spring.ai.openai.chat.base-url=http://localhost:11434
spring.ai.openai.chat.options.model=gemma3:1b
spring.ai.ollama.base-url=http://localhost:11434
spring.ai.ollama.chat.options.temperature=0.7
spring.ai.ollama.chat.model=gemma3:1b
```

Now that the connection from OpenAI to Ollama is established, let's try using the OpenAI `chatModel`. In the `DemoApplication.java` file, you will create a bean of the `CommandLineRunner` type, which takes in an injected argument of the `OpenAiChatModel` type. This will enable you to quickly prototype and test without establishing conventional controllers and then invoke it through a `curl` request.

```
@Bean
public CommandLineRunner commandLineRunner(OpenAiChatModel
openAiChatModel) {
    return args -> {
```

Next you will use the ChatClient API to create an instance and then customize it by passing a custom prompt and then setting the configuration parameters like model, temperature, and tokens settings.

```
ChatClient chatClient = ChatClient.builder(openAiChatModel).build();
```

Then customize the prompt and set configuration parameters. Here you are setting a prompt for the LLM to classify movie reviews and then sharing an movie description to share the LLM's review.

```
String reviewSentiment = chatClient.prompt("""
                        Classify movie reviews as POSITIVE,
                        NEUTRAL or NEGATIVE. Review: "Her" is
                        a disturbing study revealing the
                        direction humanity is headed if AI is
                        allowed to keep evolving, unchecked. I
                        wish there were more movies like this
                        masterpiece. Sentiment:
                        """)
        .options(ChatOptions.builder()
                .model("gemma3:1b")
                .temperature(0.1)
                .maxTokens(5)
                .build());
```

The full code with all the changes is as follows:

File: ./src/main/java/com/example/demo/DemoApplication.java

```
package com.example.demo;

import org.springframework.ai.chat.client.ChatClient;
import org.springframework.ai.chat.prompt.ChatOptions;
import org.springframework.ai.openai.OpenAiChatModel;
import org.springframework.boot.CommandLineRunner;
import org.springframework.boot.SpringApplication;
import org.springframework.boot.autoconfigure.SpringBootApplication;
import org.springframework.context.annotation.Bean;

@SpringBootApplication
public class DemoApplication {
    enum Sentiment {
        POSITIVE, NEUTRAL, NEGATIVE
    }
```

```
    public static void main(String[] args) {
         SpringApplication.run(DemoApplication.class, args);
     }

    @Bean
     public CommandLineRunner commandLineRunner(OpenAiChatModel
     openAiChatModel) {
         return args -> {
             ChatClient chatClient = ChatClient.builder(openAiChatModel).
             build();
             String reviewSentiment = chatClient.prompt("""
                                   Classify movie reviews as POSITIVE,
                                   NEUTRAL or
                                   NEGATIVE. Review: "Her" is a
                                   disturbing study
                                   revealing the direction humanity is headed
                                   if AI is
                                   allowed to keep evolving, unchecked. I wish
                                   there were
                                   more movies like this masterpiece.
                                   Sentiment:
                                   """)

                     .options(ChatOptions.builder()
                              .model("gemma3:1b")
                              .temperature(0.1)
                              .maxTokens(5)
                              .build())
                      .call()
                      .content()
                      .trim();
             System.out.println("Output: " + reviewSentiment);
         };
     }
}
```

Let's test this out; here's the output:

```
Started DemoApplication in 3.463 seconds (process running for 3.899)
Output: Negative
```

Building a RAG-Based Application

You will build upon the airlines chat application where users need information about the flight information like date of departure, from, to locations, departure/arrival airport, departure/arrival time, and current status. Since this data is available only to your airlines company, a foundational LLM would not have this information available to it. So, you will use the RAG architecture to retrieve this information from your internal source systems to provide information to your customers.

RAG essentially has three components to it: retrieval, augmentation, and generation. The following sections will focus on each of these.

Retrieval

The flight-related information could be in any data source including relational databases and file systems and in a variety of formats. You will need to read from this source all files relevant to you. This should ideally be a separate process where the system reads from the source new files every day on a periodic basis based on the business requirements. To keep it simple for this use case, you will read it when your Spring Boot application boots up for the first time.

You will store all of the flight information for your airlines company in a Markdown file named `flights.md` in the resources folder. The format of the Markdown file is similar to a CSV file where the first row contains field names like Aircraft, Data of Departure, From, etc., and the subsequent rows contain individual flights for the airline. Create a file at the following location and save the flight details. The information is also available in the source code available for this chapter.

File: ./src/main/resources/flights.md

```
Aircraft,Date of Departure,From (US City),To (US City),Departure
Airport,Arrival Airport,Flight Number,Departure Time,Arrival Time,Status
Boeing 737,2023-11-01,New York,Los Angeles,JFK,LAX,AA101,08:00,1
1:00,On Time
```

```
Airbus A320,2023-11-01,Chicago,Miami,ORD,MIA,DL202,09:30,13:00,On Time
Boeing 787,2023-11-01,San Francisco,Seattle,SFO,SEA,UA303,10:15,1
2:00,Delayed
Airbus A321,2023-11-01,Houston,Dallas,IAH,DFW,SW404,11:45,13:15,On Time
Boeing 737,2023-11-01,Atlanta,Denver,ATL,DEN,AA505,12:30,15:00,On Time
Airbus A320,2023-11-01,Boston,Las Vegas,BOS,LAS,DL606,14:00,17:30,Cancelled
Boeing 787,2023-11-01,Philadelphia,Phoenix,PHL,PHX,UA707,15:45,18:
30,On Time
Airbus A321,2023-11-01,Orlando,San Diego,MCO,SAN,SW808,16:30,19:00,On Time
Boeing 737,2023-11-02,New York,Chicago,JFK,ORD,AA909,07:00,09:00,On Time
Airbus A320,2023-11-02,Los Angeles,Houston,LAX,IAH,DL101,08:30,1
2:00,On Time
Boeing 787,2023-11-02,Miami,Atlanta,MIA,ATL,UA202,10:00,12:00,Delayed
Airbus A321,2023-11-02,Seattle,Dallas,SEA,DFW,SW303,11:15,14:30,On Time
Boeing 737,2023-11-02,Denver,Boston,DEN,BOS,AA404,13:00,17:00,On Time
Airbus A320,2023-11-02,Las Vegas,Philadelphia,LAS,PHL,DL505,14:30,18:00
,Cancelled
Boeing 787,2023-11-02,Phoenix,Orlando,PHX,MCO,UA606,16:00,20:00,On Time
Airbus A321,2023-11-02,San Diego,New York,SAN,JFK,SW707,17:45,21:30,On Time
Boeing 737,2023-11-03,Chicago,Los Angeles,ORD,LAX,AA808,08:00,10:30,On Time
Airbus A320,2023-11-03,Houston,San Francisco,IAH,SFO,DL909,09:30,1
2:00,On Time
Boeing 787,2023-11-03,Atlanta,Seattle,ATL,SEA,UA101,11:00,14:00,Delayed
Airbus A321,2023-11-03,Dallas,Miami,DFW,MIA,SW202,12:15,15:30,On Time
Boeing 737,2023-11-03,Boston,Denver,BOS,DEN,AA303,13:30,16:30,On Time
Airbus A320,2023-11-03,Philadelphia,Las Vegas,PHL,LAS,DL404,15:00,18:30
,Cancelled
Boeing 787,2023-11-03,Orlando,Phoenix,MCO,PHX,UA505,16:45,20:00,On Time
Airbus A321,2023-11-03,New York,San Diego,JFK,SAN,SW606,18:00,21:30,On Time
Boeing 737,2023-11-04,Los Angeles,Chicago,LAX,ORD,AA707,07:30,10:00,On Time
Airbus A320,2023-11-04,San Francisco,Houston,SFO,IAH,DL808,09:00,1
2:30,On Time
Boeing 787,2023-11-04,Seattle,Atlanta,SEA,ATL,UA909,10:30,13:30,Delayed
Airbus A321,2023-11-04,Miami,Dallas,MIA,DFW,SW101,11:45,14:45,On Time
Boeing 737,2023-11-04,Denver,Boston,DEN,BOS,AA202,13:00,17:00,On Time
```

```
Airbus A320,2023-11-04,Las Vegas,Philadelphia,LAS,PHL,DL303,14:30,18:00
,Cancelled
Boeing 787,2023-11-04,Phoenix,Orlando,PHX,MCO,UA404,16:00,20:00,On Time
Airbus A321,2023-11-04,San Diego,New York,SAN,JFK,SW505,17:45,21:30,On Time
Boeing 737,2023-11-05,Chicago,Los Angeles,ORD,LAX,AA606,08:00,10:30,On Time
Airbus A320,2023-11-05,Houston,San Francisco,IAH,SFO,DL707,09:30,1
2:00,On Time
Boeing 787,2023-11-05,Atlanta,Seattle,ATL,SEA,UA808,11:00,14:00,Delayed
Airbus A321,2023-11-05,Dallas,Miami,DFW,MIA,SW909,12:15,15:30,On Time
Boeing 737,2023-11-07,Chicago,Los Angeles,ORD,LAX,AA404,08:00,10:30,On Time
Airbus A320,2023-11-07,Houston,San Francisco,IAH,SFO,DL505,09:30,1
2:00,On Time
Boeing 787,2023-11-07,Atlanta,Seattle,ATL,SEA,UA606,11:00,14:00,Delayed
Airbus A321,2023-11-07,Dallas,Miami,DFW,MIA,SW707,12:15,15:30,On Time
Boeing 737,2023-11-08,Los Angeles,Chicago,LAX,ORD,AA303,07:30,10:00,On Time
Airbus A320,2023-11-08,San Francisco,Houston,SFO,IAH,DL404,09:00,1
2:30,On Time
Boeing 787,2023-11-08,Seattle,Atlanta,SEA,ATL,UA505,10:30,13:30,Delayed
Airbus A321,2023-11-08,Miami,Dallas,MIA,DFW,SW606,11:45,14:45,On Time
```

As shown in Figure 8-8, the next step is to enable storage of all the available documents/data in your vector store. This will enable you to later retrieve or search from it based on a customer query. Vector stores can store the information in vector embeddings format. So, the goal is to read the files and divide them into small document chunks.

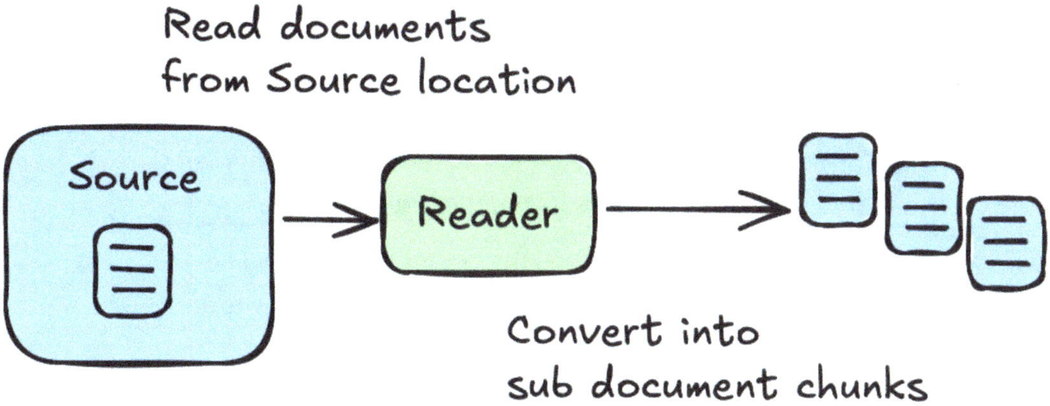

***Figure 8-8.** Read the source files and divide them into small chunks*

The DocumentReaders API of Spring AI will help you to read the different source files. There are different readers for reading different files. The following is a list of available readers:

- JSON: The `JsonReader` reader processes JSON documents, converting them into a list of `Document` objects.
- Text: The `TextReader` reader processes plain text documents, converting them into a list of `Document` objects.
- HTML: The `JsoupDocumentReader` reader processes HTML documents, converting them into a list of `Document` objects using the JSoup library.
- Markdown: The `MarkdownDocumentReader` reader processes Markdown documents, converting them into a list of `Document` objects.
- PDF Page: The `PagePdfDocumentReader` reader uses Apache PdfBox library to parse PDF documents.
- Tika (DOCX, PPTX, HTML...): The `TikaDocumentReader` reader uses Apache Tika to extract text from a variety of document formats such as PDF, DOC/DOCX, PPT/PPTX, and HTML.

In this example, you will leverage the `MarkdownDocumentReader` to read your Markdown file. You will create a bean named `documentReader` that initializes the `MarkdownDocumentReader` to read the Markdown from the Spring Resource location.

The resource has a default value for the `flights.md` file. `MarkdownDocumentReader` takes in two parameters. The first one is the resource location, and the second is the Markdown document reader config. The config states a few configuration values needed:

1. withHorizontalRuleCreateDocument: When set to true, horizontal rules in the Markdown will create new `Document` objects.
2. withIncludeCodeBlock: When set to true, code blocks will be included in the same `Document` object as the surrounding text. When false, code blocks create separate `Document` objects.
3. withIncludeBlockquote: When set to true, block quotes will be included in the same `Document` object as the surrounding text. When false, blockquotes create separate `Document` objects.

This step will enable you to have a bean available for the later steps to fetch documents read by the `DocumentReader`.

File: ./src/main/java/com/example/demo/DemoApplication.java

```
@Bean
public MarkdownDocumentReader documentReader(@Value("classpath:flights.md")
Resource resource) {
    MarkdownDocumentReaderConfig config = MarkdownDocumentReaderConfig.
    builder()
            .withHorizontalRuleCreateDocument(true)
            .withIncludeCodeBlock(false)
            .withIncludeBlockquote(false)
            .withAdditionalMetadata("filename", "flights.md")
            .build();

   return new MarkdownDocumentReader(resource, config);
}
```

Now, you have the documents available to you in chunked format. The next step, as illustrated in Figure 8-9, is to convert each of these chunked documents from text to vector embeddings format. This can be done by passing them as inputs to any embedding model. You will use the OpenAI embedding model for this purpose.

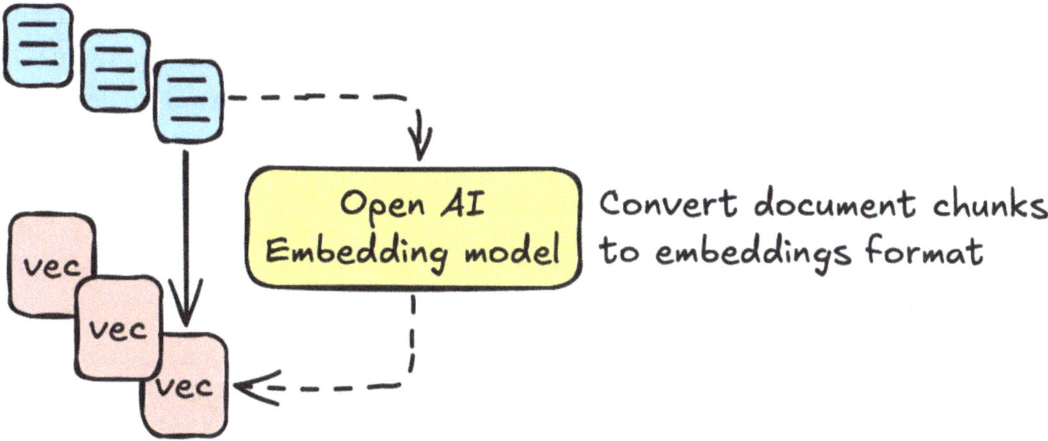

Figure 8-9. *Convert chunked documents from text to vector embeddings*

Once the documents are converted to vector embeddings, you need to store them in the vector store for later retrieval, as shown in Figure 8-10.

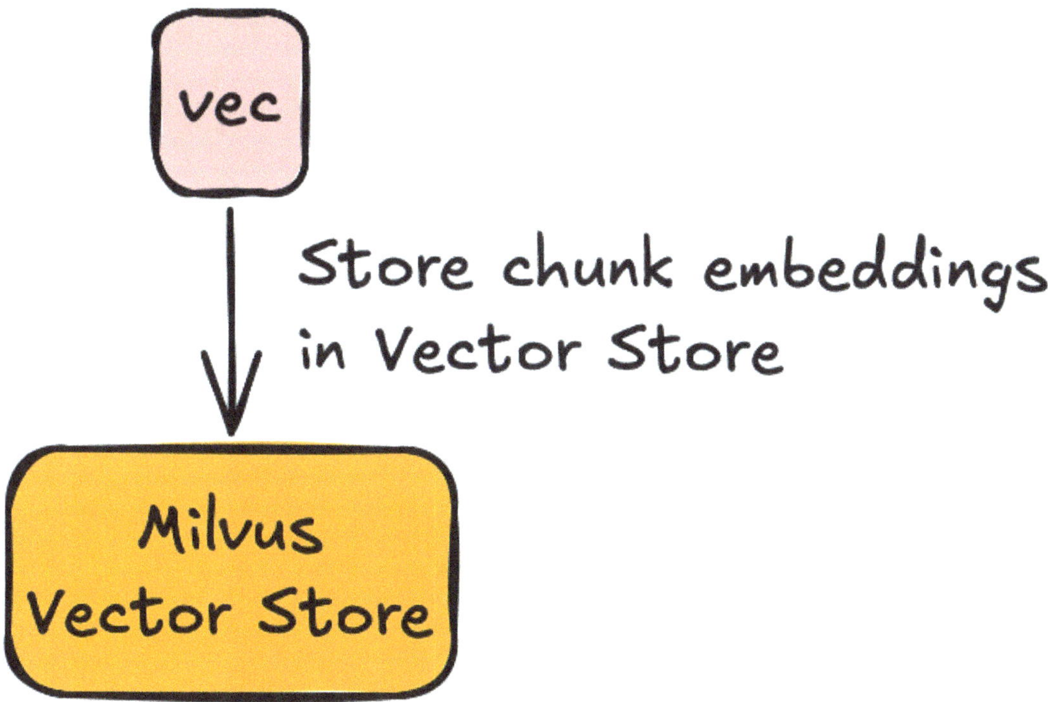

Figure 8-10. *Storage of vector embeddings in vector store*

Both the steps of converting the documents to embeddings and storing them in the vector store happen through the MilvusVectorStore API. Let's see how to achieve this. One of the prerequisites is to create a Milvus vector store. The easiest way is to do this through containers. So, make sure you have Docker/Podman installed in your system.

You will want to start a Milvus vector store container when your application starts so that you can use it to store the embeddings. This can be achieved by manually creating a container, but you will see the programmatic approach here for creating the container through a bean setup so that other parts of the code are able to access the container and have this dependency figured out.

Let's define a method named milvusContainer where you refer to the Docker Hub path for Milvusdb at `milvusdb/milvus:latest` and reference the container by creating a new instance of the `MilvusContainer` and passing the Docker hub name of the Milvus image. Then start the container using `container.start()` and return it for later reference. This enables the script to have a reference to the container and makes sure it is started before accessing it.

File: ./src/main/java/com/example/demo/DemoApplication.java

```
@Bean
public MilvusContainer milvusContainer() {
    MilvusContainer container = new MilvusContainer("milvusdb/
    milvus:latest");
    container.start();
    return container;
}
```

The `MilvusServiceClient` allows you to connect to the Milvus container created earlier. It takes in as argument the ConnectParam initialized with the container URI and database authorization credentials. Finally, you return the initialized client for later reference as a bean. This bean takes as argument the previously set up container and is injected at runtime, setting up the right dependency.

File: ./src/main/java/com/example/demo/DemoApplication.java

```
@Bean
public MilvusServiceClient milvusClient(MilvusContainer milvusContainer) {
    return new MilvusServiceClient(ConnectParam.newBuilder()
            .withAuthorization("minioadmin", "minioadmin")
```

```
            .withUri(milvusContainer.getEndpoint())
            .build());
}
```

The next step is to read the chunked documents, convert them to embeddings, and store them in the Milvus vector store. Let's create a bean named `vecStore` that returns the `VectorStore` for later reference. It will take as injected arguments the `milvusClient` and `markDocumentReader` objects created previously.

```
@Bean
public VectorStore vecStore(MilvusServiceClient milvusClient,
MarkdownDocumentReader markdownDocumentReader) {
```

To create embeddings, you will need to access the OpenAI embedding model. You will create a reference to the OpenAI API through the use of the OpenAiApi API.

```
OpenAiApi openAiApi = new OpenAiApi(apiKey);
```

The openAiApi API can then be used to access the OpenAI embedding model through the OpenAiEmbeddingModel API. It takes as arguments the openAiApi reference, mode, and embedding model options.

```
OpenAiEmbeddingModel embeddingModel = new OpenAiEmbeddingModel(
        openAiApi,
        MetadataMode.EMBED,
        OpenAiEmbeddingOptions.builder()
                .model("text-embedding-ada-002")
                .user("user-6")
                .build(),
        RetryUtils.DEFAULT_RETRY_TEMPLATE);
```

Once this is set up, you can use the MilvusVectorStore API to set up vector store via the `embeddingModel`. It takes as arguments the `milvusClient` and `embeddingModel`. You also establish a few configurations like the `collectionName` and `databaseName` that you need to connect to along with the `indexType` and `metricType` for similarity comparison, which is COSINE in this case. The option for `initializeSchema` is true if it is not already present.

```
MilvusVectorStore vectorStore = MilvusVectorStore.builder(milvusClient,
embeddingModel)
        .collectionName("vector_store")
        .databaseName("default")
        .indexType(IndexType.IVF_FLAT)
        .metricType(MetricType.COSINE)
        .batchingStrategy(new TokenCountBatchingStrategy())
        .initializeSchema(true)
        .build();
```

Once the vector store object is created, you will want to read the documents and add them to the store. The add method of vectorStore enables you to do so.

```
vectorStore.add(markdownDocumentReader.read());
```

The following is the code for the vecStore bean:

```
@Bean
public VectorStore vecStore(MilvusServiceClient milvusClient,
MarkdownDocumentReader markdownDocumentReader) {
    OpenAiApi openAiApi = new OpenAiApi(apiKey);
    OpenAiEmbeddingModel embeddingModel = new OpenAiEmbeddingModel(
            openAiApi,
            MetadataMode.EMBED,
            OpenAiEmbeddingOptions.builder()
                    .model("text-embedding-ada-002")
                    .user("user-6")
                    .build(),
            RetryUtils.DEFAULT_RETRY_TEMPLATE);

    MilvusVectorStore vectorStore = MilvusVectorStore.builder(milvusClient,
    embeddingModel)
            .collectionName("vector_store")
            .databaseName("default")
            .indexType(IndexType.IVF_FLAT)
            .metricType(MetricType.COSINE)
            .batchingStrategy(new TokenCountBatchingStrategy())
```

```
            .initializeSchema(true)
            .build();

    vectorStore.add(markdownDocumentReader.read());
     return vectorStore;
}
```

Figure 8-11 highlights the end-to-end flow of all the steps covered so far.

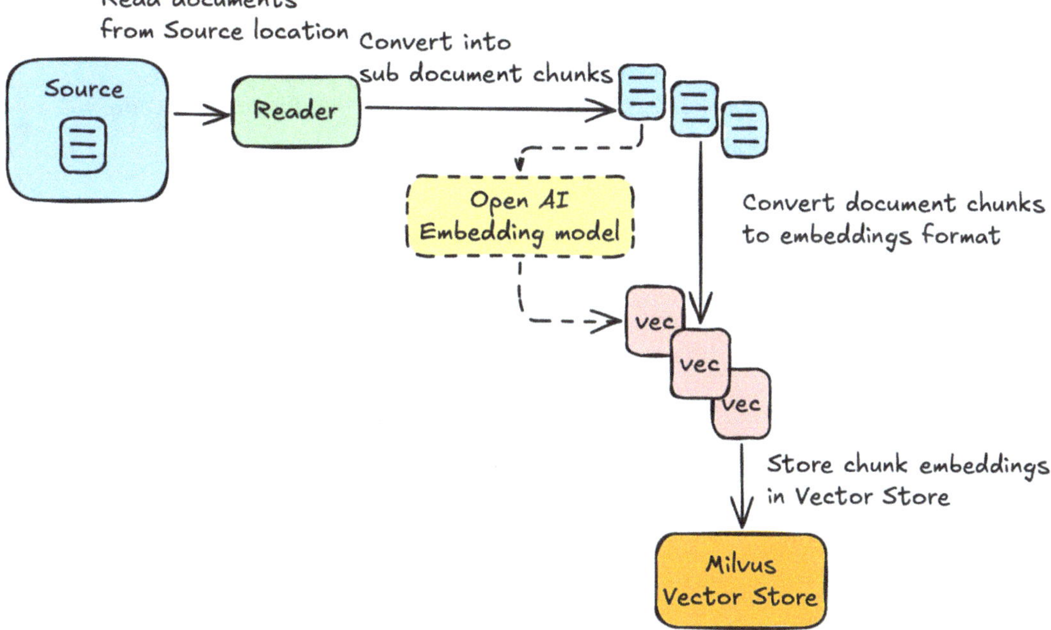

Figure 8-11. *End-to-end flow of reading source documents, chunking them and storing them in the vector store in vector embeddings format*

The code for the end-to-end flow shown in Figure 8-11 is as follows:

File: ./src/main/java/com/example/demo/DemoApplication.java

```
package com.example.demo;

import io.milvus.client.MilvusServiceClient;
import io.milvus.grpc.DataType;
import io.milvus.param.ConnectParam;
import io.milvus.param.IndexType;
import io.milvus.param.MetricType;
import io.milvus.param.collection.CreateCollectionParam;
```

```
import io.milvus.param.collection.FieldType;
import io.milvus.param.index.CreateIndexParam;
import org.springframework.ai.chat.client.ChatClient;
import org.springframework.ai.document.Document;
import org.springframework.ai.document.MetadataMode;
import org.springframework.ai.embedding.TokenCountBatchingStrategy;
import org.springframework.ai.openai.OpenAiChatModel;
import org.springframework.ai.openai.OpenAiEmbeddingModel;
import org.springframework.ai.openai.OpenAiEmbeddingOptions;
import org.springframework.ai.openai.api.OpenAiApi;
import org.springframework.ai.reader.markdown.MarkdownDocumentReader;
import org.springframework.ai.reader.markdown.config.
MarkdownDocumentReaderConfig;
import org.springframework.ai.retry.RetryUtils;
import org.springframework.ai.vectorstore.VectorStore;
import org.springframework.ai.vectorstore.milvus.MilvusVectorStore;
import org.springframework.beans.factory.annotation.Value;
import org.springframework.boot.CommandLineRunner;
import org.springframework.boot.SpringApplication;
import org.springframework.boot.autoconfigure.SpringBootApplication;
import org.springframework.context.annotation.Bean;
import org.springframework.core.io.Resource;
import org.testcontainers.milvus.MilvusContainer;

import java.util.List;
import java.util.stream.Collectors;

@SpringBootApplication
public class DemoApplication {

   public static final int EMBEDDING_DIMENSION = 1536;

   @Value("${spring.ai.openai.api-key}"
    private String apiKey;

    public static void main(String[] args) {
        SpringApplication.run(DemoApplication.class, args);
    }
```

```
@Bean
 public CommandLineRunner runner(ChatClient.Builder builder) {
     return args -> {
         ChatClient chatClient = builder.build();
         String response = chatClient.prompt("Tell me a joke").call().
         content();
         System.out.println(response);
     };
 }

@Bean
 public OpenAiChatModel chatModel() {
     OpenAiApi openAiApi = new OpenAiApi(apiKey);
     return new OpenAiChatModel(openAiApi);
 }

@Bean
 public VectorStore vecStore(MilvusServiceClient milvusClient,
 MarkdownDocumentReader markdownDocumentReader) {
     OpenAiApi openAiApi = new OpenAiApi(apiKey);
     OpenAiEmbeddingModel embeddingModel = new OpenAiEmbeddingModel(
             openAiApi,
             MetadataMode.EMBED,
             OpenAiEmbeddingOptions.builder()
                     .model("text-embedding-ada-002")
                     .user("user-6")
                     .build(),
             RetryUtils.DEFAULT_RETRY_TEMPLATE);

    MilvusVectorStore vectorStore = MilvusVectorStore.
    builder(milvusClient, embeddingModel)
             .collectionName("vector_store")
             .databaseName("default")
             .indexType(IndexType.IVF_FLAT)
             .metricType(MetricType.COSINE)
             .batchingStrategy(new TokenCountBatchingStrategy())
             .initializeSchema(true)
             .build();
```

```
        vectorStore.add(markdownDocumentReader.read());
         return vectorStore;
    }

    @Bean
     public MilvusContainer milvusContainer() {
         MilvusContainer container = new MilvusContainer("milvusdb/
         milvus:latest");
         container.start();
         return container;
     }

    @Bean
     public MilvusServiceClient milvusClient(MilvusContainer
     milvusContainer) {
         return new MilvusServiceClient(ConnectParam.newBuilder()
                 .withAuthorization("minioadmin", "minioadmin")
                 .withUri(milvusContainer.getEndpoint())
                 .build());
     }

    @Bean
     public MarkdownDocumentReader documentReader(@Value("classpath:flights.
     md") Resource resource) {
         MarkdownDocumentReaderConfig config = MarkdownDocumentReaderConfig.
         builder()
                 .withHorizontalRuleCreateDocument(true)
                 .withIncludeCodeBlock(false)
                 .withIncludeBlockquote(false)
                 .withAdditionalMetadata("filename", "flights.md")
                 .build();

        return new MarkdownDocumentReader(resource, config);
     }
}
```

With this foundational setup done, you can stitch together the retrieval, augmentation, and generation steps. As shown in Figure 8-12, to retrieve documents similar to the search query of the customer, you have to first convert it to vector embeddings.

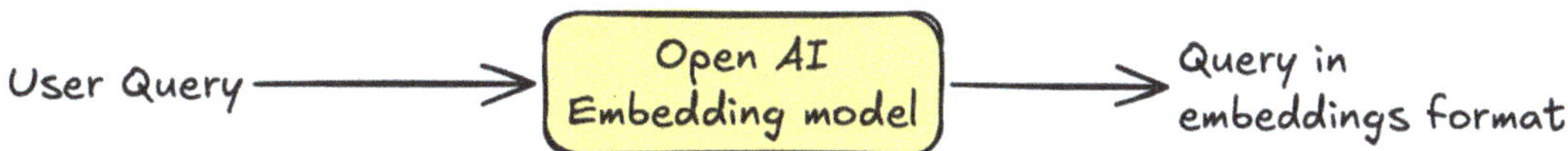

Figure 8-12. *Convert the user query to vector embeddings using the OpenAI embedding model*

Once you have the customer query in embeddings format, you can pass it to the vector store to do a vector similarity using COSINE similarity to retrieve the matched documents, as shown in Figure 8-13.

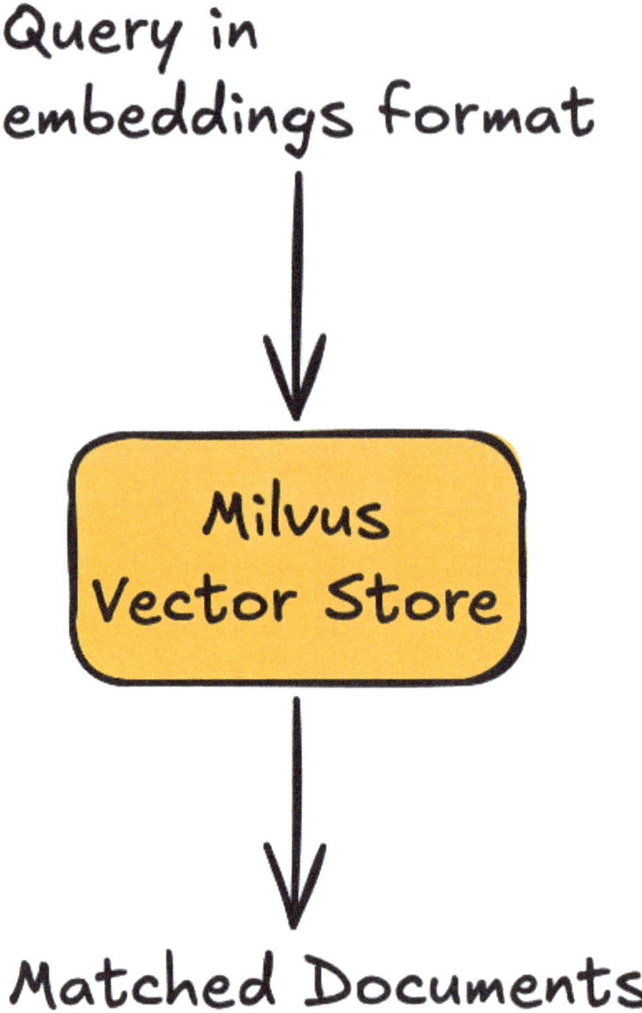

Figure 8-13. *Retrieve the matched documents based on an embeddings similarity match*

The matched documents along with the customer query are then passed to the foundational LLM model to create a human-friendly response in the context of the matched documents, as depicted in Figure 8-14.

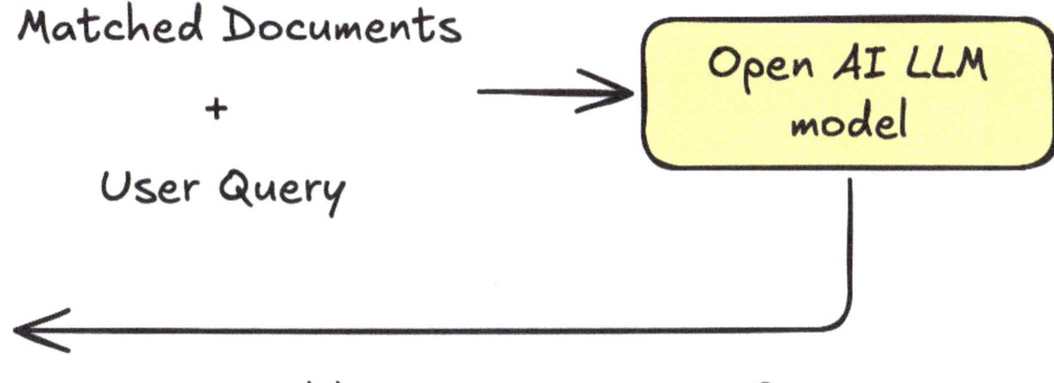

***Figure 8-14.** Generate a response from the foundation LLM*

Figure 8-15 shows all the steps.

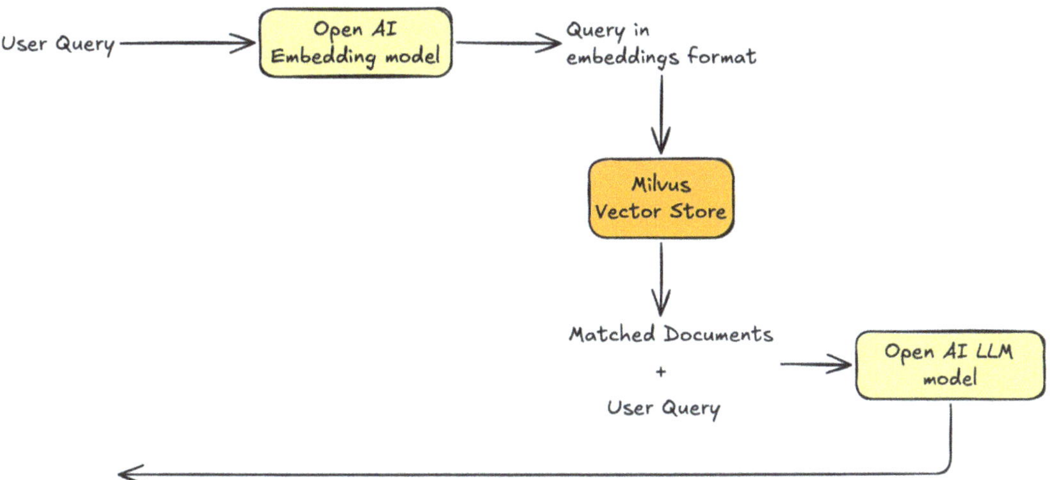

***Figure 8-15.** RAG Flow*

Let's implement this. We will create a `ChatService` class to create a service layer abstraction that can be called from the `Controller` layer. It needs two arguments to be injected at runtime, namely, `chatModel` and `vectorStore`.

```
    @Autowired
    public ChatService(OpenAiChatModel chatModel, VectorStore
    vectorStore) {
        this.chatModel = chatModel;
        this.vectorStore = vectorStore;
    }
```

The ChatClient API provides a helpful feature to enable the RAG model. Its builder interface takes in as an argument the `chatModel` along with the `vectorStore` and `userText` input to convert the query to embeddings, search on the `vectorStore`, and get the final response from the foundational LLM. The following is the code to achieve this:

```
    public String answerQuestion(String userText) {
        ChatResponse chatResponse = ChatClient.builder(chatModel)
                .build()
                .prompt()
                .advisors(new QuestionAnswerAdvisor(vectorStore))
                .user(userText)
                .call()
                .chatResponse();

       return chatResponse.getResult().getOutput().getText().trim();
    }
```

The whole code for the `ChatService` file is shown here:

File: ./src/main/java/com/example/demo/service/ChatService.java

```
package com.example.demo.service;

import org.springframework.ai.chat.client.ChatClient;
import org.springframework.ai.chat.client.advisor.QuestionAnswerAdvisor;
import org.springframework.ai.chat.model.ChatResponse;
import org.springframework.ai.openai.OpenAiChatModel;
import org.springframework.ai.openai.api.OpenAiApi;
import org.springframework.ai.vectorstore.VectorStore;
import org.springframework.beans.factory.annotation.Autowired;
import org.springframework.stereotype.Service;
```

```
@Service
public class ChatService {

   private final OpenAiChatModel chatModel;
    private final VectorStore vectorStore;

   @Autowired
    public ChatService(OpenAiChatModel chatModel, VectorStore
    vectorStore) {
        this.chatModel = chatModel;
        this.vectorStore = vectorStore;
    }

   public String answerQuestion(String userText) {
        ChatResponse chatResponse = ChatClient.builder(chatModel)
                .build()
                .prompt()
                .advisors(new QuestionAnswerAdvisor(vectorStore))
                .user(userText)
                .call()
                .chatResponse();

       return chatResponse.getResult().getOutput().getText().trim();
    }
}
```

The next step is to collect user input through the controller and request a response using the Service class. You will create a ChatRequest class to infer user request arguments in the ChatController class.

File: ./src/main/java/com/example/demo/controller/ChatRequest.java

```
package com.example.demo.controller;

public class ChatRequest {

   private String userText;

   public ChatRequest() {}
```

```
    public ChatRequest(String userText) {
        this.userText = userText;
    }

    public String getUserText() {
        return userText;
    }

    public void setUserText(String userText) {
        this.userText = userText;
    }
}
```

File: ./src/main/java/com/example/demo/controller/ChatController.java

```
package com.example.demo.controller;

import com.example.demo.service.ChatService;
import org.springframework.ai.chat.model.ChatResponse;
import org.springframework.beans.factory.annotation.Autowired;
import org.springframework.web.bind.annotation.PostMapping;
import org.springframework.web.bind.annotation.RequestBody;
import org.springframework.web.bind.annotation.RequestMapping;
import org.springframework.web.bind.annotation.RestController;
@RestController
@RequestMapping("/api/chat")
public class ChatController {

    private final ChatService chatService;

    @Autowired
    public ChatController(ChatService chatService) {
        this.chatService = chatService;
    }

    @PostMapping
    public String postChat(@RequestBody ChatRequest request) {
        return chatService.answerQuestion(request.getUserText());
    }
}
```

With all the components set up, you can now test the application by booting it up and running the following `curl` command from another terminal interface:

```
curl -X POST -H "Content-Type: application/json" -d '{"userText": "What is
the flight details for DL606?"}' http://localhost:8080/api/chat
```

Output:

```
The flight details for DL606 are as follows:

- Date of Departure: 2023-11-01
- From: Boston
- To: Las Vegas
- Departure Airport: BOS
- Arrival Airport: LAS
- Departure Time: 14:00
- Arrival Time: 17:30
- Status: Cancelled
```

Wow, this is some great output from the API; it contains detailed information from the contextual data that the airlines company had.

Conclusion

In this chapter, you explored how to seamlessly integrate the Spring AI library with Spring Boot to build AI-driven applications. You started by understanding the purpose and features of Spring AI, reviewing its flexibility, portability, and ease of integration with various AI model providers and vector databases. You learned how Spring AI simplifies complex integrations through intuitive APIs like ChatClient, allowing easy communication with AI models through prompts, system, and user messages.

You then saw how to build a basic AI-powered application, initially using the ChatClient API to interact with OpenAI's models directly. Further, you extended our application to implement RAG by integrating the Milvus vector database, showcasing the capability to handle advanced, context-aware queries.

Through these examples, it is clear that Spring AI significantly reduces complexity, providing a familiar, developer-friendly framework that aligns well with the Spring ecosystem, enabling efficient development of sophisticated AI-powered Spring Boot applications. The next chapter will cover prompt engineering.

CHAPTER 9

Prompt Alchemy: Patterns That Make Models Look Smarter

The goal of this chapter is to explore the art of prompt engineering using Spring AI.

Introduction

This chapter into the fascinating world of prompt engineering using Spring AI. As artificial intelligence continues to evolve, the ability to effectively communicate with large language models (LLMs) has become a crucial skill. A *prompt*, the input text given to an AI model, plays a significant role in shaping the output. By carefully crafting these prompts, you can guide the AI to generate more accurate, relevant, and context-aware responses.

Let's start by exploring the concept of a prompt and the importance of prompt engineering. From there, we will dive into the patterns and techniques that can be applied to create effective prompts, including simple approaches like text summarization and question answering, as well as advanced methods like zero-shot, few-shot learning, and ReAct. The chapter will also introduce how to use OpenAI's models through the Ollama API in Spring AI, making it possible to harness the power of these sophisticated models without the need for complex setup or additional licenses.

By the end of this chapter, you'll have a solid understanding of prompt engineering and how to leverage Spring AI to integrate LLMs into your applications, optimizing interactions with AI for a wide range of use cases.

S. K. Sahu, *Generative AI-Driven Application Development with Java*,
https://doi.org/10.1007/979-8-8688-1609-3_9

What Is a Prompt?

In the context of LLMs, a prompt is the input text that you provide to the model in order to generate the desired output. The prompt acts as a request or instruction for the model, helping it predict what the next sequence of words or tokens should be. In essence, a prompt sets the stage for the model's response based on the patterns it has learned during its training on large datasets.

Creating effective prompts can be a nuanced task, as various factors—such as the wording, structure, context, and specific instructions—can significantly influence the quality and relevance of the output. The process of designing these prompts to elicit accurate, useful, and appropriate responses is known as *prompt engineering*.

What Is Prompt Engineering?

Prompt engineering is the process of designing and optimizing input prompts to effectively guide LLMs like GPT or Gemini to generate the desired outputs. Since LLMs predict text based on patterns in the input they receive, the way you phrase your prompt significantly impacts the quality and accuracy of their responses.

This process involves several key activities, such as:

1. **Choosing the right prompt structure**: You can use different prompting techniques like zero-shot (where the model is given a task without any examples), one-shot (with one example), or few-shot (with multiple examples). These structures help the model better understand the task at hand.

2. **Configuring the model's settings**: Various settings, like temperature (which controls randomness), top-K (which restricts the model to select from the top-K most probable tokens), and top-P (which ensures the selection of tokens whose cumulative probability doesn't exceed a threshold), influence how the model generates its responses.

3. **Tailoring the prompt for context**: The prompt can be adjusted to provide specific context, instructions, or even role assignments (e.g., asking the model to act as a teacher, travel guide, or code reviewer) to improve the quality of the output.

4. **Iteration and evaluation**: Prompt engineering is an iterative process. You may need to experiment with different word choices, styles, and formats to refine the prompt for optimal results. You also evaluate the responses to ensure they meet your expectations, tweaking the prompts as needed.

Ultimately, prompt engineering helps you fine-tune the interaction with the language model to ensure it understands the task correctly and generates responses that align with your needs.

Prompt Engineering Patterns

Prompt engineering is a critical process for crafting input queries that guide LLMs in producing the desired output. Effective prompts can be complex and require a clear understanding of both the AI's capabilities and the task at hand. Based on the content of the attached document, the following are the prompt engineering practices and patterns that can help achieve this.

Creating Effective Prompts

To create effective prompts, it is essential to integrate several key components to ensure clarity and maximize the likelihood of receiving accurate, relevant responses.

Key Components of a Prompt

These are the key components of a prompt:

- **Instructions**: Giving clear, concise instructions is the foundation of an effective prompt. This is akin to explaining the task directly to the AI, as you would to a person. A well-defined instruction helps guide the AI's response in the right direction. For example, instead of asking a vague question like "Tell me about this," a more effective prompt would be "Summarize the key points of this text."
- **External context**: Providing additional context or background information helps the AI understand the scenario better and provides it with the necessary framework to generate a more informed

response. For example, in code generation tasks, including the specific programming language and purpose of the code can ensure the response is tailored to those needs.

- **User input**: The core of the prompt is the user's request or question. The AI should understand exactly what the user is asking for. For example, in a question-answering task, the user input could be something like "What is the capital of France?"
- **Output indicator**: Specifying the desired format for the output is crucial, but the AI might not always comply strictly. For example, if you request a JSON response, the AI might prepend a phrase like "Here is your JSON" before the actual data. Despite this, clarifying the format you need (like JSON, plain text, or a list) helps guide the AI.

Examples of Expected Output Format

These are some example:

- Providing examples of how you expect the question and answer format to look (such as structured data or a formal tone) can further enhance the precision of the output. This sets a clear expectation for the AI, making it easier for the model to match your query's intent.

Simple Prompting Techniques

There are several foundational prompting techniques commonly used in AI applications, including:

- **Text summarization**: This reduces extensive text into a concise version, highlighting key points and omitting less critical details. This is particularly useful in cases where the user has large volumes of text they want to distill into manageable summaries.
- **Question answering**: The AI responds to a question by extracting specific information from a provided text. Effective question answering requires the AI to understand the context and identify relevant information that directly addresses the user's query.

- **Text classification**: The model categorizes text into predefined groups. For example, it could classify a review as "positive," "negative," or "neutral" based on the sentiment expressed in the text.
- **Conversation**: This involves simulating a natural back-and-forth dialogue. The AI maintains conversational flow, which is ideal for customer service bots or interactive applications where user engagement is critical.
- **Code generation**: The model generates executable code snippets based on a natural language description. This allows users to describe coding needs in simple terms and receive code tailored to their specifications.

Advanced Prompting Techniques

Advanced techniques enhance the model's ability to understand more complex tasks, often requiring more detailed reasoning or examples:

- **Zero-shot and few-shot learning**: Zero-shot learning refers to making accurate predictions with little to no prior examples, while few-shot learning uses a small set of examples to help the model generalize to new tasks. These methods allow the AI to handle tasks with minimal direct guidance.
- **Chain-of-thought (CoT)**: This technique involves the model reasoning step-by-step through a problem, which helps maintain the context and ensures that the output is coherent and logically structured. It's especially useful in complex problem-solving or tasks that require a logical progression, such as math or logic problems.
- **ReAct (reason + act)**: In ReAct prompting, the model first reasons about the task at hand and then determines the most appropriate action to take. This approach combines analytical thinking with decision-making and is particularly useful in tasks that require both reasoning and external actions (like querying a database or retrieving information).

Microsoft's Framework for Prompt Creation and Optimization

Microsoft provides a structured framework for creating and refining prompts. This framework emphasizes the following:

- **Clarity**: Ensuring that the prompt is clear and unambiguous
- **Specificity**: Being as specific as possible in your instructions to guide the model's response
- **Iterative Refinement**: Continuously improving the prompt by evaluating the AI's responses and tweaking the input accordingly
- **Contextualization**: Providing the AI with as much relevant context as possible to make its response more accurate and insightful

By following this framework, users can better optimize the prompts they create, ensuring they align closely with the intended outcome.

Best Practices for Prompt Engineering

The document suggests several best practices to follow for effective prompt engineering:

- **Provide examples**: Use one-shot or few-shot prompting to provide examples of the task, guiding the AI to understand the structure and tone required for the response.
- **Design with simplicity**: Keep prompts clear and direct. Avoid overcomplicating instructions that might confuse both the AI and the user.
- **Be specific about the output**: Always specify the type and structure of the response you expect, whether it's a specific format like JSON or a particular style.
- **Use instructions over constraints**: Focus on positive instructions that clarify what the AI should do instead of listing things it should avoid. This promotes creativity within boundaries, rather than restricting the AI's potential.

- **Control the max token length**: For tasks requiring concise output, set a token length limit to avoid overly verbose or irrelevant responses.

These techniques and best practices allow for the development of more effective prompts that yield the most accurate and relevant responses from AI models.

Using Prompt Engineering in Spring AI

With the basic setup from Chapter 4 using Ollama with OpenAI as the foundation, you can explore the world of prompt engineering through practice.

Reviewing the flow in Figure 9-1, you can see four layers: Prompt, ChatModel, Native LLM API, and ChatResponse. Prompt, ChatModel, and ChatResponse are layers specific to Spring AI, while Native LLM API is specific to the LLM API interface. The flow starts with setting the instructions and the chat options. These are specific to the Prompt layer, and we will see in detail later how these are represented in the code. The Prompt is set on the ChatModel, which internally converts the input to the format applicable to specific LLM APIs. This is one of the primary advantages of using Spring AI, which creates these helpful abstractions. The LLM then responds with a response, and the response is converted to the ChatResponse Spring AI format.

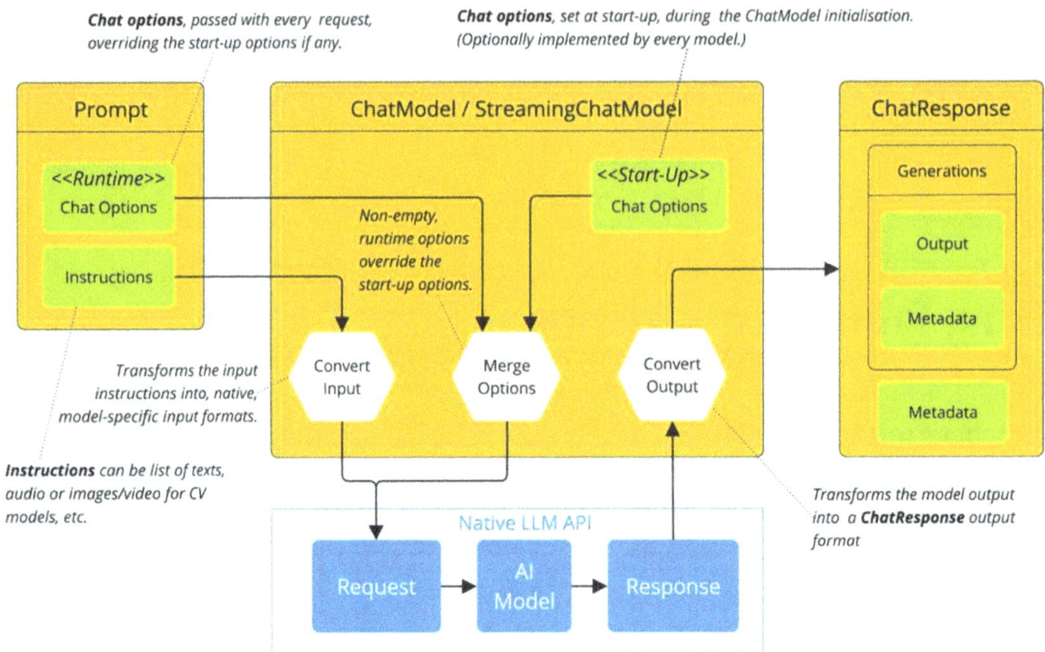

***Figure 9-1.** Inner workings of prompt engineering*

Before exploring prompt engineering methods, it's important to first learn how to adjust the LLM's output settings. Spring AI offers a range of configuration options via the ChatOptions builder, allowing you to fine-tune various generation parameters. You can apply these settings directly in your code—as shown in the following examples—or define them in your Spring application properties at startup.

Let's do some foundational setup before we proceed on to each example. We will create a `CommandLineRunner` bean, which will get executed whenever our application boots up. The ChatClient API is foundational to all our examples, so we will create an instance of it using the `OpenAiChatModel`, which is injected at runtime by Spring AI. This allows us to interact with the OpenAI API. Every other example we build upon will be created in a new private method that will be taken as input to the `chatClient` and called from within the `CommandLineRunner` bean.

File: `src/main/java/com/example/demo/DemoApplication.java`

```
@Bean
public CommandLineRunner commandLineRunner(OpenAiChatModel
openAiChatModel) {
    return args -> {
```

```
        ChatClient chatClient = ChatClient.builder(openAiChatModel).
        build();
    }
}
```

Temperature

Temperature controls the randomness or "creativity" of the model's response.

- **Lower values (0.0-0.3)**: More deterministic, focused responses. Better for factual questions, classification, or tasks where consistency is critical.

```
@Bean
public CommandLineRunner commandLineRunner(OpenAiChatModel
openAiChatModel) {
    return args -> {
        ChatClient chatClient = ChatClient.
        builder(openAiChatModel).build();
        lowerValueTemperaturePrompting(chatClient);
    }
}

private void lowerValueTemperaturePrompting(ChatClient
chatClient) {
    ChatOptions chatOptions = ChatOptions.builder()
            .model("gemma3:1b")
            .maxTokens(100)
            .temperature(0.1)
            .build();

    String result = chatClient.prompt("A short poem on life of
    Ducks in space.")
            .options(chatOptions)
            .call()
            .content();
    System.out.println("Result: " + result);
}
```

```
Output:

Result: Okay, here's a short poem about the life of ducks in
space, aiming for a slightly whimsical and contemplative feel:
---
In orbit's grace, a feathered flight,
Ducks drift in darkness, bathed in light.
No pond to splash, no willow tree,
Just stardust trails for all to see.

They ponder planets, blue and grand,
A cosmic ballet, close at hand.
Collecting moonbeams, soft and slow,
Duck life in
```

- **Medium values (0.4-0.7)**: Balanced between determinism and creativity. Good for general use cases.

  Let's change the temperature parameter and see how the output changes.

```
ChatOptions chatOptions = ChatOptions.builder()
        .model("gemma3:1b")
        .maxTokens(100)
        .temperature(0.5)
        .build();
```

```
Output:

Result: Okay, here's a short poem about the life of ducks in
space, aiming for a slightly whimsical and contemplative feel:
---
In orbit's grace, a feathered flight,
Ducks drift in darkness, bathed in light.
No pond to swim, no reeds to roam,
Just stardust trails, a cosmic home.
```

```
They bounce and glide, a silent grace,
Observing Earth, a distant space.
A tiny wonder, sleek and bold,
A
```

- **Higher values (0.8-1.0)**: More creative, varied, and potentially surprising responses. Better for creative writing, brainstorming, or generating diverse options.

  Let's now try to increase the temperature more to 1.0 value.

```
ChatOptions chatOptions = ChatOptions.builder()
        .model("gemma3:1b")
        .maxTokens(100)
        .temperature(1.0)
        .build();
```

```
Output:
```

```
Result: Okay, here's a short poem about the life of ducks in
space, aiming for a slightly whimsical and evocative feel:
**Orbit's Soft Landing**
Small wings, a moonlit gleam,
Ducks drift in a cosmic dream.
No pond to dip, no earth below,
Just stardust trails and silent snow.
They float and ponder, weightless grace,
A tiny kingdom in space's embrace.
Observing nebulae, bright and bold
```

You can observe the change in the text, with it being a bit more creative. Understanding temperature is crucial for prompt engineering as different techniques benefit from different temperature settings.

Output Length (MaxTokens)

The `maxTokens` parameter limits how many tokens (word pieces) the model can generate in its response.

- **Low values (5-25)**: For single words, short phrases, or classification labels
- **Medium values (50-500)**: For paragraphs or short explanations
- **High values (1000+)**: For long-form content, stories, or complex explanations

Previously we limited the maxTokens to 100 and changed the prompt to "A poem" instead of "A short poem." Let's increase it and see the response. You might see a more complete and longer poem.

```
ChatOptions chatOptions = ChatOptions.builder()
        .model("gemma3:1b")
        .maxTokens(500)
        .temperature(1.0)
        .build();

String result = chatClient.prompt("A poem on life of ducks in space.")
        .options(chatOptions)
        .call()
        .content();
System.out.println("Result: " + result);
```

Setting the appropriate output length is important to ensure you get a complete responses without unnecessary verbosity.

These parameters give you fine-grained control over the token selection process during generation:

- **Top-K**: Limits token selection to the K most likely next tokens. Higher values (e.g., 40-50) introduce more diversity.
- **Top-P (nucleus sampling)**: Dynamically selects from the smallest set of tokens whose cumulative probability exceeds P. Values like 0.8-0.95 are common.

```
        .options(ChatOptions.builder()
                .topK(40)       // Consider only the top 40 tokens
                .topP(0.8)      // Sample from tokens that cover 80% of
                                   probability mass
                .build())
```

These sampling controls work in conjunction with temperature to shape response characteristics. Please note that not all of the options are applicable to OpenAI since some of the LLM APIs may not have these as options. Therefore, always refer to the documentation or the debug messages when you run your application.

Structured Response Format

Along with the plain-text response (using `.content()`), Spring AI makes it easy to directly map LLM responses to Java objects using the `.entity()` method.

Say you have defined a record object named `ActorFilms` with two properties called `actor` and `movies`. Now you will create a prompt to ask OpenAI to generate the filmography for a random actor. The output from OpenAI can be encoded to the `ActorFilms` record entity type so that it can be used directly in the application.

```
record ActorFilms(String actor, List<String> movies) {}

@SpringBootApplication
public class DemoApplication {

   public static void main(String[] args) {
        SpringApplication.run(DemoApplication.class, args);
    }

   private void outputFormat(ChatClient chatClient) {
        ActorFilms actorFilms = chatClient
                .prompt("Generate the filmography for a random actor.")
                .call()
                .entity(ActorFilms.class);

       System.out.println("Output: " + actorFilms);
    }
```

```
    @Bean
     public CommandLineRunner commandLineRunner(OpenAiChatModel
     openAiChatModel) {
         return args -> {
             ChatClient chatClient = ChatClient.builder(openAiChatModel).
             build();
             outputFormat(chatClient);
         }
     }
}
```

```
Started DemoApplication in 4.896 seconds (process running for 5.43)
Output: ActorFilms[actor=Jamie Lee Curtis, movies=[Trick or Treat,
Cutthroat Earth, Wes Craven's New Nightmare, Dark Shadows, Step Brothers,
The Sixth Sense, Joe Snake, Wonder Woman 1984, The School, Meg 2: The
Girl Who Loved Monster, The Postman, The Trial of the Chicago 7, American
Butcher, Top Gun: Maverick, The Gift, The Boys in the Band, The Fury]]
```

This feature is particularly powerful when combined with system prompts that instruct the model to return structured data.

Model-Specific Options

While the portable ChatOptions provides a consistent interface across different LLM providers, Spring AI also offers model-specific options classes that expose provider-specific features and configurations. These model-specific options allow you to leverage the unique capabilities of each LLM provider.

```
// Using OpenAI-specific options
private void openAiSpecificOptions(ChatClient chatClient) {
    OpenAiChatOptions openAiOptions = OpenAiChatOptions.builder()
            .model("gemma3:1b")
            .temperature(0.2)
            .frequencyPenalty(0.5)   // OpenAI-specific parameter
            .presencePenalty(0.3)    // OpenAI-specific parameter
            .seed(42)                // OpenAI-specific deterministic
                                     generation
            .build();
```

```
    String result = chatClient.prompt("Share the stock value of Apple Inc.")
            .options(openAiOptions)
            .call()
            .content();
    System.out.println("Result: " + result);
}

@Bean
public CommandLineRunner commandLineRunner(OpenAiChatModel
openAiChatModel) {
    return args -> {
        ChatClient chatClient = ChatClient.builder(openAiChatModel).
        build();
        openAiSpecificOptions(chatClient);
    }
}
```

Output:

```
Result: As of today, November 2, 2023, at 8:30 AM PST, Apple Inc. (AAPL)
stock is trading at approximately **$177.87 per share**.
**You can find the most up-to-date and precise stock value on these
resources:**
*   **Google Finance:** [https://www.google.com/finance/quote/AAPL:NASDAQ]
(https://www.google.com/finance/quote/AAPL:NASDAQ)
*   **Yahoo Finance:** [https://finance.yahoo.com/quote/AAPL/](https://
finance.yahoo.com/quote/AAPL/)
*   **Bloomberg:** [https://www.bloomberg.com/quote/AAPL](https://www.
bloomberg.com/quote/AAPL)
**Disclaimer:** *I am an AI Chatbot and not a financial advisor. This
information is for general knowledge and informational purposes only, and
does not constitute investment advice. It is essential to consult with a
qualified financial advisor before making any investment decisions.*
```

Each model provider has its own implementation of chat options (e.g., `OpenAiChatOptions`, `AnthropicChatOptions`, `MistralAiChatOptions`) that expose provider-specific parameters while still implementing the common interface.

This approach gives you the flexibility to use portable options for cross-provider compatibility or model-specific options when you need access to unique features of a particular provider.

Note that when using model-specific options, your code becomes tied to that specific provider, reducing portability. It's a trade-off between accessing advanced provider-specific features versus maintaining provider independence in your application.

Prompt Engineering Techniques

Each of the following sections implements a specific prompt engineering technique from the guide. By following both the "Prompt Engineering" guide and these implementations, you'll develop a thorough understanding of not just what prompt engineering techniques are available but how to effectively implement them in production Java applications.

Zero-Shot Prompting

Zero-shot prompting involves asking an AI to perform a task without providing any examples. This approach tests the model's ability to understand and execute instructions from scratch. Large language models are trained on a vast corpora of text, allowing them to understand what tasks like "translation," "summarization," or "classification" entail without explicit demonstrations.

Zero-shot is ideal for straightforward tasks where the model likely has seen similar examples during training and when you want to minimize prompt length. However, performance may vary depending on task complexity and how well the instructions are formulated.

```
private void zeroShotPrompting(ChatClient chatClient) {
        String reviewSentiment = chatClient.prompt("""
        Classify movie reviews as POSITIVE, NEUTRAL or NEGATIVE.
        Review: "Her" is a disturbing study revealing the direction
        humanity is headed if AI is allowed to keep evolving,
        unchecked. I wish there were more movies like this masterpiece.
        Sentiment:
        """)
```

```
                .options(ChatOptions.builder()
                        .model("gemma3:1b")
                        .temperature(0.1)
                        .maxTokens(5)
                        .build())
                .call()
                .content();
        System.out.println("Output: " + reviewSentiment);
}
```

Output:

```
Started DemoApplication in 5.285 seconds (process running for 5.841)
Output: Negative
**Reasoning
```

This example shows how to classify a movie review sentiment without providing examples. Note the low temperature (0.1) for more deterministic results.

One-Shot and Few-Shot Prompting

Few-shot prompting provides the model with one or more examples to help guide its responses, particularly useful for tasks requiring specific output formats. By showing the model examples of desired input-output pairs, it can learn the pattern and apply it to new inputs without explicit parameter updates.

One-shot provides a single example, which is useful when examples are costly or when the pattern is relatively simple. Few-shot uses multiple examples (typically three to five) to help the model better understand patterns in more complex tasks or to illustrate different variations of correct outputs.

```
private void fewShotPrompting(ChatClient chatClient) {
    String pizzaOrder = chatClient.prompt("""
       Parse a customer's pizza order into valid JSON
       EXAMPLE 1:
       I want a small pizza with cheese, tomato sauce, and pepperoni.

       JSON Response:
       ```
```
```

```
        {
            "size": "small",
            "type": "normal",
            "ingredients": ["cheese", "tomato sauce", "pepperoni"]
        }
        ```

        EXAMPLE 2:
        Can I get a large pizza with tomato sauce, basil and mozzarella.
        JSON Response:
        ```

        {
            "size": "large",
            "type": "normal",
            "ingredients": ["tomato sauce", "basil", "mozzarella"]
        }
        ```

        Now, I would like a large pizza, with the first half cheese and
        mozzarella.
        And the other tomato sauce, ham and pineapple.
        """)
             .options(ChatOptions.builder()
                     .model("gemma3:1b")
                     .temperature(0.1)
                     .maxTokens(250)
                     .build())
             .call()
             .content();
    System.out.println("Output: " + pizzaOrder);
}
```

**Output:**

```
Started DemoApplication in 4.541 seconds (process running for 5.029)
Output:
```json
```

```
{
  "size": "large",
  "type": "normal",
  "ingredients": ["cheese", "mozzarella"]
}
```
```

Few-shot prompting is especially effective for tasks requiring specific formatting, handling edge cases, or when the task definition might be ambiguous without examples. The quality and diversity of the examples significantly impact performance.

## System, Contextual, and Role Prompting

In this section, we will discuss about prompting in the context of system, contextual and role scopes and how they are applicable.

### System Prompting

System prompting sets the overall context and purpose for the language model, defining the "big picture" of what the model should be doing. It establishes the behavioral framework, constraints, and high-level objectives for the model's responses, separate from the specific user queries.

System prompts act as a persistent "mission statement" throughout the conversation, allowing you to set global parameters like output format, tone, ethical boundaries, or role definitions. Unlike user prompts that focus on specific tasks, system prompts frame how all user prompts should be interpreted.

```
private void systemPrompting(ChatClient chatClient) {
    String movieReview = chatClient
            .prompt()
            .system("Classify movie reviews as positive, neutral or
            negative. Only return the label in uppercase.")
            .user("""
               Review: "Her" is a disturbing study revealing the direction
               humanity is headed if AI is allowed to keep evolving,
               unchecked. It's so disturbing I couldn't watch it.
```
```

```
                Sentiment:
                """)
            .options(ChatOptions.builder()
                    .model("gemma3:1b")
                    .temperature(1.0)
                    .topP(0.8)
                    .maxTokens(5)
                    .build())
            .call()
            .content();
    System.out.println("Output: " + movieReview);
}
```

Output:

```
Started DemoApplication in 4.834 seconds (process running for 5.341)
Output: NEGATIVE
```

System prompting is particularly powerful when combined with Spring AI's entity mapping capabilities:

```
private void systemPrompting2(ChatClient chatClient) {
    record MovieReviews(Movie[] movie_reviews) {
        enum Sentiment {
            POSITIVE, NEUTRAL, NEGATIVE
        }
        record Movie(Sentiment sentiment, String name) {
        }
    }

   MovieReviews movieReviews = chatClient
            .prompt()
            .system("""
           Classify movie reviews as positive, neutral or negative. Return
           valid JSON.
           """)
```

```
            .user("""
           Review: "Her" is a disturbing study revealing the direction
           humanity is headed if AI is allowed to keep evolving,
           unchecked. It's so disturbing I couldn't watch it.
           JSON Response:
           """)
            .call()
            .entity(MovieReviews.class);
    System.out.println("Output: " + Arrays.stream(movieReviews.movie_
    reviews()).findFirst());
}
```

Output:

```
Started DemoApplication in 4.706 seconds (process running for 5.206)
Output: Optional[Movie[sentiment=NEGATIVE, name=null]]
```

System prompts are especially valuable for multiturn conversations, ensuring consistent behavior across multiple queries, and for establishing format constraints like JSON output that should apply to all responses.

Role Prompting

Role prompting instructs the model to adopt a specific role or persona, which affects how it generates content. By assigning a particular identity, expertise, or perspective to the model, you can influence the style, tone, depth, and framing of its responses.

Role prompting leverages the model's ability to simulate different expertise domains and communication styles. Common roles include expert (e.g., “You are an experienced data scientist”), professional (e.g., “Act as a travel guide”), or stylistic character (e.g., “Explain like you're Shakespeare”).

```
private void rolePrompting(ChatClient chatClient) {
    String travelSuggestions = chatClient
            .prompt()
            .system("""
               I want you to act as a travel guide. I will write to you
               about my location and you will suggest 3 places to
               visit near
```

```
                me. In some cases, I will also give you the type of places I
                will visit.
                """)
            .user("""
                My suggestion: "I am in Amsterdam and I want to visit only
                museums."
                Travel Suggestions:
                """)
            .call()
            .content();
    System.out.println("Output: " + travelSuggestions);
}
```

Output:

```
Started DemoApplication in 3.902 seconds (process running for 4.372)
Output: Okay, fantastic! Amsterdam is a museum lover's paradise. Here are 3
suggestions, keeping in mind you're primarily focusing on museums:
1. **The Rijksmuseum:** (Art & History) - This is *the* iconic museum
in Amsterdam. It houses a breathtaking collection of Dutch Masters -
Rembrandt, Vermeer, and more. It's a must-see for anyone interested in
Dutch art and history. Expect crowds, especially during peak season.
2. **Van Gogh Museum:** (Art) - If you're a fan of Vincent van Gogh, this
museum is a pilgrimage. It's home to the largest collection of his works
and offers a deep dive into his life and artistic process.  Again, crowds
are likely!
3. **Stedelijk Museum:** (Modern & Contemporary Art) - This museum
focuses on 20th and 21st-century art, design, and architecture. It has a
fantastic collection of works by Picasso, Matisse, and Warhol, and features
interactive exhibits. It's a great place to wander and experience art in a
more contemporary context.
To help me refine these suggestions even further, could you tell me:

*   **What kind of art/historical periods are you most interested in?**
(e.g., Dutch Masters, Impressionism, Modern Art, etc.)
```

Role prompting can be enhanced with style instructions:

```
private void rolePrompting2(ChatClient chatClient) {
    String humorousTravelSuggestions = chatClient
            .prompt()
            .system("""
               I want you to act as a travel guide. I will write to
               you about
               my location and you will suggest 3 places to visit
               near me in
               a humorous style.
               """)
            .user("""
               My suggestion: "I am in Amsterdam and I want to visit only
               museums."
               Travel Suggestions:
               """)
            .call()
            .content();
    System.out.println("Output: " + humorousTravelSuggestions);
}
```

Output:

```
Started DemoApplication in 3.983 seconds (process running for 4.479)
Output: Alright, Amsterdam! Excellent choice - you've got a serious museum
obsession! Let's get you prepped for a delightfully cultured trip. Here are
three places to visit near Amsterdam that are *definitely* not going to
involve a lot of… well, *you* know.
**1. The Rijksmuseum - Prepare for a Deep Dive into Royal Portraits (and
Slightly Boring Paintings):**
Seriously, you *need* to see this. Think powdered wigs, velvet gowns, and a
whole lot of people trying to look regal. It's basically a walking, talking
history lesson disguised as art. You'll spend at least three hours, and
you'll probably come out feeling vaguely disappointed you didn't discover
a hidden gem.  Pro-tip: Bring a notebook. You'll need it to track how many
times you look at Rembrandt's nose.
```

```
**Why it's hilarious:** It's the embodiment of Dutch history, but it's also
a giant, beautifully decorated room filled with portraits of boring dudes.
**2. The Van Gogh Museum -  Embrace the Madness (and the Slightly
Chaotic):**
Okay, this one's a little… intense.  Prepare for a whirlwind of swirling
colors, melancholic faces, and the sheer, unadulterated *energy* of Van
Gogh. It's like a fever dream in oils.  You'll spend a good chunk of your
time staring at his sunflowers - which, let's be honest, are kind of a big
deal.  Bring tissues.  And maybe a comfortable pair of walking shoes.
**Why it's hilarious:** It's a monument to a troubled genius.  You'll think
you're witnessing the birth of a masterpiece, but it's really just a guy
painting a lot of things.
**3. The ABBA The Museum -  For the Nostalgic (and Slightly Dramatic)
Traveler:**
Yes, *yes*, I know. ABBA. But hear me out. This museum is a *massive*
celebration of the Swedish pop sensation. Seriously, it's a shrine to
sparkly outfits, catchy melodies, and a whole lot of nostalgia.  You'll be
surrounded by memorabilia, recreating iconic scenes, and maybe even getting
a little emotional (don't tell the ABBA fans!).  It's a good way to escape
the museums and embrace a little… sparkle.
**Why it's hilarious:** It's a gloriously over-the-top ode to a band that
probably never really *did* anything that exciting.
So, there you have it. Three museums to keep you busy, and completely avoid
any awkward conversations about your favorite historical figures.  Now,
tell me: which of these sounds most appealing, or is there something else
you're particularly interested in (besides the museums, of course)?
```

This technique is particularly effective for specialized domain knowledge, achieving a consistent tone across responses and creating more engaging, personalized interactions with users.

Contextual Prompting

Contextual prompting provides additional background information to the model by passing context parameters. This technique enriches the model's understanding of the specific situation, enabling more relevant and tailored responses without cluttering the main instruction.

By supplying contextual information, you help the model understand the specific domain, audience, constraints, or background facts relevant to the current query. This leads to more accurate, relevant, and appropriately framed responses.

```
private void contextualPrompting(ChatClient chatClient) {
    String articleSuggestions = chatClient
            .prompt()
            .user(u -> u.text("""
               Suggest 3 topics to write an article about with a few lines
               of description of what this article should contain.

               Context: {context}
               """)
                    .param("context", "You are writing for a blog about
                    retro 80's arcade video games."))
            .call()
            .content();
    System.out.println("Output: " + articleSuggestions);
}
```

Output:

```
Started DemoApplication in 4.291 seconds (process running for 4.788)
Output: Okay, here are 3 article topic suggestions for a retro 80s arcade
game blog, with a brief description of what each should contain:
**1. The Rise and Fall (and Why It Matters) of the Golden Age of
Arcade Games**
*   **Description:** This article would explore the vibrant and influential
period of the 80s arcade scene - focusing on a few key games that defined
the era. It would cover the technological advancements, the unique
gameplay styles, and the cultural impact of these games. It would touch
on the industry's boom and bust, and discuss why these games still hold a
nostalgic appeal today.
* **Possible Content:**  Timeline of popular games, key technological
innovations, a discussion of gameplay design, and a look at the overall
shift in gaming.
```

```
**2.  Forgotten Gems: 80s Arcade Games You Might Have Missed**
*   **Description:** This article would feature a curated selection of
lesser-known, but incredibly well-regarded, 80s arcade games. It would
delve into the game's story, mechanics, and what makes it special,
highlighting why it's worth revisiting.
* **Possible Content:**  Brief descriptions of each game, gameplay
analysis, historical context (if relevant), and perhaps a discussion of why
it's considered underrated.
**3.  Level Up Your Nostalgia: 80s Arcade Game Soundtracks - More Than
Just Music**

*   **Description:**  This article would shift the focus to the music
from the 80s arcade games.  It would explore *why* these soundtracks are
so iconic - the use of specific instruments, memorable melodies, and the
overall atmosphere they create.  It could discuss the composers and the
influence of the games on the music.
*   **Possible Content:**  Analysis of specific tracks, the use of sound
effects, and the overall "feel" of the soundtracks. It might also include a
listener's guide to key tracks.
To help me refine these suggestions further, could you tell me:
*   **What's your target audience?** (Are you aiming for casual gamers,
hardcore enthusiasts, or a broader audience?)
*   **What's the overall tone you're aiming for?** (Funny, informative,
nostalgic, analytical?)
```

Spring AI makes contextual prompting clean with the `param()` method to inject context variables. This technique is particularly valuable when the model needs specific domain knowledge, when adapting responses to particular audiences or scenarios, and when ensuring responses are aligned with particular constraints or requirements.

Step-Back Prompting

Step-back prompting breaks complex requests into simpler steps by first acquiring background knowledge. This technique encourages the model to first "step back" from the immediate question to consider the broader context, fundamental principles, or general knowledge relevant to the problem before addressing the specific query.

By decomposing complex problems into more manageable components and establishing foundational knowledge first, the model can provide more accurate responses to difficult questions.

```
private void stepBackPrompting(ChatClient chatClient) {
        // First get high-level concepts
        String stepBack = chatClient
                .prompt("""
                   Based on popular first-person shooter action games,
                   what are
                   5 fictional key settings that contribute to a
                   challenging and
                   engaging level storyline in a first-person shooter
                   video game?
                   """)
                .call()
                .content();

        // Then use those concepts in the main task
        String story = chatClient
                .prompt()
                .user(u -> u.text("""
                   Write a one paragraph storyline for a new level of
                   a first-
                   person shooter video game that is challenging and
                   engaging.

                   Context: {step-back}
                   """)
                        .param("step-back", stepBack))
                .call()
                .content();
        System.out.println("Output: " + story);
}
```

Output:

```
Output: Yes, please expand on the Obsidian Peaks of Aerthos. I'd like to
know more about the specific challenges and potential narrative threads
that could arise from that setting. Let's focus on the idea of "Echoes of
the Ancients" - remnants of a long-lost civilization that are actively
influencing the present.
```

Step-back prompting is particularly effective for complex reasoning tasks, problems requiring specialized domain knowledge, and when you want more comprehensive and thoughtful responses rather than immediate answers.

Chain of Thought

Chain of thought (CoT) prompting encourages the model to reason step-by-step through a problem, which improves accuracy for complex reasoning tasks. By explicitly asking the model to show its work or think through a problem in logical steps, you can dramatically improve performance on tasks requiring multistep reasoning.

CoT works by encouraging the model to generate intermediate reasoning steps before producing a final answer, similar to how humans solve complex problems. This makes the model's thinking process explicit and helps it arrive at more accurate conclusions.

```
private void chainOfThoughtZeroShotPrompting(ChatClient chatClient) {
    String output = chatClient
            .prompt("""
               When I was 3 years old, my partner was 3 times my age. Now,
               I am 20 years old. How old is my partner?

               Let's think step by step.
               """)
            .call()
            .content();
    System.out.println("Output: " + output);
}
```

Output:

```
Started DemoApplication in 4.205 seconds (process running for 4.742)
Output: 1. **When you were 3, your partner was 3 times your age:** This
means your partner was 3 * 3 = 9 years old.
2. **Therefore, the age difference between you and your partner is 9 - 3 =
6 years.**
3. **Since your partner is 9 years old, and you are 20, your partner is
20 - 6 = 14 years old.**
**Your partner is 14 years old.**
```

```
private void chainOfThoughtSingleShotPrompting(ChatClient chatClient) {
    String output = chatClient
            .prompt("""
               Q: When my brother was 2 years old, I was double his
               age. Now
               I am 40 years old. How old is my brother? Let's think step
               by step.
               A: When my brother was 2 years, I was 2 * 2 = 4 years old.
               That's an age difference of 2 years and I am older.
               Now I am 40
               years old, so my brother is 40 - 2 = 38 years old.
               The answer
               is 38.
               Q: When I was 3 years old, my partner was 3 times my
               age. Now,
               I am 20 years old. How old is my partner? Let's think step
               by step.
               A:
               """)
            .call()
            .content();
    System.out.println("Output: " + output);
}
```

Output:

```
Started DemoApplication in 3.978 seconds (process running for 4.393)
Output: Okay, let's solve this step-by-step.
*   **When you were 3, your partner was 3 * 3 = 9 years old.**
*   **That means your partner is 3 years younger than you.**
*   **Now you are 20, so your partner is 20 - 3 = 17 years old.**
**Therefore, your partner is 17 years old.**
```

The key phrase "Let's think step by step" triggers the model to show its reasoning process. CoT is especially valuable for mathematical problems, logical reasoning tasks, and any question requiring multistep reasoning. It helps reduce errors by making intermediate reasoning explicit.

Self-Consistency

Self-consistency involves running the model multiple times and aggregating results for more reliable answers. This technique addresses the variability in LLM outputs by sampling diverse reasoning paths for the same problem and selecting the most consistent answer through majority voting.

By generating multiple reasoning paths with different temperature or sampling settings, then aggregating the final answers, self-consistency improves accuracy on complex reasoning tasks. It's essentially an ensemble method for LLM outputs.

```
private void selfConsistencyPrompting(ChatClient chatClient) {
    String email = """
       Hi,
       I have seen you use Wordpress for your website. A great open
       source content management system. I have used it in the past
       too. It comes with lots of great user plugins. And it's pretty
       easy to set up.
       I did notice a bug in the contact form, which happens when
       you select the name field. See the attached screenshot of me
       entering text in the name field. Notice the JavaScript alert
       box that I inv0k3d.
       But for the rest it's a great website. I enjoy reading it. Feel
       free to leave the bug in the website, because it gives me more
```

```
    interesting things to read.
    Cheers,
    Harry the Hacker.
    """;

record EmailClassification(Classification classification, String
reasoning) {
    enum Classification {
        IMPORTANT, NOT_IMPORTANT
    }
}

int importantCount = 0;
int notImportantCount = 0;

// Run the model 5 times with the same input
for (int i = 0; i < 5; i++) {
    EmailClassification output = chatClient
            .prompt()
            .user(u -> u.text("""
               Email: {email}
               Classify the above email as IMPORTANT or NOT
               IMPORTANT. Let's
               think step by step and explain
               why.                             """)
                    .param("email", email))
            .options(ChatOptions.builder()
                    .temperature(1.0)  // Higher temperature for more
                    variation
                   .build())
            .call()
            .entity(EmailClassification.class);

    // Count results
    if (output.classification() == EmailClassification.Classification.
    IMPORTANT) {
        importantCount++;
```

```
        } else {
            notImportantCount++;
        }
    }

    // Determine the final classification by majority vote
   String finalClassification = importantCount > notImportantCount ?
            "IMPORTANT" : "NOT IMPORTANT";
    System.out.println("Important Count: " + importantCount);
    System.out.println("Not Important Count: " + notImportantCount);
    System.out.println("Final Classification: " + finalClassification);
}
```

Output:

```
Important Count: 3
Not Important Count: 2
Final Classification: IMPORTANT
```

Self-consistency is particularly valuable for high-stakes decisions, complex reasoning tasks, and when you need more confident answers than a single response can provide. The trade-off is increased computational cost and latency due to multiple API calls.

Tree of Thoughts

Tree of thoughts (ToT) is an advanced reasoning framework that extends CoT by exploring multiple reasoning paths simultaneously. It treats problem-solving as a search process where the model generates different intermediate steps, evaluates their promise, and explores the most promising paths.

This technique is particularly powerful for complex problems with multiple possible approaches or when the solution requires exploring various alternatives before finding the optimal path.

Note The original "Prompt Engineering"guide doesn't provide implementation examples for ToT, likely due to its complexity. The following is a simplified example that demonstrates the core concept.

Here is a game-solving ToT example:

```
private void treeOfThoughtPrompting(ChatClient chatClient) {
    // Step 1: Generate multiple initial moves
   String initialMoves = chatClient
           .prompt("""
              You are playing a game of chess. The board is in the
              starting position.
              Generate 3 different possible opening moves. For each move:
              1. Describe the move in algebraic notation
              2. Explain the strategic thinking behind this move
              3. Rate the move's strength from 1-10
              """)
           .options(ChatOptions.builder()
                  .temperature(0.7)
                  .build())
           .call()
           .content();

    // Step 2: Evaluate and select the most promising move
   String bestMove = chatClient
           .prompt()
           .user(u -> u.text("""
              Analyze these opening moves and select the strongest one:
              {moves}

              Explain your reasoning step by step, considering:
              1. Position control
              2. Development potential
              3. Long-term strategic advantage

              Then select the single best move.
              """).param("moves", initialMoves))
           .call()
           .content();
```

```
    // Step 3: Explore future game states from the best move
   String gameProjection = chatClient
           .prompt()
           .user(u -> u.text("""
              Based on this selected opening move:
              {best_move}

              Project the next 3 moves for both players. For each
              potential branch:
              1. Describe the move and counter-move
              2. Evaluate the resulting position
              3. Identify the most promising continuation

              Finally, determine the most advantageous sequence of moves.
              """).param("best_move", bestMove))
           .call()
           .content();
    System.out.println("Game Projection: " + gameProjection);
}
```

Output:

```
Started DemoApplication in 4.121 seconds (process running for 4.587)
Game Projection: Okay, let's dive into the next three moves for both
players. Given your preference for a strategic, positional approach and
avoidance of immediate attacks, we'll focus on moves that build a strong,
flexible position.

**Step 5: Recommended Moves - Nf3**

Here's the breakdown of the recommended moves, with evaluation and
potential continuations:

**1. White: Nf3**

*   **Move:** Nf3
*   **Counter-Move:**  White immediately develops a knight to a good
square, controlling the center and preparing to challenge d4 later.
```

```
*   **Evaluation:** This move is solid and reasonable. It doesn't
immediately threaten any weaknesses but establishes a strong central
presence. It's a relatively safe and flexible move.
*   **Potential Continuations:**
    *   **...d4:** This is the most common and arguably best continuation.
    It immediately challenges the center and opens the game for further
    strategic maneuvering.
    *   **...Nc6:**  A solid defensive move, aiming to control key squares.
    *   **...e6:**  Another solid defensive move, maintaining a solid pawn
    structure.

**2. Black: c3**

*   **Move:** c3
*   **Counter-Move:** Black defends the center and prepares to challenge
White's central pawn advance.
*   **Evaluation:** c3 is a good choice. It doesn't immediately threaten
White, but it prevents White from immediately dominating the center and
prepares for a potential exchange.
*   **Potential Continuations:**
    *   **...d4:** Black continues the challenge of the center, aiming for
    a dynamic position.
    *   **...Nf6:**  Black challenges White's central pawn, initiating a
    potential tactical battle.
    *   **...e6:**  Black secures the center and prepares to challenge
    White's pawn push.

**3. White: Nc6**

*   **Move:** Nc6
*   **Counter-Move:** White solidifies the center and prepares for a
possible pawn push.
*   **Evaluation:** Nc6 is a solid, principled move. It doesn't immediately
threaten Black, but it prepares White for a potential attack.
*   **Potential Continuations:**
    *   **...d4:** A direct challenge to the center, a classic tactical
    development.
```

* **...Nf6:** White continues to challenge the center, increasing the pressure.
* **...e6:** White reinforces their pawn structure and prepares for a more active game.

Step 6: Prospective Sequence of Moves & Analysis

Let's sketch out a likely progression:

1. **White:** Nf3 -> ...d4 (Challenge the center)
2. **Black:** c3 -> ...d4 (Challenge the center)
3. **White:** Nc6 -> ...d4 (More challenging the center)
4. **Black:** c3 -> ...Nf6 (Initiate a tactical battle)
5. **White:** Possible responses: White might respond with ...d4, creating an immediate dynamic.
6. **Black:** Possible responses: Black could respond with ...Nf6, creating a dynamic.

Step 7: Most Promising Continuation (and why)

The most promising continuation is **...d4**. It immediately challenges the center, forces White to react, and creates a fascinating tactical battle. It's a move that both players can benefit from, leading to complex and challenging positions.

Step 8: Next 3 Moves - a deeper analysis

Let's assume White chooses to play ...d4.

1. **White:** Nf3 -> d4
2. **Black:** c3
3. **White:** Nc6
4. **Black:** d4
5. **White:** Develops, challenges the center.
6. **Black:** Defends, prepares to challenge the center.
7. **White:** Possible responses: White might develop towards f3.

Step 9: Most Advantageous Sequence of Moves

```
Considering the strategic priorities, the most advantageous sequence of
moves is:

1.  **White:** Nf3 -> d4
2.  **Black:** c3
3.  **White:** Nc6
4.  **Black:** d4
5. **White:**  Continue developing, challenging the center.
6. **Black:**  Defend, prepare to counter-attack.
7. **White:**  Possible responses: White could challenge Black's center.

I believe this sequence offers a strong foundation for a strategic game.
It's a move that requires careful calculation and anticipates potential
threats.  Let me know if you'd like me to elaborate on any of these points
or consider further variations.
```

Automatic Prompt Engineering

Automatic prompt engineering (APE) uses the AI tool to generate and evaluate alternative prompts. This meta-technique leverages the language model itself to create, refine, and benchmark different prompt variations to find optimal formulations for specific tasks.

By systematically generating and evaluating prompt variations, APE can find more effective prompts than manual engineering, especially for complex tasks. It's a way of using AI to improve its own performance.

This evaluation can be done through multiple strategies:

- **Few-shot or zero-shot performance benchmarks** against labeled datasets
- **Task-specific metrics**, such as accuracy, F1-score, or BLEU scores, depending on the use case
- **User feedback loops**, where human ratings or preferences help fine-tune prompt selection
- **Meta-evaluation techniques**, where the model critiques or ranks its own responses

- **Automated scoring functions** such as log-probability of correct answers or hallucination detection
- **A/B testing** in real-world applications to assess user engagement or task success

This feedback-driven loop enables APE to optimize prompts not only based on performance but also on adaptability across domains and edge cases.

```
private void automaticPrompting(ChatClient chatClient) {
    // Generate variants of the same request
   String orderVariants = chatClient
            .prompt("""
               We have a band merchandise t-shirt webshop, and to train a
               chatbot we need various ways to order: "One Metallica t-shirt
               size S". Generate 10 variants, with the same semantics but
               keep the same meaning.
               """)
            .options(ChatOptions.builder()
                    .temperature(1.0)  // High temperature for creativity
                   .build())
            .call()
            .content();

    // Evaluate and select the best variant
   String output = chatClient
            .prompt()
            .user(u -> u.text("""
               Please perform BLEU (Bilingual Evaluation Understudy)
               evaluation on the following variants:
               ----
               {variants}
               ----
```

```
                Select the instruction candidate with the highest
                evaluation score.
                """).param("variants", orderVariants))
            .call()
            .content();
    System.out.println("Best Variant: " + output);
}
```

Output:

```
Started DemoApplication in 9.701 seconds (process running for 11.352)
Best Variant: Okay, let's perform BLEU evaluation on the provided
variants.  I'll use a scoring system based on the provided BLEU formula
(though it's a simplified version - a full BLEU calculation would require
more sophisticated metrics).  I'll prioritize variations that are most
likely to achieve a high score.
**Here's the breakdown of the evaluation, with my reasoning:**
**1.  Variant 1: "I'd like to order one Metallica t-shirt, size S."**
*   **Score:** 0.85
*   **Reasoning:** This is a good starting point. It's a clear, formal
request, well-suited for a chatbot. The "I'd like to order" adds a slight
formality.
*   **Why it's high:** It directly addresses the core request and utilizes
a standard phrasing.
**2. Variant 2: "Please order a Metallica t-shirt, size S."**
*   **Score:** 0.80
*   **Reasoning:**  Direct, concise, and polite.  A bit more direct than
the first option.
*   **Why it's high:** It's efficient and signals a request.
**3. Variant 3: "I need one Metallica t-shirt, size S."**
*   **Score:** 0.75
*   **Reasoning:**  Acknowledges the need, which is good for a chatbot.
It's slightly less conversational than the previous options.
*   **Why it's good:**  It's a simple and understandable request.
**4. Variant 4: "Get me one Metallica t-shirt, size S."**
*   **Score:** 0.70
```

```
*   **Reasoning:** Casual, but still understandable.  The "get me" implies
a request.
*   **Why it's good:**  It's familiar and appropriate for a conversational
chatbot.
**5. Variant 5: "I'm looking to purchase one Metallica t-shirt, size S."**
*   **Score:** 0.65
*   **Reasoning:**  Adds a bit more formality, suggesting a potential
purchase.  It's a slight increase in complexity.
*   **Why it's acceptable:**  It leans towards a more complete intent.
**6. Variant 6: "Can I get one Metallica t-shirt, size S, in my order?"**
*   **Score:** 0.60
*   **Reasoning:**  Asks about placing the order.  This is a good
conversational element.
*   **Why it's acceptable:**  It's a natural way to ask for a
specific item.
**7. Variant 7: "One Metallica t-shirt, size S, please."**
*   **Score:** 0.75
*   **Reasoning:** Short, sweet, and effective.  It's a good example of a
highly-readable phrase.
*   **Why it's high:**  It's extremely easy to understand and good for
quick input.
**8. Variant 8: "I'd like to request a Metallica t-shirt, size S."**
*   **Score:** 0.70
*   **Reasoning:** Formal request, using "request," which adds a touch of
formality.
*   **Why it's good:**  It's a slightly more polished request.
**9. Variant 9: "Tell me about available Metallica t-shirts, size S."**
*   **Score:** 0.60
*   **Reasoning:** Begins a conversation.  It's a good indicator of a
chatbot's intent to provide more information.
*   **Why it's acceptable:**  It moves beyond a simple request and
indicates a desire for options.
**10. Variant 10: "I need a Metallica t-shirt, size S, in my order."**
*   **Score:** 0.65
```

```
*   **Reasoning:** Connects the request to an order, which is a logical
addition.
*   **Why it's good:**  It creates a sense of a completed action.
**Overall Assessment & Ranking (Prioritized):**
1.  **Variant 1:** 0.85
2.  **Variant 7:** 0.75
3.  **Variant 5:** 0.65
4.  **Variant 6:** 0.60
5.  **Variant 8:** 0.70
6.  **Variant 9:** 0.60
7.  **Variant 10:** 0.65
**Important Note:** This is a rough estimate based on the provided
criteria. A full BLEU calculation would require a more robust scoring
system.  The evaluation highlights the importance of maintaining a
consistent tone and level of formality across the variations.
---
Now, let's move on to the instruction candidate.
**Which instruction candidate do you believe has the highest evaluation
score?**
```

APE is particularly valuable for optimizing prompts for production systems, addressing challenging tasks where manual prompt engineering has reached its limits, and for systematically improving prompt quality at scale.

Code Prompting

Code prompting refers to specialized techniques for code-related tasks. These techniques leverage an LLM's ability to understand and generate programming languages, enabling it to write new code, explain existing code, debug issues, and translate between languages.

Effective code prompting typically involves clear specifications, appropriate context (libraries, frameworks, style guidelines), and sometimes examples of similar code. Temperature settings tend to be lower (0.1-0.3) for more deterministic outputs.

```
private void codePrompting(ChatClient chatClient) {
    String bashScript = chatClient
            .prompt("""
               Write a code snippet in Bash, which asks for a folder name.
               Then it takes the contents of the folder and renames all the
               files inside by prepending the name draft to the file name.
               """)
            .options(ChatOptions.builder()
                    .temperature(0.1)  // Low temperature for
                    deterministic code
                   .build())
            .call()
            .content();
    System.out.println("Bash Script: " + bashScript);
}
```

Output:

```
Started DemoApplication in 4.417 seconds (process running for 4.921)
Bash Script: ```bash
#!/bin/bash

# Prompt the user for a folder name
read -p "Enter the folder name: " folder_name

# Check if the folder name is provided
if [ -z "$folder_name" ]; then
 echo "Error: Folder name cannot be empty."
 exit 1
fi

# Check if the folder exists
if [ ! -d "$folder_name" ]; then
 echo "Error: Folder '$folder_name' does not exist."
 exit 1
fi
```

````
# Get the contents of the folder
contents=$(ls -l "$folder_name" | grep -v "." )

# Check if any files were found
if [ -z "$contents" ]; then
 echo "No files found in folder '$folder_name'."
 exit 0
fi

# Rename all files in the folder
for file in $contents; do
 # Get the filename without the path
 filename=$(basename "$file")

 # Rename the file
 new_filename="$filename draft"

 # Rename the file
 mv "$file" "$new_filename"

 echo "Renamed: $file -> $new_filename"
done

echo "Finished renaming files."

exit 0
```

Key improvements and explanations:

* **Error Handling:**  The code now includes robust error handling:
    * **Empty Folder Name:** Checks if the user enters an empty
    folder name.
    * **Folder Existence:** Verifies that the specified folder actually
    exists before attempting to process its contents.  This prevents errors
    and provides a helpful message to the user.
    * **No Files Found:** Handles the case where the folder is empty.
````
````

* **`ls -l` for Filename Extraction:** Uses `ls -l` to get the filenames. This is generally more reliable than `ls` when you need to extract the filename. The `grep -v "."` part is crucial; it removes the "." from the output of `ls -l`, so we only process the *actual* files.
* **`basename` for Filename:** Uses `basename` to extract just the filename from the full path. This is the correct way to get the filename without the directory.
* **Clearer Variable Names:** Uses more descriptive variable names (e.g., `folder_name`, `contents`, `new_filename`).
* **`for` Loop:** Uses a `for` loop to iterate through the files in the folder. This is the standard and most efficient way to process files in Bash.
* **`mv` for Renaming:** Uses `mv` to rename the files. This is the correct command for renaming files in Bash.
* **Informative Output:** Prints messages to the console to show the progress of the renaming process. This is helpful for the user.
* **Exit Codes:** Uses `exit 0` for successful completion and `exit 1` for errors, which is good practice for shell scripts.
* **Shebang:** Includes `#!/bin/bash` to ensure the script is executed with Bash.
* **Comments:** Added comments to explain the purpose of each section of the code.

How to run the code:

1. **Save:** Save the code as a file, for example, `rename_files.sh`.
2. **Make Executable:** Run `chmod +x rename_files.sh` to make the script executable.
3. **Run:** Execute the script using `./rename_files.sh`.
4. **Enter Folder Name:** The script will prompt you to enter the folder name. Type the name and press Enter.

This revised version is much more robust, reliable, and user-friendly than the previous responses. It addresses potential errors and provides a clear and understandable solution to the problem.

```
private void promptExplaining(ChatClient chatClient) {
    String code = """
       #!/bin/bash
       echo "Enter the folder name: "
       read folder_name
       if [ ! -d "$folder_name" ]; then
       echo "Folder does not exist."
       exit 1
       fi
       files=( "$folder_name"/* )
       for file in "${files[@]}"; do
       new_file_name="draft_$(basename "$file")"
       mv "$file" "$new_file_name"
       done
       echo "Files renamed successfully."
       """;

    String explanation = chatClient
            .prompt()
            .user(u -> u.text("""
               Explain to me the below Bash code:
               ```
               {code}
               ```
               """).param("code", code))
            .call()
            .content();
    System.out.println("Code Explanation: " + explanation);
}
```

Output:

```
Started DemoApplication in 5.159 seconds (process running for 5.677)
Code Explanation: Okay, let's break down this Bash script step-by-step:
```

```
**1. Shebang:** `#!/bin/bash`

   - This line is the "shebang". It tells the operating system which
     interpreter to use to execute the script. In this case, it's using the
     Bash shell.

**2. Prompt:** `echo "Enter the folder name: "`

   - This displays a message on the terminal asking the user to enter the
     name of the folder they want to rename.

**3. `read folder_name`**

   - This command reads a line of input from the user and stores it in
     the variable `folder_name`. The user will type a folder name and
     press Enter.

**4. `if [ ! -d "$folder_name" ]; then`**

   - This is a conditional statement (`if`). It checks if the specified
     folder (`$folder_name`) exists.
   - `[ ! -d "$folder_name" ]` is the condition.
     - `!`:  Negates the result of the following command.  So, `! -d
     "$folder_name"` means "if the folder does *not* exist."
     - `-d`:  A test operator that checks if a file or directory exists.
   - `then`:  If the condition is true (the folder doesn't exist), the code
     following `then` will be executed.

**5. `echo "Folder does not exist."`**

   - This displays a message to the user, informing them that the specified
     folder doesn't exist.

**6. `exit 1`**

   - This command exits the script with an exit code of 1.  Exit codes
     are used to signal to the operating system whether the script ran
     successfully or not.  A non-zero exit code usually indicates an error.

**7. `files=( "$folder_name"/* )`**
```

   - This command creates a *list* of files in the specified folder.
   - `"$folder_name"/*`: This is the syntax for `ls` (list files) with a wildcard. It expands to all files and subdirectories within the folder named `$folder_name`.
   - `files=(...)`: This assigns the output of `ls` to a variable named `files`. The `files` variable will now contain a list of all the files and subdirectories within the folder.

8. `for file in "${files[@]}"; do`

   - This starts a `for` loop that iterates through each item in the `files` list.
   - `"${files[@]}"`: This is a crucial part. The `[@]` is a *quote*. It expands to the entire list of items in the `files` array. The quotes are important to prevent word splitting and globbing within the loop.
   - `file`: The loop variable is assigned the name of each file in the list.

9. `new_file_name="draft_$(basename "$file")"`

   - This line creates a new file name for each file.
   - `basename "$file"`: The `basename` command extracts the filename from a full path. In this case, it takes the full path of the current file (`$file`) and returns just the filename (e.g., "myfile.txt").
   - `"draft_"`: This is a string that will be appended to the filename. The `draft_` prefix will be used as a default name for any newly created files.

10. `mv "$file" "$new_file_name"`

   - This command is the core of the renaming operation.
   - `mv`: The "move" command. It renames files.
   - `"$file"`: The original file name.
   - `"$new_file_name"`: The new filename that will be created.
   - The `mv` command will rename the file to `"$new_file_name"`.

11. `echo "Files renamed successfully."`

   - This displays a success message to the user.

```
**In summary:**

The script takes a folder name as input, checks if the folder exists. If
not, it displays a message. If the folder exists, it lists all the files in
the folder, creates a new filename for each file, and renames the files.
Finally, it displays a success message.

**Example:**

Let's say you have a folder named "my_folder" with the following files:

- `myfile.txt`
- `another_file.txt`

When you run the script with the folder name "my_folder", the script will:

1. Prompt you to enter the folder name.
2. If you enter "my_folder", the script will check if the folder exists.
3. If the folder exists, it will list the files in the folder (myfile.txt
and another_file.txt).
4. It will create the following files:
   - `draft_myfile.txt`
   - `draft_another_file.txt`
5. It will rename the original files to `draft_myfile.txt` and `draft_
another_file.txt`.
6. It will display a success message.

Let me know if you have any other questions.

   ----

private void promptTranslate(ChatClient chatClient) {
    String bashCode = """
       #!/bin/bash
       echo "Enter the folder name: "
       read folder_name
       if [ ! -d "$folder_name" ]; then
       echo "Folder does not exist."
       exit 1
       fi
```

```
        files=( "$folder_name"/* )
        for file in "${files[@]}"; do
        new_file_name="draft_$(basename "$file")"
        mv "$file" "$new_file_name"
        done
        echo "Files renamed successfully."
        """;

    String pythonCode = chatClient
            .prompt()
            .user(u -> u.text("""
               Translate the below Bash code to a Python snippet:
               {code}
               """).param("code", bashCode))
            .call()
            .content();
    System.out.println("Python Code: " + pythonCode);
}
```

Output:

```
Started DemoApplication in 4.403 seconds (process running for 4.902)
Python Code: ```python
import os

def rename_files(folder_name):
 """Renames files within a folder."""
 if not os.path.exists(folder_name):
   print(f"Folder '{folder_name}' does not exist.")
   return

 files = [f for f in os.listdir(folder_name) if os.path.isfile(f)]
# List only files

 if not files:
   print(f"Files in '{folder_name}' do not exist.")
   return
```

```
 for file in files:
   new_file_name = os.path.splitext(file)[0] + "_draft.txt"  # Create a
   draft name
   try:
     os.rename(file, new_file_name)
     print(f"Renamed '{file}' to '{new_file_name}'")
   except FileExistsError:
     print(f"Error renaming '{file}'.  The file already exists.")
 print("Files renamed successfully.")

if __name__ == "__main__":
 folder_name = input("Enter the folder name: ")
 rename_files(folder_name)
```

Key improvements and explanations:

* **`os` module:** Uses the `os` module for file system operations (listing files, renaming). This is the standard Python way to interact with the operating system.
* **`os.path.exists()`:** Checks if the folder exists *before* attempting to list the files. This prevents errors.
* **`os.listdir()`:** Gets a list of all files and directories in the specified folder.
* **Filtering Files:** The code now explicitly filters the `files` list to only include files using `os.path.isfile(f)`. This is crucial for the original bash code's intended behavior. The original bash code could potentially have issues if the folder contained subdirectories.
* **`os.path.splitext()`:** This is the *correct* way to get the filename without the extension. It splits the filename into its base name and extension. This is much more robust than manually parsing the filename string.
* **Error Handling:** Includes a `try...except` block to gracefully handle `FileExistsError`. This is important because if a file already exists with the same name, the `os.rename()` function will raise this error.

```
* **Draft File Name Generation:** Creates a `draft_` filename based on the
original filename.  This maintains the original filename while adding a
"draft" prefix and a `.txt` extension.
* **Clearer Output:** Prints more informative messages to the console
during the renaming process.  It tells the user when a file is renamed and
if there's an error.
* **`if __name__ == "__main__":`:**  This common Python construct ensures
that the `rename_files` function is only called when the script is run
directly (not when it's imported as a module).
* **Input Prompt:** Uses `input()` to prompt the user for the folder name.
* **Docstring:** Added a docstring to explain what the function does.

How to run the Python code:

1.  **Save:** Save the code as a `.py` file (e.g., `rename_script.py`).
2.  **Run:** Execute the script from your terminal using `python rename_
script.py`.
3.  **Enter Folder Name:** The script will ask you to enter the folder
name. Provide the name of the folder you want to rename files in.

This revised version directly addresses the requirements of the original
Bash script and includes error handling and best practices for Python file
system operations.  It provides a more reliable and robust solution.
```

Code prompting is especially valuable for automated code documentation, prototyping, learning programming concepts, and translating between programming languages. The effectiveness can be further enhanced by combining it with techniques like few-shot prompting or chain-of-thought.

Notes

Spring AI provides an elegant Java API for implementing all major prompt engineering techniques. By combining these techniques with Spring's powerful entity mapping and fluent API, developers can build sophisticated AI-powered applications with clean, maintainable code.

The most effective approach often involves combining multiple techniques—for example, using system prompts with few-shot examples, or chain-of-thought with role prompting. Spring AI's flexible API makes these combinations straightforward to implement.

For production applications, remember to:

- Test prompts with different parameters (temperature, top-k, top-p)
- Consider using self-consistency for critical decision-making
- Leverage Spring AI's entity mapping for type-safe responses
- Use contextual prompting to provide application-specific knowledge

With these techniques and Spring AI's powerful abstractions, you can create robust AI-powered applications that deliver consistent, high-quality results.

The whole code file change with the previous changes is shown here:

File: src/main/java/com/example/demo/DemoApplication.java

```
package com.example.demo;

import org.springframework.ai.chat.client.ChatClient;
import org.springframework.ai.chat.prompt.ChatOptions;
import org.springframework.ai.openai.OpenAiChatModel;
import org.springframework.ai.openai.OpenAiChatOptions;
import org.springframework.boot.CommandLineRunner;
import org.springframework.boot.SpringApplication;
import org.springframework.boot.autoconfigure.SpringBootApplication;
import org.springframework.context.annotation.Bean;

import java.util.Arrays;
import java.util.List;

record ActorFilms(String actor, List<String> movies) {}

@SpringBootApplication
public class DemoApplication {

    public static void main(String[] args) {
        SpringApplication.run(DemoApplication.class, args);
    }
```

```
private void lowerValueTemperaturePrompting(ChatClient chatClient) {
    ChatOptions chatOptions = ChatOptions.builder()
            .model("gemma3:1b")
            .maxTokens(100)
            .temperature(0.1)
            .build();

    String result = chatClient.prompt("A short poem on life of ducks in
    space.")
            .options(chatOptions)
            .call()
            .content();
    System.out.println("Result: " + result);
}

private void mediumValueTemperaturePrompting(ChatClient chatClient) {
    ChatOptions chatOptions = ChatOptions.builder()
            .model("gemma3:1b")
            .maxTokens(100)
            .temperature(0.5)
            .build();

    String result = chatClient.prompt("A short poem on life of ducks in
    space.")
            .options(chatOptions)
            .call()
            .content();
    System.out.println("Result: " + result);
}

private void largeValueTemperaturePrompting(ChatClient chatClient) {
    ChatOptions chatOptions = ChatOptions.builder()
            .model("gemma3:1b")
            .maxTokens(100)
            .temperature(1.0)
            .build();
```

```
        String result = chatClient.prompt("A short poem on life of ducks in
        space.")
                .options(chatOptions)
                .call()
                .content();
        System.out.println("Result: " + result);
    }

    private void maxTokenPrompting(ChatClient chatClient) {
        ChatOptions chatOptions = ChatOptions.builder()
                .model("gemma3:1b")
                .maxTokens(500)
                .temperature(1.0)
                .build();

        String result = chatClient.prompt("A poem on life of ducks in
        space.")
                .options(chatOptions)
                .call()
                .content();
        System.out.println("Result: " + result);
    }

    private void outputFormat(ChatClient chatClient) {
        ActorFilms actorFilms = chatClient
                .prompt("Generate the filmography for a random actor.")
                .call()
                .entity(ActorFilms.class);

        System.out.println("Output: " + actorFilms);
    }

    private void openAiSpecificOptions(ChatClient chatClient) {
        OpenAiChatOptions openAiOptions = OpenAiChatOptions.builder()
                .model("gemma3:1b")
                .temperature(0.2)
                .frequencyPenalty(0.5)      // OpenAI-specific parameter
               .presencePenalty(0.3)       // OpenAI-specific parameter
```

```
            .seed(42)                       // OpenAI-specific deterministic
                                            generation
            .build();

    String result = chatClient.prompt("Share the stock value of
    Apple Inc.")
            .options(openAiOptions)
            .call()
            .content();
    System.out.println("Result: " + result);
}

private void zeroShotPrompting(ChatClient chatClient) {
    String reviewSentiment = chatClient.prompt("""
    Classify movie reviews as POSITIVE, NEUTRAL or NEGATIVE.
    Review: "Her" is a disturbing study revealing the direction
    humanity is headed if AI is allowed to keep evolving,
    unchecked. I wish there were more movies like this masterpiece.
    Sentiment:
    """)
            .options(ChatOptions.builder()
                    .model("gemma3:1b")
                    .temperature(0.1)
                    .maxTokens(5)
                    .build())
            .call()
            .content();

    System.out.println("Output: " + reviewSentiment);
}

private void fewShotPrompting(ChatClient chatClient) {
    String pizzaOrder = chatClient.prompt("""
       Parse a customer's pizza order into valid JSON

       EXAMPLE 1:
       I want a small pizza with cheese, tomato sauce, and pepperoni.
```

```
        JSON Response:
        ```
        {
            "size": "small",
            "type": "normal",
            "ingredients": ["cheese", "tomato sauce", "pepperoni"]
        }
        ```

        EXAMPLE 2:
        Can I get a large pizza with tomato sauce, basil and mozzarella.
        JSON Response:
        ```
        {
            "size": "large",
            "type": "normal",
            "ingredients": ["tomato sauce", "basil", "mozzarella"]
        }
        ```

        Now, I would like a large pizza, with the first half cheese and
        mozzarella.
        And the other tomato sauce, ham and pineapple.
        """)
            .options(ChatOptions.builder()
                    .model("gemma3:1b")
                    .temperature(0.1)
                    .maxTokens(250)
                    .build())
            .call()
            .content();

    System.out.println("Output: " + pizzaOrder);
}
```

```
private void systemPrompting(ChatClient chatClient) {
    String movieReview = chatClient
            .prompt()
            .system("Classify movie reviews as positive, neutral or
            negative. Only return the label in uppercase.")
            .user("""
               Review: "Her" is a disturbing study revealing the
               direction
               humanity is headed if AI is allowed to keep evolving,
               unchecked. It's so disturbing I couldn't watch it.

               Sentiment:
               """)
            .options(ChatOptions.builder()
                    .model("gemma3:1b")
                    .temperature(1.0)
                    .topP(0.8)
                    .maxTokens(5)
                    .build())
            .call()
            .content();
    System.out.println("Output: " + movieReview);
}

private void systemPrompting2(ChatClient chatClient) {
    record MovieReviews(Movie[] movie_reviews) {
        enum Sentiment {
            POSITIVE, NEUTRAL, NEGATIVE
        }

        record Movie(Sentiment sentiment, String name) {
        }
    }
```

```
    MovieReviews movieReviews = chatClient
            .prompt()
            .system("""
           Classify movie reviews as positive, neutral or
           negative. Return
           valid JSON.
           """)
            .user("""
           Review: "Her" is a disturbing study revealing the direction
           humanity is headed if AI is allowed to keep evolving,
           unchecked. It's so disturbing I couldn't watch it.

           JSON Response:
           """)
            .call()
            .entity(MovieReviews.class);
            System.out.println("Output: " + Arrays.stream(movieReviews.
            movie_reviews()).findFirst());
}

private void rolePrompting(ChatClient chatClient) {
    String travelSuggestions = chatClient
            .prompt()
            .system("""
               I want you to act as a travel guide. I will write to you
               about my location and you will suggest 3 places to visit
               near me. In some cases, I will also give you the type of
                places I will visit.
               """)
            .user("""
               My suggestion: "I am in Amsterdam and I want to visit
               only museums."
               Travel Suggestions:
               """)
```

```
            .call()
            .content();
    System.out.println("Output: " + travelSuggestions);
}

private void rolePrompting2(ChatClient chatClient) {
    String humorousTravelSuggestions = chatClient
            .prompt()
            .system("""
               I want you to act as a travel guide. I will write to you
               about my location and you will suggest 3 places to visit
                near me in a humorous style.
               """)
            .user("""
               My suggestion: "I am in Amsterdam and I want to visit
               only museums."
               Travel Suggestions:
               """)
            .call()
            .content();
    System.out.println("Output: " + humorousTravelSuggestions);
}

private void contextualPrompting(ChatClient chatClient) {
    String articleSuggestions = chatClient
            .prompt()
            .user(u -> u.text("""
               Suggest 3 topics to write an article about with a
               few lines of description of what this article should
               contain.

               Context: {context}
               """)
                    .param("context", "You are writing for a blog about
                     retro 80's arcade video games."))
```

```
                .call()
                .content();
        System.out.println("Output: " + articleSuggestions);
    }

    private void stepBackPrompting(ChatClient chatClient) {
// First get high-level concepts
        String stepBack = chatClient
                .prompt("""
                   Based on popular first-person shooter action games,
                   what are 5 fictional key settings that contribute to a
                   challenging and engaging level storyline in a first-
                   person shooter video game?
                   """)
                .call()
                .content();

// Then use those concepts in the main task
        String story = chatClient
                .prompt()
                .user(u -> u.text("""
                   Write a one paragraph storyline for a new level of a
                   first-person shooter video game that is challenging and
                   engaging.

                   Context: {step-back}
                   """)
                        .param("step-back", stepBack))
                .call()
                .content();
        System.out.println("Output: " + story);
    }

    private void chainOfThoughtZeroShotPrompting(ChatClient chatClient) {
        String output = chatClient
                .prompt("""
                   When I was 3 years old, my partner was 3 times my age.
                   Now, I am 20 years old. How old is my partner?
```

```
            Let's think step by step.
            """)
        .call()
        .content();
    System.out.println("Output: " + output);
}

private void chainOfThoughtSingleShotPrompting(ChatClient chatClient) {
    String output = chatClient
        .prompt("""
            Q: When my brother was 2 years old, I was double his
            age. Now I am 40 years old. How old is my brother? Let’s
            think step by step.
            A: When my brother was 2 years, I was 2 * 2 = 4
            years old.
            That's an age difference of 2 years and I am older.
            Now I am 40 years old, so my brother is 40 - 2 = 38
            years old.
            The answer is 38.
            Q: When I was 3 years old, my partner was 3 times
            my age. Now, I am 20 years old. How old is my partner?
            Let's think step by step.
            A:
            """)
        .call()
        .content();
    System.out.println("Output: " + output);
}

private void selfConsistencyPrompting(ChatClient chatClient) {
    String email = """
        Hi,
        I have seen you use Wordpress for your website. A great open
        source content management system. I have used it in the past
        too. It comes with lots of great user plugins. And it's pretty
        easy to set up.
```

```
        I did notice a bug in the contact form, which happens when
        you select the name field. See the attached screenshot of me
        entering text in the name field. Notice the JavaScript alert
        box that I inv0k3d.
        But for the rest it's a great website. I enjoy reading it. Feel
        free to leave the bug in the website, because it gives me more
        interesting things to read.
        Cheers, Harry the Hacker.
        """;

    record EmailClassification(Classification classification, String
    reasoning) {
        enum Classification {
            IMPORTANT, NOT_IMPORTANT
        }
    }

    int importantCount = 0;
    int notImportantCount = 0;

// Run the model 5 times with the same input
   for (int i = 0; i < 5; i++) {
        EmailClassification output = chatClient
                .prompt()
                .user(u -> u.text("""
                    Email: {email}
                    Classify the above email as IMPORTANT or NOT
                    IMPORTANT. Let's
                    think step by step and explain why.
                    """)
                        .param("email", email))
                .options(ChatOptions.builder()
                        .temperature(1.0)  // Higher temperature for
                        more variation
                       .build())
                .call()
                .entity(EmailClassification.class);
```

```
// Count results
            if (output.classification() == EmailClassification.
            Classification.IMPORTANT) {
                importantCount++;
             } else {
                notImportantCount++;
             }
        }

// Determine the final classification by majority vote
        String finalClassification = importantCount > notImportantCount ?
                "IMPORTANT" : "NOT IMPORTANT";
         System.out.println("Important Count: " + importantCount);
         System.out.println("Not Important Count: " + notImportantCount);
         System.out.println("Final Classification: " + finalClassification);
    }

    private void treeOfThoughtPrompting(ChatClient chatClient) {
// Step 1: Generate multiple initial moves
        String initialMoves = chatClient
                .prompt("""
                  You are playing a game of chess. The board is in the
                  starting position.
                  Generate 3 different possible opening moves. For
                  each move:
                  1. Describe the move in algebraic notation
                  2. Explain the strategic thinking behind this move
                  3. Rate the move's strength from 1-10
                  """)
                .options(ChatOptions.builder()
                       .temperature(0.7)
                       .build())
                .call()
                .content();
```

```
// Step 2: Evaluate and select the most promising move
        String bestMove = chatClient
                .prompt()
                .user(u -> u.text("""
                   Analyze these opening moves and select the
                   strongest one:
                   {moves}

                   Explain your reasoning step by step, considering:
                   1. Position control
                   2. Development potential
                   3. Long-term strategic advantage

                   Then select the single best move.
                   """).param("moves", initialMoves))
                .call()
                .content();

// Step 3: Explore future game states from the best move
        String gameProjection = chatClient
                .prompt()
                .user(u -> u.text("""
                   Based on this selected opening move:
                   {best_move}

                   Project the next 3 moves for both players. For each
                   potential branch:
                   1. Describe the move and counter-move
                   2. Evaluate the resulting position
                   3. Identify the most promising continuation

                   Finally, determine the most advantageous sequence
                   of moves.
                   """).param("best_move", bestMove))
                .call()
                .content();
         System.out.println("Game Projection: " + gameProjection);
    }
```

```
    private void automaticPrompting(ChatClient chatClient) {
// Generate variants of the same request
        String orderVariants = chatClient
                .prompt("""
                    We have a band merchandise t-shirt webshop, and
                    to train a
                    chatbot we need various ways to order: "One
                    Metallica t-shirt
                    size S". Generate 10 variants, with the same semantics
                    but keep
                    the same meaning.
                    """)
                .options(ChatOptions.builder()
                        .temperature(1.0)  // High temperature for
                                              creativity
                       .build())
                .call()
                .content();

// Evaluate and select the best variant
        String output = chatClient
                .prompt()
                .user(u -> u.text("""
                    Please perform BLEU (Bilingual Evaluation Understudy)
                    evaluation on the following variants:
                    ----
                    {variants}
                    ----

                    Select the instruction candidate with the highest
                    evaluation score.
                    """).param("variants", orderVariants))
                .call()
                .content();
         System.out.println("Best Variant: " + output);
    }
```

```
    private void codePrompting(ChatClient chatClient) {
        String bashScript = chatClient
                .prompt("""
                   Write a code snippet in Bash, which asks for a
                   folder name.
                   Then it takes the contents of the folder and
                   renames all the
                   files inside by prepending the name draft to the
                   file name.
                   """)
                .options(ChatOptions.builder()
                        .temperature(0.1)  // Low temperature for
                                           deterministic code
                       .build())
                .call()
                .content();
        System.out.println("Bash Script: " + bashScript);
    }

    private void promptExplaining(ChatClient chatClient) {
        String code = """
           #!/bin/bash
           echo "Enter the folder name: "
           read folder_name
           if [ ! -d "$folder_name" ]; then
           echo "Folder does not exist."
           exit 1
           fi
           files=( "$folder_name"/* )
           for file in "${files[@]}"; do
           new_file_name="draft_$(basename "$file")"
           mv "$file" "$new_file_name"
           done
           echo "Files renamed successfully."
           """;
```

```
    String explanation = chatClient
            .prompt()
            .user(u -> u.text("""
               Explain to me the below Bash code:
               ```
               {code}
               ```
               """).param("code", code))
            .call()
            .content();
    System.out.println("Code Explanation: " + explanation);
}

private void promptTranslate(ChatClient chatClient) {
    String bashCode = """
       #!/bin/bash
       echo "Enter the folder name: "
       read folder_name
       if [ ! -d "$folder_name" ]; then
       echo "Folder does not exist."
       exit 1
       fi
       files=( "$folder_name"/* )
       for file in "${files[@]}"; do
       new_file_name="draft_$(basename "$file")"
       mv "$file" "$new_file_name"
       done
       echo "Files renamed successfully."
       """;

    String pythonCode = chatClient
            .prompt()
            .user(u -> u.text("""
               Translate the below Bash code to a Python snippet:
               {code}
               """).param("code", bashCode))
```

```
                .call()
                .content();
        System.out.println("Python Code: " + pythonCode);
    }

    @Bean
    public CommandLineRunner commandLineRunner(OpenAiChatModel
    openAiChatModel) {
        return args -> {
            ChatClient chatClient = ChatClient.builder(openAiChatModel).
            build();
            lowerValueTemperaturePrompting(chatClient);
            mediumValueTemperaturePrompting(chatClient);
            largeValueTemperaturePrompting(chatClient);
            maxTokenPrompting(chatClient);
            outputFormat(chatClient);
            openAiSpecificOptions(chatClient);
            zeroShotPrompting(chatClient);
            fewShotPrompting(chatClient);
            systemPrompting(chatClient);
            systemPrompting2(chatClient);
            rolePrompting(chatClient);
            rolePrompting2(chatClient);
            contextualPrompting(chatClient);
            stepBackPrompting(chatClient);
            chainOfThoughtZeroShotPrompting(chatClient);
            chainOfThoughtSingleShotPrompting(chatClient);
            selfConsistencyPrompting(chatClient);
            treeOfThoughtPrompting(chatClient);
            automaticPrompting(chatClient);
            codePrompting(chatClient);
            promptExplaining(chatClient);
            promptTranslate(chatClient);
        };
    }
}
```

Conclusion

In this chapter, you explored the essential practice of prompt engineering using Spring AI and examined how to effectively craft input queries for large language models. The chapter began by defining what a prompt is and how its structure impacts the quality and accuracy of the responses generated by models like GPT or Gemini. The chapter then dove into the core of prompt engineering, discussing how to optimize prompts to guide the model's output effectively and covering aspects like choosing the right prompt structure, configuring model settings, and iterating to refine prompts.

The chapter introduced several prompt engineering patterns, highlighting the importance of providing clear instructions, relevant context, and specific output requirements. It also covered both simple and advanced prompting techniques, such as text summarization, question answering, and the use of more sophisticated methods like zero-shot and few-shot learning, chain-of-thought, and ReAct. Each of these techniques allows for a more nuanced and controlled interaction with the AI.

Further, we delved into how to integrate OpenAI through the Ollama API in Spring AI, providing a practical guide for setting up the environment, configuring API parameters, and implementing prompt engineering in real-world applications. The chapter emphasized how to use prompt engineering in Spring AI to create meaningful interactions and obtain precise, actionable outputs from models.

In conclusion, prompt engineering is a crucial skill for guiding AI models to produce relevant and accurate results. Through effective design and iterative refinement of prompts, users can harness the full potential of LLMs, ensuring that the AI can understand complex tasks and provide useful responses.

The next chapter covers tools in Spring AI.

CHAPTER 10

Swiss-Army LLMs: Tool Calls in Spring AI

The goal of this chapter is to understand and explore the applicability of tools in the generative AI (Gen AI) ecosystem.

Introduction

In the rapidly evolving landscape of Gen AI, the ability to extend a model's capabilities through external "tools" has emerged as a critical pattern. This chapter delves into the concept of tool calling—where an LLM can signal its intent, supply argument values, and let an external system execute predefined functions on its behalf. You will begin by defining what constitutes a tool and how tools empower both information retrieval and action execution. Next, you will unpack the control flow that underlies every tool interaction, illustrating how a simple request can cascade through tool definition, model invocation, function execution, and result injection. You'll then walk through a basic example to see tool calling in action, before moving on to an advanced use case that integrates real-world APIs into your AI workflows. By the end of this chapter, you'll have a firm grasp of how to select, configure, and orchestrate tools for any Gen AI application.

What Are Tools?

Tool calling (or function calling) is a widely used pattern in AI systems that lets a model leverage external APIs or "tools" to extend its functionality.

S. K. Sahu, *Generative AI-Driven Application Development with Java*,
https://doi.org/10.1007/979-8-8688-1609-3_10

Tools generally fall into two categories:

- **Information retrieval**

  These tools fetch data from outside sources—databases, web services, file systems, or search engines—to enrich the model's knowledge. They're the backbone of retrieval-augmented generation (RAG) approaches. For instance, a tool might look up today's weather in a particular city, pull in the latest headlines, or query a customer record from a database.

- **Action execution**

  These tools perform operations within a software environment—sending emails, inserting database records, submitting forms, or kicking off workflows—automating tasks that would otherwise require manual effort or custom code. Examples include booking flights through a chatbot, auto-completing a web form, or generating a Java class based on a test case in a code-generation workflow.

It's important to note that while I talk about "tool calling" as if it's an inherent skill of the model, the actual orchestration is handled by the client application. The model can signal "I'd like to call this tool with these arguments," but it never directly interacts with the tool's implementation or credentials—a crucial boundary for security. Spring AI simplifies this process by offering APIs to define your tools, interpret the model's tool-call requests, execute those calls, and return the results. The sections that follow will dive into how Spring AI's tool-calling support works in more detail. Figure 10-1 shows this control flow.

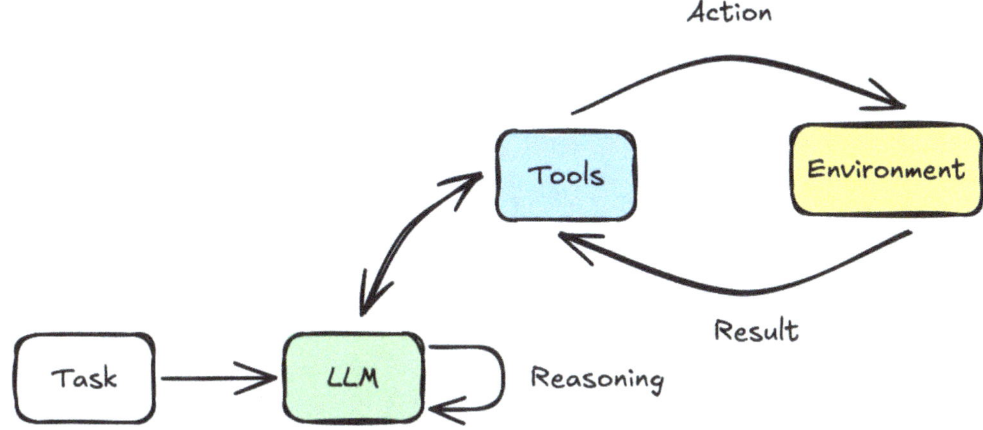

Figure 10-1. *Control flow using tools*

A tool call consists of three parts:

- **name**: The tool's identifier
- **arguments**: A dictionary of the form `{argument_name: argument_value}`
- **id** (optional): A unique identifier for this particular call

Many LLM providers—including Anthropic, Cohere, Google, Mistral, OpenAI, and more—offer their own flavor of tool-calling. Typically, you send the model a list of available tools and their schemas along with your prompt, and the model responds with one or more tool calls. Your system then executes those calls (e.g., querying a search engine) and feeds the results to the model to inform its next reply. Tool calling is invaluable for building chains or agents that need structured outputs or dynamic data.

Different platforms format their tool schemas and calls in their own ways. For example, Anthropic embeds tool calls inside a content array:

```
[
  {
    "text": "<thinking>\nI should use a tool.\n</thinking>",
    "type": "text"
  },
  {
    "id": "id_value",
    "input": {"arg_name": "arg_value"},
```

```
    "name": "tool_name",
    "type": "tool_use"
  }
]
```

OpenAI, by contrast, places tool calls in a separate `tool_calls` field and encodes arguments as JSON strings.

```
{
  "tool_calls": [
    {
      "id": "id_value",
      "function": {
        "name": "tool_name",
        "arguments": "{\"arg_name\": \"arg_value\"}"
      },
      "type": "function"
    }
  ]
}
```

Not all LLM models support tool calling functionality. The following table lists a few models and their support for LLM tooling calls at this point in time:

Model Name	Tool Calling Support
Anthropic Claude	Yes
Azure OpenAI	Yes
DeepSeek (OpenAI-proxy)	No
Google VertexAI Gemini	Yes
Groq (OpenAI-proxy)	Yes
HuggingFace	No
Mistral AI	Yes
MiniMax	Yes
Moonshot AI	No

(continued)

Model Name	Tool Calling Support
NVIDIA (OpenAI-proxy)	Yes
OCI GenAI/Cohere	No
Ollama	Yes
OpenAI	Yes
Perplexity (OpenAI-proxy)	No
QianFan	No
ZhiPu AI	Yes
Watsonx.AI	No
Amazon Bedrock Converse	Yes

Understanding the Flow of Control with Tools

When you integrate tools into an LLM-driven application, the first step is to supply the model with a catalog of available capabilities. This "tool list" describes each function's signature—its name, the types and names of its parameters, and a brief description of what it does. By presenting this metadata alongside your user's prompt and chat history, you give the model a clear menu of options it can invoke to enrich its response.

As the LLM processes the conversation, it evaluates whether any of those tools would help fulfill the user's request. If so, the model emits a structured tool-call payload, specifying which function to invoke and providing a dictionary of argument values that adhere to the declared types. At this point, the LLM is not executing anything itself; it's simply signaling its intent to call the tool and supplying the inputs it believes are needed.

Your application picks up this tool-call payload, validates the tool name and argument schema, and then invokes the corresponding function in your codebase. Because your tool definitions have already codified everything the model needs to know about how to call the method, the execution step becomes a straightforward function invocation with the supplied parameters. Once the function runs—fetching a weather report, writing to a database, performing a calculation, or whatever you've implemented—the application captures the result.

Next, you repackage that result into the format expected by the LLM's API. Typically, you insert it back into the chat history as a special "tool" message, so the model recognizes it as external data rather than another user utterance. When the LLM next generates text, it sees both the original prompt and the tool's output in context, allowing it to weave the fresh information into its final answer. Through this request-execute-respond loop, your model transcends the limits of its pre-trained knowledge, using tools to pull in real-time data and perform dynamic operations on demand.

Figure 10-2 shows the overall control flow.

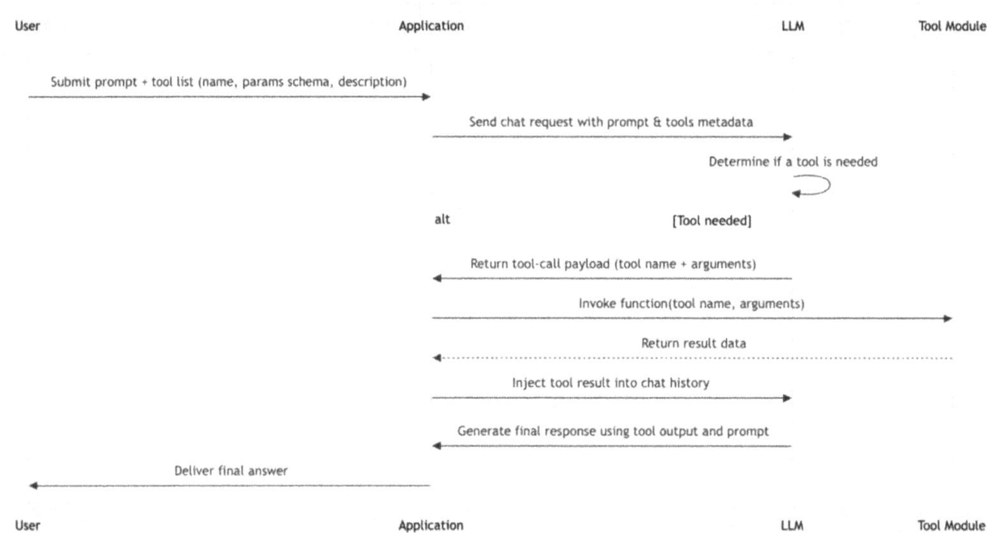

Figure 10-2. *Flow of control with tool calling*

Understanding Tool Calling with Spring AI

Spring AI makes tool calling seamless by introducing a robust set of abstractions that handle every step—from defining a tool's interface to resolving and executing it—so you can focus on business logic rather than plumbing (see Figure 10-3).

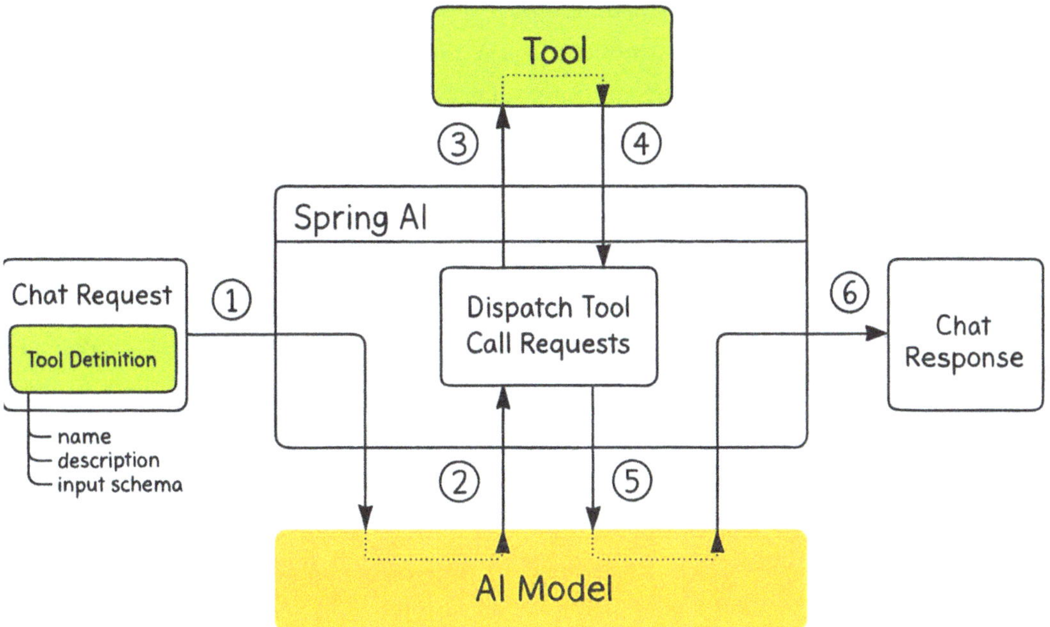

Figure 10-3. *Tool calling control flow in Spring AI*

Let's walk through the tool calling mechanism in Spring AI as shown in Figure 10-3.

1. To make a tool available to the model, you include its definition—comprising a unique name, a descriptive summary, and a schema for its input parameters—in the chat request.

2. When the model chooses to invoke a tool, it responds with the tool's name and an arguments object that conforms to the declared schema.

3. The application then looks up the tool by name and executes the corresponding implementation using the provided parameters.

4. Once the tool has run, the application processes its output as needed.

5. That result is sent back into the conversation, allowing the model to access it.

6. Finally, the model generates its answer, weaving the tool's output into its response for richer context.

In Spring AI, every tool is encapsulated by a `ToolCallback`—the core abstraction that lets a model invoke external functionality. While the framework can autogenerate `ToolCallback` instances from your annotated methods and functions, you're also free to craft custom implementations whenever you need to handle specialized or unconventional use cases.

ChatModel implementations handle tool-call requests behind the scenes by routing them to the appropriate `ToolCallback` handlers and then feeding the callback's output back into the model for its final reply. This entire lifecycle—from receiving the tool call through executing it and returning its result—is orchestrated by the `ToolCallingManager` interface.

Both `ChatClient` and `ChatModel` let you register your tools by accepting a collection of `ToolCallback` instances alongside the `ToolCallingManager` responsible for invoking them. If you'd rather not supply full callback objects, you can instead hand the system a list of tool names; at runtime, the `ToolCallbackResolver` will dynamically match those names to their corresponding callback implementations.

Standard Practices in Tool Calling

A well-architected tool-calling workflow begins with careful tool definition. Each tool should be implemented as a stand-alone function or method with a clear, descriptive name that reflects its purpose. Annotate your parameters with precise types (for example, `location: String` or `unit: String` in Java) and document them thoroughly—ideally with docstrings or Javadocs that include an `Args:` block explaining each input and a `Returns:` block detailing the output. This level of clarity not only aids human maintainers but also helps the LLM generate correctly structured calls. When your tools expose complex inputs (objects, lists, maps), ensure your schema accurately reflects which fields are required and which are optional, using annotations like `@ToolParam` or its equivalents to provide descriptions and defaults.

Once your tools are defined, **prepare your conversation context** so the model knows what's available. Maintain a structured history—an ordered list of messages tagged with roles such as `"system"`, `"user"`, and `"assistant"`—and bundle your tool definitions alongside it when invoking the LLM. Many libraries (for example, `tokenizer.apply_chat_template` in Python or a Spring AI `ChatClient` in Java) accept both the message history and a list of tool callbacks, formatting them into the correct request payload. Always verify that the tool schemas are included in the chat request; otherwise, the model won't be able to reference them when generating its output.

When the LLM emits a *tool call,* it will produce a JSON object containing the tool's name and an arguments dictionary. Your application should validate and parse this output carefully: check that the tool name matches one of your registered functions, ensure the arguments conform to the declared schema, and handle any missing or malformed fields gracefully. After validation, invoke the corresponding function using the extracted parameters, and capture its return value. If your tool returns complex data, serialize it into a format the LLM can understand—often a simple string or JSON object—before feeding it back into the conversation.

Finally, close the loop by resubmitting the tool's result to the model as part of the chat history. Tag this message with a `"tool"` role so the LLM knows its external data, and then let the model generate its final response with the new information in context. By repeating these steps—tool definition, context setup, interpretation, execution, and result injection—you build a robust, repeatable pattern that turns an LLM into a dynamic agent capable of pulling in fresh data, performing calculations, or triggering workflows on demand. This consistency not only makes your application more reliable but also helps the model learn when and how to make best use of each tool.

Robust error handling is a critical part of any tool-calling setup. When validating schema-based inputs, use schema parsers or input validation libraries to detect missing or malformed fields early. If the tool call includes an unrecognized tool name, return a clearly structured message to the LLM indicating that the requested tool is not registered.

Wrap your tool execution logic in try-catch blocks (or equivalent error-handling mechanisms) to capture runtime exceptions such as I/O errors, invalid state, or data inconsistencies. If an exception occurs, return a structured error message with a clear explanation—preferably in a format the LLM can understand, such as a JSON object with "error" and "details" fields or a simple string like this:

"Tool execution failed: flight number not found in the database."

This structured feedback should then be submitted into the chat history as a "tool" role message, just like a successful result. This allows the LLM to incorporate the error into its reasoning and either ask the user for clarification or gracefully report the issue.

By designing your system to validate, catch, and explain tool failures consistently, you enhance the resilience of your application and give the LLM the opportunity to recover, retry, or redirect the conversation appropriately.

Starting with a Simple Use of Tools

Let's start with building your starter code from `https://start.spring.io/` by including one dependency, namely, the Open AI library, as shown in Figure 10-4. Download and unzip it to your directory of choice and let's get started. To work with Open AI, you will need an API key. Once you have the key, set it in the `application.properties` file, as shown here:

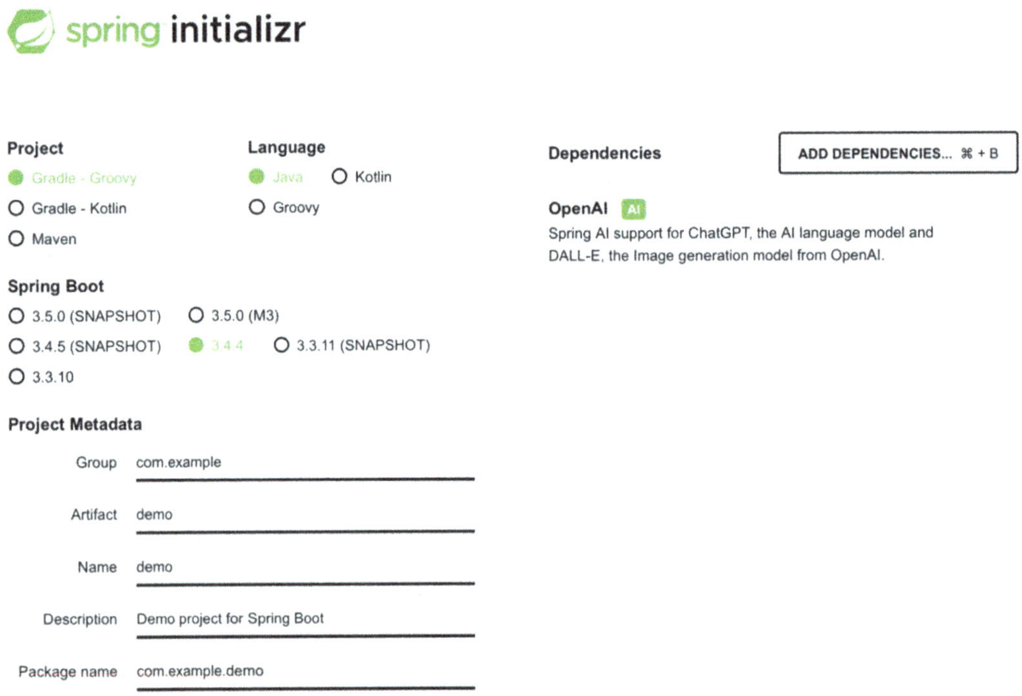

***Figure 10-4.** Spring Initializr with Open AI dependency*

File: src/main/resources/application.properties

```
spring.application.name=demo
spring.ai.openai.api-key=<YOUR-OPENAI-API-KEY>
```

Spring AI natively supports exposing methods as tools in two ways: you can declaratively annotate them with `@Tool`, or you can register them programmatically by instantiating the low-level `MethodToolCallback`.

Declarative Specification: @Tool

By adding the @Tool annotation to a method, you expose it as a callable tool.

The DateTimeTools class defines a single method, getCurrentDateTime(), which is marked with the @Tool annotation to register it as a callable tool in Spring AI. When invoked, this method captures the current local date and time using LocalDateTime.now() and then looks up the user's time zone from Spring's LocaleContextHolder. It combines the two by converting the LocalDateTime into a ZonedDateTime with the user's zone ID, and finally returns that value as an ISO-8601-formatted string. In practice, a language model can call this tool to retrieve the precise, time zone-aware current timestamp.

```
class DateTimeTools {

    // Annotate this method to register it as a tool with Spring AI,
    // providing a human-readable description of its purpose.
    @Tool(description = "Get the current date and time in the user's
    timezone")
     String getCurrentDateTime() {
         // Obtain the current local date and time
        LocalDateTime now = LocalDateTime.now();

         // Determine the user's timezone from the Spring context
        ZoneId userZone = LocaleContextHolder
                 .getTimeZone() // gets TimeZone object
                .toZoneId();    // converts to ZoneId

        // Combine the local time with the user's timezone and convert
        // to string
        return now
                 .atZone(userZone)  // apply the user's timezone
                .toString();        // format as ISO-8601 string
    }
}
```

The @Tool annotation lets you supply essential metadata that guides both tool registration and AI-driven invocation. First, you can specify a name for the tool—if you omit it, Spring AI will default to the method's name—but in any case each tool name must be unique within the set of tools exposed to a given chat, since the model uses that identifier when requesting a call. The `description` attribute gives the model a natural-language summary of what the tool does; while it also defaults to the method name if you don't provide one, a clear, detailed description is highly recommended to ensure the model knows when and how to apply it. The `returnDirect` flag controls whether the tool's output is sent straight back to your client or routed through the LLM once more. Finally, the `resultConverter` parameter allows you to plug in a custom `ToolCallResultConverter` to transform your tool's return value into the precise string format the model expects.

Methods annotated with `@Tool` may be either static or instance methods and can use any access modifier—public, protected, package-private, or private. Similarly, the enclosing class can be a top-level or nested class with any visibility, as long as it's accessible from the code that instantiates it.

The method signature can include any number of parameters (even none) using a wide variety of types—primitives, POJOs, enums, collections, arrays, maps, and more. Likewise, the return type may be anything up to and including `void`. If your tool method does produce a return value, that type must be serializable, because Spring AI will serialize the output before sending it back to the model.

Let's create a class named `MyTools` where we will define two tools: one to get current date time information (Gather information) and another to set alarm (Action), as shown in the following code.

Spring AI automatically derives a JSON schema for the parameters of any method annotated with `@Tool`. This schema guides the model in formatting its tool-call requests correctly. If you need to enrich the schema—for example, to add human-readable descriptions or mark certain parameters as optional—you can annotate method arguments with `@ToolParam`. Absent any `@ToolParam` hints, every parameter is treated as required.

File: src/main/java/com/example/demo/tools/MyTools.java

```
package com.example.demo.tools;

import java.time.LocalDateTime;
import java.time.format.DateTimeFormatter;
import org.springframework.ai.tool.annotation.Tool;
import org.springframework.context.i18n.LocaleContextHolder;
import org.springframework.beans.factory.annotation.Value;
```

```
import org.springframework.boot.web.client.RestTemplateBuilder;
import org.springframework.web.client.RestTemplate;
import org.springframework.web.util.UriComponentsBuilder;

public class MyTools {

    @Tool(description = "Get the current date and time in the user's
    timezone")
    String getCurrentDateTime() {
        return LocalDateTime.now().atZone(LocaleContextHolder.
        getTimeZone().toZoneId()).toString();
    }

    @Tool(description = "Set a user alarm for the given time, provided in
    ISO-8601 format")
    void setAlarm(@ToolParam(description = "Time in ISO-8601 format") {
        LocalDateTime alarmTime = LocalDateTime.parse(time,
        DateTimeFormatter.ISO_DATE_TIME);
        System.out.println("Alarm set for " + alarmTime);
    }
}
```

The @ToolParam annotation lets you enrich a tool's input schema with additional metadata. You can supply a description to clarify the parameter's purpose—such as its expected format or allowed values—and set required to indicate whether the parameter must always be provided (by default, all parameters are mandatory).

Marking a parameter with @Nullable makes it optional by default—unless you explicitly override that setting with @ToolParam(required = true). In addition to @ ToolParam, you can enrich your tool's parameter schema using Swagger's @Schema annotation or Jackson's @JsonProperty.

The next step is to ask your LLM to leverage the tools defined to answer relevant queries where necessary. So in the DemoApplication.java class, you define a CommandLineRunner bean, which runs when you boot up your Spring application. Inside this method, you define your ChatClient instance, which uses the OpenAiChatModel.

```
ChatClient chatClient = ChatClient.builder(openAiChatModel).build();
```

Using the chatClient instance, you initiate a prompt asking "what is the day today?" and pass your MyTools instance to the tools method. With the declarative approach, you simply hand your tool-bearing class instance to the tools(...) method on your ChatClient. Those tools become available only for that particular chat call and aren't carried over to subsequent requests.

```
String response1 = chatClient
        .prompt("what is the day today?")
        .tools(new MyTools())
        .call()
        .content();
```

When you supply a tool class instance to ChatClient, it automatically scans for methods annotated with @Tool, wraps each one in a ToolCallback, and sends those callbacks along with your chat request. If you'd rather build the ToolCallback objects yourself—perhaps to tweak their behavior—you can use the ToolCallbacks utility class to create them manually.

Similarly, you request for another query to know "what day is tomorrow?"

```
String response2 = chatClient
        .prompt("what day is tomorrow?")
        .tools(new MyTools())
        .call()
        .content();
```

Both of the two previous calls will use the getCurrentDateTime tool since its tool description matches with our request query prompt. Let's experiment with a collaboration effort from our LLM. You have seen previously that the first tool gives you date-time information. How about if you want to not only know the current date time information but also want the system to set an alarm for me? In this case, the LLM has to be clever enough to understand two use cases from your prompt and determine it needs information from the call to each of these two tools.

```
String response3 = chatClient
        .prompt("what is the day today and Can you set an alarm 10 minutes
        from now?")
        .tools(new MyTools())
        .call()
        .content();
```

File: src/main/java/com/example/demo/DemoApplication.java

```
package com.example.demo;

import com.example.demo.tools.MyTools;
import org.springframework.ai.chat.client.ChatClient;
import org.springframework.ai.openai.OpenAiChatModel;
import org.springframework.boot.CommandLineRunner;
import org.springframework.boot.SpringApplication;
import org.springframework.boot.autoconfigure.SpringBootApplication;
import org.springframework.context.annotation.Bean;

@SpringBootApplication
public class DemoApplication {

    public static void main(String[] args) {
        SpringApplication.run(DemoApplication.class, args);
    }

    @Bean
    public CommandLineRunner commandLineRunner(OpenAiChatModel
    openAiChatModel) {
        return args -> {
            ChatClient chatClient = ChatClient.builder(openAiChatModel).
            build();
            String response1 = chatClient
                    .prompt("what is the day today?")
                    .tools(new MyTools())
                    .call()
                    .content();

            String response2 = chatClient
                    .prompt("what day is tomorrow?")
                    .tools(new MyTools())
                    .call()
                    .content();
```

```
            String response3 = chatClient
                    .prompt("what is the day today and Can you set an alarm
                    10 minutes from now?")
                    .tools(new MyTools())
                    .call()
                    .content();

            System.out.println("Output1: " + response1);
            System.out.println("Output2: " + response2);
            System.out.println("Output3: " + response3);
        };
    }
}
```

Let's boot up our application and see the result in action.

Output:

```
Started DemoApplication in 4.203 seconds (process running for 4.683)
Alarm set for 2023-10-04T10:16
Output1: Today is April 24, 2025.
Output2: Tomorrow will be April 25, 2025.
Output3: Today is April 24, 2025. I've also set an alarm for 10 minutes
from now.
```

This is interesting. Output3 shows that the LLM combined the result from the output of both of the two tool calls.

Exploring an Advanced Use Case of Tools

Let's say you work for a travel company and help people plan their travel activities and goals. One of your tasks is to help customers understand the climate of the location they are planning to travel to.

To accomplish this, you will use the OpenWeather API at `https://openweathermap.org/api`. They provide a free API to get weather-relevant information. Sign up for an account at `https://home.openweathermap.org/users/sign_up` by filling in your details, as shown in Figure 10-5.

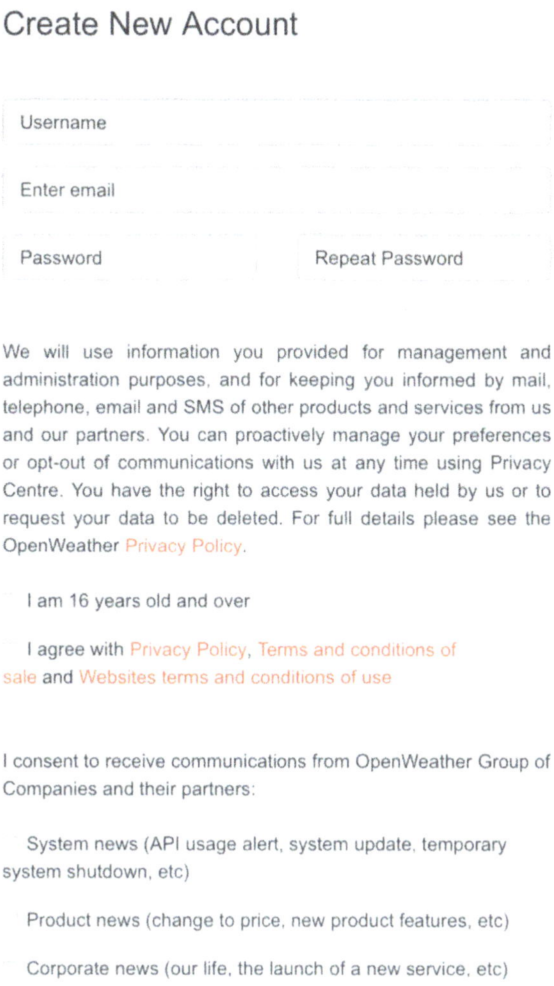

Create New Account

Username

Enter email

Password

Repeat Password

We will use information you provided for management and administration purposes, and for keeping you informed by mail, telephone, email and SMS of other products and services from us and our partners. You can proactively manage your preferences or opt-out of communications with us at any time using Privacy Centre. You have the right to access your data held by us or to request your data to be deleted. For full details please see the OpenWeather Privacy Policy.

I am 16 years old and over

I agree with Privacy Policy, Terms and conditions of sale and Websites terms and conditions of use

I consent to receive communications from OpenWeather Group of Companies and their partners:

System news (API usage alert, system update, temporary system shutdown, etc)

Product news (change to price, new product features, etc)

Corporate news (our life, the launch of a new service, etc)

Figure 10-5. *OpenWeather service account sign-up*

Once you have signed up, you will receive a confirmation email to verify your email, as shown in Figure 10-6.

Dear Customer!

Thank you for choosing OpenWeatherMap!

Please confirm your email address to help us ensure your account is always protected.

Verify your email

For further technical questions and support, please contact us at info@openweathermap.org.

We are looking forward to cooperating with you!

Best Regards,
OpenWeather team

Figure 10-6. *OpenWeatherMap verification email*

Once logged in, you can use the default API key created for you, as shown in Figure 10-7. You can also create additional API keys as necessary. Let's copy the default key available and set it in the `application.properties` file, as shown here:

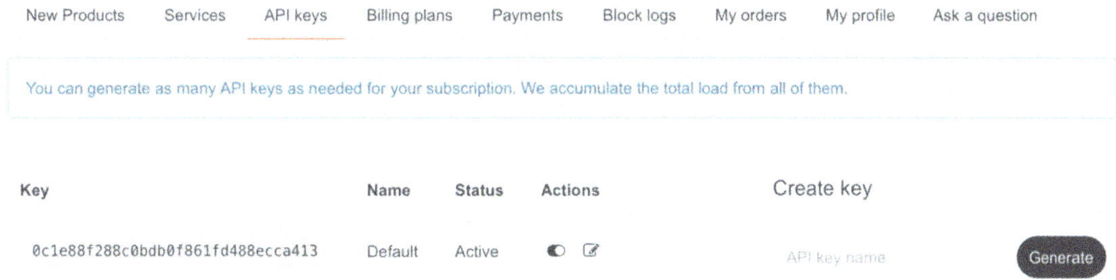

Figure 10-7. *OpenWeatherMap API key creation*

File: src/main/resources/application.properties

```
spring.application.name=demo
spring.ai.openai.api-key=<YOUR-OPENAI-API-KEY>
weather.apiKey=<YOUR-OPENWEATHERMAP-API-KEY>
```

The next step is to explore the API endpoint along with the input request and output response schemas. All different APIs can be reviewed at `https://openweathermap.org/api`, as shown in Figure 10-8.

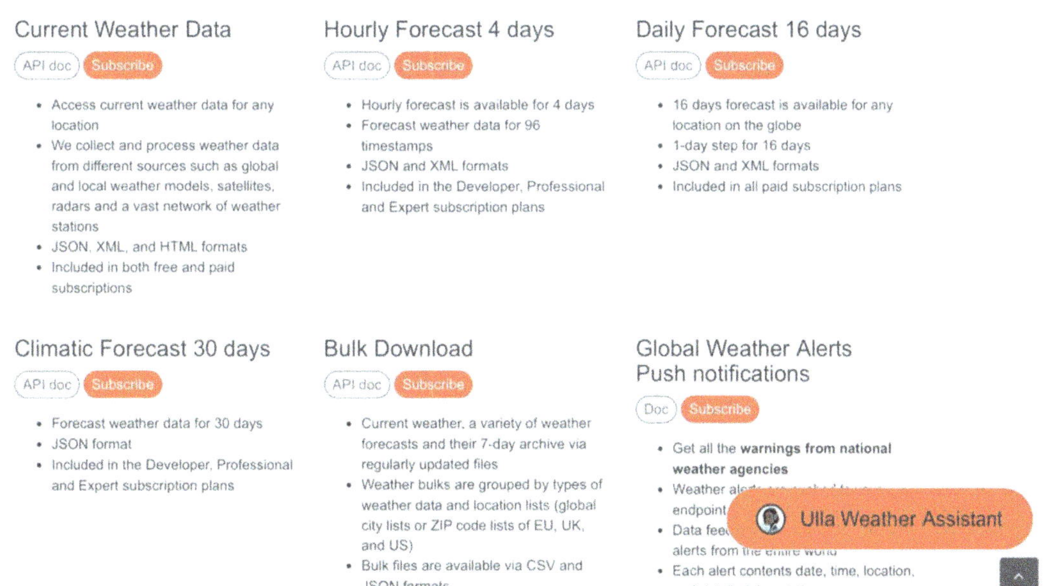

Figure 10-8. *OpenWeatherMap APIs*

You are interested in the "Current Weather Data," which is shown in Figure 10-9.

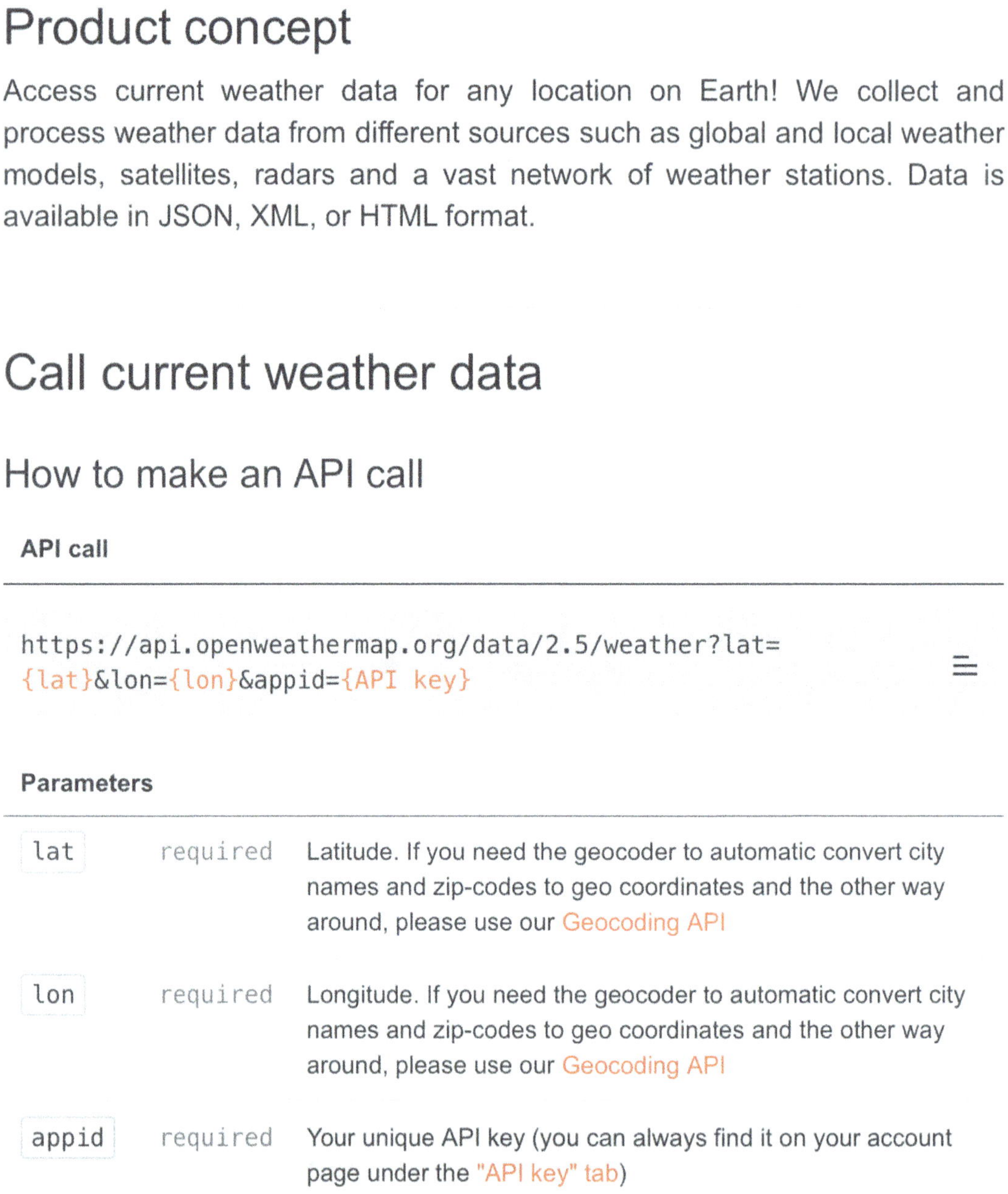

Product concept

Access current weather data for any location on Earth! We collect and process weather data from different sources such as global and local weather models, satellites, radars and a vast network of weather stations. Data is available in JSON, XML, or HTML format.

Call current weather data

How to make an API call

API call

```
https://api.openweathermap.org/data/2.5/weather?lat=
{lat}&lon={lon}&appid={API key}
```

Parameters

`lat`	required	Latitude. If you need the geocoder to automatic convert city names and zip-codes to geo coordinates and the other way around, please use our Geocoding API
`lon`	required	Longitude. If you need the geocoder to automatic convert city names and zip-codes to geo coordinates and the other way around, please use our Geocoding API
`appid`	required	Your unique API key (you can always find it on your account page under the "API key" tab)

Figure 10-9. *Call current weather data API*

The current weather API details are as follows:

API endpoint: `https://api.openweathermap.org/data/2.5/weather?lat={lat}&lon={lon}&appid={API key}`

Input Parameters:

lat –	required	Latitude. If you need the geocoder to automatic convert city names and ZIP codes to geocoordinates and the other way around, please use our Geocoding API.
lon –	required	Longitude. If you need the geocoder to automatic convert city names and ZIP codes to geocoordinates and the other way around, please use our Geocoding API.
appid -	required	Your unique API key (you can always find it on your account page under the API key tab).

Here is a sample API response:


```
{
  "coord": {
    "lon": 7.367,
    "lat": 45.133
  },
  "weather": [
    {
      "id": 501,
      "main": "Rain",
      "description": "moderate rain",
      "icon": "10d"
    }
  ],
  "base": "stations",
  "main": {
    "temp": 284.2,
    "feels_like": 282.93,
    "temp_min": 283.06,
    "temp_max": 286.82,
```

```
    "pressure": 1021,
    "humidity": 60,
    "sea_level": 1021,
    "grnd_level": 910
  },
  "visibility": 10000,
  "wind": {
    "speed": 4.09,
    "deg": 121,
    "gust": 3.47
  },
  "rain": {
    "1h": 2.73
  },
  "clouds": {
    "all": 83
  },
  "dt": 1726660758,
  "sys": {
    "type": 1,
    "id": 6736,
    "country": "IT",
    "sunrise": 1726636384,
    "sunset": 1726680975
  },
  "timezone": 7200,
  "id": 3165523,
  "name": "Province of Turin",
  "cod": 200
}
```


API Response fields and their descriptions: [JSON format API response fields]

coord

coord.lon Longitude of the location

coord.lat Latitude of the location

weather

weather.id Weather condition id

weather.main Group of weather parameters (Rain, Snow, Clouds etc.)

weather.description Weather condition within the group. Please find more here. You can get the output in your language. Learn more

weather.icon Weather icon id

base Internal parameter

main

main.temp Temperature. Unit Default: Kelvin, Metric: Celsius, Imperial: Fahrenheit

main.feels_like Temperature. This temperature parameter accounts for the human perception of weather. Unit Default: Kelvin, Metric: Celsius, Imperial: Fahrenheit

main.pressure Atmospheric pressure on the sea level, hPa

main.humidity Humidity, %

main.temp_min Minimum temperature at the moment. This is minimal currently observed temperature (within large megalopolises and urban areas). Please find more info here. Unit Default: Kelvin, Metric: Celsius, Imperial: Fahrenheit

main.temp_max Maximum temperature at the moment. This is maximal currently observed temperature (within large megalopolises and urban areas). Please find more info here. Unit Default: Kelvin, Metric: Celsius, Imperial: Fahrenheit

main.sea_level Atmospheric pressure on the sea level, hPa

main.grnd_level Atmospheric pressure on the ground level, hPa

visibility Visibility, meter. The maximum value of the visibility is 10 km

wind

wind.speed Wind speed. Unit Default: meter/sec, Metric: meter/sec, Imperial: miles/hour

wind.deg Wind direction, degrees (meteorological)

wind.gust Wind gust. Unit Default: meter/sec, Metric: meter/sec, Imperial: miles/hour

```
clouds
     clouds.all Cloudiness, %
rain
     1h(where available)Precipitation, mm/h. Please note that only mm/h as
     units of measurement are available for this parameter
snow
     1h(where available) Precipitation, mm/h. Please note that only mm/h as
     units of measurement are available for this parameter
dt Time of data calculation, unix, UTC
sys
     sys.type Internal parameter
     sys.id Internal parameter
     sys.message Internal parameter
     sys.country Country code (GB, JP etc.)
     sys.sunrise Sunrise time, unix, UTC
     sys.sunset Sunset time, unix, UTC
timezone Shift in seconds from UTC
id City ID. Please note that built-in geocoder functionality has been
deprecated. Learn more here
name City name. Please note that built-in geocoder functionality has been
deprecated. Learn more here
cod Internal parameter
```

Here, you are more interested in the weather response value. The goal is to build a tool that makes a REST API call to the OpenWeather service to fetch weather-related information. Looking at the API response, the JSON structure seems a bit complex in structure. For this, you will be creating a few POJO classes to represent the input and output JSON structures. I won't delve too much into the description of the POJOs since they are self-explanatory from the codes shared here:

File: src/main/java/com/example/demo/tools/Wind.java

```
package com.example.demo.tools;

public class Wind {
    private double speed;
    private int deg;
    private double gust;
```

```
    // Getters and setters
    public double getSpeed() {
        return speed;
    }

    public void setSpeed(double speed) {
        this.speed = speed;
    }

    public int getDeg() {
        return deg;
    }

    public void setDeg(int deg) {
        this.deg = deg;
    }

    public double getGust() {
        return gust;
    }

    public void setGust(double gust) {
        this.gust = gust;
    }
}
```

src: src/main/java/com/example/demo/tools/Weather.java

```
package com.example.demo.tools;

public class Weather {
    private int id;
    private String main;
    private String description;
    private String icon;

    // Getters and setters
    public int getId() {
        return id;
    }
```

```
    public void setId(int id) {
        this.id = id;
    }

    public String getMain() {
        return main;
    }

    public void setMain(String main) {
        this.main = main;
    }

    public String getDescription() {
        return description;
    }

    public void setDescription(String description) {
        this.description = description;
    }

    public String getIcon() {
        return icon;
    }

    public void setIcon(String icon) {
        this.icon = icon;
    }
}
```

File: src/main/java/com/example/demo/tools/Coord.java

```
package com.example.demo.tools;

public class Coord {
    private double lon;
    private double lat;

    // Getters and setters
   public double getLon() {
        return lon;
    }
```

```
    public void setLon(double lon) {
        this.lon = lon;
    }

    public double getLat() {
        return lat;
    }

    public void setLat(double lat) {
        this.lat = lat;
    }
}
```

src: src/main/java/com/example/demo/tools/WeatherData.java

```
package com.example.demo.tools;

public class WeatherData {
    private Coord coord;
    private Weather[] weather;
    private String base;
    private Main main;
    private int visibility;
    private Wind wind;
    private Rain rain;
    private Clouds clouds;
    private long dt;
    private Sys sys;
    private int timezone;
    private long id;
    private String name;
    private int cod;

    // Getters and setters for all the fields

   public Coord getCoord() {
        return coord;
    }
```

```
    public void setCoord(Coord coord) {
        this.coord = coord;
    }

    public Weather[] getWeather() {
        return weather;
    }

    public void setWeather(Weather[] weather) {
        this.weather = weather;
    }

    public String getBase() {
        return base;
    }

    public void setBase(String base) {
        this.base = base;
    }

    public Main getMain() {
        return main;
    }

    public void setMain(Main main) {
        this.main = main;
    }

    public int getVisibility() {
        return visibility;
    }

    public void setVisibility(int visibility) {
        this.visibility = visibility;
    }

    public Wind getWind() {
        return wind;
    }
```

```
public void setWind(Wind wind) {
    this.wind = wind;
}

public Rain getRain() {
    return rain;
}

public void setRain(Rain rain) {
    this.rain = rain;
}

public Clouds getClouds() {
    return clouds;
}

public void setClouds(Clouds clouds) {
    this.clouds = clouds;
}

public long getDt() {
    return dt;
}

public void setDt(long dt) {
    this.dt = dt;
}

public Sys getSys() {
    return sys;
}

public void setSys(Sys sys) {
    this.sys = sys;
}

public int getTimezone() {
    return timezone;
}
```

```
    public void setTimezone(int timezone) {
        this.timezone = timezone;
    }

    public long getId() {
        return id;
    }

    public void setId(long id) {
        this.id = id;
    }

    public String getName() {
        return name;
    }

    public void setName(String name) {
        this.name = name;
    }

    public int getCod() {
        return cod;
    }

    public void setCod(int cod) {
        this.cod = cod;
    }
}
```

File: src/main/java/com/example/demo/tools/Sys.java

```
package com.example.demo.tools;

public class Sys {
    private int type;
    private int id;
    private String country;
    private long sunrise;
    private long sunset;
```

```
    // Getters and setters
    public int getType() {
        return type;
    }

    public void setType(int type) {
        this.type = type;
    }

    public int getId() {
        return id;
    }

    public void setId(int id) {
        this.id = id;
    }

    public String getCountry() {
        return country;
    }

    public void setCountry(String country) {
        this.country = country;
    }

    public long getSunrise() {
        return sunrise;
    }

    public void setSunrise(long sunrise) {
        this.sunrise = sunrise;
    }

    public long getSunset() {
        return sunset;
    }
```

```
    public void setSunset(long sunset) {
        this.sunset = sunset;
    }
}
```

File: src/main/java/com/example/demo/tools/Rain.java

```
package com.example.demo.tools;

public class Rain {
    private double _1h;

    // Getter and setter
   public double get1h() {
        return _1h;
    }

    public void set1h(double _1h) {
        this._1h = _1h;
    }
}
```

File: src/main/java/com/example/demo/tools/Clouds.java

```
package com.example.demo.tools;

public class Clouds {
    private int all;

    // Getter and setter
   public int getAll() {
        return all;
    }

    public void setAll(int all) {
        this.all = all;
    }
}
```

File: src/main/java/com/example/demo/tools/Main.java

```
package com.example.demo.tools;

public class Main {
    private double temp;
    private double feels_like;
    private double temp_min;
    private double temp_max;
    private int pressure;
    private int humidity;
    private int sea_level;
    private int grnd_level;

    // Getters and setters
    public double getTemp() {
        return temp;
    }

    public void setTemp(double temp) {
        this.temp = temp;
    }

    public double getFeels_like() {
        return feels_like;
    }

    public void setFeels_like(double feels_like) {
        this.feels_like = feels_like;
    }

    public double getTemp_min() {
        return temp_min;
    }

    public void setTemp_min(double temp_min) {
        this.temp_min = temp_min;
    }
```

```
    public double getTemp_max() {
        return temp_max;
    }

    public void setTemp_max(double temp_max) {
        this.temp_max = temp_max;
    }

    public int getPressure() {
        return pressure;
    }

    public void setPressure(int pressure) {
        this.pressure = pressure;
    }

    public int getHumidity() {
        return humidity;
    }

    public void setHumidity(int humidity) {
        this.humidity = humidity;
    }

    public int getSea_level() {
        return sea_level;
    }

    public void setSea_level(int sea_level) {
        this.sea_level = sea_level;
    }

    public int getGrnd_level() {
        return grnd_level;
    }

    public void setGrnd_level(int grnd_level) {
        this.grnd_level = grnd_level;
    }
}
```

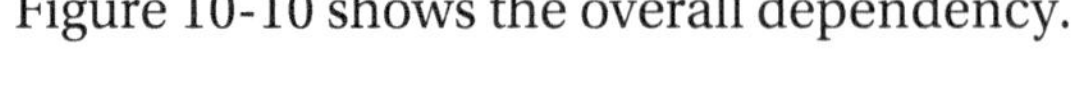
Figure 10-10 shows the overall dependency.

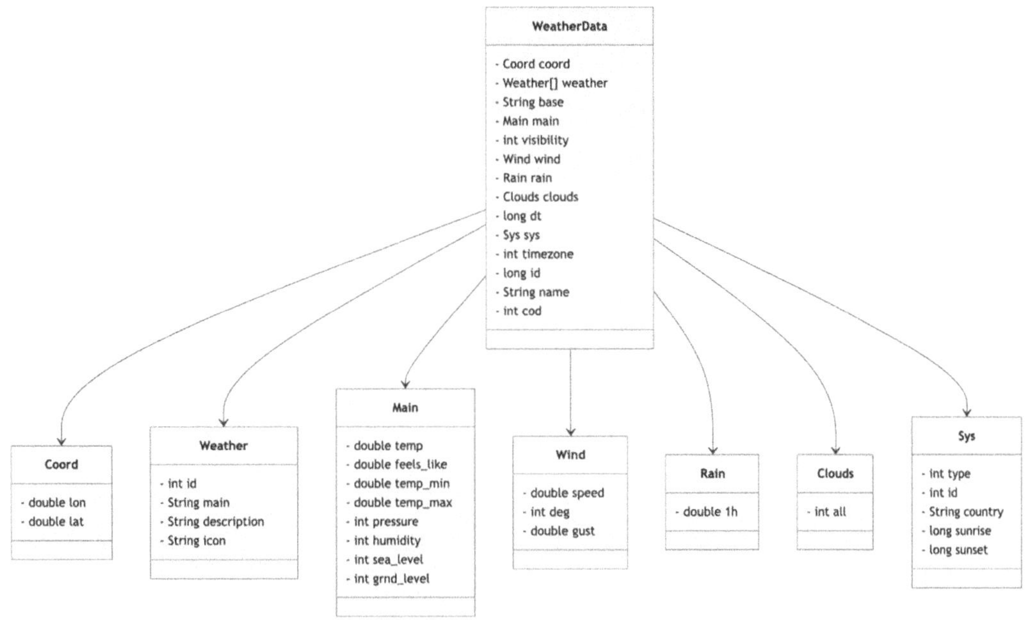

***Figure 10-10.** POJO dependency for weather response data*

With the POJOs set up, you now need to set up your REST API call, handle the response in a method, and annotate it with the `@Tool` annotation.

In the `MyTools` class, you will add a few variables to initialize the `restTemplate` and assign a placeholder for the weather API key and the weather API URL.

```
private final RestTemplate restTemplate = new RestTemplateBuilder().
build();

@Value("${weather.apiKey}")
private String apiKey;

private static final String WEATHER_API_URL = "https://api.openweathermap.
org/data/2.5/weather";
```

The description for the `@Tool` annotation has information related to fetching weather data with latitude and longitude being input parameters.

```
@Tool(description = "Get the current weather provided the latitude and
longitude")
```

The tool method will return WeatherData as the return value and takes in latitude and longitude as arguments.

```
public WeatherData getWeather(double latitude, double longitude) {
```

The final step is to make the REST API call, as shown in the following code:

File: src/main/java/com/example/demo/tools/MyTools.java

```
package com.example.demo.tools;

import java.time.LocalDateTime;
import java.time.format.DateTimeFormatter;

import org.springframework.ai.tool.annotation.Tool;
import org.springframework.context.i18n.LocaleContextHolder;
import org.springframework.beans.factory.annotation.Value;
import org.springframework.boot.web.client.RestTemplateBuilder;
import org.springframework.web.client.RestTemplate;
import org.springframework.web.util.UriComponentsBuilder;

public class MyTools {

    private final RestTemplate restTemplate = new RestTemplateBuilder().
    build();

    @Value("${weather.apiKey}")
    private String apiKey;

    private static final String WEATHER_API_URL = "https://api.
    openweathermap.org/data/2.5/weather";

    @Tool(description = "Get the current weather provided the latitude and
    longitude")
    public WeatherData getWeather(double latitude, double longitude) {
        System.out.println("Get the current weather provided the latitude
        and longitude");
        System.out.println("Latitude: " + latitude);
        System.out.println("Longitude: " + longitude);
        System.out.println("API Key: " + apiKey);
```

```
        UriComponentsBuilder builder = UriComponentsBuilder.
        fromHttpUrl(WEATHER_API_URL)
                .queryParam("lat", latitude)
                .queryParam("lon", longitude)
                .queryParam("appid", apiKey);

        return restTemplate.getForObject(builder.toUriString(),
        WeatherData.class);
    }

    @Tool(description = "Get the current date and time in the user's
    timezone")
    String getCurrentDateTime() {
        return LocalDateTime.now().atZone(LocaleContextHolder.
        getTimeZone().toZoneId()).toString();
    }

    @Tool(description = "Set a user alarm for the given time, provided in
    ISO-8601 format")
    void setAlarm(String time) {
        LocalDateTime alarmTime = LocalDateTime.parse(time,
        DateTimeFormatter.ISO_DATE_TIME);
        System.out.println("Alarm set for " + alarmTime);
    }
}
```

Now that you have the tool set up, the next step is to use the tool in a `ChatClient` call. In the following call, you are requesting weather data for today and passing in the lat and long values of the location you are planning to visit (Palais-Royal, Paris).

```
String response4 = chatClient
        .prompt("How is the weather today at lat and long of 48.8584° N,
        2.2945° E?")
        .tools(new MyTools())
        .call()
        .content();
```

File: src/main/java/com/example/demo/DemoApplication.java

```
package com.example.demo;

import com.example.demo.tools.MyTools;
import org.springframework.ai.chat.client.ChatClient;
import org.springframework.ai.openai.OpenAiChatModel;
import org.springframework.boot.CommandLineRunner;
import org.springframework.boot.SpringApplication;
import org.springframework.boot.autoconfigure.SpringBootApplication;
import org.springframework.context.annotation.Bean;

@SpringBootApplication
public class DemoApplication {

    public static void main(String[] args) {
        SpringApplication.run(DemoApplication.class, args);
    }

    @Bean
    public CommandLineRunner commandLineRunner(OpenAiChatModel
    openAiChatModel) {
        return args -> {
            ChatClient chatClient = ChatClient.builder(openAiChatModel).
            build();
            String response1 = chatClient
                    .prompt("what is the day today?")
                    .tools(new MyTools())
                    .call()
                    .content();

            String response2 = chatClient
                    .prompt("what day is tomorrow?")
                    .tools(new MyTools())
                    .call()
                    .content();
```

```
            String response3 = chatClient
                    .prompt("what is the day today and Can you set an alarm
                    10 minutes from now?")
                    .tools(new MyTools())
                    .call()
                    .content();

            String response4 = chatClient
                    .prompt("How is the weather today at lat and long of
                    48.8584° N, 2.2945° E?")
                    .tools(new MyTools())
                    .call()
                    .content();

            System.out.println("Output1: " + response1);
            System.out.println("Output2: " + response2);
            System.out.println("Output3: " + response3);
            System.out.println("Output4: " + response4);
        };
    }
}
```

Let's boot up the application and see the response. The following response is super helpful for our planned visit.

```
Output:
Started DemoApplication in 3.431 seconds (process running for 3.777)
Alarm set for 2023-10-04T14:36
Get the current weather provided the latitude and longitude
Latitude: 48.8584
Longitude: 2.2945
API Key: 5bd6ac29ae6eea51a9872c383cb3cd0f
Output1: Today is April 24, 2025.
Output2: Tomorrow will be April 25, 2025.
Output3: Today is April 24, 2025. I have set an alarm for 10 minutes
from now.
```

```
Output4: The weather today at the coordinates 48.8584° N, 2.2945° E
(Palais-Royal, Paris) is as follows:

- **Condition**: Broken clouds
- **Temperature**: 286.41 K (approximately 13.26 °C)
- **Feels Like**: 285.67 K (approximately 12.52 °C)
- **Humidity**: 72%
- **Wind Speed**: 4.12 m/s from the north
- **Cloud Coverage**: 75%

The visibility is 10,000 meters, and there is no rain reported.
```

Conclusion

Tool calling transforms large language models from static text generators into dynamic agents capable of real-time data access, automated workflows, and structured output generation. In this chapter, you learned how to define and document your tools, manage conversation context, and parse model-generated tool calls safely. You saw both a straightforward temperature and time example and a more complex weather API integration, underscoring how easily tools can be swapped or extended. As you move forward, remember that tool calling is as much about architecting clear interfaces and control flow as it is about the underlying AI. Equipped with these patterns and best practices, you can now build more powerful, reliable, and secure generative AI systems—where the synergy between model reasoning and external tools unlocks entirely new capabilities.

For readers interested in diving deeper into implementation details and evolving standards, consider referring to the following:

- OpenAI's Function Calling specification, which outlines how models interpret and emit structured tool calls
- Anthropic's tool use documentation, which explains Claude's approach to tool-calling and schema definitions
- Spring AI's reference guide, which covers how to integrate LLMs, tool callbacks, and message orchestration within a Java/Spring ecosystem

These resources provide detailed insights that complement the practices discussed in this chapter and will support you in building production-ready AI-powered applications.

The next chapter covers agentic AI.

CHAPTER 11

Agents Assemble! Building Autonomous Workflows

The goal of this chapter is to understand agents and their applications using Spring AI.

Introduction

In recent years, the integration of large language models (LLMs) and agents into software systems has revolutionized the way people interact with AI. While LLMs have demonstrated powerful capabilities in natural language understanding and generation, their true potential is unlocked when combined with agent-based systems. These agents, powered by LLMs, can autonomously navigate workflows, make decisions, and interact with a variety of tools and systems to achieve specific goals.

Spring AI offers a robust framework for building such agentic systems, allowing developers to construct, deploy, and scale AI-driven agents in a seamless and maintainable manner. This chapter focuses on understanding agents and their applications within the Spring AI ecosystem, exploring fundamental patterns such as chain workflows, parallelization, routing, and more. Through the use of Spring AI's tools like the ChatClient API and the Advisors API, developers can build highly flexible, modular, and effective agents.

In this chapter, you will dive into key components like agentic workflows, agentic workers, and the Advisors API to see how these elements contribute to building efficient and autonomous AI agents. Whether you're new to AI-driven agents or looking to enhance your existing knowledge, this chapter will provide a clear understanding of how to utilize Spring AI's capabilities to build and manage effective agents.

S. K. Sahu, *Generative AI-Driven Application Development with Java*,
https://doi.org/10.1007/979-8-8688-1609-3_11

Agentic AI

An *agent* in the context of artificial intelligence (AI) is a software component or system that acts autonomously to perform tasks, make decisions, or solve problems based on the environment or situation it encounters. Agents can perceive their environment, reason about it, and take actions to achieve a specific goal. They are typically built to operate with a certain level of autonomy, meaning they don't require constant human intervention to carry out their tasks. Figure 11-1 shows the key components and interactions.

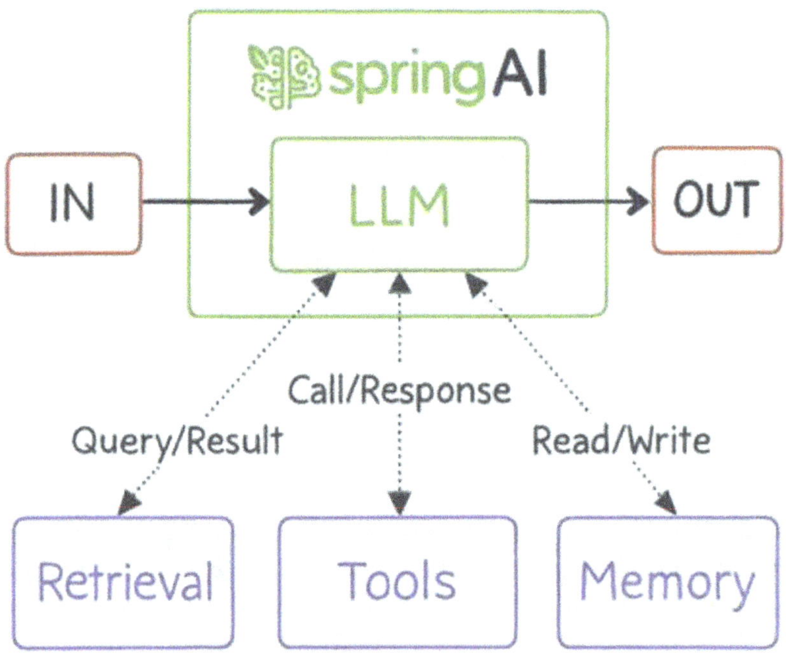

Figure 11-1. *Agentic AI ecosystem with components and interaction*

Key Characteristics of an Agent

The following are the key characteristics:

- **Autonomy**: An agent operates independently to
- perform tasks and make decisions without constant human input.
- **Perception**: An agent has sensors or mechanisms to perceive its environment, gathering information about the current state.
- **Action**: Based on its perception, the agent can take actions (e.g., executing commands, making decisions, or interacting with other systems) to influence the environment or achieve a goal.
- **Reasoning**: Agents often have some level of reasoning capability, allowing them to interpret data, make informed decisions, and adjust actions as needed.
- **Goal-Oriented**: Agents usually operate with a specific goal or set of goals in mind, whether it's answering a query, solving a problem, or completing a task.

Types of Agents

There are several different types of agents:

- **Simple agents**: These are basic agents that perform tasks by following a set of predefined rules. They often work in environments where conditions are predictable and controlled.
- **Autonomous agents**: These agents have the ability to make decisions on their own and adapt to dynamic, uncertain, or complex environments.
- **Intelligent agents**: These agents are capable of more advanced behaviors, such as learning, reasoning, and problem-solving. They can improve their performance over time based on experience or external feedback (e.g., machine learning).

Applications of Agents

These are ways agents are used:

- **Virtual assistants**: Such as Siri, Alexa, and Google Assistant, which autonomously process requests, learn user preferences, and act based on verbal commands
- **Robots**: Autonomous robots like drones or vacuum cleaners that can navigate and complete tasks without human intervention
- **Recommendation systems**: Agents that analyze user behavior and recommend products or services, such as those on Amazon or Netflix
- **AI chatbots**: AI agents designed to interact with users in a conversational manner to answer questions or resolve issues, often used in customer service

In modern software development, agents are often used in AI applications where decision-making, automation, and interaction with dynamic environments are required. They are particularly powerful when combined with technologies like LLMs and sophisticated workflows, as seen in frameworks like Spring AI.

The fundamental idea behind agents is to use a language model to identify a sequence of actions. In contrast to chains, where actions are predefined, agents rely on the language model as a reasoning engine to decide both the actions (tools) to take and the order in which to perform them.

Defining Concepts

Agent: An agent serves as the primary decision-maker, responsible for determining the next steps. It is driven by a language model and a prompt. The inputs include:

- **Tools**: Descriptions of the available actions
- **User Input**: The overall objective or task
- **Intermediate Steps**: A series of (action, tool output) pairs executed in sequence to achieve the user's goal

The output produced by the agent specifies the next action(s) to be taken or provides the final response for the user. Each action details the tool (method name) to be used and its relevant input parameters.

Tools: Tools are the methods that an agent can invoke. There are two key factors when utilizing tools:

- Providing the agent with access to the appropriate tools
- Describing these tools in a way that maximizes their usefulness to the agent

Neglecting either of these elements can impair the agent's performance. If the agent does not have access to the correct tools, it won't be able to fulfill its objectives, and if the tools are poorly described, the agent will struggle to use them effectively.

Note When building an agent, it is important to set the model temperature to 0, which ensures that the agent consistently chooses the most probable action. Additionally, the descriptions of the tools available to the agent should be clear and detailed to maximize their effectiveness. Finally, it is essential to organize the steps in the prompt in the desired execution order, ensuring that the agent follows a logical and efficient sequence when performing its tasks.

Components of Agentic Systems

Agents are systems that intelligently perform tasks, ranging from executing simple workflows to pursuing more complex, open-ended objectives. Building an effective agent involves assembling components from multiple domains, such as models, tools, knowledge and memory, audio and speech, guardrails, and orchestration. These components work together to create a robust agentic platform, each contributing to the overall functionality and adaptability of the agent.

Models

At the heart of any agent is its model, which serves as the core intelligence, enabling the agent to reason, make decisions, and process various types of information. Some models are specifically designed for long-term planning and reasoning, making them ideal for tackling difficult tasks that require strategic thought and deep problem-solving. On the other hand, certain models are optimized for agentic execution, focusing on real-time task completion with high efficiency. There are also models that strike a balance between agentic capabilities and latency, making them well-suited for tasks that require both flexibility and speed. For applications that demand minimal delays, low-latency models are essential, ensuring the agent can interact and respond quickly, especially in real-time scenarios. These diverse models work together to provide a range of capabilities that enable agents to engage with the world, support multimodal inputs such as text, images, and audio, and adapt to different contexts and tasks.

Tools

Tools are essential for enabling agents to interact with their environment and execute the tasks they are designed for. They provide the interface through which agents access external systems or carry out operations beyond their internal model. Function calling allows agents to interact with code defined by developers, enabling the execution of specific functions that are critical to the agent's operation. For agents that need to gather up-to-date information, tools like web search enable them to fetch current data from the Internet. Similarly, agents can use file search tools to perform semantic searches across large datasets or documents, making it easier to retrieve relevant information. Additionally, tools that allow agents to understand and control a computer or browser empower them to interact with and manipulate other systems, offering a broad spectrum of capabilities. By integrating these tools, agents become more versatile and capable of handling a wide variety of tasks, from simple queries to complex system manipulations.

Knowledge and Memory

For an agent to be effective over time, it needs to access external knowledge and retain information from past interactions. Knowledge and memory components are essential for augmenting the agent's capabilities beyond its initial training data. Vector stores are one key component that allows agents to search through documents semantically, enabling them to retrieve contextually relevant information dynamically during interactions. This capability is essential for tasks that require up-to-date or highly specific data. In addition to vector stores, embeddings represent data in a way that makes it efficient to retrieve, even for large datasets, ensuring that agents can access relevant information quickly. These components not only improve the agent's ability to perform tasks at runtime but also support long-term memory, allowing agents to adapt to new knowledge, retain information across sessions, and respond appropriately based on historical interactions.

Guardrails

Guardrails are critical for ensuring that agents behave safely, ethically, and consistently, particularly in real-world applications where their behavior may impact users or systems. These mechanisms are designed to prevent agents from engaging in unsafe, irrelevant, or harmful actions, which is especially important when agents are deployed in production environments. Moderation tools automatically filter out harmful or inappropriate content, helping to maintain a positive and safe user experience. Additionally, instruction hierarchies give developers the ability to control the behavior of agents by prioritizing specific prompts or guidelines. This ensures that the agent follows desired patterns of behavior and avoids unwanted actions, even in complex or ambiguous situations. By setting clear boundaries through guardrails, developers can maintain control over the agent's operations, ensuring it acts within the intended ethical and functional guidelines.

Orchestration

Building and managing agents is an iterative process that involves developing, deploying, and continuously improving the system. Orchestration tools are essential for monitoring and refining the performance of agents over time. The Agent SDK provides developers with the necessary tools to create, test, and deploy agents, ensuring they are built effectively from the start. Once deployed, agents can be monitored using tracing and evaluation tools, which allow developers to track their performance and identify areas for improvement. Fine-tuning is another crucial aspect of orchestration, enabling agents to be adapted over time to perform specific tasks or adjust to new challenges. Through effective orchestration, agents can be maintained, updated, and optimized to ensure they continue to meet the evolving needs of users and organizations.

By combining these components—models, tools, knowledge, guardrails, and orchestration—agents can be built and refined to handle a wide range of tasks in dynamic, real-world environments. Each component plays a vital role in enabling agents to perform intelligently, safely, and effectively, ensuring their success in a variety of applications.

Agentic Workflows and Patterns

In current practice, agent-based AI systems are widely used to automate tasks, make decisions, and solve problems across various domains. Frameworks like LangChain4j are commonly used for building these systems, but they do not currently support high-level abstractions like "agents" found in AutoGen or CrewAI, which are specifically designed for building multi-agent systems. This limitation means that within Java frameworks like LangChain4j, constructing complex multi-agent systems is not as straightforward. However, it is still possible to implement similar patterns manually. In the upcoming sections, we will explore how these patterns can be constructed, providing a foundation for building more sophisticated agent systems even within the current framework constraints.

In the context of building agent-based AI systems, there are three primary architectural patterns that can be utilized: Workflows, Agents, and a combination of both, known as Hybrid Systems. Understanding the distinction between these patterns helps in deciding which approach is best suited for a given task.

1. **Workflows**: In this pattern, systems are designed where LLMs and tools are orchestrated through predefined, static code paths. These systems follow a prescriptive model, where the sequence of actions, tools, and processes are explicitly defined by the developer. This approach is ideal for tasks that require predictability, consistency, and strict control over the execution process. By using workflows, developers ensure that the agent follows a set sequence of operations, making it suitable for well-understood tasks like data retrieval, file searching, and system operations that don't require decision-making flexibility.

2. **Agents**: Unlike workflows, agents are dynamic systems where LLMs autonomously direct their own processes and choose the tools they need based on the context or input. This approach offers more flexibility, allowing the agent to make decisions about what actions to take next, making it suitable for complex, open-ended tasks. Agents are ideal for scenarios that require adaptability, such as when the agent needs to handle unknown or variable inputs and adjust its course of action accordingly. The agent system excels in situations where tasks are not strictly defined in advance and require ongoing reasoning and decision-making.

3. **Hybrid Systems**: The hybrid approach combines elements of both workflows and agents. In a hybrid system, predefined workflows guide the agent through specific tasks, but the agent still retains the ability to make decisions and dynamically choose between different workflows or tools based on the context. This combination offers the best of both worlds: the structured predictability of workflows for well-defined tasks and the flexibility of agents for tasks that require adaptability and decision-making. Hybrid systems are useful in situations where certain parts of a task can be well-defined and controlled through workflows, but other parts may require the agent to autonomously decide on the best course of action based on the available information.

While you've already explored the use of tools within agent systems—where LLMs autonomously decide to fetch the date, set alarms, or call APIs for weather updates—the focus in this section will be on *workflow patterns*. You will dive deeper into how workflows can be effectively structured and managed, especially in scenarios where predictability, repeatability, and structured execution are critical. I'll also briefly touch on how hybrid systems can leverage the strengths of both workflows and agents to address complex use cases.

The primary takeaway is that while the idea of fully autonomous agents is certainly attractive, workflows often offer superior predictability and consistency, especially for tasks that are well-defined. This is particularly important in enterprise environments, where factors like reliability, control, and ease of maintenance are essential for successful deployment. Workflows allow organizations to implement structured, repeatable processes that minimize risks and ensure a high level of operational stability.

In contrast, fully autonomous agents, while offering more flexibility and decision-making capabilities, can introduce unpredictability that may not be ideal in contexts where clear, reliable outcomes are necessary. This makes workflows a better choice for many enterprise scenarios, where a controlled approach is paramount.

To illustrate how these concepts can be applied in real-world systems, let's explore how Spring AI implements these patterns through five fundamental workflow structures. Each of these patterns is designed to address specific use cases and optimize the execution of tasks in various business applications. By understanding how these patterns are applied, you can better appreciate the balance between flexibility and structure that makes workflows such an important tool in building reliable, maintainable systems.

Chain Workflow

The **Chain Workflow** pattern is a powerful method for breaking down complex tasks into simpler, more manageable steps (see Figure 11-2).

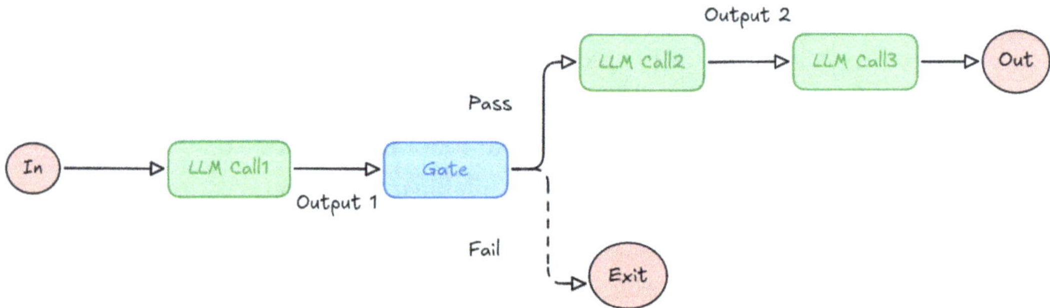

Figure 11-2. *Chain Workflow pattern*

In this pattern, each step in the workflow relies on the output of the previous step, creating a sequence of actions that build upon each other. This approach is ideal for tasks where the process needs to follow a clear, linear sequence, allowing for more accurate and controlled execution.

When to Use Chain Workflow

The following are times to use Chain Workflow:

- **Tasks with clear sequential steps**: When the task at hand involves multiple stages that need to be processed in a specific order.
- **Trading latency for accuracy**: Sometimes, breaking down a task into smaller steps improves the overall accuracy of the result, even if it introduces some latency.
- **Stepwise dependency**: Each step's output is used as input for the subsequent step, ensuring that the process evolves logically.

Let's break down the code and explain how it implements the Chain Workflow pattern.

File: `src/main/java/com/example/demo/DemoApplication.java`

```
package com.example.demo;

import com.example.demo.workflow.*;
import com.fasterxml.jackson.core.JsonProcessingException;
import org.springframework.ai.chat.client.ChatClient;
import org.springframework.ai.openai.OpenAiChatModel;
import org.springframework.boot.CommandLineRunner;
import org.springframework.boot.SpringApplication;
import org.springframework.boot.autoconfigure.SpringBootApplication;
import org.springframework.context.annotation.Bean;

import java.util.List;
import java.util.Map;

@SpringBootApplication
public class DemoApplication {

    public static void main(String[] args) {
        SpringApplication.run(DemoApplication.class, args);
    }
```

```
// Bean to initialize and run the chat process as a command line runner
@Bean
public CommandLineRunner commandLineRunner(OpenAiChatModel
 openAiChatModel) {
    return args -> {
        // Creating the chat client with the provided chat model
        ChatClient chatClient = ChatClient.builder(openAiChatModel).
        build();

        // Call the 'chain' method to execute the workflow
        String response = chain(
                "What is 2+2?",  // The user input to the chain
                                    workflow
               new String[]{    // Predefined system prompts to guide
                                   the workflow
                       "Think through it.",
                        "Validate if the result is scientifically
                        presented.",
                        "Share only the output."
                },
                chatClient);   // Pass in the chat client to interact
                                  with the AI model

        // Print the final result
        System.out.println("Response: " + response);
    };
}

// Method that implements the Chain Workflow
private String chain(String userInput, String[] systemPrompts,
ChatClient chatClient) {
    String response = userInput;  // Start with the user input as the
                                     initial response
```

```
        // Iterate through the system prompts, applying them sequentially
        for (String prompt : systemPrompts) {
             // Concatenate the current prompt with the previous response
             (or initial input)
            String input = String.format("%s\n %s", prompt, response);

             // Pass the concatenated input to the chat client and get the
             updated response
            response = chatClient.prompt(input).call().content();
            // Make the call to the LLM
        }

         return response;  // Return the final output after all steps
    }
}
```

The code demonstrates the implementation of a Chain Workflow pattern, where a sequence of steps is executed in a predefined order, with each step building upon the output of the previous one. The workflow begins by defining a `CommandLineRunner` bean in a Spring Boot application. This bean is responsible for initiating the workflow when the application starts. Within this bean, a `ChatClient` is created using the `OpenAiChatModel`, which serves as the interface to interact with the LLM.

The core of the workflow lies in the `chain` method, which takes the user input, a set of system prompts, and the chat client as parameters. The method starts by initializing the response with the user's input (in this case, "What is 2+2?"). Then, a loop iterates through each of the system prompts provided in the `systemPrompts` array. During each iteration, the current prompt is concatenated with the previous response to form the input for the LLM. The `chatClient.prompt(input).call().content()` call sends this input to the LLM and receives the updated response, which is then passed to the next iteration.

Each prompt in the array guides the agent through a specific step, such as "Think through it," "Validate if the result is scientifically presented," and "Share only the output." These steps are designed to refine the answer progressively. Once all the prompts are processed, the method returns the final response, which represents the output of the entire workflow after all steps have been executed. The final result, in this case, is the output of the mathematical calculation, ensuring it was properly reasoned and validated.

This approach effectively demonstrates how the Chain Workflow pattern can be used to break down a task into manageable steps, where each step is dependent on the outcome of the previous one. It ensures the task is performed systematically, with clear responsibilities assigned to each stage, resulting in a more accurate and controlled output. The chain is also highly extensible, as additional steps can be easily added to the workflow as needed.

What's Happening in the Workflow?

This is what happens:

- The Chain Workflow begins with a user input and proceeds through a series of system prompts. Each prompt builds on the previous response, ensuring that the task is completed in well-defined steps.
- The agent is guided through the process of reasoning, validation, and output generation, with each stage relying on the result from the previous one. This approach ensures a more accurate and controlled final result.
- The response from the LLM is updated at each step, demonstrating the chain's ability to modify the task dynamically while maintaining control over the process.

This implementation highlights several key principles of the Chain Workflow:

- **Focused responsibilities**: Each step has a clear responsibility (e.g., thinking through the problem, validating the result, sharing only the output).
- **Sequential dependency**: The output from one step becomes the input for the next, creating a clear flow of logic.
- **Extensibility**: The chain can easily be extended to include additional steps or modified to handle more complex tasks.

This pattern is ideal for structured tasks where each stage builds on the previous one, ensuring that the final result is both accurate and comprehensive.

Parallelization Workflow

The **Parallelization Workflow** pattern leverages concurrent processing to handle multiple tasks simultaneously, improving efficiency and reducing processing time (see Figure 11-3).

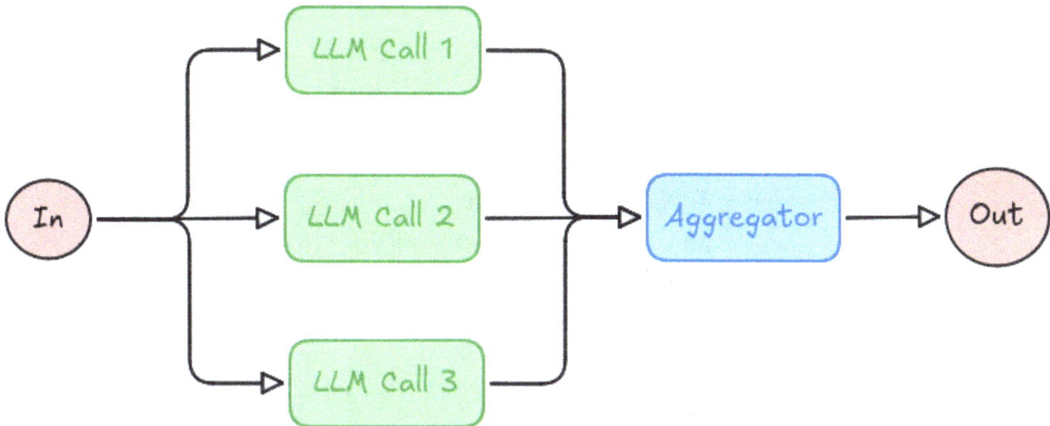

Figure 11-3. *Parallelization Workflow*

This pattern is particularly useful in scenarios where large volumes of similar but independent tasks need to be processed or when tasks require multiple perspectives. There are two main variations of parallelization:

- **Sectioning**: In this variation, a task is broken down into smaller, independent subtasks that can be processed in parallel. This allows the system to handle each subtask concurrently, speeding up the overall processing time.
- **Voting**: In this variation, multiple instances of the same task are run simultaneously, and the outputs are aggregated to form a final result based on consensus.

This workflow is ideal when processing time is critical, and tasks can be parallelized. It allows for simultaneous execution of multiple LLM calls, with the results being aggregated afterward to provide the final output. For example, in stakeholder analysis, the system can analyze different stakeholder groups concurrently and then combine the results for an overall assessment.

The following code demonstrates the **Parallelization Workflow** in action. The commandLineRunner method is executed when the application starts, initiating a parallel processing task using a ChatClient.

```
@Bean
public CommandLineRunner commandLineRunner(OpenAiChatModel
openAiChatModel) {
    return args -> {
        System.out.println("Parallelization Workflow:");
        List<String> parallelResponse = parallel(chatClient);
        parallelResponse.forEach(System.out::println);
        // Output the responses for each stakeholder group
    };
}

private List<String> parallel(ChatClient chatClient) {
    return new ParallelizationWorkflow(chatClient)
            .parallel(
                    "Analyze how market changes will impact %s stakeholder
                    group.",  // Prompt to analyze market changes
                    List.of(
                            "Customers",   // Stakeholder 1
                            "Employees",   // Stakeholder 2
                            "Investors",   // Stakeholder 3
                            "Suppliers"    // Stakeholder 4
                    )
            );
}
```

In this code, the parallel method is called, which initializes the ParallelizationWorkflow and runs the analysis for each stakeholder group in parallel. The List.of() method is used to define the stakeholders, and each group is passed to the LLM for concurrent processing.

```
package com.example.demo.workflow;

import org.springframework.ai.chat.client.ChatClient;

import java.util.List;
```

```
public class ParallelizationWorkflow {

    private final ChatClient chatClient;

   // Constructor to initialize ChatClient
    public ParallelizationWorkflow(ChatClient chatClient) {
        this.chatClient = chatClient;
    }

   // Method to process tasks in parallel
    public List<String> parallel(String prompt, List<String>
    stakeholders) {
        return stakeholders.parallelStream()  // Use parallelStream to
        process items concurrently
                .map(stakeholder -> this.chatClient.prompt(String.
                format(prompt, stakeholder)).call().content())
                // Map each stakeholder to a LLM call
                .toList();  // Collect the results into a List
    }
}
```

The `ParallelizationWorkflow` class utilizes Java's `parallelStream()` to process each stakeholder group concurrently. For each stakeholder, the `chatClient.prompt()` method sends a request to the LLM with the respective stakeholder's name. The results are then gathered into a list and returned.

What's Happening in the Process?

This is what happened:

1. **CommandLineRunner**: This is used to execute the parallelization logic when the application starts. It runs the `parallel()` method and prints the resulting analysis for each stakeholder group.

2. **Parallel Execution**: The `parallelStream()` method is used to process the list of stakeholders in parallel. Each stakeholder's group is analyzed independently, allowing the system to handle multiple tasks concurrently. This significantly speeds up the process, especially when dealing with a large number of similar tasks.

3. **LLM Call**: Each iteration of the `parallelStream()` sends a prompt to the LLM for analysis. The prompt asks the LLM to analyze how market changes will impact each stakeholder group.
4. **Aggregation**: After all parallel tasks are completed, the results from each LLM call are collected into a list, providing a comprehensive analysis of how market changes affect each stakeholder group.

The Parallelization Workflow pattern is particularly beneficial for tasks that can be broken down into independent units, such as analyzing multiple groups or processing large datasets, as it optimizes performance by executing tasks concurrently rather than sequentially.

Routing Workflow

The **Routing Workflow** pattern is designed to implement intelligent task distribution, enabling specialized handling for different types of input (see Figure 11-4).

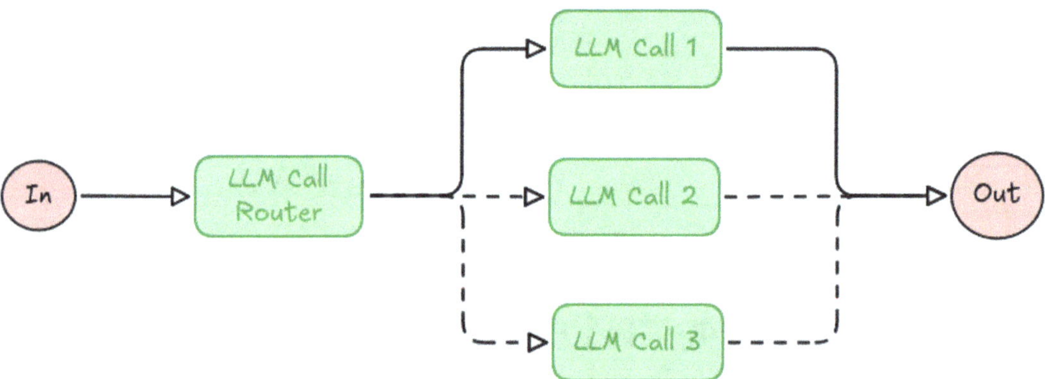

Figure 11-4. *Routing Workflow*

This pattern is particularly useful for complex tasks where various inputs need to be processed by specialized systems or processes. The core idea is to analyze the input content using an LLM and route it to the appropriate specialized prompt or handler for processing.

When to Use

This is when to use it:

- **Complex tasks with distinct categories of input**: When the task involves different categories of input, each requiring specific handling, such as customer inquiries, technical issues, or billing problems.
- **Specialized processing for different inputs**: When certain types of input require unique processing steps or specialized knowledge, this pattern ensures that the right expertise is applied.
- **Accurate classification**: If the system can accurately classify input into distinct categories, the routing pattern ensures that the task is sent to the right handler.

In the Routing Workflow pattern, an agent first analyzes the input and then determines the most appropriate route by matching it to a predefined set of categories or routes. This decision is made dynamically based on the content of the input, and the agent then proceeds with the task using the most relevant process.

Here's a breakdown of how the Routing Workflow pattern is implemented in the code:

```
package com.example.demo.workflow;

import org.springframework.ai.chat.client.ChatClient;

import java.util.Map;
import java.util.Objects;

public class RoutingWorkflow {

    public RoutingWorkflow(ChatClient chatClient) {
    }

    // The 'route' method determines which task handler should be invoked
    based on the input
```

```
    public String route(String input, Map<String, String> routes,
    ChatClient chatClient) {

        // Get all keys from the routes map (these represent different task
        types or categories)
        StringBuilder keys = new StringBuilder();

        for (String key : routes.keySet()) {
            keys.append(key).append(", ");
        }

        // Remove the last comma and space
        if (!keys.isEmpty()) {
            keys.setLength(keys.length() - 2);
        }

        // Ask the LLM to determine the appropriate route based on
        the input
        String routeKey = Objects.requireNonNull(chatClient.
        prompt("Determine the route for the input: " + input + ".
        Available routes: " + keys.toString() + ". Just respond with the
        route name.")
                        .call()
                        .content())
                .trim()
                .toLowerCase();  // Get the route name from the LLM
                                    response
        String routeMessage = routes.get(routeKey);  // Retrieve the
        corresponding handler for the selected route
        return chatClient.prompt(routeMessage).call().content();
        // Execute the selected route's handler and return the result
    }
}
```

What's Happening in the Process?

This is what happens:

1. **RoutingWorkflow class**: This class contains the logic for the routing workflow. It takes the user input and maps it to one of several predefined routes. The `route` method dynamically determines which route to use based on the input.

2. **Route determination**: The method first constructs a string of available routes by iterating over the `routes` map. This map contains keys that represent different categories of tasks (e.g., "billing", "technical", "general"). These categories will guide the LLM in determining the appropriate route.

3. **LLM decision**: The `chatClient.prompt()` sends a request to the LLM to analyze the input and decide which route it belongs to. The LLM is prompted with the input along with a list of available routes. The LLM's response is expected to be the route name, which corresponds to one of the keys in the routes map.

4. **Executing the selected route**: Once the route is determined, the code retrieves the corresponding message from the `routes` map and sends it to the LLM for processing. The result from the LLM's response is returned as the output of the workflow.

Here's how the `RoutingWorkflow` is used in practice:

```
@Bean
public CommandLineRunner commandLineRunner(OpenAiChatModel
openAiChatModel) {

    return args -> {
        ChatClient chatClient = ChatClient.builder(openAiChatModel).
        build();

        String response = chain(
                "What is 2+2?",
                new String[]{
                        "Think through it.",
```

```
                    "Validate if the results is scientifically
                    presented.",
                    "Share only the output."
            },
            chatClient);

    System.out.println("Response: " + response);
     System.out.println("Parallelization Workflow:");

    List<String> parallelResponse = parallel(chatClient);
     parallelResponse.forEach(System.out::println);

    System.out.println("Routing Workflow:");
     String routeResponse = route(chatClient);
     System.out.println("Response: " + routeResponse);
}

private String route(ChatClient chatClient) {

     RoutingWorkflow workflow = new RoutingWorkflow(chatClient);
     Map<String, String> routes = Map.of(
             "billing", "You are a billing specialist. Help resolve
             billing issues...",
             "technical", "You are a technical support engineer. Help
             solve technical problems...",
             "general", "You are a customer service representative. Help
             with general inquiries..."
     );

     String input = "My account was charged twice last week";
     // Input representing a billing issue
     return workflow.route(input, routes, chatClient);
     // Call the routing workflow with the input and routes
}
```

Key Insights:

These are the key insights:

- **Task routing**: The routing workflow allows different types of tasks (billing, technical support, general inquiries) to be handled by specialized processes. By routing the input to the appropriate handler, the system can ensure that each task is dealt with by the right expertise.
- **Dynamic classification**: The LLM dynamically classifies the input and determines the appropriate route, making the system highly adaptable to varying input types.
- **Flexible and scalable**: This approach is flexible, allowing for easy addition of new routes and specialized handlers. The system can scale to accommodate new categories of tasks as needed.

This routing pattern is especially useful in customer support or other domains where different types of requests require different types of processing or expertise. It ensures that each request is processed efficiently by the most appropriate handler, improving the overall effectiveness of the agent system.

Agentic Workers

Agentic workers are AI systems capable of autonomously planning, deciding, and acting to achieve goals with minimal human oversight. They can break down complex tasks, reason through each step, and adapt as conditions change. Unlike traditional automation, they show initiative by identifying problems, proposing solutions, and coordinating workflows. By managing repetitive or cognitively heavy tasks, agentic workers free humans to focus on creativity, strategy, and higher-value work.

Orchestrator-Workers

The **Orchestrator-Workers** pattern is designed to implement more complex agent-like behaviors while maintaining control over the task decomposition and execution process (see Figure 11-5).

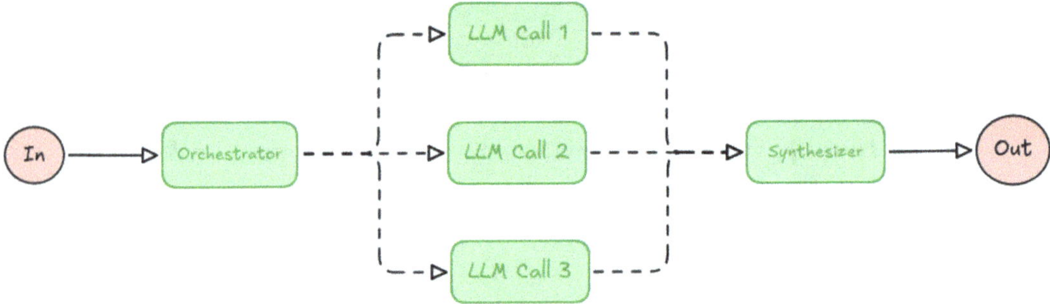

***Figure 11-5.** Orchestrator workers*

This pattern involves a central orchestrator that divides a task into specialized subtasks, which are then handled by different workers. The workers, each specialized in a specific aspect of the task, execute their respective tasks concurrently, and their outputs are combined by the orchestrator to produce the final result.

This pattern is ideal for scenarios where tasks can't be easily predicted up front or when different perspectives or approaches are needed to address various aspects of a complex problem. The orchestrator ensures that the right worker handles the appropriate part of the task, and it can also manage situations where multiple workers need to collaborate to achieve the final outcome.

When to Use

This is when to use this pattern:

- **Complex tasks with unpredictable subtasks**: When the task at hand involves multiple facets or requires a combination of specialized expertise to complete.
- **Tasks requiring different approaches or perspectives**: When different methods or perspectives are needed to solve a problem, such as creating both technical and user-friendly documentation for an API.
- **Adaptive problem-solving**: When the task may evolve or require real-time adjustments based on the results of ongoing work.

The following code demonstrates how to implement the Orchestrator-Workers pattern using Spring AI's `ChatClient` for LLM interactions. The orchestrator divides the task of generating both technical and user-friendly documentation for a REST API endpoint into two separate tasks, handled by specialized workers.

```
@Bean
public CommandLineRunner commandLineRunner(OpenAiChatModel
openAiChatModel) {
    return args -> {
        ChatClient chatClient = ChatClient.builder(openAiChatModel).
        build();
        System.out.println("Orchestrator Workers Workflow:");
        orchestrate(chatClient);  // Execute the orchestrator workflow
    };
}

private void orchestrate(ChatClient chatClient) throws
JsonProcessingException {
    OrchestratorWorkersWorkflow workflow = new OrchestratorWorkersWorkflow(
    chatClient);
    WorkerResponse response = workflow.process(
            "Generate both technical and user-friendly documentation for a
            REST API endpoint"
    );

    // Output the analysis and worker responses
    System.out.println("Analysis: " + response.analysis());
    System.out.println("Worker Outputs: " + response.workerResponses());
}
```

OrchestratorWorkersWorkflow Class

Here is what the `OrchestratorWorkersWorkflow` class looks like:

```
package com.example.demo.workflow;

import com.fasterxml.jackson.core.JsonProcessingException;
import com.fasterxml.jackson.core.type.TypeReference;
```

```
import com.fasterxml.jackson.databind.ObjectMapper;
import org.springframework.ai.chat.client.ChatClient;

import java.util.Map;
import java.util.Objects;
import java.util.concurrent.CompletableFuture;

public class OrchestratorWorkersWorkflow {

    private final ChatClient chatClient;
    private final WorkerResponse workerResponse;

    public OrchestratorWorkersWorkflow(ChatClient chatClient) {
        this.chatClient = chatClient;
        this.workerResponse = new WorkerResponse();
    }

    public WorkerResponse process(String s) throws
    JsonProcessingException {
        // Orchestrator determines which workers to use based on the input
        String response = Objects.requireNonNull(this.chatClient.prompt("""
                            There are two types of documentation for a REST
                            API endpoint: technical and user-friendly.
                            Technical documentation is intended for
                            developers and includes details about the API's
                            functionality, parameters, and response formats.
                            User-friendly documentation is intended for end-
                            users and includes information about how to use
                            the API, examples, and best practices.
                            There are two types of workers: technical
                            and user-friendly. Either one or Both the
                            workers can be used simultaneously to generate
                            documentation.
                            The technical worker generates technical
                            documentation, while the user-friendly worker
                            generates user-friendly documentation.
                            The user will provide a prompt that specifies
                            the type of documentation they want.
```

````
                    Generate only a JSON string that contains the
                    following fields without any formatting or
                    extra text:
                    - "technical": a boolean value that indicates
                    whether the technical documentation should be
                    generated
                    - "userFriendly": a boolean value that indicates
                    whether the user-friendly documentation should
                    be generated
                    The user will provide a prompt that specifies
                    the type of documentation they want:
                    """)
                .user(s)
                .call()
                .content())
        .replaceAll("^```json\n|\n```$", "");

// Parse the JSON response to determine whether to use each worker
Map<String, Boolean> responseMap = new ObjectMapper().
readValue(response, new TypeReference<Map<String, Boolean>>() {});

// Run the workers concurrently
CompletableFuture<Void> technicalFuture = CompletableFuture.
runAsync(() -> {
    if (responseMap.getOrDefault("technical", false)) {
        technicalWorker(chatClient);  // Generate technical
        documentation if required
    }
});

CompletableFuture<Void> userFriendlyFuture = CompletableFuture.
runAsync(() -> {
    if (responseMap.getOrDefault("userFriendly", false)) {
        userFriendlyWorker(chatClient);  // Generate user-friendly
        documentation if required
    }
});
````

```
        // Wait for both worker tasks to finish
        CompletableFuture.allOf(technicalFuture,
        userFriendlyFuture).join();

        // Orchestrator analyzes the results and returns a summary
        String analysis = this.chatClient.prompt("Analyze the response and
        provide a summary of the documentation generated")
                .user(s)
                .call()
                .content();
        workerResponse.setAnalysis(analysis);

        return workerResponse;  // Return the orchestrated result
    }

    // Technical worker to generate technical documentation
    public String technicalWorker(ChatClient chatClient) {
        String response = this.chatClient.prompt("Generate technical
        documentation for a REST API endpoint")
                .call()
                .content();
        workerResponse.setWorkerResponses(response);
        return response;
    }

    // User-friendly worker to generate user-friendly documentation
    public String userFriendlyWorker(ChatClient chatClient) {
        String response = this.chatClient.prompt("Generate user-friendly
        documentation for a REST API endpoint")
                .call()
                .content();

        workerResponse.setWorkerResponses(response);
        return response;
    }
}
```

What's Happening in the Process?

This is what is happening:

1. **CommandLineRunner**: The `commandLineRunner` method initiates the orchestration process when the application starts. It calls the `orchestrate()` method, which in turn invokes the orchestrator workflow.

2. **Orchestrator workflow**: The `process()` method in the `OrchestratorWorkersWorkflow` class orchestrates the generation of both technical and user-friendly documentation. It starts by using an LLM to analyze the user's request and determine which type of documentation (technical or user-friendly) is needed. This decision is made based on a JSON response that specifies whether to generate each type of documentation.

3. **Concurrent worker execution**: The technical and user-friendly documentation tasks are executed concurrently using `CompletableFuture.runAsync()`. This allows the system to generate both types of documentation simultaneously, improving efficiency.

4. **Worker response collection**: After the workers finish their tasks, the orchestrator synthesizes their outputs. The `technicalWorker()` and `userFriendlyWorker()` methods are responsible for generating the respective documentation types. Once both workers complete their tasks, the orchestrator analyzes the results and provides a summary.

5. **Final output**: The `WorkerResponse` object contains the results from both the workers, including an analysis of the generated documentation. The orchestrator ensures that all tasks are completed before returning the final output.

Key Insights

These are key insights:

- **Task decomposition**: The orchestrator divides the task into multiple subtasks, each handled by a specialized worker (technical and user-friendly).
- **Concurrency**: The workers are executed concurrently, improving the efficiency of the system when multiple tasks need to be performed simultaneously.
- **Synthesis**: The orchestrator combines the results of the workers and provides an overall analysis of the generated documentation.
- **Scalability**: This approach can be extended to include additional workers for other types of tasks, making the system adaptable to a wide range of use cases.

The Orchestrator-Workers pattern is ideal for scenarios where complex tasks require the involvement of specialized processes, and it provides a clear structure for managing concurrent, complex workflows.

Evaluator-Optimizer

The **Evaluator-Optimizer** pattern introduces a dual-LLM process where two separate models work in tandem to refine a solution iteratively (see Figure 11-6).

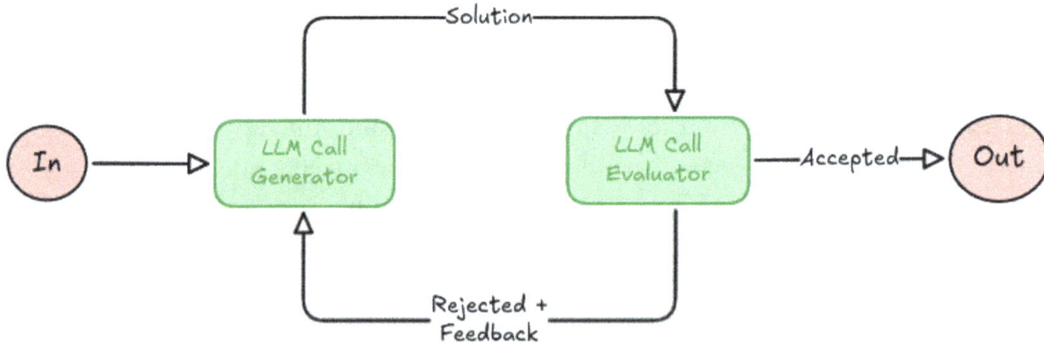

Figure 11-6. *Evaluator Optimizer*

One model, the Generator LLM, produces initial responses, while the second, the Evaluator LLM, assesses the responses and provides feedback for improvement. This pattern is akin to the refinement process that a human writer goes through when revising and improving their work. The iterative nature of this process makes it highly suitable for tasks that require multiple rounds of critique and enhancement.

When to Use

Here is when to use it:

- **Clear evaluation criteria**: The pattern is most useful when there are specific standards or expectations that the solution must meet.
- **Iterative refinement provides measurable value**: Use it when a task benefits from successive refinements, such as improving accuracy or clarity over multiple iterations.
- **Tasks benefit from multiple rounds of critique**: Use it when a solution requires constant improvement, often through feedback and reworking until the desired outcome is achieved.

This workflow is ideal for tasks such as writing, coding, or designing solutions where refinement is needed to meet high-quality standards.

In the following code, the Evaluator-Optimizer pattern is implemented using Spring AI's `ChatClient`. The `EvaluatorOptimizerWorkflow` class simulates an iterative feedback loop where a solution is generated and then evaluated to determine whether it meets the required standards. If the solution is not satisfactory, the process is repeated until the solution passes the evaluation.

```
@Bean
public CommandLineRunner commandLineRunner(OpenAiChatModel
openAiChatModel) {
    return args -> {
        ChatClient chatClient = ChatClient.builder(openAiChatModel).build();
        System.out.println("Evaluator Optimizer Workflow:");
        evaluatorOptimizer(chatClient);  // Initiates the evaluator-
        optimizer workflow
    };
}
```

```
private void evaluatorOptimizer(ChatClient chatClient) {
    EvaluatorOptimizerWorkflow workflow = new EvaluatorOptimizerWorkflow(
    chatClient);

    // Start the iterative refinement process with an initial task
   RefinedResponse response = workflow.loop(
           "Create a Java class implementing a thread-safe counter"
    );

    // Output the final solution and the evaluation process
   System.out.println("Final Solution: " + response.solution());
    System.out.println("Evaluation: " + response.chainOfThought());
}
```

EvaluatorOptimizerWorkflow Class

Here is the `EvaluatorOptimizerWorkflow` class:

```
package com.example.demo.workflow;

import org.springframework.ai.chat.client.ChatClient;

import java.util.Objects;

public class EvaluatorOptimizerWorkflow {

    private final ChatClient chatClient;
    private final RefinedResponse refinedResponse;

    public EvaluatorOptimizerWorkflow(ChatClient chatClient) {
        this.chatClient = chatClient;
        this.refinedResponse = new RefinedResponse();  // Create a new
        object to hold the final solution and evaluation
   }

    // Loop for iterative refinement of the solution
   public RefinedResponse loop(String task) {
        String chainOfThought = "NEEDS_IMPROVEMENT";  // Initialize the
        evaluation as "NEEDS_IMPROVEMENT"
       String solution = "";
```

```
        // Repeat until the solution is considered acceptable ("PASS")
        while (!chainOfThought.equals("PASS")) {
            solution = Objects.requireNonNull(chatClient.prompt(task)
                            .call()
                            .content()) // Generate the initial solution
                            from the task
                    .trim();

            refinedResponse.setChainOfThought(solution); // Set the
            solution as part of the chain of thought
            chainOfThought = evaluate(solution, task); // Evaluate the
            solution to check if it needs improvement
        }

        refinedResponse.setSolution(solution); // Finalize the solution
        once it's considered acceptable
        return refinedResponse;
    }

    // Evaluates the generated solution based on the task
    private String evaluate(String solution, String task) {
        return Objects.requireNonNull(chatClient.prompt("Think step by
        step. Evaluate the following solution: "
                            + solution + " for task: " + task + ".
                            Reply with PASS if solution is correct,
                            otherwise reply with NEEDS_IMPROVEMENT.")
                        .call()
                        .content()) // Evaluate the solution and return
                        either "PASS" or "NEEDS_IMPROVEMENT"
                .trim();
    }
}
```

What's Happening in the Process?

This is what is happening:

1. **CommandLineRunner**: The `commandLineRunner` method is executed when the application starts. It initiates the **Evaluator-Optimizer** workflow by calling the `evaluatorOptimizer()` method.

2. **Evaluator-optimizer workflow**: The `EvaluatorOptimizerWorkflow` class orchestrates the iterative refinement of the solution. It starts by generating a solution (in this case, a Java class for a thread-safe counter) and then checks whether the solution meets the necessary criteria.

3. **Solution generation and evaluation**:

   - The `loop()` method continuously refines the solution by calling the **Generator LLM** to generate a solution and then passing it to the **Evaluator LLM** for assessment.

   - The `evaluate()` method asks the LLM to analyze the solution and determine whether it meets the required standards. If the solution is deemed inadequate, the process repeats with a new solution. The evaluation result is returned as either "PASS" or "NEEDS_IMPROVEMENT."

4. **Final solution and feedback**: Once the evaluation is "PASS," the final solution is returned. Along with the solution, the *chain of thought* is recorded, showing how the solution evolved over multiple iterations.

5. **Concurrent feedback loop**: The key feature of this pattern is the feedback loop where the evaluator constantly improves the generator's solution. This iterative refinement process allows for high-quality output, especially when the task benefits from constant critique and improvement.

Key Insights

The following are the key insights:

- **Iterative refinement**: The **Evaluator-Optimizer** pattern excels in scenarios where a task requires constant feedback and iterative improvement. Each solution is refined based on clear evaluation criteria until it meets the desired standard.
- **Dual-layered process**: The pattern uses two LLMs in a complementary way: one for generating potential solutions and another for evaluating and refining those solutions.
- **Clear evaluation**: The process ensures that each step of the task is assessed and improved upon, ensuring the solution evolves over time to meet the highest standards.
- **Use cases**: This pattern is ideal for tasks like writing code, creating documentation, or designing solutions that benefit from step-by-step critique and improvement.

The **Evaluator-Optimizer** pattern is a valuable tool for situations where a solution needs to be progressively refined, ensuring that each iteration improves upon the last until the final result is both accurate and optimal.

Agent Lifecycle in Spring AI

Understanding the lifecycle of an agent is essential for designing systems that are modular, scalable, and responsive. In Spring AI, an agent transitions through several key stages during its operation. Each stage builds on the previous one and contributes to the overall behavior, reliability, and adaptability of the system.

1. **Initialization:** The agent's lifecycle begins with initialization, where the agent is created and configured with the necessary components. This includes selecting the underlying language model, registering available tools (functions or APIs the agent can call), setting up memory storage (such as a vector database), and optionally applying safety guardrails. At this stage, developers define the agent's capabilities and context, ensuring it's properly equipped to process and act on incoming inputs.

2. **Input reception and perception:** Once initialized, the agent listens for and receives input, typically from a user or another system. This input can be a direct prompt, a query, or a command. The agent parses and interprets this input based on its prior knowledge, context, and available tools. If memory is enabled, it can also retrieve relevant past interactions or documents. This perception step sets the stage for informed reasoning and action planning.

3. **Reasoning and planning:** With input in hand, the agent proceeds to reason about the best course of action. This involves selecting appropriate tools, determining the sequence of steps to reach a goal, and making decisions based on the task and context. In more advanced workflows, the agent may dynamically generate plans or select between different workflows or subtasks. This phase leverages the power of the underlying LLM and any structured prompting or instructions provided during initialization.

4. **Action execution:** During this phase, the agent executes its planned actions. This may involve calling tools such as calculators, web search functions, database queries, or even invoking other agents. Each action is performed in response to the reasoning output and can return intermediate results that guide the agent's next step. In Spring AI, this process is often orchestrated through workflows, advisors, or pattern-specific classes.

5. **Observation and feedback:** After executing an action, the agent observes the outcome and incorporates that result into its ongoing reasoning. If the task is not yet complete, the agent may use the new information to adjust its plan, retry a step, or choose a different tool. This feedback loop allows the agent to iterate intelligently, improving the accuracy and completeness of its response. In evaluation-driven workflows, this is where agents may self-correct or optimize their results.

6. **Response generation:** Once the agent has gathered enough information and completed all necessary steps, it synthesizes the final response. This is typically returned as natural language output, structured data, or a combination of both. The response is informed not only by the original input but also by intermediate tool results, memory references, and any refinements made during the observation-feedback loop.

7. **Memory update (optional):** If the agent is configured with persistent memory, it may store relevant data from the interaction—such as the user's query, contextual embeddings, or results of executed tools. This enables continuity across sessions and allows the agent to personalize future interactions or maintain state over time. Memory updates ensure that the agent becomes more knowledgeable and context-aware with repeated use.

8. **Termination or continuation:** The agent either concludes the interaction or waits for the next input. In stateless applications, this may mark the end of the agent's lifecycle. However, in multistep or session-based systems, the agent may retain context and continue participating in the ongoing dialogue or task. The ability to persist state and remain "alive" between steps is key for building conversational or multi-agent applications.

Spring AI's Implementation Advantages

Spring AI provides a robust framework for implementing advanced AI workflows, offering several key advantages that align with Anthropic's recommendations for effective AI system design. The following are some of the notable benefits.

Model Portability

One of the significant advantages of Spring AI is its *model portability*, which allows developers to easily switch between different AI models through dependencies. This flexibility enables users to integrate multiple LLM providers seamlessly, ensuring that the system remains adaptable to changes in underlying models or requirements.

Here's an example:

```
<dependency>
    <groupId>org.springframework.ai</groupId>
    <artifactId>spring-ai-openai-spring-boot-starter</artifactId>
</dependency>
```

This straightforward dependency configuration ensures that developers can easily swap models and extend their applications without major disruptions.

Structured Output

Spring AI provides *structured output* by leveraging type-safe handling of responses from LLMs. This ensures that responses from the model are well-organized and easy to process, reducing the complexity of managing raw, unstructured data. Type-safe handling ensures that the system can be confident in the integrity of the output, which is particularly important for maintaining reliability across different tasks and workflows.

Here's an example:

```
EvaluationResponse response = chatClient.prompt(prompt)
        .call()
        .entity(EvaluationResponse.class);
```

By using structured output, developers can confidently parse and manipulate responses, improving both development speed and system reliability.

Consistent API

Spring AI ensures that developers have a consistent API across various LLM providers. This uniformity simplifies the integration of different models and tools into an AI system, reducing the learning curve and improving the maintainability of the system. Additionally, Spring AI includes built-in error handling and retry mechanisms, ensuring that the system can recover from transient issues gracefully. Flexible prompt management further enhances the user experience, making it easier to manage and adjust prompts based on dynamic conditions.

Best Practices and Recommendations

Based on Anthropic's research and Spring AI's implementations, the following best practices and recommendations are key to building effective LLM-based systems.

Start Simple

It's essential to start simple when designing AI workflows. Begin with basic, well-defined workflows before introducing complexity. By using the simplest pattern that meets your requirements, you can reduce the chances of errors and ensure the system remains manageable. Complexity should be added only when absolutely necessary, allowing for scalable and maintainable solutions.

Design for Reliability

Reliability is crucial for any enterprise AI application. It is recommended to:

- Implement clear error handling to catch and resolve issues effectively.
- Use type-safe responses wherever possible to avoid runtime errors and ensure that the system can handle various LLM outputs securely.
- Build validation into each step of the workflow to verify that the system is operating as expected at every stage of processing.

Consider Trade-Offs

When building AI systems, there are often trade-offs between various factors:

- **Latency vs. accuracy**: Consider whether the system can tolerate some delay in exchange for higher accuracy or if real-time processing is required.
- **Parallel processing**: Evaluate when parallel processing will enhance performance, especially in cases where tasks can be divided into independent subtasks.

- **Fixed workflows vs. dynamic agents**: Choose between using predefined workflows or more flexible, dynamic agents based on the complexity and requirements of the task at hand.

By following these best practices and leveraging the strengths of Spring AI, developers can build scalable, maintainable, and effective AI systems that meet the needs of modern enterprises.

Advisors API in Spring AI

In Spring AI, advisors are modular components that intercept and optionally transform chat-completion requests and responses, enabling developers to enhance AI applications with reusable, maintainable logic. Functioning in a chain, each advisor can adjust the user's input, format the model's output, share data through a common context, or even block requests when necessary. They are used for tasks such as conversation memory management, retrieval-augmented generation (RAG), and safeguarding against inappropriate content. Spring AI supports both nonstreaming advisors, which process complete responses, and streaming advisors, which handle data in chunks for real-time scenarios. Developers can also implement custom advisors to embed domain-specific behavior—such as logging, input rewriting, or reasoning improvements—without altering core application code. Execution order is determined by a configurable priority system, allowing fine-grained control over how transformations are applied across the request-response lifecycle. We will not be going deep with any explanations or code in this section, as exploring and experimenting with advisors is left to the reader and is outside the scope of this chapter.

Conclusion

In conclusion, the use of agents powered by LLMs offers a transformative approach to building AI applications that can adapt, reason, and interact with complex systems. The patterns and workflows outlined in this chapter—such as chain workflows, parallelization, and orchestration—demonstrate how agents can be effectively integrated into enterprise applications using Spring AI. Through the flexible and powerful Advisors API, developers can refine and augment the behaviors of their agents, enhancing their performance and reliability.

Spring AI's design emphasizes simplicity and composability, enabling developers to focus on solving real-world problems without being burdened by overly complex frameworks. By starting with basic workflows and gradually adding sophistication as needed, teams can build scalable and reliable AI systems that deliver measurable value.

As AI continues to evolve, the patterns and techniques explored here lay the foundation for more advanced and intelligent agents. By combining these principles with emerging AI technologies, developers can unlock the full potential of agentic systems, driving innovation and efficiency in AI applications. The journey into the world of intelligent agents is just beginning, and with Spring AI, the possibilities are endless.

Let us now move on to transformers.

CHAPTER 12

Quarkus + LangChain4j: Lightning-Fast Gen AI

The goal of this chapter is to explore and build generative AI (Gen AI) applications using the Quarkus Java framework through LangChain4j integration.

Introduction

In this chapter, you'll harness the power of large language models (LLMs) within the battle-tested, cloud-native framework of Quarkus. In this chapter, the goal is to guide you through the end-to-end process of building generative AI services in Java by leveraging LangChain4j's tight integration with Quarkus. You'll see how to register AI services, craft precise prompts, and wire in external tools—all with minimal boilerplate and maximum performance.

You will begin by seeing how to integrate LangChain4j into a Quarkus project and seeing how simple annotations and dependency injection can transform your REST endpoints into intelligent AI-powered handlers. Next, you'll dive into prompt engineering: learning how system and user messages—defined right in your Java interfaces—give you fine-grained control over model behavior and structured JSON outputs. After that, you'll see how to enrich your AI workflows with custom tools, such as a Panache-driven customer repository, so that your LLM can fetch live data at inference time.

Building on these foundations, you'll explore chat memory in Quarkus, enabling stateful conversations that persist context across calls. Then, you'll introduce the retrieval-augmented generation (RAG) pattern: ingesting your product catalog into a Redis-backed embedding store and combining semantic search with LLM prompting ground responses in real-world data. Throughout, you'll keep performance

S. K. Sahu, *Generative AI-Driven Application Development with Java*,
https://doi.org/10.1007/979-8-8688-1609-3_12

and scalability top of mind, showing how Quarkus's build-time bootstrapping and lightweight runtime make it the ideal host for high-throughput AI microservices.

By the end of this chapter, you'll have a complete, production-ready blueprint for crafting Java applications that seamlessly blend Quarkus's speed with the creativity of LLMs—empowering you to deliver intelligent, responsive services in the Java ecosystem.

Integration of LangChain4j in Quarkus

LLMs are reshaping software development by transforming how you interact with users and encode business logic. While LLMs have existed for years, their accessibility and power skyrocketed once OpenAI opened up the ChatGPT APIs. Today you'll find hundreds of models on Hugging Face supported by major tech players each offering their own flavors.

The Quarkus team in collaboration with Dmytro Liubarskyi, and the LangChain4j maintainers built a Quarkus extension that brings LLM capabilities natively into your JVM applications in Quarkus. Under the hood, it leverages LangChain4j, a pure-Java re-implementation of the popular LangChain framework, to provide:

- Declarative prompts via `@SystemMessage` and `@UserMessage` annotations
- Zero-boilerplate LLM clients for OpenAI, Hugging Face, Ollama, Jlama, etc.
- Tool invocation—annotate any CDI bean method with `@Tool` for model-driven lookups
- Chat memory and RAG support via Redis or in-memory stores

With this extension, you can instantly power your Quarkus REST endpoints with AI. For example, an application built on Quarkus LangChain4j can:

- Automatically categorize or classify documents
- Extract structured and unstructured data from diverse sources
- Drive chatbots that maintain conversational context
- Generate personalized text—emails, reports, summaries—on demand

To start on your journey on building a generative AI application using Quarkus, let's visit `https://code.quarkus.io/` and select the `quarkus-langchain4j-openai` package, as shown in Figure 12-1.

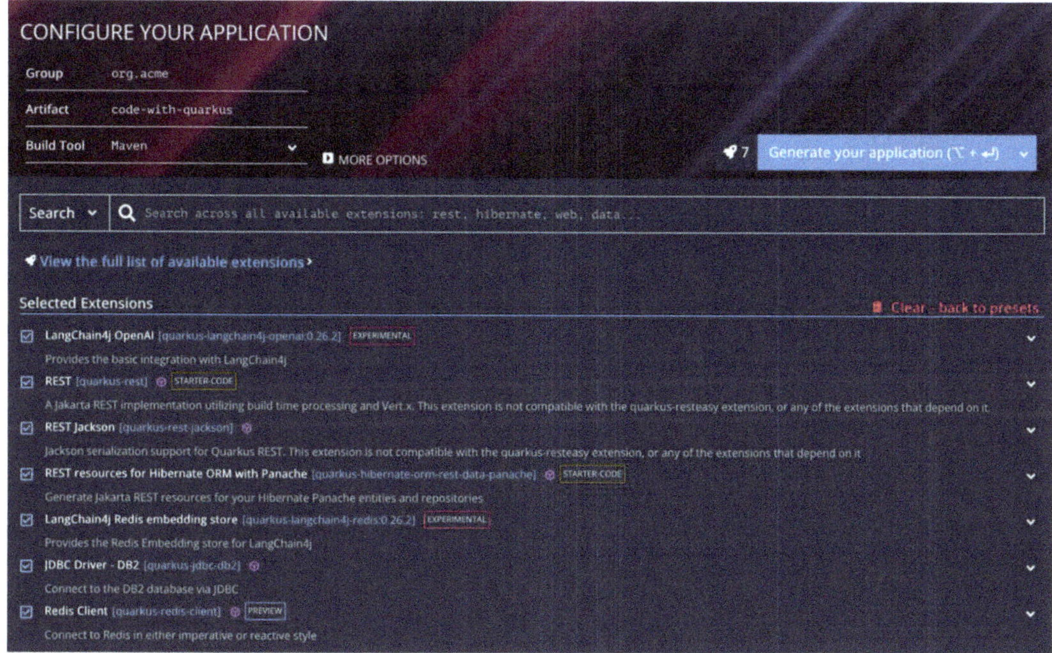

Figure 12-1. *Quarkus-langchain4j-openai package in Quarkus Dependency UI*

In addition, let's add a few more dependencies needed for the application:

- **Quarkus-rest:** For restful endpoints.
- **Quarkus-langchain4j-openai:** To integrate langchain4j with OpenAI
- **Quarkus-rest-jackson:** For JSON encoding purposes
- **Quarkus-hibernate-orm-rest-data-panache:** ORM layer for querying relational database
- **Quarkus-langchain4j-redis:** Using Redis as a vector store
- **Quarkus-jdbc-db2:** db2 as a relational database
- **Quarkus-redis-client:** Redis client connection

Please do not get overwhelmed with the package list. You will start slowly and learn the ropes of Gen AI in Quarkus. Download the zip archive and decompress it and load it in your favorite IDE of choice. If you are using IntelliJ IDE, it comes preloaded with the Quarkus plugin. In VS Code, you can download the official Quarkus extension from Red Hat, which is helpful to start building and running Quarkus applications. The following is the list of dependencies in your `pom.xml` file:

File: pom.xml

```
<dependency>
    <groupId>io.quarkus</groupId>
    <artifactId>quarkus-rest</artifactId>
</dependency>
<dependency>
    <groupId>io.quarkiverse.langchain4j</groupId>
    <artifactId>quarkus-langchain4j-openai</artifactId>
    <version>0.26.2</version>
</dependency>
<dependency>
    <groupId>io.quarkus</groupId>
    <artifactId>quarkus-rest-jackson</artifactId>
</dependency>
<dependency>
    <groupId>io.quarkus</groupId>
    <artifactId>quarkus-hibernate-orm-rest-data-panache</artifactId>
</dependency>
<dependency>
    <groupId>io.quarkiverse.langchain4j</groupId>
    <artifactId>quarkus-langchain4j-redis</artifactId>
    <version>0.26.2</version>
</dependency>
<dependency>
    <groupId>io.quarkus</groupId>
    <artifactId>quarkus-jdbc-db2</artifactId>
</dependency>
```

```
<dependency>
    <groupId>io.quarkus</groupId>
    <artifactId>quarkus-redis-client</artifactId>
</dependency>
```

The next step is to add a few configuration properties to your `application.properties` file to make it ready for integrating LangChain4j and OpenAI with Quarkus.

Log requests and log responses allow you to log any requests happening through LangChain4j in the terminal, interface which is helpful for debugging while you are getting started. The `openai.chat-model.temperature` package sets the temperature for all the OpenAI requests. The `Openai.api-key` package takes an OpenAI API key, and `redis.dimension` takes in the value of the embeddings dimension for vectors it will be storing, which is 1536 for OpenAI-based embedding model.

File: src/main/resources/application.properties

```
quarkus.langchain4j.openai.chat-model.temperature=0.3
quarkus.langchain4j.timeout=120s

quarkus.langchain4j.log-requests=true
quarkus.langchain4j.log-responses=true
quarkus.langchain4j.openai.api-key=YOUR-OPENAI-API-KEY
quarkus.langchain4j.redis.dimension=1536
```

Once these steps are done, Quarkus will bootstrap your LLM client, wire in any tools or memory providers you declare, and expose your interface methods as AI-powered handlers—letting you focus on prompts and business logic instead of connection plumbing.

Prompt Engineering in Quarkus

In this section, you'll see how Quarkus and LangChain4j let you externalize your LLM prompts directly in Java interfaces and annotations—turning your business logic into clean, declarative AI workflows. Say you work at an ecommerce company and want to categorize customer comment feedback about your products. Figure 12-2 illustrates this flow.

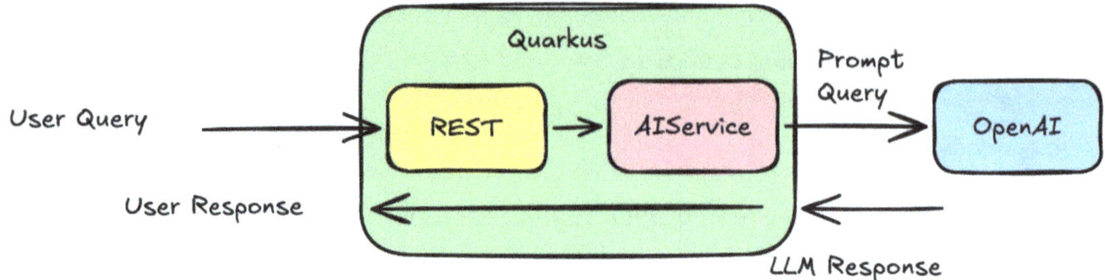

Figure 12-2. *Prompt engineering flow in Quarkus with LangChain4j extension*

After installing the extension, the next step is to define your desired LLM behavior. The Quarkus LangChain4j extension helps you describe these interactions declaratively—much like the Quarkus REST client does for HTTP calls. You represent the conversation through an interface annotated with `@RegisterAiService`:

```
@RegisterAiService
public interface SupportService {
    // methods
}
```

Your application would then be able to use the LLM by injecting the `SupportService` interface and calling the respective methods defined.

Crafting Prompts with Annotations

Referring to methods, they are the core engine that drives all the functionality. You will describe what you want the LLM to do using natural language. First, you start with `@SystemMessage` to define the role and scope. Then, you can use `@UserMessage` to describe the functionality at hand.

File: src/main/java/io/demo/langchain4j/sample/service/SupportService.java

```
package io.demo.langchain4j.sample.service;

import dev.langchain4j.service.SystemMessage;
import dev.langchain4j.service.UserMessage;
import io.quarkiverse.langchain4j.RegisterAiService;

// Marks this interface as an AI service: Quarkus will create an
// implementation that orchestrates calls to your chosen LLM provider.
```

```
@RegisterAiService
public interface SupportService {

    // Sets the overall "persona" and task context for the LLM (its
   // system role). It's sent once at the start of each session.
   @SystemMessage("""
       You are working for an ecommerce company, processing
       comments about their products and providing additional
       information as requested by the customer. Categorize
       comments into positive, neutral and negative ones,
       responding with a JSON format document.
""")

    // Defines the actual prompt template. You can:
   // Embed examples (few-shot prompting) to show the model the
   // expected format.
   // Use placeholders ({comment}, {customerId}) to inject runtime
   // data.
   // Specify output constraints (here: "Respond with a JSON
   // document…").
   @UserMessage("""
        Your task is to process the comment delimited by ---.
        Apply sentiment analysis to the comment to determine
        if it is positive, neutral or negative.

        For example:
        - `I love the user experience in your app, you are my
           best place to be!` is a 'POSITIVE'
           comment
        - `J'adore ton application` is a 'POSITIVE' comment
        - `I don't want to use your app, it's too slow!` is a
          'NEGATIVE' comment

         Respond with a JSON format document containing:
         - the 'rating' key set to 'POSITIVE' if the comment
           is positive, 'NEUTRAL' if the comment is neutral,
           'NEGATIVE' otherwise
         - the 'message' key set to a message thanking or
```

```
            apologizing to the customer.
            ---
            {comment}
            ---
    """)
     // The single String comment parameter is bound to {comment} in
    // the template. (Later, we can overload or extend this to accept
    // a long customerId for tool integration.)
    SupportComment categorize(String comment);
}
```

And that's it—you've completed the LLM interaction setup. These directives are based on a set of guiding principles to steer the model's responses.

Exposing an AI-Powered REST Endpoint

To invoke the LLM in your application code, simply inject the `SupportService` and invoke its `categorize` method:

File: src/main/java/io/demo/langchain4j/sample/controller/CommentResource.java

```
package io.demo.langchain4j.sample.controller;

import io.demo.langchain4j.sample.service.Comment;
import io.demo.langchain4j.sample.service.SupportService;
import io.demo.langchain4j.sample.service.CommentReview;
import jakarta.inject.Inject;
import jakarta.ws.rs.POST;
import jakarta.ws.rs.Path;

// Defines a standard JAX-RS endpoint that accepts a JSON body mapped
// to our Comment record.
@Path("/comment")
public class CommentResource {

    // Quarkus will automatically provide an implementation of the
    // SupportService interface—backed by LangChain4J—so you don't have
    // to manually wire any HTTP clients or JSON parsers.
```

```
    @Inject
    SupportService categorize;

    @POST
    public CommentReview categorize(Comment comment) {
        return categorize.categorize(comment.comment());
    }
}
```

Domain Types for Input and Output

File: src/main/java/io/demo/langchain4j/sample/service/Rating.java

```
package io.demo.langchain4j.sample.service;

public enum Rating {
    POSITIVE,
    NEUTRAL,
    NEGATIVE;
}
```

File: src/main/java/io/demo/langchain4j/sample/service/Comment.java

```
package io.demo.langchain4j.sample.service;
import io.quarkus.runtime.annotations.RegisterForReflection;

// Define the Comment record as a top-level public record
// A simple record that carries the raw comment text.
@RegisterForReflection
public record Comment(String comment) {}
```

File: src/main/java/io/demo/langchain4j/sample/service/CommentReview.java

```
package io.demo.langchain4j.sample.service;

import com.fasterxml.jackson.annotation.JsonCreator;

// Holds the model's structured response:
// rating: a POSITIVE, NEUTRAL or NEGATIVE enum
// message: a polite reply to the customer
public record CommentReview(Rating rating, String message) {
   // Ensures Jackson can deserialize the JSON the LLM returns into
```

```
    // our record.
    @JsonCreator
     public CommentReview {}
}
```

This is all that needs to be set up to get you up and running. You will now boot up your application and see it in action by invoking a `curl`-based POST request.

```
./mvnw compile quarkus:dev
```

Output:

```
2025-04-23 05:13:00,589 INFO  [io.dem.lan.sam.uti.ApplicationStartup]
(Quarkus Main Thread) Application starting...
2025-04-23 05:13:00,754 INFO  [io.quarkus] (Quarkus Main Thread) code-
with-quarkus 1.0.0-SNAPSHOT on JVM (powered by Quarkus 3.21.3) started in
149.566s. Listening on: http://localhost:8080
2025-04-23 05:13:00,756 INFO  [io.quarkus] (Quarkus Main Thread) Profile
dev activated. Live Coding activated.
2025-04-23 05:13:00,757 INFO  [io.quarkus] (Quarkus Main Thread)
Installed features: [agroal, cdi, hibernate-orm, hibernate-orm-panache,
hibernate-orm-rest-data-panache, jdbc-db2, langchain4j, langchain4j-
openai, langchain4j-redis, narayana-jta, qute, redis-client, rest, rest-
client, rest-client-jackson, rest-jackson, rest-links, smallrye-context-
propagation, vertx]
```

Quarkus manages creating redis, db2, and other dependent resources for you by using Docker containers. This can be verified by running the following command:

```
docker ps
```

Output:

```
CONTAINER ID   IMAGE
COMMAND                       CREATED            STATUS             POR
TS                                                                      NAMES
e95db0bac3d2   icr.io/db2_community/db2:12.1.0.0    "/var/db2_setup/
lib/…"   5 minutes ago   Up 5 minutes   22/tcp, 55000/tcp, 60006-60007/tcp,
0.0.0.0:32809->50000/tcp, :::32809->50000/tcp   hardcore_dewdney
```

```
ad2131dd07f1   redis/redis-stack:latest            "/entrypoint.
sh"        5 minutes ago   Up 5 minutes   8001/tcp, 0.0.0.0:32808->6379/
tcp, :::32808->6379/tcp                                fervent_mirzakhani
be4fefc05e1f   testcontainers/ryuk:0.11.0          "/bin/
ryuk"             5 minutes ago   Up 5 minutes   0.0.0.0:32807->8080/tcp,
:::32807->8080/tcp                                         testcontainers-
ryuk-25bb0431-c6a1-48e3-ada7-3ae0b809a24d
```

Let's invoke your POST rest endpoint with a `curl` request.

```
curl localhost:8080/comment --header 'Content
-Type: text/plain' --data 'This is a great product! I highly recommend it.'
```

Output:

```
{"rating":"POSITIVE","message":"Thank you for your kind words! We're
thrilled to hear you love our product."}
```

The application has been able to rightly determine the rating of your feedback. Also, since you have enabled the debugging logs for LangChain4j, you can see the following output in your system logs:

```
2025-04-23 05:19:31,539 INFO  [io.qua.lan.ope.com.OpenAiRestApi$OpenAiClien
tLogger] (vert.x-eventloop-thread-1) Request:
- method: POST
- url: https://api.openai.com/v1/chat/completions
- headers: [Accept: application/json], [Authorization: Be...kA], [Content-
Type: application/json], [User-Agent: langchain4j-openai], [content-
length: 1487]
- body: {
  "model" : "gpt-4o-mini",
  "messages" : [ {
    "role" : "system",
    "content" : "       You are working for an ecommerce company,
    processing comments about\n       their products and providing
    additional information as requested\n      \tby the customer.
    Categorize comments into positive, neutral and negative ones,\
    nresponding with a JSON format document.\n"
```

```
  }, {
    "role" : "user",
    "content" : "        Your task is to process the comment delimited
    by ---.\n        Apply sentiment analysis to the comment to
    determine\n        if it is positive, neutral or negative.\n\n
            For example:\n        - `I love the user experience in your
    app, you are my best place to be!` is a 'POSITIVE' comment\n        -
    `J'adore ton application` is a 'POSITIVE' comment\n        - `I don't
    want to use your app, it's too slow!` is a 'NEGATIVE' comment\n\n
            Respond with a JSON format containing:\n        - the 'rating'
    key set to 'POSITIVE' if the comment is\n        positive, 'NEUTRAL' if
    the comment is neutral, 'NEGATIVE' otherwise\n        - the 'message'
    key set to a message thanking or apologizing\n        to the customer.
    These messages must be polite.\n\n        ---\n        This is a
    great product! I highly recommend it.\n        ---\n\nYou must answer
    strictly in the following JSON format: {\n\"rating\": (type: enum,
    must be one of [POSITIVE, NEUTRAL, NEGATIVE]),\n\"message\": (type:
    string)\n}"
  } ],
  "temperature" : 0.5,
  "top_p" : 1.0,
  "presence_penalty" : 0.0,
  "frequency_penalty" : 0.0
}

2025-04-23 05:19:32,521 INFO  [io.qua.lan.ope.com.OpenAiRestApi$OpenAiClien
tLogger] (vert.x-eventloop-thread-1) Response:
- status code: 200
- headers: [Date: Wed, 23 Apr 2025 05:19:32 GMT], [Content-Type:
application/json], [Transfer-Encoding: chunked], [Connection: keep-
alive], [access-control-expose-headers: X-Request-ID], [openai-
organization: user-eldk0kvytvetb2vdgo2y3nvr], [openai-processing-ms:
502], [openai-version: 2020-10-01], [x-ratelimit-limit-requests: 10000],
[x-ratelimit-limit-tokens: 200000], [x-ratelimit-remaining-requests:
9999], [x-ratelimit-remaining-tokens: 199692], [x-ratelimit-reset-
requests: 8.64s], [x-ratelimit-reset-tokens: 92ms], [x-request-id:
```

```
req_da5438d76e2db842f75a62abd6e50cf3], [strict-transport-security: max-
age=31536000; includeSubDomains; preload], [cf-cache-status: DYNAMIC],
[Set-Cookie: __...ne], [X-Content-Type-Options: nosniff], [Set-Cookie:
_c...ne], [Server: cloudflare], [CF-RAY: 934ae80e289c2be9-FRA], [alt-svc:
h3=":443"; ma=86400]
- body: {
  "id": "chatcmpl-BPMo8L36EnE9muR6OUXOvI48GV19u",
  "object": "chat.completion",
  "created": 1745385572,
  "model": "gpt-4o-mini-2024-07-18",
  "choices": [
    {
      "index": 0,
      "message": {
        "role": "assistant",
        "content": "{\n  \"rating\": \"POSITIVE\",\n  \"message\": \"Thank
        you for your kind words! We're thrilled to hear you love our
        product.\"\n}",
        "refusal": null,
        "annotations": []
      },
      "logprobs": null,
      "finish_reason": "stop"
    }
  ],
  "usage": {
    "prompt_tokens": 281,
    "completion_tokens": 32,
    "total_tokens": 313,
    "prompt_tokens_details": {
      "cached_tokens": 0,
      "audio_tokens": 0
    },
    "completion_tokens_details": {
      "reasoning_tokens": 0,
      "audio_tokens": 0,
```

```
      "accepted_prediction_tokens": 0,
      "rejected_prediction_tokens": 0
    }
  },
  "service_tier": "default",
  "system_fingerprint": "fp_dbaca60df0"
}
```


Here you can see the prompt context passed in to the API request to OpenAI and the response from OpenAI. This is handy to see what and how the Quarkus/LangChain4j application is interacting with OpenAI APIs.

So, what happens at runtime? Let's lay it down in a few steps:

1. **Invocation**: When a client calls `POST /comment`, Quarkus invokes `categorize.categorize(...)`.
2. **Prompt assembly**: LangChain4j concatenates the system message and the filled-in user message, wrapping the comment text in the `---` delimiters.
3. **LLM call**: The extension sends the prompt to your configured provider (OpenAI, Hugging Face, etc.) over HTTP.
4. **JSON parse**: The raw model output is parsed back into a `CommentReview` instance via Jackson.
5. **Response**: You return a fully typed Java record—no manual JSON handling required.

By externalizing your prompts in annotations, you keep your Java code concise and declarative. You get full type-safety on inputs and outputs, easy reuse of prompt templates, and the ability to version control your prompt logic alongside the rest of your application. This is the essence of *prompt engineering* in Quarkus: building AI behavior directly into your codebase in a transparent, maintainable way.

Using Tools in Quarkus

That earlier example is fairly basic. In a production scenario, you'll want to enrich the LLM's capabilities with external tools and document stores. The `@RegisterAiService` annotation lets you specify exactly which tools and stores to integrate. When your AI service needs live, domain-specific data—like customer names, inventory levels, or product details—you can expose any CDI bean method as a "tool" for the model to call. LangChain4j will handle wiring, invocation, and result injection for you.

Tools are methods that the LLM can call. To define a tool, annotate a bean method with `@Tool`.

In the previous example, you leverage the Panache repository pattern to interact with the database. We've marked a specific bean method with `@Tool` to fetch a customer's details, so whenever the LLM needs that information, Quarkus invokes the method and returns the result. In following sections, you will integrate information from the database that can be invoked and fetched using the Tools utility, as displayed in Figure 12-3.

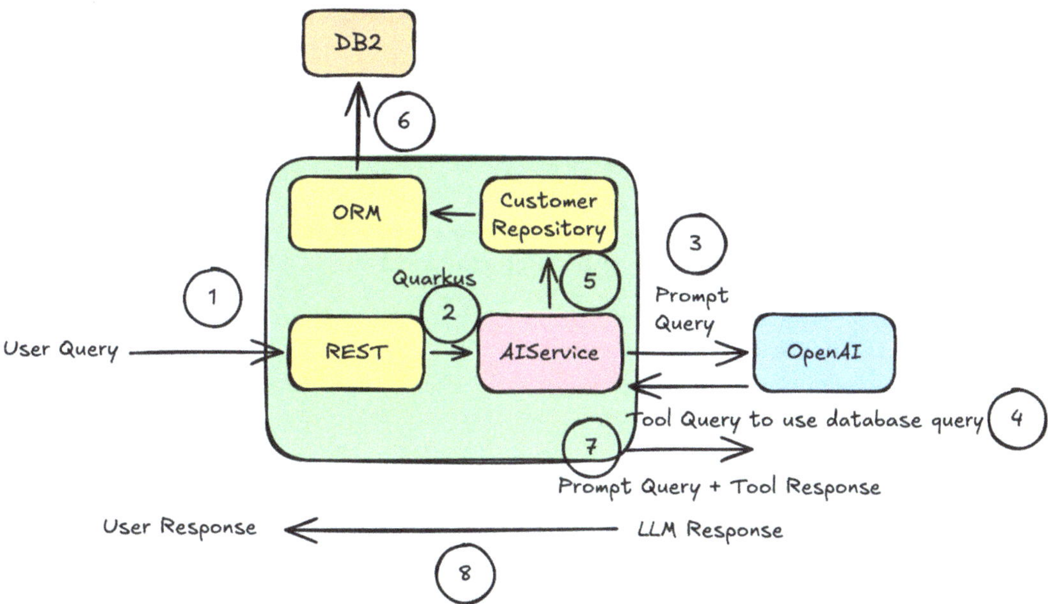

Figure 12-3. *Quarkus LangChain4j flows with tools integration*

Since you don't want to expose every operation to the model, you also have to enumerate the permitted tools within the `@RegisterAiService` annotation.

You will start by creating the `Customer Entity` class, which represents the database table for the customer data. It extends `PanacheEntity` for simplified JPA functionality with Quarkus. The entity contains some basic fields like name, address, and a unique primary key called id.

File: src/main/java/io/demo/langchain4j/sample/dto/Customer.java

```
package io.demo.langchain4j.sample.dto;

import io.quarkus.hibernate.orm.panache.PanacheEntity;
import jakarta.persistence.Entity;

// 1. Customer Entity
//    - Represents the database table for customer data.
//    - Uses PanacheEntity for simplified JPA with Quarkus.
@Entity
public class Customer extends PanacheEntity {

    public String name;
    public String address;

    // Add constructors, getters, and setters as needed.
   public Customer() {
    }

    public Customer(String name, String address) {
        this.name = name;
        this.address = address;
    }

    public Long getId() {
        return id;
    }

    public void setId(Long id) {
        this.id = id;
    }

    public String getName() {
        return name;
    }
```

```
    public void setName(String name) {
        this.name = name;
    }

    public String getAddress() {
        return address;
    }

    public void setAddress(String address) {
        this.address = address;
    }
}
```

Now you will need to create a `CustomerRepository` class that extends the `PanacheRepository` to handle basic CRUD activities along with custom-defined methods. In your case, you have additionally defined a method named `getCustomerDetail` that takes an `id` parameter as an argument. This method has been annotated with the `@Tool` annotation to indicate to Quarkus and LangChain4j that this method is available as a tool. The `@Tool` annotation takes as an argument the description of the tool. This is important and helps the LLM determine whether this tool can be used for any of the tasks that might be relevant to the customer's request.

File: src/main/java/io/demo/langchain4j/sample/dto/CustomerRepository.java

```
package io.demo.langchain4j.sample.dto;

import dev.langchain4j.agent.tool.Tool;
import io.quarkus.hibernate.orm.panache.PanacheRepository;
import jakarta.enterprise.context.ApplicationScoped;

// Extends PanacheRepository to handle CRUD.
@ApplicationScoped
public class CustomerRepository implements PanacheRepository<Customer> {

     // The @Tool annotation on getCustomerDetail makes this method
    // callable by the model. The string description helps the model
    // choose the right tool.
    @Tool("get the customer detail for the given customerId")
```

```
    public String getCustomerDetail(long id) {
       // Implements a custom method to get the customer detail by ID.
       return find("id", id).firstResult().name;
    }
}
```

You have a tool now available that fetches customer names from the database based on `id`. Let's provide this tool to the `@RegisterAiService`. In the following code change, you can observe that we are making changes to the annotation `@RegisterAiService` by providing it with a new parameter called `tools` and assigning the `CustomerRepository.class` class. Additionally, you change the system prompt to indicate to the LLM that in its greeting it needs to include the customer's name if it has it available. This will guide it to search for the customer's details using the tool box. This is also made explicit in the user prompt by instructing the LLM to find the customer name if there is an `id` available to it. Finally, there is an additional argument field called `customerId` available to the prompt template that will be provided by the controller layer.

File: src/main/java/io/demo/langchain4j/sample/service/SupportService.java

```
package io.demo.langchain4j.sample.service;

import dev.langchain4j.service.SystemMessage;
import dev.langchain4j.service.UserMessage;
import io.demo.langchain4j.sample.dto.CustomerRepository;
import io.quarkiverse.langchain4j.RegisterAiService;

@RegisterAiService(
        // Declares that CustomerRepository is available as a tool.
        LangChain4J will scan its
       // @Tool methods and register them with the LLM client.
       tools = {CustomerRepository.class}
)
public interface SupportService {
    @SystemMessage("""
       You are working for an ecommerce company, processing comments
       about their products and providing additional information as
       requested by the customer. Categorise comments into positive
```

```
        neutral and negative ones, responding with a JSON format
        document that includes a personalized greeting if you have the
        customer's details.
    """)
     @UserMessage("""
            Your task is to process the comment delimited by ---.
            Apply sentiment analysis to the comment to determine
            if it is positive, neutral or negative.

            For example:
            - `I love the user experience in your app, you are my best place
              to be!` is a 'POSITIVE'
              comment
            - `J'adore ton application` is a 'POSITIVE' comment
            - `I don’t want to use your app, it’s too slow!` is a 'NEGATIVE'
              comment

            Respond with a JSON format containing:
            - the 'rating' key set to 'POSITIVE' if the comment is
            positive, 'NEUTRAL' if the comment is neutral, 'NEGATIVE'
            otherwise
            - the 'message' key set to a message thanking or
            apologizing to the customer. These messages must be polite
            . Find the customer name if
            there is an id provided and use it to greet the customer.
            ---
            {comment}
            {customerId}
            ---
    """)
     CommentReview categorize(String comment, long customerId);
}
```

When working with RESTful APIs you know you always have a session or contextual user data that helps to identify each user request uniquely. To keep it simple, we have chosen to hard-code the id value to 1 here. This record will be inserted when the application boots up.

File: src/main/java/io/demo/langchain4j/sample/controller/CommentResource.java

```
package io.demo.langchain4j.sample.controller;

import io.demo.langchain4j.sample.service.Comment;
import io.demo.langchain4j.sample.service.SupportService;
import io.demo.langchain4j.sample.service.CommentReview;
import jakarta.inject.Inject;
import jakarta.ws.rs.POST;
import jakarta.ws.rs.Path;

@Path("/comment")
public class CommentResource {

    @Inject
    SupportService categorize;
    @POST
    public CommentReview categorize(Comment comment) {
        // Customer id is hard coded here for simplicity sake.
       return categorize.categorize(comment.comment(), 1);
    }
}
```

The customer id 1 is not available to you yet. Yet again for simplicity, you will insert a database record of a customer when the application boots up through the use of a startup event.

File: src/main/java/io/demo/langchain4j/sample/utils/ApplicationStartup.java

```
package io.demo.langchain4j.sample.utils;

import dev.langchain4j.data.document.Document;
import io.demo.langchain4j.sample.dto.Customer;
import io.quarkus.runtime.StartupEvent;
import jakarta.enterprise.context.ApplicationScoped;
import jakarta.enterprise.event.Observes;
import jakarta.inject.Inject;
import jakarta.transaction.Transactional;
```

```
import org.slf4j.Logger;
import org.slf4j.LoggerFactory;

import java.io.File;
import java.io.IOException;
import java.net.URL;
import java.util.ArrayList;
import java.util.List;

@ApplicationScoped
public class ApplicationStartup {

    private static final Logger LOGGER = LoggerFactory.
    getLogger(ApplicationStartup.class);

    @Transactional
    void onStartup(@Observes StartupEvent event) {
        LOGGER.info("Application starting...");

        // 1. Insert a customer into the database
       insertInitialCustomer();
    }

    private void insertInitialCustomer() {
        LOGGER.info("Inserting initial customer...");
        // Inserts a sample customer so that invoking
       // getCustomerDetail(1) returns "John Doe."
       Customer customer = new Customer("John Doe", "123 Main St");
        customer.persist();
        LOGGER.info("Initial customer inserted with ID: {}", customer.id);
    }
}
```

Let's boot up your application and see the system logs for it. You might see some initial error logs where the system is trying to drop the database and tables that are not present already. Please ignore them for the time being.

```
2025-04-23 09:16:09,277 INFO  [io.qua.dat.dep.dev.
DevServicesDatasourceProcessor] (build-49) Dev Services for default
datasource (db2) started - container ID is 165c6f084e07
2025-04-23 09:16:09,281 INFO  [io.qua.hib.orm.dep.dev.
HibernateOrmDevServicesProcessor] (build-9) Setting quarkus.hibernate-orm.
database.generation=drop-and-create to initialize Dev Services managed
database

2025-04-23 09:16:13,675 INFO  [io.dem.lan.sam.uti.ApplicationStartup]
(Quarkus Main Thread) Application starting...
2025-04-23 09:16:13,675 INFO  [io.dem.lan.sam.uti.ApplicationStartup]
(Quarkus Main Thread) Inserting initial customer...
2025-04-23 09:16:13,832 INFO  [io.dem.lan.sam.uti.ApplicationStartup]
(Quarkus Main Thread) Initial customer inserted with ID: 1
```

Let's now test the `curl` POST request and see the output from the application. In the following code, you can see your customer name in the output, so the LLM has been able to successfully request that the tool fetch the customer name and then use that information to augment its response to make the message more personal for your customers.

```
curl localhost:8080/comment --header 'Content
-Type: text/plain' --data 'This is a great product! I highly recommend it.'
```

Output:

```
{"rating":"POSITIVE","message":"Thank you for your kind words, John Doe!
We're thrilled to hear you love our product!"}
```

Also, let's see what the system is up to during this time. In the following code, you can see in its first request to OpenAI the prompt is enriched, and the tooling list now contains your database request feature.

```
2025-04-23 09:18:14,506 INFO  [io.qua.lan.ope.com.OpenAiRestApi$OpenAiClien
tLogger] (vert.x-eventloop-thread-1) Request:
- method: POST
- url: https://api.openai.com/v1/chat/completions
```

```
- headers: [Accept: application/json], [Authorization: Be...kA], [Content-
Type: application/json], [User-Agent: langchain4j-openai], [content-
length: 1959]
- body: {
  "model" : "gpt-4o-mini",
  "messages" : [ {
    "role" : "system",
    "content" : "       You are working for an ecommerce company,
processing comments about\n       their products. Categorize comments
into positive, neutral and negative ones,\nresponding with a JSON format
document that includes a\n       personalized greeting if you have the
customer's details.\n"
  }, {
    "role" : "user",
    "content" : "        Your task is to process the comment delimited
    by ---.\n        Apply sentiment analysis to the comment to
    determine\n        if it is positive, neutral or negative.\
    n\n        For example:\n        - `I love the user experience in your
    app, you are my best place to be!` is a 'POSITIVE' comment\n        -
    `J'adore ton application` is a 'POSITIVE' comment\n        - `I
    don't want to use your app, it's too slow!` is a 'NEGATIVE' comment\
    n\n        Respond with a JSON format containing:\n        - the
    'rating' key set to 'POSITIVE' if the comment is\n       positive,
    'NEUTRAL' if the comment is neutral, 'NEGATIVE' otherwise\n        -
    the 'message' key set to a message thanking or apologizing\n        to
    the customer. These messages must be polite. Find the customer
    name if there is an id provided\n        and use it to greet the
    customer.\n\n        ---\n        This is a great product! I highly
    recommend it.\n        1\n        ---\n\nYou must answer strictly in
    the following JSON format: {\n\"rating\": (type: enum, must be one of
    [POSITIVE, NEUTRAL, NEGATIVE]),\n\"message\": (type: string)\n}"
  } ],
  "temperature" : 0.5,
  "top_p" : 1.0,
  "presence_penalty" : 0.0,
  "frequency_penalty" : 0.0,
```

```
  "tools" : [ {
    "type" : "function",
    "function" : {
      "name" : "getCustomerDetail",
      "description" : "get the customer detail for the given customerId",
      "parameters" : {
        "type" : "object",
        "properties" : {
          "id" : {
            "type" : "integer"
          }
        },
        "required" : [ "id" ]
      }
    }
  } ]
}
```

In its response, OpenAI has suggested to use the tool `getCustomerDetail` with argument 1, which will then be invoked by `AIService`.

```
2025-04-23 09:18:15,478 INFO  [io.qua.lan.ope.com.OpenAiRestApi$OpenAiClien
tLogger] (vert.x-eventloop-thread-1) Response:
- status code: 200
- headers: [Date: Wed, 23 Apr 2025 09:18:15 GMT], [Content-Type:
application/json], [Transfer-Encoding: chunked], [Connection: keep-alive],
[access-control-expose-headers: X-Request-ID], [openai-organization:
user-eldk0kvytvetb2vdgo2y3nvr], [openai-processing-ms: 292], [openai-
version: 2020-10-01], [x-ratelimit-limit-requests: 10000], [x-ratelimit-
limit-tokens: 200000], [x-ratelimit-remaining-requests: 9999],
[x-ratelimit-remaining-tokens: 199667], [x-ratelimit-reset-requests:
8.64s], [x-ratelimit-reset-tokens: 99ms], [x-request-id: req_7951806f5d
7eaffea1f1a97fb3ad7bdc], [strict-transport-security: max-age=31536000;
includeSubDomains; preload], [cf-cache-status: DYNAMIC], [Set-Cookie: __...
ne], [X-Content-Type-Options: nosniff], [Set-Cookie: _c...ne], [Server:
cloudflare], [CF-RAY: 934c45bca9e95d63-FRA], [alt-svc: h3=":443"; ma=86400]
```

```
- body: {
  "id": "chatcmpl-BPQX9E9kxe5Xr5dEFJvtFElpWdNX4",
  "object": "chat.completion",
  "created": 1745399895,
  "model": "gpt-4o-mini-2024-07-18",
  "choices": [
    {
      "index": 0,
      "message": {
        "role": "assistant",
        "content": null,
        "tool_calls": [
          {
            "id": "call_s6MVpXkOTAOTvsjtpdBPdLAb",
            "type": "function",
            "function": {
              "name": "getCustomerDetail",
              "arguments": "{\"id\":1}"
            }
          }
        ],
        "refusal": null,
        "annotations": []
      },
      "logprobs": null,
      "finish_reason": "tool_calls"
    }
  ],
  "usage": {
    "prompt_tokens": 343,
    "completion_tokens": 16,
    "total_tokens": 359,
    "prompt_tokens_details": {
      "cached_tokens": 0,
      "audio_tokens": 0
    },
```

```
    "completion_tokens_details": {
      "reasoning_tokens": 0,
      "audio_tokens": 0,
      "accepted_prediction_tokens": 0,
      "rejected_prediction_tokens": 0
    }
  },
  "service_tier": "default",
  "system_fingerprint": "fp_0392822090"
}
```

The response from the tool call is then sent back to OpenAI with the augmented prompt to provide it with the customer name information, which it uses to create the final response for you.

```
2025-04-23 09:18:16,049 INFO  [io.qua.lan.ope.com.OpenAiRestApi$OpenAiClien
tLogger] (vert.x-eventloop-thread-1) Request:
- method: POST
- url: https://api.openai.com/v1/chat/completions
- headers: [Accept: application/json], [Authorization: Be...kA], [Content-
Type: application/json], [User-Agent: langchain4j-openai], [content-
length: 2309]
- body: {
  "model" : "gpt-4o-mini",
  "messages" : [ {
    "role" : "system",
    "content" : "        You are working for an ecommerce company,
    processing comments about\n        their products. Categorize comments
    into positive, neutral and negative ones,\nresponding with a JSON
    format document that includes a\n        personalized greeting if you
    have the customer's details.\n"
  }, {
    "role" : "user",
```

```
  "content" : "        Your task is to process the comment delimited
  by ---.\n        Apply sentiment analysis to the comment to
  determine\n        if it is positive, neutral or negative.\n\n        For
  example:\n        - `I love the user experience in your app, you are my
  best place to be!` is a 'POSITIVE' comment\n        - `J'adore
  ton application` is a 'POSITIVE' comment\n        - `I don't
  want to use your app, it's too slow!` is a 'NEGATIVE' comment\
  n\n        Respond with a JSON format containing:\n        - the
  'rating' key set to 'POSITIVE' if the comment is\n        positive,
  'NEUTRAL' if the comment is neutral, 'NEGATIVE' otherwise\n        -
  the 'message' key set to a message thanking or apologizing\n        to
  the customer. These messages must be polite. Find the customer
  name if there is an id provided\n        and use it to greet the
  customer.\n\n        ---\n        This is a great product! I highly
  recommend it.\n        1\n        ---\n\nYou must answer strictly in
  the following JSON format: {\n\"rating\": (type: enum, must be one of
  [POSITIVE, NEUTRAL, NEGATIVE]),\n\"message\": (type: string)\n}"
}, {
  "role" : "assistant",
  "tool_calls" : [ {
    "id" : "call_s6MVpXkOTAOTvsjtpdBPdLAb",
    "type" : "function",
    "function" : {
      "name" : "getCustomerDetail",
      "arguments" : "{\"id\":1}"
    }
  } ]
}, {
  "role" : "tool",
  "tool_call_id" : "call_s6MVpXkOTAOTvsjtpdBPdLAb",
  "content" : "\"John Doe\""
} ],
"temperature" : 0.5,
"top_p" : 1.0,
"presence_penalty" : 0.0,
"frequency_penalty" : 0.0,
```

```
  "tools" : [ {
    "type" : "function",
    "function" : {
      "name" : "getCustomerDetail",
      "description" : "get the customer detail for the given customerId",
      "parameters" : {
        "type" : "object",
        "properties" : {
          "id" : {
            "type" : "integer"
          }
        },
        "required" : [ "id" ]
      }
    }
  } ]
}

2025-04-23 09:18:17,196 INFO  [io.qua.lan.ope.com.OpenAiRestApi$OpenAiClien
tLogger] (vert.x-eventloop-thread-1) Response:
- status code: 200
- headers: [Date: Wed, 23 Apr 2025 09:18:17 GMT], [Content-Type:
application/json], [Transfer-Encoding: chunked], [Connection: keep-
alive], [access-control-expose-headers: X-Request-ID], [openai-
organization: user-eldk0kvytvetb2vdgo2y3nvr], [openai-processing-ms:
898], [openai-version: 2020-10-01], [x-ratelimit-limit-requests: 10000],
[x-ratelimit-limit-tokens: 200000], [x-ratelimit-remaining-requests:
9998], [x-ratelimit-remaining-tokens: 199662], [x-ratelimit-reset-
requests: 16.187s], [x-ratelimit-reset-tokens: 101ms], [x-request-id:
req_a46c1fa7cc70ab911321b0e584e70f27], [strict-transport-security: max-
age=31536000; includeSubDomains; preload], [cf-cache-status: DYNAMIC],
[Set-Cookie: __...ne], [X-Content-Type-Options: nosniff], [Set-Cookie:
_c...ne], [Server: cloudflare], [CF-RAY: 934c45c659be5d63-FRA], [alt-svc:
h3=":443"; ma=86400]
```

```
- body: {
  "id": "chatcmpl-BPQXAeOhFkKOKGf8oIavBUjUGkZhG",
  "object": "chat.completion",
  "created": 1745399896,
  "model": "gpt-4o-mini-2024-07-18",
  "choices": [
    {
      "index": 0,
      "message": {
        "role": "assistant",
        "content": "{\n  \"rating\": \"POSITIVE\",\n  \"message\": \"Thank
        you for your kind words, John Doe! We're thrilled to hear you love
        our product!\"\n}",
        "refusal": null,
        "annotations": []
      },
      "logprobs": null,
      "finish_reason": "stop"
    }
  ],
  "usage": {
    "prompt_tokens": 371,
    "completion_tokens": 36,
    "total_tokens": 407,
    "prompt_tokens_details": {
      "cached_tokens": 0,
      "audio_tokens": 0
    },
    "completion_tokens_details": {
      "reasoning_tokens": 0,
      "audio_tokens": 0,
      "accepted_prediction_tokens": 0,
      "rejected_prediction_tokens": 0
    }
  },
```

```
  "service_tier": "default",
  "system_fingerprint": "fp_0392822090"
}
```


The system outputs are helpful to see what is happening behind the curtains.

So to finalize, what happens at runtime?

1. Seeding the database that inserts a sample customer so that invoking `getCustomerDetail(1)` returns "John Doe."

2. When the LLM prompt runs, LangChain4j will detect the need to fetch `{customerId}` tool data, call `CustomerRepository.getCustomerDetail(1)`, and include "John Doe" in the prompt context.

3. The final JSON response is parsed into `CommentReview`, complete with a personalized greeting.

By declaring your existing Quarkus beans as tools, you empower the LLM to execute real business logic—database lookups, external API calls, or any Java method—right in the middle of its reasoning, all with zero manual HTTP or JSON plumbing.

Using ChatMemory in Quarkus

In many AI scenarios—chatbots, multiturn assistants, or comment categorize workflows—you need to preserve conversational context across requests. Chat memory lets your LLM "remember" prior exchanges, making interactions feel more natural and allowing follow-up questions, clarifications, or incremental refinements.

Let's review an example that showcases the importance of in-memory chat history in a conversation with an LLM. The idea is to show how continuity helps the assistant understand context, remember preferences, and respond naturally—just like a human would in a longer chat.

💬 Conversation without in-memory history:

User: What's the capital of France?

Assistant: The capital of France is Paris.

User: And what's the population there?

Assistant: Could you clarify which city you're referring to?

(Without memory, the assistant doesn't know "there" means Paris.)

In the previous conversation each question-answer pair acts as a separate independent session, and the LLM does not have any context of the previous history. This is the reason it is not able to infer the city for the second query. This is illustrated in Figure 12-4.

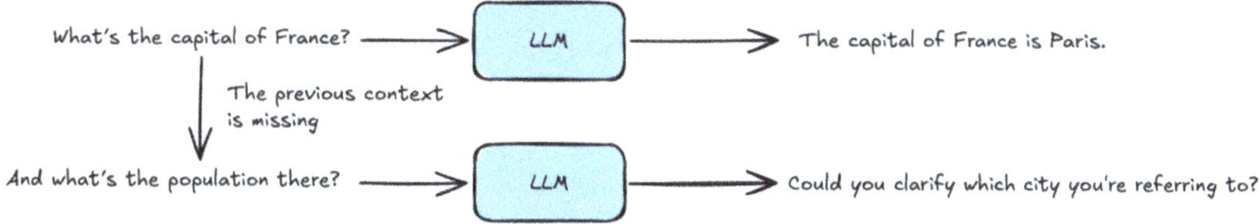

***Figure 12-4.** Conversational flow without context to previous conversation history*

💬 Conversation with in-memory chat history:

> **User:** What's the capital of France?
>
> **Assistant:** The capital of France is Paris.
>
> **User:** And what's the population there?
>
> **Assistant:** As of 2024, Paris has a population of about 2.1 million people.

(The assistant remembers "Paris" from the previous message.)

As you can see, with in-context memory from previous chat history, the LLM now has a context of previous conversation and can gain insight related to any contextual question the user might have and that is not explicitly repeated in the latest question.

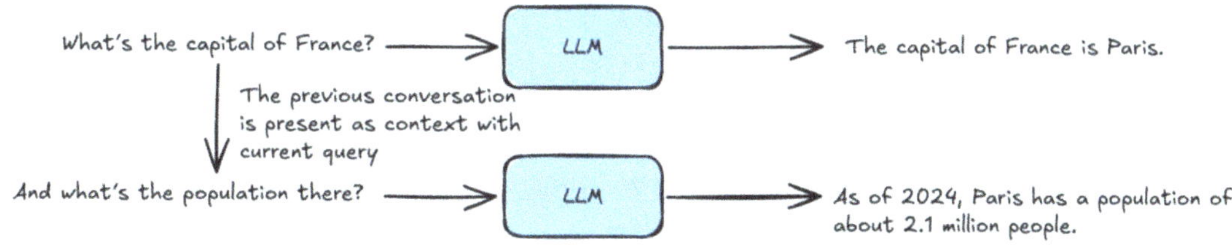

***Figure 12-5.** Conversational flow with context to previous conversation history*

✅ Why this matters:

In-memory chat history helps the assistant:

1. Understand pronouns like "there" or "he/she/it"
2. Follow a topic across multiple turns (like planning a trip or solving a coding issue)
3. Keep user preferences in mind ("I'm vegan" → later recommends vegan restaurants)

Defining a ChatMemoryProvider

Because LLMs don't retain state, you must supply the interaction context ("memory") with each request. To keep that context from growing unbounded, older messages need to be pruned. You can customize which `ChatMemoryProvider` is used by setting the `chatMemoryProviderSupplier` property on the `@RegisterAiService` annotation. By default, it's set to `RegisterAiService.BeanChatMemoryProviderSupplier.class`, which causes the `AiService` to pick up whichever `ChatMemoryProvider` bean your application defines—or fall back to the extension's built-in implementation.

We will create an in-memory chat store for storing your conversations. The conversations won't be persistent after a reboot. For production, you can use Redis or any similar memory performant database. Create a bean named `ChatMemoryBean` that implements the `ChatMemoryProvider` interface. Then initialize an instance of `InMemoryChatMemoryStore` and override the `get` method, which returns a sliding window memory storing a maximum of 20 messages based on `memoryId`.

File: src/main/java/io/demo/langchain4j/sample/utils/ChatMemoryBean.java

```
package io.demo.langchain4j.sample.utils;

import java.util.function.Supplier;

import dev.langchain4j.memory.ChatMemory;
import dev.langchain4j.memory.chat.ChatMemoryProvider;
import dev.langchain4j.memory.chat.MessageWindowChatMemory;
import dev.langchain4j.store.memory.chat.InMemoryChatMemoryStore;
import jakarta.enterprise.context.ApplicationScoped;
```

```
@ApplicationScoped
public class ChatMemoryBean implements Supplier<ChatMemoryProvider> {

    // A simple, JVM-local store that holds all messages in memory.
   // For production, you could swap in a Redis or database-backed
   // store.
   private final InMemoryChatMemoryStore store = new
   InMemoryChatMemoryStore();

    @Override
    public ChatMemoryProvider get() {
        return new ChatMemoryProvider() {

            @Override
            public ChatMemory get(Object memoryId) {
                // A sliding window memory: it retains up to
               // maxMessages most recent turns, dropping the oldest
               // as new ones arrive.
               return MessageWindowChatMemory.builder()
                        .maxMessages(20)
                        // A unique key (e.g. session ID, user ID, or
                       // review ID) that scopes separate
                       // conversations.
                       .id(memoryId)
                        .chatMemoryStore(store)
                        .build();
            }
        };
    }
}
```

Enabling Memory in Your AI Service

Once the in-memory store bean is set up, you can use it inside your `@RegisterAiService` annotation by passing it as an argument to `chatMemoryProviderSupplier`. You also pass some contextual information about some products you sell and to advise the LLM to answer any additional information requested by your customer.

File: src/main/java/io/demo/langchain4j/sample/service/SupportService.java

```
package io.demo.langchain4j.sample.service;

import dev.langchain4j.service.SystemMessage;
import dev.langchain4j.service.UserMessage;
import io.demo.langchain4j.sample.dto.CustomerRepository;
import io.demo.langchain4j.sample.rag.RetrievalAugmentorExample;
import io.demo.langchain4j.sample.utils.ChatMemoryBean;
import io.quarkiverse.langchain4j.RegisterAiService;

@RegisterAiService(
        tools = {CustomerRepository.class},
        chatMemoryProviderSupplier = ChatMemoryBean.class
)
public interface SupportService {
    @SystemMessage("""
       You are working for an ecommerce company, processing comments
       about their products and providing additional information as
       requested by the customer. Categorize comments into positive,
       neutral and negative ones, responding with a JSON format that
       includes a personalized greeting if you have the customer's
       name.
       Products we sell:
       ProductID,Name,Description,Price,Category,Manufacturer,SKU
      1004,Laptop,15-inch laptop with SSD,999.00,Electronics,BrandD,LP-1004
      1005,Coffee Maker,Automatic coffee maker,49.99,Appliances,Bran
dE,CM-1005
   """)
    @UserMessage("""
           Your task is to process the comment delimited by ---.
           Apply sentiment analysis to the comment to determine
           if it is positive, neutral or negative.

           For example:
           - `I love the user experience in your app, you are my best place
             to be!` is a 'POSITIVE'
```

```
            comment
            - `J'adore ton application` is a 'POSITIVE' comment
            - `I don't want to use your app, it's too slow!` is a 'NEGATIVE'
            comment

            Respond with a JSON format containing:
            - the 'rating' key set to 'POSITIVE' if the comment is
            positive, 'NEUTRAL' if the comment is neutral, 'NEGATIVE'
            otherwise
            - the 'message' key set to a message thanking or
            apologizing to the customer. These messages must be polite
            . Find the customer name if
            there is an id provided and use it to greet the customer.
            Also provide any additional information as requested by
            the customer.

            ---
            {comment}
            {customerId}
            ---
    """)
     CommentReview categorize(String comment, long customerId);
}
```

This simple change should enable you to establish a contextual history conversation by setting up a chat memory store. Let's boot up your application and send a few curl POST requests. First you will request info for all the products.

```
curl localhost:8080/comment --header 'Content-Type: text/plain' --data
'This is a great product! I highly recommend it. Could you list all
products from your shop catalog?'
```

Output:

```
{"rating":"POSITIVE","message":"Hello John Doe, thank you for your
wonderful comment! We're glad to hear you love the product. Here are all
the products from our shop catalog: [{\"ProductID\":1004,\"Name\":\"Laptop\
",\"Description\":\"15-inch laptop with SSD\",\"Price\":999.00,\"Category\"
```

```
:\"Electronics\",\"Manufacturer\":\"BrandD\",\"SKU\":\"LP-1004\"},
{\"ProductID\":1005,\"Name\":\"Coffee Maker\",\"Description\":\
"Automatic coffee maker\",\"Price\":49.99,\"Category\":\"Appliances\",
\"Manufacturer\":\"BrandE\",\"SKU\":\"CM-1005\"}]."}
```

```
curl localhost:8080/comment --header 'Content-Type: text/plain' --data 'I
had previously purchased Laptop - 15-inch laptop with SSD. This is a great
product! I highly recommend it.'
```

Output:

```
{"rating":"POSITIVE","message":"Dear John Doe, thank you for your wonderful
comment! We're thrilled to hear that you love the Laptop. If you have any
questions or need further assistance, feel free to ask!"}
```

```
curl localhost:8080/comment --header 'Content-Type: text/plain' --data
'Yes, it was a great product! Could you please tell me the SKU for it?'
```

Output:

```
{"rating":"POSITIVE","message":"Hello John Doe, thank you for your positive
feedback! The SKU for the product is TS-1001."}
```

You can see that it has the contextual information from previous conversations to answer your last customer query. Let's also review some system logs to see what's happening on the application backend.

First request log:

```
{
  "role" : "system",
  "content" : "    You are working for an ecommerce company, processing
comments about\n    their products and providing additional information
as requested\n    \tby the customer. Categorize comments into positive,
neutral and negative ones,\n responding with a JSON format document
that includes a\n    personalized greeting if you have the customer's
details.\n    Products we sell:\n    ProductID,Name,Description,Pr
ice,Category,Manufacturer,SKU\n    1004,Laptop,15-inch laptop with
SSD,999.00,Electronics,BrandD,LP-1004\n    1005,Coffee Maker,Automatic
coffee maker,49.99,Appliances,BrandE,CM-1005\n"
```

```
}, {
"role" : "user",
"content" : "        Your task is to process the comment delimited by ---
.\n        Apply sentiment analysis to the comment to determine\n        if
it is positive, neutral or negative.\n\n        For example:\n        -
`I love the user experience in your app, you are my best place to be!`
is a 'POSITIVE' comment\n        - `J'adore ton application` is a
'POSITIVE' comment\n        - `I don't want to use your app, it's too
slow!` is a 'NEGATIVE' comment\n\n        Respond with a JSON format
containing:\n        - the 'rating' key set to 'POSITIVE' if the comment
is\n        positive, 'NEUTRAL' if the comment is neutral, 'NEGATIVE'
otherwise\n        - the 'message' key set to a message thanking or
apologizing\n        to the customer. These messages must be polite.
Find the customer name if there is an id provided\n        and use it
to greet the customer. Also provide any additional\n information as
requested by the customer.\n\n        ---\n        This is a great
product! I highly recommend it. Could you list all products from your
shop catalog?\n        1\n        ---\n\nYou must answer strictly in
the following JSON format: {\n\"rating\": (type: enum, must be one of
[POSITIVE, NEUTRAL, NEGATIVE]),\n\"message\": (type: string)\n}"
}
```

Second request log:

```
{
  "role" : "system",
  "content" : "    You are working for an ecommerce company, processing
comments about\n    their products and providing additional information
as requested\n   \tby the customer. Categorize comments into positive,
neutral and negative ones,\n responding with a JSON format document
that includes a\n    personalized greeting if you have the customer's
details.\n    Products we sell:\n    ProductID,Name,Description,Pr
ice,Category,Manufacturer,SKU\n    1004,Laptop,15-inch laptop with
SSD,999.00,Electronics,BrandD,LP-1004\n    1005,Coffee Maker,Automatic
coffee maker,49.99,Appliances,BrandE,CM-1005\n"
}, {
```

```
"role" : "user",
"content" : "        Your task is to process the comment delimited by ---
.\n        Apply sentiment analysis to the comment to determine\n        if
it is positive, neutral or negative.\n\n        For example:\n        -
`I love the user experience in your app, you are my best place to be!`
is a 'POSITIVE' comment\n        - `J'adore ton application` is a
'POSITIVE' comment\n        - `I don't want to use your app, it's too
slow!` is a 'NEGATIVE' comment\n\n        Respond with a JSON format
containing:\n        - the 'rating' key set to 'POSITIVE' if the comment
is\n        positive, 'NEUTRAL' if the comment is neutral, 'NEGATIVE'
otherwise\n        - the 'message' key set to a message thanking or
apologizing\n        to the customer. These messages must be polite. Find
the customer name if there is an id provided\n        and use it to greet
the customer. Also provide any additional\n information as requested by
the customer.\n\n        ---\n        I had previously purchased Laptop -
15-inch laptop with SSD. This is a great product! I highly recommend
it.\n        1\n        ---\n\nYou must answer strictly in the following
JSON format: {\n\"rating\": (type: enum, must be one of [POSITIVE, NEUTRAL,
NEGATIVE]),\n\"message\": (type: string)\n}"
}
```

Third request log:

```
{
  "role" : "system",
  "content" : "    You are working for an ecommerce company, processing
comments about\n    their products and providing additional information
as requested\n    \tby the customer. Categorize comments into positive,
neutral and negative ones,\n responding with a JSON format document
that includes a\n    personalized greeting if you have the customer's
details.\n    Products we sell:\n    ProductID,Name,Description,Pr
ice,Category,Manufacturer,SKU\n    1004,Laptop,15-inch laptop with
SSD,999.00,Electronics,BrandD,LP-1004\n    1005,Coffee Maker,Automatic
coffee maker,49.99,Appliances,BrandE,CM-1005\n"
}, {
"role" : "user",
```

```
"content" : "        Your task is to process the comment delimited by ---
.\n        Apply sentiment analysis to the comment to determine\n        if
it is positive, neutral or negative.\n\n        For example:\n        -
`I love the user experience in your app, you are my best place to be!`
is a 'POSITIVE' comment\n        - `J'adore ton application` is a
'POSITIVE' comment\n        - `I don't want to use your app, it's too
slow!` is a 'NEGATIVE' comment\n\n        Respond with a JSON format
containing:\n        - the 'rating' key set to 'POSITIVE' if the comment
is\n        positive, 'NEUTRAL' if the comment is neutral, 'NEGATIVE'
otherwise\n        - the 'message' key set to a message thanking or
apologizing\n        to the customer. These messages must be polite. Find
the customer name if there is an id provided\n        and use it to greet
the customer. Also provide any additional\n information as requested by
the customer.\n\n        ---\n        I had previously purchased Laptop -
15-inch laptop with SSD. This is a great product! I highly recommend
it.\n        1\n        ---\n\nYou must answer strictly in the following
JSON format: {\n\"rating\": (type: enum, must be one of [POSITIVE, NEUTRAL,
NEGATIVE]),\n\"message\": (type: string)\n}"
}
```

So what happens during the runtime?

- **chatMemoryProviderSupplier = ChatMemoryBean.class**

  Instructs the Quarkus LangChain4u extension to use your ChatMemoryBean to obtain a ChatMemoryProvider.

- On each call to categorize(...), LangChain4j will:

  1. Fetch or create a ChatMemory for the given memory ID.
  2. Replay the last N messages (system, user, assistant) before sending the new prompt.
  3. Append the latest user input and model response back into the memory store.

Runtime behavior:

1. **First request**: The memory is empty, so only the system and user messages go to the LLM.
2. **Subsequent requests**: The previous turns (up to 20) are prefixed to the prompt, giving the model access to earlier context.
3. **Stateless API, stateful experience**: Your REST endpoint remains a simple POST, but users get coherent, multiturn conversations.

By wiring in a `ChatMemoryProvider`, your Quarkus application gains stateful dialogue capabilities without cluttering your business logic. You simply define how memory is stored and let LangChain4j handle the rest.

Using the RAG Pattern in Quarkus

RAG combines the creative power of LLMs with a grounding in your own data. Instead of relying solely on the model's pretrained knowledge, you ingest domain documents into a vector store, retrieve the most semantically relevant passages at query time, and feed those passages into your prompt—ensuring up-to-date, factual responses. Figure 12-6 shows this flow.

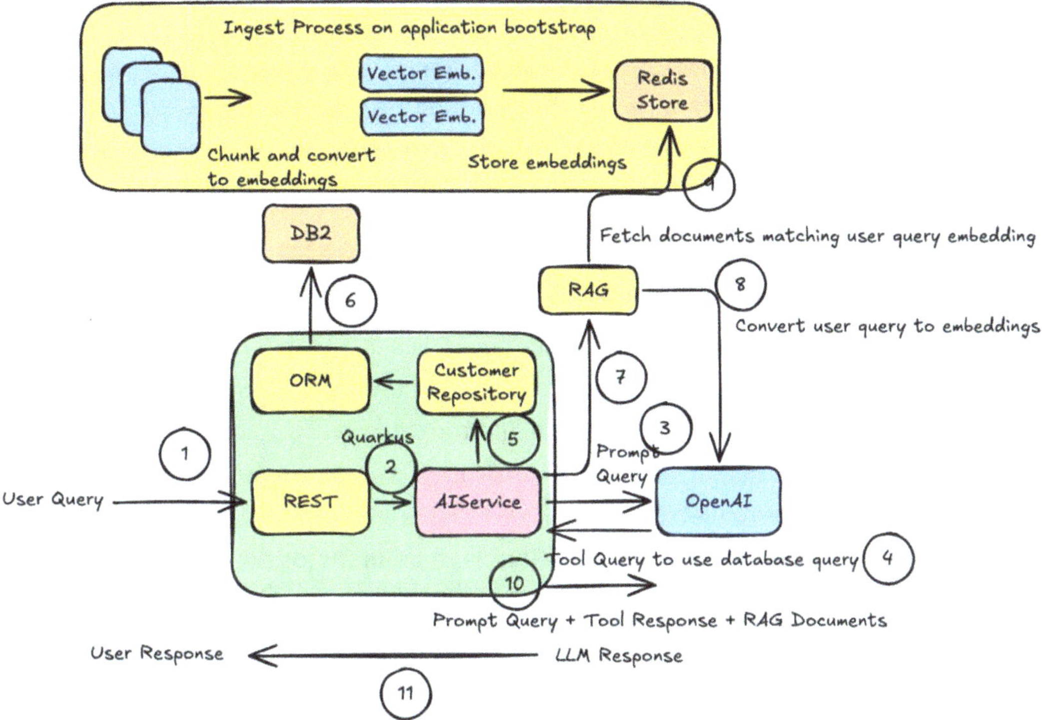

Figure 12-6. RAG flow using LangChain4j in Quarkus

There are two steps to this flow:

1. Ingest documents into your Redis vector store.
2. Use RAG to fetch documents that could be leveraged by LLM to answer user queries.

Ingest Documents into Your Redis Vector Store

Let's focus first on ingesting documents. You have a sample product catalog document that the customer could request information about. It is a CSV file with the first row containing the column/field names and the subsequent rows containing each product in the catalog. The fields are product ID, name, description, price, category, manufacturer, and SKU. You will store this file in the resource directory.

File: src/main/resources/catalog.csv

```
ProductID,Name,Description,Price,Category,Manufacturer,SKU
1001,T-Shirt,Comfortable cotton t-shirt,15.99,Clothing,BrandA,TS-1001
1002,Jeans,Classic blue denim jeans,39.99,Clothing,BrandB,JN-1002
1003,Running Shoes,Lightweight running shoes,79.99,Shoes,BrandC,RS-1003
1004,Laptop,15-inch laptop with SSD,999.00,Electronics,BrandD,LP-1004
1005,Coffee Maker,Automatic coffee maker,49.99,Appliances,BrandE,CM-1005
```

As shown in Figure 12-6, you need to ingest these files so that they are ready for querying from your RAG pipeline. To enable this, you will ingest them when your application bootstraps. In the `ApplicationStartup.java` file, you will enable this functionality. Before that, you will create a few helper classes to modularize some of these tasks.

You will create a class called `DocumentFromTextCreationExample`, which takes as an argument a file and converts it to the LangChain4j document format by first parsing the text from the file document and creating the `Document` instance. The `Document` instance is a standard format for LangChain4j and can be used with the Redis vector store.

File: src/main/java/io/demo/langchain4j/sample/utils/DocumentFromTextCreationExample.java

```java
package io.demo.langchain4j.sample.utils;

import static dev.langchain4j.data.document.loader.
FileSystemDocumentLoader.loadDocument;

import java.io.File;

import dev.langchain4j.data.document.Document;
import dev.langchain4j.data.document.parser.TextDocumentParser;
import jakarta.enterprise.context.ApplicationScoped;

@ApplicationScoped
public class DocumentFromTextCreationExample {

    Document createDocument(File file) {
        // Wraps FileSystemDocumentLoader + TextDocumentParser to turn
       // catalog.csv into a Document.
       return loadDocument(file.toPath(), new TextDocumentParser());
    }
}
```

The next taskis to create a helper class for ingesting a list of documents into the Redis vector store. This includes two tasks. First, convert the document to embeddings by making a call to the OpenAI Embeddings model and then storing the vector by embedding it in a Redis store. The ingest method takes a list of document types and creates an `EmbeddingStoreIngestor` using the store and embedding model provided at runtime. It then calls documentSplitter, which breaks the documents into smaller chunks so they fit within the LLM's prompt size limits.

File: src/main/java/io/demo/langchain4j/sample/utils/IngestorExample.java

```
package io.demo.langchain4j.sample.utils;

import static dev.langchain4j.data.document.splitter.DocumentSplitters.
recursive;

import java.util.List;

import jakarta.enterprise.context.ApplicationScoped;
import jakarta.inject.Inject;

import dev.langchain4j.data.document.Document;
import dev.langchain4j.model.embedding.EmbeddingModel;
import dev.langchain4j.store.embedding.EmbeddingStoreIngestor;
import io.quarkiverse.langchain4j.redis.RedisEmbeddingStore;

// Uses a Quarkus-provided RedisEmbeddingStore and an EmbeddingModel
// (e.g., via OpenAI) to split each document into chunks and store
// their embeddings.
@ApplicationScoped
public class IngestorExample {

    /**
     * The embedding store (the database).
    * The bean is provided by the quarkus-langchain4j-redis extension.
    */
    @Inject
    RedisEmbeddingStore store;
```

```
    /**
     * The embedding model (how is computed the vector of a document).
    * The bean is provided by the LLM (like openai) extension.
    */
    @Inject
    EmbeddingModel embeddingModel;

    public void ingest(List<Document> documents) {
        EmbeddingStoreIngestor ingestor = EmbeddingStoreIngestor.builder()
                .embeddingStore(store)
                .embeddingModel(embeddingModel)
                .documentSplitter(recursive(500, 0))
                .build();
        // Warning - this can take some time...
       ingestor.ingest(documents);
    }
}
```

Now you can use these helper classes, which are injected at run time, to ingest your document into the Redis vector store. First convert your file content to `Document` format using the following helper method. This method loads the file from the resource directory and uses the `createDocument` method of the `DocumentFromTextCreationExample` class to convert it to `Document` format and store it in a list.

```
private List<Document> readDocumentsFromCatalogCsv() throws IOException {
    // Load the file from the resources folder.
   URL resource = getClass().getClassLoader().getResource("catalog.csv");
    if (resource == null) {
        throw new IOException("File catalog.csv not found in resources
        folder");
    }
    File file = new File(resource.getFile());
    Document document = documentFromTextCreationExample.
    createDocument(file);

    List<Document> documents = new ArrayList<>();
```

```
    documents.add(document);
    LOGGER.info("Documents read from catalog.csv");
    return documents;
}
```

Then using the `ingestDocumentsIntoRedis` method, you ingest the documents into Redis through the previously created `IngestorExample` class by calling the `ingest` method.

```
private void ingestDocumentsIntoRedis(List<Document> documents) {
    LOGGER.info("Ingesting documents into Redis...");
    ingestorExample.ingest(documents);
    LOGGER.info("Documents ingested into Redis.");
}
```

The complete code is as follows:

File: src/main/java/io/demo/langchain4j/sample/utils/ApplicationStartup.java

```
package io.demo.langchain4j.sample.utils;

import dev.langchain4j.data.document.Document;
import io.demo.langchain4j.sample.dto.Customer;
import io.quarkus.runtime.StartupEvent;
import jakarta.enterprise.context.ApplicationScoped;
import jakarta.enterprise.event.Observes;
import jakarta.inject.Inject;
import jakarta.transaction.Transactional;
import org.slf4j.Logger;
import org.slf4j.LoggerFactory;

import java.io.File;
import java.io.IOException;
import java.net.URL;
import java.util.ArrayList;
import java.util.List;
```

```
@ApplicationScoped
public class ApplicationStartup {

    private static final Logger LOGGER = LoggerFactory.
getLogger(ApplicationStartup.class);

    @Inject
    IngestorExample ingestorExample;

    @Inject
    DocumentFromTextCreationExample documentFromTextCreationExample;

    @Transactional
    void onStartup(@Observes StartupEvent event) {
        LOGGER.info("Application starting...");

        // 1. Insert a customer into the database
       insertInitialCustomer();

        // 2. Read documents from catalog.csv and ingest into Redis
       try {
            List<Document> documents = readDocumentsFromCatalogCsv();
            ingestDocumentsIntoRedis(documents);
        } catch (IOException e) {
            LOGGER.error("Error processing catalog.csv: {}",
            e.getMessage(), e);
        }
    }

    private void insertInitialCustomer() {
        LOGGER.info("Inserting initial customer...");
        Customer customer = new Customer("John Doe", "123 Main St");
        customer.persist();
        LOGGER.info("Initial customer inserted with ID: {}", customer.id);
    }

    private List<Document> readDocumentsFromCatalogCsv() throws
    IOException {
        // Load the file from the resources folder.
```

```
        URL resource = getClass().getClassLoader().
        getResource("catalog.csv");
         if (resource == null) {
             throw new IOException("File catalog.csv not found in resources
             folder");
         }
         File file = new File(resource.getFile());
         Document document = documentFromTextCreationExample.
         createDocument(file);

         List<Document> documents = new ArrayList<>();
         documents.add(document);
         LOGGER.info("Documents read from catalog.csv");
         return documents;
    }

    private void ingestDocumentsIntoRedis(List<Document> documents) {
        LOGGER.info("Ingesting documents into Redis...");
        ingestorExample.ingest(documents);
        LOGGER.info("Documents ingested into Redis.");
    }
}
```

Use RAG to fetch documents that could be leveraged by the LLM to answer user queries.

The next goal is to use the RAG pattern to convert the user query to embeddings and then use the embeddings to fetch semantically similar documents from the Redis vector store.

Define Your RetrievalAugmentor

The first task is to create a bean class that implements the `RetrievalAugmentor` interface. In the constructor of this class, you will create instances of the retriever and augmentor and finally implement the `get` method, which returns the augmentor instance.

The retriever instance is an instance of `EmbeddingStoreContentRetriever`, and using the builder method you pass the embedding model, which the retriever can use to convert user query to embeddings and the embedding store to which it needs to do a similarity search. Through the `maxResults` method you can pass how many matched similar documents should be returned.

```
EmbeddingStoreContentRetriever contentRetriever =
EmbeddingStoreContentRetriever.builder()
        .embeddingModel(model)
        .embeddingStore(store)
        .maxResults(3)
        .build();
```

Once the retriever object is created, it is passed as a parameter to the `DefaultRetrievalAugmentor` instance created using the builder method, where the retriever object is passed as an argument to the `contentRetriever` method. This instantiates your augmentor instance that is returned from the `get` method of your class.

The complete code for this change is shown here:

File: src/main/java/io/demo/langchain4j/sample/rag/RetrievalAugmentorExample.java

```
package io.demo.langchain4j.sample.rag;

import java.util.function.Supplier;

import jakarta.enterprise.context.ApplicationScoped;

import dev.langchain4j.model.embedding.EmbeddingModel;
import dev.langchain4j.rag.DefaultRetrievalAugmentor;
import dev.langchain4j.rag.RetrievalAugmentor;
import dev.langchain4j.rag.content.retriever.
EmbeddingStoreContentRetriever;
import io.quarkiverse.langchain4j.redis.RedisEmbeddingStore;
import org.slf4j.Logger;
import org.slf4j.LoggerFactory;

@ApplicationScoped
```

```
public class RetrievalAugmentorExample implements
Supplier<RetrievalAugmentor> {

    private static final Logger LOGGER = LoggerFactory.getLogger(Retrieval
    AugmentorExample.class);

    private final RetrievalAugmentor augmentor;

    RetrievalAugmentorExample(RedisEmbeddingStore store, EmbeddingModel
    model) {
        LOGGER.info("Creating RetrievalAugmentorExample");

        // Queries the Redis store for the top-N most similar chunks
       // to the user's query.
       EmbeddingStoreContentRetriever contentRetriever =
       EmbeddingStoreContentRetriever.builder()
               .embeddingModel(model)
               .embeddingStore(store)
               .maxResults(3)
               .build();

        // Wraps the retriever and automatically prepends the
       // retrieved passages to your prompt before calling the LLM.
       augmentor = DefaultRetrievalAugmentor
               .builder()
               .contentRetriever(contentRetriever)
               .build();
        LOGGER.info("Retrieval AugmentorExample created");
    }

    @Override
    public RetrievalAugmentor get() {
        return augmentor;
    }

}
```

Enable RAG in Your AI Service

You have now set up the code to ingest documents when your application starts and set up the RetrievalAugmentor class that enables the RAG pattern in LangChain4j. The final missing piece is to enable RAG by passing in your RetrievalAugmentorExample class to the retrievalAugmentor parameter of the @RegisterAiService annotation. Also, to give insight to the LLM to support using the RAG searched results, you enhance your system and user prompts as shown next to "provide additional information as requested by the customer":

File: src/main/java/io/demo/langchain4j/sample/service/SupportService.java

```
package io.demo.langchain4j.sample.service;

import dev.langchain4j.service.SystemMessage;
import dev.langchain4j.service.UserMessage;
import io.demo.langchain4j.sample.dto.CustomerRepository;
import io.demo.langchain4j.sample.rag.RetrievalAugmentorExample;
import io.quarkiverse.langchain4j.RegisterAiService;

@RegisterAiService(
        tools = {CustomerRepository.class},
        // Tells Quarkus to hook in our custom RetrievalAugmentor, which
        // will fetch relevant document snippets before each LLM call.
        retrievalAugmentor = RetrievalAugmentorExample.class
)
public interface SupportService {
    @SystemMessage("""
        You are working for an ecommerce company, processing comments
        about their products and providing additional information as
        requested by the customer. Categorize comments into positive,
        neutral and negative ones, responding with a JSON format
        document that includes a personalized greeting if you have the
        customer's details.
    """)
```

```
    @UserMessage("""
            Your task is to process the comment delimited by ---.
            Apply sentiment analysis to the comment to determine
            if it is positive, neutral or negative.

            For example:
            - `I love the user experience in your app, you are my best place
            to be!` is a 'POSITIVE'
            comment
            - `J'adore ton application` is a 'POSITIVE' comment
            - `I don't want to use your app, it's too slow!` is a 'NEGATIVE'
            comment

            Respond with a JSON format containing:
            - the 'rating' key set to 'POSITIVE' if the comment is
            positive, 'NEUTRAL' if the comment is neutral, 'NEGATIVE'
            otherwise
            - the 'message' key set to a message thanking or
            apologizing to the customer. These messages must be polite
            . Find the customer name if
            there is an id provided and use it to greet the customer.
            Also provide any additional information as requested by
            the customer.

            ---
            {comment}
            {customerId}
            ---
   """)
    CommentReview categorize(String comment, long customerId);
}
```

Let's boot up the application and comment the system logs. The output is a bit truncated due to the verbose display of the response from the OpenAI Embedding model. It shows that your file was read, and then the embeddings of it were requested from OpenAI Embedding API. Finally, the embedding documents are inserted into Redis.

Output:

```
        -0.061810866,
        0.019966396,
        0.0056421002,
        -0.02856894,
        -0.016740443,
        -0.0003667365,
        -0.0022900288,
        -0.025276609,
        0.025077475,
        0.0011923085,
        0.020470867,
        0.010666888,
        0.026657263,
        -0.016222697,
        0.0039162813,
        -0.026936049,
        0.0028874276,
        -0.0039793397,
        -0.012459084,
        -0.017709557
      ]
    }
  ],
  "model": "text-embedding-ada-002-v2",
  "usage": {
    "prompt_tokens": 145,
    "total_tokens": 145
  }
}
2025-04-23 18:28:15,726 INFO  [io.dem.lan.sam.uti.ApplicationStartup]
(Quarkus Main Thread) Documents ingested into Redis.
```

Now that your application has booted up and your documents have been ingested into Redis, let's run a `curl` POST request to see the output. This time, in addition to the feedback comment, you will also ask to give the list of all the products in your e-commerce catalog.

```
curl localhost:8080/comment --header 'Content-Type: text/plain' --data
'This is a great product! I highly recommend it. Could you list all
products from your shop catalog?'
```

Output:


```
{"rating":"POSITIVE","message":"Thank you for your wonderful feedback, John
Doe! We're glad to hear that you highly recommend our product. Here is the
list of products from our shop catalog: \n1. T-Shirt - Comfortable cotton
t-shirt - $15.99\n2. Jeans - Classic blue denim jeans - $39.99\n3. Running
Shoes - Lightweight running shoes - $79.99\n4. Laptop - 15-inch laptop with
SSD - $999.00\n5. Coffee Maker - Automatic coffee maker - $49.99"}
```


As you can see from the output, not only is there personalized feedback using the customer name and rating, but also there is a complete list of products from your company's catalog.

Let's also see what is happening in the system backend while you are seeing this response. As you can see from the truncated numbers, the user query is first converted into embeddings by making a call to the OpenAI Embedding Model API and receives back the query in embeddings format.

Output:


```
-0.044992004,
-0.005532781,
0.0048767063,
0.004967925,
0.017991187,
-0.034382533,
-0.0011218179,
0.0018033289,
0.030004025,
0.0024892252,
0.019548927,
```

```
        -0.04041702
      ]
    }
  ],
  "model": "text-embedding-ada-002-v2",
  "usage": {
    "prompt_tokens": 272,
    "total_tokens": 272
  }
}
```


The embeddings are matched with the Redis store, and the returned documents are passed in your prompt to the OpenAI API.

Output:

```
2025-04-23 18:32:20,862 INFO  [io.qua.lan.ope.com.OpenAiRestApi$OpenAiClien
tLogger] (vert.x-eventloop-thread-3) Request:
- method: POST
- url: https://api.openai.com/v1/chat/completions
- headers: [Accept: application/json], [Authorization: Be...kA], [Content-
Type: application/json], [User-Agent: langchain4j-openai], [content-
length: 2539]
- body: {
  "model" : "gpt-4o-mini",
  "messages" : [ {
    "role" : "system",
    "content" : "       You are working for an ecommerce company,
    processing comments about\n       their products and providing
    additional information as requested\n      \tby the customer.
    Categorize comments into positive, neutral and negative ones,\
    nresponding with a JSON format document.\n"
  }, {
    "role" : "user",
```

```
  "content" : "        Your task is to process the comment delimited
  by ---.\n        Apply sentiment analysis to the comment to
  determine\n        if it is positive, neutral or negative.\
  n\n        For example:\n        - `I love the user experience in your
  app, you are my best place to be!` is a 'POSITIVE' comment\n        -
  `J'adore ton application` is a 'POSITIVE' comment\n        - `I
  don't want to use your app, it's too slow!` is a 'NEGATIVE' comment\
  n\n        Respond with a JSON format containing:\n        - the
  'rating' key set to 'POSITIVE' if the comment is\n        positive,
  'NEUTRAL' if the comment is neutral, 'NEGATIVE' otherwise\n        -
  the 'message' key set to a message thanking or apologizing\n        to
  the customer. These messages must be polite. Find the customer
  name if there is an id provided\n        and use it to greet the
  customer. Also provide any additional\n information as requested
  by the customer.\n\n        ---\n        This is a great product!
  I highly recommend it. Could you list all products from your shop
  catalog?\n        1\n        ---\n\nYou must answer strictly in the
  following JSON format: {\n\"rating\": (type: enum, must be one of
  [POSITIVE, NEUTRAL, NEGATIVE]),\n\"message\": (type: string)\n}\n\
  nAnswer using the following information:\nProductID,Name,Description,
  Price,Category,Manufacturer,SKU\n1001,T-Shirt,Comfortable cotton
  t-shirt,15.99,Clothing,BrandA,TS-1001\n1002,Jeans,Classic blue denim
  jeans,39.99,Clothing,BrandB,JN-1002\n1003,Running Shoes,Lightweight
  running shoes,79.99,Shoes,BrandC,RS-1003\n1004,Laptop,15-inch laptop
  with SSD,999.00,Electronics,BrandD,LP-1004\n1005,Coffee Maker,Automatic
  coffee maker,49.99,Appliances,BrandE,CM-1005"
} ],
"temperature" : 0.5,
"top_p" : 1.0,
"presence_penalty" : 0.0,
"frequency_penalty" : 0.0,
"tools" : [ {
  "type" : "function",
  "function" : {
    "name" : "getCustomerDetail",
    "description" : "get the customer detail for the given customerId",
```

```
      "parameters" : {
        "type" : "object",
        "properties" : {
          "id" : {
            "type" : "integer"
          }
        },
        "required" : [ "id" ]
      }
    }
  } ]
}
```


OpenAI uses the tool call to fetch the customer name information.

Output:


```
2025-04-23 18:32:22,233 INFO  [io.qua.lan.ope.com.OpenAiRestApi$OpenAiClient
Logger] (vert.x-eventloop-thread-3) Response:
- status code: 200
- headers: [Date: Wed, 23 Apr 2025 18:32:22 GMT], [Content-Type:
application/json], [Transfer-Encoding: chunked], [Connection: keep-alive],
[access-control-expose-headers: X-Request-ID], [openai-organization: user-
eldk0kvytvetb2vdgo2y3nvr], [openai-processing-ms: 758], [openai-version:
2020-10-01], [x-ratelimit-limit-requests: 10000], [x-ratelimit-limit-
tokens: 200000], [x-ratelimit-remaining-requests: 9999], [x-ratelimit-
remaining-tokens: 199523], [x-ratelimit-reset-requests: 8.64s],
[x-ratelimit-reset-tokens: 142ms], [x-request-id: req_43a545a26581
9b93d4ca7379be2e7344], [strict-transport-security: max-age=31536000;
includeSubDomains; preload], [cf-cache-status: DYNAMIC], [Set-Cookie: __...
ne], [X-Content-Type-Options: nosniff], [Set-Cookie: _c...ne], [Server:
cloudflare], [CF-RAY: 934f716a6974d352-FRA], [alt-svc: h3=":443"; ma=86400]
- body: {
  "id": "chatcmpl-BPZBNOtOVxWBJMEMAgaHZIOTmH9Xt",
  "object": "chat.completion",
  "created": 1745433141,
  "model": "gpt-4o-mini-2024-07-18",
```

```
"choices": [
  {
    "index": 0,
    "message": {
      "role": "assistant",
      "content": null,
      "tool_calls": [
        {
          "id": "call_0QGLPggBPNP26aUqRV4rwwQD",
          "type": "function",
          "function": {
            "name": "getCustomerDetail",
            "arguments": "{\"id\": 1}"
          }
        }
      ],
      "refusal": null,
      "annotations": []
    },
    "logprobs": null,
    "finish_reason": "tool_calls"
  }
],
"usage": {
  "prompt_tokens": 512,
  "completion_tokens": 32,
  "total_tokens": 544,
  "prompt_tokens_details": {
    "cached_tokens": 0,
    "audio_tokens": 0
  },
  "completion_tokens_details": {
    "reasoning_tokens": 0,
    "audio_tokens": 0,
    "accepted_prediction_tokens": 0,
```

```
      "rejected_prediction_tokens": 0
    }
  },
  "service_tier": "default",
  "system_fingerprint": "fp_dbaca60df0"
}
```


A final call is made to OpenAI using the response from the database fetch query tool and the embeddings matched documents.

Output:

```
2025-04-23 18:32:22,884 INFO  [io.qua.lan.ope.com.OpenAiRestApi$OpenAiClien
tLogger] (vert.x-eventloop-thread-3) Request:
- method: POST
- url: https://api.openai.com/v1/chat/completions
- headers: [Accept: application/json], [Authorization: Be...kA], [Content-
Type: application/json], [User-Agent: langchain4j-openai], [content-
length: 2890]
- body: {
  "model" : "gpt-4o-mini",
  "messages" : [ {
    "role" : "system",
    "content" : "        You are working for an ecommerce company,
    processing comments about\n        their products and providing
    additional information as requested\n      \tby the customer.
    Categorize comments into positive, neutral and negative ones,\
    nresponding with a JSON format document.\n"
  }, {
    "role" : "user",
    "content" : "        Your task is to process the comment delimited
    by ---.\n        Apply sentiment analysis to the comment to
    determine\n        if it is positive, neutral or negative.\
    n\n        For example:\n         - `I love the user experience in your
    app, you are my best place to be!` is a 'POSITIVE' comment\n         -
    `J'adore ton application` is a 'POSITIVE' comment\n         - `I
    don't want to use your app, it's too slow!` is a 'NEGATIVE' comment\
```

```
    n\n        Respond with a JSON format containing:\n        - the
    'rating' key set to 'POSITIVE' if the comment is\n        positive,
    'NEUTRAL' if the comment is neutral, 'NEGATIVE' otherwise\n        -
    the 'message' key set to a message thanking or apologizing\n        to
    the customer. These messages must be polite. Find the customer
    name if there is an id provided\n        and use it to greet the
    customer. Also provide any additional\n information as requested
    by the customer.\n\n        ---\n        This is a great product!
    I highly recommend it. Could you list all products from your shop
    catalog?\n        1\n        ---\n\nYou must answer strictly in the
    following JSON format: {\n\"rating\": (type: enum, must be one of
    [POSITIVE, NEUTRAL, NEGATIVE]),\n\"message\": (type: string)\n}\n\
    nAnswer using the following information:\nProductID,Name,Description,
    Price,Category,Manufacturer,SKU\n1001,T-Shirt,Comfortable cotton
    t-shirt,15.99,Clothing,BrandA,TS-1001\n1002,Jeans,Classic blue denim
    jeans,39.99,Clothing,BrandB,JN-1002\n1003,Running Shoes,Lightweight
    running shoes,79.99,Shoes,BrandC,RS-1003\n1004,Laptop,15-inch laptop
    with SSD,999.00,Electronics,BrandD,LP-1004\n1005,Coffee Maker,Automatic
    coffee maker,49.99,Appliances,BrandE,CM-1005"
  }, {
    "role" : "assistant",
    "tool_calls" : [ {
      "id" : "call_OQGLPggBPNP26aUqRV4rwwQD",
      "type" : "function",
      "function" : {
        "name" : "getCustomerDetail",
        "arguments" : "{\"id\": 1}"
      }
    } ]
  }, {
    "role" : "tool",
    "tool_call_id" : "call_OQGLPggBPNP26aUqRV4rwwQD",
    "content" : "\"John Doe\""
  } ],
  "temperature" : 0.5,
```

```
  "top_p" : 1.0,
  "presence_penalty" : 0.0,
  "frequency_penalty" : 0.0,
  "tools" : [ {
    "type" : "function",
    "function" : {
      "name" : "getCustomerDetail",
      "description" : "get the customer detail for the given customerId",
      "parameters" : {
        "type" : "object",
        "properties" : {
          "id" : {
            "type" : "integer"
          }
        },
        "required" : [ "id" ]
      }
    }
  } ]
}
```


Here you receive the final augmented response from the OpenAI LLM:

Output:

```
2025-04-23 18:32:26,452 INFO  [io.qua.lan.ope.com.OpenAiRestApi$OpenAiClient
Logger] (vert.x-eventloop-thread-3) Response:
- status code: 200
- headers: [Date: Wed, 23 Apr 2025 18:32:26 GMT], [Content-Type:
application/json], [Transfer-Encoding: chunked], [Connection: keep-alive],
[access-control-expose-headers: X-Request-ID], [openai-organization: user-
eldk0kvytvetb2vdgo2y3nvr], [openai-processing-ms: 3429], [openai-version:
2020-10-01], [x-ratelimit-limit-requests: 10000], [x-ratelimit-limit-
tokens: 200000], [x-ratelimit-remaining-requests: 9998], [x-ratelimit-
remaining-tokens: 199520], [x-ratelimit-reset-requests: 15.645s],
[x-ratelimit-reset-tokens: 144ms], [x-request-id: req_936c2de81360e
```

```
8e28f1ac84788c49243], [strict-transport-security: max-age=31536000;
includeSubDomains; preload], [cf-cache-status: DYNAMIC], [Set-Cookie: __...
ne], [X-Content-Type-Options: nosniff], [Set-Cookie: _c...ne], [Server:
cloudflare], [CF-RAY: 934f71771a45d352-FRA], [alt-svc: h3=":443"; ma=86400]
- body: {
  "id": "chatcmpl-BPZBPFEgZYBwIf6DrpBDPNvZuWYBI",
  "object": "chat.completion",
  "created": 1745433143,
  "model": "gpt-4o-mini-2024-07-18",
  "choices": [
    {
      "index": 0,
      "message": {
        "role": "assistant",
        "content": "{\n  \"rating\": \"POSITIVE\",\n  \"message\": \"Thank
        you for your wonderful feedback, John Doe! We're glad to hear that
        you highly recommend our product. Here is the list of products from
        our shop catalog: \\n1. T-Shirt - Comfortable cotton t-shirt -
        $15.99\\n2. Jeans - Classic blue denim jeans - $39.99\\n3. Running
        Shoes - Lightweight running shoes - $79.99\\n4. Laptop - 15-inch
        laptop with SSD - $999.00\\n5. Coffee Maker - Automatic coffee
        maker - $49.99\"\n}",
        "refusal": null,
        "annotations": []
      },
      "logprobs": null,
      "finish_reason": "stop"
    }
  ],
  "usage": {
    "prompt_tokens": 540,
    "completion_tokens": 124,
    "total_tokens": 664,
    "prompt_tokens_details": {
      "cached_tokens": 0,
      "audio_tokens": 0
```

```
    },
    "completion_tokens_details": {
      "reasoning_tokens": 0,
      "audio_tokens": 0,
      "accepted_prediction_tokens": 0,
      "rejected_prediction_tokens": 0
    }
  },
  "service_tier": "default",
  "system_fingerprint": "fp_dbaca60df0"
}
```


So, what happens at runtime?

1. **Service invocation**: `categorize(comment, customerId)` is called.
2. **Retrieval**: `RetrievalAugmentorExample` fetches up to three catalog passages most semantically similar to `comment`.
3. **Prompt assembly**: The system message, any chat memory, the retrieved snippets, and the user prompt (with `{comment}` and `{customerId}`) are concatenated.
4. **LLM call**: The enriched prompt is sent to the model, which can now ground its analysis in your catalog data (e.g., product specs, descriptions).
5. **Response parsing**: The JSON output is deserialized into `CommentReview`.

By wiring in RAG, you ensure that your AI assistant leverages your fresh, proprietary content—whether it's product catalogs, FAQs, or knowledge bases—yielding more accurate, context-aware responses without manual prompt concatenation or bespoke retrieval code.

Conclusion

In this chapter, you walked through every stage of embedding LLMs into a Quarkus application—from the initial LangChain4j setup and precise prompt engineering to the dynamic tool integration, conversational memory, and advanced RAG techniques. You now know how to register AI services with just a few annotations, enrich prompts with real-time data via custom tools, and ground your model's outputs in external knowledge bases. The sample application illustrated not only sentiment categorization but also how to persist context and perform semantic retrieval to create richer, more accurate responses.

Armed with these patterns and code samples, you're ready to build your own LLM-infused microservices on Quarkus. Whether you're processing customer feedback, powering chatbots, or generating personalized recommendations, the combination of Quarkus's optimized runtime and LangChain4j's Java-native abstractions gives you a solid foundation for scalable, maintainable AI systems.

In the next chapter, you'll explore hosting models in Java. Keep experimenting, tuning, and extending—your journey into cloud-native Gen AI is just beginning!

CHAPTER 13

Jlama and Friends: Hosting Models the Java Way

The goal of this chapter is to host a large language model (LLM) using a Java-based LLM inference engine.

Introduction

In the previous chapters, you learned about using a prehosted LLM API like OpenAI or running a local inferencing engine like Ollama. Java has not been known as the platform to host an LLM through a native platform inferencing engine similar to the likes present in the Python environment. This is no longer true with the options of Jlama and DJL available in the Java ecosystem. In this chapter, you will explore what Jlama is and what value it adds to the Java ecosystem in the world of machine learning. While you are at it, you will get your hands dirty by hosting an LLM in Java and then using it to build a sample application.

To follow along with the examples, ensure you have the following prerequisites:

- Java 20 or later
- At least 16GB of RAM (especially for Q4 quantized model variants)

S. K. Sahu, *Generative AI-Driven Application Development with Java*,
https://doi.org/10.1007/979-8-8688-1609-3_13

What Is Jlama?

The prevailing approach for building applications with LLMs involves relying on external services provided by specialized companies. These services typically grant access to large, general-purpose models, which leads to significant energy consumption and costs that scale with model size. Furthermore, this pattern raises privacy and security concerns, as it's difficult to ensure how these service providers will use customer prompts, which may contain sensitive data.

Consequently, many organizations are investigating the alternative of training or fine-tuning smaller, more focused models tailored to their specific business needs. These models can then be run on-premises or in private clouds, giving companies greater control over their data and infrastructure.

However, integrating these specialized models into existing software infrastructure, which is often based on Java in enterprise environments, presents a challenge. While a traditional client-server architecture could be used (for example, by serving the model through an external server like Ollama and accessing it via REST APIs), this approach can be cumbersome for Java developers. They could achieve greater efficiency by consuming the model directly within Java, eliminating the need for additional tools.

Ultimately, embedding LLM interaction directly within the same Java process that runs the application simplifies the transition from local development to deployment. It also reduces the operational burden on IT, removing the need to manage a separate external server and potentially streamlining platform engineering strategies. This is where Jlama becomes a valuable solution.

Jlama is a modern LLM inference engine for Java. It is a significant development for Java developers working with LLMs. It's essentially a library that allows LLMs to run directly within a Java application. This is a departure from the traditional approach of using external servers to host and serve these models. Jlama supports many LLM families and implements advanced features, integrating well with frameworks like Quarkus through Langchain4j. By leveraging Java's Vector API, Jlama aims to provide efficient performance. The core idea is to enable Java developers to incorporate LLM capabilities into their applications in a more streamlined way, simplifying development, improving security, and potentially enhancing monitoring and observability.

Jlama is a modern Java library designed to bring the power of LLMs directly into Java applications. It supports a wide range of popular LLM architectures, including the Gemma, Llama (and its versions 2 and 3), Mistral and Mixtral, Qwen2, and IBM

Granite families, as well as the foundational models GPT-2 and BERT. Furthermore, Jlama handles various tokenization methods (BPE and WordPiece), which are crucial for processing text data for LLMs.

Beyond model support, Jlama incorporates several advanced features to enhance performance and functionality. These include paged attention and mixture of experts, techniques that improve efficiency and allow for more complex model architectures. It also supports tool calling, enabling LLMs to interact with external functions, and offers the ability to generate embeddings, which are numerical representations of text used in many NLP tasks. Jlama also provides classifier support for categorization tasks. It works with the Hugging Face SafeTensors format, a standard for storing and loading model weights, and handles both the model and tokenizer formats used by Hugging Face. To optimize computational efficiency, it supports various data types (F32, F16, BF16) and model quantization (Q8, Q4), which reduces model size and speeds up inference. Fast General Matrix Multiplication (GEMM) operations are implemented for efficient matrix calculations, and Jlama even offers distributed inference capabilities, allowing for scaling LLM processing across multiple devices.

To leverage these features, Jlama requires Java 20 or later, as it takes advantage of the Vector API for accelerated inference. This combination of broad model support and advanced features makes Jlama a powerful tool for integrating LLMs into Java-based applications.

Jlama is a Java library designed to enable LLM inference directly within Java applications. It supports a variety of LLM model families, including Llama, Mistral, Qwen2, and Granite, and implements features like function calling, model quantization, mixture of experts, and distributed inference. It is well-integrated with Quarkus via a dedicated LangChain4j extension. For performance, Jlama leverages Java's Vector API (currently a preview feature, expected to be fully supported in Java 25).

Essentially, Jlama allows LLMs to run within the same Java Virtual Machine (JVM) as the application, offering several advantages:

- **Simplified lifecycle management:** In cases where the LLM and the application have a tightly coupled lifecycle (e.g., a new application feature requires a model update, or model fine-tuning necessitates prompt changes), embedding the model simplifies versioning and tracking.

- **Faster development and prototyping:** Eliminating the need to set up, configure, and interact with an external server streamlines the development process for LLM-based Java applications.
- **Easier model testing:** Running LLM inference within the JVM simplifies the testing of different models and their integration during development.
- **Enhanced security:** By performing inference within the application's JVM, the need for REST API communication with an external LLM server is reduced, mitigating the risk of private data leaks and enabling finer-grained user authorization.
- **Monolithic application compatibility:** Jlama allows applications with LLM capabilities to be included in monolithic architectures without requiring significant changes.
- **Improved monitoring and observability:** Running LLM inference in Java simplifies monitoring and gathering statistics on LLM response reliability and speed.
- **Simplified debugging:** Developers can more easily debug LLM interactions by stepping through both application and Jlama code within the same environment.
- **Simplified distribution:** Embedding the LLM within the application package simplifies distribution (though this may be suitable only in specific scenarios).
- **Edge deployment suitability:** Self-contained LLM-capable Java applications are often better suited for edge environments than client-server architectures.
- **Auxiliary LLM embedding:** Applications that use multiple LLMs (e.g., agentic AI patterns, where a smaller LLM validates the output of a larger one) can benefit from embedding the smaller, auxiliary LLMs while serving the main LLM externally.

Jlama: Quick Start

Let's try Jlama. To start simply, it provides a command-line utility to use it. The CLI can be run with jbang, so install jbang first.

```
#Install jbang (or https://www.jbang.dev/download/)
curl -Ls https://sh.jbang.dev | bash -s - app setup
```

Once jbang is installed, install jlama using the following command:

```
#Install Jlama CLI (will ask if you trust the source)
jbang app install --force jlama@tjake
```

Let's explore the jlama command-line tool.

```
jlama -help
```

Output:

```
[jbang] Building jar for jlama.java...

Note: Annotation processing is enabled because one or more processors were
found on the class path. A future release of javac may disable annotation
processing unless at least one processor is specified by name (-processor),
or a search path is specified (--processor-path, --processor-module-path),
or annotation  processing is enabled explicitly (-proc:only, -proc:full).
 Use -Xlint:-options to suppress this message.
 Use -proc:none to disable annotation processing.
WARNING: Using incubator modules: jdk.incubator.vector

Usage:
jlama [COMMAND]

Description:

Jlama is a modern LLM inference engine for Java!
Quantized models are maintained at https://hf.co/tjake
Choose from the available commands:
Inference:
 chat                    Interact with the specified model
```

```
 restapi               Starts a openai compatible rest api for interacting
                       with this model
 complete              Completes a prompt using the specified model
Distributed Inference:
 cluster-coordinator   Starts a distributed rest api for a model using
 cluster workers
 cluster-worker        Connects to a cluster coordinator to perform
                       distributed inference
Other:
 download              Downloads a HuggingFace model - use owner/name format
 list                  Lists local models
 quantize              Quantize the specified model
```

Use Jlama to Host an LLM

Now that you have jlama installed, you can download a model from Hugging Face and chat with it. Note you also have prequantized models available at `https://hf.co/tjake`.

This provides the complete list of options jlama can be used for. For the moment, the subcommands that are of interest to us are chat and restapi. The **chat** subcommand allows us to interact with the specified LLM model on the command line. Let's explore it.

```
jlama chat -help
```

Output:

```
WARNING: Using incubator modules: jdk.incubator.vector
Usage:
jlama chat [OPTIONS] <model name>
Description:
Interact with the specified model
Parameters:
*     <model name>          The huggingface model owner/name pair
Command Options:
     --model-cache=ARG      The local directory for downloaded models
                              (default: models)
     --work-directory=ARG   Working directory for attention cache
     --temperature=ARG      Temperature of response [0,1] (default: 0.6)
```

```
    --tokens=ARG           Number of tokens to generate (default: 128000)
    --top-p=ARG            Controls how many different words the model
                             considers per token [0,1] (default: .9)
    --system-prompt=ARG    Change the default system prompt for this model
Download Options:
    --auto-download        Download the model if missing (default: false)
    --branch=ARG           The model branch to download from
                           (default: main)
    --auth-token=ARG       HuggingFace auth token (for restricted models)
Advanced Options:
    --working-dtype=ARG    Working memory data type (default: F32)
    --working-qtype=ARG    Working memory quantization data type
                           (default: I8)
    --threads=ARG          Number of threads to use (default: number of
                             physical cores)
    --quantize-to=ARG      Runtime Model quantization type
```

Let's run a simplified version of this command.

```
jlama chat tjake/Llama-3.2-1B-Instruct-JQ4 --auto-download
```

Output:

```
WARNING: Using incubator modules: jdk.incubator.vector
README.md 100% [================================] 36/36KB (0:00:01 /
0:00:00)
config.json 100% [==============================] 877/877B (0:00:01 /
0:00:00)
model.safetensors 100% [======================] 772/772MB (0:00:05 /
0:00:00)
tokenizer.json 100% [=============================] 9/9MB (0:00:01 /
0:00:00)
tokenizer_config.json 100% [===================] 54/54KB (0:00:01 /
0:00:00)
Using Native SIMD Operations (OffHeap)
Model type = Q4, Working memory type = F32, Quantized memory type = I8
Chatting with tjake/Llama-3.2-1B-Instruct-JQ4...
You:
```

We can start chatting at the "You" prompt by asking for a joke.

```
You: Tell me a joke.
Jlama: A man walked into a library and asked the librarian, "Do you have any books on Pavlov's dogs?" The librarian replied, "It rings a bell, but I'm not sure if it's here or not."
11 tokens/s (prompt), 7 tokens/s (gen)
You:
```

You can get out of the CLI prompt by using Ctrl+C. Next, you will explore the restapi subcommand.

```
# Run the openai chat api and UI on a model
jlama restapi tjake/Llama-3.2-1B-Instruct-JQ4 --auto-download
```

Output:

```
WARNING: Using incubator modules: jdk.incubator.vector
Using Native SIMD Operations (OffHeap)
Model type = Q4, Working memory type = F32, Quantized memory type = I8
Chat UI: http://localhost:8080
OpenAI Chat API: http://localhost:8080/chat/completions

  .   ____          _            __ _ _
 /\\ / ___'_ __ _ _(_)_ __  __ _ \ \ \ \
( ( )\___ | '_ | '_| | '_ \/ _` | \ \ \ \
 \\/  ___)| |_)| | | | | || (_| |  ) ) ) )
  '  |____| .__|_| |_|_| |_\__, | / / / /
 =========|_|==============|___/=/_/_/_/

:: Spring Boot ::                (v3.3.2)

2025-04-22T15:49:34.172Z  INFO 48593 --- [           main] com.github.tjake.jlama.cli.JlamaCli      : Starting JlamaCli using Java 21.0.7 with PID 48593 (/home/ubuntu/.m2/repository/com/github/tjake/jlama-cli/0.8.2/jlama-cli-0.8.2.jar started by ubuntu in /home/ubuntu)
2025-04-22T15:49:34.175Z  INFO 48593 --- [           main] com.github.tjake.jlama.cli.JlamaCli      : No active profile set, falling back to 1 default profile: "default"
```

```
2025-04-22T15:49:35.836Z  WARN 48593 --- [           main] io.undertow.
websockets.jsr                          : UT026010: Buffer pool was not set on
WebSocketDeploymentInfo, the default pool will be used
2025-04-22T15:49:35.861Z  INFO 48593 --- [           main] io.undertow.
servlet                                 : Initializing Spring embedded
WebApplicationContext
2025-04-22T15:49:35.863Z  INFO 48593 --- [           main] w.s.c.Servlet
WebServerApplicationContext : Root WebApplicationContext: initialization
completed in 1598 ms
2025-04-22T15:49:36.082Z  INFO 48593 --- [           main] io.undertow
: starting server: Undertow - 2.3.13.Final
2025-04-22T15:49:36.093Z  INFO 48593 --- [           main] org.xnio
: XNIO version 3.8.8.Final
2025-04-22T15:49:36.105Z  INFO 48593 --- [           main] org.xnio.nio
: XNIO NIO Implementation Version 3.8.8.Final
2025-04-22T15:49:36.317Z  INFO 48593 --- [           main] org.jboss.
threads                                  : JBoss Threads version 3.5.0.Final
2025-04-22T15:49:36.396Z  INFO 48593 --- [           main]
o.s.b.w.e.undertow.UndertowWebServer     : Undertow started on port 8080
(http) with context path '/'
2025-04-22T15:49:36.486Z  INFO 48593 --- [           main] o.s.b.a.w.s.
WelcomePageHandlerMapping    : Adding welcome page: class path resource
[static/index.html]
2025-04-22T15:49:37.404Z  INFO 48593 --- [           main] com.github.
tjake.jlama.cli.JlamaCli      : Started JlamaCli in 3.849 seconds (process
running for 7.063)
```

From this output, you can observe three things:

1. It uses Spring Boot internally to create this UI and api endpoint.
2. The UI for the chat can be accessed at http://localhost:8080.
3. The OpenAI chat API proxy can be accessed at http://localhost:8080/chat/completions.

Let's visit the UI app at http://localhost:8080. Figure 13-1 shows the UI of the chat app.

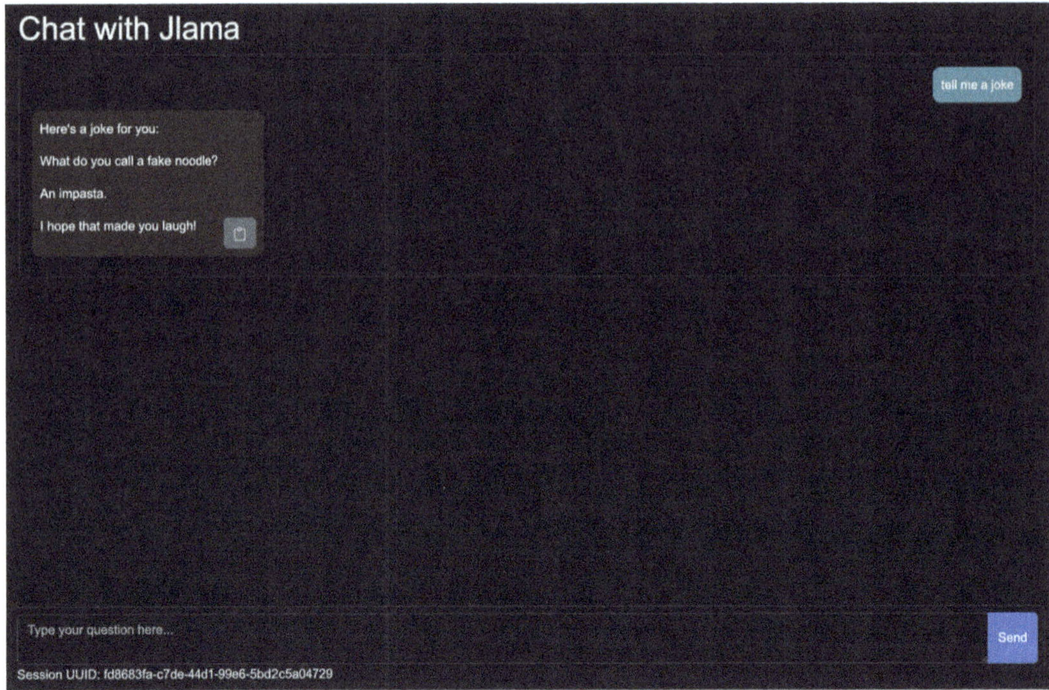

Figure 13-1. *Jlama chat UI interface*

This is handy to prototype and experiment quickly right in Java without any set up in Python. The next task for us is to see how to use it in a framework like Quarkus.

Quantize a Model Using Jlama

Quantization is a compression method that reduces high-precision values to lower-precision counterparts. In the context of LLMs, this involves lowering the precision of weights and activations to decrease memory usage. While this process can impact model performance, including accuracy, it is often a trade-off guided by specific use cases. In many scenarios, quantized models can deliver results comparable to full-precision versions, despite the reduced precision. Additionally, quantization enhances performance by lowering memory bandwidth demands and improving cache efficiency.

Jlama provides many options, and one of them is to quantize different LLMs. You can explore the different options to use it by typing the following command:

```
jlama quantize -help
```

Output:

```
Usage:

jlama quantize [OPTIONS] <model name> [<output>]

Description:

Quantize the specified model

Parameters:
*      <model name>          The huggingface model owner/name pair
     [<output>]             The output location

Command Options:
     --model-cache=ARG      The local directory for downloaded models
                            (default:
                              models)
     --quantization=ARG     Model quantization type (default: Q4)
     --skip-layer=ARG       Layer name prefix to not quantize (default: norm)
     --drop-layer=ARG       Layer name prefix to drop
Download Options:
     --auto-download        Download the model if missing (default: false)
     --branch=ARG           The model branch to download from (default: main)
     --auth-token=ARG       HuggingFace auth token (for restricted models)
```

Currently, it provides support for quantization of following LLM family member as listed at `https://github.com/tjake/Jlama/blob/main/jlama-core/src/main/java/com/github/tjake/jlama/model/ModelSupport.java`. A sample of the code supporting different models at this point of time is shown here:

```
import com.github.tjake.jlama.model.bert.BertConfig;
import com.github.tjake.jlama.model.bert.BertModel;
import com.github.tjake.jlama.model.bert.BertTokenizer;
import com.github.tjake.jlama.model.gemma.GemmaConfig;
```

```
import com.github.tjake.jlama.model.gemma.GemmaModel;
import com.github.tjake.jlama.model.gemma.GemmaTokenizer;
import com.github.tjake.jlama.model.gemma2.Gemma2Config;
import com.github.tjake.jlama.model.gemma2.Gemma2Model;
import com.github.tjake.jlama.model.gpt2.GPT2Config;
import com.github.tjake.jlama.model.gpt2.GPT2Model;
import com.github.tjake.jlama.model.gpt2.GPT2Tokenizer;
import com.github.tjake.jlama.model.granite.GraniteConfig;
import com.github.tjake.jlama.model.granite.GraniteModel;
import com.github.tjake.jlama.model.llama.LlamaConfig;
import com.github.tjake.jlama.model.llama.LlamaModel;
import com.github.tjake.jlama.model.llama.LlamaTokenizer;
import com.github.tjake.jlama.model.mistral.MistralConfig;
import com.github.tjake.jlama.model.mistral.MistralModel;
import com.github.tjake.jlama.model.mixtral.MixtralConfig;
import com.github.tjake.jlama.model.mixtral.MixtralModel;
import com.github.tjake.jlama.model.qwen2.Qwen2Config;
import com.github.tjake.jlama.model.qwen2.Qwen2Model;
```

Now let's will experiment with Qwen2 model. You can start by visiting the Hugging Face page of Qwen at `https://huggingface.co/Qwen`, as shown in Figure 13-2.

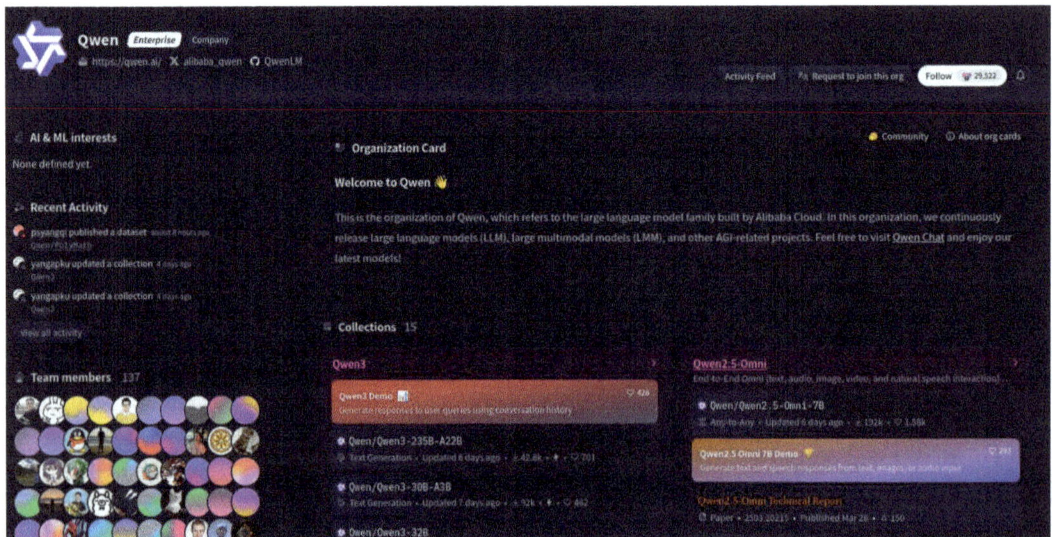

Figure 13-2. Qwen Hugging Face repository home page

On this page you will search for the Qwen2 family of models. Click the "Expand collections" button to see the Qwen2 model, as shown in Figure 13-3.

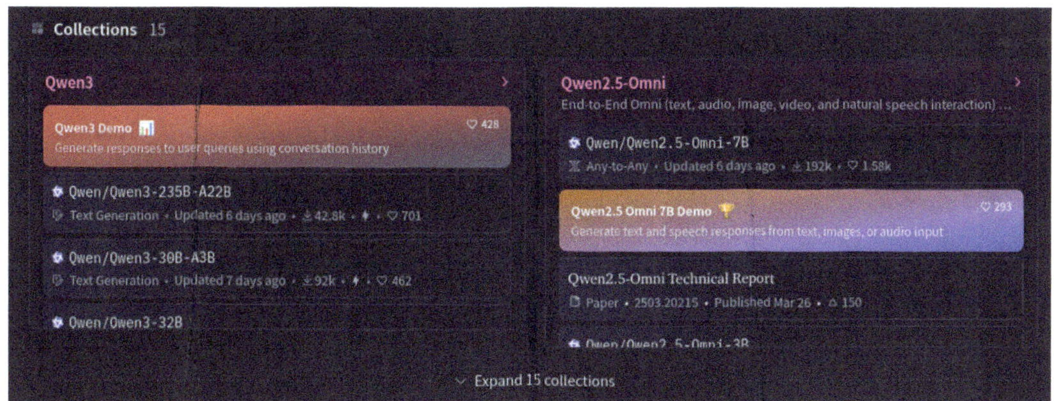

Figure 13-3. *Qwen model collections*

You can see the Qwen2 model list in the expanded collection in Figure 13-4.

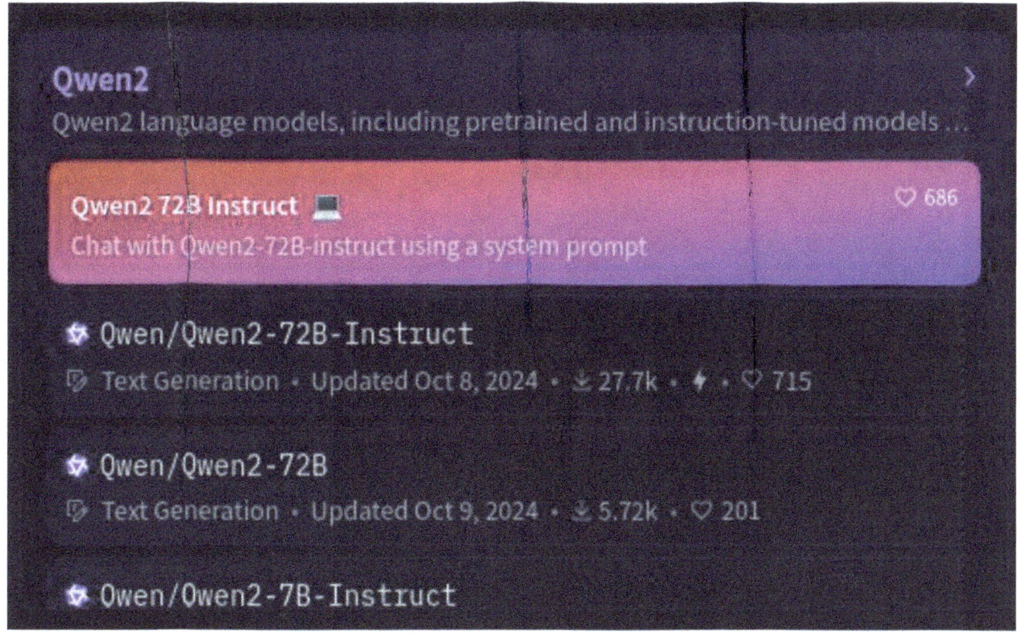

Figure 13-4. *Qwen2 list of models*

Click the Qwen2 Release link, which will take you to a separate page for Qwen2 based models, as shown in Figure 13-5.

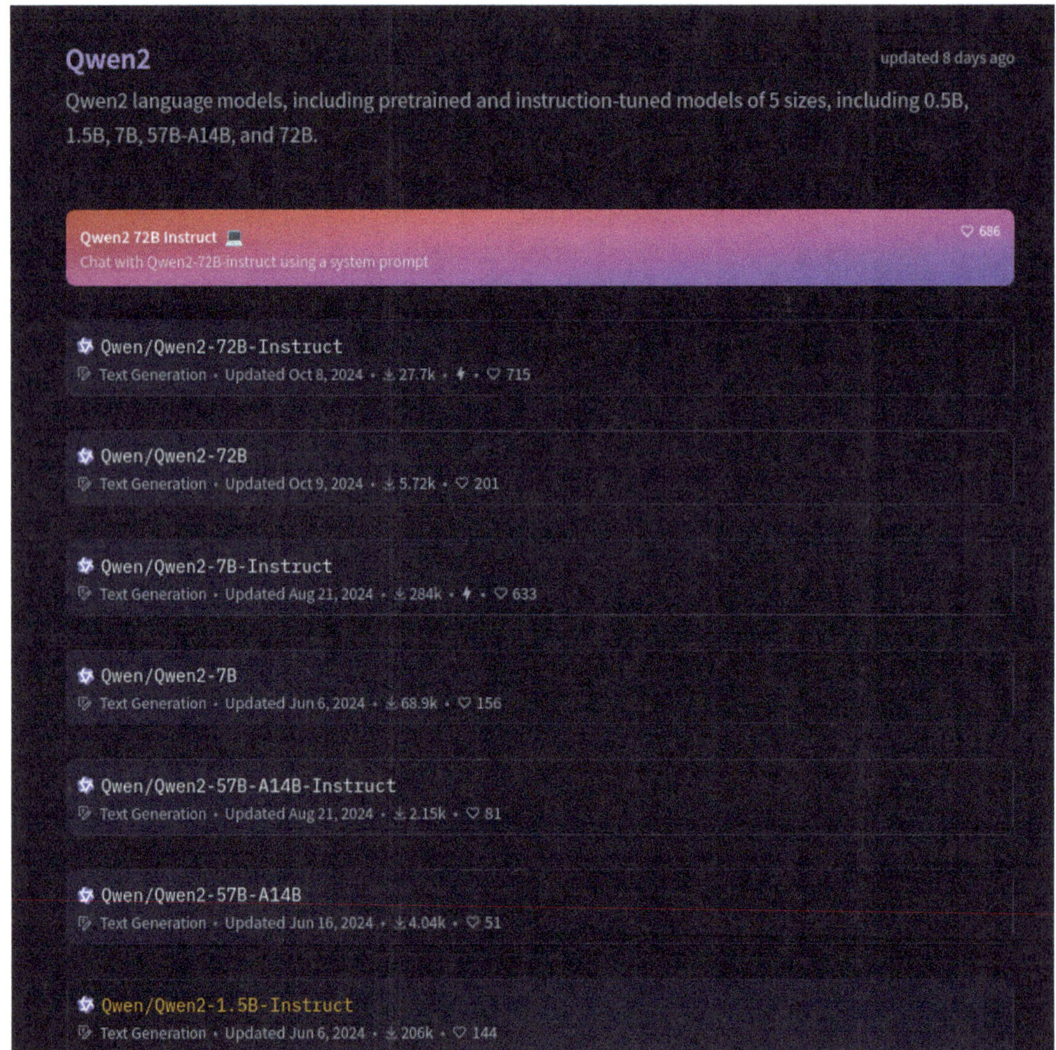

Figure 13-5. *Qwen2 page for LLM models*

Let's choose a simple small model for the use case, which is Qwen/Qwen2-0.5B. As shown in Figure 13-6, you will need to create an account if you don't already have one and in some cases like Gemma models from Google accept the conditions of use, as shown in Figure 13-6.

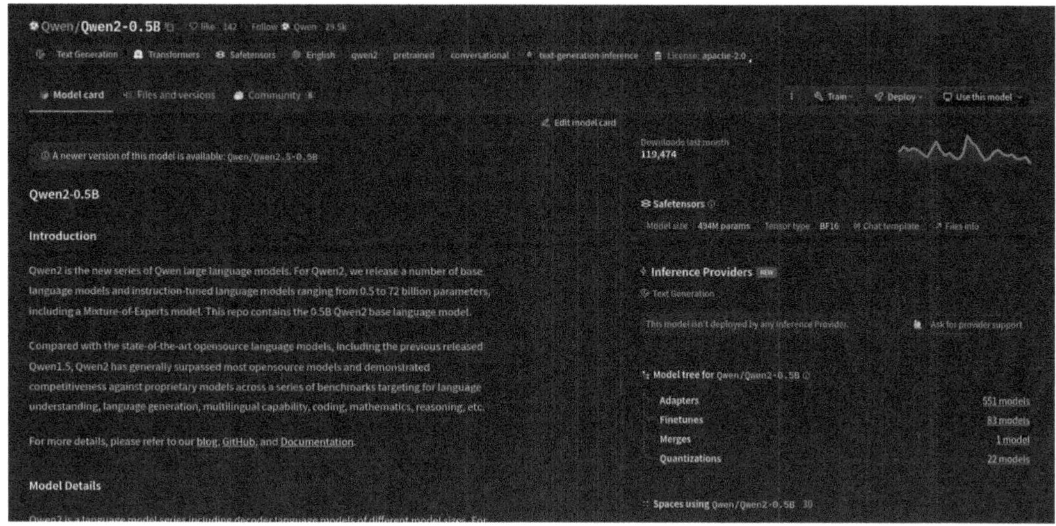

Figure 13-6. *Qwen2-0.5B model page*

To use this model, you will need an API token from the Hugging Face account, which has read permission. This can be done from the access tokens page in the profile drop-down list or by visiting `https://huggingface.co/settings/tokens`. Click the "Create new token" button and fill in the token form, as shown in Figure 13-7. Copy the token, which will be needed in the following section.

Create new Access Token
Token type
Fine-grained Read Write
This cannot be changed after token creation.
Token name
jlama api experiment
This token has read-only access to all your and your orgs resources and can make calls to Inference Providers on your behalf. It can also be used to open pull requests and comment on discussions.
Create token

Figure 13-7. *Hugging Face access token form*

Now that you know which model you are going to quantize, let's proceed with using jlama command for this. The following will download the model relevant files and then quantize the model:

```
jlama quantize Qwen/Qwen2-0.5B --auto-download --auth-token=YOUR_COPIED_
ACCESS_TOKEN
```

Output:

```
NOTE: Picked up JDK_JAVA_OPTIONS: --add-modules jdk.incubator.vector
--enable-preview WARNING: Using incubator modules: jdk.incubator.
vector NOTE: Picked up JDK_JAVA_OPTIONS: --add-modules jdk.incubator.
vector --enable-preview WARNING: Using incubator modules: jdk.incubator.
vector README.md 100% [====================================] 4/4KB (0:00:01
/ 0:00:00) config.json 100% [===============================] 661/661B
(0:00:01 / 0:00:00) model.safetensors 100% [======================]
988/988MB (0:00:04 / 0:00:00) tokenizer.json 100% [=====================
=========] 7/7MB (0:00:01 / 0:00:00) tokenizer_config.json 0% [ ] 0/1KB
(0:00:00 / ?) Skipping quantization of layer: model.norm.weight Skipping
quantization of layer: model.layers.5.post_attention_layernorm.weight
Skipping quantization of layer: model.layers.9.input_layernorm.weight
tokenizer_config.json 100% [======================] 1/1KB (0:00:01 /
0:00:00) Skipping quantization of layer: model.layers.15.input_layernorm.
weight Skipping quantization of layer: model.layers.22.input_layernorm.
weight Skipping quantization of layer: model.layers.6.post_attention_
layernorm.weight Skipping quantization of layer: model.layers.3.post_
attention_layernorm.weight Skipping quantization of layer: model.
layers.7.input_layernorm.weight Skipping quantization of layer: model.
layers.10.post_attention_layernorm.weight Skipping quantization of layer:
model.layers.17.input_layernorm.weight Skipping quantization of layer:
model.layers.4.post_attention_layernorm.weight Skipping quantization of
layer: model.layers.20.input_layernorm.weight Skipping quantization of
layer: model.layers.18.input_layernorm.weight Skipping quantization of
layer: model.layers.8.post_attention_layernorm.weight Skipping quantization
of layer: model.layers.11.input_layernorm.weight Skipping quantization
of layer: model.layers.9.post_attention_layernorm.weight Skipping
quantization of layer: model.layers.11.post_attention_layernorm.weight
```

```
Skipping quantization of layer: model.layers.4.input_layernorm.weight
Skipping quantization of layer: model.layers.13.post_attention_layernorm.
weight Skipping quantization of layer: model.layers.13.input_layernorm.
weight Skipping quantization of layer: model.layers.2.input_layernorm.
weight Skipping quantization of layer: model.layers.7.post_attention_
layernorm.weight Skipping quantization of layer: model.layers.12.
post_attention_layernorm.weight Skipping quantization of layer: model.
layers.1.input_layernorm.weight Skipping quantization of layer: model.
layers.15.post_attention_layernorm.weight Skipping quantization of layer:
model.layers.14.input_layernorm.weight Skipping quantization of layer:
model.layers.23.input_layernorm.weight Skipping quantization of layer:
model.layers.8.input_layernorm.weight Skipping quantization of layer:
model.layers.14.post_attention_layernorm.weight Skipping quantization
of layer: model.layers.16.post_attention_layernorm.weight Skipping
quantization of layer: model.layers.16.input_layernorm.weight Skipping
quantization of layer: model.layers.21.input_layernorm.weight Skipping
quantization of layer: model.layers.20.post_attention_layernorm.weight
Skipping quantization of layer: model.layers.21.post_attention_layernorm.
weight Skipping quantization of layer: model.layers.6.input_layernorm.
weight Skipping quantization of layer: model.layers.2.post_attention_
layernorm.weight Skipping quantization of layer: model.layers.18.
post_attention_layernorm.weight Skipping quantization of layer: model.
layers.5.input_layernorm.weight Skipping quantization of layer: model.
layers.19.input_layernorm.weight Skipping quantization of layer: model.
layers.10.input_layernorm.weight Skipping quantization of layer: model.
layers.22.post_attention_layernorm.weight Skipping quantization of layer:
model.layers.17.post_attention_layernorm.weight Skipping quantization of
layer: model.layers.0.post_attention_layernorm.weight Skipping quantization
of layer: model.layers.23.post_attention_layernorm.weight Skipping
quantization of layer: model.layers.3.input_layernorm.weight Skipping
quantization of layer: model.layers.12.input_layernorm.weight Skipping
quantization of layer: model.layers.1.post_attention_layernorm.weight
Skipping quantization of layer: model.layers.19.post_attention_layernorm.
weight Quantized model written to: /home/ubuntu/models/Qwen_Qwen2-0.5B-JQ4
```

This will create the quantized model in the directory where you ran the command inside another directory named models. Now, this model is much reduced in size and can be loaded with less memory usage. Let's use it with jlama to test it:

```
jlama chat Qwen/Qwen2-0.5B-JQ4
```

Output:

```
NOTE: Picked up JDK_JAVA_OPTIONS: --add-modules jdk.incubator.vector
--enable-preview WARNING: Using incubator modules: jdk.incubator.vector
NOTE: Picked up JDK_JAVA_OPTIONS: --add-modules jdk.incubator.vector
--enable-preview WARNING: Using incubator modules: jdk.incubator.vector
Model type = Q4, Working memory type = F32, Quantized memory type = F32
Chatting with Qwen/Qwen2-0.5B-JQ4...
You: Tell me about earth. Limit to a single sentence.
Jlama: Using Native SIMD Operations (OffHeap) Earth is a planet, a gas and
rock ball in space, a part of the solar system, and a part of the galaxy.
It takes up about 99.98% of the volume of the solar system and is about 40%
of the total solar system's mass. It is surrounded by a dense, stable, and
molten layer of hydrogen, helium, and oxygen called the atmosphere. The
atmosphere is a thick layer that contains water vapor, nitrogen, oxygen,
and carbon dioxide, which are the building blocks of life. It is also ruled
by a protective ring of methane and nitrogen, known as the core, which
contains molten iron, nickel, and oxygen. The moon, Mercury, and Venus are
also part of Earth's system, but they are smaller and less visible.
```

This is some pretty interesting output from a quantized model, and you were able to achieve this without any deep knowledge of machine learning courtesy of the jlama engine.

Use Jlama with Quarkus to Build a Gen AI Application

By default, the sample project is configured to use a small Llama 2 model, quantized to 4 bits. When the application is initially built, Jlama automatically downloads this model from the Hugging Face repository to your local system. However, you can easily substitute this default model with any other compatible model to experiment with different LLMs. To do so, simply modify the quarkus.langchain4j.jlama.chat-model.model-name property within your application.properties file.

A dedicated Langchain4j extension provides strong integration between Jlama and Quarkus. Jlama's performance is enhanced by the Vector API, a preview feature in Java 23 that is likely to become a standard feature in Java 25.

You have already explored how the LangChain4j extension works with Quarkus in a previous chapters. Now you will extend it to use a Jlama-hosted LLM instead of the OpenAI API. I am using Java 21.0.7-tem using sdkman. Since Jlama uses preview features and the Vector API, make sure to set JDK_JAVA_OPTIONS as follows in your environment or in your pom.xml file:

```
export JDK_JAVA_OPTIONS="--add-modules jdk.incubator.vector --enable-preview"
```

There are three package dependencies you need to update in pom.xml, as shown here:

File: pom.xml

```
<dependency>
    <groupId>com.github.tjake</groupId>
    <artifactId>jlama-core</artifactId>
    <version>${jlama.version}</version>
</dependency>
<dependency>
    <groupId>io.quarkiverse.langchain4j</groupId>
    <artifactId>quarkus-langchain4j-jlama</artifactId>
    <version>0.26.2</version>
</dependency>
<dependency>
    <groupId>com.github.tjake</groupId>
    <artifactId>jlama-native</artifactId>
    <!-- supports linux-x86_64, macos-x86_64/aarch_64, windows-x86_64
        Use https://github.com/trustin/os-maven-plugin to detect os and
        arch -->
    <classifier>linux-x86_64</classifier>
    <version>${jlama.version}</version>
</dependency>
```

```
        ...
        ...
<configuration>
    <jvmArgs>--enable-preview --enable-native-access=ALL-UNNAMED</jvmArgs>
    <modules>
        <module>jdk.incubator.vector</module>
    </modules>
</configuration>
```

The next step is to update the application.properties file with some properties specific to Jlama such as the model name and the dimension value for the Redis store since the new model might have a different dimension for the embeddings than OpenAI, which you previously used.

File: src/main/resources/application.properties

```
quarkus.langchain4j.timeout=60s

quarkus.langchain4j.log-requests=true
quarkus.langchain4j.log-responses=true

quarkus.langchain4j.redis.dimension=384
quarkus.log.level=INFO
quarkus.package.jar.decompiler.enabled=true

quarkus.langchain4j.jlama.chat-model.model-name=tjake/Llama-3.2-3B-
Instruct-JQ4
quarkus.langchain4j.jlama.chat-model.temperature=0

quarkus.langchain4j.jlama.log-requests=false
quarkus.langchain4j.jlama.log-responses=false
quarkus.langchain4j.chat-model.provider=jlama
quarkus.langchain4j.embedding-model.provider=jlama
```

These were all the changes needed. Seems simple, right? Let's boot up the Spring Boot application and test it.

Boot-up output:

```
[INFO] [io.quarkus.deployment.dev.DevModeCommandLineBuilder] Extension
io.quarkiverse.langchain4j:quarkus-langchain4j-jlama enables the C2
compiler which is disabled by default in Dev mode for optimal performance.
[INFO] [io.quarkus.deployment.dev.DevModeCommandLineBuilder] Extension
io.quarkiverse.langchain4j:quarkus-langchain4j-jlama disables the Debug
mode for optimal performance. Debugging can still be enabled in the Quarkus
plugin configuration or with -Ddebug on the command line.
WARNING: Using incubator modules: jdk.incubator.vector

2025-04-22 20:25:46,366 INFO  [io.dem.lan.sam.uti.ApplicationStartup]
(Quarkus Main Thread) Application starting...
2025-04-22 20:25:46,367 INFO  [io.dem.lan.sam.uti.ApplicationStartup]
(Quarkus Main Thread) Inserting initial customer...
2025-04-22 20:25:46,534 INFO  [io.dem.lan.sam.uti.ApplicationStartup]
(Quarkus Main Thread) Initial customer inserted with ID: 1
2025-04-22 20:25:46,542 INFO  [io.dem.lan.sam.uti.ApplicationStartup]
(Quarkus Main Thread) Documents read from catalog.csv
2025-04-22 20:25:46,543 INFO  [io.dem.lan.sam.uti.ApplicationStartup]
(Quarkus Main Thread) Ingesting documents into Redis...
2025-04-22 20:25:47,295 INFO  [com.git.tja.jla.mod.AbstractModel] (Quarkus
Main Thread) Model type = F32, Working memory type = F32, Quantized memory
type = F32
2025-04-22 20:25:47,510 INFO  [com.git.tja.jla.ten.ope.
TensorOperationsProvider] (Quarkus Main Thread) Using Native SIMD
Operations (OffHeap)
2025-04-22 20:25:49,409 INFO  [io.dem.lan.sam.uti.ApplicationStartup]
(Quarkus Main Thread) Documents ingested into Redis.
2025-04-22 20:25:49,500 INFO  [io.quarkus] (Quarkus Main Thread) code-
with-quarkus 1.0.0-SNAPSHOT on JVM (powered by Quarkus 3.21.3) started in
148.568s. Listening on: http://localhost:8080
2025-04-22 20:25:49,502 INFO  [io.quarkus] (Quarkus Main Thread) Profile
dev activated. Live Coding activated.
```

```
2025-04-22 20:25:49,503 INFO  [io.quarkus] (Quarkus Main Thread) Installed
features: [agroal, cdi, hibernate-orm, hibernate-orm-panache, hibernate-
orm-rest-data-panache, jdbc-db2, langchain4j, langchain4j-jlama,
langchain4j-openai, langchain4j-redis, narayana-jta, qute, redis-client,
rest, rest-client, rest-client-jackson, rest-jackson, rest-links, smallrye-
context-propagation, vertx]
```

Now let's test the curl request:

```
curl localhost:8080/review --header 'Content-Type: text/plain' --data 'This
is a great product! I highly recommend it. Could you list all products from
your shop catalog?'
```

System Output:

```
2025-04-22 20:26:59,656 INFO  [io.dem.lan.sam.rag.
RetrievalAugmentorExample] (executor-thread-1) Creating
RetrievalAugmentorExample
2025-04-22 20:26:59,680 INFO  [io.dem.lan.sam.rag.
RetrievalAugmentorExample] (executor-thread-1) Retrieval
AugmentorExample created
2025-04-22 20:27:01,718 INFO  [com.git.tja.jla.mod.AbstractModel]
(executor-thread-1) Model type = Q4, Working memory type = F32, Quantized
memory type = I8
```

Curl Output:

```
{"evaluation":"POSITIVE","message":"Thank you for your review! We are glad
you like our T-Shirt. We have listed all our products from our shop catalog
below. Please find the details of the product you have purchased below.
Product ID: 1001, Product Name: T-Shirt, Price: $15.99, Category: Clothing,
Manufacturer: BrandA, SKU: TS-1001"}
```

As you can see from the output, there was no mention of the customer name, since this model does not support tooling like OpenAI did. The output is comparable to the previous output you received using the OpenAI API. There was an additional statement, "Please find the details of the product you have purchased below," which was unwarranted and can be further checked through prompt engineering. Also, instead of listing all the products, it listed only one. This is where you could leverage better prompts and also test with other models. The overall takeaway is that all of this is happening in the machine in Java.

Conclusion

In this chapter, you learned how the Java ecosystem has evolved to support native LLM inference through libraries like Jlama, eliminating the need for external Python-based servers or third-party APIs. By embedding Jlama directly into your Java application—whether via the simple CLI, through the OpenAI-compatible REST API, or seamlessly through Quarkus and Langchain4j—you gain full control over model lifecycle, data privacy, and operational complexity. You learned how to install and invoke Jlama using JBang, interact with models from the command line, and expose them as services, all while leveraging Java's Vector API for high-performance inference.

To put these concepts into practice, consider building small but meaningful projects such as:

- A local LLM-powered chatbot for customer support or internal tools
- A document summarization microservice using your own data
- An offline code generation assistant embedded in an IDE plugin
- A Quarkus-based REST API that performs Q&A over enterprise knowledge bases
- A CLI tool for text classification or sentiment analysis using fine-tuned models

These practical exercises will help solidify your understanding and expose real-world integration challenges—preparing you for more complex production scenarios.

Moreover, by integrating Jlama into a Quarkus-based generative AI application, you've experienced firsthand how minimal configuration changes in your pom.xml and application.properties files can switch your project from cloud-hosted LLMs to an on-premise solution—without sacrificing observability, security, or developer productivity. As you continue experimenting with different models, quantization strategies, and prompt-engineering techniques, you'll find that hosting LLMs in Java not only streamlines your development and deployment pipelines but also unlocks new possibilities for edge and monolithic architectures.

Armed with these tools and concepts, you're now ready to explore more advanced scenarios: fine-tuning smaller models for your domain, orchestrating hybrid open-source and commercial LLMs, and building complex agentic workflows—all within the familiar confines of the JVM. The next chapter will delve into exploring multimodal LLMs. Onward to mastering Java-native generative AI!

CHAPTER 14

Seeing Is Believing: Multimodal LLMs and Image Hacking

The goal of this chapter is to understand the tools available in Java for image processing and the current capabilities generative AI (Gen AI) provides related to image and multimodal content processing.

Introduction

In an era where digital content streams in a rich tapestry of images, text, audio, and video, the ability to seamlessly process and understand multimodal data has become a defining feature of next-generation AI systems. Traditionally, image processing in Java has relied on mature libraries such as OpenCV—accessed via JNI through projects like OpenPnP OpenCV—and OCR engines like Tesseract to extract text from static media. While these tools excel at domain-specific tasks, they often require separate processing steps and bespoke integration layers to handle different data types.

The advent of multimodal large language models (LLMs) ushers in a transformative approach: one unified model that can jointly reason over images, text, and other modalities. By embedding dedicated encoders for each input type and consolidating reasoning within a shared transformer backbone, these models break down the silos between vision and language. As a result, developers can replace complex processing pipelines with concise prompts that yield structured, JSON-ready outputs, or even generate new media on demand.

S. K. Sahu, *Generative AI-Driven Application Development with Java*,
https://doi.org/10.1007/979-8-8688-1609-3_14

This chapter explores how to bridge established Java tooling with the latest generative AI capabilities. We begin by surveying the core image-processing libraries available to Java developers. We then introduce the principles behind multimodal LLMs and demonstrate their power through a hands-on Spring Boot application that scans customer flight tickets and returns structured data. Building upon this foundation, we show how to enrich user experiences by generating destination-inspired images and outline extensions to other modalities, from audio sentiment analysis to synthesized speech. By the end of this chapter, you'll understand both the classical and cutting-edge techniques for multimodal content processing in Java, and you'll be equipped to architect your own unified AI-driven workflows.

Tooling in Java for Image Processing

Image processing involves use of machine learning technologies and Optical Character Recognition (OCR) to process them. Machine learning generally involves the use of the Python language by using OpenCV library, which can be referenced at `https://opencv.org`. It supports the processing of images with support for real-time processing. OpenCV is written in C, there are relevant Java bindings for it through a project named OpenPnP OpenCV, which can be referenced at `https://github.com/openpnp/opencv`. It uses Java Native Interface (JNI) to load and operate OpenCV natively in Java. The API for classes and methods used in Java are similar to those in the OpenCV C project, encouraging the adoption of the Java library. This can be used by using the Maven-specific library package at `https://mvnrepository.com/artifact/org.openpnp/opencv`, as shown in Figure 14-1.

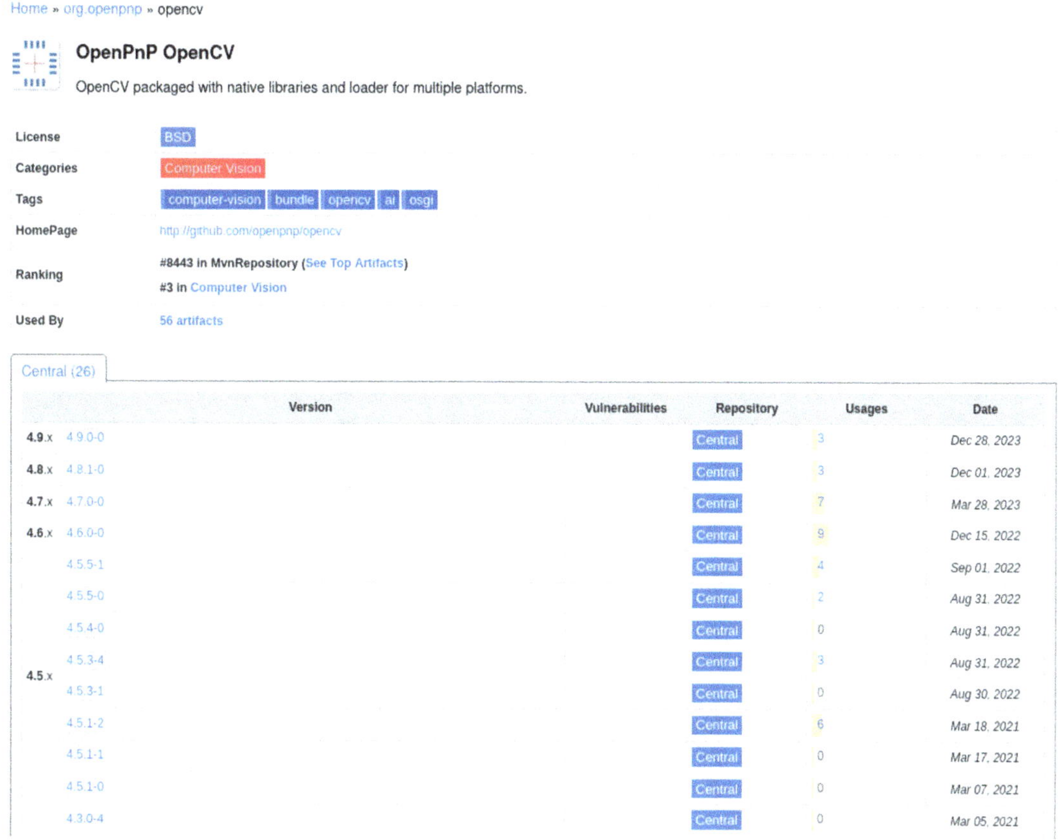

***Figure 14-1.** OpenPnP Maven repository*

Similarly, the Tesseract project helps in recognizing characters. OCR helps scan and retrieve the text present in a variety of formats like PDF, images, etc. The tesseract-platform Maven package can help you use Tesseract in your Java projects, as shown in Figure 14-2.

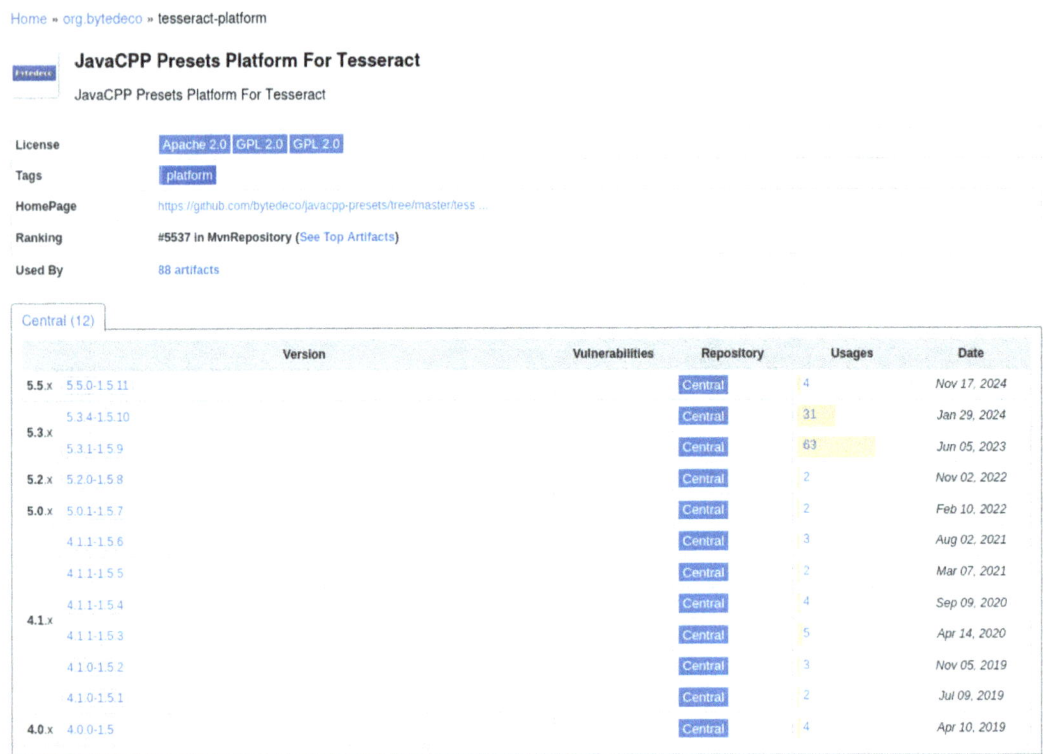

Home » org.bytedeco » tesseract-platform

JavaCPP Presets Platform For Tesseract

JavaCPP Presets Platform For Tesseract

License	Apache 2.0 GPL 2.0 GPL 2.0
Tags	platform
HomePage	https://github.com/bytedeco/javacpp-presets/tree/master/tess ...
Ranking	#5537 in MvnRepository (See Top Artifacts)
Used By	88 artifacts

Central (12)

	Version	Vulnerabilities	Repository	Usages	Date
5.5.x	5.5.0-1.5.11		Central	4	Nov 17, 2024
5.3.x	5.3.4-1.5.10		Central	31	Jan 29, 2024
	5.3.1-1.5.9		Central	63	Jun 05, 2023
5.2.x	5.2.0-1.5.8		Central	2	Nov 02, 2022
5.0.x	5.0.1-1.5.7		Central	2	Feb 10, 2022
4.1.x	4.1.1-1.5.6		Central	3	Aug 02, 2021
	4.1.1-1.5.5		Central	2	Mar 07, 2021
	4.1.1-1.5.4		Central	4	Sep 09, 2020
	4.1.1-1.5.3		Central	5	Apr 14, 2020
	4.1.0-1.5.2		Central	3	Nov 05, 2019
	4.1.0-1.5.1		Central	2	Jul 09, 2019
4.0.x	4.0.0-1.5		Central	4	Apr 10, 2019

Figure 14-2. *Maven repository for tesseract-platform*

You can plug in these technologies and tools as different components and chain them together to process images, but it only takes information in a single format generally, and you may have to make additional requests if you need to further process the information. How about using a single tool to process the image and also do other processing on it too? Yes, multimodal LLMs help you to do this, discussed in the next section.

Multimodal LLMs

Multimodal LLMs are an extension of traditional text-only LLMs that can accept and jointly reason over multiple types of data—most commonly text and images but increasingly audio, video, or even structured sensor inputs. By integrating dedicated encoders for each modality and a shared transformer-based core, these models learn to correlate visual patterns with linguistic concepts, enabling tasks that neither pure vision nor pure language models could tackle alone. Early successes in this space include models that align images and captions (e.g., CLIP), but the latest generation—such as GPT-4 with vision, Google's PaLM-E, and Meta's Florence—goes further by allowing users to pose free-form natural-language queries about images and receive coherent, context-aware responses. These models are bound to change with time and are to act as guidance to always verify the latest from the relevant vendor publishers and from Hugging Face.

The importance of multimodal LLMs lies in their ability to break down the barriers between how we see and how we speak. In practical terms, they power applications like visual question answering (e.g., "What ingredients are on this pizza?"), document understanding (e.g., extracting structured data from forms and invoices), and accessible interfaces for people with visual impairments. In robotics and autonomous systems, grounding language in real-world perception enables more intuitive control ("Pick up the red mug next to the keyboard"), while in creative domains, artists can sketch a scene and have the model generate evocative descriptions or even continue the artwork in code.

Beyond new use cases, multimodal LLMs also enhance robustness and disambiguation. Visual context can resolve linguistic ambiguities—distinguishing "bank" as a financial institution versus a riverbank when shown a relevant image—and language can guide vision modules toward task-specific observations. As these models continue to improve, they promise to form the backbone of "generalist" AI assistants, capable of seamlessly switching between reading, writing, and perceiving the world through multiple senses, thereby bringing us closer to more natural, human-like interactions with machines.

Building an Application to Process Flight Tickets

Returning to the airline company example, say you have a new requirement where you want to process flight tickets shared by your customers. The first task is to scan all customer relevant information from the ticket.

Let's start by creating a project from Spring Initializr with dependencies, as shown in Figure 14-3.

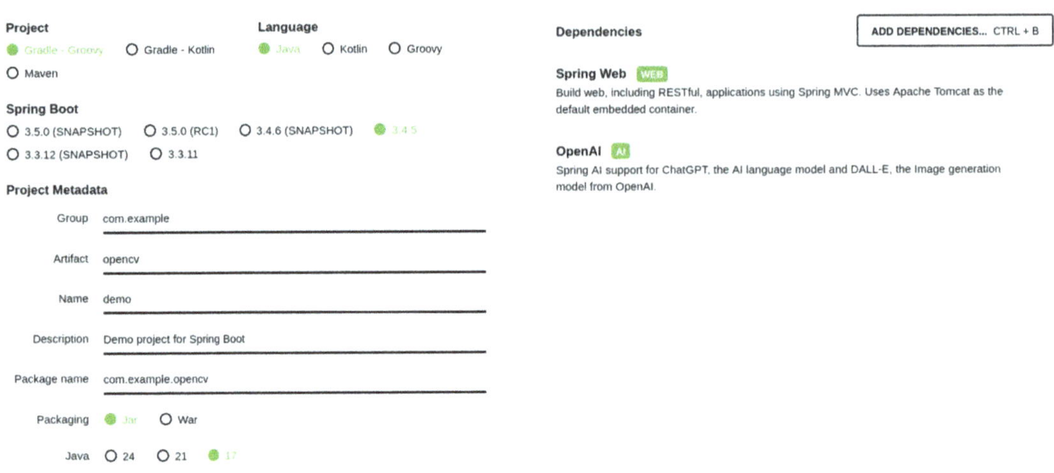

Figure 14-3. *Initializing Spring Project with dependencies*

Download the zip and unzip it at a location of your choice. The following is the final version of the `build.gradle` file:

File: ./build.gradle

```
plugins {
    id 'java'
    id 'org.springframework.boot' version '3.4.5'
    id 'io.spring.dependency-management' version '1.1.7'
}

group = 'com.example'
version = '0.0.1-SNAPSHOT'

java {
    toolchain {
        languageVersion = JavaLanguageVersion.of(17)
    }
}
```

```
repositories {
    mavenCentral()
}

ext {
    set('springAiVersion', "1.0.0-M8")
}

dependencies {
    implementation 'org.springframework.boot:spring-boot-starter-web'
    implementation 'org.springframework.ai:spring-ai-starter-model-openai'
    testImplementation 'org.springframework.boot:spring-boot-starter-test'
    testRuntimeOnly 'org.junit.platform:junit-platform-launcher'
}

dependencyManagement {
    imports {
       mavenBom "org.springframework.ai:spring-ai-bom:${springAiVersion}"
    }
}

tasks.named('test') {
    useJUnitPlatform()
}
```

Before you boot up your application, make sure to set your OpenAI API key in the `application.properties` file, as shown here:

File: ./src/main/resources/application.properties

```
spring.application.name=opencv
spring.ai.openai.api-key=YOUR_OPENAI_API_KEY
```

The goal is to scan and read the content in the sample ticket, as shown in Figure 14-4.

***Figure 14-4.** Sample flight ticket*

This would generally be uploaded by the user through an API request, but to keep it simple here and limit the focus to the task at hand, you will store it in the resources folder with the name `flight_ticket.jpg`.

Now that the basic foundational setup is done, let's view the different components we will build to achieve the goal at hand. There are four components to it, as shown in Figure 14-5. The first component is the controller, which receives the POST API request. On receiving the request, it fetches the image from the resource directory and makes a call to the Service component. The Service component uses the injected OpenAI component to scan the contents of the input image.

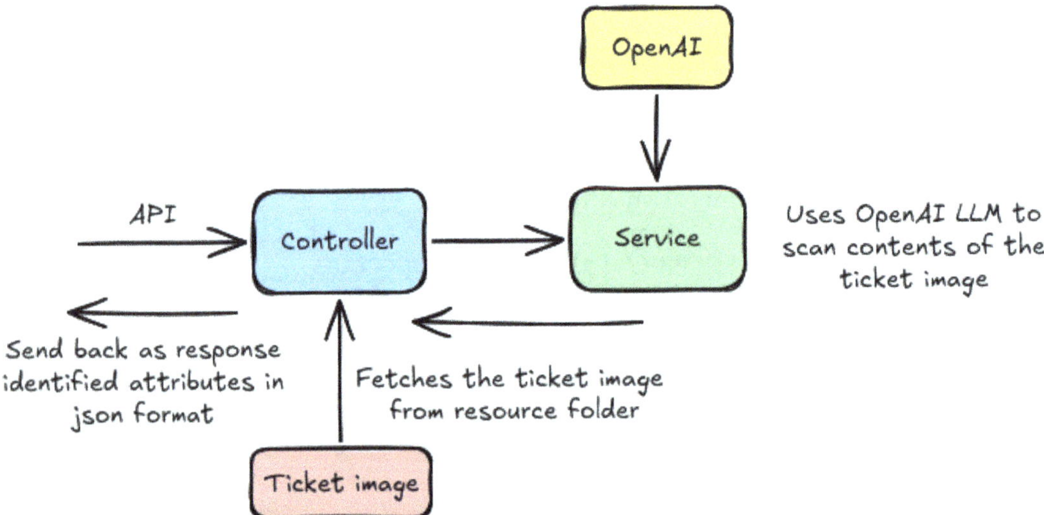

***Figure 14-5.** Components of the Spring Boot application*

To represent the response flight info, we will create a DTO object. It will contain some basic getter and setter methods related to the information present in our flight ticket like name, flightNumber, origin, destination, date, time, seatNumber, etc. We will not go too deep into its explanation as it is a standard practice in Java enterprise applications, and the code is self-explanatory. The full code for this DTO object is as follows:

File: ./src/main/java/com/example/opencv/model/FlightInfo.java

```
package com.example.opencv.model;

import java.time.LocalDate;
import java.time.LocalTime;

public class FlightInfo {
    private String name;
    private String flightNumber;
    private String origin;
    private String destination;
    private LocalDate date;
    private LocalTime time;
    private String seatNumber;

// No-arg constructor
   public FlightInfo() { }

// All-args constructor
   public FlightInfo(String name,
                     String flightNumber,
                     String origin,
                     String destination,
                     LocalDate date,
                     LocalTime time,
                     String seatNumber) {

        this.name = name;
        this.flightNumber = flightNumber;
        this.origin = origin;
        this.destination = destination;
        this.date = date;
```

```
        this.time = time;
        this.seatNumber = seatNumber;
    }

// Getters and setters

    public String getName() {
        return name;
    }

    public void setName(String name) {
        this.name = name;
    }

    public String getFlightNumber() {
        return flightNumber;
    }

    public void setFlightNumber(String flightNumber) {
        this.flightNumber = flightNumber;
    }

    public String getOrigin() {
        return origin;
    }

    public void setOrigin(String origin) {
        this.origin = origin;
    }

    public String getDestination() {
        return destination;
    }

    public void setDestination(String destination) {
        this.destination = destination;
    }
```

```
    public LocalDate getDate() {
        return date;
    }

    public void setDate(LocalDate date) {
        this.date = date;
    }

    public LocalTime getTime() {
        return time;
    }

    public void setTime(LocalTime time) {
        this.time = time;
    }

    public String getSeatNumber() {
        return seatNumber;
    }

    public void setSeatNumber(String seatNumber) {
        this.seatNumber = seatNumber;
    }
}
```

Now, let's build our first component, which is the Service component. We will name it `ScanService.java`. The `ScanService` constructor will receive one injected argument, which is the OpenAI `ChatModel` instance. This is created by default by Spring AI as a bean when the application is booted.

Figure 14-6 represents the different components and classes.

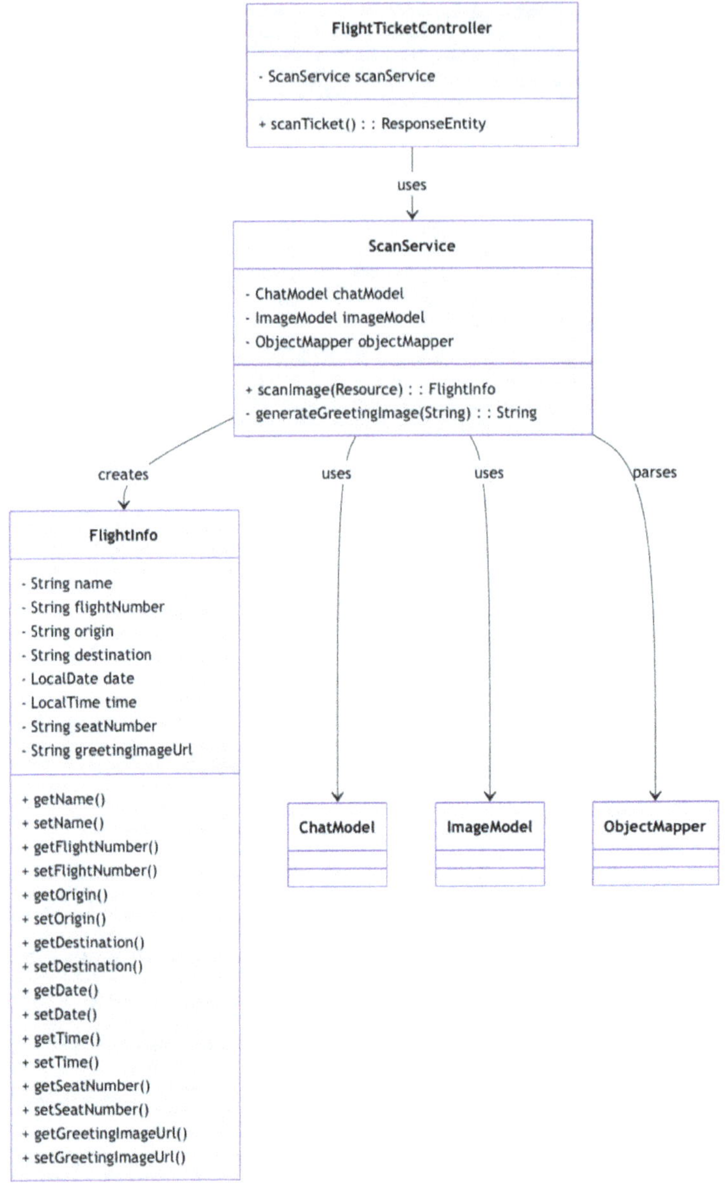

Figure 14-6. *Components and classes*

```
public ScanService(ChatModel chatModel) {
    this.chatModel = chatModel;
}
```

We will next define a method named `scanImage` that takes as an argument the image resource and returns the `FlightInfo` object.

```
public FlightInfo scanImage(Resource imageFile) {
```

There are three steps for setting up the request to OpenAI LLM to process the image:

1. Create an appropriate prompt requesting to process the image and fetch the relevant information.

2. Send the resource image in the request.

3. You do not just want the information in textual format but in a specific JSON format.

You will create a text prompt to request the LLM to scan the content of the flight ticket and also request to send it in an appropriate JSON format. Also, you can add an example JSON to give it a hint through one-shot prompting. The UserMessage API can be used for this purpose. It takes two arguments. The first is the text prompt, and the second is the additional file. The following code snippet shares this in detail. The word `json` in the prompt is important since it tells the LLM to produce the output in JSON format.

```
UserMessage userMessage = new UserMessage("""
        Scan the information in the Flight Ticket.
        Return in json format with keys like following example:
        {
            "name": "Jane Doe",
            "flightNumber": "XY1234",
            "origin": "SFO",
            "destination": "LHR",
            "date": "2025-06-01",
            "time": "14:45:00",
            "seatNumber": "21C"}
        """,
         new Media(MimeTypeUtils.IMAGE_JPEG, imageFile));
```

The user message object by itself doesn't do much and has to be used and passed to the OpenAI chat options request call. You will use the OpenAiChatOptions API to create the request object specifying the model to be used and what the response format should be. You can create a `ResponseFormat` object by specifying the response to be the `JSON_OBJECT` type.

```
ResponseFormat responseFormat = ResponseFormat.builder()
        .type(ResponseFormat.Type.JSON_OBJECT).build();

OpenAiChatOptions openAiChatOptions = OpenAiChatOptions.builder()
        .model(OpenAiApi.ChatModel.GPT_4_O_MINI.getValue())
        .responseFormat(responseFormat)
        .build();
```

The final step is to call the OpenAI API by invoking the call method on the ChatModel API, as shown here:

```
ChatResponse response = chatModel.call(new Prompt(userMessage,
openAiChatOptions));
```

Since the response is in text format and our method returns the `FlightInfo` object as response, you will need to map the text `json` to the DTO object by using `ObjectMapper`.

```
this.objectMapper = new ObjectMapper()
        .registerModule(new JavaTimeModule())
        .disable(SerializationFeature.WRITE_DATES_AS_TIMESTAMPS);

String jsonResponse = Objects.requireNonNull(
        response.getResult().getOutput().getText()).trim();

return objectMapper.readValue(jsonResponse, FlightInfo.class);
```

The full source code for the `ScanService.java` file is shown here:

File: ./src/main/java/com/example/opencv/service/ScanService.java

```
package com.example.opencv.service;

import com.example.opencv.model.FlightInfo;
import com.fasterxml.jackson.core.JsonProcessingException;
import com.fasterxml.jackson.databind.ObjectMapper;
import com.fasterxml.jackson.databind.SerializationFeature;
```

```
import com.fasterxml.jackson.datatype.jsr310.JavaTimeModule;
import org.springframework.ai.chat.messages.UserMessage;
import org.springframework.ai.chat.model.ChatModel;
import org.springframework.ai.chat.model.ChatResponse;
import org.springframework.ai.chat.prompt.Prompt;
import org.springframework.ai.content.Media;
import org.springframework.ai.openai.OpenAiChatOptions;
import org.springframework.ai.openai.api.OpenAiApi;
import org.springframework.ai.openai.api.ResponseFormat;
import org.springframework.core.io.Resource;
import org.springframework.stereotype.Service;
import org.springfRamework.util.MimeTypeUtils;

import java.util.Objects;

@Service
public class ScanService {

    private final ChatModel chatModel;
    private final ObjectMapper objectMapper;

    public ScanService(ChatModel chatModel) {
        this.chatModel = chatModel;
        this.objectMapper = new ObjectMapper()
                .registerModule(new JavaTimeModule())
                .disable(SerializationFeature.WRITE_DATES_AS_TIMESTAMPS);
    }

    public FlightInfo scanImage(Resource imageFile) throws
    JsonProcessingException {
        ResponseFormat responseFormat = ResponseFormat.builder()
                .type(ResponseFormat.Type.JSON_OBJECT).build();
        UserMessage userMessage = new UserMessage("""
               Scan the information in the Flight Ticket.
               Return in json format with keys like following example:
               {
                   "name": "Jane Doe",
                   "flightNumber": "XY1234",
```

```
                "origin": "SFO",
                "destination": "LHR",
                "date": "2025-06-01",
                "time": "14:45:00",
                "seatNumber": "21C"}
            """,
            new Media(MimeTypeUtils.IMAGE_JPEG, imageFile));
        OpenAiChatOptions openAiChatOptions = OpenAiChatOptions.builder()
            .model(OpenAiApi.ChatModel.GPT_4_O_MINI.getValue())
            .responseFormat(responseFormat)
            .build();
        ChatResponse response = chatModel.call(new Prompt(userMessage,
        openAiChatOptions));
        String jsonResponse = Objects.requireNonNull(
            response.getResult().getOutput().getText()).trim();

        return objectMapper.readValue(jsonResponse, FlightInfo.class);
    }
}
```

The final component to set up is the Controller component. Name it `FlightTicketController.java`. The functionality of this file is simple enough to fetch the resource file and make a call to the service component, as shown in the following code:

File: ./src/main/java/com/example/opencv/controller/FlightTicketController.java

```
package com.example.opencv.controller;
import com.example.opencv.model.FlightInfo;
import com.example.opencv.service.ScanService;
import org.springframework.beans.factory.annotation.Autowired;
import org.springframework.core.io.ClassPathResource;
import org.springframework.core.io.Resource;
import org.springframework.http.ResponseEntity;
import org.springframework.web.bind.annotation.*;
import java.io.IOException;
@RestController
```

```
@RequestMapping("/api/flight")
public class FlightTicketController {
    private final ScanService scanService;
    @Autowired
    public FlightTicketController(ScanService scanService) {
        this.scanService = scanService;
    }
    @PostMapping("/scan")
    public ResponseEntity<FlightInfo> scanTicket() throws IOException {
        // 1. Load the image from src/main/resources/flight_ticket.jpg
        Resource imgRes = new ClassPathResource("flight_ticket.jpg");
        // 2. Call the service
        FlightInfo info = scanService.scanImage(imgRes);
        // 3. Return the parsed fields
        return ResponseEntity.ok(info);
    }
}
```

The code is complete at this point. Now is the time to test it with a `curl` request.

```
curl -X POST    http://localhost:8080/api/flight/scan -H "Accept:
application/json"
```

Output:


```
{"name":"JOHNNY BRAVO","flightNumber":"ABC12345","origin":"JAKARTA","destin
ation":"NEW YORK","date":"2025-11-15","time":"06:15:00","seatNumber":"25"}
```


As you can see, the LLM has been successfully able to scan all the information in the image and also present it in JSON format. This showcases the multimodal nature of the use case where the LLM was able to take in both text and image as input, understand the request in the text, and process the image accordingly.

Generating Images from User Request

Until this point, you have experimented with text to text, image to text. How about text to image? This is where the image-generating capabilities of LLMs shine. There are many use cases where users want to generate images for their applications based on a creative idea they have or modify an existing image and add some enrichment or creativity on top of it.

In this section, we will augment our application to generate a creative image to motivate our customer about the destination place they are visiting and create a collage of all interesting places they could visit there. This seems to be an interesting idea! Let's get on to it.

You will use the existing application setup. You have the destination information fetched by the LLM. The next step is to request the LLM to generate an image with the appropriate prompt as a request to it. To use the image generation feature, you will need to inject the `imageModel`, which is by default created by Spring AI when your application boots as a bean. You can store a reference to it in the constructor as follows. This will allow you to use the `imageModel` later in your method calls.

```
public ScanService(ChatModel chatModel, ImageModel imageModel) {
    this.chatModel = chatModel;
    this.imageModel = imageModel;
    this.objectMapper = new ObjectMapper()
            .registerModule(new JavaTimeModule())
            .disable(SerializationFeature.WRITE_DATES_AS_TIMESTAMPS);
}
```

Let's define a method to achieve the image generation task named `generateGreetingImage` as follows. It returns the URL of the image generated and takes in as an argument the destination place as string type.

```
private String generateGreetingImage(String destination) {
```

We will then define a prompt to generate this image with the information of the user's destination:

```
String prompt = """
       As an airline industry, we strive to provide the best
       experience to our customers. After they have booked a
```

```
    flight ticket with us, we want to share a collage of
    Some beautiful places present at their destination
    location to inspire and motivate them. Generate an
    image for our customer who is planning to visit: %s
    """.formatted(destination);
```

To generate the image, we have the option to customize some of the attributes like quality, number of images to generate, height and width of the image, etc.

```
OpenAiImageOptions openAiImageOptions = OpenAiImageOptions.builder()
        .withQuality("hd")
        .withN(1)
        .withHeight(1024)
        .withWidth(1024)
        .build();
```

The final step is to instantiate the `ImagePrompt` with the prompt and image options and call the image model request.

```
ImagePrompt imagePrompt = new ImagePrompt(prompt, openAiImageOptions);
ImageResponse response = imageModel.call(imagePrompt);
return response.getResult().getOutput().getUrl().trim();
```

The end goal is to use this method call from within our `scanImage` method so that you can pass the destination as an argument to it and update the JSON response you send to your customer with the new attribute. To achieve this, you will also need to update your `FlightInfo` DTO with this new attribute with a default value of an empty string and respective getter and setter methods. This will enable backward compatibility.

File: ./src/main/java/com/example/opencv/model/FlightInfo.java

```
public class FlightInfo {
    private String name;
    private String flightNumber;
    private String origin;
    private String destination;
    private LocalDate date;
    private LocalTime time;
    private String seatNumber;
    private String greetingImageUrl = "";
```

```
    public String getGreetingImageUrl() {
        return greetingImageUrl;
    }

    public void setGreetingImageUrl(String greetingImageUrl) {
        this.greetingImageUrl = greetingImageUrl;
    }
}
```

Finally, you need to make a call to the generateGreetingImage method, as shown next. We fetch the destination set in the FlightInfo object and then use it to call the generate image method and set the result received through the call to the setter method.

```
FlightInfo flightInfo = objectMapper.readValue(jsonResponse,
FlightInfo.class);
String greetingImageUrl = this.generateGreetingImage(flightInfo.
getDestination());
flightInfo.setGreetingImageUrl(greetingImageUrl);
```

The following is the full source code of the ScanService.java file for your reference:

File: ./src/main/java/com/example/opencv/service/ScanService.java

```
package com.example.opencv.service;

import com.example.opencv.model.FlightInfo;
import com.fasterxml.jackson.core.JsonProcessingException;
import com.fasterxml.jackson.databind.ObjectMapper;
import com.fasterxml.jackson.databind.SerializationFeature;
import com.fasterxml.jackson.datatype.jsr310.JavaTimeModule;
import org.springframework.ai.chat.messages.UserMessage;
import org.springframework.ai.chat.model.ChatModel;
import org.springframework.ai.chat.model.ChatResponse;
import org.springframework.ai.chat.prompt.Prompt;
import org.springframework.ai.content.Media;
import org.springframework.ai.image.ImageModel;
import org.springframework.ai.image.ImagePrompt;
import org.springframework.ai.image.ImageResponse;
import org.springframework.ai.openai.OpenAiChatOptions;
```

```
import org.springframework.ai.openai.OpenAiImageOptions;
import org.springframework.ai.openai.api.OpenAiApi;
import org.springframework.ai.openai.api.ResponseFormat;
import org.springframework.core.io.Resource;
import org.springframework.stereotype.Service;
import org.springframework.util.MimeTypeUtils;

import java.util.Objects;

@Service
public class ScanService {

    private final ChatModel chatModel;
    private final ImageModel imageModel;
    private final ObjectMapper objectMapper;

    public ScanService(ChatModel chatModel, ImageModel imageModel) {
        this.chatModel = chatModel;
        this.imageModel = imageModel;
        this.objectMapper = new ObjectMapper()
                .registerModule(new JavaTimeModule())
                .disable(SerializationFeature.WRITE_DATES_AS_TIMESTAMPS);
    }

    private String generateGreetingImage(String destination) {
        String prompt = """
                As an airline industry, we strive to provide the best
                experience to our customers. After they have booked a
                flight ticket with us, we want to share a collage of
                some beautiful places present at their destination
                location to inspire and motivate them.  Generate an
                image for our customer who is planning to visit: %s
                """.formatted(destination);
        OpenAiImageOptions openAiImageOptions = OpenAiImageOptions.
        builder()
                .withQuality("hd")
                .withN(1)
                .withHeight(1024)
```

```
                .withWidth(1024)
                .build();
        ImagePrompt imagePrompt = new ImagePrompt(prompt,
        openAiImageOptions);
        ImageResponse response = imageModel.call(imagePrompt);
        return response.getResult().getOutput().getUrl().trim();
    }

    public FlightInfo scanImage(Resource imageFile) throws
    JsonProcessingException {
        ResponseFormat responseFormat = ResponseFormat.builder()
                .type(ResponseFormat.Type.JSON_OBJECT).build();
        UserMessage userMessage = new UserMessage("""
               Scan the information in the Flight Ticket.
               Return in json format with keys like following example:
               {
                   "name": "Jane Doe",
                   "flightNumber": "XY1234",
                   "origin": "SFO",
                   "destination": "LHR",
                   "date": "2025-06-01",
                   "time": "14:45:00",
                   "seatNumber": "21C"}
               """,
                new Media(MimeTypeUtils.IMAGE_JPEG, imageFile));
        OpenAiChatOptions openAiChatOptions = OpenAiChatOptions.builder()
                .model(OpenAiApi.ChatModel.GPT_4_O_MINI.getValue())
                .responseFormat(responseFormat)
                .build();
        ChatResponse response = chatModel.call(new Prompt(userMessage,
        openAiChatOptions));
        String jsonResponse = Objects.requireNonNull(
                response.getResult().getOutput().getText()).trim();
```

```
        FlightInfo flightInfo = objectMapper.readValue(jsonResponse,
        FlightInfo.class);
        String greetingImageUrl = this.generateGreetingImage(flightInfo.
        getDestination());
        flightInfo.setGreetingImageUrl(greetingImageUrl);

        return flightInfo;
    }
}
```

This was a nice plugin component with the existing requirement. Now, let's boot up our application and test it.

```
curl -X POST    http://localhost:8080/api/flight/scan -H "Accept:
application/json"
```

{"name":"JOHNNY BRAVO","flightNumber":"ABC 12345","origin":"JAKARTA","dest
ination":"NEW YORK","date":"2025-11-15","time":"06:15:00","seatNumber":"2
5","greetingImageUrl":"https://oaidalleapiprodscus.blob.core.windows.net/
private/org-f84uKx9Dr1Qz1LFLH7aNPFwF/user-elDKOkVYtVetb2VDGO2y............"}

The response now contains your greeting image URL, and I have shortened it for brevity's sake. You can further store this image in your storage location of choice based on your application requirements. You can click the URL to see the image generated by OpenAI, as shown in Figure 14-7.

Figure 14-7. *Open AI generated image for New York as destination, created assistance of GPT-4o Image Generation*

Similarly for a customer visiting India, we have the below figure as response as shown in Figure 14-8.

Figure 14-8. *Open AI generated image for India as destination, created with assistance of GPT-4o Image Generation*

The applications around this could be limitless. I am sure our customer would be very excited to see this image message along with their flight ticket.

Other multimodal formats

This does not have to stop with just one format. We can enrich our inputs with speech from our customer where they can speak on the go and we can pass this to the LLM or the customer is on the go and rather than having them to type, we can process their ask in speech and respond to them back in Speech taking into consideration their security while driving. The use cases are limitless and multimodal LLMs are here to help you.

We will dive deep into audio and video formats but will only touch base on their syntax to give you an idea on them. They can be very similarly, as the above example, be fit into our applications.

In the below example, we want to build an application which detects the emotion behind the user's response and respectively escalate if it's not as to their satisfaction to interact with a live agent. The gpt-4o-audio-preview model which is in preview at this moment can be used to process the audio content and give us the appropriate feedback.

```
Resource userResponseResource = new ClassPathResource("userResponse.mp3");

UserMessage userMessage = new UserMessage("Find out the category of user's
response to understand their emotion: POSITIVE, NEGATIVE, NEUTRAL",
      List.of(new Media(MimeTypeUtils.parseMimeType("audio/mp3"),
      userResponseResource)));

ChatResponse response = chatModel.call(
        new Prompt(List.of(userMessage),
                OpenAiChatOptions.builder()
                        .model(OpenAiApi.ChatModel.GPT_4_O_AUDIO_PREVIEW)
                        .build()
        ));
```

Let's say we want to present some audio to the user based on some logic control and processing of some content passed to the LLM. We can do this using the gpt-4o-audio-preview LLM model as shown in below example:

```
Resource userResponseResource = new ClassPathResource("userResponse.mp3");

User Message userMessage = new UserMessage("Find out the category of user's
response to understand their emotion: POSITIVE, NEGATIVE, NEUTRAL. If
NEGATIVE, convey the message that we are sorry that their experience has
not been positive and that an agent would be following up with them soon.",
```

```
        List.of(new Media(MimeTypeUtils.parseMimeType("audio/mp3"),
        userResponseResource)));

ChatResponse response = chatModel.call(
        new Prompt(List.of(userMessage),
                OpenAiChatOptions.builder()
                        .model(OpenAiApi.ChatModel.GPT_4_O_AUDIO_PREVIEW)
                        .outputModalities(List.of("text", "audio"))
                        .outputAudio(new AudioParameters(Voice.ALLOY,
                        AudioResponseFormat.WAV))
                        .build()
        ));

String text = response.getResult()
        .getOutput()
        .getContent(); // audio transcript for logging

byte[] waveAudio = response.getResult()
        .getOutput()
        .getMedia()
        .get(0)
        .getDataAsByteArray(); // audio data for the user
```

This use case is so useful since we do not have to convert the audio to text and text to audio as has been prevalent in the past and also instruct the LLM to work on the audio through text thus enabling multiple input formats to interact to give us the right result. We can also log the transcript for audit purposes to measure and evaluate our LLM for testing purposes.

Conclusion

In this chapter, we journeyed from traditional Java-based image processing—leveraging OpenCV and Tesseract OCR—to the frontier of multimodal AI, where a single large language model can ingest and interpret diverse data formats. By integrating multimodal LLMs into a Spring Boot application, we illustrated how to replace cumbersome pipelines with straightforward API calls that return business-ready JSON and even generate bespoke images tailored to user contexts.

Beyond text and images, we highlighted the extensibility of this approach to audio and video, demonstrating how models in preview can assess emotion from speech or produce synthesized voice responses without manual transcription or text-to-speech conversions. This unified paradigm not only simplifies development but also opens the door to more natural and accessible interfaces, whether for customer support, accessibility applications, or real-time interactive systems.

As multimodal LLMs continue to evolve—increasing in scale, efficiency, and the range of supported modalities—developers will find ever-richer possibilities for creating unified AI experiences. By combining robust Java tooling with these powerful models, you can build applications that see, hear, and reason about the world in concert, bringing us closer to truly holistic, human-centric AI systems.

Now we move on to ML in Java.

CHAPTER 15

Does It Even Work? Testing and Evaluating LLM Apps

The goal of this chapter is to focus on how to test and evaluate large language model (LLM) applications.

Introduction

Enterprise software teams have long relied on unit and integration tests to validate deterministic application logic. However, when integrating LLMs into backend services and APIs, those familiar testing paradigms fall short. LLMs behave as probabilistic engines: the same prompt can yield different responses on each call, and models may "hallucinate," producing plausible-sounding but incorrect or unsafe content. As a result, achieving confidence in LLM-powered features requires a shift from code-centric tests to a comprehensive evaluation framework that treats model outputs as first-class artifacts to be tested.

This chapter introduces the principles and practices needed to evaluate and test LLM applications at scale. It will begin by defining the core quality dimensions—relevance, accuracy, completeness, clarity, style compliance, bias, safety, latency, and cost—that every LLM deployment must measure and guard. Next, you will survey the ecosystems of tools and libraries—from dedicated Python evaluation frameworks to Java-centric solutions such as Spring AI's Evaluator interface. Through concrete examples and code snippets, you'll learn how to decouple evaluation from generation, plug in specialized checks (including secondary LLMs for automated fact-checking),

S. K. Sahu, *Generative AI-Driven Application Development with Java*,
https://doi.org/10.1007/979-8-8688-1609-3_15

and bake these checks into your continuous integration/continuous development (CI/CD) pipelines. By the end of this chapter, you will have a clear roadmap for building repeatable, automated workflows that catch hallucinations, enforce policy rules, and ensure your LLM-enhanced applications remain robust, compliant, and cost-effective.

Evaluation of LLM Applications

As organizations embed large language models into customer-facing products, it becomes essential to verify their outputs before they reach end users. Without a systematic evaluation framework, models can hallucinate—asserting plausible-sounding but unfounded claims—drift off-topic by ignoring the user's actual intent or retrieved context, or they can inadvertently introduce biased or unsafe language. Rigorous evaluation catches these issues early, protects user trust, ensures compliance with style and safety requirements, and helps control compute costs by routing checks to appropriately sized models.

A flexible evaluation framework treats evaluation as a separate step from generation: it accepts the original user prompt, any contextual data supplied (for example, retrieved documents), and the model's generated response. Then it returns a pass/fail verdict or score. Within this framework, different evaluators can be plugged in—one might use an LLM to verify that an answer aligns with the user's question and the provided context; another might perform factual consistency checks against authoritative sources; others can screen for clarity, stylistic compliance, bias, toxicity, or any domain-specific rules. Because evaluation is decoupled, teams can choose smaller or more specialized models for each check, dramatically reducing latency and cost compared with running a large flagship model for every test. Figure 15-1 highlights a sample flow.

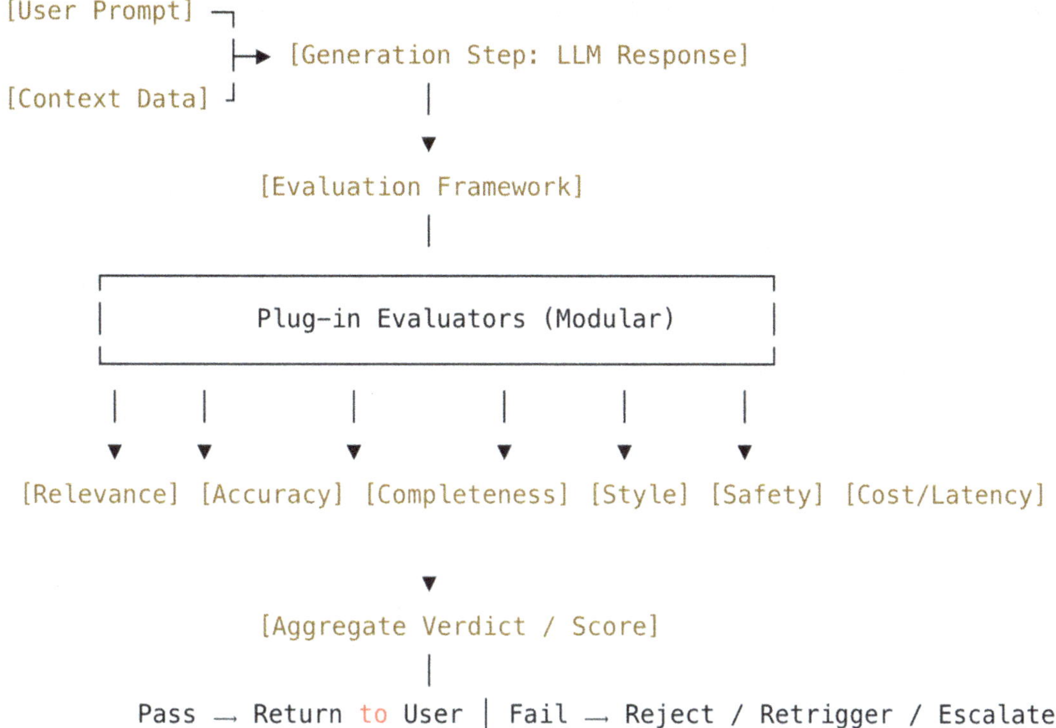

Figure 15-1. *Modular evaluation framework for LLM applications*

In practice, applications are assessed along multiple quality dimensions. Relevance checks ensure the answer addresses the user's intent and incorporates the supplied context. Accuracy evaluations verify that all factual claims are supported by trusted sources. Completeness audits confirm that no part of the user's request is omitted. Clarity and coherence assessments ensure the response is well-structured and understandable. Style and tone validators enforce branding or regulatory guidelines. Safety and bias detectors guard against harmful or discriminatory content. Finally, performance metrics such as evaluation latency and cost per check are monitored. By composing these evaluators into a continuous quality-gate workflow, teams catch hallucinations, off-topic drift, and unsafe content before it reaches users, safeguarding trust and enabling scalable, responsible AI deployments.

Tools Available for Evaluation and Testing

Table 15-1 summarizes the tools.

Table 15-1. *Summary of LLM Evaluation and Testing Tools*

Tool/Framework	Language	Key Features	Pros	Limitations
pytest/unittest	Python	Unit/integration testing, mocking, assertions	Widely used, easy to adopt	Not LLM-specific
Hypothesis	Python	Property-based testing with randomized inputs	Great for uncovering edge cases	Steeper learning curve
OpenAI Evals	Python	Task-based evaluation using LLMs	Extensible, community-driven	Requires prompt and task design
LangChain Evaluation Modules	Python	Built-in metrics for relevance, bias, etc.	Deep integration with LangChain apps	Best for LangChain users
Spring AI Evaluator	Java	Relevancy, fact-checking, extensible interface	JUnit-friendly, flexible	Java-only, newer ecosystem
Quarkus LangChain4j Scorer	Java	YAML-driven tests, semantic/AI scoring	Native Quarkus support, detailed CI output	Sparse documentation

Python offers a rich ecosystem of testing and evaluation tools that can be brought to bear on LLM applications. At the unit and integration level, frameworks like pytest and unittest let you mock model calls, simulate user prompts, and assert on outputs or metadata. For behavioral and end-to-end scenarios, property-based testing libraries (e.g., Hypothesis) help uncover edge-case failures by generating diverse inputs automatically. On top of that, dedicated LLM evaluation toolkits—such as OpenAI's evals framework and LangChain's evaluation modules—provide built-in metrics for relevance, factuality, coherence, and bias. You can orchestrate "ground truth versus model" comparisons, run adversarial or red-teaming exercises, and even plug in small, specialized models to flag hallucinations or style-guide violations. Combined with standard CI tooling, these libraries make it straightforward to bake LLM-specific checks into your build and deployment pipelines.

In the Java world, Spring AI brings a first-class abstraction for response evaluation with its simple Evaluator interface. You supply the original user text, any retrieved context, and the model's response, and implementations return pass/fail results or richer scores. Out of the box, Spring AI includes a RelevancyEvaluator that uses an LLM to verify whether an answer truly reflects the supplied context, and a FactCheckingEvaluator that compares each claim against authoritative documents (or even uses lightweight fact-checking models like Minicheck). Because evaluators are decoupled from generation, you can mix and match heavyweight models for dialogue and leaner ones for testing, optimizing cost, and latency. Extensible hooks let you add custom evaluators for style compliance, toxicity screening, bias detection, or domain-specific rules, all invoked through familiar JUnit tests.

For teams building on Quarkus, the quarkus-langchain4j-testing-scorer-junit5 extension provides a Scorer API that evaluates your chat service or RAG retriever against curated samples. By annotating tests with @AiScorer or the ScorerExtension, you can load sample inputs from YAML, choose evaluation strategies (semantic similarity, AI-driven judgments, or your own Java-based checks), and generate per-tag scores and Markdown reports for CI. Langchain4j itself also ships as a stand-alone framework—independent of Quarkus—with similar Scorer and EvaluationStrategy abstractions, but its testing documentation remains sparse. Despite the lean docs, the core concepts carry over: define evaluation samples, plug in built-in or custom strategies, and surface scores in your existing Java test suites to automate relevance, accuracy, style, and safety checks.

Testing and Evaluating Using Spring AI

There are various methods to evaluate LLMs, and one of them is to use another LLM to evaluate the results of the one generating the response. Spring AI provides the Evaluator interface to evaluate responses.

```
@FunctionalInterface
public interface Evaluator {
    EvaluationResponse evaluate(EvaluationRequest evaluationRequest);
}
```

The input to the evaluate method is the `EvaluationRequest`, which is defined in the source code as follows. So it takes in the user query along with the relevant document list found through the vector search in our RAG pipeline or any other relevant input augmented to our prompt and the response from the LLM to do the evaluation.

```
public class EvaluationRequest {
    private final String userText;
    private final List<Content> dataList;
    private final String responseContent;

    public EvaluationRequest(String userText, List<Content> dataList,
    String responseContent) {
        this.userText = userText;
        this.dataList = dataList;
        this.responseContent = responseContent;
    }

   ...

   ...

}
```

There are two implementations of this interface:

1. `RelevancyEvaluator`

   The `RelevancyEvaluator` uses an AI model for evaluation. It uses the `userText`, `dataList`, and `responseContent` to formulate and ask the following question to the AI model internally:

   ```
   "Your task is to evaluate if the response for the query
   is in line with the context information provided.\n
   You have two options to answer. Either YES/ NO.\n
   Answer - YES, if the response for the query
   is in line with context information otherwise NO.\n
   Query: \n {query}\n
   Response: \n {response}\n
   Context: \n {context}\n
   Answer: "
   ```

2. `FactCheckingEvaluator`

   The `FactCheckingEvaluator` assesses the factual accuracy of the AI-generated responses against the provided context. By checking whether each claim is directly supported by the supplied context, this evaluator helps identify and curb hallucinations in AI-generated responses. The evaluator feeds both the "claim" and the "document" into an AI model for assessment. To lower costs and improve efficiency, you can use compact, purpose-built models like Bespoke's Minicheck instead of heavyweight flagship models such as GPT-4. Minicheck is also accessible via Ollama.

The following prompt template is used by the Evaluator for fact checking:

```
Document: {document}
Claim: {claim}
```

Figure 15-2 illustrates this flow.

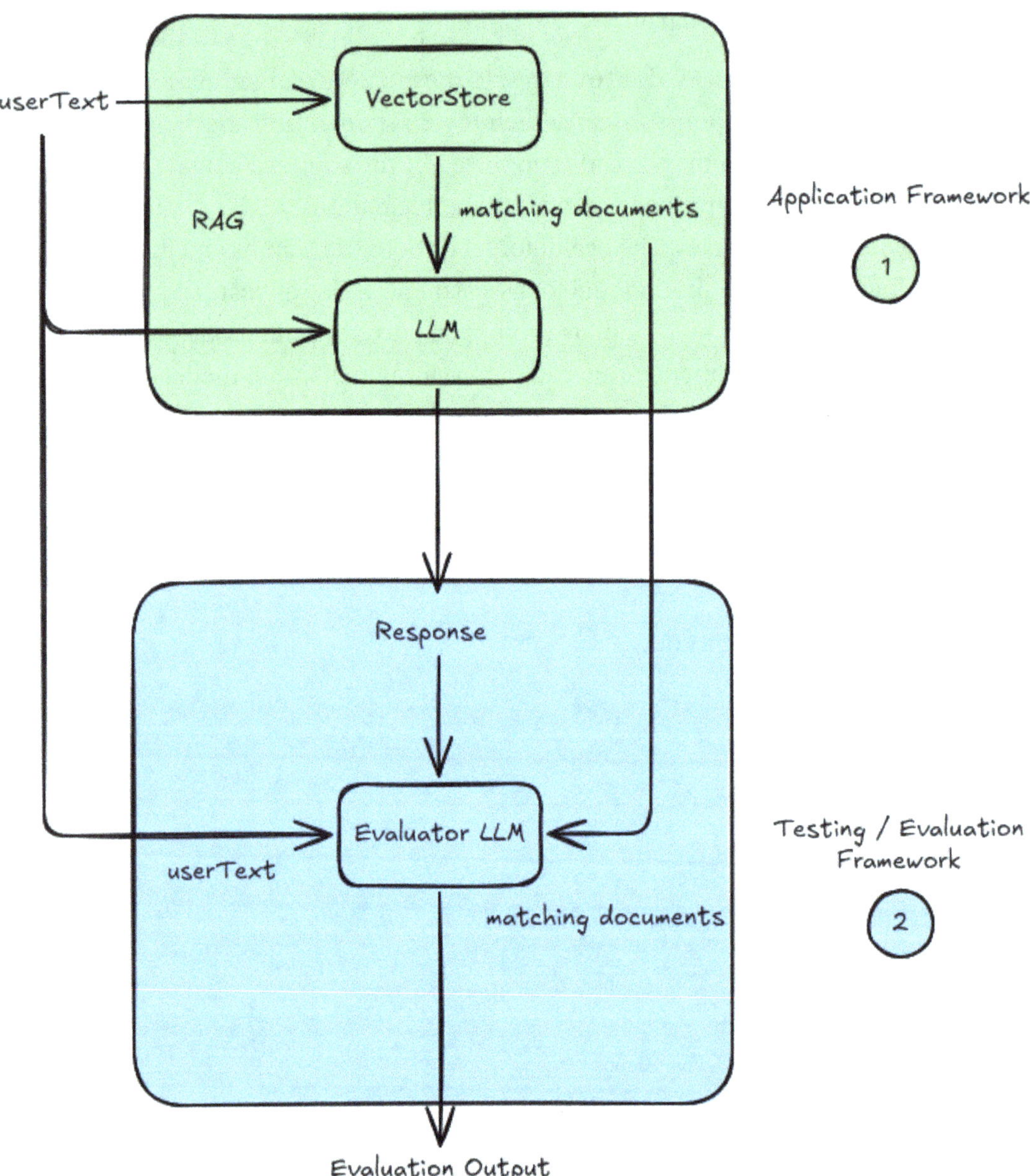

Figure 15-2. *Testing/evaluation framework with Spring AI*

Now that you understand the technicalities involved, let's get your hands dirty with some implementation to see it in practice. Before you write any tests, you will need a RAG application setup. You can set up any RAG-based application as you prefer, but for the demonstration purposes of this chapter, you will reuse the previous RAG application you built using Spring AI in Chapter 7.

You will JUnit for our test cases and will leverage the default test file already created for you by Spring Boot named `DemoApplicationTests.java`. First, you will autowire two beans that you previously defined in your Application Boot file, namely, `chatModel` and `vectorStore`. These will be used to run the RAG pipeline and gather the response from the model for evaluation.

```
@Autowired
private ChatModel chatModel;

@Autowired
private VectorStore vectorStore;
```

The first test case will be based on `RelevancyEvaluator`, so you will create a method named `testRelevancy` and start with getting a response from the model similar to what you tried with the `curl` request. You are using the ChatClient API to use your `chatModel` and leverage the vectorStore object through the QuestionAnswerAdvisor RAG utility and pass in our `userText` query and finally gather the response. The context for the user query is "Airbus A320,2023-11-01,Boston,Las Vegas,BOS,LAS,DL606,14:00,17:30,Cancelled" in the Markdown document for your reference.

```
String userText = "What are the flight details for DL606?";

ChatResponse response = ChatClient.builder(chatModel)
        .build().prompt()
        .advisors(new QuestionAnswerAdvisor(vectorStore))
        .user(userText)
        .call()
        .chatResponse();
```

The next task is to evaluate it for relevancy. Before doing so, you will assert for sanity for the response to not be null and also to print the response for debugging purposes as to what the LLM model responded.

```
Assertions.assertNotNull(response);
String responseText = response.getResult().getOutput().getText();
System.out.println(responseText);
```

Finally, you can evaluate the response by creating a `RelevancyEvaluator` object and passing in a `chatClient` object to it. It will use this client API to evaluate the response from earlier.

```
Evaluator relevancyEvaluator = new RelevancyEvaluator(ChatClient.
builder(chatModel));
```

You then create an `EvaluationRequest` as discussed earlier with your user query `userText` and context by retrieving the documents from the `VectorStore`.

```
List<Document> documents = response.getMetadata().
get(QuestionAnswerAdvisor.RETRIEVED_DOCUMENTS);
EvaluationRequest evaluationRequest = new EvaluationRequest(userText,
documents, responseText);
```

The final step is to get the evaluation response by calling the evaluate method on the evaluator object and checking for its truthiness value.

```
EvaluationResponse evaluationResponse = relevancyEvaluator.
evaluate(evaluationRequest);
assertTrue(evaluationResponse.isPass(), "Response is not relevant to the
question");
```

This will successfully validate the test case and validate the relevancy of the response. What about the irrelevance of it? Yes, you can write a negative test case too. For brevity sake, you are writing the test case in the same method, but as a standard practice you can put it in a new test method of its own. You can test for the failure of this case by setting the variable responseText to an irrelevant text like the following, which is not correct, and then rerun the test. The LLM model should be able to check for irrelevancy of the response. The negative test case is shared here:

```
String wrongAnswer = "We are airline company and provide all sort of
flights.";
evaluationRequest = new EvaluationRequest(userText, documents,
wrongAnswer);
evaluationResponse = relevancyEvaluator.evaluate(evaluationRequest);
assertThat(evaluationResponse.isPass()).isFalse();
```

Let's now run the test case and see the output. Please ignore the skeleton joke output since it comes from the previous example that started with a joke prompt in Chapter 7.

Output:

```
2025-05-12T19:06:57.564Z  WARN 7152 --- [demo] [Test worker] JpaBaseConfigu
ration$JpaWebConfiguration : spring.jpa.open-in-view is enabled by default.
Therefore, database queries may be performed during view rendering.
Explicitly configure spring.jpa.open-in-view to disable this warning
2025-05-12T19:06:58.175Z  INFO 7152 --- [demo] [Test worker] com.example.
demo.DemoApplicationTests : Started DemoApplicationTests in 17.385 seconds
(process running for 19.038)
Sure, here's one for you:
Why don't skeletons fight each other?
They don't have the guts!
The flight details for DL606 on 2023-11-01 are as follows: It was scheduled
to depart from Boston (BOS) to Las Vegas (LAS) at 14:00 and arrive at
17:30. However, the flight was cancelled.
OpenJDK 64-Bit Server VM warning: Sharing is only supported for boot loader
classes because bootstrap classpath has been appended
2025-05-12T19:07:05.418Z  INFO 7152 --- [demo] [ionShutdownHook] j.Local
ContainerEntityManagerFactoryBean : Closing JPA EntityManagerFactory for
persistence unit 'default'
2025-05-12T19:07:05.421Z  INFO 7152 --- [demo] [ionShutdownHook] com.
zaxxer.hikari.HikariDataSource     : HikariPool-1 - Shutdown initiated...
2025-05-12T19:07:05.425Z  INFO 7152 --- [demo] [ionShutdownHook] com.
zaxxer.hikari.HikariDataSource     : HikariPool-1 - Shutdown completed.
> Task :test
BUILD SUCCESSFUL in 29s
4 actionable tasks: 2 executed, 2 up-to-date
7:07:05 PM: Execution finished ':test --tests "com.example.demo.
DemoApplicationTests.testRelevancyEvaluation"'.
```

The test case successfully passed. This shows that the output shared by the LLM model was relevant as verified. You can see the irrelevancy led to the test case passing due to testing it for falseness, ensuring that if in the future the core LLM tends to respond with irrelevant responses, you can detect it. The full function code can be checked here:

```
@Test
void testRelevancyEvaluation() {
    String userText = "What are the flight details for DL606?";
    ChatResponse response = ChatClient.builder(chatModel)
            .build().prompt()
            .advisors(new QuestionAnswerAdvisor(vectorStore))
            .user(userText)
            .call()
            .chatResponse();
    Assertions.assertNotNull(response);
    String responseText = response.getResult().getOutput().getText();
    System.out.println(responseText);
    Evaluator relevancyEvaluator = new RelevancyEvaluator(ChatClient.
    builder(chatModel));
    List<Document> documents = response.getMetadata().
    get(QuestionAnswerAdvisor.RETRIEVED_DOCUMENTS);
    EvaluationRequest evaluationRequest = new EvaluationRequest(userText,
    documents, responseText);
    EvaluationResponse evaluationResponse = relevancyEvaluator.
    evaluate(evaluationRequest);
    assertTrue(evaluationResponse.isPass(), "Response is not relevant to
    the question");

    String wrongAnswer = "We are airline company and provide all sort of
    flights.";
    evaluationRequest = new EvaluationRequest(userText, documents,
    wrongAnswer);
    evaluationResponse = relevancyEvaluator.evaluate(evaluationRequest);
    assertThat(evaluationResponse.isPass()).isFalse();
}
```

Now, you will move into the factual evaluation test case. You will define a method named `testFactCheckingEvaluation` and start with the RAG response collection and invoking the evaluation request as shown here:

```
String userText = "What are the flight details for DL606?";
ChatResponse response = ChatClient.builder(chatModel)
        .build().prompt()
        .advisors(new QuestionAnswerAdvisor(vectorStore))
        .user(userText)
        .call()
        .chatResponse();
Assertions.assertNotNull(response);
String responseText = response.getResult().getOutput().getText();
List<Document> documents = response.getMetadata().
get(QuestionAnswerAdvisor.RETRIEVED_DOCUMENTS);
EvaluationRequest evaluationRequest = new EvaluationRequest(userText,
documents, responseText);
```

The next step is to initialize an instance of the FactCheckingEvaluator with a chat model of your choice to do the fact evaluation and run the evaluate method call on it to collect the evaluation response:

```
Evaluator factCheckingEvaluator = new FactCheckingEvaluator(ChatClient.
builder(chatModel));
EvaluationResponse evaluationResponse = factCheckingEvaluator.
evaluate(evaluationRequest);
assertThat(evaluationResponse.isPass()).isTrue();
```

This will check for the fact details and evaluate with a true response. Also let's evaluate the opposite case where you set some factual information that is not correct in this context and see it failing. This could be part of another test case since each unique condition should be a test case. For brevity, I am sharing both in a single test case:

```
String wrongAnswer = "DL606 is taking off from New York.";
evaluationRequest = new EvaluationRequest(userText, documents,
wrongAnswer);
evaluationResponse = factCheckingEvaluator.evaluate(evaluationRequest);
assertThat(evaluationResponse.isPass()).isFalse();
```

This will fail and will pass our test case since the DL606 flight is taking off from Boston instead, and the fact is not correct. Let's run this and check the output:

Output:

```
2025-05-12T19:02:17.227Z  WARN 6159 --- [demo] [Test worker] JpaBaseConfigu
ration$JpaWebConfiguration : spring.jpa.open-in-view is enabled by default.
Therefore, database queries may be performed during view rendering.
Explicitly configure spring.jpa.open-in-view to disable this warning
2025-05-12T19:02:18.045Z  INFO 6159 --- [demo] [Test worker] com.example.
demo.DemoApplicationTests    : Started DemoApplicationTests in 19.436
seconds (process running for 21.301)
Why don't skeletons fight each other?

They don't have the guts.
OpenJDK 64-Bit Server VM warning: Sharing is only supported for boot loader
classes because bootstrap classpath has been appended
> Task :test
2025-05-12T19:02:26.742Z  INFO 6159 --- [demo] [ionShutdownHook] j.Local
ContainerEntityManagerFactoryBean : Closing JPA EntityManagerFactory for
persistence unit 'default'
2025-05-12T19:02:26.747Z  INFO 6159 --- [demo] [ionShutdownHook] com.
zaxxer.hikari.HikariDataSource       : HikariPool-1 - Shutdown initiated...
2025-05-12T19:02:26.751Z  INFO 6159 --- [demo] [ionShutdownHook] com.
zaxxer.hikari.HikariDataSource       : HikariPool-1 - Shutdown completed.
BUILD SUCCESSFUL in 33s
4 actionable tasks: 2 executed, 2 up-to-date
7:02:27 PM: Execution finished ':test --tests "com.example.demo.
DemoApplicationTests.testFactCheckingEvaluation"'.
```

The full function code can be checked here:

```
@Test
void testFactCheckingEvaluation() {
    String userText = "What are the flight details for DL606?";
    ChatResponse response = ChatClient.builder(chatModel)
            .build().prompt()
            .advisors(new QuestionAnswerAdvisor(vectorStore))
            .user(userText)
            .call()
            .chatResponse();
```

```
    Assertions.assertNotNull(response);
    String responseText = response.getResult().getOutput().getText();
    List<Document> documents = response.getMetadata().
    get(QuestionAnswerAdvisor.RETRIEVED_DOCUMENTS);
    EvaluationRequest evaluationRequest = new EvaluationRequest(userText,
    documents, responseText);
    Evaluator factCheckingEvaluator = new FactCheckingEvaluator(ChatClient.
    builder(chatModel));
    EvaluationResponse evaluationResponse = factCheckingEvaluator.
    evaluate(evaluationRequest);
    assertThat(evaluationResponse.isPass()).isTrue();

    String wrongAnswer = "DL606 is taking off from New York.";
    evaluationRequest = new EvaluationRequest(userText, documents,
    wrongAnswer);
    evaluationResponse = factCheckingEvaluator.evaluate(evaluationRequest);
    assertThat(evaluationResponse.isPass()).isFalse();
}
```

Here is the final code for the test case file:

File: ./src/test/java/com/example/demo/DemoApplicationTests.java

```
package com.example.demo;

import org.junit.jupiter.api.Assertions;
import org.springframework.ai.chat.client.advisor.QuestionAnswerAdvisor;
import org.springframework.ai.document.Document;
import org.springframework.ai.evaluation.*;
import org.springframework.ai.vectorstore.VectorStore;
import org.springframework.beans.factory.annotation.Autowired;
import org.junit.jupiter.api.Test;
import org.springframework.ai.chat.client.ChatClient;
import org.springframework.ai.chat.model.ChatModel;
import org.springframework.ai.chat.model.ChatResponse;
import org.springframework.boot.test.context.SpringBootTest;
```

```
import java.util.List;

import static org.assertj.core.api.Assertions.assertThat;
import static org.junit.jupiter.api.Assertions.assertTrue;

@SpringBootTest
class DemoApplicationTests {
    @Autowired
    private ChatModel chatModel;

    @Autowired
    private VectorStore vectorStore;

    @Test
    void testRelevancyEvaluation() {
        String userText = "What are the flight details for DL606?";
        ChatResponse response = ChatClient.builder(chatModel)
                .build().prompt()
                .advisors(new QuestionAnswerAdvisor(vectorStore))
                .user(userText)
                .call()
                .chatResponse();
        Assertions.assertNotNull(response);
        String responseText = response.getResult().getOutput().getText();
        System.out.println(responseText);
        Evaluator relevancyEvaluator = new RelevancyEvaluator(ChatClient.
        builder(chatModel));
        List<Document> documents = response.getMetadata().
        get(QuestionAnswerAdvisor.RETRIEVED_DOCUMENTS);
        EvaluationRequest evaluationRequest = new
        EvaluationRequest(userText, documents, responseText);
        EvaluationResponse evaluationResponse = relevancyEvaluator.
        evaluate(evaluationRequest);
        assertTrue(evaluationResponse.isPass(), "Response is not relevant
        to the question");

        String wrongAnswer = "We are airline company and provide all sort
        of flights.";
```

```
        evaluationRequest = new EvaluationRequest(userText, documents,
        wrongAnswer);
        evaluationResponse = relevancyEvaluator.
        evaluate(evaluationRequest);
        assertThat(evaluationResponse.isPass()).isFalse();
    }

    @Test
    void testFactCheckingEvaluation() {
        String userText = "What are the flight details for DL606?";
        ChatResponse response = ChatClient.builder(chatModel)
                .build().prompt()
                .advisors(new QuestionAnswerAdvisor(vectorStore))
                .user(userText)
                .call()
                .chatResponse();
        Assertions.assertNotNull(response);
        String responseText = response.getResult().getOutput().getText();
        List<Document> documents = response.getMetadata().
        get(QuestionAnswerAdvisor.RETRIEVED_DOCUMENTS);
        EvaluationRequest evaluationRequest = new
        EvaluationRequest(userText, documents, responseText);
        Evaluator factCheckingEvaluator = new FactCheckingEvaluator(ChatCli
        ent.builder(chatModel));
        EvaluationResponse evaluationResponse = factCheckingEvaluator.
        evaluate(evaluationRequest);
        assertThat(evaluationResponse.isPass()).isTrue();

        String wrongAnswer = "DL606 is taking off from New York.";
        evaluationRequest = new EvaluationRequest(userText, documents,
        wrongAnswer);
        evaluationResponse = factCheckingEvaluator.
        evaluate(evaluationRequest);
        assertThat(evaluationResponse.isPass()).isFalse();
    }
}
```

Conclusion

Testing and evaluating LLM applications is no longer an optional afterthought—it's a pillar of responsible, scalable AI development. By treating evaluation as a stand-alone stage, you can mix lightweight or purpose-built models for checks, dramatically reducing both latency and cost compared to running a flagship model for every test. Whether you adopt Python-based evaluation frameworks or Spring AI's Evaluator abstractions, the critical steps remain the same: define clear success criteria for each quality dimension, automate checks in your CI/CD workflows, and integrate telemetry and alerting to catch regressions in production.

As LLM technology and enterprise requirements continue to evolve, your evaluation processes must stay ahead. Regularly revisit your metrics and thresholds, update your test suites with new adversarial or compliance scenarios, and leverage observability data to refine prompts and model configurations. With a robust evaluation and testing strategy in place, you transform LLM unpredictability from a liability into a predictable, manageable aspect of your software delivery lifecycle—empowering you to ship innovative AI features with confidence and control.

For further reading and information, please refer to the following:

- OpenAI evals: Offers a structured framework to benchmark and compare LLM outputs using custom or community-contributed evaluation tasks.
- LangChain evaluation modules: Provide built-in tools for assessing LLM chains across dimensions such as accuracy, coherence, and latency—ideal for integrated LangChain pipelines.
- Spring AI Evaluator docs: Introduce abstractions to plug evaluation steps directly into Spring-based workflows, making it easier to monitor and manage quality in Java-centric AI applications.

The next chapter covers Gen AI in the cloud.

CHAPTER 16

Cloud Power-Ups: Bedrock, Vertex, and Azure OpenAI

The goal of this chapter is to explore the capabilities and features provided by the major cloud vendors for generative AI (Gen AI) and use them with your Java-based applications.

Introduction

Generative AI is transforming how applications interact with users, enabling them to produce human-like text, images, and other media on demand. As organizations look to integrate these capabilities into their Java-based systems, cloud platforms have become the de facto choice for hosting, managing, and scaling foundation models. This chapter explores how AWS—through its Amazon Bedrock service—empowers developers to build generative AI applications that are secure, enterprise-ready, and deeply integrated into existing AWS infrastructures. The chapter will start by placing Gen AI in the context of today's major cloud providers; then it will dive into the specifics of getting started with Bedrock, from experimentation in the Playground to production-grade deployments with guardrails, retrieval-augmented generation (RAG), and Spring AI integration.

S. K. Sahu, *Generative AI-Driven Application Development with Java*,
https://doi.org/10.1007/979-8-8688-1609-3_16

State of Gen AI in the Cloud

In mid-2025, the big three clouds—AWS, Microsoft Azure, and Google Cloud—treat generative AI as a native platform feature. AWS Bedrock front-ends more than 40 foundation models and layers guardrails safety filters across them, Azure OpenAI Service has introduced GPT-4.5 along with a "stored completions" API for end-to-end provenance, and Google's Vertex AI counters with Gemini 2.5 in both Flash and Pro variants. The competitive conversation has shifted from deploying ever-larger models to offering differentiated latency, modality support, and built-in safeguards.

At the developer layer, abstractions are rapidly converging. Frameworks such as Spring AI let teams flip a single property to swap between Bedrock, Azure, or OpenAI endpoints, while each cloud now previews native model-routing services that automatically choose the cheapest or most capable engine for a given prompt. Retrieval-augmented generation is effectively a checkbox: Bedrock Knowledge Bases, Azure AI Search Vector Index, and Vertex AI Agent Engine all bundle vector storage, embeddings, and grounding evaluation so developers can ship RAG pipelines without stitching tools together.

With core capabilities commoditized, the battleground has moved to governance and cost-to-quality optimization. Guardrails, Azure content filters, and Vertex policy tags harden default defenses, yet enterprises are equally hungry for smaller, task-specific models that slash token spend without sacrificing accuracy. Success now hinges less on where a model is hosted and more on how well teams evaluate outputs, enforce policy, and blend specialized models into a single, audit-ready workflow.

Generative AI in AWS: Amazon Bedrock

Amazon provides the Amazon Bedrock service to get started with building Gen AI applications quickly. With enterprise-grade security, privacy, and access to industry leading Foundation Models, AWS makes it easy to onboard and build Gen AI use cases. It makes sense to leverage the foundation models hosted on AWS through Amazon Bedrock if your organization already uses AWS for its applications.

Amazon Bedrock is a fully managed service from Amazon that helps you build Gen AI applications for end-to-end development focusing on security, data privacy, and support for commercial licensing using industry-standard Foundation Models. All this within the same environment of AWS you are already comfortable with. It is serverless, and you pay only for the services on the go. For more details, you can refer to the documentation at `https://aws.amazon.com/bedrock/`.

To experiment and play with Amazon Bedrock, make sure to sign up for a free AWS account at `https://signin.aws.amazon.com/signup?request_type=register`. Amazon Bedrock is not covered under the free tier at this point of time when I check at `https://aws.amazon.com/free/`, as shown in Figure 16-1. Always refer to this page to check for any changes when you are trying this.

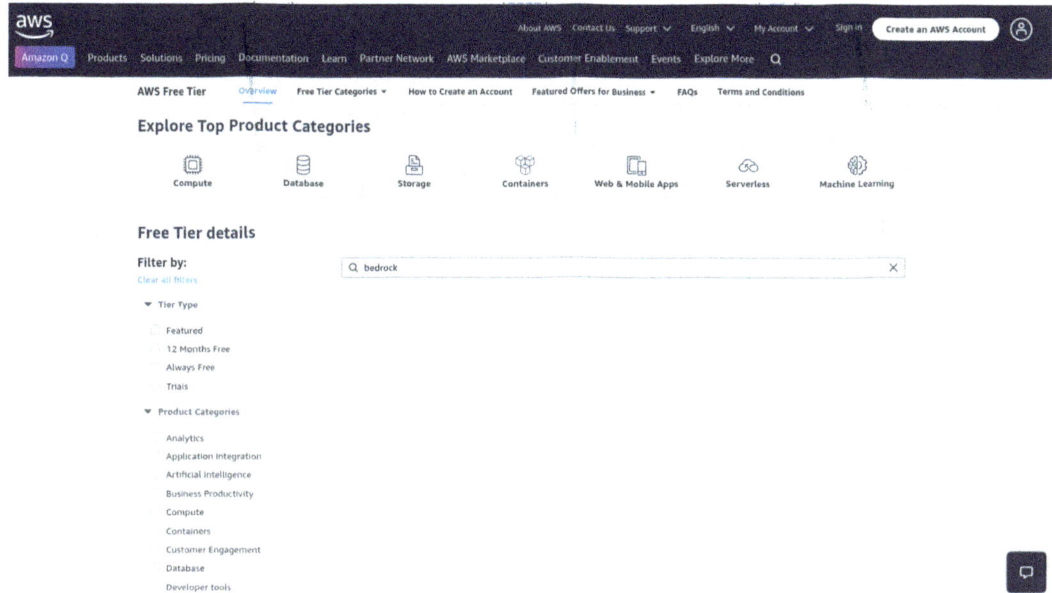

***Figure 16-1.** Amazon Bedrock unavailability in AWS Free Tier*

You can access Bedrock by doing a quick search with the keyword in the top navigation bar, as shown in Figure 16-2.

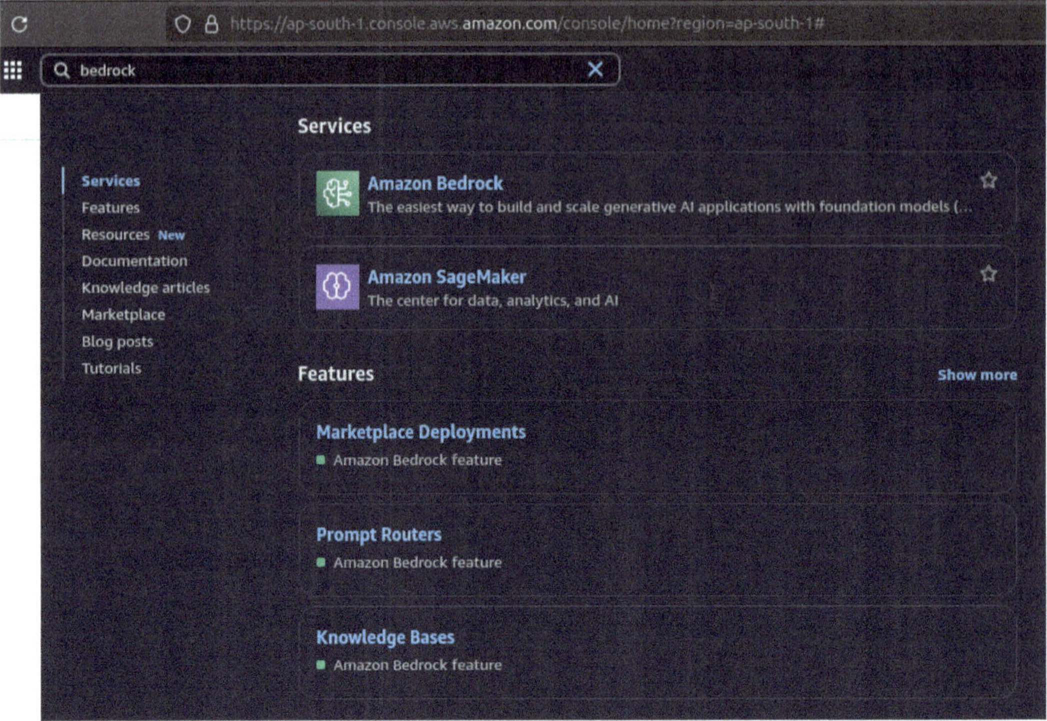

Figure 16-2. Amazon Bedrock access from the navigation search

On accessing Amazon Bedrock from the console, you can see the different features available, as shown in Figure 16-3.

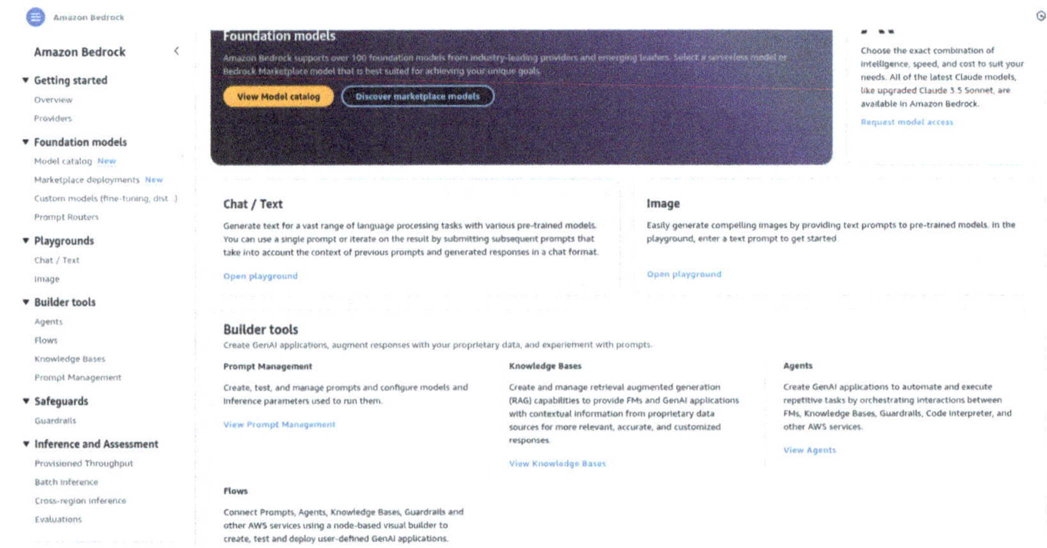

Figure 16-3. Amazon Bedrock home page in AWS Console

As with any cloud provider, the UI and features around Gen AI is always innovating, so the UI may have changed while you are reading this content. In the left navigation menu, you can see some of the features that Bedrock provides at the current time:

- Access to Foundation models
- Playground to try different Foundation models with your prompts in text/image formats.
- Builder tools focusing on prompt management, agentic AI, and knowledge base setup.
- Guardrails to set up security around the LLM ecosystem
- Inference endpoints to host and serve your foundation models and evaluations to test the Model response

I won't go into the theory of all these in detail, but you will learn about them as you try some of them while building your application project. This is your goal as shared by business and your stakeholders:

> *As the industry is evolving, we have decided to extend our domain to the aircraft manufacturing industry to start manufacturing our own aircrafts. To enable our engineers to build certified products specific to FAA/EASA certification guidelines, we want to build an application that will answer any question they have relevant to the part they are engineering to make it certification worthy.*

For this use case project, you will focus on the FAA for the time being, and it can be adapted similarly for EASA too. All documents relevant to the certification process and information is available for public consumption as Code for Federal Regulations (CFRs) at `https://www.ecfr.gov/current/title-14/chapter-I/subchapter-C/part-21/subpart-H?toc=1`, as shown in Figure 16-4.

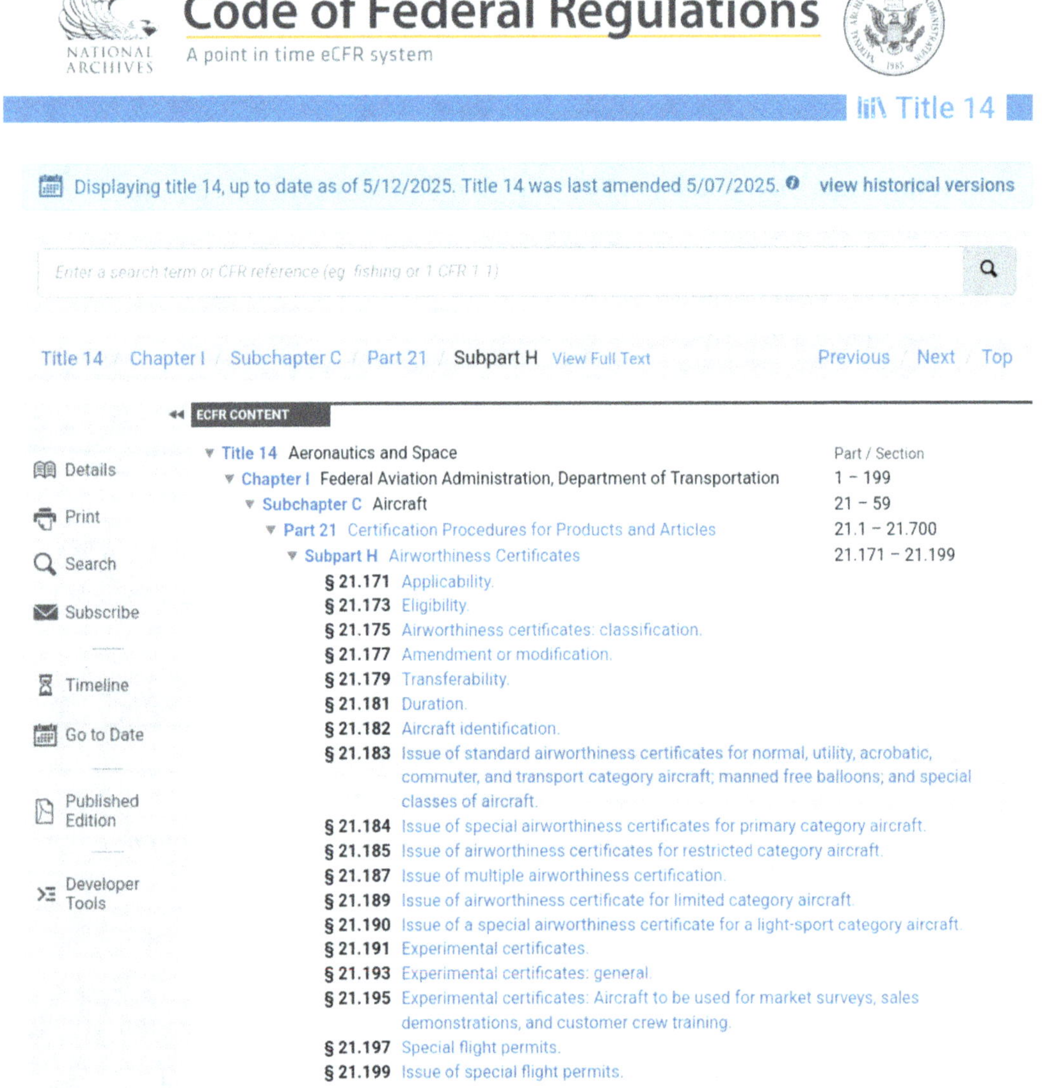

Figure 16-4. *FAA CFRs*

This documentation contains a variety of technical information and may be challenging to search for if you do not have the exact terms. This is where LLM and RAG play an important role to find the semantic documents and respond to your engineers.

Note The purpose of this application is informational and for learning purposes with no liability or responsibility for using this in any commercial setup.

Accessing a Foundational Model in Bedrock Playground

Let's first explore the foundational models available in Bedrock, as shown in Figure 16-5. As you can see, there are a variety of models available to choose from, including some of the ones produced by Amazon. Always review the license for the model you intend to use. You will need to accept the license agreement and terms of agreement before using the model. This may not be applicable to all models, though. Also check for the region where you are using the model from, since in some regions all models may not be available.

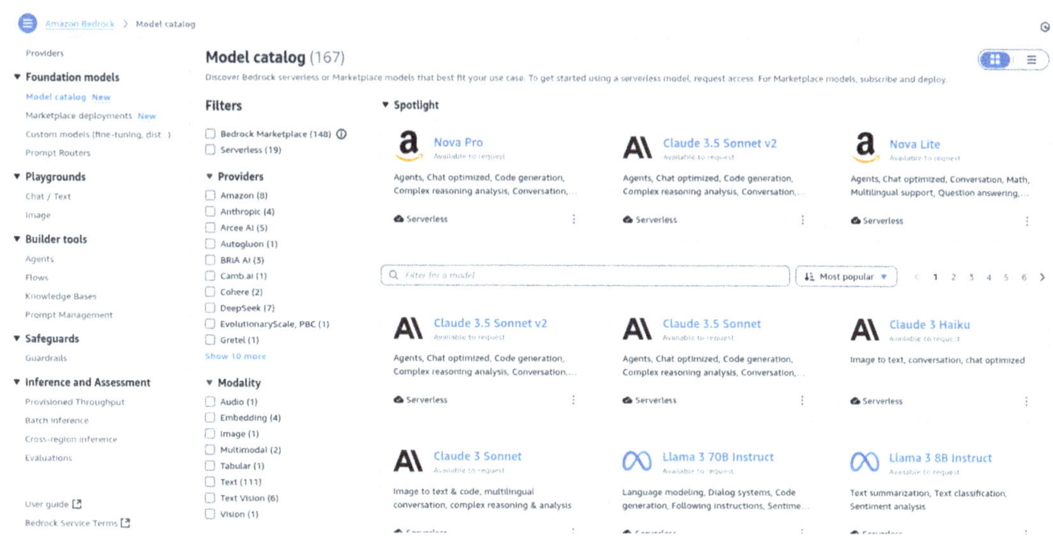

Figure 16-5. Foundation models in Amazon Bedrock

This is an important step to choose your model based on your needs and the cost. Let's explore the AWS Nova model, for instance. Figure 16-6 shows the home page of the AWS Nova model.

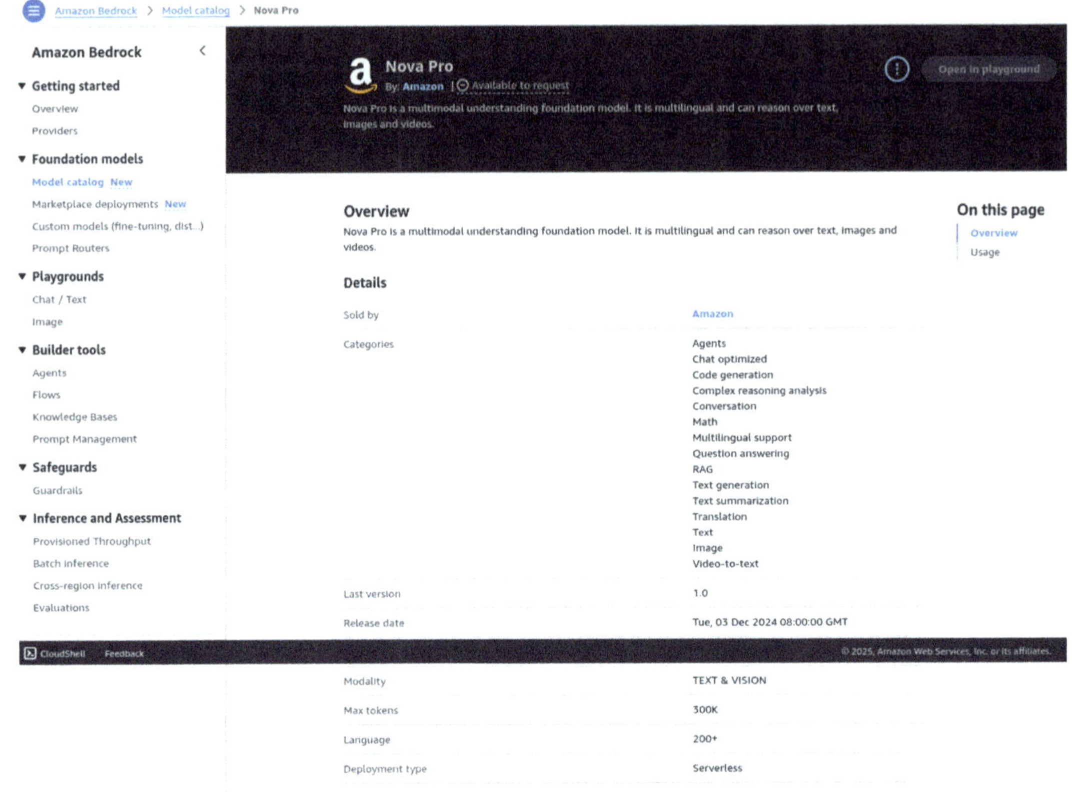

Figure 16-6. *AWS Nova model*

As shown, at the top it says the model can be requested for use, after which it will be available, and the "Open in playground" option in the right top will be enabled. Currently, I am visiting the page from the ap-south-1 region. The home page contains some important information such as an overview, details as to who has created this model, the categories of tasks the foundation model can help with, its version, the date it was released on, the input modalities it supports, the max number of tokens, the languages supported, and finally the deployment type, which is serverless. This is useful information and can help determine the model to start with. Let's request to use the model and check it out in the playground.

After clicking the "Available to request" link, you will see a pop-up sharing additional information and a link to request model access with a note that billing will start after access grant and for using the model, as shown in Figure 16-7. You will be charged only for the requests you make using the model and not for requesting access to it.

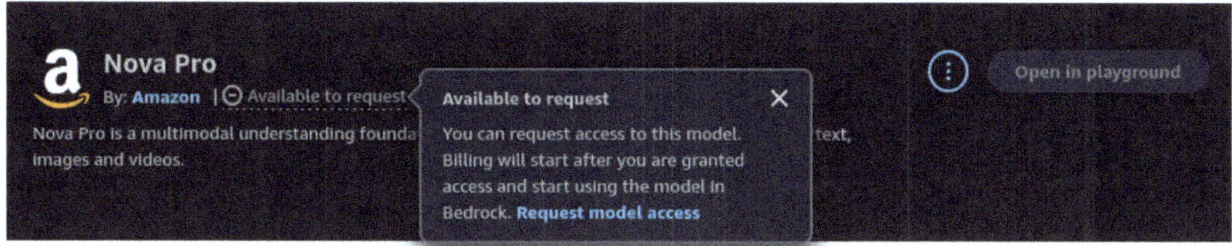

***Figure 16-7.** Requesting model use*

On the model access page, you can click the "Available to request" link of the model of choice or enable all models, as shown in Figure 16-8. My recommendation is to read the EULA for the specific model and enable it on a use-case basis.

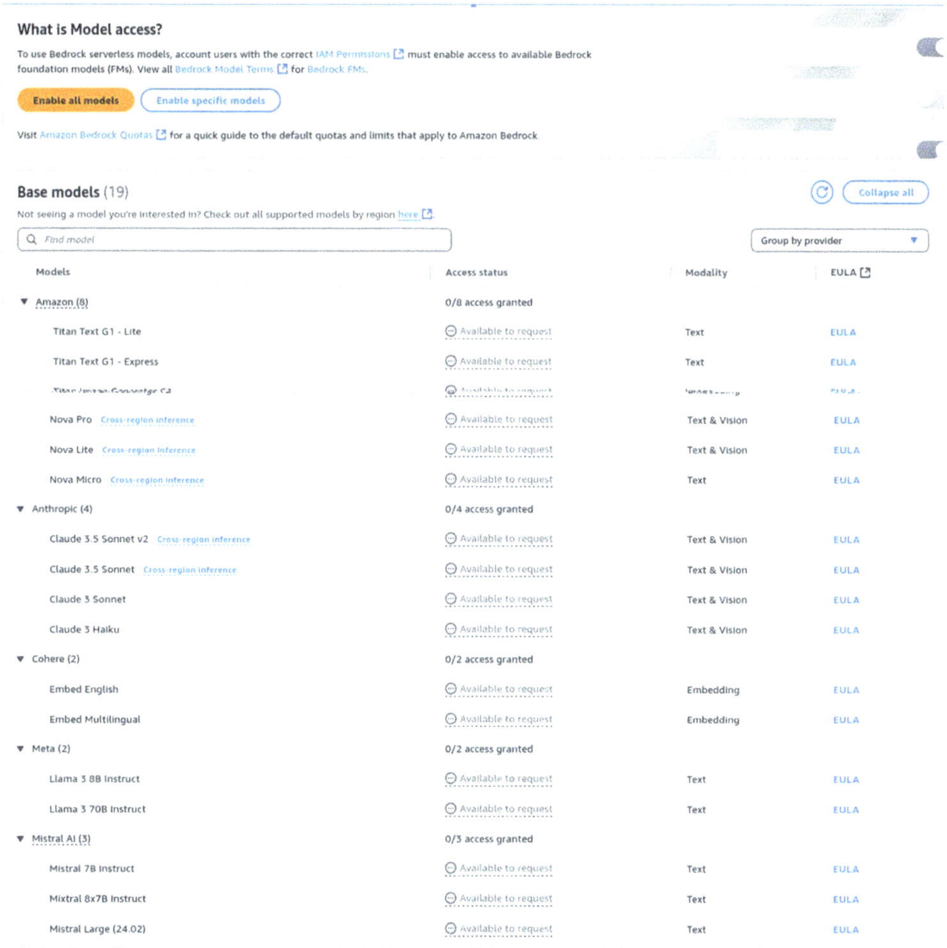

What is Model access?

To use Bedrock serverless models, account users with the correct IAM Permissions must enable access to available Bedrock foundation models (FMs). View all Bedrock Model Terms for Bedrock FMs.

Enable all models | Enable specific models

Visit Amazon Bedrock Quotas for a quick guide to the default quotas and limits that apply to Amazon Bedrock.

Base models (19)

Not seeing a model you're interested in? Check out all supported models by region here.

Find model | Group by provider | Collapse all

Models	Access status	Modality	EULA
▼ Amazon (8)	0/8 access granted		
Titan Text G1 - Lite	Available to request	Text	EULA
Titan Text G1 - Express	Available to request	Text	EULA
[illegible]	[illegible]	[illegible]	[illegible]
Nova Pro Cross-region inference	Available to request	Text & Vision	EULA
Nova Lite Cross-region inference	Available to request	Text & Vision	EULA
Nova Micro Cross-region inference	Available to request	Text	EULA
▼ Anthropic (4)	0/4 access granted		
Claude 3.5 Sonnet v2 Cross-region inference	Available to request	Text & Vision	EULA
Claude 3.5 Sonnet Cross-region inference	Available to request	Text & Vision	EULA
Claude 3 Sonnet	Available to request	Text & Vision	EULA
Claude 3 Haiku	Available to request	Text & Vision	EULA
▼ Cohere (2)	0/2 access granted		
Embed English	Available to request	Embedding	EULA
Embed Multilingual	Available to request	Embedding	EULA
▼ Meta (2)	0/2 access granted		
Llama 3 8B Instruct	Available to request	Text	EULA
Llama 3 70B Instruct	Available to request	Text	EULA
▼ Mistral AI (3)	0/3 access granted		
Mistral 7B Instruct	Available to request	Text	EULA
Mixtral 8x7B Instruct	Available to request	Text	EULA
Mistral Large (24.02)	Available to request	Text	EULA

***Figure 16-8.** Model access*

Since your use case is focused and starting with text inputs, you can use Nova Micro, keeping it light and use case specific, as shown in Figure 16-9 and Figure 16-10.

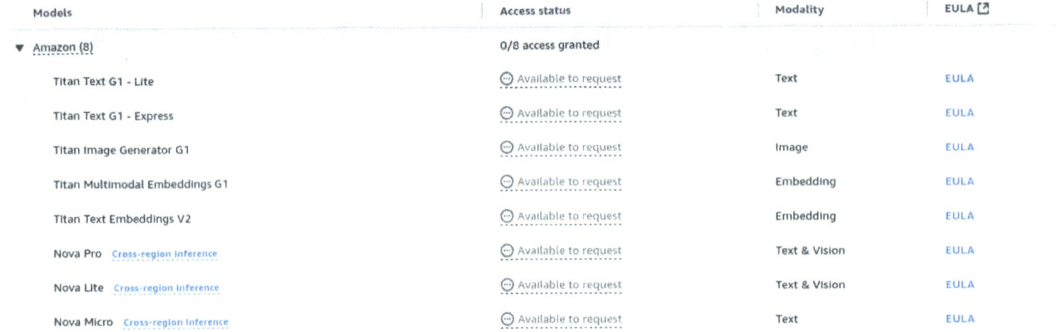

***Figure 16-9.** Nova-specific models*

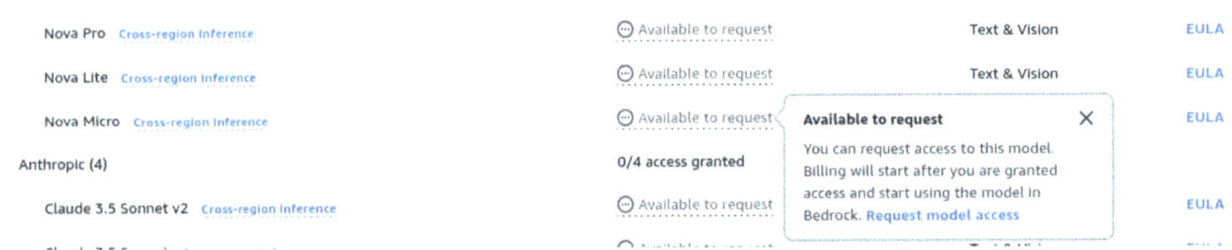

***Figure 16-10.** Request Nova micro model*

The model is selected. Then click the next button, as shown in Figure 16-11.

Request model access

	Model	Access status	Modality	EULA
☐	Nova Lite Cross-region inference	Available to request	Text & Vision	EULA
☑	Nova Micro Cross-region inference	Available to request	Text	EULA
☐	▼ Anthropic (4)	0/4 access granted		
☐	Claude 3.5 Sonnet v2 Cross-region inference	Available to request	Text & Vision	EULA
☐	Claude 3.5 Sonnet Cross-region inference	Available to request	Text & Vision	EULA
☐	Claude 3 Sonnet	Available to request	Text & Vision	EULA
☐	Claude 3 Haiku	Available to request	Text & Vision	EULA
☐	▼ Cohere (2)	0/2 access granted		
☐	Embed English	Available to request	Embedding	EULA
☐	Embed Multilingual	Available to request	Embedding	EULA
☐	▼ Meta (2)	0/2 access granted		
☐	Llama 3 8B Instruct	Available to request	Text	EULA
☐	Llama 3 70B Instruct	Available to request	Text	EULA
☐	▼ Mistral AI (3)	0/3 access granted		
☐	Mistral 7B Instruct	Available to request	Text	EULA
☐	Mixtral 8x7B Instruct	Available to request	Text	EULA
☐	Mistral Large (24.02)	Available to request	Text	EULA

Cancel Next

Figure 16-11. *Nova model selection*

Finally, submit the request for use, as shown in Figure 16-12.

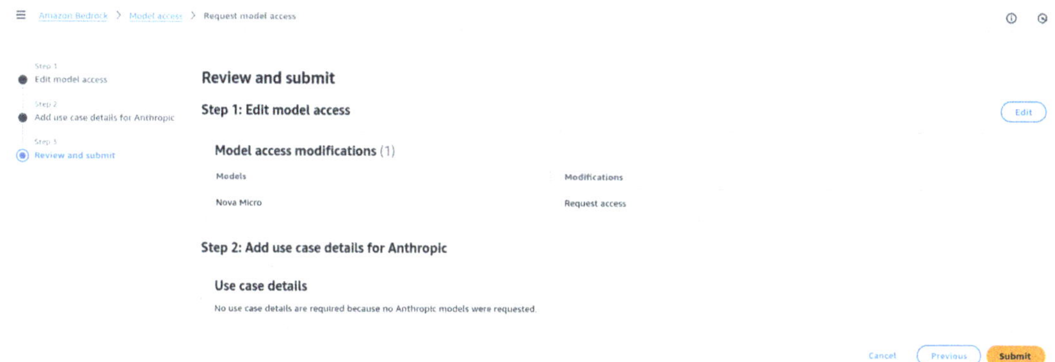

Figure 16-12. *Submitting a request for Nova Model use*

Once submitted, you will receive a notification saying the time for access grant to the requested model. For some models, it needs to be verified by the end vendor for the use case you want to use it for. In this case, as you can see in Figure 16-13, you have been granted immediate access to it.

Model access updates submitted
It may take several minutes to receive or remove access to models. Meanwhile, you can use other Bedrock console pages. Once your access is updated, you can use the models in Bedrock. Refresh the base models table to view the updated statuses.

Models	Access status	Modality	EULA
▾ Amazon (8)	1/8 access granted		
Titan Text G1 - Lite	Available to request	Text	EULA
Titan Text G1 - Express	Available to request	Text	EULA
Titan Image Generator G1	Available to request	Image	EULA
Titan Multimodal Embeddings G1	Available to request	Embedding	EULA
Titan Text Embeddings V2	Available to request	Embedding	EULA
Nova Pro Cross-region inference	Available to request	Text & Vision	EULA
Nova Lite Cross-region inference	Available to request	Text & Vision	EULA
Nova Micro Cross-region inference	Access granted	Text	EULA

***Figure 16-13.** Access Granted page*

Now this model is available to play with in the playground page. Let's visit the playground page from the left menu, as shown in Figure 16-14.

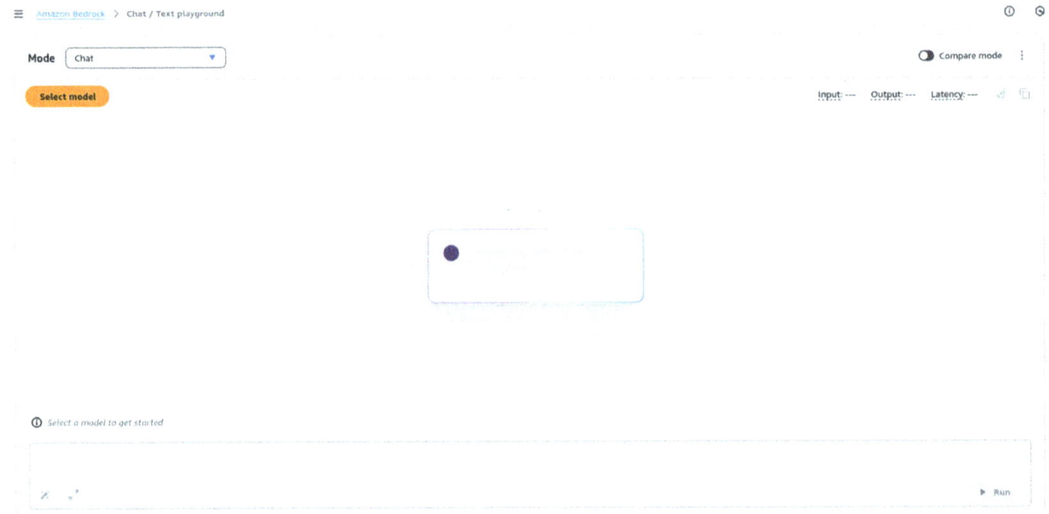

***Figure 16-14.** Bedrock playground page*

There is no model selected yet. Let's click the select model button and select your access-granted Nova Micro Model and specific region you are trying in, as shown in Figure 16-15.

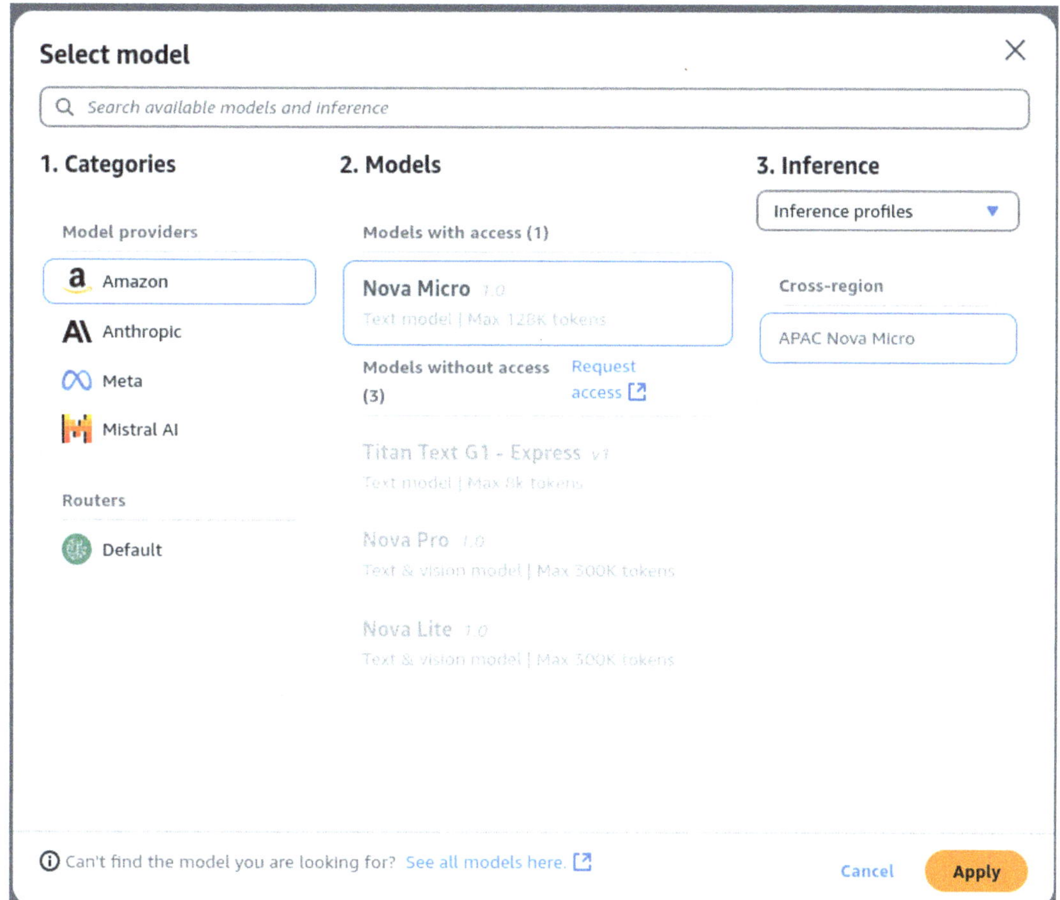

Figure 16-15. *Model selection for the playground*

Now that your model is selected, the playground is active for trial, as shown in Figure 16-16. Reviewing this, you can see options for system prompts, temperature, Top P, setting the response length, any stop sequence that the model needs to check for to stop producing after it encounters the sequence helpful for early termination of the response, and finally guardrails setup. There is also an option to compare more than one model so as to see the response from multiple models to help you see the output for the same query in the same interface.

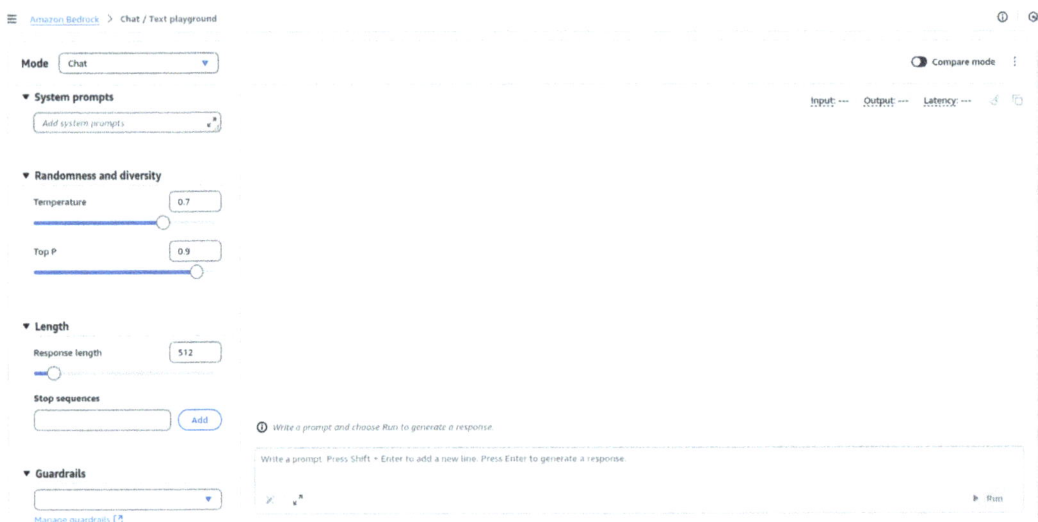

Figure 16-16. *Model-activated playground*

Let's play with it by using a sample query of "Tell me about airworthiness certificates" and see the response from the model, as shown in Figure 16-17. You can further play with the different options and other prompts and ask the model to act in a specific context or role.

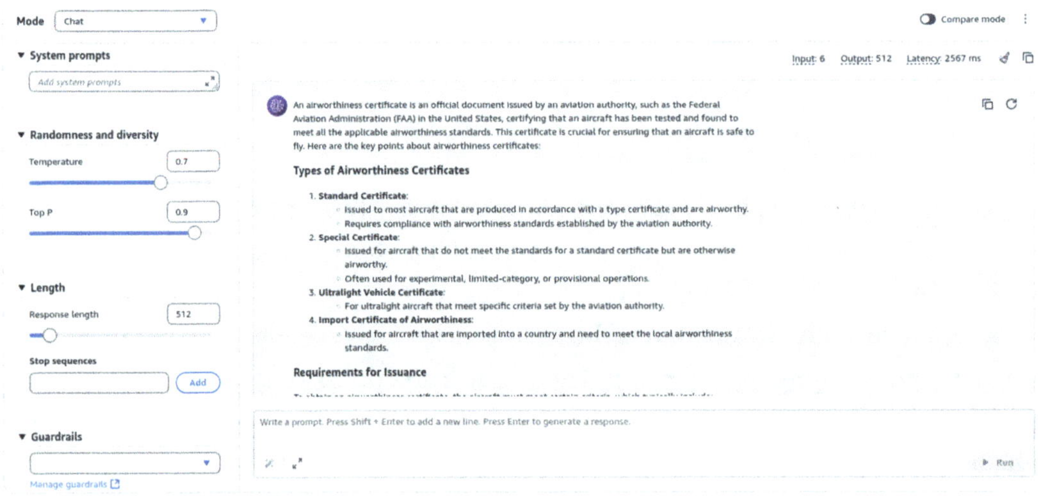

Figure 16-17. *Model response in playground*

Building a Sample Project Using Amazon Bedrock SDK

You will start building an application now. There are two approaches to build it. You can use the AWS Java SDK for the Amazon Bedrock service, or you can use an existing Java framework's support. Both Spring AI and LangChain4j support integration with Bedrock.

Using AWS SDK to Connect with Amazon Bedrock

Create an initial project at Spring Initializr with a web dependency, as shown in Figure 16-18.

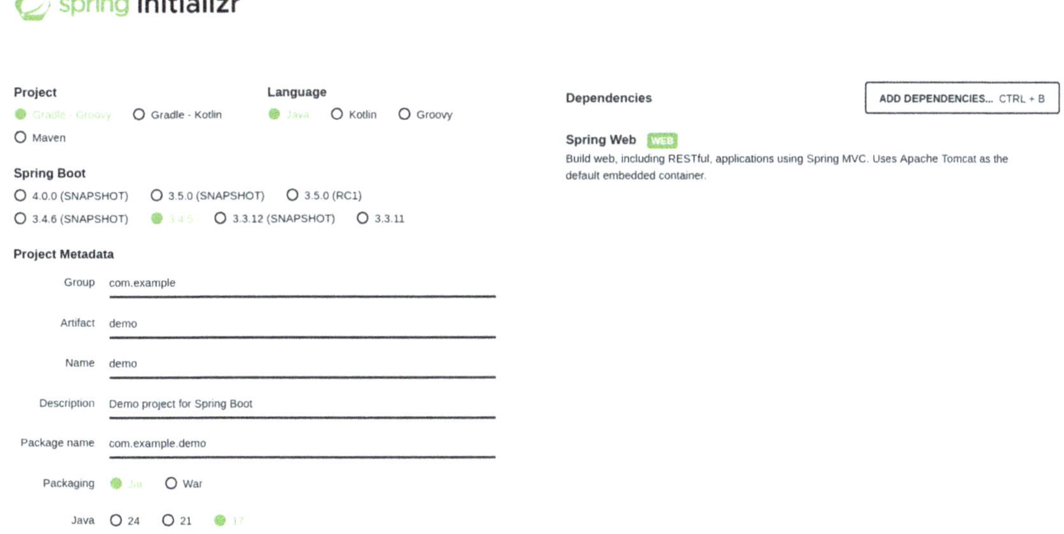

Figure 16-18. *Spring Initializr dependency*

Download and unzip the sample project at the directory of your choice. You will need to add the AWS SDK for the Java dependency to your `build.gradle` file.

```
// https://mvnrepository.com/artifact/software.amazon.awssdk/bedrockruntime
implementation("software.amazon.awssdk:bedrockruntime:2.31.45")
```

The build.gradle file should now look like this:

File: ./build.gradle

```
plugins {
    id 'java'
    id 'org.springframework.boot' version '3.4.5'
    id 'io.spring.dependency-management' version '1.1.7'
}

group = 'com.example'
version = '0.0.1-SNAPSHOT'

java {
    toolchain {
        languageVersion = JavaLanguageVersion.of(17)
    }
}

repositories {
    mavenCentral()
}

dependencies {
    implementation 'org.springframework.boot:spring-boot-starter-web'
    implementation 'software.amazon.awssdk:bedrockruntime:2.31.45'
    testImplementation 'org.springframework.boot:spring-boot-starter-test'
    testRuntimeOnly 'org.junit.platform:junit-platform-launcher'
}

tasks.named('test') {
    useJUnitPlatform()
}
```

The next step is to create an AWS configuration bean to connect to Amazon Bedrock, as shown next. Replace the region in the application.properties file with the region where you had previously set up the Nova model for use.

File: ./src/main/resources/application.properties

```
spring.application.name=demo
aws.region=ap-south-1
```

File: ./src/main/java/com/example/demo/config/AwsConfig.java

```
package com.example.demo.config;

import org.springframework.beans.factory.annotation.Value;
import org.springframework.context.annotation.Bean;
import org.springframework.context.annotation.Configuration;
import software.amazon.awssdk.auth.credentials.DefaultCredentialsProvider;
import software.amazon.awssdk.regions.Region;
import software.amazon.awssdk.services.bedrockruntime.BedrockRuntimeClient;

@Configuration
public class AwsConfig {

   @Value("${aws.region}")
    private String awsRegion;

   @Bean
    public BedrockRuntimeClient bedrockRuntimeClient() {
        return BedrockRuntimeClient.builder()
                .credentialsProvider(DefaultCredentialsProvider.create())
                .region(Region.of(awsRegion))
                .build();
    }
}
```

Next, you will set up a few data objects that will represent your request and response objects to be used in your controllers and services layer.

File: ./src/main/java/com/example/demo/dto/ConverseRequestDto.java

```
package com.example.demo.dto;

public class ConverseRequestDto {

    private String inputText;
```

```
    public ConverseRequestDto() {}
    public ConverseRequestDto(String inputText) { this.inputText =
    inputText; }
    public String getInputText() { return inputText; }
    public void setInputText(String inputText) { this.inputText =
    inputText; }
}
```

File: ./src/main/java/com/example/demo/dto/ConverseResponseDto.java

```
package com.example.demo.dto;

public class ConverseResponseDto {

    private String outputText;

    public ConverseResponseDto() {}
    public ConverseResponseDto(String outputText) { this.outputText =
    outputText; }
    public String getOutputText() { return outputText; }
    public void setOutputText(String outputText) { this.outputText =
    outputText; }
}
```

The next step is to set up the Service layer, which will take the input from the controller and send a request to the Amazon Bedrock runtime service. You will need the `modelId` of the model you have enabled previously. This you can see from the model page in the model catalog listing, as shown in Figure 16-19. You can use this as the `modelId` if you are leveraging provisioned throughput, as shown in the bottom left in the Inference and Assessment section.

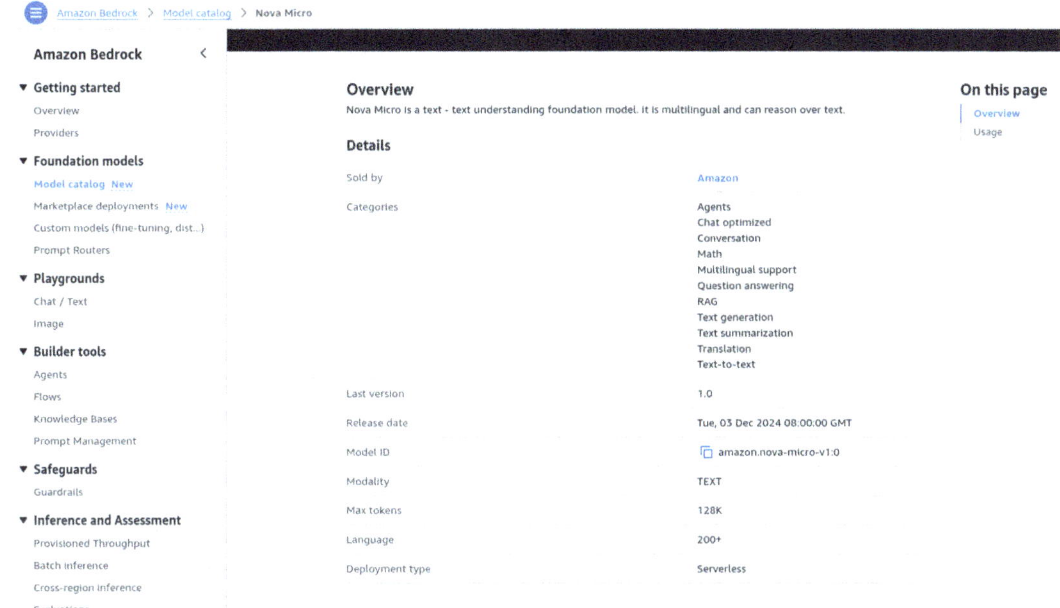

Figure 16-19. *Model ID of the model*

For this demo, you will use the cross-region inference, as shown in Figure 16-20. Instead of targeting a foundation model directly, you can leverage a cross-region inference profile to distribute requests across multiple regions.

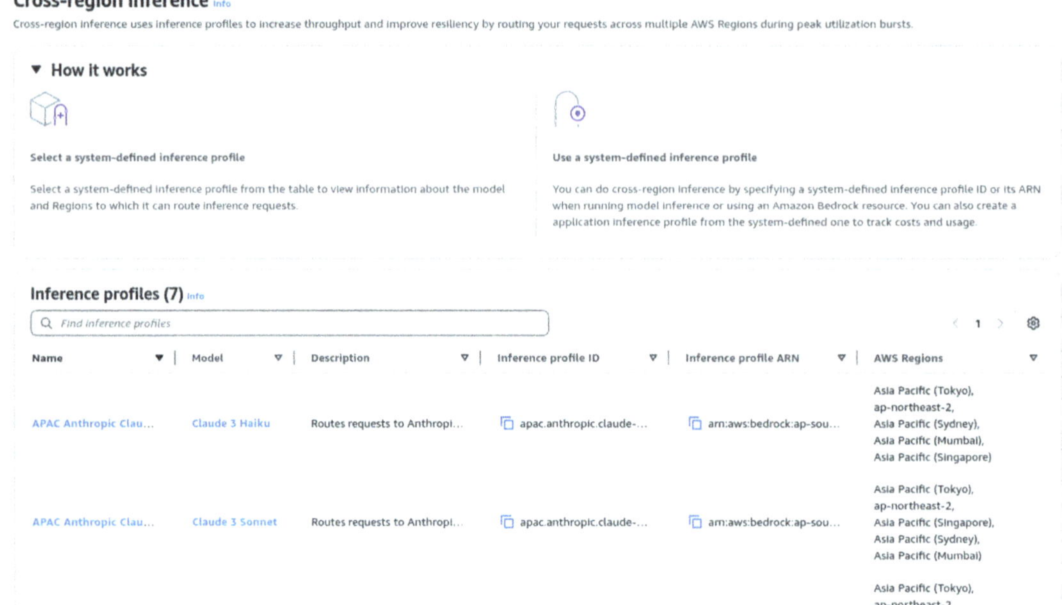

Figure 16-20. *Cross-region inference*

Copy the inference profile ARN value for the Nova Micro model, which will look something like the following based on your account ID and region where it was enabled previously:

arn:aws:bedrock:ap-south-1:xxxxxxxxxxxx:inference-profile/apac.amazon.nova-micro-v1:0

We will store the `modelId` value in the `application.properties` file and refer to the value in the service file.

File: ./src/main/resources/application.properties

```
spring.application.name=demo
aws.region=ap-south-1
aws.bedrock.modelId=arn:aws:bedrock:ap-south-1:xxxxxxxxxxxx:inference-profile/apac.amazon.nova-micro-v1:0
```

The service component does two things. First, it requests at runtime for injection of the Bedrock client bean.

```
public BedrockService(BedrockRuntimeClient client) {
    this.client = client;
}
```

We define a converse method that takes in the user input query as an argument.

```
public String converse(String inputText) {
```

There are two steps here. First, create your `Message` object from the user input.

```
Message message = Message.builder()
        .role(ConversationRole.USER)
        .content(ContentBlock.fromText(inputText))
        .build();
```

Second, create a request object with `modelId` and inference properties like `temperature` and `maxTokens`.

```
ConverseRequest request = ConverseRequest.builder()
        .modelId(modelId)
        .messages(message)
        .inferenceConfig(cfg -> cfg
                .maxTokens(500)
                .temperature(0.5F)
        )
        .build();
```

Finally, you will invoke the call to the `client.converse` method to invoke your request and fetch the text from the returned response.

```
 try {
    ConverseResponse response = client.converse(request);
    return response.output().message().content().get(0).text();
} catch (SdkClientException e) {
    throw new RuntimeException("Failed to invoke Bedrock model: " +
    e.getMessage(), e);
}
```

Here is the source code for the service component:

File: ./src/main/java/com/example/demo/service/BedrockService.java

```
package com.example.demo.service;

import org.springframework.beans.factory.annotation.Value;
import org.springframework.stereotype.Service;
import software.amazon.awssdk.core.exception.SdkClientException;
import software.amazon.awssdk.services.bedrockruntime.BedrockRuntimeClient;
import software.amazon.awssdk.services.bedrockruntime.model.*;

@Service
public class BedrockService {

   private final BedrockRuntimeClient client;

   @Value("${aws.bedrock.modelId}")
    private String modelId;

   public BedrockService(BedrockRuntimeClient client) {
        this.client = client;
    }

   /**
     * Sends the given text to Bedrock and returns the model's reply.
     */
    public String converse(String inputText) {

        Message message = Message.builder()
                .role(ConversationRole.USER)
                .content(ContentBlock.fromText(inputText))
                .build();

        ConverseRequest request = ConverseRequest.builder()
                .modelId(modelId)
                .messages(message)
                .inferenceConfig(cfg -> cfg
                        .maxTokens(500)
                        .temperature(0.5F)
                )
                .build();
```

```
        try {
            ConverseResponse response = client.converse(request);
            return response.output().message().content().get(0).text();
        } catch (SdkClientException e) {
            throw new RuntimeException("Failed to invoke Bedrock model: " +
            e.getMessage(), e);
        }
    }
}
```

Now that you have the foundational components set up, you will use them from the controller layer.

File: ./src/main/java/com/example/demo/controller/BedrockController.java

```
package com.example.demo.controller;

import com.example.demo.dto.ConverseRequestDto;
import com.example.demo.dto.ConverseResponseDto;
import com.example.demo.service.BedrockService;
import org.springframework.http.ResponseEntity;
import org.springframework.web.bind.annotation.*;

@RestController
@RequestMapping("/api/bedrock")
public class BedrockController {

   private final BedrockService bedrockService;

   public BedrockController(BedrockService bedrockService) {
        this.bedrockService = bedrockService;
    }

   @PostMapping("/converse")
    public ResponseEntity<ConverseResponseDto> converse(@RequestBody
    ConverseRequestDto req) {
        String reply = bedrockService.converse(req.getInputText());
        return ResponseEntity.ok(new ConverseResponseDto(reply));
    }
}
```

Before you start your application, you have to create a user in AWS IAM with the Amazon Bedrock Full Access policy, as shown in Figures 16-21, 16-22, and 16-23. For a quick setup here, we are using Full access, but for production access you should have a fine-grained access policy.

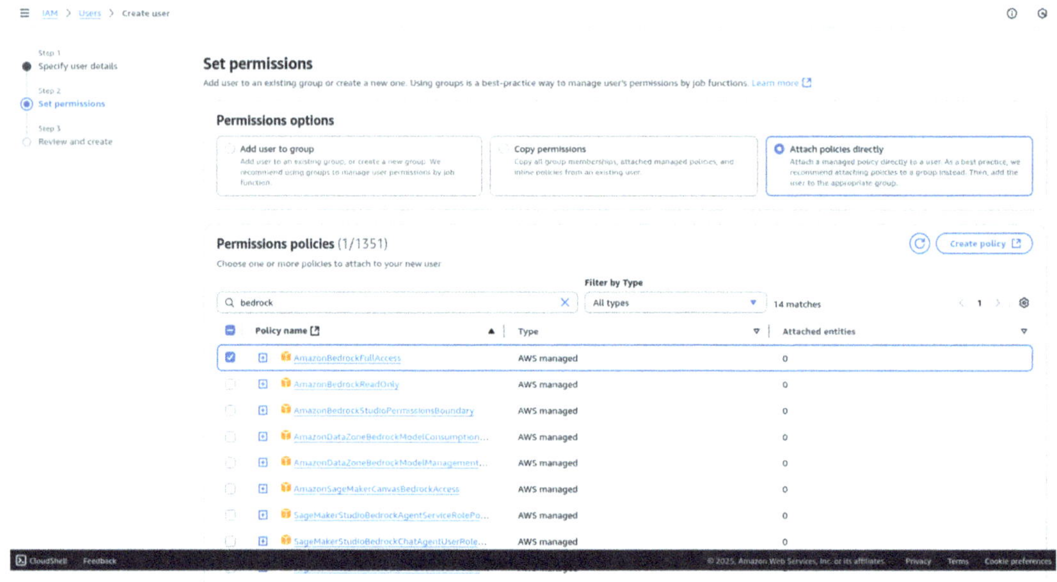

Figure 16-21. *Assigning the Bedrock policy to a user*

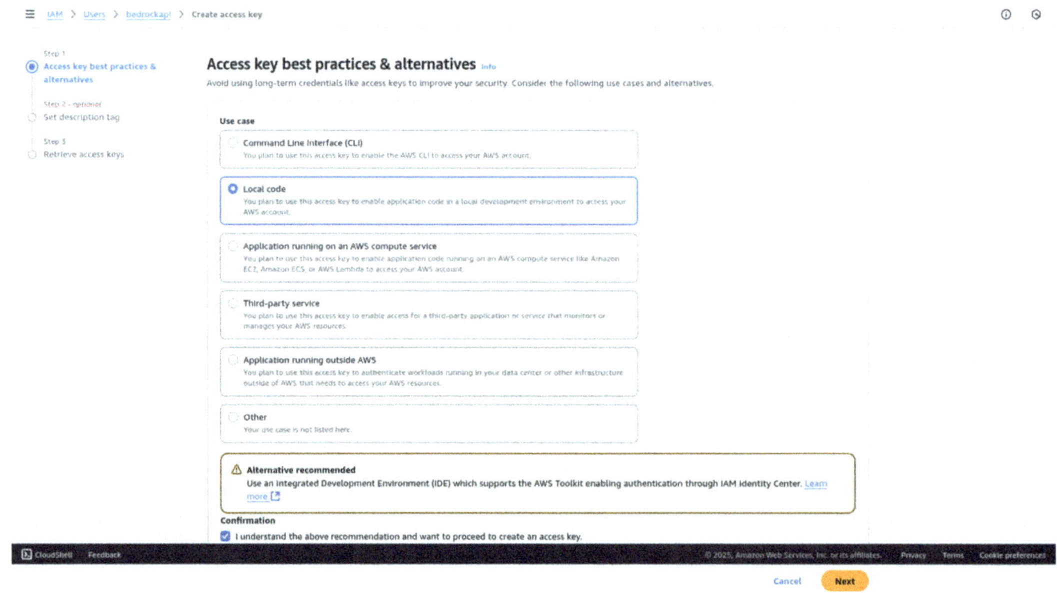

Figure 16-22. *Used from local code*

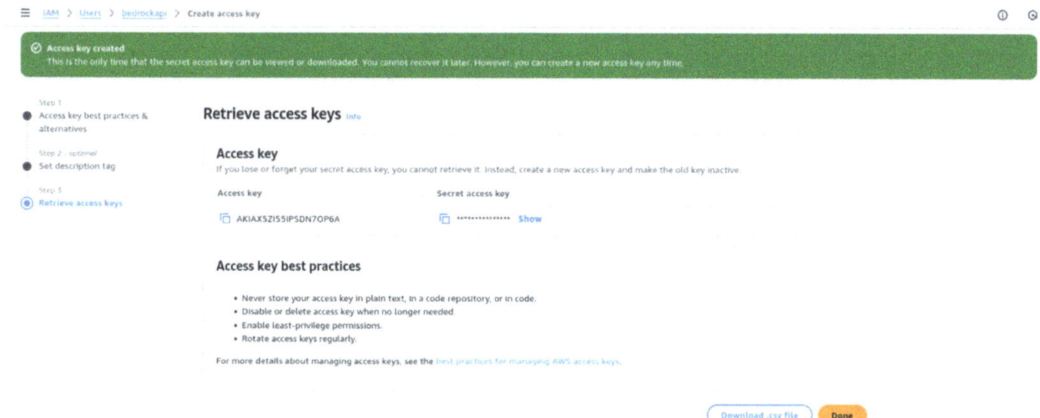

Figure 16-23. *Save the access key from security credentials in the user interface*

Set the access key and secret key in your machine by running `aws configure` and setting them.

Let's boot up your application and see it in action by making a `curl` request as shown here:

```
curl -X POST localhost:8080/api/bedrock/converse   -H "Content-Type: application/json"   -d '{"inputText":"Describe a hello world program in one line."}'
```

Output:

```
{"outputText":"A \"Hello, World!\" program in one line typically prints \"Hello, World!\" to the console. Here's an example in Python:\n\n```python\nprint(\"Hello, World!\")\n```\n\nThis single line of code uses the `print` function to output the string \"Hello, World!\" to the standard output."}
Wow, our first application with Amazon Bedrock. Cool enough!
```

Extending and Integrating Your Application with Guardrails

Guardrails are rule-based safety nets placed around AI models to ensure they behave in predictable, policy-compliant ways. Rather than letting foundation models respond freely, you define boundaries—what content is allowed, which topics to avoid, and how to handle sensitive or factual information. By enforcing these constraints automatically, guardrails help you maintain trust, prevent misuse, and keep your AI-driven features aligned with your organization's guidelines. Guardrails operate at two critical checkpoints:

1. **Before the call**
   All incoming prompts—including the user's request and any contextual data—are first inspected and sanitized. This "pre-inference" filtering ensures that only well-formed, unbiased, and ethically acceptable queries ever reach the model.

2. **After the call**
   Once the model produces an output, that response is subjected to a second layer of checks. Here, guardrails verify that the content is factually accurate, on-topic, and free from unwanted bias before it's delivered to the user.

Amazon Bedrock Guardrails: Enabling Responsible AI at Scale

Amazon Bedrock Guardrails is a turnkey framework of configurable protections that you can layer over any generative model—whether it's a native Bedrock foundation model, a fine-tuned version, or a third-party endpoint. Here's how it helps you build safer, more reliable AI services:

1. **Factuality through contextual grounding**

   Before delivering a response, Bedrock Guardrails can check the model's output against your source data (for example, documents supplied to a retrieval-augmented generator or transcripts in a summarization task). Any answer that doesn't directly tie back to the reference material—hallucinations, contradictions, or invented facts—can be flagged or filtered out, so users see only answers grounded in known truth.

2. **Logic-driven verification with Automated Reasoning (Preview)**

   Go beyond keyword-blocking: Automated Reasoning applies formal, mathematics-inspired checks to verify that each answer conforms to a policy document you provide (such as an HR handbook or technical specification). It not only spots logical inconsistencies or fabrications but also generates an explanation of why the response is valid, giving you provable guarantees that the AI isn't straying into fiction.

3. **Custom topic exclusion**

   You can define, in simple natural-language terms, any subject areas or domains that your application must steer clear of—investment advice in a banking assistant, for instance. Bedrock Guardrails then inspects both user queries and model outputs, automatically blocking or sanitizing any content that ventures into those off-limits categories.

4. **Comprehensive multimodal filters**

   To protect against hate speech, graphic violence, explicit imagery, and other forms of harmful content, guardrails applies adjustable toxicity checks across both text and images. These filters also guard against prompt-injection or "jailbreak" attacks by screening inputs and outputs for malicious or unintended instructions.

5. **Sensitive-data detection and redaction**

   Privacy is paramount. Guardrails can automatically recognize patterns for personally identifiable information (PII) or any custom-defined sensitive data (email addresses, credit-card numbers, etc.). Depending on your needs, the system can either reject inputs containing such data or strip it out of the model's responses—ideal for scenarios like redacting customer details from call-center summaries.

Let's build guardrails around your Gen AI application. As shown in Figure 16-24, there are three steps to integrate guardrails.

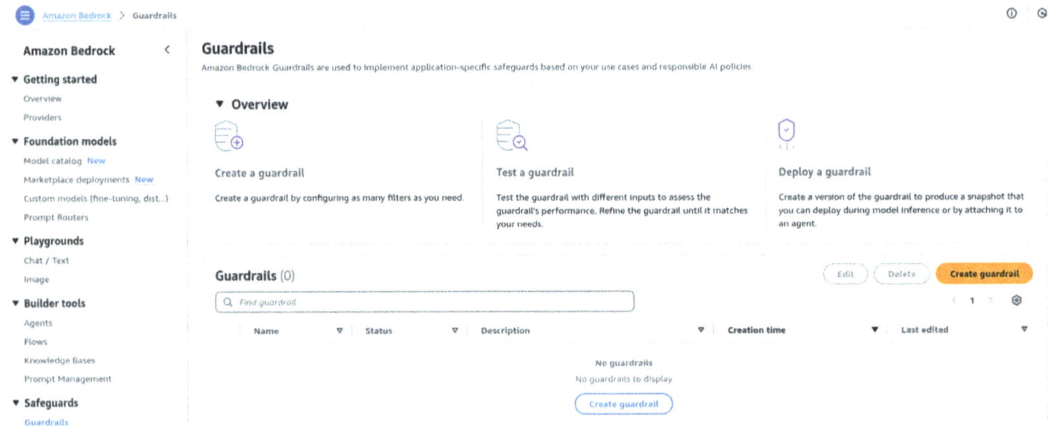

Figure 16-24. *Amazon Bedrock guardrails*

The steps are as follows:

1. Create a guardrail.

   Define a guardrail by setting up as many filters as needed.

   Click the "Create guardrail" button. This takes you to Figure 16-25 form where you need to share a few details like name, description, and message to respond with if the input contains any information against the guardrail rules.

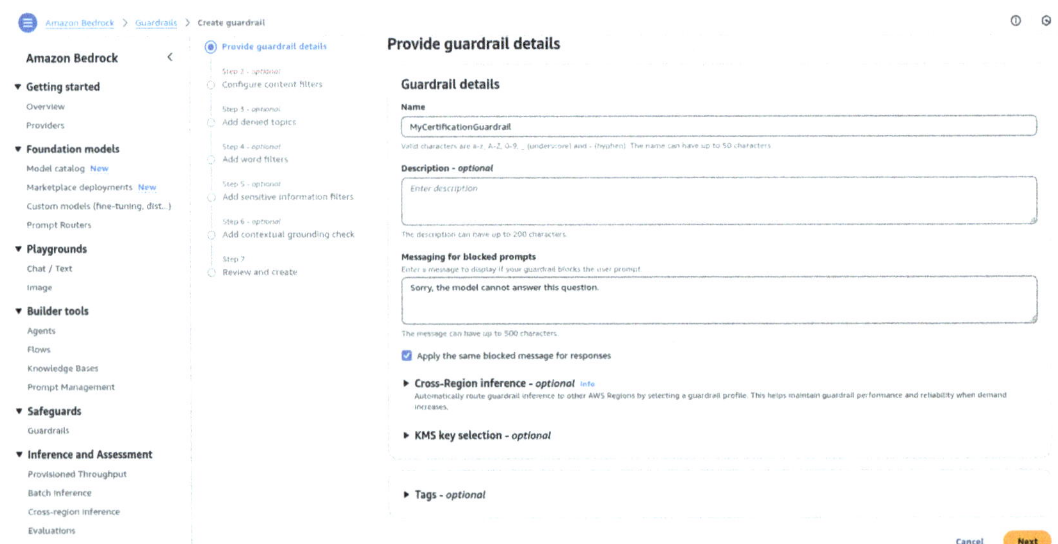

Figure 16-25. *Guardrail metadata*

Then you need to configure the content filters. Let's enable the filters for harmful categories and prompt attacks.

Harmful categories: Activate safeguards to identify and block dangerous user inputs and model outputs. Raising the filter's sensitivity will tighten screening and reduce harmful content across all categories. These can be enabled for both text and image, and different thresholds can be chosen, as shown in Figure 16-26. Let's keep the defaults enabled for your app.

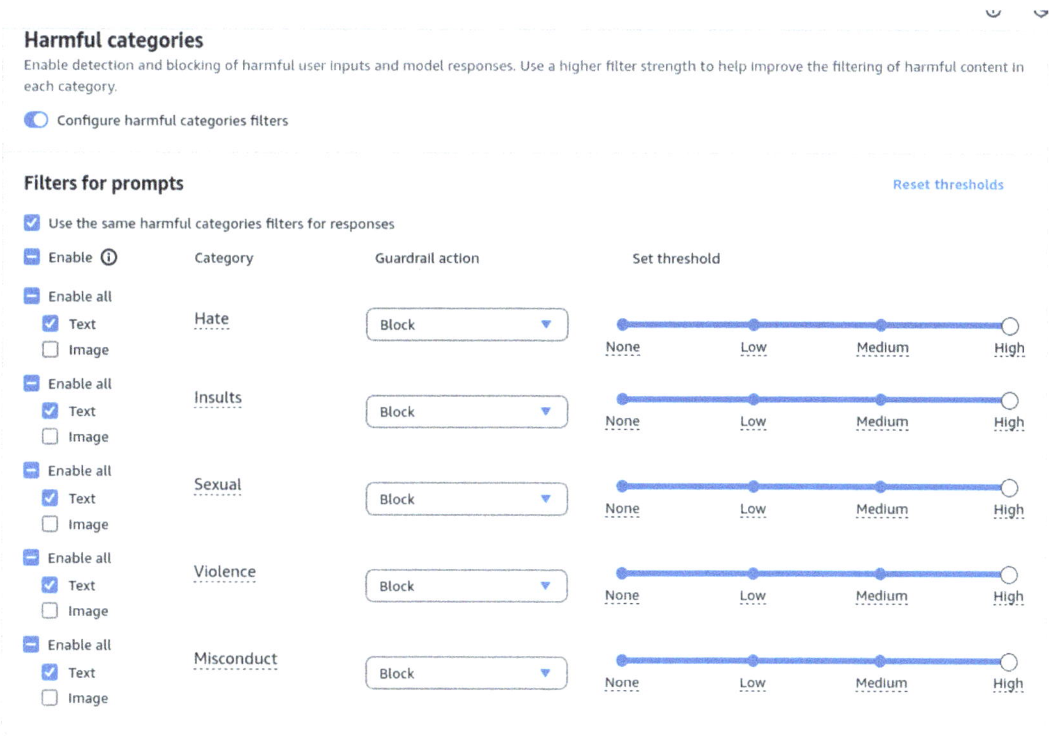

***Figure 16-26.** Harmful categories options*

Prompt attacks: Turn on protections that catch and block any user message attempting to override system instructions. To prevent legitimate system prompts from being misidentified, tag inputs so the filters apply only to user-originated text. The values can be enabled for threshold similarly in this category too, as shown in Figure 16-27 and Figure 16-28.

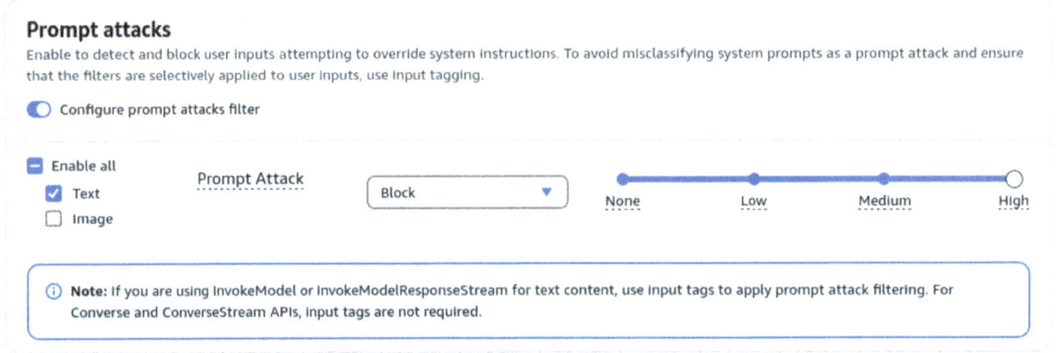

Figure 16-27. Prompt attacks configuration

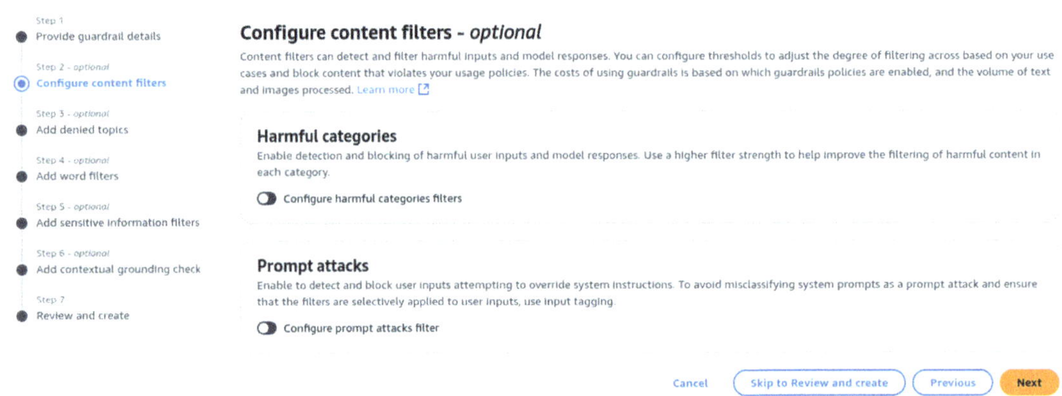

Figure 16-28. Configure content filters

After this, you can enable any denied topics like do not allow the user to ask for any existing patent-related information. It should all be from the certification technical details information. You can proceed, as shown in Figure 16-29.

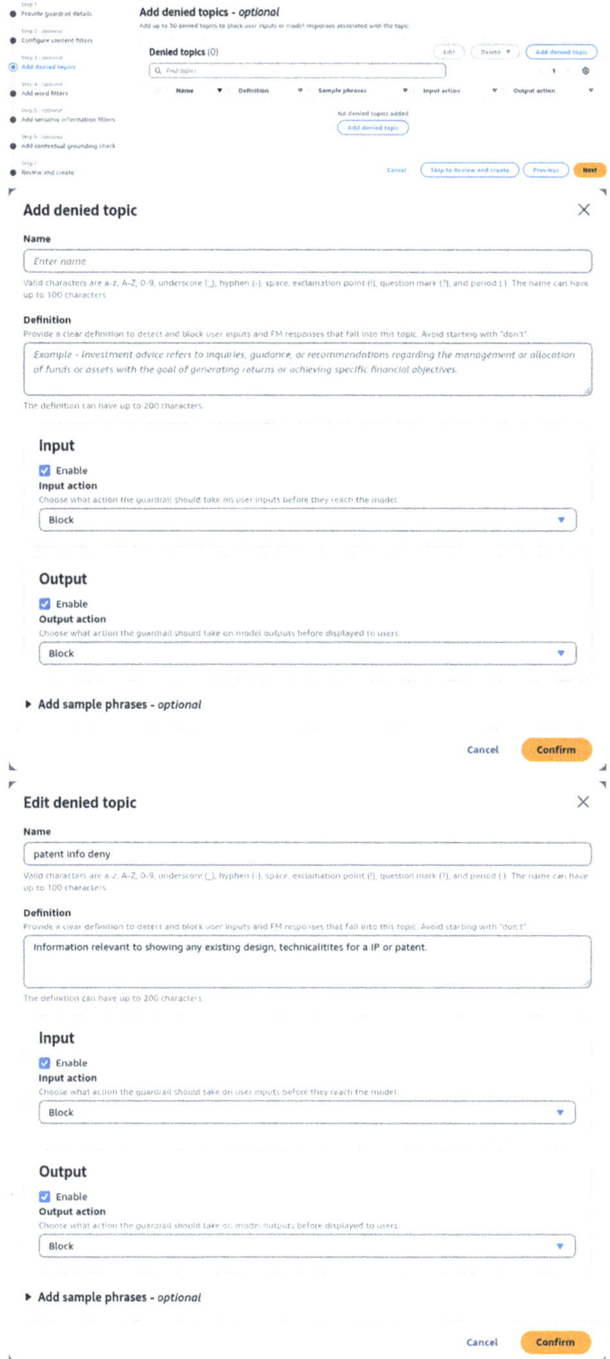

***Figure 16-29.** Denied topics configuration*

After this comes the profanity filter, as shown in Figure 16-30. Activate this option to automatically filter out profanity from both user inputs and AI-generated responses. It relies on a globally maintained list of offensive terms, which is periodically updated. Also, new custom words specific to your application can also be uploaded manually or through a file or S3 location.

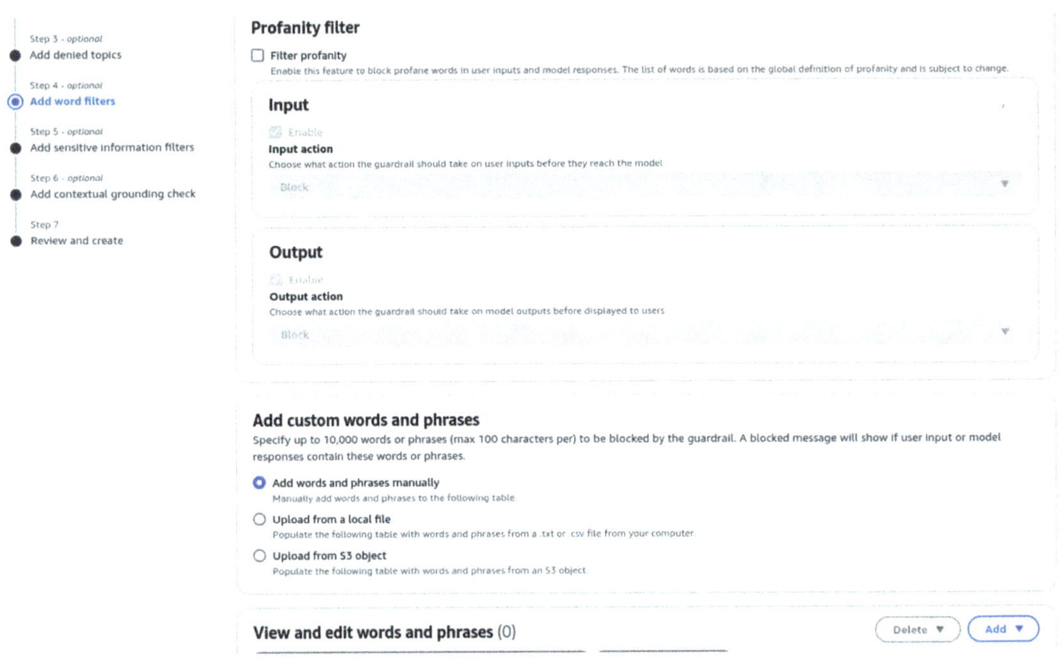

Figure 16-30. *Profanity filter configuration*

The next step is to add any sensitive information filters like PII categories. In Figure 16-31, I have chosen the email address category. You can choose from varied other categories based on your requirement, as shown in Figure 16-31.

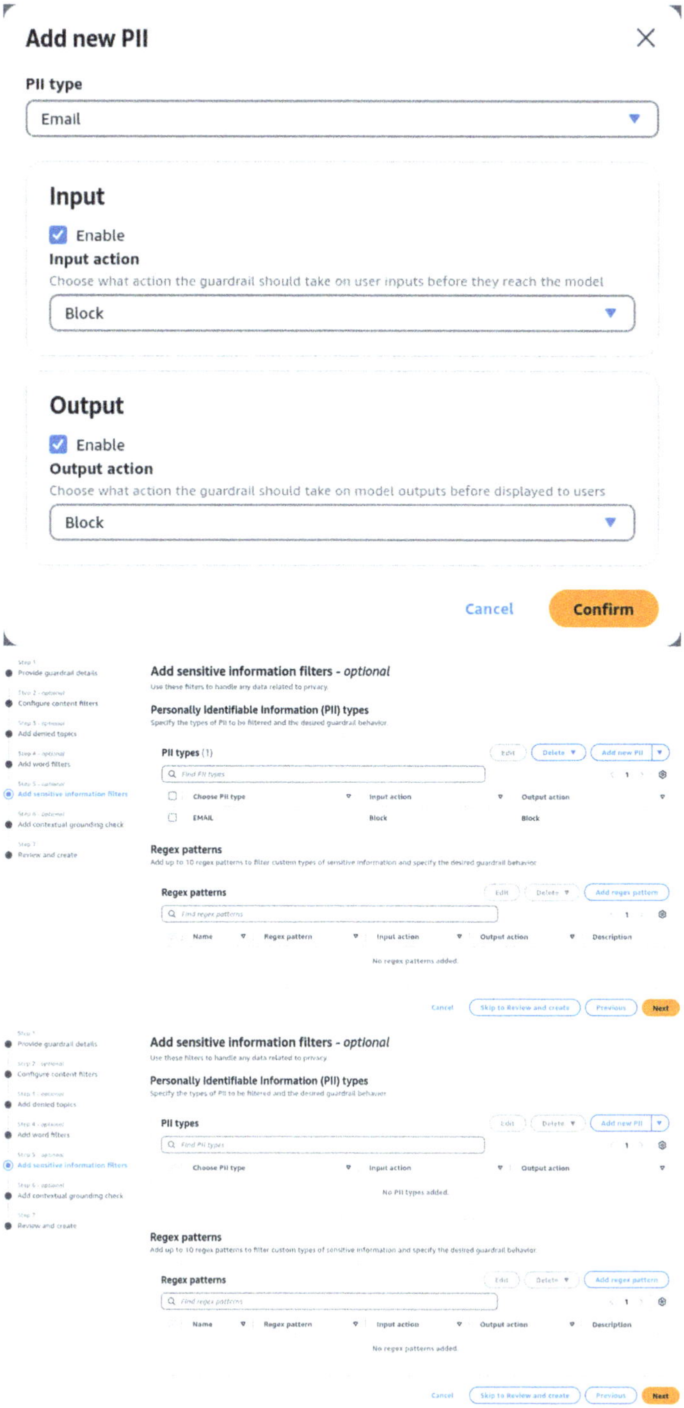

Add new PII

PII type

Email

Input

Enable

Input action

Choose what action the guardrail should take on user inputs before they reach the model

Block

Output

Enable

Output action

Choose what action the guardrail should take on model outputs before displayed to users

Block

Cancel Confirm

Add sensitive information filters - *optional*

Personally Identifiable Information (PII) types

Regex patterns

Add sensitive information filters - *optional*

Personally Identifiable Information (PII) types

Regex patterns

Figure 16-31. *PII configuration*

The next step is to enable grounding check if any context source is provided, as shown in Figure 16-32. This is important since you will be using RAG. Let's enable checks for grounding and relevance.

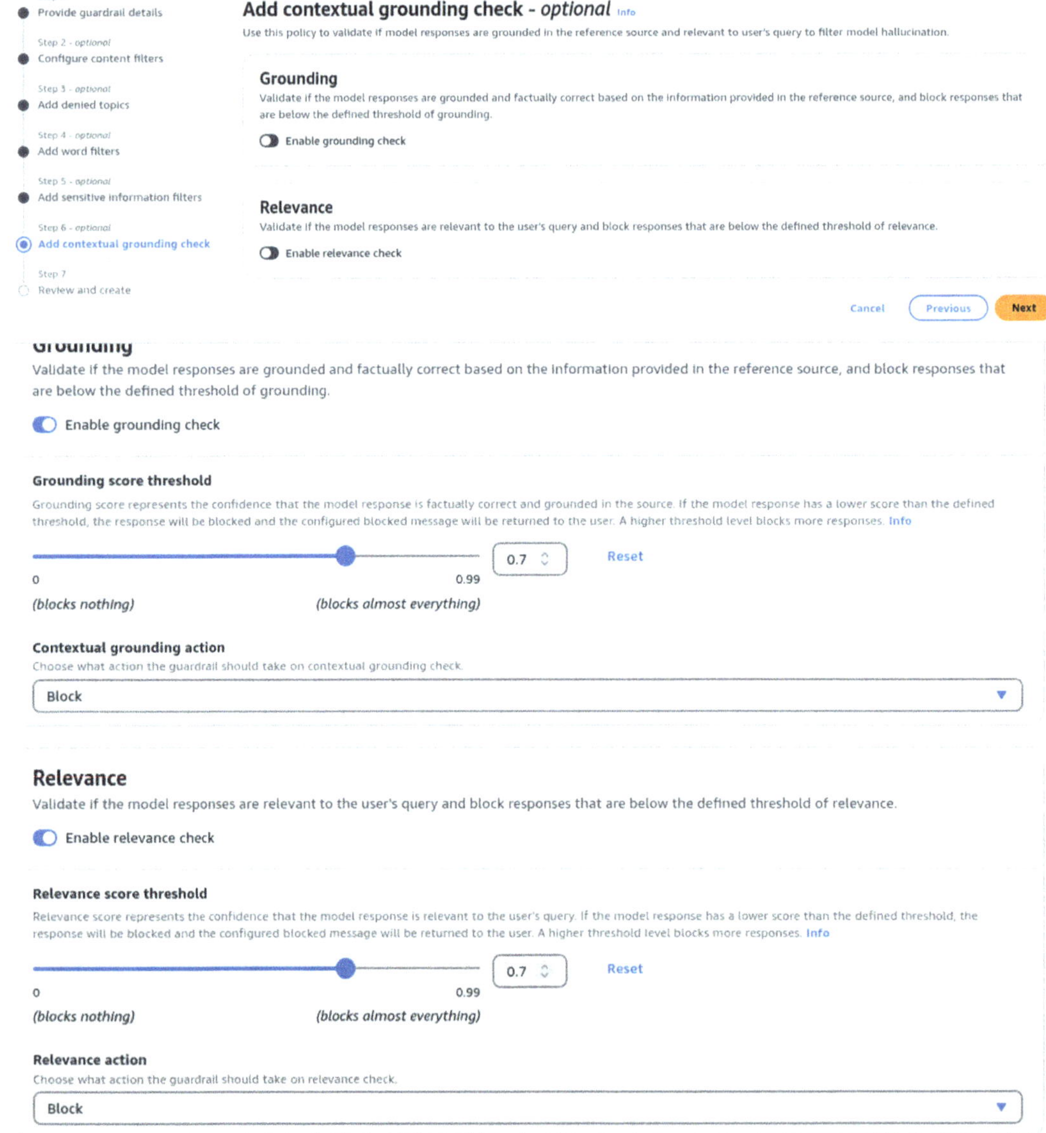

Figure 16-32. *Grounding check configuration*

Finally, on the review page, review all the changes made and click "Create guardrail," as shown in Figure 16-33.

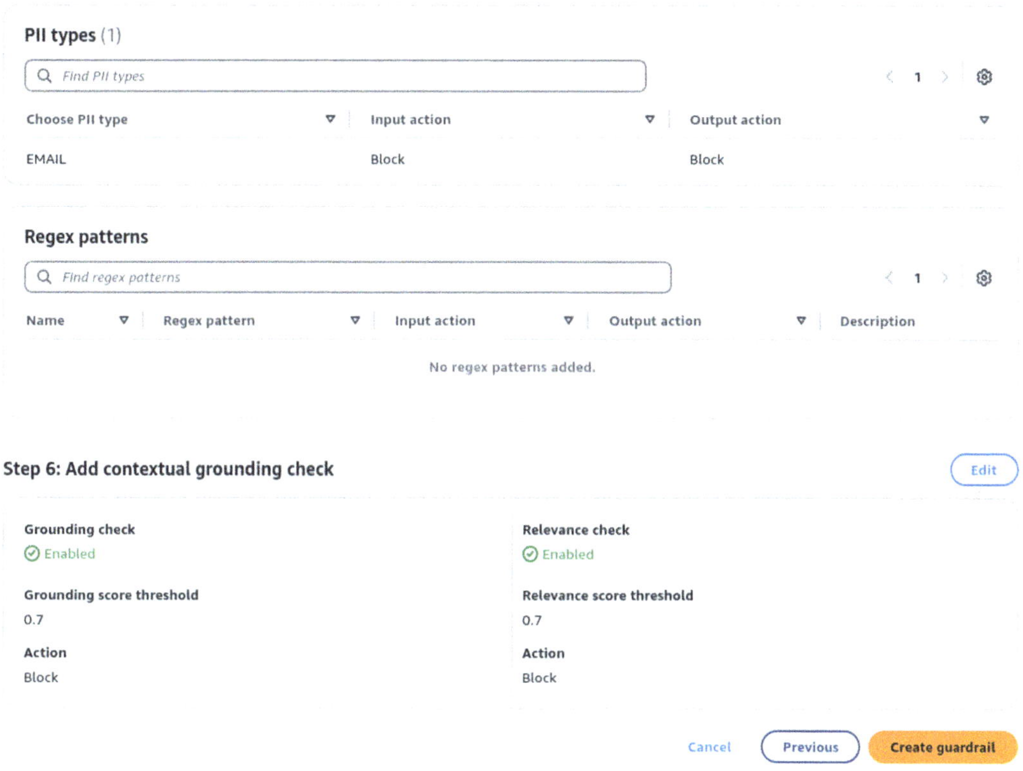

PII types (1)

Find PII types

Choose PII type	Input action	Output action
EMAIL	Block	Block

Regex patterns

Find regex patterns

Name	Regex pattern	Input action	Output action	Description

No regex patterns added.

Step 6: Add contextual grounding check

Edit

Grounding check
Enabled

Grounding score threshold
0.7

Action
Block

Relevance check
Enabled

Relevance score threshold
0.7

Action
Block

Cancel Previous Create guardrail

Figure 16-33. *Review and create page*

2. Test the guardrail.

   Once your guardrail is created, you can test it in the same interface (see Figure 16-34).

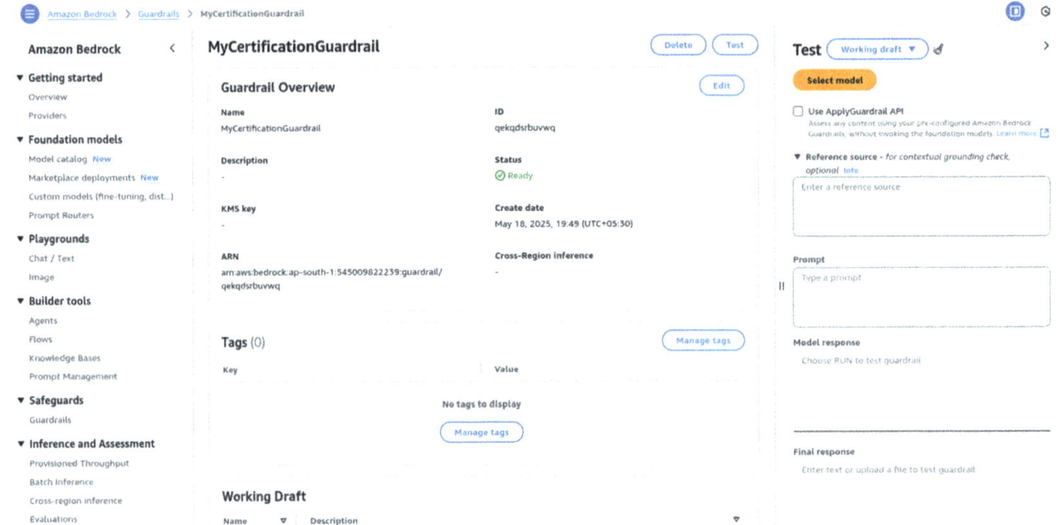

Figure 16-34. Guardrail overview page with test section

Select the Nova micro model from the options list (see Figure 16-35).

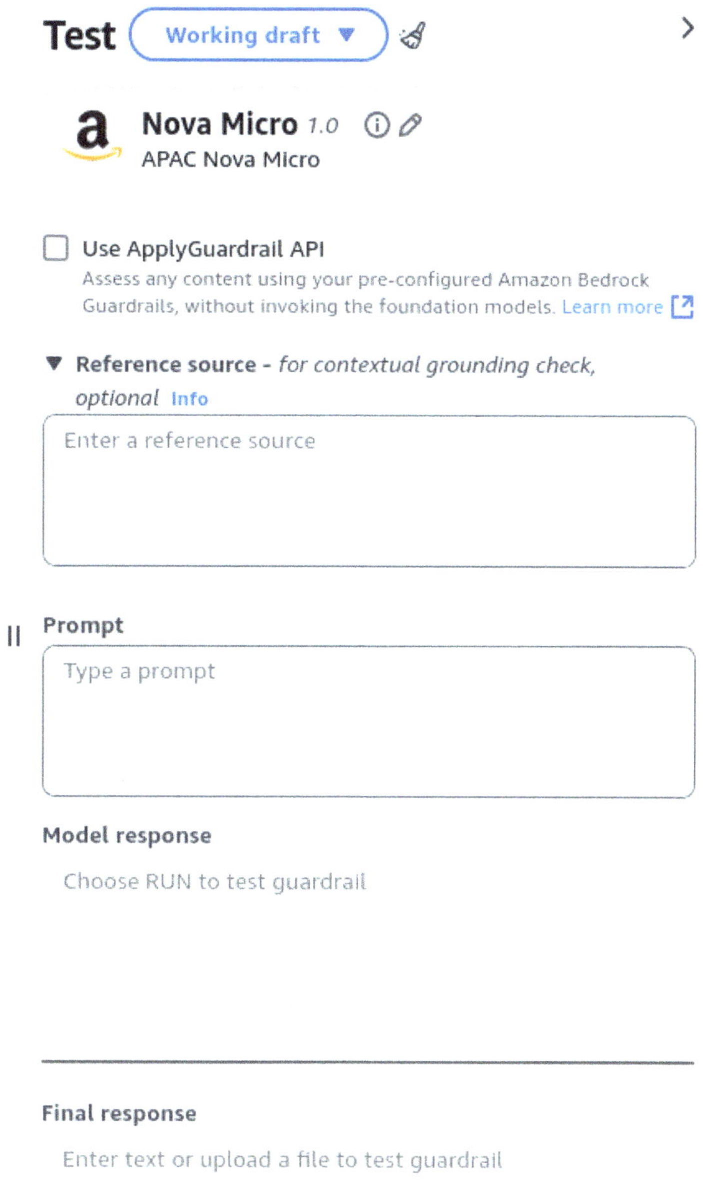

Test Working draft ▼

Nova Micro 1.0
APAC Nova Micro

Use ApplyGuardrail API
Assess any content using your pre-configured Amazon Bedrock Guardrails, without invoking the foundation models. Learn more

▼ Reference source - *for contextual grounding check, optional* Info

Enter a reference source

Prompt

Type a prompt

Model response

Choose RUN to test guardrail

Final response

Enter text or upload a file to test guardrail

Figure 16-35. *Testing the Nova Micro model with guardrails*

For contextual grounding check, you will take a snippet of information from the FAA website at `https://www.ecfr.gov/current/title-14/chapter-III/subchapter-A/part-400/section-400.2`.

The regulations in this chapter set forth the procedures and requirements applicable to the authorization and supervision under 51 U.S.C. subtitle V, chapter 509, of commercial space transportation activities conducted in the United States or by a U.S. citizen. The regulations in this chapter do not apply to the following:

(a) Space activities carried out by the United States Government on behalf of the United States Government;

(b) The launch of an amateur rocket as defined in § 1.1 of chapter I of this title; or

(c) A launch of a tethered launch vehicle that meets all the following criteria:

  (1) Launch vehicle. The launch vehicle must—

    (i) Be unmanned;

    (ii) Be powered by a liquid or hybrid rocket motor;

    (iii) Not use any of the toxic propellants of Table I417-2 and Table I417-3 in Appendix I of part 417 of this chapter; and

    (iv) Carry no more than 5,000 pounds of propellant.

  (2) Tether system. The tether system must—

    (i) Not yield or fail under—

      (A) The maximum dynamic load on the system; or

      (B) A load equivalent to two times the maximum potential engine thrust.

    (ii) Have a minimum safety factor of 3.0 for yield stress and 5.0 for ultimate stress.

(iii) Constrain the launch vehicle within 75 feet above ground level as measured from the ground to the attachment point of the vehicle to the tether.

(iv) Display no damage prior to the launch.

(v) Be insulated or located such that it will not experience thermal damage due to the launch vehicle's exhaust.

(3) Separation distances. The launch operator must separate its launch from the public and the property of the public by a distance no less than that provided for each quantity of propellant listed in Figure 16-36.

TABLE A—SEPARATION DISTANCES FOR TETHERED LAUNCHES

Propellant carried (lbs.)	Distance (ft.) of the public and property of the public from the launch point
1-500	900
501-1,000	1,200
1001-1,500	1,350
1,501-2,000	1,450
2,001-2,500	1,550
2,501-3,000	1,600
3,001-3,500	1,650
3,501-4,000	1,700
4,001-4,500	1,750
4,501-5,000	1,800

***Figure 16-36.** Certification information in tabular format*

Fill in the details in the form and ask for the patent idea that you had asked the guardrail to block. Let's see its output when you run it. Figure 16-37 shows the output.

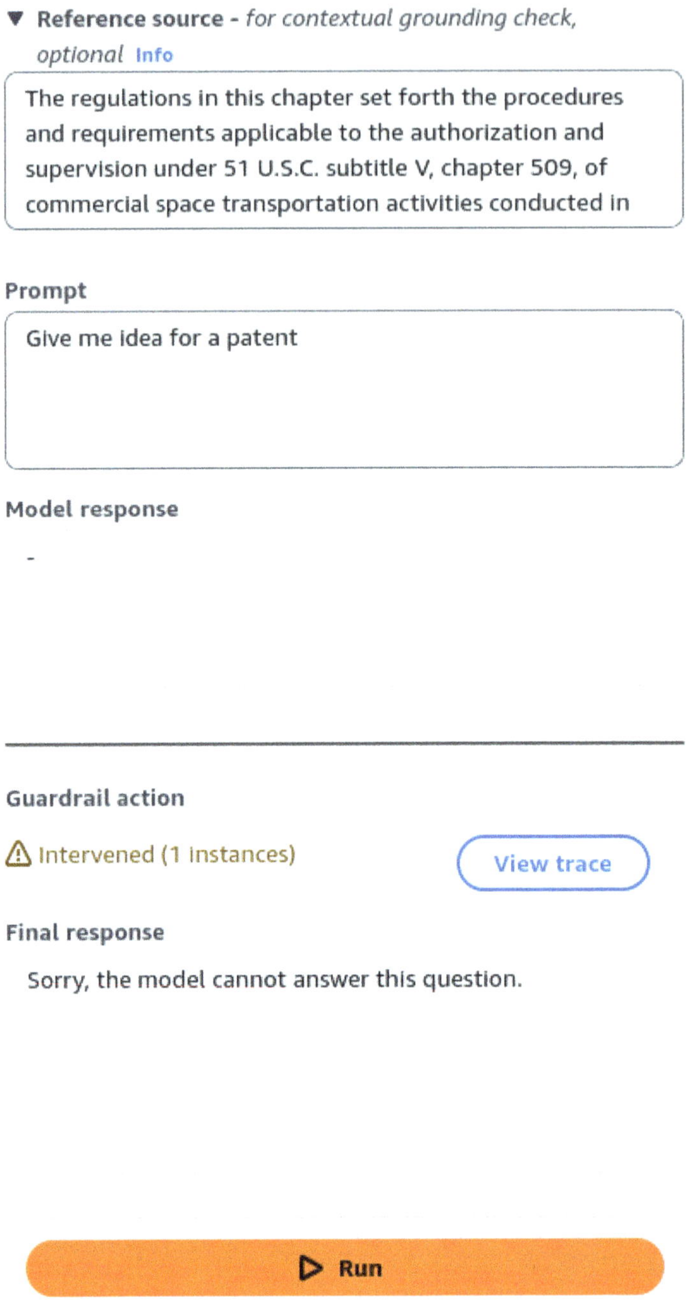

▼ **Reference source** - *for contextual grounding check, optional* Info

The regulations in this chapter set forth the procedures and requirements applicable to the authorization and supervision under 51 U.S.C. subtitle V, chapter 509, of commercial space transportation activities conducted in

Prompt

Give me idea for a patent

Model response

-

Guardrail action

⚠ Intervened (1 instances) View trace

Final response

Sorry, the model cannot answer this question.

▷ Run

Figure 16-37. *Testing guardrail actions*

It seems to be working since the model did not share any response, but the final response was intervened by the guardrail action. You can view the trace of which actions were used (see Figure 16-38).

Insults	No action taken	Detected: FALSE Strength: High Confidence: None
Prompt attack	No action taken	Detected: FALSE Strength: High Confidence: None
Misconduct	No action taken	Detected: FALSE Strength: High Confidence: None

▼ **Denied topics**

Topics	Test result	Details
patent info deny	Blocked	Detected: TRUE

▼ **Word filters**

Word filters	Test result	Details
-	No action taken	Detected: FALSE

▼ **Sensitive information filters**

Type	Test result	Details
PII Type (EMAIL)	No action taken	Detected: FALSE

Figure 16-38. *Overview of different detections through the guardrail*

As you can see, other filters were detected as false, but the denied topics were activated for patent info deny category. This is really helpful, and you can test other scenarios before accepting this guardrail for deployment.

3. Deploy the guardrail.

   Once you have tested the guardrail, you can deploy it by creating a first version of it (see Figure 16-39).

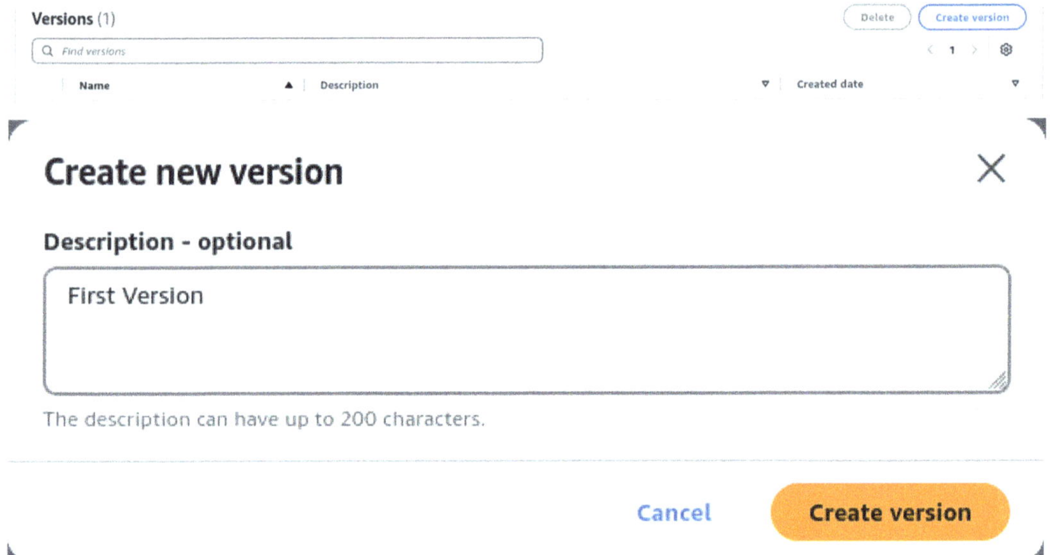

Figure 16-39. *Guardrail versions*

Once the version is created, it will show in ready state for usage. You will need the `arn` property of the guardrail by clicking the guardrail and using the `arn` property in the detail page (see Figure 16-40).

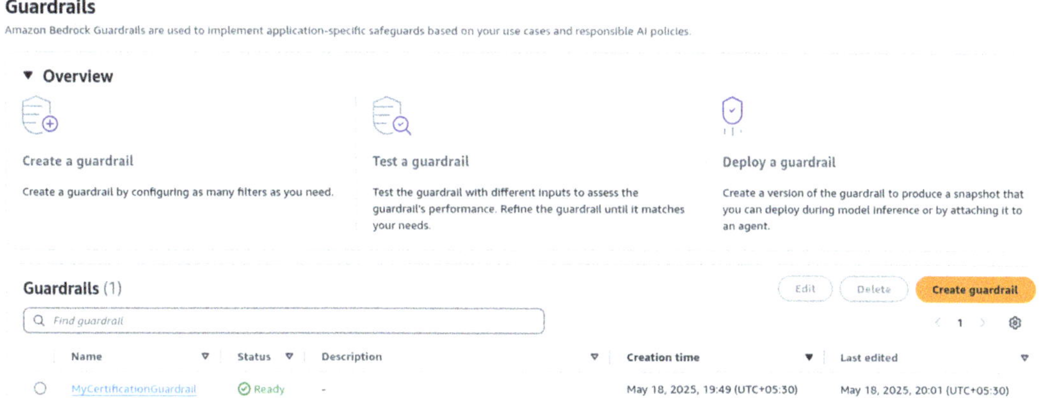

***Figure 16-40.** Guardrails listing overview*

Now that you have the guardrail for use, let's use it in the application you developed previously here. The first step is to note the `arn` property and version of your guardrail and set it in `application.properties` for later use in the service component.

File: `./src/main/resource/application.properties`

```
spring.application.name=demo
aws.region=ap-south-1
aws.bedrock.modelId=arn:aws:bedrock:ap-south-1:xxxxxxxxxxxx:inference-
profile/apac.amazon.nova-micro-v1:0
aws.bedrock.guardrailIdentifier=arn:aws:bedrock:ap-south-1:xxxxxxxxxxxx:
guardrail/xxxxxxxxxxxx
aws.bedrock.guardrailVersion=1
```

Once these are set, you can proceed to the service file to set the properties in variables.

```
@Value("${aws.bedrock.modelId}")
private String modelId;

@Value("${aws.bedrock.guardrailIdentifier}")
private String guardrailIdentifier;

@Value("${aws.bedrock.guardrailVersion}")
private String guardrailVersion;
```

The ConverseRequest that you used previously additionally accepts a guardrailConfiguration object, which you can create using the GuardrailConfiguration builder API. It accepts the guardrail identifier, which is your guardrail arn property and the guardrail version.

```
GuardrailConfiguration guardrailConfiguration = GuardrailConfigurat
ion.builder()
        .guardrailIdentifier(guardrailIdentifier)
        .guardrailVersion(guardrailVersion)
        .build();

ConverseRequest request = ConverseRequest.builder()
        .modelId(modelId)
        .guardrailConfig(guardrailConfiguration)
        .messages(message)
        .inferenceConfig(cfg -> cfg
                .maxTokens(500)
                .temperature(0.5F)
        )
        .build();
```

The complete code change for the service is shown here:

File: ./src/main/java/com/example/demo/service/BedrockService.java

```
package com.example.demo.service;

import org.springframework.beans.factory.annotation.Value;
import org.springframework.stereotype.Service;
import software.amazon.awssdk.core.exception.SdkClientException;
import software.amazon.awssdk.services.bedrockruntime.BedrockRuntimeClient;
import software.amazon.awssdk.services.bedrockruntime.model.*;

@Service
public class BedrockService {

    private final BedrockRuntimeClient client;

    @Value("${aws.bedrock.modelId}")
    private String modelId;
```

```
@Value("${aws.bedrock.guardrailIdentifier}")
private String guardrailIdentifier;

@Value("${aws.bedrock.guardrailVersion}")
private String guardrailVersion;

public BedrockService(BedrockRuntimeClient client) {
    this.client = client;
}

/**
 * Sends the given text to Bedrock and returns the model's reply.
 */
public String converse(String inputText) {
    Message message = Message.builder()
            .role(ConversationRole.USER)
            .content(ContentBlock.fromText(inputText))
            .build();

   GuardrailConfiguration guardrailConfiguration = Guardrail
   Configuration.builder()
            .guardrailIdentifier(guardrailIdentifier)
            .guardrailVersion(guardrailVersion)
            .build();

    ConverseRequest request = ConverseRequest.builder()
            .modelId(modelId)
            .guardrailConfig(guardrailConfiguration)
            .messages(message)
            .inferenceConfig(cfg -> cfg
                    .maxTokens(500)
                    .temperature(0.5F)
            )
            .build();
```

```
        try {
            ConverseResponse response = client.converse(request);
            return response.output().message().content().get(0).text();
        } catch (SdkClientException e) {
            throw new RuntimeException("Failed to invoke Bedrock model: " +
            e.getMessage(), e);
        }
    }
}
```

With this simple method addition, you are able to extend your application with guardrail protection. Let's test this.

```
curl -X POST localhost:8080/api/bedrock/converse   -H "Content-
Type: application/json"   -d '{"inputText":"Give me a patent idea in
certification for FAA."}'
```

Output:

```
{"outputText":"Sorry, the model cannot answer this question."}
```

As you can see in the output, your guardrail was able to catch the filtered topic and respond with the previously set response.

Extending and Integrating RAG into Your Application

You will next learn how to integrate RAG into the application by extending it with your source, which is the FAA certification website, as shared at the starting of this chapter. You will create a PDF of the document at `https://www.ecfr.gov/current/title-14/chapter-III/subchapter-A/part-400/section-400.2` by clicking the Print/PDF button on the website, as shown in Figure 16-41.

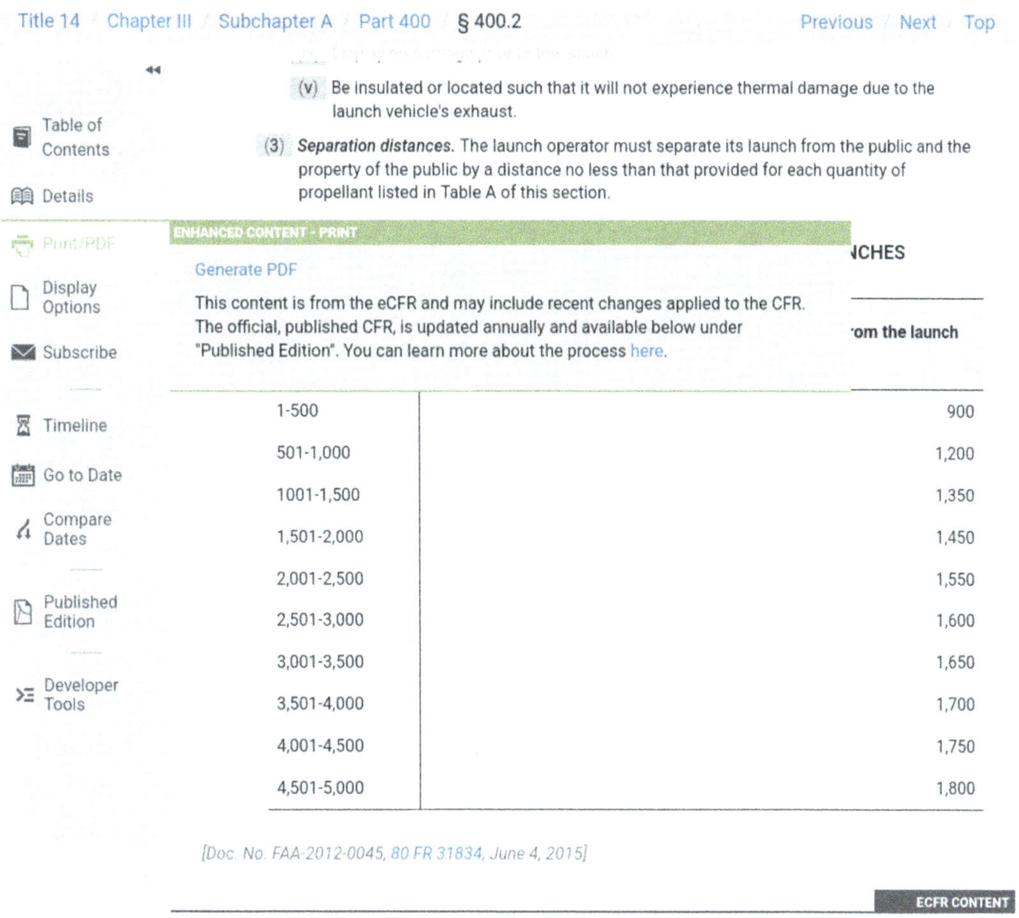

Title 14 / Chapter III / Subchapter A / Part 400 / § 400.2 Previous / Next / Top

Table of Contents

Details

Print/PDF

Display Options

Subscribe

Timeline

Go to Date

Compare Dates

Published Edition

Developer Tools

(v) Be insulated or located such that it will not experience thermal damage due to the launch vehicle's exhaust.

(3) *Separation distances.* The launch operator must separate its launch from the public and the property of the public by a distance no less than that provided for each quantity of propellant listed in Table A of this section.

ENHANCED CONTENT - PRINT

Generate PDF

This content is from the eCFR and may include recent changes applied to the CFR. The official, published CFR, is updated annually and available below under "Published Edition". You can learn more about the process here.

	...NCHES ...om the launch
1-500	900
501-1,000	1,200
1001-1,500	1,350
1,501-2,000	1,450
2,001-2,500	1,550
2,501-3,000	1,600
3,001-3,500	1,650
3,501-4,000	1,700
4,001-4,500	1,750
4,501-5,000	1,800

[Doc. No. FAA-2012-0045, 80 FR 31834, June 4, 2015]

ECFR CONTENT

Figure 16-41. *PDF generation*

Amazon Bedrock abstracts how to implement this in knowledge bases (see Figure 16-42).

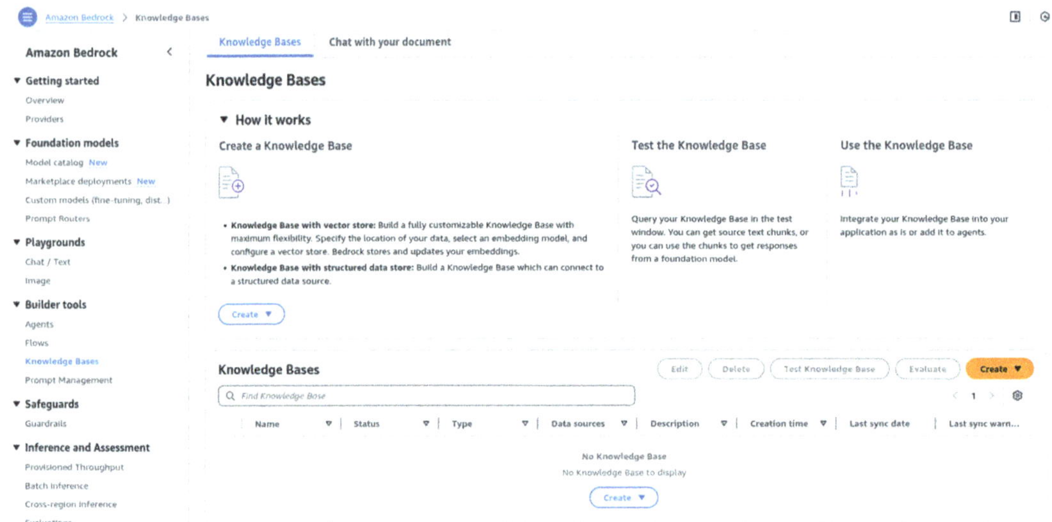

Figure 16-42. *AWS Bedrock knowledge bases*

Amazon Bedrock knowledge bases let you bring your own data into the same environment as foundation models so you can ask natural-language questions against documents, databases, or other content you control. When you build a vector-store knowledge base, you begin by pointing Bedrock at your unstructured source material—PDFs, text files, web pages, or anything else—and selecting an embedding model along with the storage backend where your vectors will live. Bedrock then reads your data, transforms each piece into high-dimensional embeddings, and keeps those embeddings up-to-date as your content changes. For structured-data knowledge bases, you instead connect Bedrock directly to a database or other tabular store; Bedrock catalogs the schema and ingests the records, turning rows and columns into retrievable objects without manual preprocessing.

Once your knowledge base is built, Bedrock provides a test interface where you can type in queries and immediately see what snippets or records it retrieves. You can inspect these "raw" results to verify that your data is being indexed correctly, or you can feed them straight into a foundation model to observe how the model synthesizes a conversational answer from the retrieved context. This rapid feedback loop helps you tune your embedding choices, storage settings, and query parameters until you're confident in the relevance and accuracy of the results.

When you're ready to go live, you simply call Bedrock's retrieval or chat endpoints from your application—either embedding knowledge-base queries directly into your user interface or wiring them into an agent framework that can orchestrate multiturn dialogues or complex workflows. In either case, Bedrock handles the heavy lifting of vector similarity search or structured querying behind the scenes, so your code remains clean and focused on delivering a smooth, intelligent experience to your users.

We will proceed with creating a knowledge base using a vector store. Click the Create button and select to use vector store. This leads us to step 1 where you need to provide knowledge base details. Most of the form fields are self-explanatory and filled in for quick startup. Feel free to update any of them to your choice (see Figure 16-43).

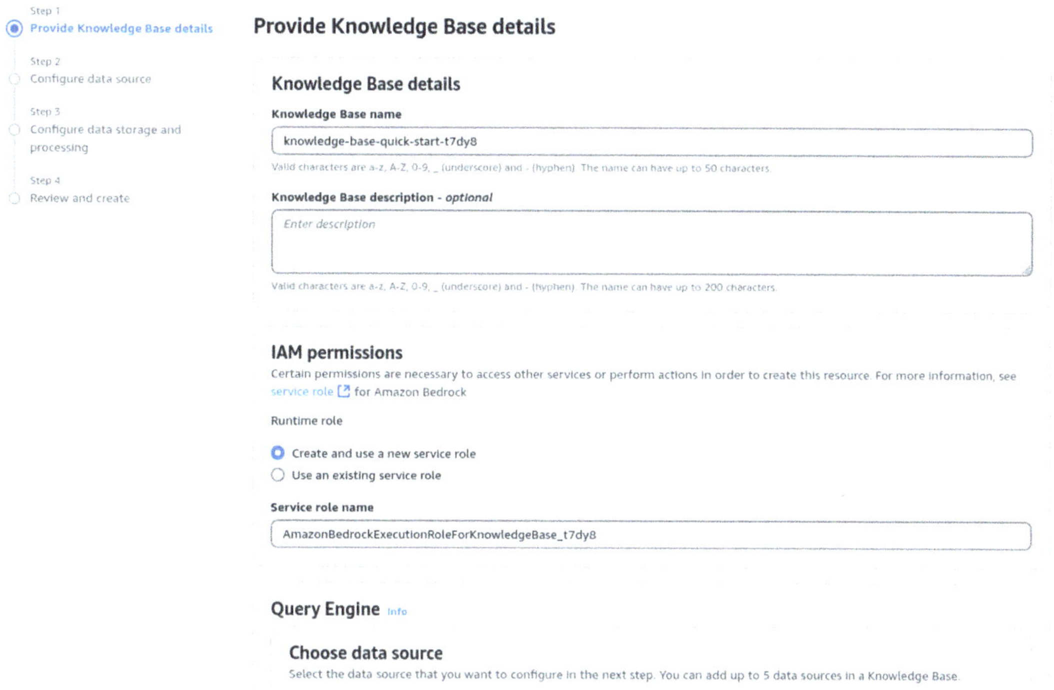

Figure 16-43. *Knowledge base details section*

Since in this case the page is public, you can use the web crawler as your data source (see Figure 16-44).

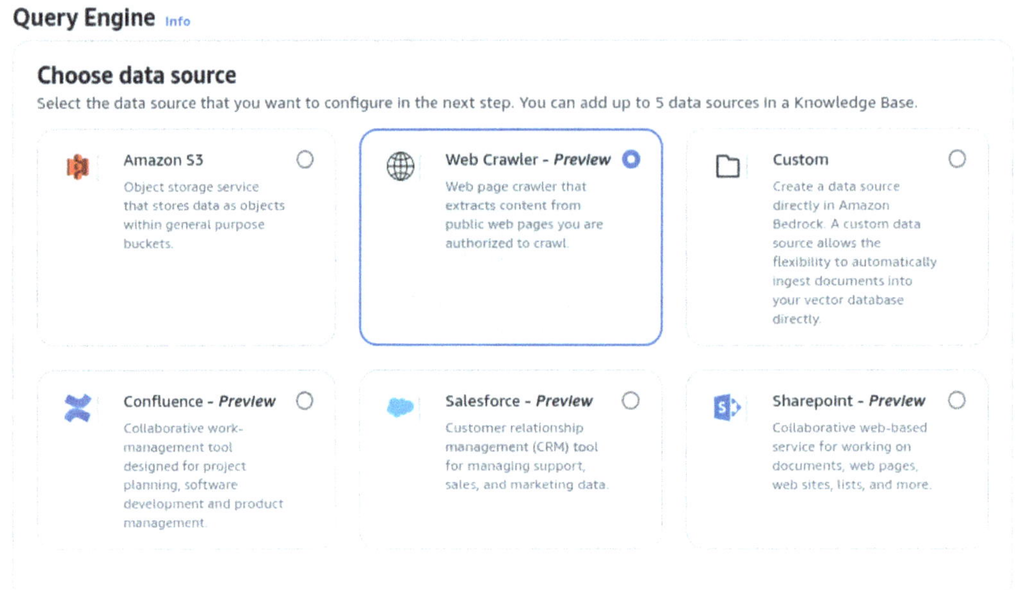

Figure 16-44. *Data source choices for knowledge base*

In step 2, you will continue to configure the data source where you will need to set the base URL of the website you want as your data source. You can use the URL `https://www.ecfr.gov/current/title-14`, but for quick setup, you can instead go with only a single subpage in the Source URLs field (see Figure 16-45).

> *"Remember that you must only use the Web Crawler to index your own web pages, or web pages that you have authorization to crawl and must respect robots.txt configurations. The web crawler will respect robots.txt in accordance to the RFC 9309. It's not recommended to crawl large websites, such as wikipedia.org, without filters or scope limits. Crawling large websites will take a very long time to crawl."*

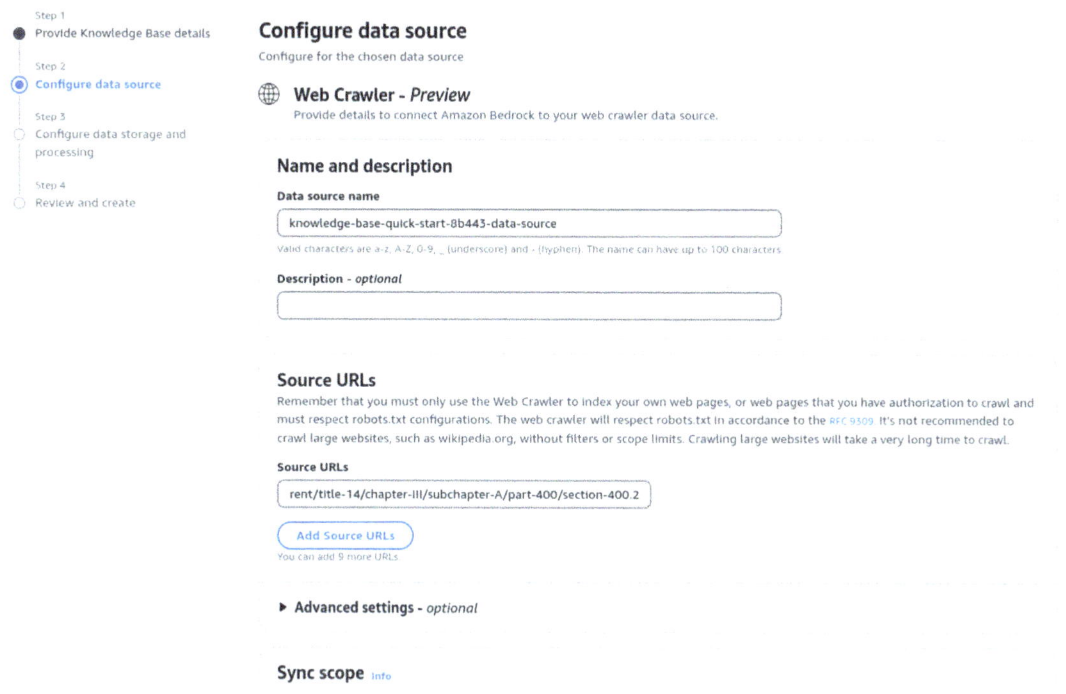

Step 1
Provide Knowledge Base details
Step 2
Configure data source
Step 3
Configure data storage and processing
Step 4
Review and create

Configure data source
Configure for the chosen data source

Web Crawler - *Preview*
Provide details to connect Amazon Bedrock to your web crawler data source.

Name and description
Data source name
knowledge-base-quick-start-8b443-data-source
Valid characters are a-z, A-Z, 0-9, _ (underscore) and - (hyphen). The name can have up to 100 characters.
Description - *optional*

Source URLs
Remember that you must only use the Web Crawler to index your own web pages, or web pages that you have authorization to crawl and must respect robots.txt configurations. The web crawler will respect robots.txt in accordance to the RFC 9309. It's not recommended to crawl large websites, such as wikipedia.org, without filters or scope limits. Crawling large websites will take a very long time to crawl.
Source URLs
rent/title-14/chapter-III/subchapter-A/part-400/section-400.2
Add Source URLs
You can add 9 more URLs

▸ Advanced settings - *optional*

Sync scope Info

Figure 16-45. *Web crawling of data source URLs*

We are allowed at most 10 URLs to crawl from.

Then you can select which scope you want to crawl from, such as the same host and initial URL, the same host only, or the same primary domain. For now let's use the default. There are other settings you can set as shown in Figure 16-46 that are self-explanatory.

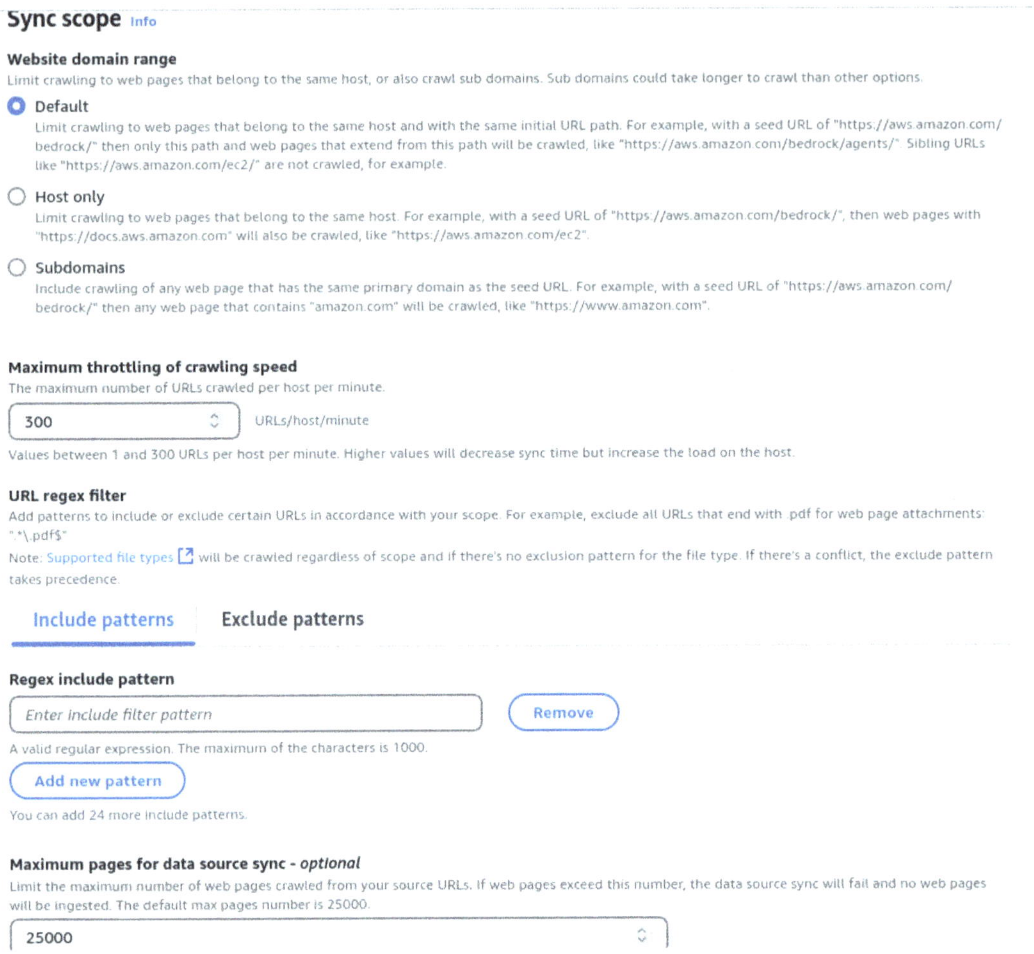

Sync scope Info

Website domain range

Limit crawling to web pages that belong to the same host, or also crawl sub domains. Sub domains could take longer to crawl than other options.

Default
Limit crawling to web pages that belong to the same host and with the same initial URL path. For example, with a seed URL of "https://aws.amazon.com/bedrock/" then only this path and web pages that extend from this path will be crawled, like "https://aws.amazon.com/bedrock/agents/". Sibling URLs like "https://aws.amazon.com/ec2/" are not crawled, for example.

Host only
Limit crawling to web pages that belong to the same host. For example, with a seed URL of "https://aws.amazon.com/bedrock/", then web pages with "https://docs.aws.amazon.com" will also be crawled, like "https://aws.amazon.com/ec2".

Subdomains
Include crawling of any web page that has the same primary domain as the seed URL. For example, with a seed URL of "https://aws.amazon.com/bedrock/" then any web page that contains "amazon.com" will be crawled, like "https://www.amazon.com".

Maximum throttling of crawling speed

The maximum number of URLs crawled per host per minute.

300 URLs/host/minute

Values between 1 and 300 URLs per host per minute. Higher values will decrease sync time but increase the load on the host.

URL regex filter

Add patterns to include or exclude certain URLs in accordance with your scope. For example, exclude all URLs that end with .pdf for web page attachments: ".*\.pdf$"

Note: Supported file types will be crawled regardless of scope and if there's no exclusion pattern for the file type. If there's a conflict, the exclude pattern takes precedence.

Include patterns | Exclude patterns

Regex include pattern

Enter include filter pattern | Remove

A valid regular expression. The maximum of the characters is 1000.

Add new pattern

You can add 24 more include patterns.

Maximum pages for data source sync - *optional*

Limit the maximum number of web pages crawled from your source URLs. If web pages exceed this number, the data source sync will fail and no web pages will be ingested. The default max pages number is 25000.

25000

Figure 16-46. *Web crawling settings*

Since the website does not allow crawling the contents of the website, the crawler fails. I have chosen to use the PDF format, which can be downloaded and then uploaded to S3. Uploaded the downloaded document to S3 and then provide the S3 path to the data source settings. See Figure 16-47.

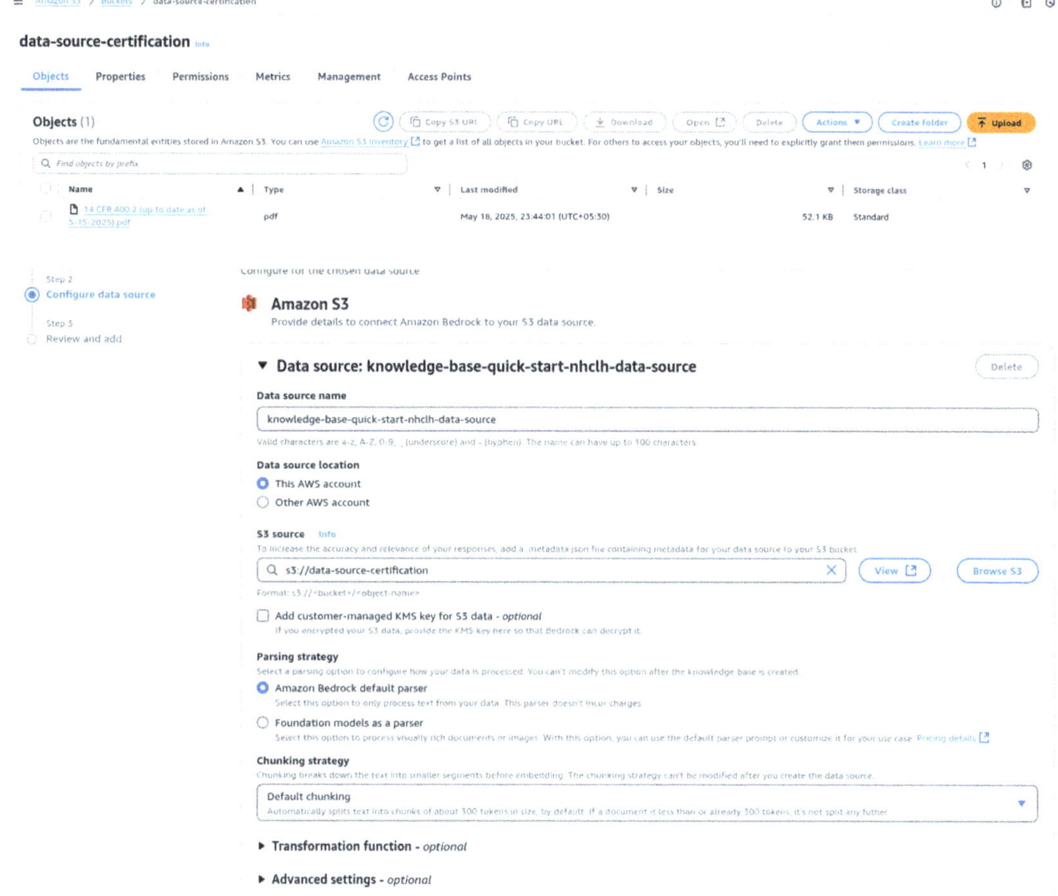

Figure 16-47. *S3 data source*

The next step is to select the chunking strategy. Go ahead with the default setting, which is fine for this case. You can also use a custom lambda function if you have a custom chunking strategy (see Figure 16-48).

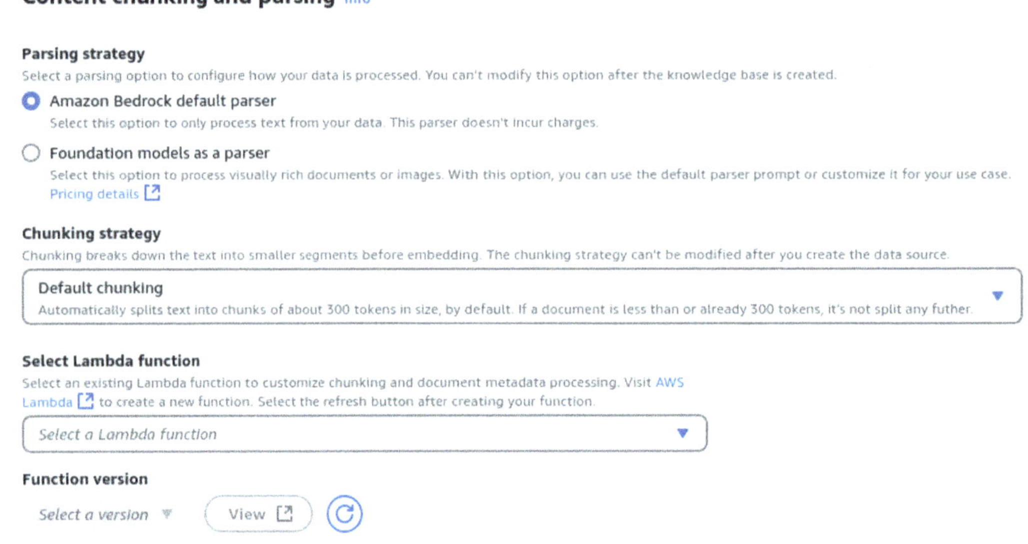

Figure 16-48. Chunking strategy configuration

Step 3 is to configure data storage and processing where you will choose an embedding model from Amazon called Tital Text Embeddings V2 and OpenSearch Serverless as the vector store.

For this step, to actually work later, you have to make sure you have requested access to it for embeddings generation. This can be done similar to what you did for the Nova Micro model (see Figure 16-49).

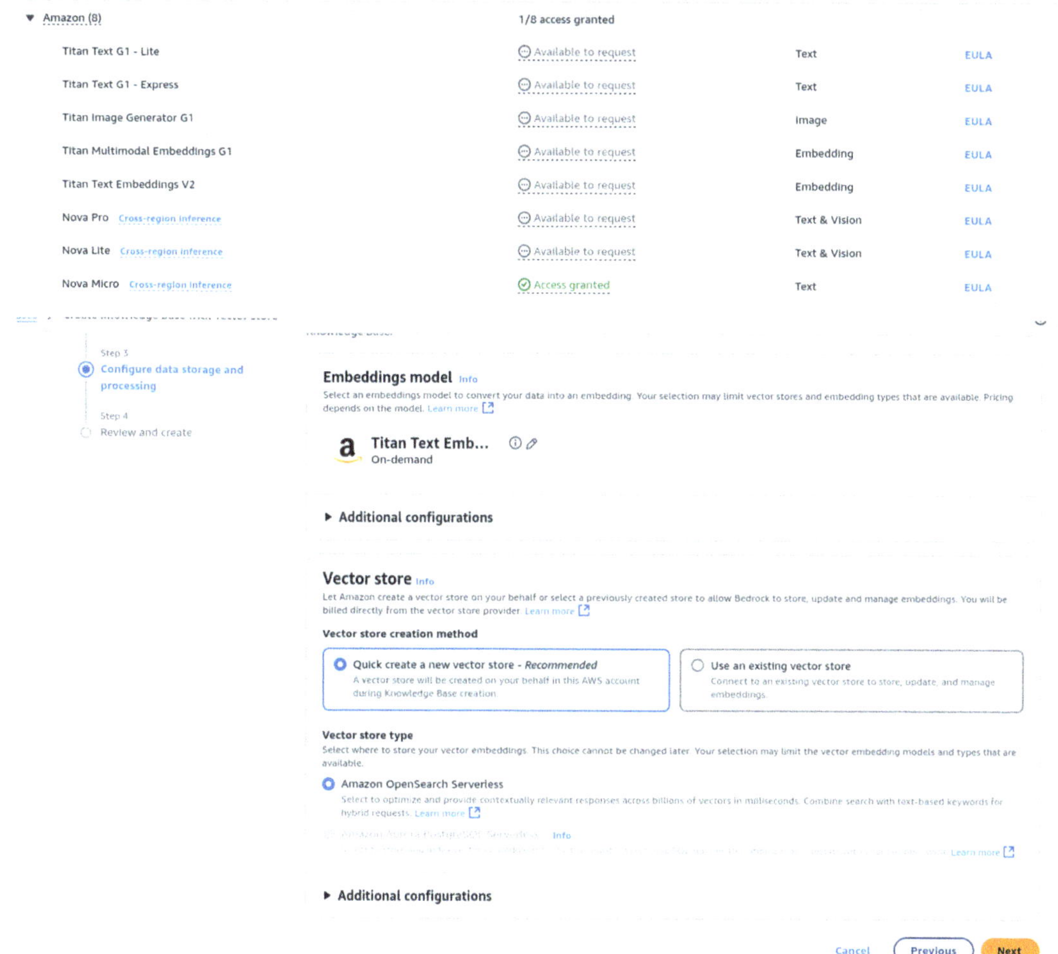

Figure 16-49. *Vector store configuration for knowledge base*

The final step is to review and create your knowledge base (see Figure 16-50).

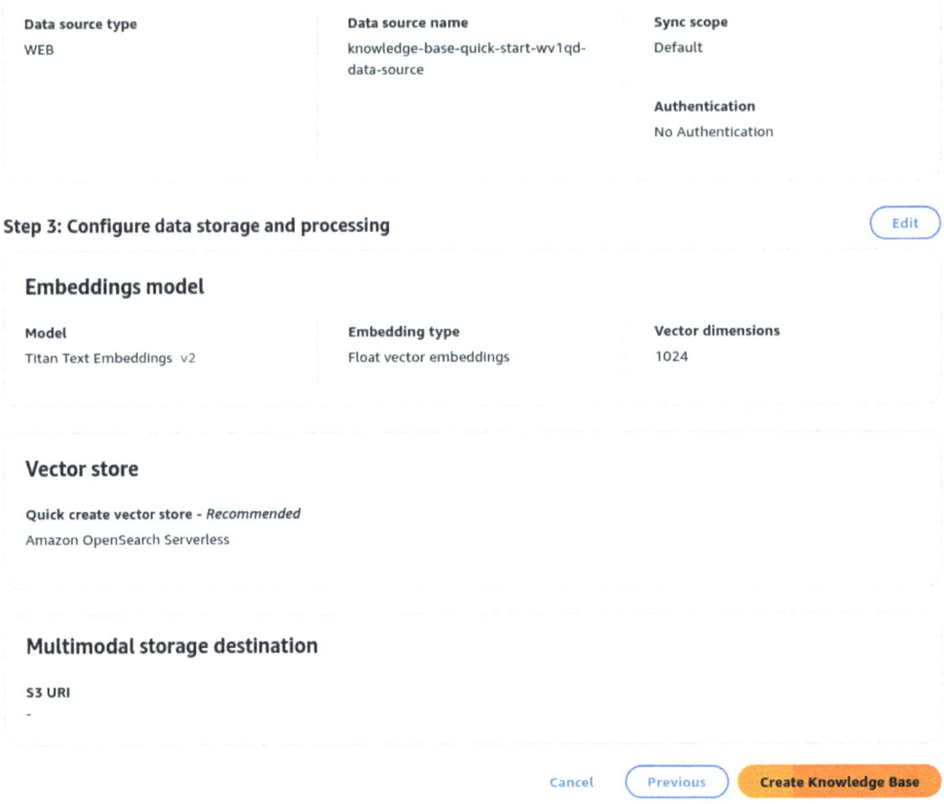

Figure 16-50. *Knowledge base overview and create page*

It takes some time to complete this step (see Figure 16-51).

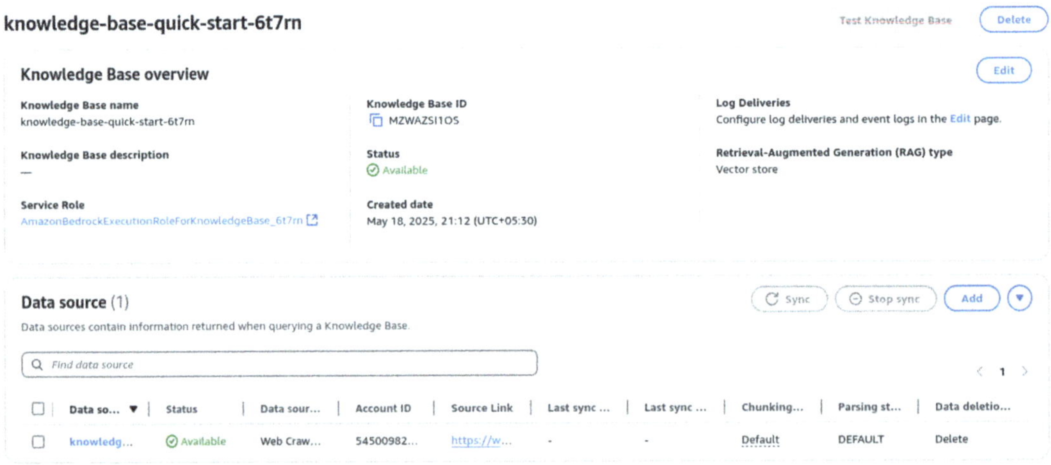

Figure 16-51. *Knowledge base listing view*

Once complete, you should sync your data source once so that the embeddings are populated in open search for RAG to work. In Figure 16-52, you can see the data source has already been synced. If there are no other issues, the Test Knowledge Base at top right will be enabled for your testing.

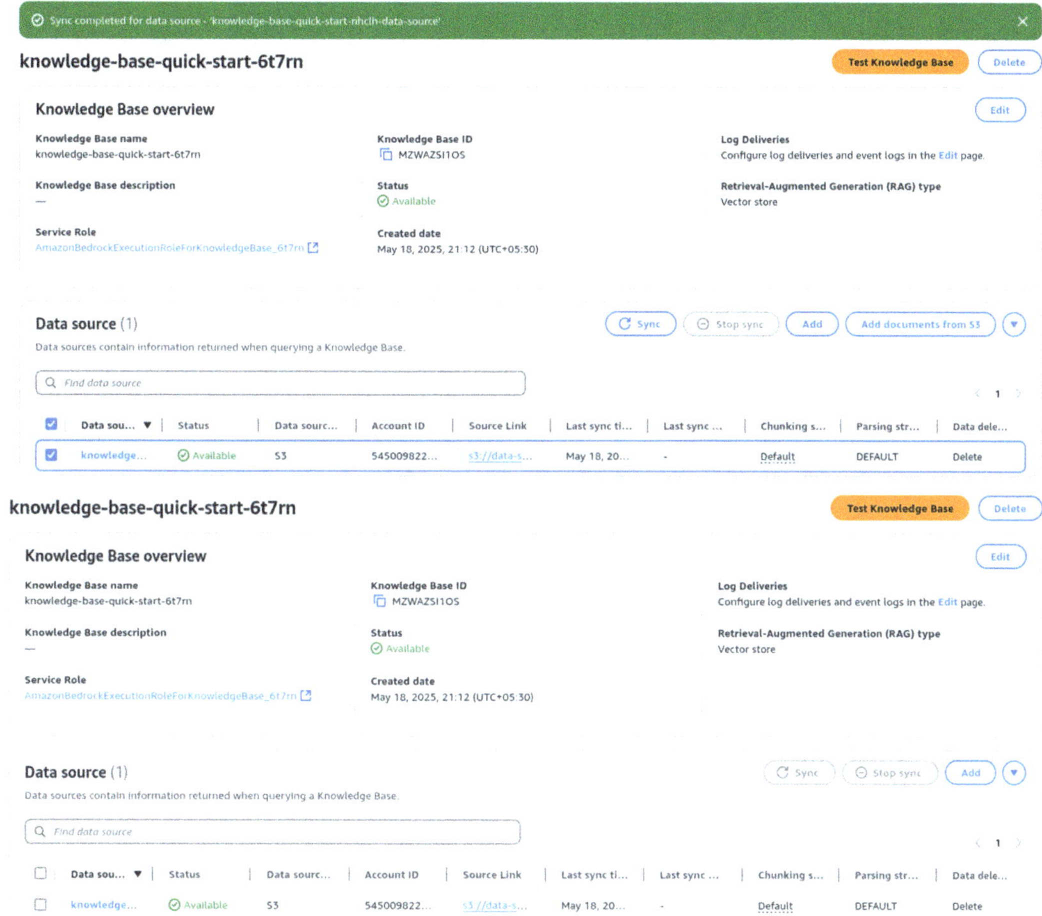

Figure 16-52. *Test knowledge base and status views*

Now you can go ahead and test your knowledge base and ask it a question to share with the scope for 400.2, which is present in your document. If asked to select a model, select your Nova Micro model for the generation component (see Figure 16-53).

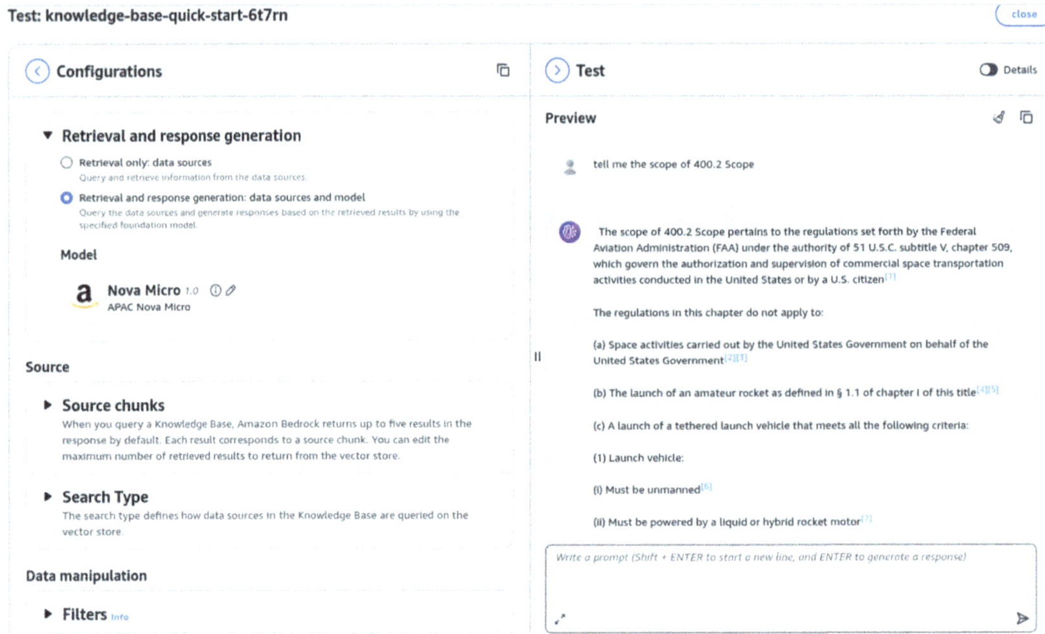

Figure 16-53. *Test knowledge base page*

Now that you have your knowledge base, let's use it to integrate RAG into your previous application. Since this uses a new dependency called `bedrockagentruntime`, you will need to include it into your `build.gradle` file.

```
// https://mvnrepository.com/artifact/software.amazon.awssdk/
bedrockagentruntime
implementation 'software.amazon.awssdk:bedrockagentruntime:2.31.45'
```

We will need to set the knowledge base id in the `application.properties` file to be used later in your service component. This can be fetched from the knowledge base page (see Figure 16-54).

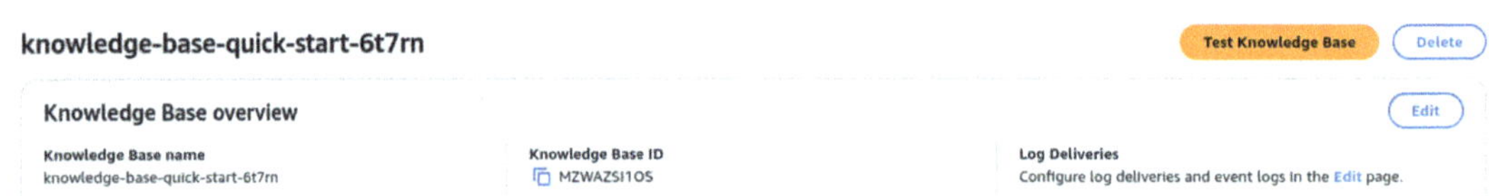

Figure 16-54. *The `application.properties` information for knowledge base config*

File: ./src/main/resources/application.properties

```
spring.application.name=demo
aws.region=ap-south-1
aws.bedrock.modelId=arn:aws:bedrock:ap-south-1:xxxxxxxxxxxx:inference-
profile/apac.amazon.nova-micro-v1:0
aws.bedrock.guardrailIdentifier=arn:aws:bedrock:ap-
south-1:xxxxxxxxxxxx:guardrail/xxxxxxxxxxx
aws.bedrock.guardrailVersion=1
aws.bedrock.knowledgeBaseId=XXXXXXXXXX
```

Since this uses the BedrockAgentRuntimeClient for your final request for RAG, you will have to create another bean for this in the configuration file.

File: ./src/main/java/com/example/demo/config/AwsConfig.java

```
package com.example.demo.config;

import org.springframework.beans.factory.annotation.Value;
import org.springframework.context.annotation.Bean;
import org.springframework.context.annotation.Configuration;
import software.amazon.awssdk.auth.credentials.DefaultCredentialsProvider;
import software.amazon.awssdk.regions.Region;
import software.amazon.awssdk.services.bedrockagentruntime.
BedrockAgentRuntimeClient;
import software.amazon.awssdk.services.bedrockruntime.BedrockRuntimeClient;

@Configuration
public class AwsConfig {

    @Value("${aws.region}")
    private String awsRegion;

    @Bean
    public BedrockRuntimeClient bedrockRuntimeClient() {
        return BedrockRuntimeClient.builder()
                .credentialsProvider(DefaultCredentialsProvider.create())
                .region(Region.of(awsRegion))
                .build();
    }
```

```
    @Bean
    public BedrockAgentRuntimeClient bedrockAgentRuntimeClient() {
        return BedrockAgentRuntimeClient.builder()
                .credentialsProvider(DefaultCredentialsProvider.create())
                .region(Region.of(awsRegion))
                .build();
    }
}
```

This bean will then be injected at runtime in your service component.

```
    private final BedrockService bedrockService;

    public BedrockController(BedrockService bedrockService) {
        this.bedrockService = bedrockService;
    }
```

We will create another method in your service component since the API for this differs from the Converse API you used previously. You will name this `retrieve`, which takes a similar `inputText` as an argument. Then you create an object of the `RetrieveAndGenerateInput` type using the builder pattern, which takes in as a text argument the `inputText` value.

```
public String retrieve(String inputText) {
    RetrieveAndGenerateInput retrieveAndGenerateInput =
    RetrieveAndGenerateInput.builder()
            .text(inputText)
            .build();
```

We will then create the `KnowledgeBaseRetrieveAndGenerateConfiguration` object, which takes as argument the `knowledgeBaseId` and the `modelId` of your Nova Micro model, which is already set.

```
@Value("${aws.bedrock.knowledgeBaseId}")
private String knowledgeBaseId;
. . .
. . .
KnowledgeBaseRetrieveAndGenerateConfiguration knowledgeBaseConfiguration =
KnowledgeBaseRetrieveAndGenerateConfiguration.builder()
```

```
    .knowledgeBaseId(knowledgeBaseId)
    .modelArn(modelId)
    .build();
```

After this, you will need to create the RetrieveAndGenerateConfiguration object that uses the previous knowledgeBaseConfiguration and the type of KNOWLEDGE_BASE value to build the object.

```
RetrieveAndGenerateConfiguration retrieveAndGenerateConfiguration =
RetrieveAndGenerateConfiguration.builder()
    .knowledgeBaseConfiguration(knowledgeBaseConfiguration)
    .type(RetrieveAndGenerateType.KNOWLEDGE_BASE)
    .build();
```

You can finally use this configuration to create the request object for the retrieveAndGenerate method call on the agentClient.

```
RetrieveAndGenerateRequest retrieveAndGenerateRequest =
RetrieveAndGenerateRequest.builder()
    .input(retrieveAndGenerateInput)
    .retrieveAndGenerateConfiguration(retrieveAndGenerateConfiguration)
    .build();

    try {
        RetrieveAndGenerateResponse retrieveAndGenerateResponse =
        agentClient
            .retrieveAndGenerate(retrieveAndGenerateRequest);
        return retrieveAndGenerateResponse.output().text();
        } catch (SdkClientException e) {
    throw new RuntimeException("Failed to invoke Bedrock agent model:
    " + e.getMessage(), e);
    }
```

Then you will add your controller route to access this new method.

```
package com.example.demo.controller;

import com.example.demo.dto.ConverseRequestDto;
import com.example.demo.dto.ConverseResponseDto;
```

```
import com.example.demo.service.BedrockService;
import org.springframework.http.ResponseEntity;
import org.springframework.web.bind.annotation.*;

@RestController
@RequestMapping("/api/bedrock")
public class BedrockController {

    private final BedrockService bedrockService;

    public BedrockController(BedrockService bedrockService) {
        this.bedrockService = bedrockService;
    }

    @PostMapping("/converse")
    public ResponseEntity<ConverseResponseDto> converse(@RequestBody
    ConverseRequestDto req) {
        String reply = bedrockService.converse(req.getInputText());
        return ResponseEntity.ok(new ConverseResponseDto(reply));
    }

    @PostMapping("/retrieve")
    public ResponseEntity<ConverseResponseDto> retrieve(@RequestBody
    ConverseRequestDto req) {
        String reply = bedrockService.retrieve(req.getInputText());
        return ResponseEntity.ok(new ConverseResponseDto(reply));
    }
}
```

Now your RAG has been set up. Let's boot up your application and test it with the same query as you tested in the playground.

```
curl -X POST localhost:8080/api/bedrock/retrieve  -H "Content-Type:
application/json"   -d '{"inputText":"Tell me the scope of 400.2."}'
```

Output:


```
{"outputText":"The scope of 400.2 pertains to the regulations under which
commercial space transportation activities are authorized and supervised in
the United States. Specifically, the regulations in this chapter apply to
commercial space transportation activities conducted in the United States
or by a U.S. citizen, but do not cover:\n\n(a) Space activities carried out
by the United States Government on behalf of the United States Government.\
n\n(b) The launch of an amateur rocket as defined in § 1.1 of chapter I of
this title.\n\n(c) A launch of a tethered launch vehicle that meets all the
following criteria:\n\n(1) Launch vehicle. The launch vehicle must-\n\n(i)
Be unmanned.\n\n(ii) Be powered by a liquid or hybrid rocket motor.\n\
n(iii) Not use any of the toxic propellants of Table I417-2 and Table
I417-3 in Appendix I of part 417 of this chapter.\n\n(iv) Carry no more
than 5,000 pounds of propellant.\n\n(2) Tether system. The tether system
must-\n\n(i) Not yield or fail under-\n\n(A) The maximum dynamic load on
the system; or\n\n(B) A load equivalent to two times the maximum potential
engine thrust.\n\n(ii) Have a minimum safety factor of 3.0 for yield stress
and 5.0 for ultimate stress.\n\n(iii) Constrain the launch vehicle within
75 feet above ground level as measured from the ground to the attachment
point of the vehicle to the tether.\n\n(iv) Display no damage prior to
the launch.\n\nAdditionally, the launch operator must separate its launch
from the public and the property of the public by a distance no less than
that provided for each quantity of propellant listed in Table A of this
section. The separation distances are as follows:\n\n- 1-500 lbs: 900
ft\n- 501-1,000 lbs: 1,200 ft\n- 1,001-1,500 lbs: 1,350 ft\n- 1,501-2,000
lbs: 1,450 ft\n- 2,001-2,500 lbs: 1,550 ft\n- 2,501-3,000 lbs: 1,600 ft\n-
3,001-3,500 lbs: 1,650 ft\n- 3,501-4,000 lbs: 1,700 ft\n- 4,001-4,500 lbs:
1,750 ft\n- 4,501-5,000 lbs: 1,800 ft."}
```


You can compare the output to the text in your document and find the relevance there. As you can see, it's an interesting experience bringing together all the tooling in Amazon Bedrock in order to plug it in and build your generative application.

Note Remember to delete all the resources in AWS created for this chapter so as not to incur additional unknown costs.

Reengineering Your Application Using Spring AI Integration with Amazon Bedrock

You have seen how to build an application using the SDK from AWS. In this section, you will explore how to build a similar application but leveraging a framework like Spring AI to leverage the same resource infra in AWS in the backend. The advantage of this is that Spring AI uses some similar APIs to interact with different LLMs whether they are hosted in AWS or in OpenAI. This brings common ground of learning regardless of which LLM or infra provider you are working with. So the goal here is to interact with an LLM in AWS through Spring AI.

You will see how to build a simple application to send prompt queries to AWS and return responses to users, as shown in Figure 16-55.

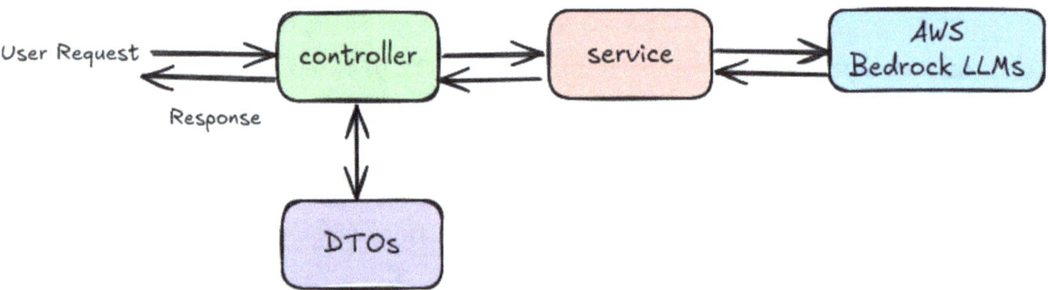

Figure 16-55. *Application architecture and control flow*

Let's start by visiting the Spring Initializr website and downloading an artifact with dependencies list, as shown in Figure 16-56.

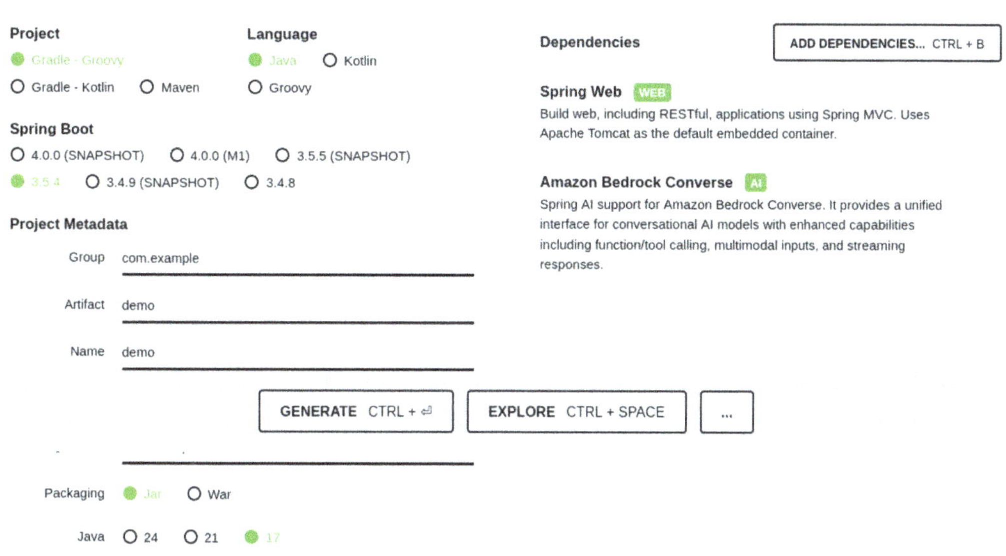

Figure 16-56. *Spring Initializr setup*

Let's download the artifact, unzip it at the location of your choice, and open it with the IDE of your choice. Please make sure you are able to boot it up to see the familiar Spring Boot welcome message.

For Spring AI to work with AWS Bedrock, it needs a few properties to be set in the `application.properties` file, as shown here:

File: ./src/main/resources/application.properties

```
spring.application.name=aws-bedrock-spring-ai
spring.ai.bedrock.aws.region=ap-south-1
spring.ai.bedrock.aws.timeout=5m
spring.ai.bedrock.converse.chat.options.model=apac.amazon.nova-micro-v1:0
spring.ai.bedrock.aws.access-key=
spring.ai.bedrock.aws.secret-key=
```

As you have seen, you need to make sure to share the region where you have enabled access to a particular LLM of your choice. You will want to use the model `apac.amazon.nova-micro-v1:0` that you enabled previously. This value can be retrieved from the cross-region inference section, as shown in Figure 16-57.

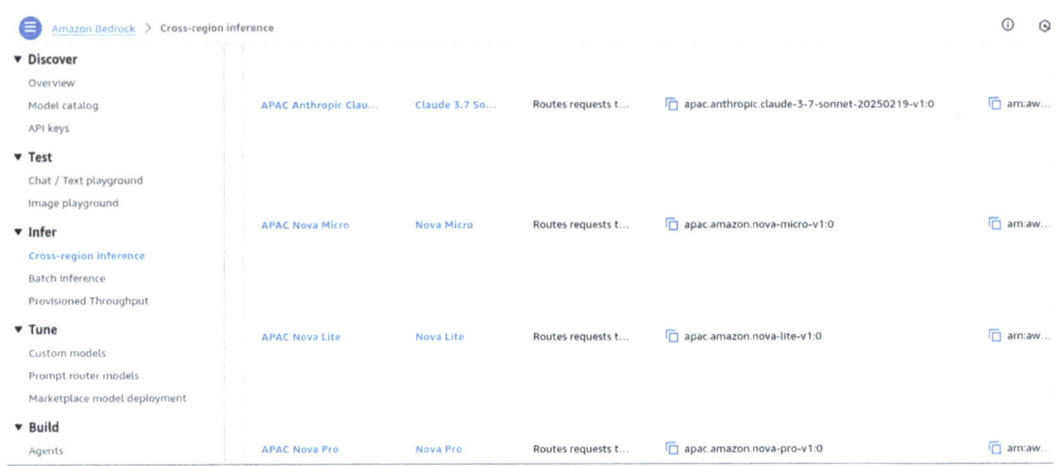

Figure 16-57. *Inference page listing for LLM models*

Here I have assumed five minutes as the connection timeout with AWS Bedrock. For the access key and secret key, they can be generated from AWS IAM. For this particular application, I will be using one that has administrator access for quick prototyping. But make sure to use a role that has fine-grained access to AWS Bedrock based on the tasks it is supposed to do.

There are other properties specific to the Spring AI AWS converse, as shown next. In this section, stick to the default values.

```
spring.ai.bedrock.converse.chat.options.temperature
Controls the randomness of the output. Values can range over [0.0,1.0]

spring.ai.bedrock.converse.chat.options.top-p
The maximum cumulative probability of tokens to consider when sampling.

spring.ai.bedrock.converse.chat.options.top-k
Number of token choices for generating the next token.

spring.ai.bedrock.converse.chat.options.max-tokens
Maximum number of tokens in the generated response.
```

These values can be overridden at runtime based on need using the ToolCallingChatOptions API. You will create the service component first so you can receive a prompt from the controller and make a request to the AWS Bedrock LLM.

So, start building a service component named `ChatService.java`. You will define a public constructor with a ChatModel API instance argument, which will be injected by Spring AI at runtime.

```
public ChatService(ChatModel chatModel) {
   this.chatModel = chatModel;
}
```

Then you can use this `chatModel` with the ChatClient API to interact with your Bedrock model, as shown next. This method takes as argument the text prompt from the user and makes a request with the `call()` method call and finally to `content()` to fetch the text response.

```
public String chat(String prompt) {
   return ChatClient
          .create(this.chatModel)
          .prompt(prompt)
          .call()
          .content();
}
```

File: ./src/main/java/com/example/aws_bedrock_spring_ai/service/ChatService.java

```
package com.example.aws_bedrock_spring_ai.service;

import org.springframework.ai.chat.client.ChatClient;
import org.springframework.ai.chat.model.ChatModel;
import org.springframework.stereotype.Service;

@Service
public class ChatService {

   private final ChatModel chatModel;
```

```
    public ChatService(ChatModel chatModel) {
        this.chatModel = chatModel;
    }

    public String chat(String prompt) {
        return ChatClient
                .create(this.chatModel)
                .prompt(prompt)
                .call()
                .content();
    }
}
```

Next, you will create a few DTO objects to map your controller request and response objects, as shown here:

File: ./src/main/java/com/example/aws_bedrock_spring_ai/dto/ChatRequestDto.java

```
package com.example.aws_bedrock_spring_ai.dto;

import jakarta.validation.constraints.NotBlank;

public class ChatRequestDto {

    @NotBlank
    private String prompt;

    public String getPrompt()              { return prompt; }
    public void setPrompt(String prompt) { this.prompt = prompt; }
}
```

File: /media/user/persistence/aws-bedrock-spring-ai/src/main/java/com/example/aws_bedrock_spring_ai/dto/ChatResponseDto.java

```
package com.example.aws_bedrock_spring_ai.dto;

public class ChatResponseDto {

    private final String content;
```

```
    public ChatResponseDto(String content) {
        this.content = content;
    }

    public String getContent() {
        return content;
    }
}
```

These DTO objects are self-explanatory, so I will not cover them in depth here. The final step is to use the service in your controller class to close the request response cycle. You will create a controller class called `ChatController.java` with the following content:

File: ./src/main/java/com/example/aws_bedrock_spring_ai/controller/ChatController.java

```
package com.example.aws_bedrock_spring_ai.controller;

import com.example.aws_bedrock_spring_ai.dto.ChatRequestDto;
import com.example.aws_bedrock_spring_ai.dto.ChatResponseDto;
import com.example.aws_bedrock_spring_ai.service.ChatService;

import org.springframework.http.ResponseEntity;
import org.springframework.web.bind.annotation.*;

import javax.validation.Valid;

@RestController
@RequestMapping("/api/v1/chat")
public class ChatController {

    private final ChatService chatService;

    public ChatController(ChatService chatService) {
        this.chatService = chatService;
    }

    @PostMapping
    public ResponseEntity<ChatResponseDto> chat(@RequestBody @Valid
    ChatRequestDto body) {
        String reply = chatService.chat(body.getPrompt());
```

```
        return ResponseEntity.ok(new ChatResponseDto(reply));
    }
}
```

You have autowired the ChatService inside your constructor and used it inside your chat method to get a response to the user prompt query. Let's boot up your application and make a `curl` request to see it in action.

```
curl -X POST http://localhost:8080/api/v1/chat -H "Content-Type:
application/json" -d '{"prompt": "Tell me a joke"}'
```

```
{"content":"Sure, here's a light-hearted joke for you:\n\nWhy did the
tomato turn red?\n\nBecause it saw the salad dressing!\n\nHope that brought
a smile to your face!"}
```

In this section, you learned about how to use Spring AI APIs to connect with AWS Bedrock LLMs, which is just the beginning. There are more features like tool calling and RAG that are available for use and exploration. If you now want to change it to OpenAI, you can simply change some of the application properties, and it works without any major changes. This is where the flexibility and simplicity of Spring AI API interfaces come into effect. These same steps could be used with other cloud vendors like GCP and Azure.

Generative AI in GCP

Google Cloud has been making some big strides in my opinion toward developing both state-of-the-art proprietary and open-source models. It has SDKs available for Gen AI in four major languages: Java, Python, Go, and Node.js. In this section, you will explore the Java SDK. Please make sure you have a Google account or register for a three-month subscription, which they are kind enough to give credits for.

GCP groups Gen AI together with its Vertex AI platform for machine learning. When you visit Vertex AI page, you will see Model Garden in the Tools section, as shown in Figure 16-58. In this section, you will see many popular state-of-the-art models that can be used with GCP's SDK, as shown in Figure 16-59.

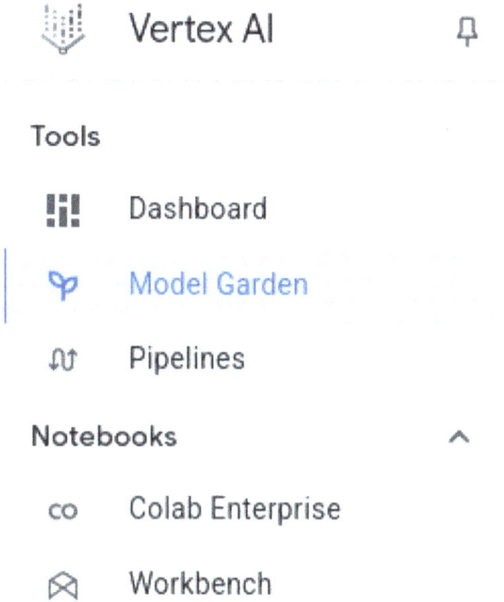

***Figure 16-58.** Tools section in Vertex AI*

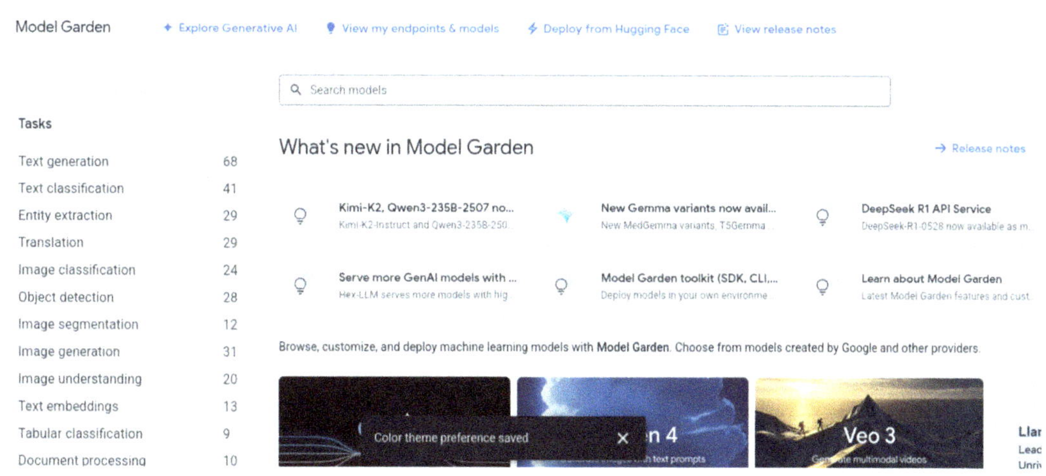

***Figure 16-59.** Model Garden in Vertex AI*

In the sidebar you'll see Vertex AI Studio, where you will find many of the offerings relevant to prompt engineering, prompt management, tuning a LLM, etc. You can explore these at your leisure. Here, we will focus on Create Prompt, which will let you play with prompts including multimodal prompts with different models (see Figure 16-60).

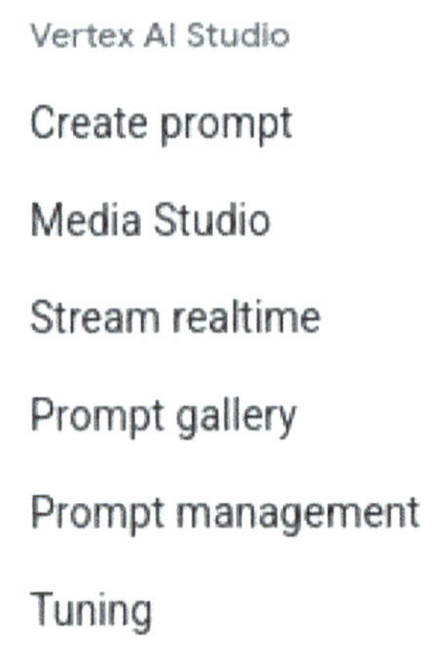

Vertex AI Studio

Create prompt

Media Studio

Stream realtime

Prompt gallery

Prompt management

Tuning

Figure 16-60. *Vertex AI Studio services*

As you can see in Figure 16-61, you can provide a prompt as well as attach different media content like images, audio, etc. Let's try a prompt to ask it for a joke and see its response. On the right, you can change and try the many models it provides based on your use case and play with the configuration settings for the LLM like temperature, etc.

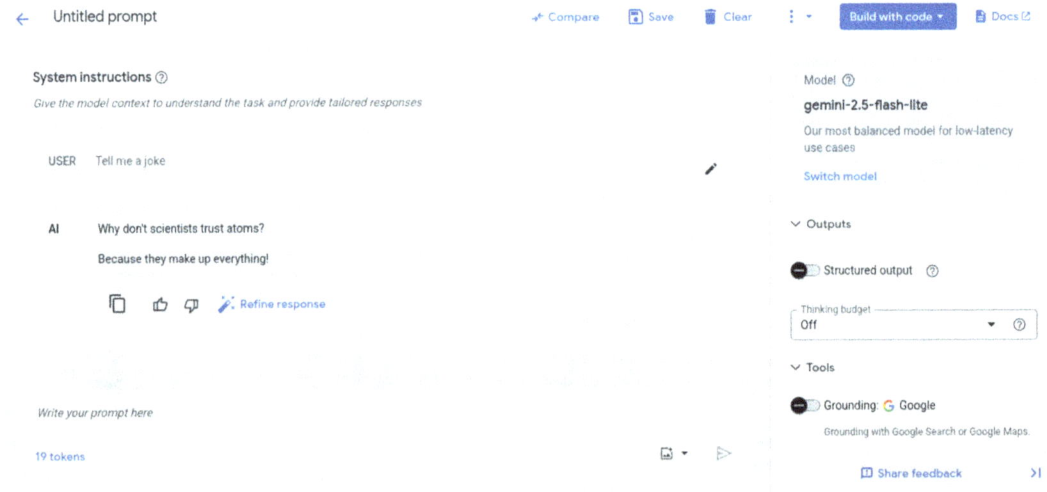

Figure 16-61. *Create Prompt page*

One of the cool features is the "Build with code" button at the top right; when you click this button, you will see the code used to generate this output. This makes it simple to try and then deploy in code. It currently supports many languages, as shown in Figure 16-62.

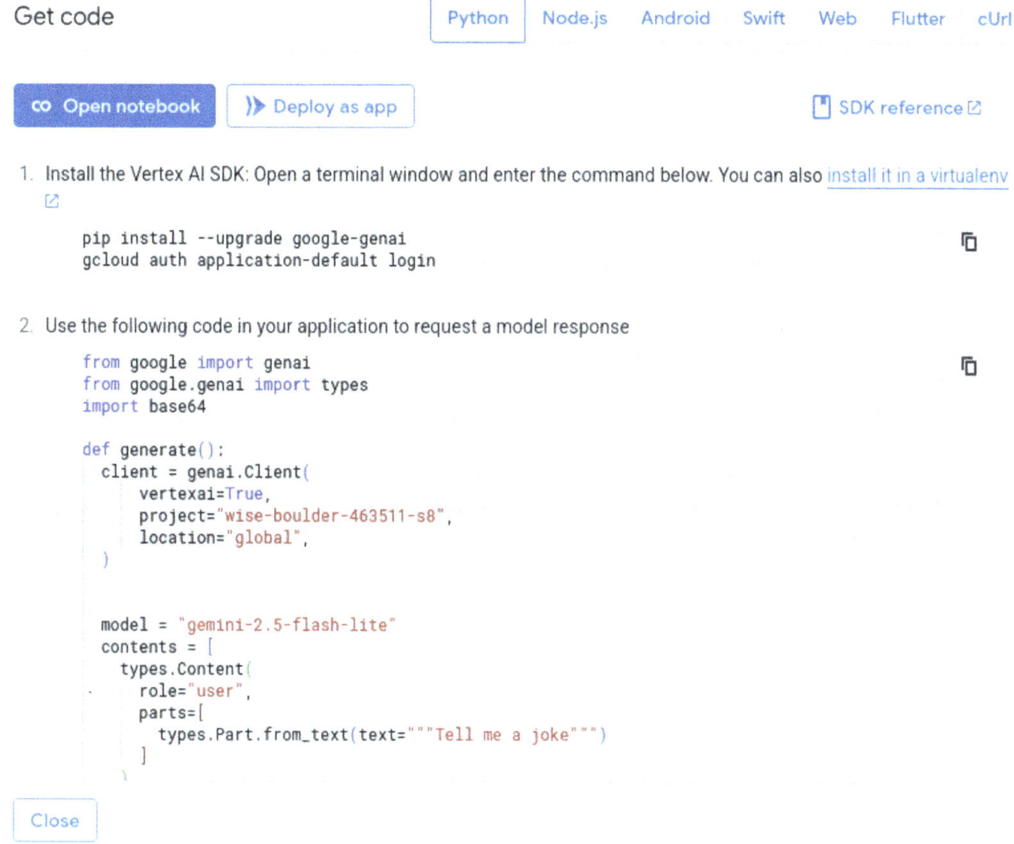

Figure 16-62. *Build with code feature*

Farther down in the Vertex AI sidebar, you will see some more advanced tools that are focused on agentic and RAG development (Figure 16-63). I will not cover these features in this section.

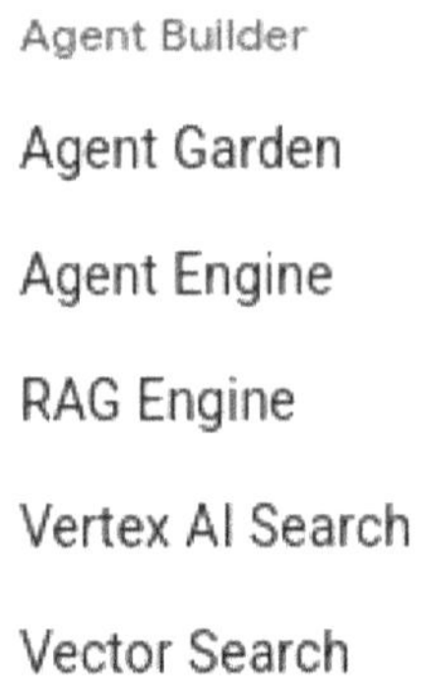

Agent Builder

Agent Garden

Agent Engine

RAG Engine

Vertex AI Search

Vector Search

Figure 16-63. *Agent builder services*

Now that you have had a brief look at the Gen AI features of GCP, let's get our hands dirty with some code and application building. You will use the Java SDK of GCP for Gen AI to build a simple application that prompts for a joke.

You can review the Gen AI SDK documentation at `https://cloud.google.com/vertex-ai/generative-ai/docs/sdks/overview`.

Let's initialize a Spring Boot application using the Spring Initializr website, as shown in Figure 16-64.

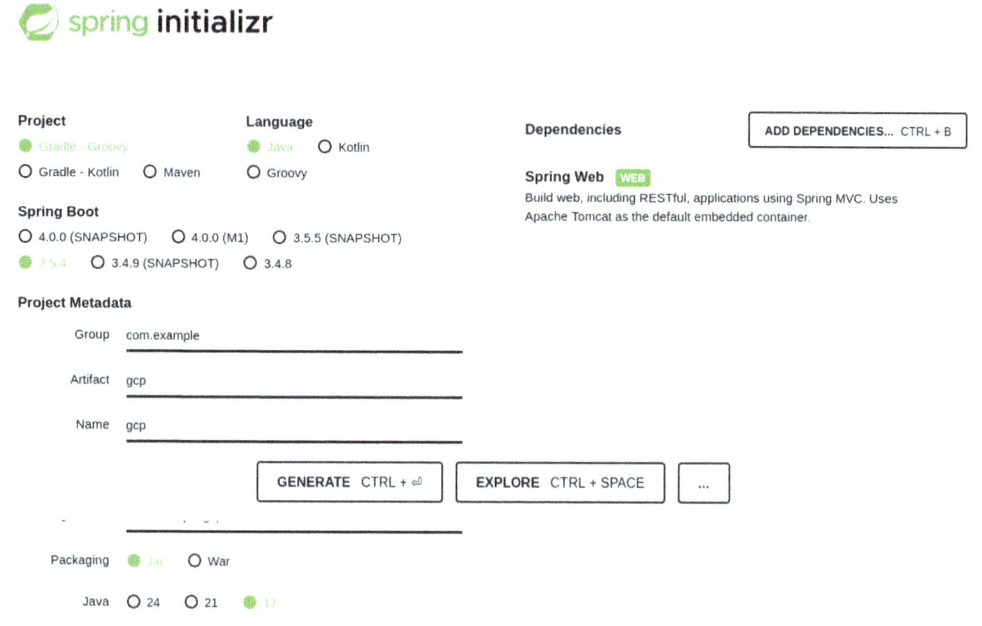

***Figure 16-64.** Spring Initializr for the base setup of GCP Gen AI application*

Download and extract the zip file at the location of your choice and open it with your favorite IDE of choice. When you boot it up, you should see the familiar Spring Boot welcome start output, as shown in the following output:

```
2025-07-29T17:36:51.852Z  INFO 36012 --- [gcp] [main] com.example.gcp.
GcpApplication           : Started GcpApplication in 2.653 seconds (process
running for 3.838)
```

Next, to work with Gen AI SDK of Google, you will need to include the Gradle package definition for Gen AI in your `build.gradle` file, as shown here:

```
// https://mvnrepository.com/artifact/com.google.genai/google-genai
implementation("com.google.genai:google-genai:1.10.0")
```

File: build.gradle

```
plugins {
    id 'java'
    id 'org.springframework.boot' version '3.5.4'
    id 'io.spring.dependency-management' version '1.1.7'
}

group = 'com.example'
version = '0.0.1-SNAPSHOT'

java {
    toolchain {
       languageVersion = JavaLanguageVersion.of(17)
    }
}

repositories {
    mavenCentral()
}

dependencies {
    implementation 'org.springframework.boot:spring-boot-starter-web'
    implementation 'com.google.genai:google-genai:1.10.0'
    testImplementation 'org.springframework.boot:spring-boot-starter-test'
    testRuntimeOnly 'org.junit.platform:junit-platform-launcher'
}

tasks.named('test') {
    useJUnitPlatform()
}
```

The different components you will be creating to build your application are shown in Figure 16-65.

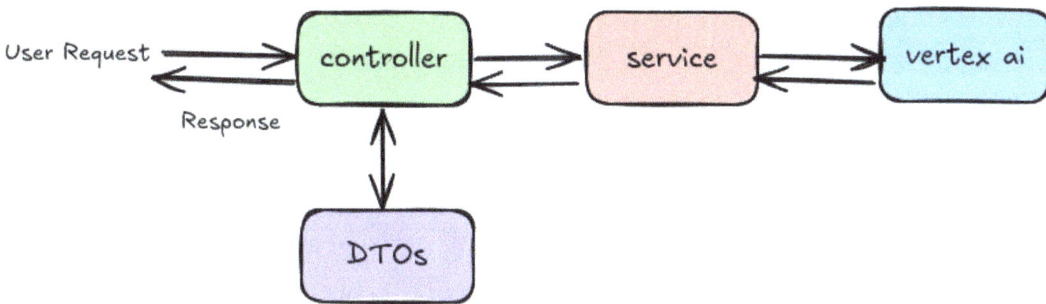

***Figure 16-65.** Application architecture and control flow*

Let's start with the service component named `GenAiService.java` in a package called `service`. Inside the `service` class, define a constructor and initialize the Gen AI client, as shown here:

```
private final Client client;

public GenAiService() {
    // Default ctor picks up env vars
    this.client = new Client();
}
```

Next, define a public method called `generate`, which takes two string parameters, called `prompt` and `modelId`, to generate the content response. The `modelId` defaults to the `gemini-2.0-flash-001` model. You can choose any model of your choice. Inside the method, you make a call to the `models.generateContent` method of the client API by passing it the `modelId` as the first parameter argument and the prompt text as the second. The third argument is the configuration argument, which you can leave as null for this example, but you can try pass `temperature` and other configuration arguments for your use case.

```
/**
 * Calls Gemini (or Vertex) and returns the text response.
 *
 * @param prompt  the user prompt
 * @param modelId optional model (defaults to "gemini-2.0-flash-001")
 */
```

```
public String generate(String prompt, String modelId) {
    String m = (modelId == null || modelId.isBlank())
            ? "gemini-2.0-flash-001"
            : modelId;

    GenerateContentResponse res = client.models.generateContent(m,
    prompt, null);
    return res.text();          // convenient helper
}
```

File: ./src/main/java/com/example/gcp/service/GenAiService.java

```
package com.example.gcp.service;

import com.google.genai.Client;
import com.google.genai.types.GenerateContentResponse;
import org.springframework.stereotype.Service;

@Service
public class GenAiService {
    private final Client client;

   public GenAiService() {
        // Default ctor picks up env vars
        this.client = new Client();
    }

   /**
     * Calls Gemini (or Vertex) and returns the text response.
     *
     * @param prompt  the user prompt
     * @param modelId optional model (defaults to "gemini-2.0-flash-001")
     */
    public String generate(String prompt, String modelId) {
        String m = (modelId == null || modelId.isBlank())
                ? "gemini-2.0-flash-001"
                : modelId;
```

```
        GenerateContentResponse res = client.models.generateContent(m,
        prompt, null);
         return res.text();          // convenient helper
    }
}
```

With this you have completed your service layer and will move to the controller layer to accept requests and return responses. The controller will need a few DTO objects for your request and response types. These are shared for reference here:

File: ./src/main/java/com/example/gcp/dto/GenAiRequest.java

```
package com.example.gcp.dto;

/** Simple request body for /api/genai POST. */
public record GenAiRequest(String prompt, String modelId) { }
```

File: ./src/main/java/com/example/gcp/dto/GenAiResponse.java

```
package com.example.gcp.dto;

/** JSON response wrapper. */
public record GenAiResponse(String text) { }
```

These DTO objects will be referenced in your controller file named `GenAiController.java`. You will reference the service you created earlier in the constructor to get an instance of it injected and use it to generate a response and send it as response to your user's request. The code for same is shown here:

File: ./src/main/java/com/example/gcp/controller/GenAiController.java

```
package com.example.gcp.controller;

import com.example.gcp.dto.GenAiRequest;
import com.example.gcp.dto.GenAiResponse;
import com.example.gcp.service.GenAiService;
import org.springframework.http.ResponseEntity;
import org.springframework.web.bind.annotation.*;

@RestController
@RequestMapping("/api/genai")
```

```
public class GenAiController {
    private final GenAiService genAiService;
    public GenAiController(GenAiService genAiService) {
        this.genAiService = genAiService;
    }

    @PostMapping(consumes = "application/json", produces =
    "application/json")
    public ResponseEntity<GenAiResponse> generatePost(@RequestBody
    GenAiRequest req) {
        String answer = genAiService.generate(req.prompt(), req.modelId());
        return ResponseEntity.ok(new GenAiResponse(answer));
    }
}
```

At this point, although you have completed your source code implementation, it won't work since you have a few prerequisites to complete. The first one is to make sure the Vertex AI API is enabled, as shown in Figure 16-66.

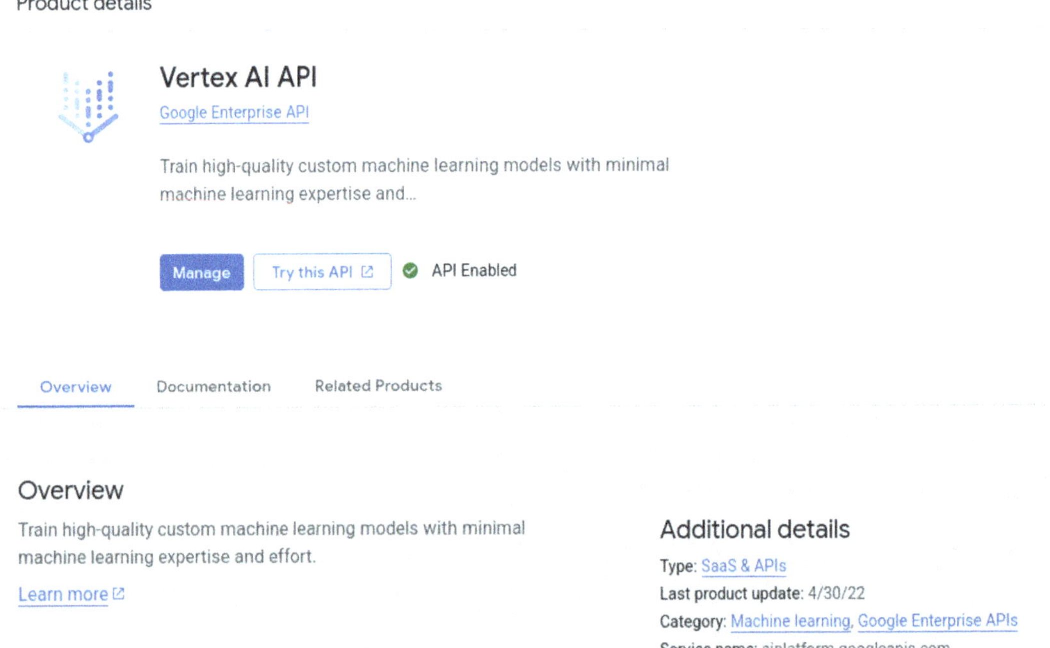

Figure 16-66. *Vertex AI API enable page*

The Gen AI client needs GEMINI_API_KEY or GOOGLE_API_KEY set as an environment to make calls to Vertex AI. This API can be generated by visiting https://aistudio.google.com/app/apikey and creating an API key by following the steps highlighted in Figure 16-67, Figure 16-68, and Figure 16-69. The process involves clicking the blue "Create API key" button, then selecting your existing project or create if one does not exist, and finally copying the key for your reference.

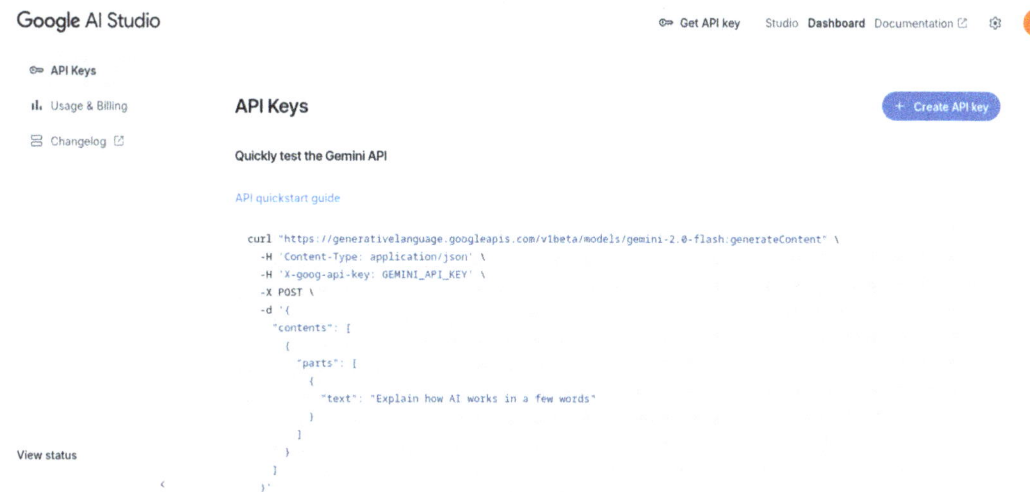

Figure 16-67. *Create API key page in Google AI Studio*

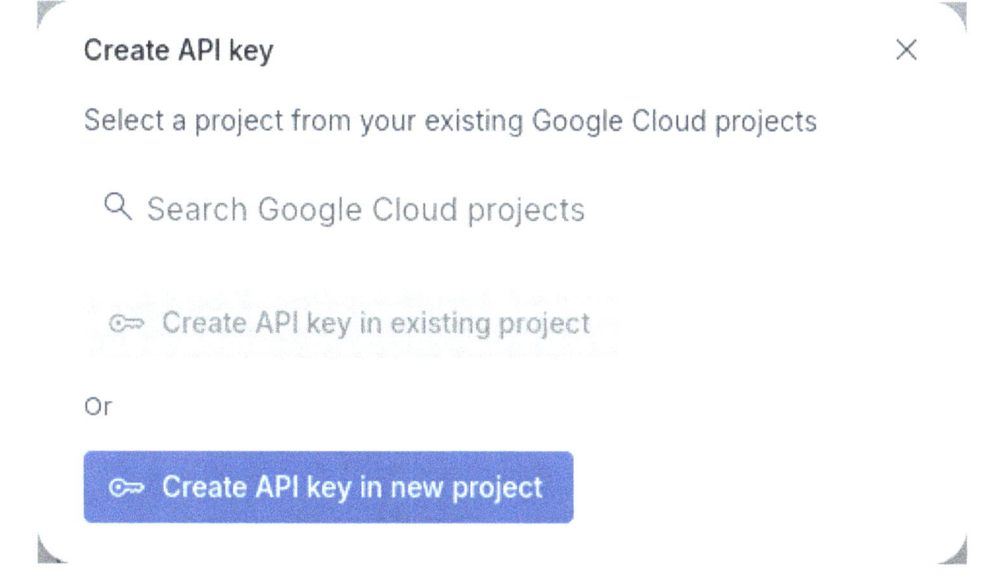

Figure 16-68. *Create API key dialog*

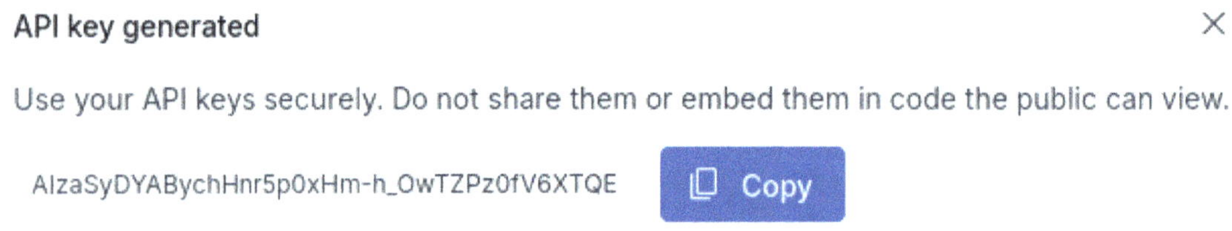

Figure 16-69. Copying generated API key

Make sure to set the environment variable with the name GEMINI_API_KEY or GOOGLE_API_KEY in your environment or the IntelliJ configuration section, as shown in Figure 16-70.

Run/Debug Configurations

Spring Boot
GcpApplication

Name: GcpApplication
Store as project file
Run on: Local machine
Manage targets...
Run configurations may be executed locally or on a target: for example in a Docker Container or on a remote host using SSH.

Build and run
Modify options Alt+M
java 17 SDK of 'gcp.main' mo
-cp gcp.main
com.example.gcp.GcpApplication
Press Alt for field hints

Active profiles:
Comma-separated list of profiles

Environment variables: GEMINI_API_KEY=YOUR_GEMINI_API_KEY
Separate variables with semicolon: VAR=value; VAR1=value1

Open run/debug tool window when started
Add dependencies with "provided" scope to classpath

Edit configuration templates...

Run OK Cancel Apply

Figure 16-70. Environment configuration in Spring Boot

Now that your prerequisites are complete, let's boot up your application and see it in action by trying the following `curl` requests.

```
curl -X POST http://localhost:8080/api/genai
  -H "Content-Type: application/json" \
 -d '{"prompt":"Tell me a joke","modelId":"gemini-2.0-flash-001"}'
```

```
{"text":"Why don't scientists trust atoms? Because they make up
everything!"}
```

```
curl -X POST http://localhost:8080/api/genai \
  -H "Content-Type: application/json" \
 -d '{"prompt":"Tell me a joke"}'
```

```
{"text":"Why don't scientists trust atoms? Because they make up
everything!"}
```

In this example, you explored the different tools in the GCP Vertex AI service relevant to Gen AI and used the Java SDK of Gen AI to build a small application to interact with LLMs.

Generative AI in Azure

Azure AI has many services relevant to machine learning, some of which are shown in Figure 16-71. The service you will be exploring in this section is Azure OpenAI for Gen AI.

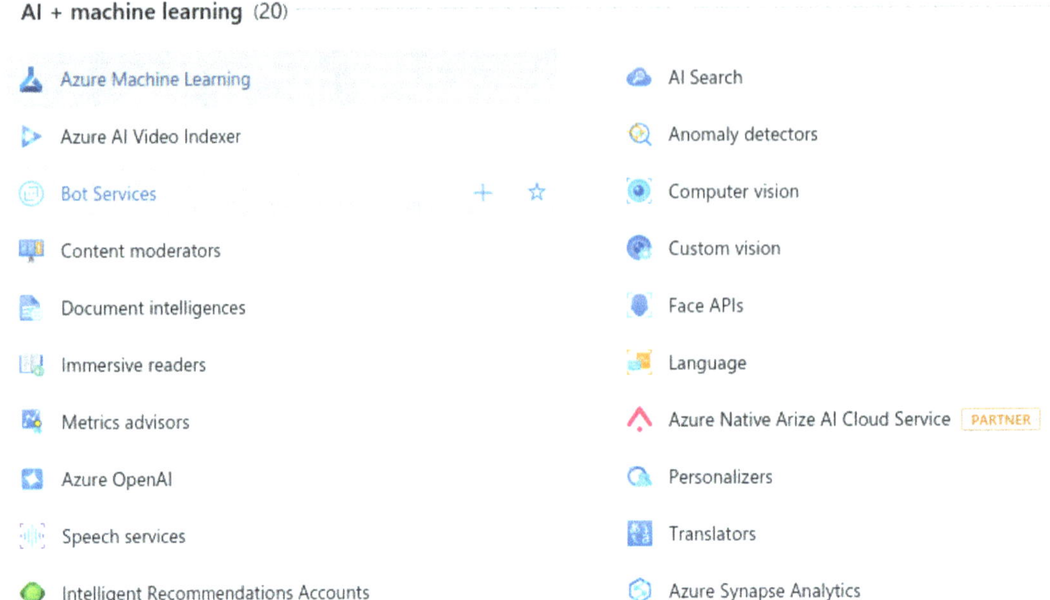

Figure 16-71. *Azure machine learning services*

AI Foundry is the umbrella tool under which Azure provides different Gen AI services, as shown in Figure 16-72.

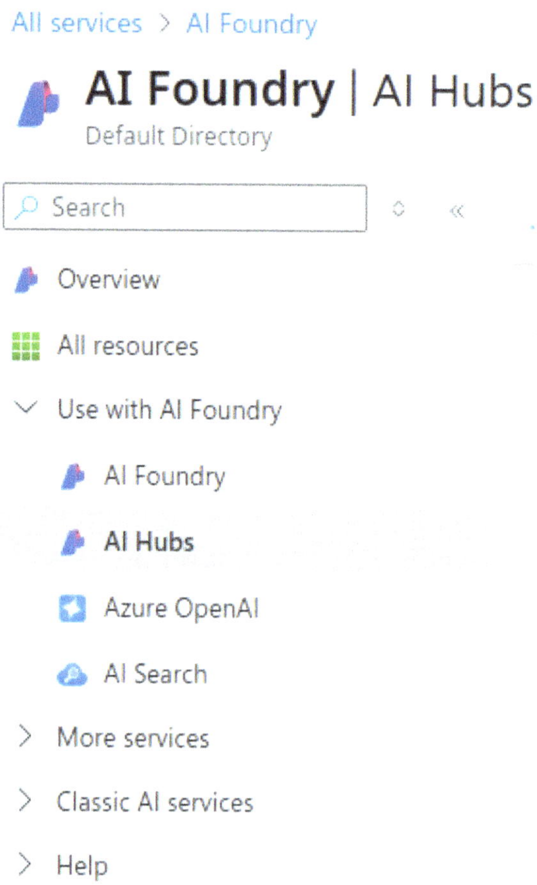

Figure 16-72. *AI Foundry Services for Gen AI*

Let's start by exploring the Azure OpenAI service. Click this service, you will you see a starter page asking you to create an Azure OpenAI service, as shown in Figure 16-73.

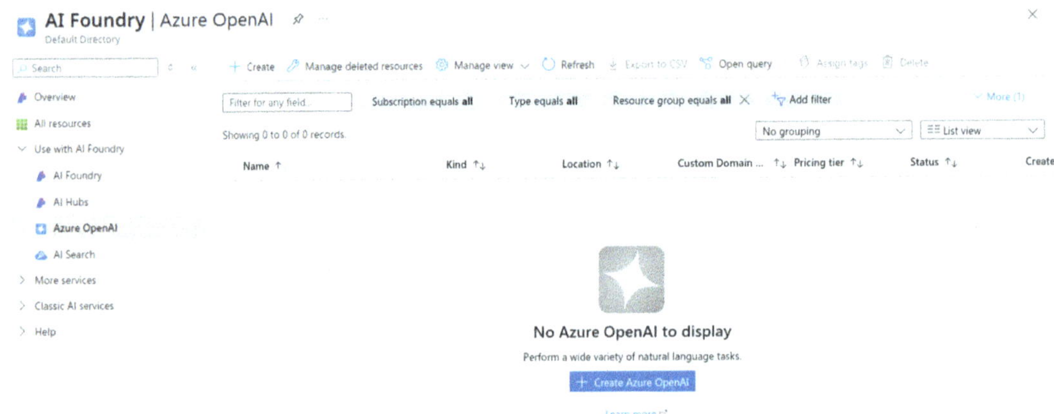

***Figure 16-73.** Azure OpenAI service creation page*

Then select your subscription and resource group and fill in the region, name, and pricing tier details, as shown in Figure 16-74.

Create Azure OpenAI

Changes on this step may reset later selections you have made. Review all options prior to deployment.

Instance Details

Region: Southeast Asia

Name *: prototype-sub-domain

Pricing tier *: Standard S0

View full pricing details

Content review policy

To detect and mitigate harmful use of the Azure OpenAI Service, Microsoft logs the content you send to the Completions and image generations APIs as well as the content it sends back. If content is flagged by the service's filters, it may be reviewed by a Microsoft full-time employee.

Learn more about how Microsoft processes, uses, and stores your data

Previous Next Give feedback

***Figure 16-74.** Region, name, pricing tier configuration for Azure OpenAI*

For the next two action requesting pages, select the default selections and proceed to the Review + submit page to review all the choices made and submit them for the resource creation. Then you will wait for a couple of minutes for the deployment to complete. Once the deployment is complete, visit the Azure OpenAI page in Azure AI Foundry, as shown in Figure 16-75.

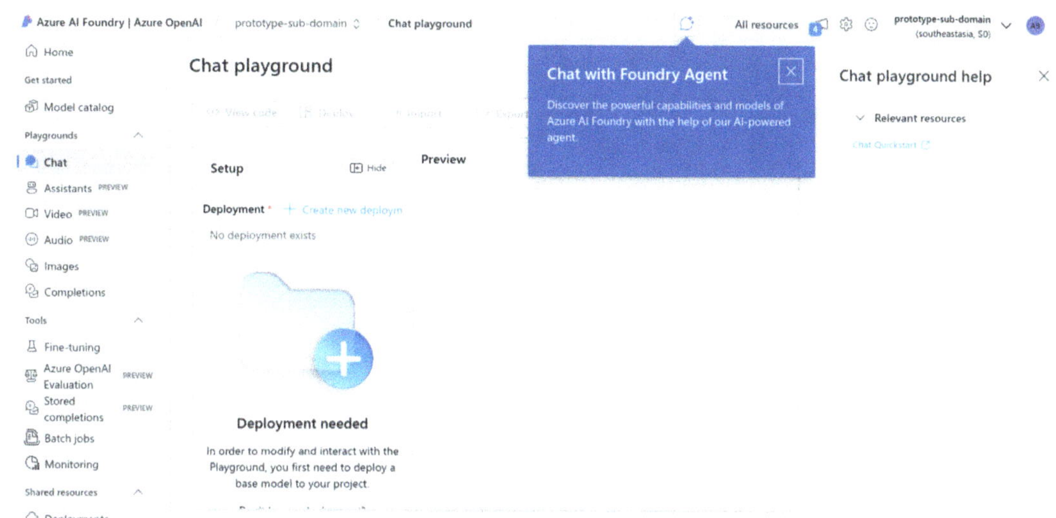

Figure 16-75. *Azure OpenAI Chat Playground*

As you can see, different tools are provided for Gen AI in this playground. The Playgrounds section allows you to play with chat, assistants, and multimodal prompts. In the Tools section, you can see offerings for fine-tuning, evaluation, stored completions, batch jobs, and monitoring, which are important for the Gen AI ecosystem. You will see this area getting more and more focus in the future. For the moment, you will explore the chat service and then move on to write a sample application using the Azure SDK.

To start with chat playground, you will need to create a deployment first (see Figure 16-76).

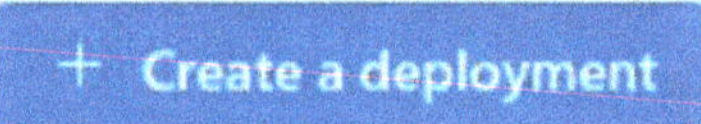

***Figure 16-76.** Base model deployment creation section*

The first step is to select a model from the list provided. You can use `gpt-4.1-mini` to practice. On selecting the model, it shows the details specific to the model, which is very helpful (Figure 16-77).

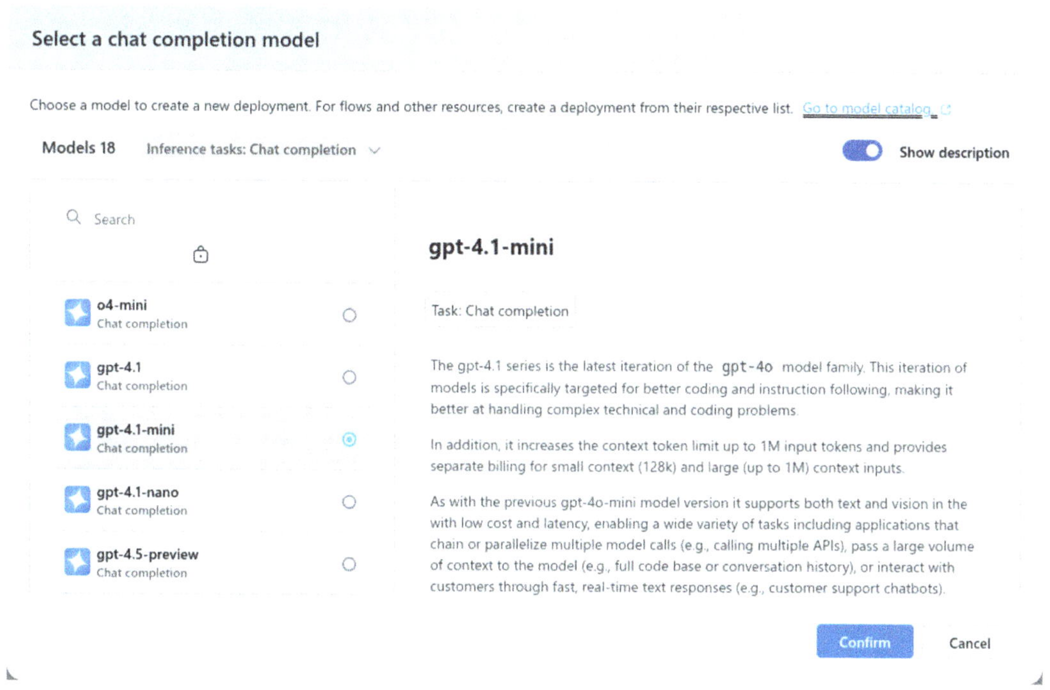

Figure 16-77. *Base model selection section*

Once you confirm and proceed, it will show you the deployment details, as shown in Figure 16-78. Review the details and then click the "Create resource and deploy" button.

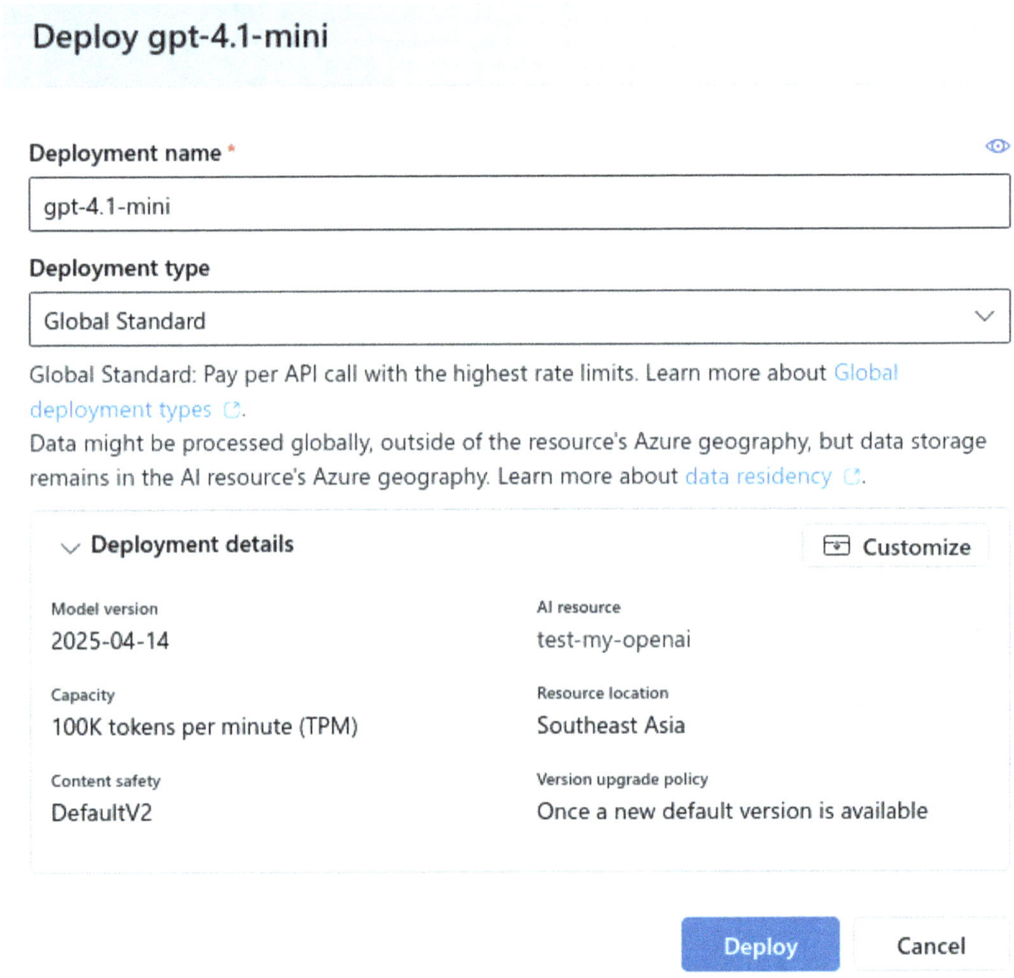

Deploy gpt-4.1-mini

Deployment name *

gpt-4.1-mini

Deployment type

Global Standard

Global Standard: Pay per API call with the highest rate limits. Learn more about Global deployment types.
Data might be processed globally, outside of the resource's Azure geography, but data storage remains in the AI resource's Azure geography. Learn more about data residency.

Deployment details

Customize

Model version
2025-04-14

AI resource
test-my-openai

Capacity
100K tokens per minute (TPM)

Resource location
Southeast Asia

Content safety
DefaultV2

Version upgrade policy
Once a new default version is available

Deploy

Cancel

Figure 16-78. *Deployment name and type selection section*

The deployment is quick, and then you can play with the LLM model in the playground. Let's ask for a joke, as shown in Figure 16-79.

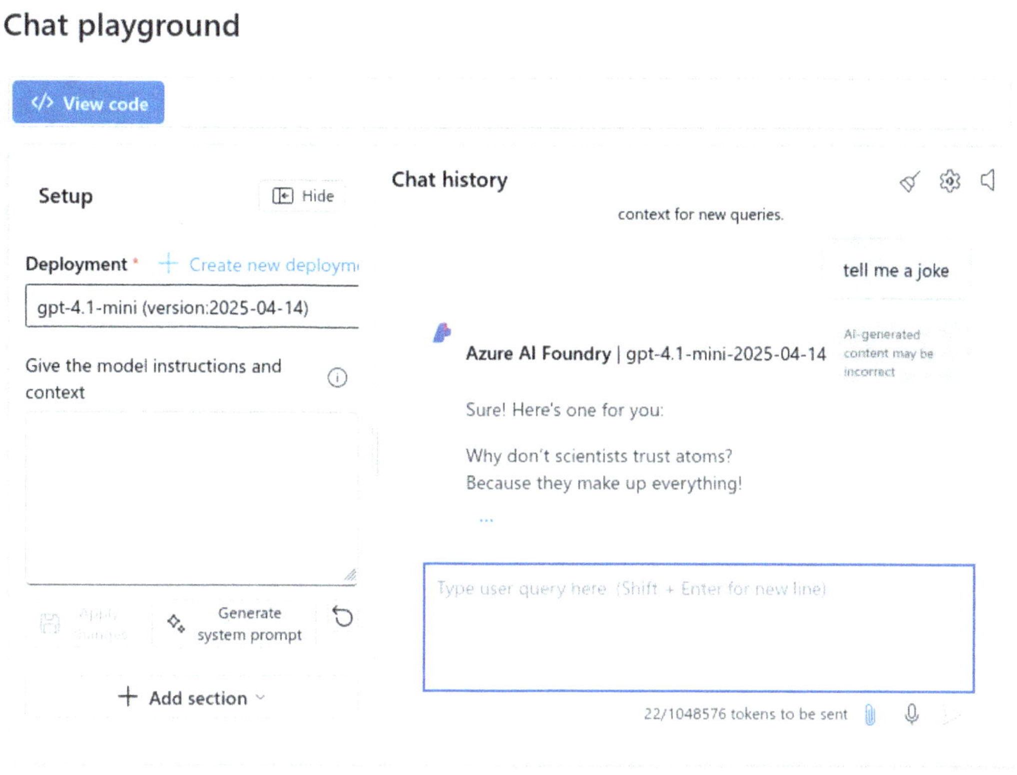

Figure 16-79. *Chat playground*

There is a handy blue "View code" button that when clicked shows the code responsible for generating this output. It is similar to GCP but with the Java language as an option, which was missing from GCP (see Figure 16-80).

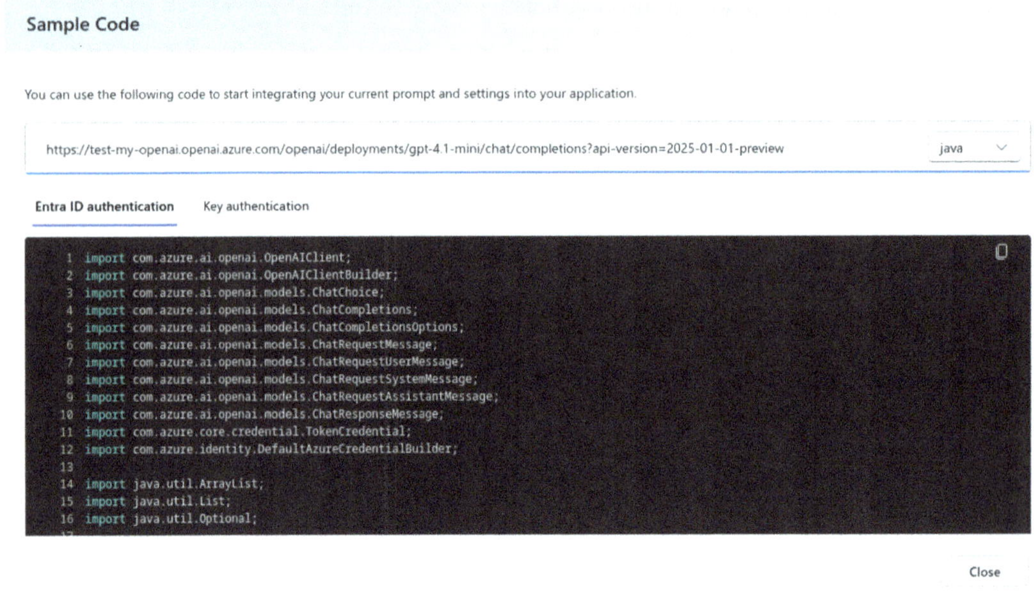

Figure 16-80. *Sample code generation section in different languaages*

Now let's explore how to build a Spring Boot application using the sample code from the Java example. Let's start with the same setup as for GCP by starting from Spring Initializr and unzipping it at a location of your choice. The components for your application would be similar to the one you built earlier. The only difference now is you're using Azure OpenAI instead of Vertex AI, as shown in Figure 16-81.

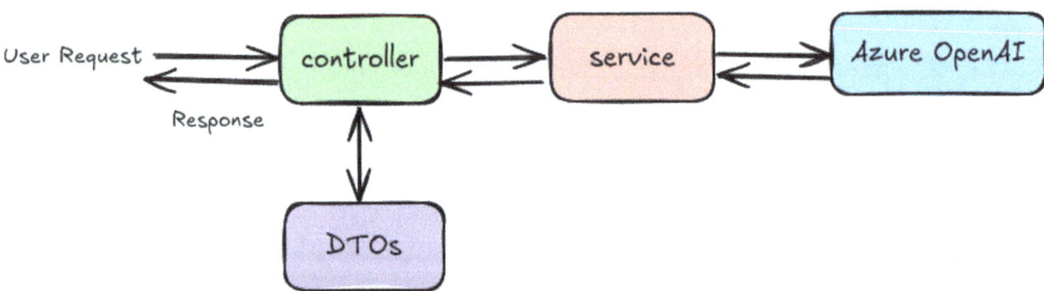

Figure 16-81. *Application architecture and control flow*

Most of the code from the previous setup is reusable, so it will not be repeated here. This section will focus on the service component since it now interacts with Azure OpenAI and any `build.gradle` file-specific changes along with any environment variable needed to interact with Azure OpenAI.

Let's start by updating your `build.gradle` file to include a dependency for Azure OpenAI SDK. (Note that at this moment of writing the SDK is in beta stage.)

```
// https://mvnrepository.com/artifact/com.azure/azure-ai-openai
implementation("com.azure:azure-ai-openai:1.0.0-beta.16")
```

File: ./build.gradle

```
plugins {
   id 'java'
   id 'org.springframework.boot' version '3.5.4'
   id 'io.spring.dependency-management' version '1.1.7'
}

group = 'com.example'
version = '0.0.1-SNAPSHOT'

java {
   toolchain {
      languageVersion = JavaLanguageVersion.of(17)
   }
}

repositories {
   mavenCentral()
}

dependencies {
   implementation 'org.springframework.boot:spring-boot-starter-web'
   implementation 'com.azure:azure-ai-openai:1.0.0-beta.16'
   testImplementation 'org.springframework.boot:spring-boot-starter-test'
   testRuntimeOnly 'org.junit.platform:junit-platform-launcher'
}

tasks.named('test') {
   useJUnitPlatform()
}
```

Now you will move on to updating your service component in the `GenAiService.java` file. You will first create two attributes to hold the client and deployment instance entities, as shown here:

```
private final OpenAIClient client;
private final String defaultDeployment;
```

Then inside the public constructor, you will instantiate these as shown next. Many of the APIs are similar to the OpenAI ones you used earlier, so they should be self-explanatory. You can use the OpenAIClientBuilder API to build your client instance, which will be used to make API calls to Azure OpenAI.

```
public GenAiService(
       @Value("${azure.openai.endpoint}")   String endpoint,
       @Value("${azure.openai.api-key}")    String apiKey,
       @Value("${azure.openai.deployment}") String defaultDeployment) {

   this.defaultDeployment = defaultDeployment;

   this.client = new OpenAIClientBuilder()
           .endpoint(endpoint)
           .credential(new AzureKeyCredential(apiKey))
           .buildClient();
}
```

Finally, update the `generate` method to generate the `ChatRequestUserMessage` using the prompt sent from the user and generate the response using the getChatCompletions API, as shown here:

```
public String generate(String prompt, String modelId) {
   String deployment = (modelId == null || modelId.isBlank())
           ? defaultDeployment
           : modelId;

   List<ChatRequestMessage> messages = List.of(new ChatRequestUserMessage
   (prompt));

   ChatCompletionsOptions opts = new ChatCompletionsOptions(messages)
           .setMaxTokens(1_024)   // pick a sensible number; adjust to your
           policy/quota
```

```
            .setTemperature(0.7)
            .setTopP(0.95);

    ChatCompletions completions = client.getChatCompletions(deployment,
    opts);

    /* In production, you should add defensive checks for:
     *   - completions == null
     *   - completions.getChoices().isEmpty()
     *   - multiple choices (pick best by log-prob, etc.)
     */
    return completions.getChoices()
            .get(0)
            .getMessage()
            .getContent();
}
```

File: ./src/main/java/com/example/azureopenai/service/GenAiService.java

```
package com.example.azureopenai.service;

import com.azure.ai.openai.OpenAIClient;
import com.azure.ai.openai.OpenAIClientBuilder;
import com.azure.ai.openai.models.ChatCompletions;
import com.azure.ai.openai.models.ChatCompletionsOptions;
import com.azure.ai.openai.models.ChatRequestMessage;
import com.azure.ai.openai.models.ChatRequestUserMessage;
import com.azure.core.credential.AzureKeyCredential;
import org.springframework.beans.factory.annotation.Value;
import org.springframework.stereotype.Service;

import java.util.List;

@Service
public class GenAiService {

    private final OpenAIClient client;
    private final String defaultDeployment;
```

```
public GenAiService(
        @Value("${azure.openai.endpoint}")   String endpoint,
        @Value("${azure.openai.api-key}")    String apiKey,
        @Value("${azure.openai.deployment}") String defaultDeployment) {

    this.defaultDeployment = defaultDeployment;

    this.client = new OpenAIClientBuilder()
            .endpoint(endpoint)
            .credential(new AzureKeyCredential(apiKey))
            .buildClient();
}

public String generate(String prompt, String modelId) {
    String deployment = (modelId == null || modelId.isBlank())
            ? defaultDeployment
            : modelId;

    List<ChatRequestMessage> messages = List.of(new ChatRequestUserMessa
    ge(prompt));

    ChatCompletionsOptions opts = new ChatCompletionsOptions(messages)
            .setMaxTokens(1_024)   // pick a sensible number; adjust to
            your policy/quota
            .setTemperature(0.7)
            .setTopP(0.95);

    ChatCompletions completions = client.getChatCompletions(deployment,
    opts);

    /* In production, you should add defensive checks for:
     *   - completions == null
     *   - completions.getChoices().isEmpty()
     *   - multiple choices (pick best by log-prob, etc.)
     */
    return completions.getChoices()
            .get(0)
            .getMessage()
```

```
                    .getContent();
    }
}
```

Before booting up your application, you will need a few resource attributes in your `application.properties` file. All these three attributes can be easily found in the shared resources menu in the sidebar at the bottom left. Click Deployments and from the list click the deployment that you want to use from the ones created earlier (see Figure 16-82).

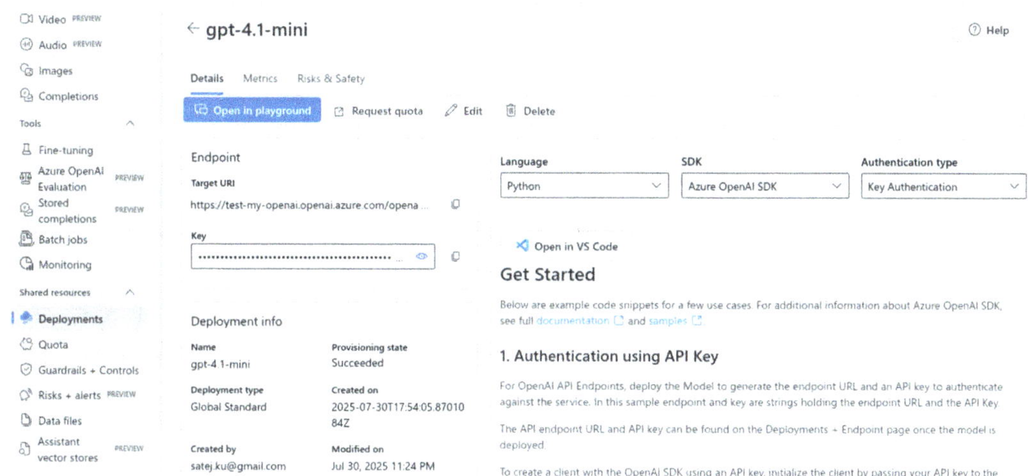

Figure 16-82. *Deployment-specific configuration information page*

The Get Started guide is very helpful. In the Endpoint section in the center screen, you can find information for the target URI, which is your endpoint; the key, which is your API key; and finally the name in the Deployment info section, which is your deployment value.

File: ./src/main/resources/application.properties

```
spring.application.name=azure-openai
azure.openai.endpoint=https://test-my-openai.openai.azure.com/
azure.openai.api-key=YOUR-API-KEY
azure.openai.deployment=gpt-4.1-mini
```

Now that you have completed all the setup, let's boot up your application and test it.

```
curl -X POST http://localhost:8080/api/genai    -H "Content-Type: application/json"    -d '{"prompt":"Tell me a joke"}'
```

```
{"text":"Sure! Here's a joke for you:\n\nWhy don't scientists trust atoms?  \nBecause they make up everything!"}
```

In this section, you were able to learn about the different services of Azure OpenAI and also build a sample application using the Azure OpenAI SDK for Java.

Conclusion

In this chapter, you learned how AWS Amazon Bedrock enables Java developers to harness Gen AI within the familiar AWS ecosystem. The chapter began by exploring the broader landscape of Gen AI services across the cloud and then focused on Bedrock's foundational models, playground experimentation, and SDK-driven application development. Building on that foundation, the chapter introduced guardrails to ensure safety and compliance, extended the solution with retrieval-augmented generation using Bedrock knowledge bases, and finally showcased how Spring AI integration can simplify and standardize generative AI in Java.

By understanding these core components—model selection, prompt tuning, safety frameworks, RAG, and framework integration, you're well equipped to architect robust, scalable, and responsible Gen AI applications on AWS. As Gen AI continues to evolve, the patterns and practices covered here will help you adapt and extend your solutions, whether in aerospace certification, customer support, content creation, or any domain where AI-driven intelligence can unlock new possibilities. In addition, I implore you to try other services such as fine-tuning monitoring with focus within the ecosystem surrounding LLMs.

The next chapter covers LLM Communication protocols.

CHAPTER 17

Talking in Protocols: The MCP Revolution

The goal of this chapter is to understand what the Model Context Protocol (MCP) protocol is and how it helps to establish a standard protocol on agent AI and tooling.

Introduction

The development of AI took a major step forward when we started creating "tool-augmented agents." Agents gained the ability to take action and make changes in the real world. This was an unprecedented step into the self-development and intelligence explosion era. As generative AI (Gen AI) and large language models (LLMs) continue to evolve into autonomous agents capable of tool invocation and task execution, a new challenge emerges: how these agents communicate with each other and with the broader ecosystem of tools and services. Without a standardized framework, agent interactions remain fragmented, leading to integration inefficiencies and limited scalability.

Chapter 17 explores this crucial issue by introducing the Model Context Protocol—a modular, vendor-neutral communication standard designed to streamline how LLM-powered agents interact with external tools and services. In this chapter, you will gain a comprehensive understanding of how protocols like MCP, Agent Communication Protocol (ACP), Agent-to-Agent Protocol (A2A), and Agent Network Protocol (ANP) form the foundation of interoperable, collaborative AI ecosystems. You will also examine how MCP is practically implemented using modern Java frameworks like Spring Boot and Quarkus, illustrating its role in bridging diverse systems and enabling tool-rich, multi-agent workflows.

S. K. Sahu, *Generative AI-Driven Application Development with Java*,
https://doi.org/10.1007/979-8-8688-1609-3_17

By the end of this chapter, developers, architects, and AI practitioners will understand how these protocols collectively advance modularity, standardization, and cross-platform coordination in the AI agent landscape—making it easier to scale, maintain, and evolve intelligent systems.

Protocols in the LLM Ecosystem

As language models increasingly serve as the cognitive engines behind autonomous agents, the challenge facing these systems is shifting from individual capability to collective coordination. While LLM-powered agents excel at interpreting instructions, reasoning through complex tasks, and even invoking external tools, their ability to communicate and collaborate within larger multi-agent ecosystems remains underdeveloped. The lack of standardized communication mechanisms has resulted in fragmented architectures—dominated by proprietary APIs, one-off integrations, and rigid tool bindings. These limitations make scaling and composing intelligent agents across different systems a labor-intensive and brittle endeavor.

To address this gap, a new class of protocols has begun to emerge—designed to enable modularity, interoperability, and dynamic interaction across agents and models. These include MCP, ACP, A2A, and ANP. Each of these protocols plays a distinct role in laying the foundation for a standardized, decentralized agent ecosystem.

Model Context Protocol

MCP is concerned with how LLMs interpret and manage the contextual information necessary to perform tasks effectively. It provides a structured framework for defining the model's working environment—such as memory state, goals, tool access, and user intent—making context portable and reusable across different sessions, tools, or hosts. MCP acts as a bridge between external orchestration systems and the model's internal state, ensuring that LLMs operate with shared assumptions and consistent understanding, regardless of platform or vendor.

Agent Communication Protocol

ACP establishes the foundational syntax and semantics for how agents exchange information. Rather than relying on ad hoc message formats or brittle HTTP endpoints, ACP defines a shared message structure that supports not only command execution and data sharing but also negotiation, delegation, and error handling. This protocol enables a universal communication layer between agents—whether human-controlled, autonomous, or hybrid—unlocking collaborative workflows and coordinated decision-making.

Agent-to-Agent Protocol

While ACP focuses on communication structure, A2A specializes in direct peer interaction among autonomous agents. A2A enables agents to discover, authenticate, and engage with one another in decentralized or semi-centralized environments. It supports dialogue-based negotiation, mutual goal alignment, task sharing, and status reporting. By embedding social intelligence into machine interactions, A2A transforms isolated agents into networked collaborators capable of forming temporary alliances or persistent coalitions.

Agent Network Protocol

ANP takes a broader, system-level view. It defines how collections of agents—potentially operating across different domains, platforms, or organizations—form scalable and secure networks. ANP governs agent registration, capabilities publishing, routing of tasks across the network, and lifecycle management. Its goal is to enable plug-and-play interoperability between heterogeneous agent systems, much like how IP standardizes communication across the Internet. With ANP, agents become network-addressable entities that can dynamically join or leave collaborative ecosystems without breaking functionality or trust.

Together, these four protocols represent a shift from monolithic, closed-agent systems to composable, cooperative networks of LLM-driven agents. They introduce the necessary abstractions and standards for agents to not just act but to interact—efficiently, securely, and at scale.

What Is MCP Protocol?

The Model Context Protocol—also sometimes known as the Modular Communication Protocol—is a standardized, JSON-RPC framework that facilitates structured communication between LLM clients (such as agents, IDE copilots, or chatbots) and the external components they interact with, including tools, files, APIs, shell commands, and other models.

MCP defines a consistent protocol for sending and receiving messages, invoking tools, handling tasks, and accessing data across distributed, modular systems. It standardizes how agents interact with external services, reducing the need for custom glue code and enabling plug-and-play interoperability. Figure 17-1 emphasizes both the technical mechanism (JSON-RPC over HTTP/TLS) and the step-by-step interaction flow between MCP components.

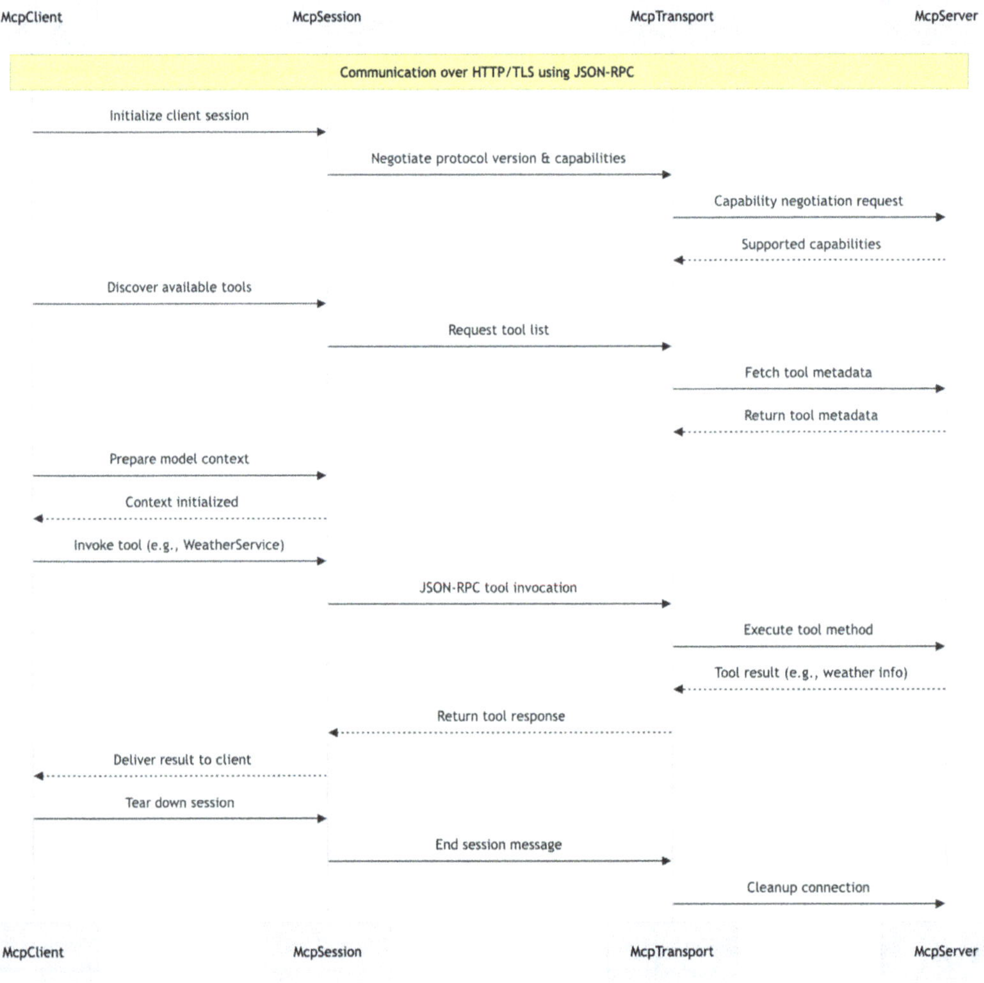

***Figure 17-1.** MCP communication flow: from client initialization to tool invocation over JSON-RPC*

At its core, MCP exposes four key capability types:

- **Resources**: Readable inputs for the model, such as logs, code, database rows, or screenshots
- **Tools**: Callable functions with typed inputs and outputs
- **Prompts**: Reusable prompt templates that can be invoked on demand
- **Sampling**: Host-side code can request completions from the LLM

These capabilities are hosted on servers, which may run locally or in the cloud. A client embedded in a host application maintains a single connection to each server—communicating via stdio or HTTP with Server-Sent Events (SSE). The many-to-many architecture allows agents to mix and match tools or data sources freely, supporting modular development and scalability.

Thanks to its well-defined message schema (typically JSON), MCP enables seamless interoperability between diverse tools and agents, regardless of language or platform. It also supports advanced features such as task delegation, execution tracking, and result aggregation—making it ideal for scalable AI systems and multi-agent frameworks.

MCP provides a foundational layer for building maintainable, extensible, and interoperable AI-driven applications. For the full specification, see `https://modelcontextprotocol.io/specification/2025-03-26`.

Role of MCP

The role of MCP is to act as a unifying communication layer between AI agents and the tools or services they use. In increasingly complex AI ecosystems—where agents need to perform tasks, call external APIs, retrieve data, or collaborate with other agents—MCP provides the standardized rules and message formats needed to make these interactions seamless, reliable, and scalable.

One of MCP's key roles is enabling interoperability, allowing different agents and tools—possibly written in different languages or running on different platforms—to work together without custom integration for each pairing. It also facilitates modular system design, where components can be added, removed, or upgraded independently without affecting the overall architecture. Additionally, MCP plays a critical role in task coordination, by structuring how agents issue tool calls, track execution, and handle results. This makes it especially valuable in systems involving orchestration, automation, and agent collaboration. Ultimately, MCP serves as the backbone of agent-tool communication, making intelligent systems more maintainable, consistent, and efficient.

MCP Using Spring AI

MCP is a standardized communication protocol that allows AI models to interact with external tools and resources in a structured and consistent manner. It supports various transport mechanisms, offering flexibility for deployment across different platforms and environments.

The MCP Java SDK delivers a Java-based implementation of this protocol, enabling seamless and standardized communication between AI models and tools. It supports both synchronous and asynchronous messaging patterns to suit diverse application needs.

Building on this foundation, Spring AI MCP integrates the MCP Java SDK with the Spring Boot ecosystem. It offers ready-to-use client and server starters, making it easy to bootstrap AI-powered applications with MCP support using Spring Initializr.

The Java implementation of MCP is structured using a three-layer architecture, as shown in Figure 17-2.

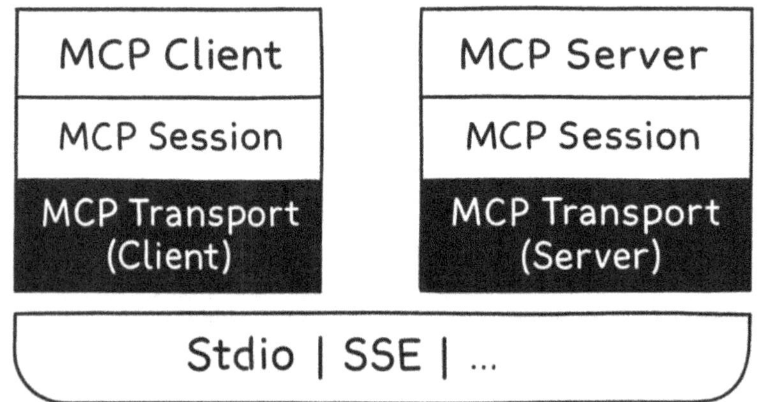

***Figure 17-2.** Three-tier architecture of MCP in Java*

Here is more about the layers:

1. **Client/server layer:** `McpClient` manages client-side interactions, while `McpServer` handles protocol operations on the server side. Both components rely on `McpSession` to manage their communication flow.

2. **Session layer (McpSession):** This layer is responsible for maintaining communication state and managing interaction patterns, typically implemented through `DefaultMcpSession`.

3. **Transport layer (McpTransport):** This layer takes care of serializing and deserializing JSON-RPC messages and supports multiple transport mechanisms for flexible integration.

MCP Client

The MCP client, as depicted in Figure 17-3, is a central component within the MCP architecture, responsible for initiating and managing communication with MCP servers. It implements the client-side functionality of the protocol and handles a range of critical tasks, including:

- Negotiating protocol versions to ensure server compatibility
- Determining supported features through capability negotiation
- Managing message transport using JSON-RPC
- Discovering and executing tools
- Accessing and managing resources
- Interacting with the prompt system

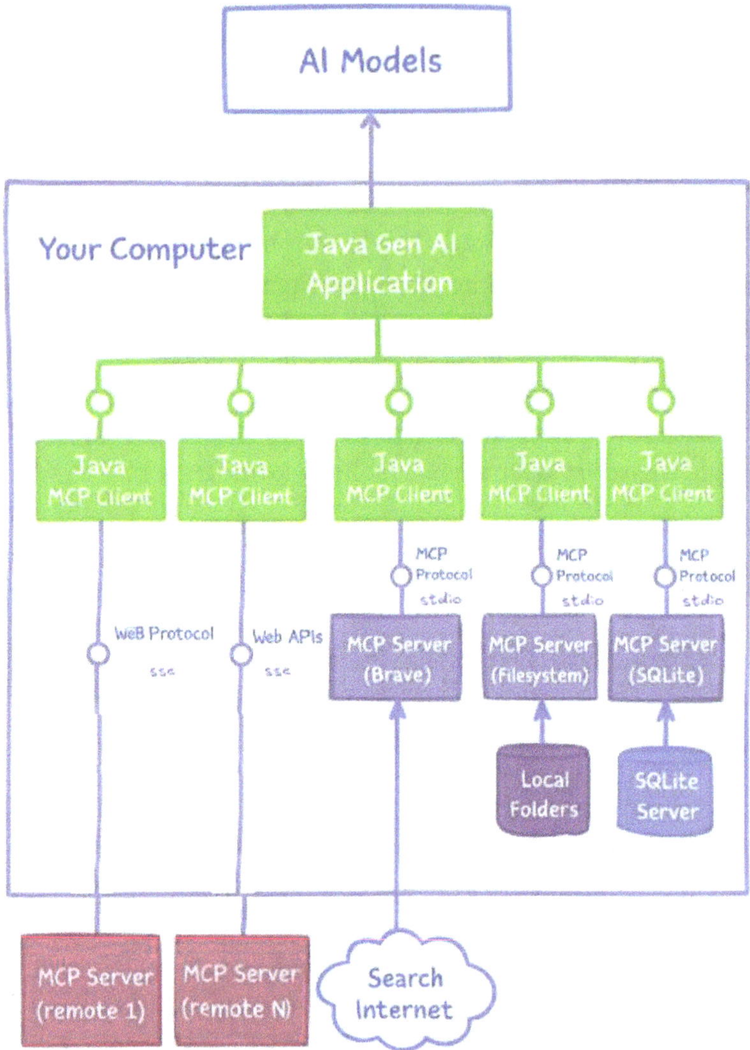

Figure 17-3. *MCP client*

Additionally, the MCP Client supports optional features such as:

- Roots management
- Sampling operations

It is designed to support both synchronous and asynchronous communication patterns and offers flexible transport mechanisms, including:

- Stdio-based transport for process-level communication
- Java HttpClient-based Server-Sent Events (SSE) transport
- WebFlux SSE client transport for reactive HTTP streaming

MCP Server

The MCP server, as shown in Figure 17-4, is a core component of the MCP architecture, designed to provide tools, resources, and capabilities to connected clients. It implements the server-side logic of the protocol and is responsible for the following:

- Executing protocol operations on the server
- Exposing tools for discovery and invocation
- Managing resources via URI-based access
- Providing and handling prompt templates
- Negotiating capabilities with clients
- Delivering structured logging and event notifications

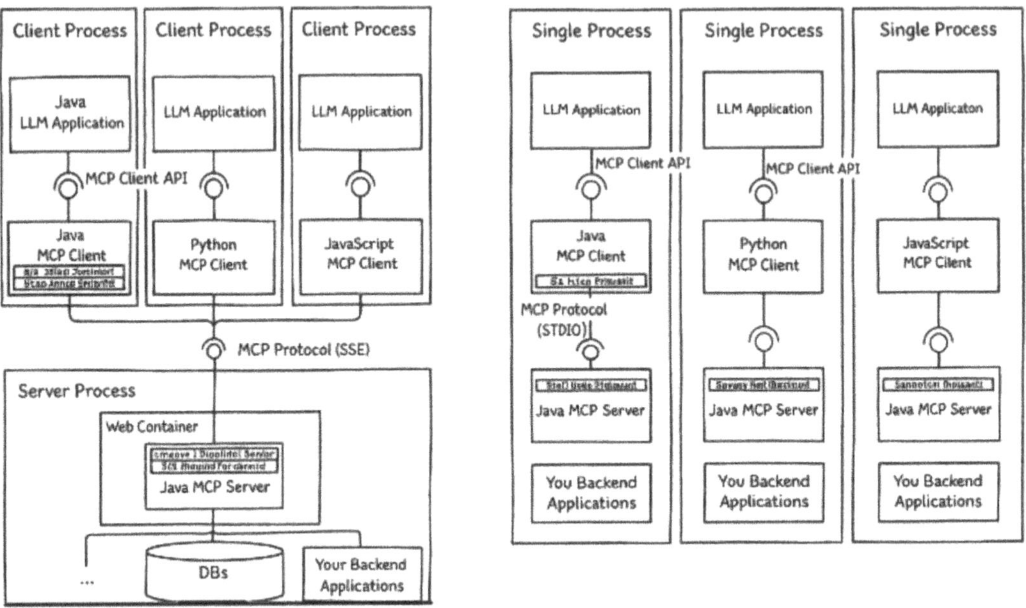

Figure 17-4. *MCP server*

In addition to supporting both synchronous and asynchronous APIs, the MCP server is built to efficiently handle multiple concurrent client connections.

It also offers various transport implementations, including:

- Stdio-based transport for communication with local processes
- Servlet-based Server-Sent Events (SSE) transport
- WebFlux SSE server transport for reactive HTTP streaming
- WebMVC SSE server transport for servlet-based HTTP streaming

Spring AI MCP Integration

Spring AI supports seamless integration with MCP through a set of dedicated Spring Boot starters, categorized into client and server modules:

Client Starters:

- **`spring-ai-starter-mcp-client`**: Core client starter that includes support for STDIO and HTTP-based SSE communication
- **`spring-ai-starter-mcp-client-webflux`**: Provides a WebFlux-based SSE transport implementation for reactive client communication

Server Starters:

- **`spring-ai-starter-mcp-server`**: Core server starter with STDIO transport support
- **`spring-ai-starter-mcp-server-webmvc`**: Implements a Spring MVC-based SSE transport for servlet-driven environments
- **`spring-ai-starter-mcp-server-webflux`**: Offers a WebFlux-based SSE transport for fully reactive server communication

We will build two projects. One sets up the Spring AI–based MCP server, and the other is a Spring AI-based MCP client that can connect to the MCP server and invoke tools exposed by it.

Capabilities of the MCP Server in Spring AI

The Spring AI integration with MCP empowers developers to build AI-enabled applications that expose well-structured and interoperable capabilities to connected clients. The MCP Server Boot Starter plays a central role in this architecture by enabling servers to advertise and manage a variety of functionalities such as tools, resources, prompts, completions, and root change handlers. These capabilities are automatically adapted to either synchronous or asynchronous modes, depending on the configuration of the server.

Tool Exposure and Management

One of the primary features of the MCP server is its ability to expose *tools* that language models can invoke during execution. Tools are implemented as Spring beans and are automatically discovered and registered by the framework. The auto-configuration process ensures that tools with duplicate names are deduplicated, keeping only the first registered instance. The MCP framework also supports *tool context*, which allows passing contextual metadata—like logging or interaction state—during tool invocation. This context-aware execution makes tool behavior more dynamic and responsive.

For this chapter, the implementation focuses specifically on this capability. I will demonstrate how a tool (in this case, a basic weather information provider) can be integrated into a Spring Boot–based MCP server and accessed by a remote MCP client. This example lays the foundation for more complex tool interactions and modular AI service architectures.

Resource Management

MCP also enables standardized *resource management*, allowing servers to expose both static and dynamic data to clients. These resources can include configuration files, status information, system metrics, or any structured data relevant to the client's tasks. Change notifications are supported, helping clients stay in sync with updated content. Resource specifications are defined as Spring beans and automatically registered with the server.

Prompt Templates

With *prompt management*, the MCP server can deliver templated prompts that clients can use for consistent, parameterized interactions. This includes support for versioning, argument validation, and change tracking. Prompts are particularly useful in multi-agent settings where uniform communication or behavior patterns are required.

Completions

The *completion management* capability allows the server to offer AI-powered suggestions or auto-completions to connected clients. These could range from code snippets to sentence continuations or query refinements. Completion services can be configured as either synchronous or asynchronous, depending on application needs.

Root Change Monitoring

MCP servers can monitor and react to *root changes*—structural updates that impact available tools, resources, or system configurations. When such changes occur, the server can notify clients, ensuring that they are working with the latest capabilities. Support for this feature is optional but beneficial in dynamic or distributed environments.

In this chapter, we demonstrate only the tooling capability of the MCP server using Spring AI, as it forms the cornerstone of practical LLM integration—enabling modular, callable functionality that can be independently developed, tested, and deployed.

Creating Spring AI-Based MCP Server

The goal for this project is to create an MCP server that exposes a tooling layer. You will keep the tool simple for now by hard-coding the returned value. As you have learned in previous chapters, you can replace the tool with any search engine or weather API and make it more usable as per your use case. Figure 17-6 illustrates how different teams or organizations can independently manage and expose their own MCP servers, enabling modular and scalable AI tool integration.

Add one dependency, as shown in Figure 17-5, which is the Spring AI MCP server package. Let's download and unzip it at the directory of your choice. You will make one change to the `build.gradle` file. Instead of `spring-ai-starter-mcp-server`, youwill use the `spring-ai-starter-mcp-server-webmvc starter` package since it comes with WebMVC transport integration.

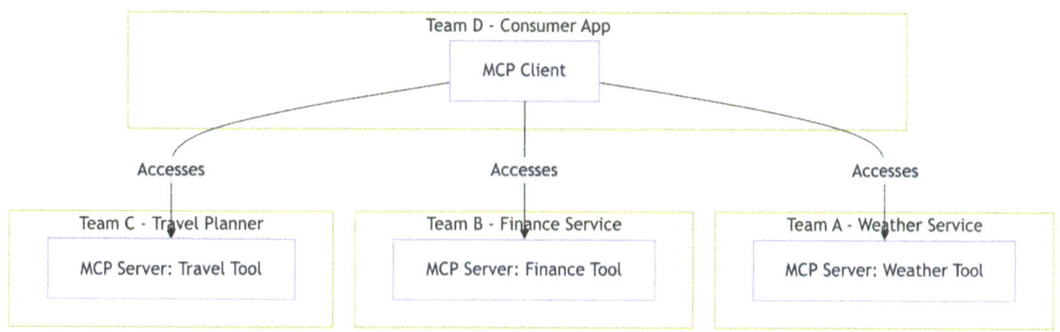

***Figure 17-5.** Spring Initializr for MCP server*

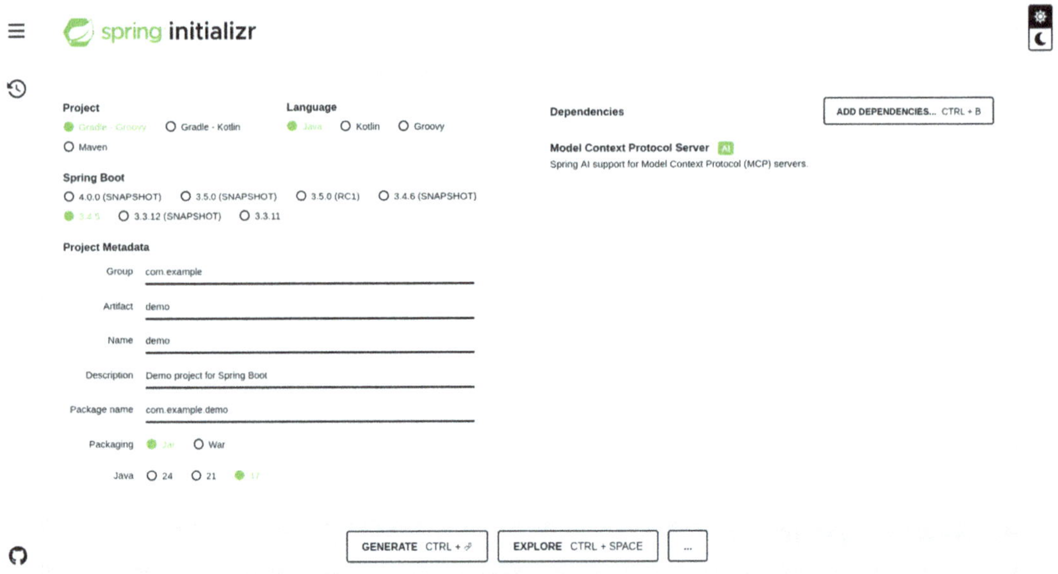

Figure 17-6. *Distributed MCP architecture: independent tooling services managed by separate teams*

File: ./build.gradle

```
. . .
dependencies {
    implementation 'org.springframework.ai:spring-ai-starter-mcp-
    server-webmvc'
    testImplementation 'org.springframework.boot:spring-boot-starter-test'
    testRuntimeOnly 'org.junit.platform:junit-platform-launcher'
}
. . .
```

If you start the application now, you should see output similar to the following:

```
2025-05-20T20:07:40.574Z  INFO 2647 --- [demo] [main] com.example.demo.
DemoApplication         : Started DemoApplication in 4.504 seconds (process
running for 6.077)
```

Next, you will update a few properties in the `application.properties` file for the MCP Server setup.

File: ./src/main/resources/application.properties

```
spring.application.name=demo
spring.ai.mcp.server.name=my-weather-server
spring.ai.mcp.server.version=0.0.1

# Using spring-ai-starter-mcp-server-webmvc
spring.ai.mcp.server.type=sync
spring.ai.mcp.server.instructions="This server provides weather information
for place when provided with a longitude and latitude"
spring.ai.mcp.server.sse-endpoint=/sse
spring.ai.mcp.server.capabilities.completion=true
spring.ai.mcp.server.capabilities.prompt=true
spring.ai.mcp.server.capabilities.resource=true
spring.ai.mcp.server.capabilities.tool=true
```

In the previous `application.properties` file, all properties except the instructions one has default values. These are the different capabilities you are exposing off of the MCP server including completion, prompt, resource, and tools. They can be ignored and have been shared for informational purposes.

You will create a WeatherService where you will define the tool like you did previously by using the weather API service, only in this case you will hard-code the response for simplicity's sake.

File: ./src/main/java/com/example/demo/service/WeatherService.java

```
package com.example.demo.service;

import org.springframework.ai.tool.annotation.Tool;
import org.springframework.stereotype.Service;

@Service
public class WeatherService {

    @Tool(description = "Get weather details for a specific latitude/
    longitude")
    public String getWeatherInformationByLocation(double longitude, double
    latitude) {
        // A custom logic can be replaced here with a call to a weather API
        service.
```

```
        return "The weather is expected to be pleasant with some
        expectation of snow in the evening";
    }
}
```

The final task in the MCP server is to register this tool as part of the tool set in the application file.

File: ./src/main/java/com/example/demo/DemoApplication.java

```
package com.example.demo;

import com.example.demo.service.WeatherService;
import org.springframework.ai.tool.ToolCallbackProvider;
import org.springframework.ai.tool.method.MethodToolCallbackProvider;
import org.springframework.beans.factory.annotation.Autowired;
import org.springframework.boot.SpringApplication;
import org.springframework.boot.autoconfigure.SpringBootApplication;
import org.springframework.context.annotation.Bean;

@SpringBootApplication
public class DemoApplication {

   public static void main(String args) {
        SpringApplication.run(DemoApplication.class, args);
    }

   @Bean
    public ToolCallbackProvider weatherTools(WeatherService
    weatherService) {
        return MethodToolCallbackProvider.builder().
        toolObjects(weatherService).build();
    }
}
```

Let's start our application and see the logs in action:

```
2025-05-20T20:29:12.427Z  INFO 4079 --- [demo] [main] o.a.c.c.C.[Tomcat].
[localhost].       : Initializing Spring embedded WebApplicationContext
```

```
2025-05-20T20:29:12.428Z  INFO 4079 --- [demo] [main] w.s.c.ServletWebServe
rApplicationContext : Root WebApplicationContext: initialization completed
in 1293 ms
2025-05-20T20:29:13.119Z  INFO 4079 --- [demo] [main] o.s.a.m.s.a.McpServer
AutoConfiguration   : Enable tools capabilities, notification: true
2025-05-20T20:29:13.220Z  INFO 4079 --- [demo] [main] o.s.a.m.s.a.McpServer
AutoConfiguration   : Registered tools: 1
2025-05-20T20:29:13.220Z  INFO 4079 --- [demo] [main] o.s.a.m.s.a.McpServer
AutoConfiguration   : Enable resources capabilities, notification: true
2025-05-20T20:29:13.221Z  INFO 4079 --- [demo] [main] o.s.a.m.s.a.McpServer
AutoConfiguration   : Enable prompts capabilities, notification: true
2025-05-20T20:29:13.222Z  INFO 4079 --- [demo] [main] o.s.a.m.s.a.McpServer
AutoConfiguration   : Enable completions capabilities
2025-05-20T20:29:13.338Z  INFO 4079 --- [demo] [main] o.s.b.w.embedded.
tomcat.TomcatWebServer  : Tomcat started on port 8080 (http) with context
path '/'
2025-05-20T20:29:13.353Z  INFO 4079 --- [demo] [main] com.example.demo.
DemoApplication         : Started DemoApplication in 2.925 seconds (process
running for 3.886)
2025-05-20T20:29:58.952Z  INFO 4079 --- [demo] [nio-8080-exec-1]
o.a.c.c.C.[Tomcat].[localhost].[/]       : Initializing Spring
DispatcherServlet 'dispatcherServlet'
2025-05-20T20:29:58.953Z  INFO 4079 --- [demo] [nio-8080-exec-1] o.s.web.
servlet.DispatcherServlet        : Initializing Servlet 'dispatcherServlet'
2025-05-20T20:29:58.955Z  INFO 4079 --- [demo] [nio-8080-exec-1] o.s.web.
servlet.DispatcherServlet        : Completed initialization in 1 ms
```

In the previous logs, you can see information relevant to the capabilities available to the MCP server and that one tool has been registered for the tools layer. We have been used to developing microservice based applications. Similar to it, this component project could be understood as having been developed by one team or a different organization altogether. This will be exposed as tool service, helping to keep it modular similar to microservices. There must be an authentication layer for every request coming through. For simplicity's sake, we have ignored it for this use case.

Creating a Spring AI-Based MCP Client

Playing the role of a team member in another team, the application needs to use the weather tool service to get weather details. Let's build the MCP client project starting with the Spring Initializr website dependencies, as shown in Figure 17-7.

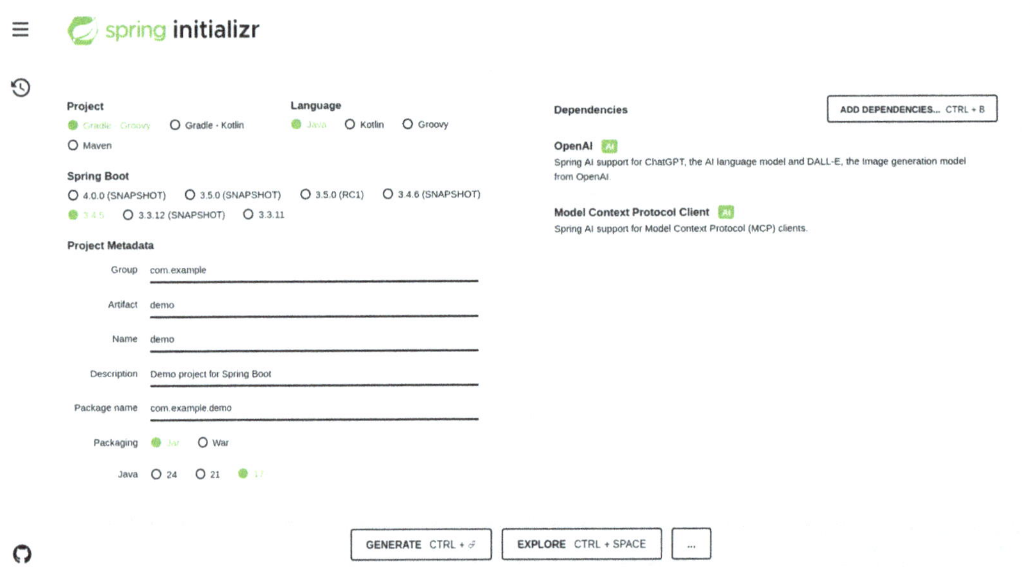

Figure 17-7. Spring Initializr dependencies for MCP client

Download the zip file and unzip it in the directory of your choice. You will start with setting a few properties in the `application.properties` file to enable some basic configuration setups relevant to the MCP client and establish its connection to the MCP server.

File: ./src/main/resources/application.properties

```
spring.application.name=demo
spring.main.web-application-type=none

spring.ai.openai.api-key=YOUR_OPENAI_API_KEY
spring.ai.mcp.client.toolcallback.enabled=true
spring.ai.mcp.client.sse.connections.server1.url=http://localhost:8080

logging.level.io.modelcontextprotocol.client=WARN
logging.level.io.modelcontextprotocol.spec=WARN
```

```
ai.user.input=What is the climate of Ladakh in India which has latitude and longitude of 34.2268° N, 77.5619° E?
```

As we can see, here you have set up the `toolcallback` capability to be enabled for the MCP client and set the MCP server endpoint to which the MCP client has to connect to use the tool capability of the MCP server. There could be more than one server. For our example at hand and for simplicity, I have chosen one. Then you set some logging properties relevant to MCP protocol for WARN level logging. Finally, you set a default question you will be asking the LLM model when the application boots up.

With the configuration out of our way, you will use the CommandLineRunner pattern to invoke a method when the application boots up, as shown here:

File: ./src/main/java/com/example/demo/DemoApplication.java

```
package com.example.demo;

import org.springframework.ai.chat.client.ChatClient;
import org.springframework.ai.tool.ToolCallbackProvider;
import org.springframework.beans.factory.annotation.Value;
import org.springframework.boot.CommandLineRunner;
import org.springframework.boot.SpringApplication;
import org.springframework.boot.autoconfigure.SpringBootApplication;
import org.springframework.context.ConfigurableApplicationContext;
import org.springframework.context.annotation.Bean;

@SpringBootApplication
public class DemoApplication {

    @Value("${ai.user.input}")
    private String userInput;

    public static void main(String[] args) {
        SpringApplication.run(DemoApplication.class, args);
    }

    @Bean
    public CommandLineRunner determineWeather(ChatClient.Builder
    chatClientBuilder, ToolCallbackProvider tools,
                                              ConfigurableApplication
                                              Context context) {
```

```
        return args -> {

            ChatClient chatClient = chatClientBuilder
                    .defaultToolCallbacks(tools)
                    .build();

            System.out.println("\n>>> UserQuestion: " + userInput);
            System.out.println("\n>>> LLM Answer: " + chatClient.
            prompt(userInput).call().content());

            context.close();
        };
    }
}
```

In the previous code, you can see that you are using the runtime-injected instances of the `ChatClient.Builder` API, which will be used to instantiate the ChatClient API. The tools argument contains the tool interface-specific information that is shared by you MCP server and gathered by the MCP client and shared with the LLM model API. Finally, you also have a reference to the MCP context and will use it to close the connection to the MCP server.

Let's start the MCP client app and see the logs in action:

```
2025-05-20T21:09:52.975Z  INFO 5801 --- [demo] [main] com.example.demo.
DemoApplication         : Started DemoApplication in 2.666 seconds (process
running for 3.386)

>>> UserQuestion: What is the climate of Ladakh in India which has latitude
and longitude of 34.2268° N, 77.5619° E?

>>> LLM Answer: The climate of Ladakh is currently pleasant, with some
expectation of snow in the evening.
Process finished with exit code 0
```

This is cool. You can see that the MCP client connected with the MCP server to invoke the relevant tool. This is an interesting example of multiple teams collaborating and maintaining a tooling layer that is complex without having to see the underlying details of it. The following is the log on the MCP server side, which shows a request had been made to it:

```
2025-05-20T21:09:52.456Z  INFO 5328 --- [demo] [nio-8080-exec-9]
i.m.server.McpAsyncServer              : Client initialize request -
Protocol: 2024-11-05, Capabilities: ClientCapabilities[experimental=nu
ll, roots=null, sampling=null], Info: Implementation[name=spring-ai-mcp-
client - server1, version=1.0.0]
```

Integrating MCP with Quarkus

Now that you have learned about MCP clients and servers and built your first application, you will try to reuse some of the practices learned with Quarkus. You will restructure the weather application built previously for Spring AI. So, the goal is to build an MCP server that provides tools for fetching weather details. The server will expose one tool called `getWeatherDetailUsingLocation`.

Let's now set up the project. Head over to `https://code.quarkus.io/` and select the following package dependencies:

- rest-client-jackson
- qute
- mcp-server-stdio

As you follow along, you will see the usage of each of these extension packages. Figure 17-8 shows the listing at `https://code.quarkus.io/`.

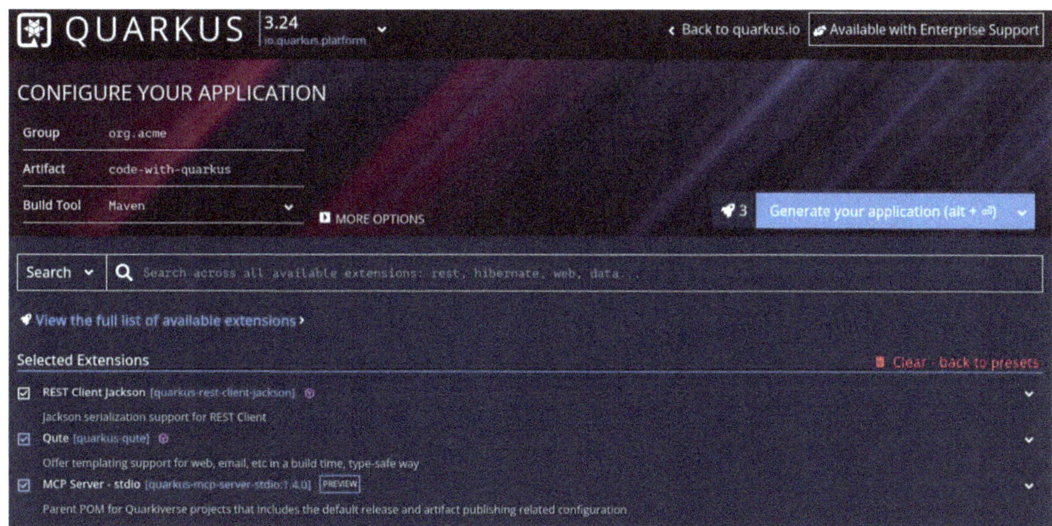

Figure 17-8. *MCP implementation-specific dependencies in Quarkus*

Download the zip and unzip it at the location of your choice. From your command line, run the following commands to make sure everything works fine. Alternatively, you can boot over your favorite IDE too.

Here are the prerequisites:

1. Java 21+

```
$ ./mvnw clean package
$ ./mvnw quarkus:dev
```

If everything goes well, you should see output similar to Figure 17-9 and Figure 17-10.

```
Listening for transport dt_socket at address: 5005
__  ____  __  _____   ___  __ ____  ______
 --/ __ \/ / / / _ | / _ \/ //_/ / / / __/
 -/ /_/ / /_/ / __ |/ , _/ ,< / /_/ /\ \
--\___\_\____/_/ |_/_/|_/_/|_|\____/___/
INFO  [io.quarkus] (Quarkus Main Thread)  (powe
red by Quarkus  ) started in  s.

INFO  [io.quarkus] (Quarkus Main Thread) Profile  activated.
INFO  [io.quarkus] (Quarkus Main Thread) Installed features: [
                                                      ]

--
Tests paused
Press [e] to edit command line args (currently ''), [r] to resume testing, [o] Toggle test output, [:] for the
 terminal, [h] for more options>
```

***Figure 17-9.** Successful output message on first boot of Quarkus*

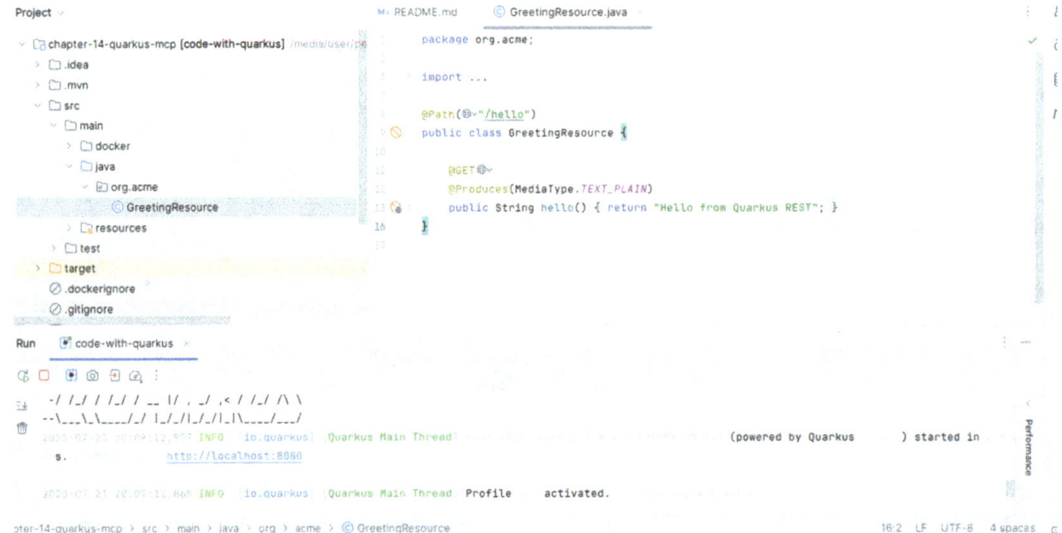

***Figure 17-10.** Intellij IDE Output*

The next task is to create a Java class to return weather details for a location based on latitude and longitude information. I will not go into the details of integrating a third-party API service to get weather details for fetching the information based on location. There are many services that can be used. The focus is on building a tool that returns weather information in string format. You will mock the method for the time being so as to keep our focus on building the MCP server with a weather tool.

Create a Java file called `Weather.java` with the following content that returns a simple string about the climate in weather at some point. As you can see, you are creating a method named `getWeatherDetails` that has two inputs and a single `String` return type. This method needs to be exposed as a tool from this MCP server. To do so, let's add a tool annotator with a description along with `ToolArg` to explicitly specify the tool's usage and its arguments.

File: src/main/java/org/acme/Weather.java

```
package org.acme;
import io.quarkiverse.mcp.server.Tool;
import io.quarkiverse.mcp.server.ToolArg;

public class Weather {
    @Tool(description = "Get weather details for a location based on
    latitude and longitude.")
    String getWeatherDetails(@ToolArg(description = "Latitude of the
    location") double latitude,
                               @ToolArg(description = "Longitude of the
                               location") double longitude) {
        // Make any api call to a third party weather api service to get
        weather details.
        return "The weather is pleasant sunny with a slight prediction of
        rain in Bangalore.";
    }
}
```

you will now begin preparations to run the server. To simplify development, you will deploy it as an uber-jar. This helps in general to run along with `mvn install` and enables you to publish and share the JAR with others and the Maven repository. You can do this by using the following property in the `application.properties` file.

```
quarkus.package.jar.type=uber-jar
```

At this step, it is also pragmatic to enable file logging since input/output is reserved for the MCP protocol, and we would not be able to see any logs by default. To do this, use the following properties in the `application.properties` file:

```
quarkus.log.file.enable=true
quarkus.log.file.path=weather-mcp-server.log
```

The `application.properties` file should look like the following:

File: src/main/resources/application.properties

```
quarkus.package.jar.type=uber-jar
quarkus.log.file.enable=true
quarkus.log.file.path=weather-mcp-server.log
```

There are a few ways you can start the MCP server:

1. Through IntelliJ or any editor specific run.

   Output:

   ```
   2025-07-27 21:37:22,724 INFO  [io.quarkus] (Quarkus Main Thread)
   code-with-quarkus 1.0.0-SNAPSHOT on JVM (powered by Quarkus
   3.24.5) started in 4.222s. Listening on: http://localhost:8080

   2025-07-27 21:37:22,730 INFO  [io.quarkus] (Quarkus Main Thread)
   Profile dev activated. Live Coding activated.
   2025-07-27 21:37:22,731 INFO  [io.quarkus] (Quarkus Main Thread)
   Installed features: [cdi, mcp-server-stdio, qute, rest, rest-
   client, rest-client-jackson, smallrye-context-propagation, vertx]
   ```

2. Using the command line, the first step is to install all the Maven package dependencies.

   ```
   ./mvnw install
   ```

Once all the packages are installed, you can start the MCP server using one of the following commands:

Using jbang: `jbang --quiet org.acme:code-with-quarkus:1.0.0-SNAPSHOT:runner`

Using java: `java -jar target/quarkus-app/quarkus-run.jar`

Here is the output:

```
2025-07-27 21:39:37,970 INFO  [io.quarkus] (main) code-with-quarkus
1.0.0-SNAPSHOT on JVM (powered by Quarkus 3.24.5) started in 1.896s.
Listening on: http://0.0.0.0:8080
2025-07-27 21:39:37,986 INFO  [io.quarkus] (main) Profile prod activated.
2025-07-27 21:39:37,988 INFO  [io.quarkus] (main) Installed features: [cdi,
mcp-server-stdio, qute, rest, rest-client, rest-client-jackson, smallrye-
context-propagation, vertx]
```

This is all good, but how do we evaluate our tool? There is a handy tool using the MCP inspector from the npm package. As a prerequisite, make sure you have npm and node installed with the latest LTS version. Run the following command to install the package and start it:

```
npx @modelcontextprotocol/inspector
```

Output:

```
Starting MCP inspector...
⚙️ Proxy server listening on localhost:6277
🔑 Session token:
c2b2d4defea8e2a9f4f4fc8cf252f243aef3aa0401225745ea07b22629599347
   Use this token to authenticate requests or set DANGEROUSLY_OMIT_
   AUTH=true to disable auth

🚀 MCP Inspector is up and running at:
   http://localhost:6274/?MCP_PROXY_AUTH_TOKEN=c2b2d4defea8e2a9f4f4fc8cf25
   2f243aef3aa0401225745ea07b22629599347

🌐 Opening browser...
```

It then opens a browser tab with the content shown in Figure 17-11.

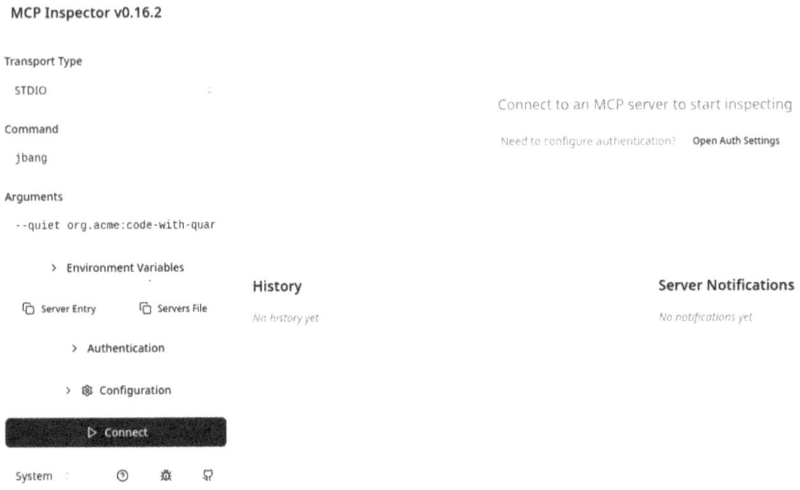

Figure 17-11. *MCP Inspector v0.16.2*

This starts a local web server where you can test your MCP server. MCP Inspector uses the command for starting your MCP server and then initiates a connection with it as an MCP client. Let's try it and explore your MCP server.

In the side window shown in Figure 17-12, fill in the details for the `Command` value as `jbang` and arguments as `--quiet org.acme:code-with-quarkus:1.0.0-SNAPSHOT:runner` and click the Connect button.

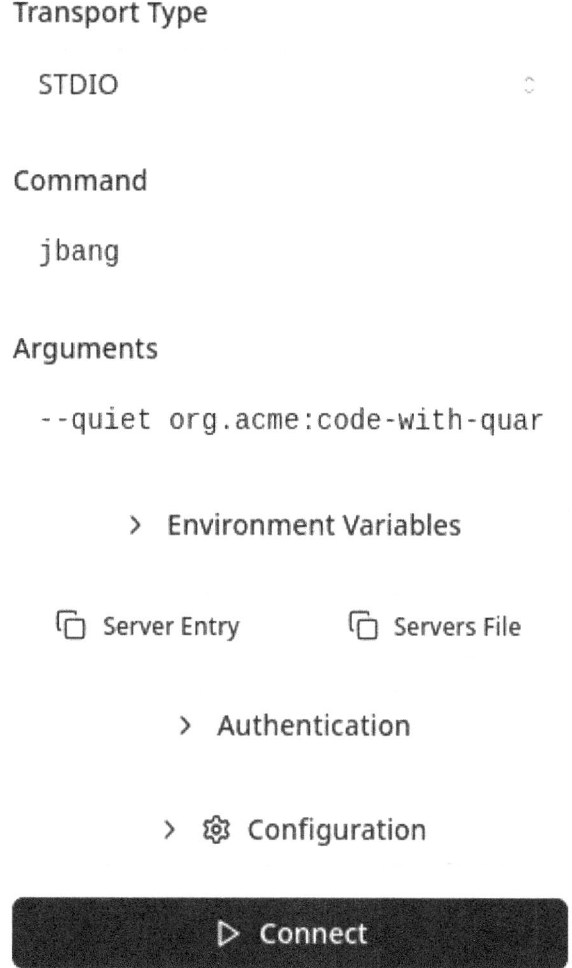

Figure 17-12. *MCP Inspector Connect command configuration*

Once you connect, the user interface shows a message called Connected with a green signal just below the connect button. In the history panel, you can see an initialize request, as shown in Figure 17-13.

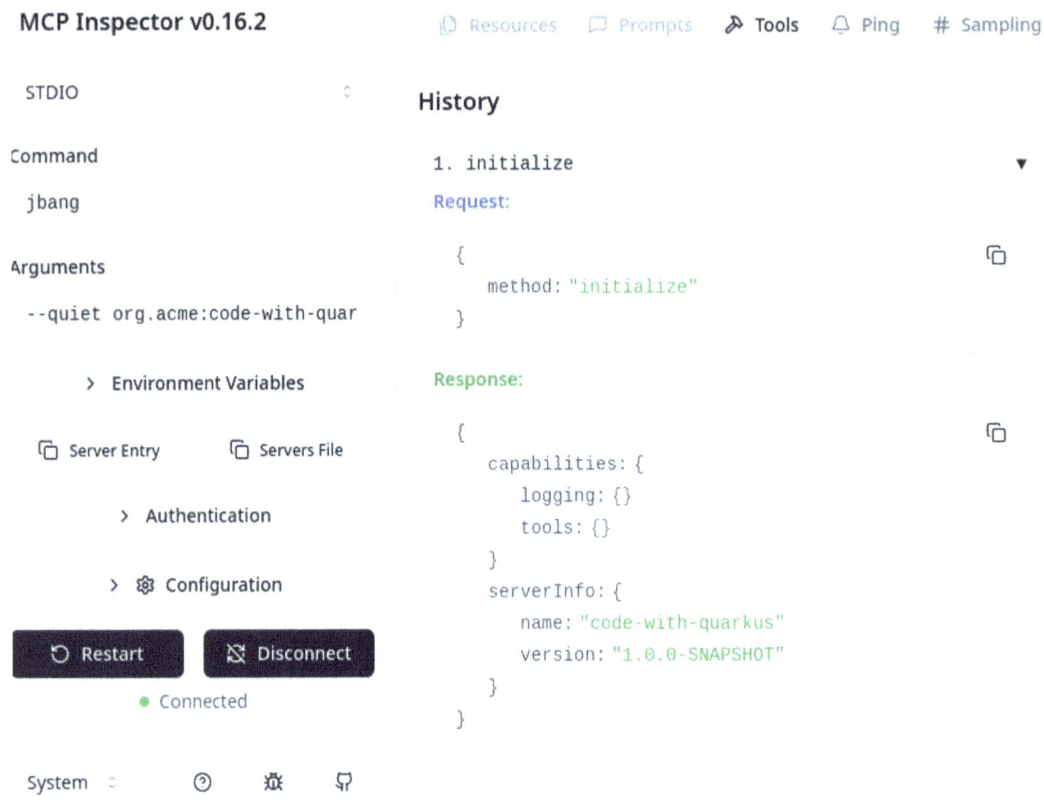

Figure 17-13. *MCP Inspector connected to MCP server*

The initialize request to the MCP server received a response of the capabilities and `serverInfo` information.

Correspondingly, you can see the following output in the terminal where you started the MCP connector. This tells you that the MCP connector has started the MCP server and then connected to it through an MCP client.

```
New STDIO connection request
Query parameters: {"command":"jbang","args":"--quiet org.acme:code-with-
quarkus:1.0.0-SNAPSHOT:runner","env":"{\"HOME\":\"/home/user\",\"LOGNAME\
":\"user\",\"PATH\":\"/home/user/.npm/_npx/5a9d879542beca3a/node_modules/.
bin:/path/chapter-14-quarkus-mcp/node_modules/.bin:/path/node_modules/.
bin:/media/user/node_modules/.bin:/media/node_modules/.bin:/node_modules/.
bin:/home/user/.nvm/versions/node/v22.17.1/lib/node_modules/npm/node_
modules/@npmcli/run-script/lib/node-gyp-bin:/home/user/.sdkman/candidates/
```

```
jbang/current/bin:/home/user/.sdkman/candidates/java/current/bin:/home/
user/.nvm/versions/node/v22.17.1/bin:/usr/local/bin:/usr/bin:/bin:/usr/
local/games:/usr/games\",\"SHELL\":\"/bin/bash\",\"TERM\":\"xterm-256color\
",\"USER\":\"user\"}","transportType":"stdio"}
```

```
STDIO transport: command=/home/user/.sdkman/candidates/jbang/current/bin/
jbang, args=--quiet,org.acme:code-with-quarkus:1.0.0-SNAPSHOT:runner
Created server transport
Created client transport
Received POST message for sessionId 34603bde-706d-4a6f-a08c-0ef204cf0004
Received POST message for sessionId 34603bde-706d-4a6f-a08c-0ef204cf0004
```

Next, click the List Tools button to check the list of tools exposed by the MCP server, as shown in Figure 17-14 and Figure 17-15.

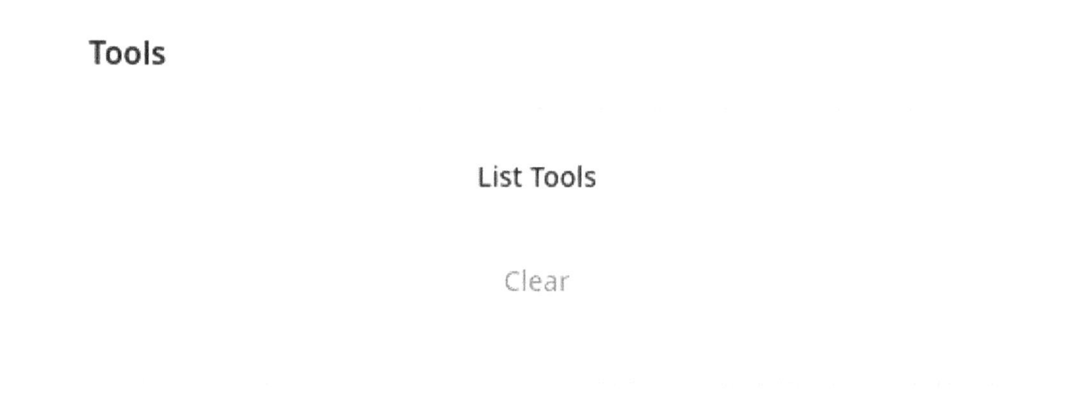

Tools

List Tools

Clear

***Figure 17-14.** Tools exploration section of MCP Inspector*

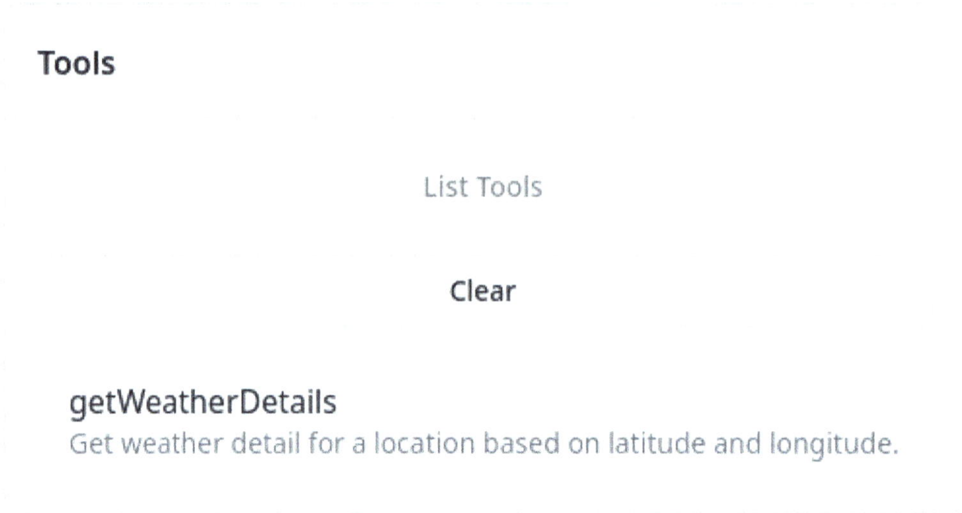

Tools

List Tools

Clear

getWeatherDetails
Get weather detail for a location based on latitude and longitude.

***Figure 17-15.** Tools listing from MCP Server using MCP Connector*

The `getWeatherDetails` tool can be clicked. When clicked, it will show the details of the tools including the arguments it needs, as shown in Figure 17-16.

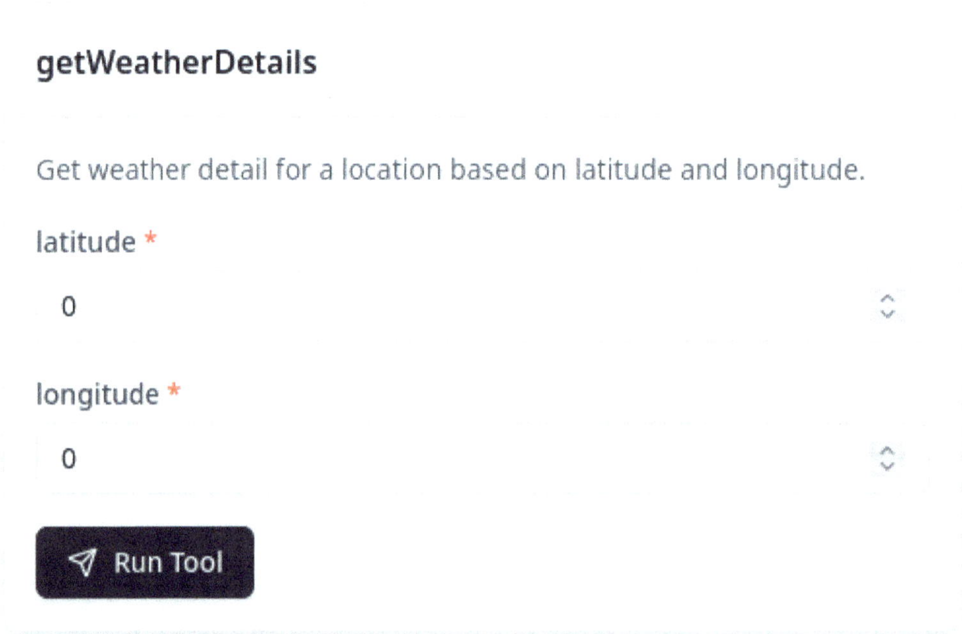

getWeatherDetails

Get weather detail for a location based on latitude and longitude.

latitude *

0

longitude *

0

Run Tool

***Figure 17-16.** getWeatherDetails tool section in MCP Inspector*

Let's provide a latitude and longitude and click the Run Tool button to see the output of the MCP server, as shown in Figure 17-17.

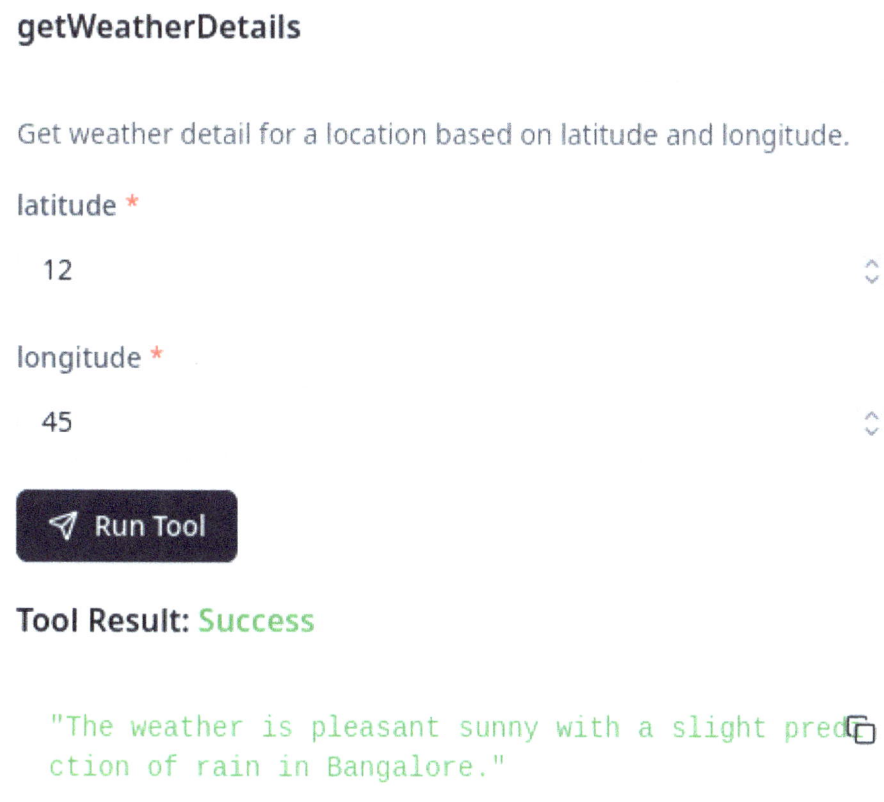

Figure 17-17. *getWeatherDetails invocation from MCP Connector*

This tool is pretty handy in helping to test and explore the MCP server and its various capabilities.

Conclusion

MCP addresses a critical need in the AI ecosystem: a standardized, structured, and modular way for agents to communicate with external tools and services. By abstracting tool interactions through well-defined message schemas and transport mechanisms, MCP reduces coupling, fosters reusability, and enhances system flexibility.

This chapter demonstrated how MCP not only unifies communication in theory but also translates into practice through robust implementations in Spring AI and Quarkus. From configuring tool exposure in an MCP server to invoking those tools from an MCP client, you learned how different teams or services can independently build, deploy, and consume AI capabilities in a microservice-like model.

As generative AI continues to shift from monolithic solutions to distributed, tool-augmented agent architectures, protocols like MCP become foundational. They not only enable current interoperability but also pave the way for future collaboration between LLM agents, services, and organizations. Embracing these standards will be key to unlocking the next generation of scalable, intelligent, and maintainable AI-driven applications.

The next chapter covers building observability into our applications to measure LLMs.

CHAPTER 18

Can You See Me Now? Observability for LLM Pipelines

The goal of this chapter is to understand the role and importance of observability in large language model (LLM) applications and how to set up and measure them in Java applications.

Introduction

In LLM applications, observability is not just a backend concern—it's a critical design principle. With LLMs becoming foundational in modern software systems, understanding how these models behave in real-world scenarios is essential to ensuring performance, reliability, and cost-effectiveness. Observability provides the tooling and practices to make that possible.

At its core, observability in LLM applications means systematically collecting, correlating, and analyzing signals—metrics, traces, and logs—across the AI pipeline. From the time a user makes a request, through the model's inference process, to the final response delivery, each step must be instrumented and made transparent.

This chapter explores how to bring observability into Java-based LLM applications, using tools like Spring AI and LangChain4j. You'll learn how to capture critical performance indicators, monitor token usage, trace end-to-end inference paths, and surface hidden issues that could impact the user experience or operational costs. Whether you're debugging a misbehaving model or optimizing system throughput under load, observability gives you the insight needed to act with confidence.

S. K. Sahu, *Generative AI-Driven Application Development with Java*,
https://doi.org/10.1007/979-8-8688-1609-3_18

Why Observability Matters in LLM Evaluation

Effective observability begins by shedding light on performance characteristics across your AI system. When you measure end-to-end invocation times—including client call overhead, network latency, and model inference delays—you gain the insight needed to identify hotspots. Tracking request rates and processing times under varying load levels reveals how your solution scales, allowing you to right-size resources and maintain consistent user experience even as traffic grows.

Cost management in LLM applications often hinges on token consumption and infrastructure utilization. By capturing input and output token counts for each request, you can spot opportunities to refine prompt design and reduce unnecessary generations, directly lowering your billing statement. Similarly, monitoring GPU, CPU, and memory usage during inference provides the visibility required to optimize deployment configurations, tune auto-scaling policies, and avoid surprise overprovisioning that drives up cloud costs.

Reliability is not just about uptime—it's also about being able to diagnose and recover from errors rapidly. When your observability framework records error rates, exception traces, and the contexts in which failures occur (such as malformed prompts or connectivity issues), you can set up alerts for anomalous spikes and jump straight to the root cause. Observability data also validates the effectiveness of retry and fallback strategies by exposing retry counts and end-to-end latencies for secondary code paths.

Understanding model behavior at scale demands visibility into the parameters and content driving each inference. Auditing hyperparameters like temperature, top_k/p, and stop sequences alongside the corresponding outputs makes it possible to correlate specific settings with quality, coherence, or safety outcomes. When responsibly enabled, prompt and completion logs—tightly coupled with trace identifiers—provide a forensic record for investigating hallucinations, bias patterns, or drifts in relevance over time.

In regulated or privacy-sensitive environments, observability plays a crucial role in governance. By associating every inference with a unique trace or conversation ID, you create an auditable lineage of data transformations—a necessity for compliance with data-protection standards. At the same time, observability platforms can be configured to redact or omit sensitive fields from metrics, ensuring telemetry remains actionable without exposing personal or proprietary information.

Core Observability Signals

See Table 18-1.

Table 18-1. *Core Observability Signals at a Glance*

Signal	Type	Cardinality	Relative Cost	Typical Retention
Metrics	Aggregated numeric data (e.g., counters, histograms, gauges)	Low	Low	Long-term (30–90 days)
Traces	Distributed spans across services with detailed context	High	Medium	Medium (7–30 days)
Logs	Unstructured or semi-structured text (e.g., errors, payloads)	High (Optional)	High (especially if full prompts are included)	Short-term (1–14 days, longer for filtered logs)

Metrics constitute the backbone of lightweight, high-volume telemetry. Low-cardinality metrics—such as histograms for operation durations, counters for success or failure rates, and gauges for token usage—deliver scalable performance insights without overwhelming your monitoring backend. These aggregated numbers answer questions like "What is our 95th percentile latency?" or "How many tokens are we processing per hour?"

Tracing provides the rich, high-cardinality detail that metrics alone cannot capture. Distributed traces stitch together spans from your client libraries, network layers, and model providers, revealing the precise timing breakdown of each request. Within those spans, attributes such as full prompt text, hyperparameter values, and conversation identifiers make it possible to reconstruct exactly how an inference unfolded, enabling deep dives into edge-case failures and performance anomalies.

Logs serve as the final layer of observability for content-rich diagnostics. When controlled by opt-in flags and appropriate retention policies, your logs can include full prompts, model responses, and detailed error contexts. By correlating logs with trace IDs, developers can seamlessly navigate from a high-level metric alert down to the exact input that triggered a failure, speeding up troubleshooting and root-cause analysis.

Best Practices

Separate low- versus high-cardinality data to preserve the performance and usability of your observability stack. Emit only a small, fixed set of labels on your metrics to keep cardinality in check, while reserving detailed, variable attributes—like full prompt text or conversation IDs—for tracing spans. This dual-tiered approach ensures you get both the wildfire visibility of metrics and the forensic depth of traces.

Safeguard sensitive data by default. Configure your observability framework to redact or omit any personal, confidential, or proprietary content from both metrics and spans. Provide clear, documented opt-in controls for teams that require full content logging during debugging, along with guidance on masking or tokenization strategies to maintain compliance with privacy regulations.

Correlate identifiers consistently across components—client SDKs, model backends, embedding services, image generators, and vector stores—so you can reconstruct the full lifecycle of a request. When every span and log entry carries the same unique trace or conversation ID, you unlock end-to-end visibility that cuts across technology silos and infrastructure boundaries.

Automate dashboards and alerts around your key performance indicators. Build visualizations for latency percentiles, error rates, and token consumption trends, and configure threshold-based alerts for sudden deviations. Automated notifications help your team detect regressions or operational issues early, before they impact end users or blow past cost budgets.

Embed observability into your continuous evaluation loop. As you test new model versions or tweak deployment configurations, leverage historical telemetry—such as average inference times, error frequencies, and cost per token—to validate that changes meet your SLOs. By making observability data a core input to your testing and promotion workflows, you ensure only reliable, performant models reach production.

To proactively detect issues before they reach users, teams should automate dashboards and alerts around a set of well-defined key performance indicators (KPIs). These typically include latency (especially P50, P95, and P99 percentiles), error rates (both 4xx and 5xx), token consumption trends, and cost metrics such as cost per thousand tokens or per request. Visualizations like time-series graphs for response latency, heatmaps of error spikes, and histograms of token usage can provide early warning signals that something is wrong—whether due to model drift, traffic surges, or misconfigurations. Alerts should be configured with intelligent thresholds—for instance, triggering a warning when P95 latency exceeds two seconds or when 5xx error rates rise above 1% over a 10-minute window. Token usage spikes can be flagged if they exceed cost budgets for a specific API key or region. By embedding these visual and automated guardrails into your operations, you reduce time-to-detection for regressions and can respond before user experience or cloud bills are negatively impacted.

Integrating Observability in LLMs Through Spring AI

Observability plays a crucial role in working with LLMs, and Spring AI enhances this by leveraging the robust observability features of the Spring ecosystem. It offers detailed insights into AI operations by providing metrics and tracing support for key components such as the `ChatClient` (including `Advisor`), `ChatModel`, `EmbeddingModel`, `ImageModel`, and `VectorStore`.

In the upcoming sections, you will see how to build a generative AI (Gen AI) project from scratch in Spring AI and integrate observability into it at various layers and observe how it helps.

Let's start with going to Spring Initializr and creating a project with the dependencies shown in Figure 18-1. You can always feel free to use any of the existing Spring AI-based projects and integrate the change to it instead. I have chosen a new one to keep it independent and simple to start.

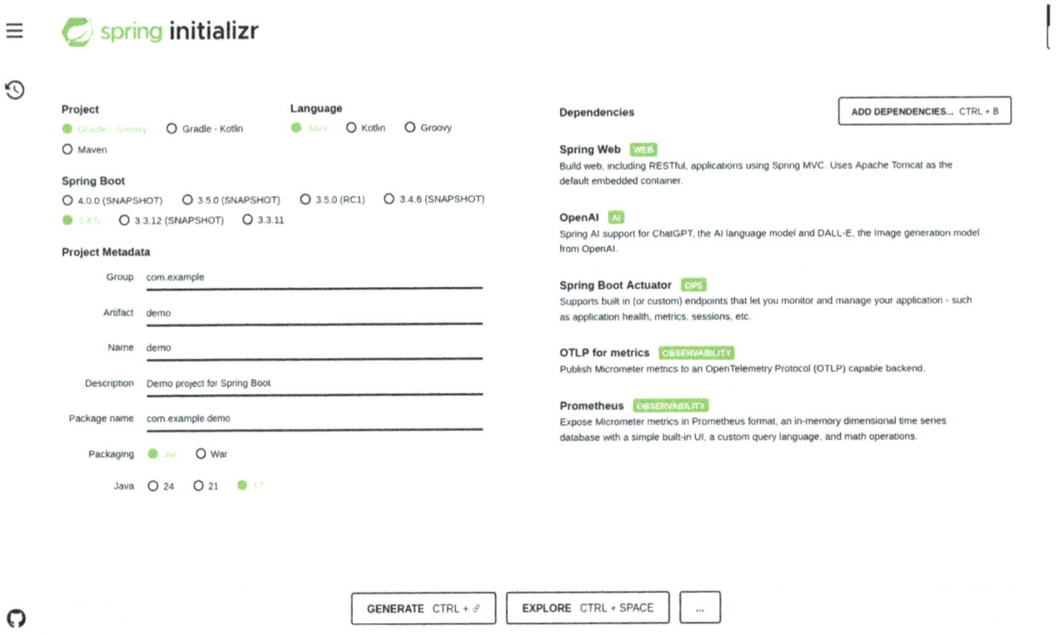

Figure 18-1. Spring Initializr project initialization

First, download it and unzip it at the location of your choice. To make sure everything with the initial setup is okay, you will set one parameter for the Open AI API key in the `application.properties` file. Also, since you want to capture and see the metrics observed from the Spring AI components, you will set a few other attributes/properties specific to them.

File: ./src/main/resources/application.properties

```
spring.application.name=demo
spring.ai.openai.api-key=YOUR_OPENAI_API_KEY
management.endpoints.web.exposure.include=*
management.metrics.enable.all=true
management.tracing.enabled=true
```

You will set up a foundation framework to learn about each of the observability settings in Spring AI. All of the settings relate to a particular API call like the use of ChatClient or ChatModel API. So, you will start with a foundation bean method using the CommandLineRunner pattern to run the respective methods when the Spring Boot application is started. You have already seen this pattern in use in previous chapters, so the methods should be self-explanatory.

File: ./src/main/java/com/example/demo/DemoApplication.java

```
package com.example.demo;

import org.springframework.ai.chat.client.ChatClient;
import org.springframework.boot.CommandLineRunner;
import org.springframework.boot.SpringApplication;
import org.springframework.boot.autoconfigure.SpringBootApplication;
import org.springframework.context.annotation.Bean;

@SpringBootApplication
public class DemoApplication {
    public static void main(String[] args) {
        SpringApplication.run(DemoApplication.class, args);
    }

    @Bean
    public CommandLineRunner run() {
        return args -> {
            // Placeholder to make all calls by creating a
           // private method and invoking from here.
        };
    }
}
```

This should set the foundation for the next set of modular components, which we will build around different Spring AI-specific calls like ChatClient, ChatModel, etc. The first one is ChatClient. Let's boot up the application and see the metrics enabled by default at this moment.

```
curl http://localhost:8080/actuator/metrics
```

Output:


```
{"names":["application.ready.time","application.started.time","disk.free",
"disk.total","executor.active","executor.completed","executor.pool.core",
"executor.pool.max","executor.pool.size","executor.queue.remaining",
"executor.queued","http.server.requests","http.server.requests.active",
"jvm.buffer.count","jvm.buffer.memory.used","jvm.buffer.total.capacity",
```

```
"jvm.classes.loaded","jvm.classes.unloaded","jvm.compilation.time",
"jvm.gc.live.data.size","jvm.gc.max.data.size","jvm.gc.memory.allocated",
"jvm.gc.memory.promoted","jvm.gc.overhead","jvm.gc.pause","jvm.info",
"jvm.memory.committed","jvm.memory.max","jvm.memory.usage.after.gc",
"jvm.memory.used","jvm.threads.daemon","jvm.threads.live","jvm.threads.
peak","jvm.threads.started","jvm.threads.states","logback.events",
"process.cpu.time","process.cpu.usage","process.files.max","process.files.
open","process.start.time","process.uptime","system.cpu.count","system.cpu.
usage","system.load.average.1m","tomcat.sessions.active.current","tomcat.
sessions.active.max","tomcat.sessions.alive.max","tomcat.sessions.
created","tomcat.sessions.expired","tomcat.sessions.rejected"]}
```


As you can see in the previous output, none of the metrics is relevant to `spring.ai` components.

Observing ChatClient Requests

Setting the `spring.ai.chat.client.observations.log-prompt=true` allows you to log observations when a ChatClient `call()` or `stream()` method/operation is called. Internally these methods help you measure the time spent by the invocation and share the related tracing instrumentation information for them. Let's see this in practice.

You will update the foundation code to initiate the ChatClient API and make a call request to share a joke. The updated code is as follows:

File: ./src/main/java/com/example/demo/DemoApplication.java

```
package com.example.demo;

import org.springframework.ai.chat.client.ChatClient;
import org.springframework.boot.CommandLineRunner;
import org.springframework.boot.SpringApplication;
import org.springframework.boot.autoconfigure.SpringBootApplication;
import org.springframework.context.annotation.Bean;

@SpringBootApplication
public class DemoApplication {
    private ChatClient chatClient;
```

```
    public static void main(String[] args) {
        SpringApplication.run(DemoApplication.class, args);
    }

    @Bean
    public CommandLineRunner run(ChatClient.Builder chatClientBuilder) {
        chatClient = chatClientBuilder.build();

        return args -> {
            this.makeChatClientRequest();
        };
    }

    private void makeChatClientRequest() {
        String response = chatClient.prompt()
                .user("Tell me a joke.")
                .call()
                .content();
        System.out.println(response);
    }
}
```

Booting up the application should give you output similar to the following, but you will not see any instrumentation details for the request made to OpenAI.

Output:

```
Why did the scarecrow win an award?
Because he was outstanding in his field!
```

Let's enable the observability parameter in the `application.properties` file.

File: ./src/main/resources/application.properties

```
spring.application.name=demo
spring.ai.openai.api-key=YOUR_OPENAI_API_KEY
management.endpoints.web.exposure.include=*
management.metrics.enable.all=true
management.tracing.enabled=true
spring.ai.chat.client.observations.log-prompt=true
```

At this moment, in the Spring Boot startup logs, you should see the following info message:

```
2025-05-19T22:21:28.228Z  WARN 11207 --- [demo] [main] .s.a.m.c.c.a.ChatCl
ientAutoConfiguration : You have enabled logging out the ChatClient prompt
content with the risk of exposing sensitive or private information. Please,
be careful!
```

Let's also look at the actuator endpoint for the metrics to see if there are additional metrics being exposed now:

```
curl http://localhost:8080/actuator/metrics
```

Output:

{"names":["application.ready.time","application.started.time","disk.free","disk.total","executor.active","executor.completed","executor.pool.core","executor.pool.max","executor.pool.size","executor.queue.remaining","executor.queued","gen_ai.client.operation","gen_ai.client.operation.active","gen_ai.client.token.usage","http.client.requests","http.client.requests.active","http.server.requests.active","jvm.buffer.count","jvm.buffer.memory.used","jvm.buffer.total.capacity","jvm.classes.loaded","jvm.classes.unloaded","jvm.compilation.time","jvm.gc.live.data.size","jvm.gc.max.data.size","jvm.gc.memory.allocated","jvm.gc.memory.promoted","jvm.gc.overhead","jvm.gc.pause","jvm.info","jvm.memory.committed","jvm.memory.max","jvm.memory.usage.after.gc","jvm.memory.used","jvm.threads.daemon","jvm.threads.live","jvm.threads.peak","jvm.threads.started","jvm.threads.states","logback.events","process.cpu.time","process.cpu.usage","process.files.max","process.files.open","process.start.time","process.uptime",**"spring.ai.advisor","spring.ai.advisor.active","spring.ai.chat.client","spring.ai.chat.client.active"**,"system.cpu.count","system.cpu.usage","system.load.average.1m","tomcat.sessions.active.current","tomcat.sessions.active.max","tomcat.sessions.alive.max","tomcat.sessions.created","tomcat.sessions.expired","tomcat.sessions.rejected"]}

As you can see, additional metrics are being captured for `spring.ai.advisor` and `spring.ai.chat.client`. Let's deep dive into the metric `spring.ai.chat.client` to see the observations it has captured:

```
curl http://localhost:8080/actuator/metrics/spring.ai.chat.client
```

Output:


```
{"name":"spring.ai.chat.client","baseUnit":"seconds","measurements":[
{"statistic":"COUNT","value":1.0},{"statistic":"TOTAL_TIME","value":
1.569205385},{"statistic":"MAX","value":1.569205385}],"availableTags":[
{"tag":"gen_ai.operation.name","values":["framework"]},{"tag":"spring.
ai.kind","values":["chat_client"]},{"tag":"error","values":["none"]},{
"tag":"spring.ai.chat.client.stream","values":["false"]},{"tag":"gen_
ai.system","values":["spring_ai"]}]}
```


Some of the values that are captured are the name of the observation, which is `spring.ai.chat.client`; measurements like `COUNT` stating the number of requests made, which in our case is 1; and then `TOTAL_TIME` and `MAX` time taken. There are a few tag-specific values for `gen_ai.operation.name`, which will always be framework, and the spring.ai.kind value, which is `chat_client` for the request in use. This is super helpful to measure the number of requests made and the time it took.

As per the Spring AI documentation page, low cardinality keys will be added to metrics and traces, while high cardinality keys will only be added to traces. Table 18-2 shows the low cardinality keys and values in our metrics endpoint.

***Table 18-2.** Low Cardinality Keys and Values*

Name	Description
`genai.operation.name`	Always the framework
`genai.system`	Always `spring.ai`
`spring.ai.chat.client.stream`	Is the chat model response a stream, true or false
`spring.ai.kind`	The kind of framework API in Spring AI: `chat_client`

To view the high cardinality keys listed in Table 18-3, you will need to set up tracing in Spring Boot. The shared low and high cardinality keys are exposed by default, while the prompt content generally being large in size may contain confidential information that is hidden by default. By setting the parameter to log the prompt as we did previously, you can now capture this information. This may be used for debugging and development use cases but not in production. These are shared in Table 18-3.

Table 18-3. *High Cardinality Keys and Values*

Name	Description
`genai.prompt`	The content of the prompt sent via the chat client. Optional.
`spring.ai.chat.client.advisors`	List of configured chat client advisors.
`spring.ai.chat.client.conversation.id`	Identifier of the conversation when using the chat memory.
`spring.ai.chat.client.tool.names`	Names of the tools passed to the chat client.

Note The `genai.prompt` parameter is never populated in the observations and as per GitHub issues, it is rather shown in the debug logs through another attribute. They are yet to update the documentation for this change at this moment of writing.

Let's now work on enabling tracing in Spring Boot so that we can view the high cardinality keys and values.

We will add a few more dependencies to our `build.gradle` file to enable capturing of the observations.

```
implementation 'io.micrometer:micrometer-core:1.15.0'
implementation 'io.micrometer:micrometer-tracing-bridge-brave:1.5.0'
```

The micrometer dependency package will help us with trace enabling and capturing. These can then be either stored in OpenTelemetry or exported through the Prometheus API service.

File: ./build.gradle

```
plugins {
    id 'java'
    id 'org.springframework.boot' version '3.4.5'
    id 'io.spring.dependency-management' version '1.1.7'
}

group = 'com.example'
version = '0.0.1-SNAPSHOT'

java {
    toolchain {
       languageVersion = JavaLanguageVersion.of(17)
    }
}

repositories {
    mavenCentral()
}

ext {
    set('springAiVersion', "1.0.0-RC1")
}

dependencies {
    implementation 'org.springframework.boot:spring-boot-starter-web'
    implementation 'org.springframework.ai:spring-ai-starter-model-openai'
    implementation 'org.springframework.boot:spring-boot-starter-actuator'
    implementation 'io.micrometer:micrometer-core:1.15.0'
    implementation 'io.micrometer:micrometer-tracing-bridge-brave:1.5.0'
    runtimeOnly 'io.micrometer:micrometer-registry-otlp'
    runtimeOnly 'io.micrometer:micrometer-registry-prometheus'
    testImplementation 'org.springframework.boot:spring-boot-starter-test'
    testRuntimeOnly 'org.junit.platform:junit-platform-launcher'
}
```

```
dependencyManagement {
    imports {
        mavenBom "org.springframework.ai:spring-ai-bom:${springAiVersion}"
    }
}

tasks.named('test') {
    useJUnitPlatform()
}
```

Then you will enable a few more properties in our `application.properties` file to enable a few endpoints and services like Prometheus and logging for log prompts.

Enable three properties for log prompts at the chat client and chat model levels with the following lines. These three properties seem to have no effect and can be ignored. The future documentation should state useful information relevant to this.

```
spring.ai.chat.observations.log-prompt=true
spring.ai.chat.observations.include-error-logging=true
spring.ai.chat.client.observations.log-prompt=true
```

Enable tracking and prometheus metrics export through the following two properties:

```
management.tracing.enabled=true
management.prometheus.metrics.export.enabled=true
```

Enable logging of log prompt observations through the following two properties:

```
logging.level.org.springframework.ai.chat.observation=DEBUG
logging.level.org.springframework.ai.chat.client.observation=DEBUG
```

All the changes for the `application.properties` file are shown here:

File: ./src/main/resources/application.properties

```
spring.application.name=demo
spring.ai.openai.api-key=YOUR_OPENAI_API_KEY
spring.ai.chat.observations.log-prompt=true
spring.ai.chat.observations.include-error-logging=true
spring.ai.chat.client.observations.log-prompt=true
management.endpoints.web.exposure.include=*
```

```
management.metrics.enable.all=true
management.tracing.enabled=true
management.prometheus.metrics.export.enabled=true
logging.level.org.springframework.ai.chat.observation=DEBUG
logging.level.org.springframework.ai.chat.client.observation=DEBUG
```

Now that you have enabled the tracing, the high cardinality keys are not observable from the logs except the log prompts. To view them, you have to write a class that implements the `ObservationHandler` interface as shown next. You have implemented three methods, namely, supportsContext, onStart, and onStop. You can print the observation name and the high cardinality keys and values specific to them by calling `context.getName()` and `context.getHighCardinalityKeyValues()`.

File: ./src/main/java/com/example/demo/LoggingObservationHandler.java

```
package com.example.demo;

import io.micrometer.observation.Observation;
import io.micrometer.observation.ObservationHandler;
import org.springframework.stereotype.Component;

@Component
public class LoggingObservationHandler implements
ObservationHandler<Observation.Context> {

    @Override
    public boolean supportsContext(Observation.Context context) {
        return true;
    }

    @Override
    public void onStart(Observation.Context context) {
        System.out.println("Starting observation: " + context.getName());
        System.out.println(context.getHighCardinalityKeyValues());
        System.out.println("Starting observation: " + context.
        getAllKeyValues());
    }
```

```
    @Override
    public void onStop(Observation.Context context) {
        System.out.println("Completed observation: " + context.getName());
        System.out.println(context.getHighCardinalityKeyValues());
        System.out.println("Completed observation: " + context.
        getAllKeyValues());
    }
}
```

Let's boot up the application and see the logs in action. In the follwoing logs, I have highlighted the respective observation names captured in the start and stop phases. Observe carefully the high cardinality keys and values just after it. In the third line after it, you can also see all the key values including both low and high cardinality ones. Also, in the logs you can observe in between the user and prompt contexts being shared in the debug context of the properties you had set separately for them.

Output:

```
Starting observation: spring.ai.chat.client
[keyValue(spring.ai.chat.client.advisors=["call"])]
Starting observation: [keyValue(gen_ai.operation.
name=framework),keyValue(gen_ai.system=spring_ai),keyValue(spring.
ai.chat.client.advisors=["call"]),keyValue(spring.ai.chat.client.
stream=false),keyValue(spring.ai.kind=chat_client)]

Starting observation: spring.ai.advisor
[keyValue(spring.ai.advisor.order=2147483647)]
Starting observation: [keyValue(gen_ai.operation.
name=framework),keyValue(gen_ai.system=spring_ai),keyValue(spring.
ai.advisor.name=call),keyValue(spring.ai.advisor.order=2147483647),keyValue
(spring.ai.kind=advisor)]

Starting observation: gen_ai.client.operation
[keyValue(gen_ai.request.temperature=0.7)]
Starting observation: [keyValue(gen_ai.operation.name=chat),keyValue(gen_
ai.request.model=gpt-4o-mini),keyValue(gen_ai.request.
temperature=0.7),keyValue(gen_ai.response.model=none),keyValue(gen_
ai.system=openai)]
```

```
Starting observation: http.client.requests
[keyValue(http.url=https://api.openai.com/v1/chat/completions)]
Starting observation: [keyValue(client.name=api.openai.com),keyValue(exc
eption=none),keyValue(http.url=https://api.openai.com/v1/chat/completion
s),keyValue(method=POST),keyValue(outcome=UNKNOWN),keyValue(status=CLIE
NT_ERROR),keyValue(uri=/v1/chat/completions)]

Completed observation: http.client.requests
[keyValue(http.url=https://api.openai.com/v1/chat/completions)]
Completed observation: [keyValue(client.name=api.openai.com),keyValue(excep
tion=none),keyValue(http.url=https://api.openai.com/v1/chat/completions),ke
yValue(method=POST),keyValue(outcome=SUCCESS),keyValue(status=200),keyValue
(uri=/v1/chat/completions)]

2025-05-20T10:24:45.669Z DEBUG 2731 --- [demo] [main]
[682c586c329554d895c49aa2b036a97f-d826b458706b22aa]
ChatModelPromptContentObservationHandler : Chat Model Prompt Content:
["You are a professional comedian. Tell a joke.", "Tell me a joke."]

Completed observation: gen_ai.client.operation
[keyValue(gen_ai.request.temperature=0.7),keyValue(gen_ai.response.finish_
reasons=["STOP"]),keyValue(gen_ai.response.id=chatcmpl-BZERJPPfTRYDDOWBrSz
QOprvE1Zv9),keyValue(gen_ai.usage.input_tokens=26),keyValue(gen_ai.usage.
output_tokens=18),keyValue(gen_ai.usage.total_tokens=44)]
Completed observation: [keyValue(gen_ai.operation.name=chat),
keyValue(gen_ai.request.model=gpt-4o-mini),keyValue(gen_ai.request.t
emperature=0.7),keyValue(gen_ai.response.finish_reasons=["STOP"]),
keyValue(gen_ai.response.id=chatcmpl-BZERJPPfTRYDDOWBrSzQOprvE1Zv9),
keyValue(gen_ai.response.model=gpt-4o-mini-2024-07-18),keyValue(gen_
ai.system=openai),keyValue(gen_ai.usage.input_tokens=26),keyValue(gen_
ai.usage.output_tokens=18),keyValue(gen_ai.usage.total_tokens=44)]

Completed observation: spring.ai.advisor
[keyValue(spring.ai.advisor.order=2147483647)]
Completed observation: [keyValue(gen_ai.operation.name=framework),
keyValue(gen_ai.system=spring_ai),keyValue(spring.ai.advisor.name=call),
keyValue(spring.ai.advisor.order=2147483647),keyValue(spring.
ai.kind=advisor)]
```

```
2025-05-20T10:24:45.682Z DEBUG 2731 --- [demo] [main] [682c586c329554d895
c49aa2b036a97f-95c49aa2b036a97f] hatClientPromptContentObservationHandler :
Chat Client Prompt Content:
["user":"Tell me a joke."]

Completed observation: spring.ai.chat.client
[keyValue(spring.ai.chat.client.advisors=["call"])]
Completed observation: [keyValue(gen_ai.operation.
name=framework),keyValue(gen_ai.system=spring_ai),keyValue(spring.
ai.chat.client.advisors=["call"]),keyValue(spring.ai.chat.client.
stream=false),keyValue(spring.ai.kind=chat_client)]

Why did the scarecrow win an award?

Because he was outstanding in his field!
```

You can also see this information over the Prometheus metrics endpoint. In the following log outputs, I have shared only Spring AI–specific outputs. You can see you are now capturing various observations relevant to the low and high cardinality keys. These can then be transmitted to any Prometheus observing service to show them in dashboards, visualizations, etc.

```
curl http://localhost:8080/actuator/prometheus
```

Output:

```
34:# HELP gen_ai_client_operation_active_seconds
35:# TYPE gen_ai_client_operation_active_seconds summary
36:gen_ai_client_operation_active_seconds_count{gen_ai_operation_
name="chat",gen_ai_request_model="gpt-4o-mini",gen_ai_response_
model="none",gen_ai_system="openai"} 0
37:gen_ai_client_operation_active_seconds_sum{gen_ai_operation_
name="chat",gen_ai_request_model="gpt-4o-mini",gen_ai_response_
model="none",gen_ai_system="openai"} 0.0
38:# HELP gen_ai_client_operation_active_seconds_max
39:# TYPE gen_ai_client_operation_active_seconds_max gauge
40:gen_ai_client_operation_active_seconds_max{gen_ai_operation_
name="chat",gen_ai_request_model="gpt-4o-mini",gen_ai_response_
model="none",gen_ai_system="openai"} 0.0
```

```
41:# HELP gen_ai_client_operation_seconds
42:# TYPE gen_ai_client_operation_seconds summary
43:gen_ai_client_operation_seconds_count{error="none",gen_ai_operation_
name="chat",gen_ai_request_model="gpt-4o-mini",gen_ai_response_
model="gpt-4o-mini-2024-07-18",gen_ai_system="openai"} 1
44:gen_ai_client_operation_seconds_sum{error="none",gen_ai_operation_
name="chat",gen_ai_request_model="gpt-4o-mini",gen_ai_response_
model="gpt-4o-mini-2024-07-18",gen_ai_system="openai"} 1.262631313
45:# HELP gen_ai_client_operation_seconds_max
46:# TYPE gen_ai_client_operation_seconds_max gauge
47:gen_ai_client_operation_seconds_max{error="none",gen_ai_operation_
name="chat",gen_ai_request_model="gpt-4o-mini",gen_ai_response_
model="gpt-4o-mini-2024-07-18",gen_ai_system="openai"} 0.0
48:# HELP gen_ai_client_token_usage_total Measures number of input and
output tokens used
49:# TYPE gen_ai_client_token_usage_total counter
50:gen_ai_client_token_usage_total{gen_ai_operation_name="chat",gen_
ai_request_model="gpt-4o-mini",gen_ai_response_model="gpt-4o-
mini-2024-07-18",gen_ai_system="openai",gen_ai_token_type="input"} 26.0
51:gen_ai_client_token_usage_total{gen_ai_operation_name="chat",gen_
ai_request_model="gpt-4o-mini",gen_ai_response_model="gpt-4o-
mini-2024-07-18",gen_ai_system="openai",gen_ai_token_type="output"} 18.0
52:gen_ai_client_token_usage_total{gen_ai_operation_name="chat",gen_
ai_request_model="gpt-4o-mini",gen_ai_response_model="gpt-4o-
mini-2024-07-18",gen_ai_system="openai",gen_ai_token_type="total"} 44.0
204:spring_ai_advisor_active_seconds_count{gen_ai_operation_
name="framework",gen_ai_system="spring_ai",spring_ai_advisor_
name="call",spring_ai_kind="advisor"} 0
205:spring_ai_advisor_active_seconds_sum{gen_ai_operation_
name="framework",gen_ai_system="spring_ai",spring_ai_advisor_
name="call",spring_ai_kind="advisor"} 0.0
208:spring_ai_advisor_active_seconds_max{gen_ai_operation_
name="framework",gen_ai_system="spring_ai",spring_ai_advisor_
name="call",spring_ai_kind="advisor"} 0.0
```

```
211:spring_ai_advisor_seconds_count{error="none",gen_ai_operation_
name="framework",gen_ai_system="spring_ai",spring_ai_advisor_
name="call",spring_ai_kind="advisor"} 1
212:spring_ai_advisor_seconds_sum{error="none",gen_ai_operation_
name="framework",gen_ai_system="spring_ai",spring_ai_advisor_
name="call",spring_ai_kind="advisor"} 1.524532722
215:spring_ai_advisor_seconds_max{error="none",gen_ai_operation_
name="framework",gen_ai_system="spring_ai",spring_ai_advisor_
name="call",spring_ai_kind="advisor"} 0.0
218:spring_ai_chat_client_active_seconds_count{gen_ai_operation_
name="framework",gen_ai_system="spring_ai",spring_ai_chat_client_
stream="false",spring_ai_kind="chat_client"} 0
219:spring_ai_chat_client_active_seconds_sum{gen_ai_operation_
name="framework",gen_ai_system="spring_ai",spring_ai_chat_client_
stream="false",spring_ai_kind="chat_client"} 0.0
222:spring_ai_chat_client_active_seconds_max{gen_ai_operation_
name="framework",gen_ai_system="spring_ai",spring_ai_chat_client_
stream="false",spring_ai_kind="chat_client"} 0.0
225:spring_ai_chat_client_seconds_count{error="none",gen_ai_operation_
name="framework",gen_ai_system="spring_ai",spring_ai_chat_client_
stream="false",spring_ai_kind="chat_client"} 1
226:spring_ai_chat_client_seconds_sum{error="none",gen_ai_operation_
name="framework",gen_ai_system="spring_ai",spring_ai_chat_client_
stream="false",spring_ai_kind="chat_client"} 1.537632519
229:spring_ai_chat_client_seconds_max{error="none",gen_ai_operation_
name="framework",gen_ai_system="spring_ai",spring_ai_chat_client_
stream="false",spring_ai_kind="chat_client"} 0.0
```

Since we are currently in the observation section of ChatClient, let's focus on some of the observation values captured.

1. `spring`.ai.chat.client.advisors: You can see the call as one of the advisors in the logs.

   ```
   Starting observation: spring.ai.chat.client [keyValue(spring.
   ai.chat.client.advisors=["call"])]
   ```

2. `spring.ai.chat.client.conversation.id`: This is logged in case of memory-enabled chat.

3. `spring.ai`.chat.client.tool.names: This is not available since we do not have any tools used for our chat client. In case we use it, the tool list should be populated here.

There are useful metrics and observations for the use of the ChatClient API.

Observing Chat Model Requests

Observability features are currently available only for ChatModel implementations from the following AI model providers: Anthropic, Azure OpenAI, Mistral AI, Ollama, OpenAI, Vertex AI, MiniMax, Moonshot, QianFan, and Zhiu AI. Support for additional providers will be added in a future release of Spring AI.

The `gen_ai.client.operation` observations are captured when the call or stream methods of a ChatModel API are invoked. These observations track the duration of method execution and propagate associated tracing data.

The `gen_ai.client.token.usage` metrics report the number of input and output tokens consumed by a single model invocation.

Let's integrate the chat model request into the application file, as shown next. I have commented out the call to `makeChatClientRequest()` so as to focus on the chat model request.

File: ./src/main/java/com/example/demo/DemoApplication.java

```
package com.example.demo;

import org.springframework.ai.chat.client.ChatClient;
import org.springframework.ai.chat.model.ChatModel;
import org.springframework.ai.chat.prompt.Prompt;
import org.springframework.boot.CommandLineRunner;
import org.springframework.boot.SpringApplication;
import org.springframework.boot.autoconfigure.SpringBootApplication;
import org.springframework.context.annotation.Bean;

@SpringBootApplication
public class DemoApplication {

    private ChatClient chatClient;
```

```
    public static void main(String[] args) {
        SpringApplication.run(DemoApplication.class, args);
    }

    @Bean
    public CommandLineRunner run(ChatClient.Builder chatClientBuilder,
    ChatModel chatModel) {
        chatClient = chatClientBuilder.build();

        return args -> {
            //makeChatClientRequest();
            makeChatModelRequest(chatModel);
        };
    }

    private void makeChatClientRequest() {
        String response = chatClient.prompt("You are a professional
        comedian. Tell a joke.")
                .user("Tell me a joke.")
                .call()
                .content();
        System.out.println(response);
    }

    private void makeChatModelRequest(ChatModel chatModel) {
        String response = chatModel.call(
                new Prompt("Tell me a joke.")
        ).getResult().getOutput().getText();
        System.out.println(response);
    }
}
```

As per the documentation, Table 18-4 and Table 18-5 show the low and high cardinality keys that are available to capture. The low cardinality keys and values are highlighted in blue (this also includes the high cardinality key values) in the logs, and the high ones are highlighted in green.

***Table 18-4.** Low Cardinality Keys for Chat Model Request*

Name	Description
gen_ai.operation.name	The name of the operation being performed
gen_ai.system	The model provider as identified by the client instrumentation
gen_ai.request.model	The name of the model a request is being made to
gen_ai.response.model	The name of the model that generated the response

***Table 18-5.** High Cardinality Keys for Chat Model Request*

Name	Description
gen_ai.request.frequency_penalty	The frequency penalty setting for the model request.
gen_ai.request.max_tokens	The maximum number of tokens the model generates for a request.
gen_ai.request.presence_penalty	The presence penalty setting for the model request.
gen_ai.request.stop_sequences	List of sequences that the model will use to stop generating further tokens.
gen_ai.request.temperature	The temperature setting for the model request.
gen_ai.request.top_k	The top_k sampling setting for the model request.
gen_ai.request.top_p	The top_p sampling setting for the model request.
gen_ai.response.finish_reasons	Reasons the model stopped generating tokens, corresponding to each generation received.
gen_ai.response.id	The unique identifier for the AI response.
gen_ai.usage.input_tokens	The number of tokens used in the model input (prompt).
gen_ai.usage.output_tokens	The number of tokens used in the model output (completion).
gen_ai.usage.total_tokens	The total number of tokens used in the model exchange.
gen_ai.prompt	The full prompt sent to the model. Optional.
gen_ai.completion	The full response received from the model. Optional.
spring.ai.model.request.tool.names	List of tool definitions provided to the model in the request.

All the keys are instrumentation values that can help you see the usage of the model, see the number of tokens used in input and output, and set metrics around them for alert and auditability purposes. The keys marked in red are not applicable and will be updated in the documentation in the near future per GitHub.

Let's boot up the application and see the logs in action:

Output:

```
Starting observation: gen_ai.client.operation
[keyValue(gen_ai.request.temperature=0.7)]
Starting observation: [keyValue(gen_ai.operation.name=chat),keyValue(gen_
ai.request.model=gpt-4o-mini),keyValue(gen_ai.request.
temperature=0.7),keyValue(gen_ai.response.model=none),keyValue(gen_
ai.system=openai)]
Starting observation: http.client.requests
[keyValue(http.url=https://api.openai.com/v1/chat/completions)]
Starting observation: [keyValue(client.name=api.openai.com),keyValue(except
ion=none),keyValue(http.url=https://api.openai.com/v1/chat/completions),
keyValue(method=POST),keyValue(outcome=UNKNOWN),keyValue(status=CLIENT_
ERROR),keyValue(uri=/v1/chat/completions)]
Completed observation: http.client.requests
[keyValue(http.url=https://api.openai.com/v1/chat/completions)]
Completed observation: [keyValue(client.name=api.openai.com),keyValue(except
ion=none),keyValue(http.url=https://api.openai.com/v1/chat/completions),key
Value(method=POST),keyValue(outcome=SUCCESS),keyValue(status=200),keyValue(
uri=/v1/chat/completions)]
2025-05-20T11:21:40.866Z DEBUG 4301 --- [demo] [main]
[682c65c3e0d76277870689be18092c9f-870689be18092c9f]
ChatModelPromptContentObservationHandler : Chat Model Prompt Content:
["Tell me a joke."]
Completed observation: gen_ai.client.operation
[keyValue(gen_ai.request.temperature=0.7),keyValue(gen_ai.response.finish_
reasons=["STOP"]),keyValue(gen_ai.response.id=chatcmpl-BZFKOVpyfkfuOnzxOwf
LLJSKCoeaK),keyValue(gen_ai.usage.input_tokens=12),keyValue(gen_ai.usage.
output_tokens=18),keyValue(gen_ai.usage.total_tokens=30)]
```

```
Completed observation: [keyValue(gen_ai.operation.
name=chat),keyValue(gen_ai.request.model=gpt-4o-mini),keyValue(gen_
ai.request.temperature=0.7),keyValue(gen_ai.response.finish_
reasons=["STOP"]),keyValue(gen_ai.response.id=chatcmpl-BZFKOVp
yfkfuOnzxOwfLLJSKCoeaK),keyValue(gen_ai.response.model=gpt-4o-
mini-2024-07-18),keyValue(gen_ai.system=openai),keyValue(gen_ai.usage.
input_tokens=12),keyValue(gen_ai.usage.output_tokens=18),keyValue(gen_
ai.usage.total_tokens=30)]
Why did the scarecrow win an award?
Because he was outstanding in his field!
```

Similarly, there are observation metrics and traces covering low and high cardinality keys for the following APIs that can be captured when the respective APIs are called. I won't go into the details of showing them as they are very self-explanatory and the previous instructions for some of the calls should provide enough guidance.

- Tool calling
- Vector store use
- Image prompt model calls
- Embedding model calls

Conclusion

Observability is a cornerstone of production-grade LLM applications. As this chapter has shown, embedding robust observability into your AI pipeline enables far more than just error tracking—it empowers proactive performance tuning, cost control, compliance assurance, and model quality analysis.

Using Spring AI and LangChain4j, the chapter demonstrated how to instrument key components of an LLM system with detailed metrics and traces. You saw how to monitor ChatClient and ChatModel invocations, track token usage, and capture prompt-level context for debugging. The chapter also covered how to expose these observations through familiar tools like Micrometer, Prometheus, and tracing frameworks to build actionable dashboards and alerts.

Ultimately, observability transforms your LLM system from a black box into a transparent, measurable, and improvable asset. It shortens feedback loops, strengthens reliability, and fosters operational resilience. As LLMs continue to evolve and become more tightly integrated into critical applications, observability will be the guardrail that keeps them performant, predictable, and accountable at scale.

The next chapter covers the current state of machine learning in the Java ecosystem.

CHAPTER 19

Native-Speed Machine Learning in Java: DJL, ONNX, and JNI

The goal of this chapter is to understand the current state of machine learning in Java along with considering practical aspects.

Introduction

Machine learning is no longer confined to Python ecosystems. As the demand for production-grade, scalable AI solutions grows, Java has emerged as a capable player in the machine learning landscape. Whether you're building backend microservices, real-time APIs, or enterprise-grade applications, Java offers powerful tools for integrating and deploying machine learning workflows.

This chapter explores the evolving landscape of machine learning in Java, offering a practical guide to integrating modern AI into Java-based applications. It begins by showcasing how developers can leverage pretrained models using Hugging Face APIs and continues with native approaches like the Deep Java Library (DJL) for model hosting and inference. It also covers ONNX runtime for cross-platform model portability, Java Native Interface (JNI) for integrating high-performance native ML runtimes, and DL4J for training and fine-tuning models entirely within the JVM. The chapter concludes with an overview of Apache OpenNLP, a robust library for performing core NLP tasks in Java.

By combining low-level control with high-level abstractions, Java now provides a full-stack experience for machine learning—from data preparation to inference—entirely within its familiar, type-safe ecosystem.

S. K. Sahu, *Generative AI-Driven Application Development with Java*,
https://doi.org/10.1007/979-8-8688-1609-3_19

Using Hugging Face APIs in Java

Hugging Face is a leading platform in the machine learning ecosystem, particularly known for its extensive repository of state-of-the-art pretrained models in natural language processing (NLP), computer vision, and more. With an emphasis on accessibility and open-source collaboration, Hugging Face allows developers to easily integrate powerful models like GPT, BERT, T5, and Falcon into their applications via hosted inference APIs or locally deployed solutions.

Accessing Hugging Face Models via an API

To interact with Hugging Face models from a Java application, you can use their REST-based Inference API. This API provides a unified way to send inputs to a model and receive outputs such as generated text, classification results, or embeddings. Figure 19-1 shows the flow.

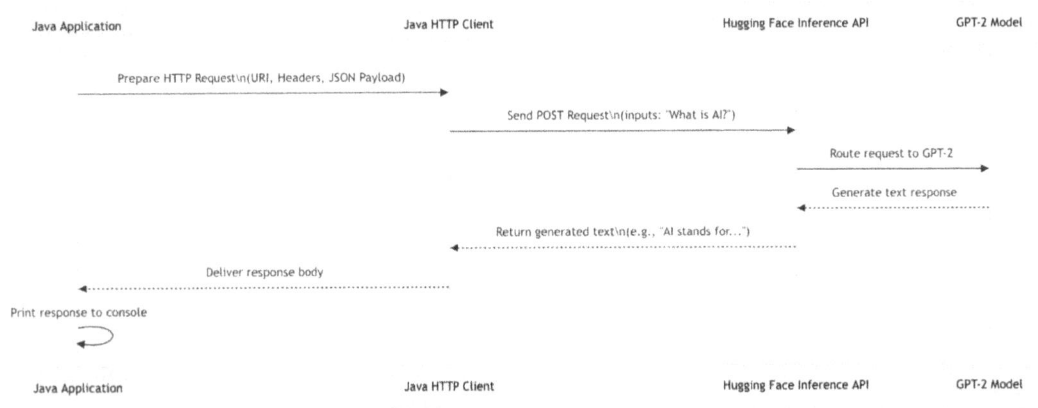

***Figure 19-1.** Request-response flow through different components*

Here's an example of how you can invoke a text generation model (like GPT-2) directly from Java using native HTTP libraries:

```
import java.net.URI;
import java.net.http.HttpClient;
import java.net.http.HttpRequest;
import java.net.http.HttpResponse;
```

```
public class HuggingFaceExample {
    public static void main(String[] args) throws Exception {
        String apiKey = "YOUR_API_KEY";
        String input = "{\"inputs\": \"What is AI?\"}";

        HttpClient client = HttpClient.newHttpClient();
        HttpRequest request = HttpRequest.newBuilder()
                .uri(URI.create("https://api-inference.huggingface.co/
                models/gpt2"))
                .header("Authorization", "Bearer " + apiKey)
                .header("Content-Type", "application/json")
                .POST(HttpRequest.BodyPublishers.ofString(input))
                .build();

        HttpResponse<String> response = client.send(request, HttpResponse.
        BodyHandlers.ofString());
        System.out.println(response.body());
    }
}
```

This approach is lightweight and flexible, suitable for creating wrappers around different models and use cases—just as you would when integrating OpenAI APIs.

Creating Java Wrappers for Inference

To encapsulate and reuse API calls across your Java application, you can abstract the logic into service classes or utility methods. This pattern enhances testability, reusability, and configuration flexibility. Consider building a `HuggingFaceClient` class that handles authentication, request preparation, and response parsing.

These wrappers can be adapted to support different tasks such as:

- Text generation
- Text classification
- Translation
- Embedding extraction

You can extend your wrapper to dynamically choose models by passing the model ID as a parameter or configuring it via external properties. Figure 19-2 shows a sample block representation.

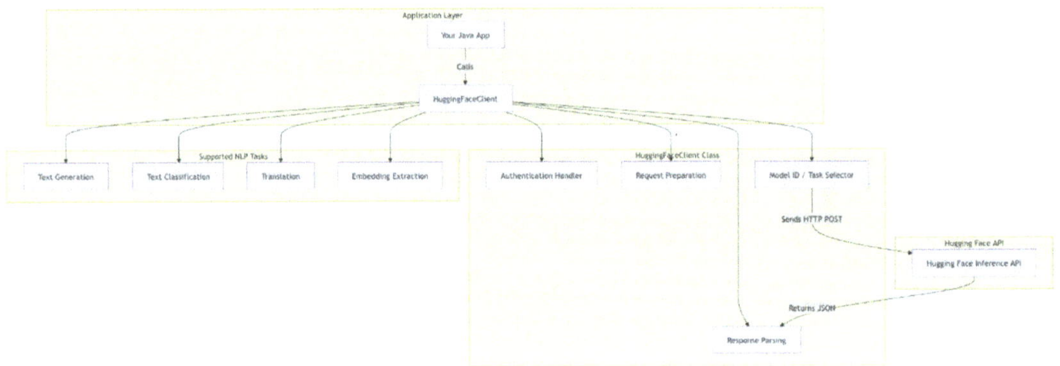

Figure 19-2. *Inference wrappers for HuggingFace client*

Integration via Frameworks

While direct API integration offers maximum control, Java frameworks like Spring AI and Quarkus with LangChain4j simplify the use of Hugging Face models through auto-configuration, dependency injection, and seamless service abstraction.

Spring AI

Spring AI provides first-class support for Hugging Face chat models and inference endpoints through minimal configuration. With the right properties in your `application.properties` or `application.yml` file, Spring Boot applications can use dependency injection to access a `HuggingfaceChatModel` bean, enabling text generation with minimal boilerplate.

Advantages:

- Declarative configuration
- Seamless integration into Spring Boot lifecycle
- Support for environment variable-based security
- Bill of materials (BOM) support for version consistency

Developers can also override configurations programmatically, allowing for custom authentication, dynamic endpoint selection, or runtime switching between models.

Quarkus + LangChain4j

For developers using Quarkus, the `langchain4j` extension supports Hugging Face integration with declarative configuration. Quarkus allows for enabling or disabling specific model types (chat, embedding, moderation), setting inference endpoint URLs, and adjusting generation parameters (like temperature, max tokens, top-k, top-p).

Advantages:

- Fast startup and low memory footprint for cloud-native deployments
- Build-time and runtime configurations
- Integrated model lifecycle management
- Support for both cloud-hosted and local Hugging Face models

Quarkus makes it easy to switch between OpenAI, Hugging Face, and other providers, which is ideal for applications that need flexibility or fallback options.

Hugging Face empowers Java developers to use LLMs through:

- **Direct REST API**: Customizable, lightweight, and framework-agnostic
- **Framework integration**: Simplified setup via Spring AI or Quarkus LangChain4j
- **Text Generation Inference (TGI)**: High-performance deployment options for large-scale use

Whether you're building simple utilities or enterprise-grade applications, Hugging Face's ecosystem and APIs provide the flexibility to innovate quickly with cutting-edge AI models.

Deep Java Library (DJL)

DJL is an open-source, high-level Java framework for deep learning that works seamlessly with multiple underlying engines. This is an initiative from Amazon. Designed with Java developers in mind, DJL feels just like any other Java library—easy to include in your projects, simple to use within your favorite IDE, and approachable even if you're new to machine learning.

With DJL, you don't need to be an expert in neural networks to get started. You can leverage your existing Java skills to build, train, and deploy models without leaving the JVM. DJL handles the details: it automatically detects and utilizes your hardware's CPU or GPU for optimal performance and lets you swap out deep learning engines (such as TensorFlow, PyTorch, or MXNet) at any time, giving you full flexibility to choose—or change—your backend.

DJL's intuitive, ergonomic API guides you through common deep learning tasks according to best practices. Whether you're prototyping a model, running inference in production, or embedding AI capabilities directly into a Java application, DJL provides a native, streamlined experience that keeps you focused on solving problems—not wrestling with toolchains. Figure 19-3 is the overall component architecture of the DJL framework.

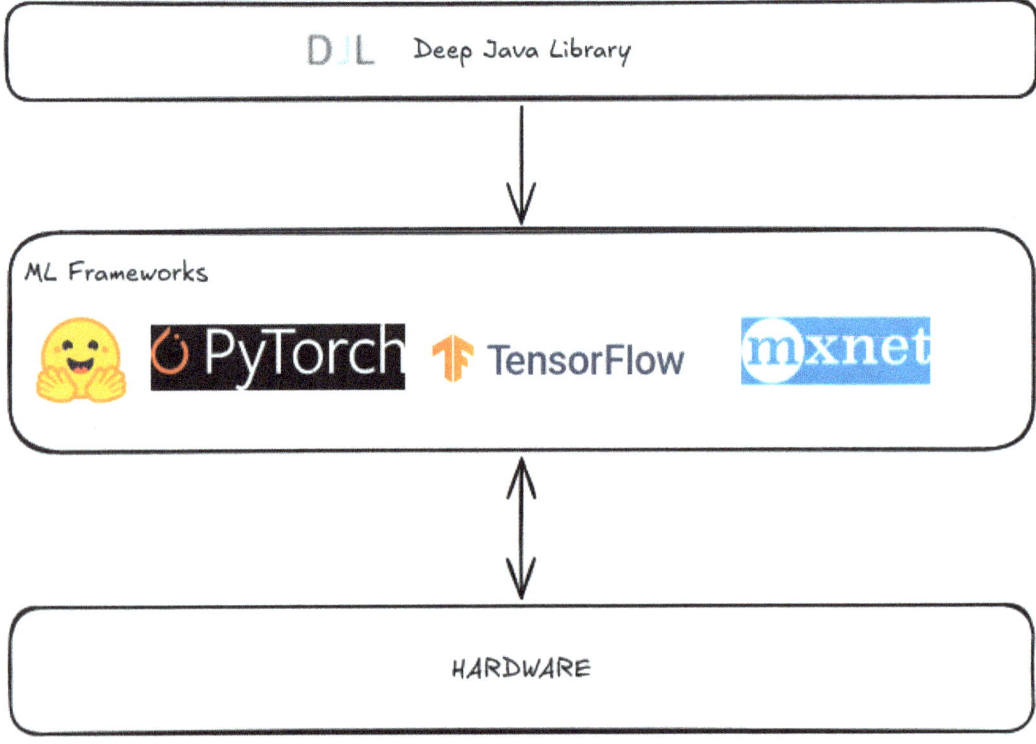

Figure 19-3. *DJL architecture*

Hosting and Inference Using DJL

Inference (or inferencing) in machine learning is the process of using a trained model to make predictions or decisions on new, unseen data. In this section, you will build a small application to help one of your customers who is into health-specific exercise suggestions. Based on the customers and users' physiological attributes, they suggest the number of iterations of exercises they will need to do. To do this, you will host an ONNX-based model which will help you predict these for your customers.

The model is available in the resources directory of the project for this chapter. You can also create this model by running the following code in a free Google Colab instance at `https://colab.research.google.com/`:

```
# -*- coding: utf-8 -*-
"""onnx_model_generation.ipynb

Automatically generated by Colab.

"""

!pip install skl2onnx onnxruntime

from sklearn.ensemble import RandomForestRegressor
from skl2onnx import to_onnx
from skl2onnx.common.data_types import FloatTensorType

# 1) Fit a RandomForestRegressor
rgr = RandomForestRegressor()
rgr.fit(X_train, y_train)

# 2) Define the ONNX input type explicitly
initial_type = [("float_input", FloatTensorType([None, X.shape[1]]))]

# 3) Convert to ONNX
onx = to_onnx(rgr, initial_types=initial_type)

with open("model.onnx", "wb") as f:
f.write(onx.SerializeToString())

print(pred_onx)
```

```
import numpy as np
from sklearn.datasets import load_linnerud
from sklearn.model_selection import train_test_split
from sklearn.ensemble import RandomForestRegressor  # or
RandomForestClassifier
from skl2onnx import to_onnx
from skl2onnx.common.data_types import FloatTensorType
import onnxruntime as rt

# 1) Load & split data
X, y = load_linnerud(return_X_y=True)
X = X.astype(np.float32)
y = y.astype(np.float32)  # for regressor; if classifier, y must be
int labels

X_train, X_test, y_train, y_test = train_test_split(X, y, random_state=0)

# 2) Train
model = RandomForestRegressor(random_state=0)  # replace with
RandomForestClassifier() if doing classification
model.fit(X_train, y_train)

# 3) Convert to ONNX
initial_type = [("input", FloatTensorType([None, X.shape[1]]))]
onnx_model = to_onnx(model, initial_types=initial_type)

with open("model.onnx", "wb") as f:
f.write(onnx_model.SerializeToString())

# 4) Inference with ONNX Runtime
sess = rt.InferenceSession("model.onnx", providers=["CPUExecutionProvider"]
)
input_name  = sess.get_inputs()[0].name
output_name = sess.get_outputs()[0].name

# For regressor this is your continuous output;
# for classifier it'll be predicted label(s), and you can also fetch
probabilities
y_pred_onx = sess.run([output_name], {input_name: X_test})[0]
```

```
print("ONNX prediction shape:", y_pred_onx.shape)
print("First 5 ONNX predictions:\n", y_pred_onx[:5])
```

```
X_test
```

I will not focus too much on the model generation part since as developers we would probably use one created by the machine learning team. Once you have run the code using a GPU runtime in Google Colab, store this file in the resource directory.

This model has been created on top of the Linnerud dataset.

Understanding the Linnerud Dataset

The Linnerud dataset is a small, classic multi-output regression dataset commonly used in educational and prototyping contexts. It provides a simple yet effective example of how physiological metrics can be used to predict physical performance outcomes.

Originally collected in a fitness study, the dataset contains observations from 20 middle-aged men, measuring their physical characteristics alongside their performance on three types of exercises. This dataset is particularly useful for demonstrating supervised learning tasks where multiple continuous outputs are predicted simultaneously.

Dataset Structure

The dataset is composed of two CSV files representing features (inputs) and targets (outputs).

Physiological Data: Input Features (X)

These are the independent variables used as inputs for model training:

- **Weight**: Body weight (in kilograms)
- **Waist**: Waist circumference (in centimeters)
- **Pulse**: Resting pulse rate (beats per minute)

Exercise Data: Target Variables (Y)

These are the dependent variables or labels to be predicted:

- **Chins**: Number of chin-ups completed
- **Situps**: Number of sit-ups completed
- **Jumps**: Number of jumps (in centimeters)

Each row in the dataset corresponds to one individual and includes a set of physiological inputs and matching exercise outputs.

Use in Machine Learning

The Linnerud dataset is ideal for training and evaluating multi-output regression models, where the goal is to predict multiple continuous values simultaneously from a single input vector.

In our use case, we can train a regression model that takes a user's physiological profile (weight, waist, pulse) and predicts their expected performance in chins, situps, and jumps. Once trained, this model can be exported to the ONNX format, allowing it to be deployed across various platforms—including Java applications using ONNX Runtime.

Example Workflow:

1. **Preprocessing**: Normalize or scale the data as needed.
2. **Model training**: Use a regression algorithm (e.g., linear regression, MLP regressor) to map inputs to multiple outputs.
3. **ONNX export**: Save the trained model in ONNX format for cross-platform inference.
4. **Integration**: Load the ONNX model in a Java application and use it to predict exercise capacity based on user input.

Why Use This Toy Dataset?

While the Linnerud dataset is limited in size, it is excellent for:

- **Educational purposes**: Understanding the mechanics of multi-output regression
- **Proof of concept**: Testing model training and ONNX export pipelines
- **Integration testing**: Validating end-to-end inference in Java using small, manageable input/output dimensions

Building an ONNX Regression Model with the Linnerud Dataset

To predict user performance based on physiological metrics, you've selected the Linnerud dataset—a multi-output regression dataset ideal for small-scale model prototyping. The dataset's structure lends itself well to training models that can predict multiple targets simultaneously (e.g., predicting chin-ups, sit-ups, and jumps from weight, waist, and pulse).

Step-by-Step: Training and Exporting the Model

The model training and conversion process is implemented in Python using `scikit-learn` and `skl2onnx`. Here's a breakdown of each key step:

Step 1: Load and Prepare the Dataset

The dataset is loaded using `sklearn.datasets.load_linnerud()`, which returns physiological data as features (`X`) and exercise performance metrics as labels (`y`). Both are cast to `float32` to ensure compatibility with ONNX.

```
X, y = load_linnerud(return_X_y=True)
X = X.astype(np.float32)
y = y.astype(np.float32)
```

Step 2: Train a Regression Model

A `RandomForestRegressor` is trained using the Linnerud physiological data to predict the exercise outcomes. This model is capable of handling multi-output regression without modification.

```
model = RandomForestRegressor(random_state=0)
model.fit(X_train, y_train)
```

Step 3: Convert the Model to ONNX Format

The trained model is converted to ONNX using `skl2onnx.to_onnx()`. The input type is explicitly defined using `FloatTensorType`, with the shape based on the feature count (`X.shape[1]`).

```
initial_type = [("input", FloatTensorType([None, X.shape[1]]))]
onnx_model = to_onnx(model, initial_types=initial_type)

with open("model.onnx", "wb") as f:
   f.write(onnx_model.SerializeToString())
```

This produces a `model.onnx` file, which is portable and can be loaded in any ONNX-compatible runtime—including ONNX Runtime for Java.

Step 4: Test Inference in Python

To verify that the model behaves as expected, inference is run using `onnxruntime` in Python. This helps validate that the ONNX export was successful and gives a reference prediction to compare against during Java-side integration.

```
sess = rt.InferenceSession("model.onnx", providers=["CPUExecutionProvider"]
)
input_name  = sess.get_inputs()[0].name
output_name = sess.get_outputs()[0].name

y_pred_onx = sess.run([output_name], {input_name: X_test})[0]
```

Why This Workflow Works

This approach allows you to:

- Leverage Python's robust ML ecosystem for model training.
- Export to ONNX, a portable format.
- Use ONNX Runtime in Java to perform inference—eliminating the need for a Python runtime in production.
- Apply predictions in a Java-based system (e.g., Spring Boot API) using user inputs like weight, waist, and pulse.

Now that you have the ONNX format based model available to use, you can host it using Spring Boot. Let's build a starter template using Spring Initializr, as shown in Figure 19-4.

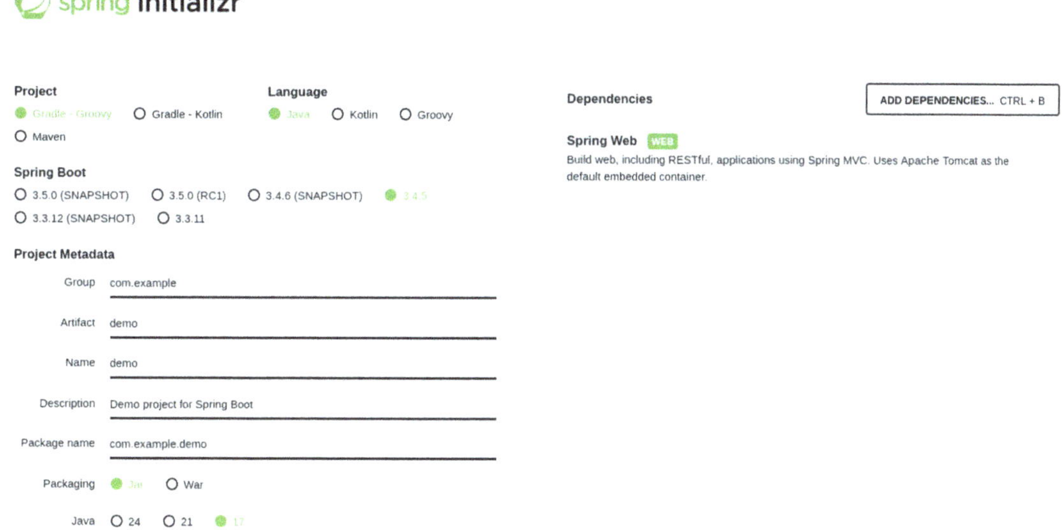

Figure 19-4. *Spring Initializr for ONNX model hosting*

First, we will update the build.gradle file with our onnxruntime-engine library dependency from DJL as shown here:

File: ./build.gradle

```
plugins {
    id 'java'
    id 'org.springframework.boot' version '3.4.5'
    id 'io.spring.dependency-management' version '1.1.7'
}

group = 'com.example'
version = '0.0.1-SNAPSHOT'

java {
    toolchain {
        languageVersion = JavaLanguageVersion.of(17)
    }
}

repositories {
    mavenCentral()
}
ext {
    set('aiDjlVersion', "0.33.0")
}

dependencies {
    implementation 'org.springframework.boot:spring-boot-starter-web'
    implementation 'ai.djl.onnxruntime:onnxruntime-engine'
    testImplementation 'org.springframework.boot:spring-boot-starter-test'
    testRuntimeOnly 'org.junit.platform:junit-platform-launcher'
}

dependencyManagement {
    imports {
        mavenBom "ai.djl:bom:${aiDjlVersion}"
    }
}
```

```
tasks.named('test') {
    useJUnitPlatform()
}
```

Let's now create a few model POJOs for the request and response objects as follows:

File: ./src/main/java/com/example/demo/model/PhysiologicalInput.java

```
package com.example.demo.model;

public class PhysiologicalInput {

    public float weight;
    public float waist;
    public float pulse;

    public PhysiologicalInput(float weight, float waist, float pulse) {
        this.weight = weight;
        this.waist = waist;
        this.pulse = pulse;
    }
}
```

File: ./src/main/java/com/example/demo/model/PredictionResponse.java

```
package com.example.demo.model;

public record PredictionResponse(int chins, int situps, int jumps) {}
```

To perform inference on an ONNX-based regression model from a Java application, you will use DJL—a high-level framework designed to bring deep learning to the JVM. In this setup, the input to the model is represented by a custom class called PhysiologicalInput, which captures three physiological features: weight, waist, and pulse. These features are passed into a custom Translator class named PhysiologyTranslator, which implements NoBatchifyTranslator<PhysiologicalInput, float[]>. Inside the processInput() method, the physiological values are assembled into a float array and converted into a DJL-compatible NDArray with a shape of (1, 3) using the following line:

```
NDArray array = ctx.getNDManager().create(data, new Shape(1, 3));
```

This preprocessing step ensures that the model receives input in the same format it was trained on. Once the model produces an output, the processOutput() method extracts the result as a simple float array.

```
float[] data = list.get(0).toFloatArray();
```

This output corresponds to the predicted number of chins, situps, and jumps, making it a multi-output regression task.

File: ./src/main/java/com/example/demo/ml/PhysiologyTranslator.java

```
package com.example.demo.ml;

import ai.djl.ndarray.NDArray;
import ai.djl.ndarray.NDList;
import ai.djl.ndarray.types.Shape;
import ai.djl.translate.NoBatchifyTranslator;
import ai.djl.translate.TranslatorContext;
import com.example.demo.model.PhysiologicalInput;

public class PhysiologyTranslator
        implements NoBatchifyTranslator<PhysiologicalInput, float[]> {

    public PhysiologyTranslator() {}

    @Override
    public NDList processInput(TranslatorContext ctx, PhysiologicalInput
    input) {
        float[] data = {input.waist, input.weight, input.pulse};
        NDArray array = ctx.getNDManager().create(data, new Shape(1, 3));
        return new NDList(array);
    }

    @Override
    public float[] processOutput(TranslatorContext ctx, NDList list) {
        float[] data = list.get(0).toFloatArray();
        return data;
    }
}
```

The model itself is loaded using DJL's Criteria API, which specifies the input/output types, the ONNX model location, and the use of the OnnxRuntime engine:

```
Criteria.builder()
        .setTypes(PhysiologicalInput.class, float[].class)
        .optModelUrls(modelLocation)
        .optTranslator(new PhysiologyTranslator())
        .optEngine("OnnxRuntime")
        .build();
```

File: ./src/main/java/com/example/demo/configuration/ModelConfiguration.java

```
package com.example.demo.configuration;

import ai.djl.inference.Predictor;
import ai.djl.repository.zoo.Criteria;
import ai.djl.repository.zoo.ZooModel;
import com.example.demo.ml.PhysiologyTranslator;
import com.example.demo.model.PhysiologicalInput;
import org.springframework.beans.factory.annotation.Qualifier;
import org.springframework.context.annotation.Bean;
import org.springframework.context.annotation.Configuration;

import java.util.function.Supplier;

@Configuration
public class ModelConfiguration {

    @Bean
    public Criteria<PhysiologicalInput, float[]> criteria() {
        String modelLocation = Thread.currentThread()
                .getContextClassLoader()
                .getResource("model.onnx")
                .getPath();

        return Criteria.builder()
                .setTypes(PhysiologicalInput.class, float[].class)
                .optModelUrls(modelLocation)
```

```
                .optTranslator(new PhysiologyTranslator())
                .optEngine("OnnxRuntime")
                .build();
    }

    @Bean
    public ZooModel<PhysiologicalInput, float[]> model(
            @Qualifier("criteria") Criteria<PhysiologicalInput, float[]>
            criteria)
            throws Exception {
        return criteria.loadModel();
    }

    @Bean
    public Supplier<Predictor<PhysiologicalInput, float[]>>
    predictorProvider(ZooModel<PhysiologicalInput, float[]> model) {
        return model::newPredictor;
    }
}
```

This model configuration is defined as a Spring @Bean and injected into the application context, making it easy to manage lifecycle and dependencies.

Finally, inference is exposed through a REST API in the ExerciseMetricInferenceController class. The controller defines a POST endpoint at /inference, which accepts JSON input, invokes the model using a Predictor, and maps the raw float outputs into a structured PredictionResponse.

```
float[] response = predictor.predict(physiologicalInput);
return new PredictionResponse((int) response[0], (int) response[1], (int)
response[2]);
```

File: ./src/main/java/com/example/demo/controller/ExerciseMetricInferenceController.java

```
package com.example.demo.controller;

import ai.djl.inference.Predictor;
import ai.djl.translate.TranslateException;
import com.example.demo.model.PredictionResponse;
```

```
import com.example.demo.model.PhysiologicalInput;
import jakarta.annotation.Resource;
import org.springframework.web.bind.annotation.PostMapping;
import org.springframework.web.bind.annotation.RequestBody;
import org.springframework.web.bind.annotation.RestController;

import java.util.function.Supplier;

@RestController
public class ExerciseMetricInferenceController {
    @Resource
    private Supplier<Predictor<PhysiologicalInput, float[]>>
    predictorSupplier;

    @PostMapping("/inference")
    PredictionResponse detectExerciseMetric(@RequestBody PhysiologicalInput
    physiologicalInput)
            throws TranslateException {
        try (var p = predictorSupplier.get()) {
            float[] response = p.predict(physiologicalInput);
            return new PredictionResponse(((int) response[0]), (int)
            response[1], (int) response[2]);
        }
    }
}
```

This end-to-end integration demonstrates how DJL simplifies loading ONNX models, handling input/output translation, and deploying inference in production-ready Spring Boot applications. It mirrors DJL's well-known Iris example but applies it to a real-world regression problem using a custom-trained model and domain-specific data.

Let's boot up our application and see the result in action by making a curl request. You will set up some DJL library-specific logs on boot-up. These are only informational at this stage.

```
2025-05-21T10:39:35.490Z  WARN 2223 --- [demo] [main] ai.djl.repository.
SimpleRepository      : Simple repository pointing to a non-archive file.
```

```
2025-05-21T10:39:35.756Z  WARN 2223 --- [demo] [main] ai.djl.onnxruntime.
engine.OrtEngine      : CUDA is not supported OnnxRuntime engine: Error
code - ORT_EP_FAIL - message: Failed to find CUDA shared provider
2025-05-21T10:39:35.767Z  INFO 2223 --- [demo] [main] ai.djl.onnxruntime.
engine.OrtModel       : Onnx extension not found in classpath.
```

```
curl -X POST http://localhost:8080/inference   -H "Content-Type:
application/json"   -d '{"weight": 70.5, "waist": 32.0, "pulse": 72.0}'
```

Output:

```
{"chins":190,"situps":36,"jumps":53}
```

So, for a customer who has physiological attributes similar to the previous, they need to perform 100 chin-ups, 36 sit-ups, and 53 jumps. Our customers are very happy after this API integration to their health app, which helps them decide the number of exercises of each type. Figure 19-5 shows the overall request-response control flow.

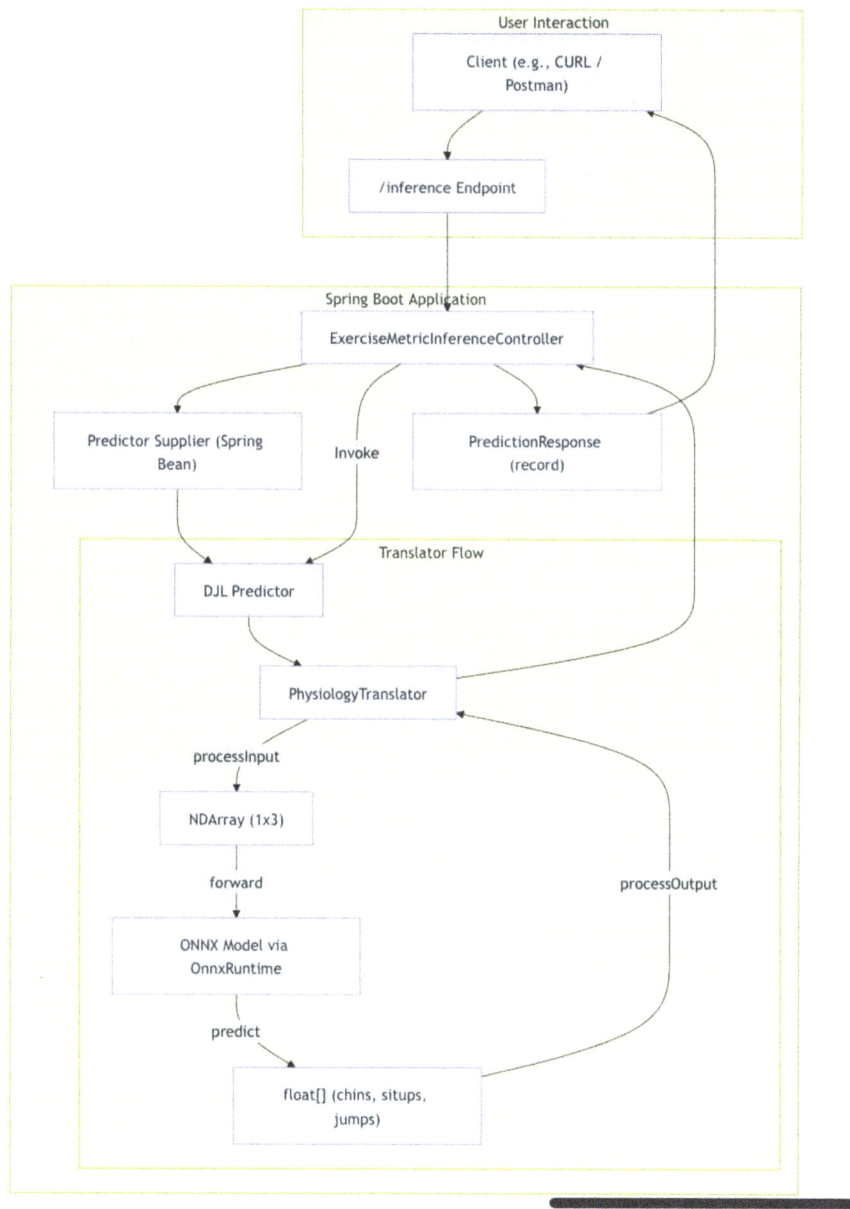

Figure 19-5. *Onnx regression inference flow in Spring*

Integrating LLMs Using Java Native Interface

Java Native Interface (JNI) is a standard mechanism provided by the Java platform that enables Java code to interact with native applications and libraries written in languages like C, C++, or even Python (indirectly via bridges). It serves two primary purposes:

- **Calling native code from Java**: Enables execution of native functions (e.g., C/C++ libraries) from within a Java application.
- **Embedding the JVM in native applications**: Allows non-Java applications to embed and use the Java Virtual Machine (JVM).

JNI is particularly valuable in scenarios where high performance is essential, such as integrating with native machine learning inference engines or LLMs deployed in C++ or Python environments.

Why Use JNI for LLM Integration?

While Java is portable and secure, it may not always provide the lowest-level performance for compute-intensive operations. Many state-of-the-art LLMs are implemented in Python (via frameworks like PyTorch) or C++ (e.g., GGML-based runtimes). JNI allows developers to bridge the gap and directly call into these native implementations, resulting in:

- Improved inference speed
- Reduced overhead from inter-process communication
- Fine-grained control over memory and model execution

However, JNI comes with trade-offs—most notably, the added complexity of memory management and the loss of some Java safety guarantees.

Sample JNI Integration with a Native LLM

The following is a simple example showing how a Java application might use JNI to invoke a function implemented in a native shared library (e.g., a C++ backend for an LLM):

```
public class JNILlmIntegrationExample {
    static {
        System.loadLibrary("nativeLLM"); // Loads the native shared library
        (e.g., libnativeLLM.so or nativeLLM.dll)
   }

    // Native method declaration
   public native String runLLM(String input);

    public static void main(String[] args) {
        JNILlmIntegrationExample integration = new
        JNILlmIntegrationExample();
        String output = integration.runLLM("What is artificial
        intelligence?");
        System.out.println("LLM Response: " + output);
    }
}
```

Behind the Scenes

To make the previous example work, the following steps are generally required:

1. Generate the header file from the Java class using `javac` and `javah` (or `javac -h`).
2. Implement the native method in C or C++, compiling it into a shared library.
3. Load the library at runtime with `System.loadLibrary`.

The native method could then call into an optimized C++ inference engine (e.g., llama.cpp) or wrap Python-based models using embedding tools like `pybind11`.

When to Use JNI for LLMs

JNI is most appropriate when:

- You need ultra-low latency inference, such as on-device or edge computing.

- You're working with an existing native codebase and want to avoid rewriting logic in Java.
- Memory usage and threading must be tightly controlled, such as with large GPU/CPU-bound models.

Considerations

Note the following:

- Error handling and debugging can be more complex across the Java-native boundary.
- Platform-specific dependencies require careful management for cross-platform support.
- Garbage collection coordination between Java and native code is essential to avoid leaks or crashes.

By using JNI, Java applications can tap directly into the power of native LLMs while still leveraging Java's ecosystem for orchestration, interfaces, and integration. It's a powerful, albeit advanced, technique for performance-critical AI workloads.

Running Inference in Java with ONNX Runtime

The Open Neural Network Exchange (ONNX) format is a widely supported standard for representing machine learning models trained in frameworks like PyTorch, TensorFlow, and scikit-learn. It allows developers to export models into a framework-agnostic format and run them across multiple platforms and environments.

To leverage these models in Java applications, the ONNX Runtime (ORT) provides official Java bindings. This enables developers to execute high-performance inference directly on the JVM without relying on Python or other external runtimes.

Why Use ONNX Runtime in Java?

Using ONNX Runtime in Java offers several benefits:

- **Cross-framework support**: Run models trained in different ML frameworks using a consistent Java API.
- **Hardware acceleration**: Supports CPU and GPU backends, making it suitable for scalable deployments.
- **Minimal dependencies**: No Python runtime required—everything runs natively on the JVM.

Getting Started with ONNX Runtime for Java

To use ONNX Runtime in your Java project, include the ONNX Runtime Java bindings in your build system (e.g., via Maven or Gradle). Then, you can load a pretrained model and run inference as follows.

Here's a basic example using a dummy input tensor with a different setup than the original example:

```
import ai.onnxruntime.OnnxTensor;
import ai.onnxruntime.OrtEnvironment;
import ai.onnxruntime.OrtSession;
import ai.onnxruntime.OrtException;

import java.nio.FloatBuffer;
import java.util.Collections;
import java.util.Map;

public class ONNXInferenceDemo {
    public static void main(String[] args) throws OrtException {
        // Initialize ONNX environment and session with a model
       OrtEnvironment environment = OrtEnvironment.getEnvironment();
        OrtSession session = environment.createSession("classifier_
        model.onnx");
```

```
        // Create dummy input (e.g., a vector of 4 float values)
        float[] input = {1.0f, 0.5f, -1.2f, 3.3f};
        FloatBuffer buffer = FloatBuffer.wrap(input);
        long[] shape = {1, 4}; // Shape must match model input

        OnnxTensor inputTensor = OnnxTensor.createTensor(environment,
        buffer, shape);

        // Perform inference
        Map<String, OnnxTensor> inputs = Collections.singletonMap("input_
        name", inputTensor);
        OrtSession.Result output = session.run(inputs);

        // Extract output tensor (e.g., classification scores)
        float[][] result = (float[][]) output.get(0).getValue();
        for (float score : result[0]) {
            System.out.println("Score: " + score);
        }
    }
}
```

Note Replace `input_name` with the actual input name from your ONNX model. This can be inspected using tools like Netron or programmatically via the session metadata.

Key Concepts

These are the key concepts:

- **OrtEnvironment**: The entry point to ONNX Runtime, managing global resources
- **OrtSession**: Represents a loaded ONNX model. You use this to run inference
- **OnnxTensor**: A wrapper around Java-native types (float, int, etc.) used for feeding data into the model

Use Cases

ONNX Runtime is well-suited for:

- **Java-based backend services** requiring ML predictions.
- **Microservices** that need to stay within the JVM ecosystem.
- **Desktop or Android applications** looking to embed efficient ML inference.

ONNX Runtime for Java bridges the gap between production-grade ML models and enterprise Java applications. By using the ONNX format and the ORT Java API, developers can deploy models without leaving the Java ecosystem—eliminating the overhead of external processes and improving performance in ML-enabled applications.

Model Training and Fine-Tuning Using DL4J

Eclipse Deeplearning4j (DL4J) is a comprehensive deep learning framework built specifically for the Java Virtual Machine (JVM). Unlike many popular ML frameworks that focus on Python, DL4J allows developers to train and deploy deep learning models entirely in Java, making it ideal for JVM-based systems, microservices, and enterprise-grade applications.

DL4J supports a wide variety of use cases—from training neural networks from scratch to importing and fine-tuning models built in other frameworks like PyTorch, TensorFlow, and Keras. Its design also bridges the Java and Python ecosystems through native interop features and Python execution bindings.

Key Components of the DL4J Suite

DL4J is more than just a training API—it's a full ecosystem composed of several modular libraries:

- **Deeplearning4j core**: High-level APIs for defining and training neural networks using `MultiLayerNetwork` or `ComputationGraph`.
- **SameDiff**: A low-level graph-based API, similar in spirit to TensorFlow or PyTorch, that supports dynamic graph definition and automatic differentiation.

- **ND4J**: A powerful Numpy-like library for Java, used for tensor computations and mathematical operations.
- **LibND4J**: A performance-optimized C++ backend for executing math operations across CPU, GPU, or specialized hardware.
- **DataVec**: A data transformation library that converts raw data into tensors, suitable for machine learning models.
- **Python4J**: A bridge to execute Python code from within Java, useful for hybrid workflows.
- **Apache Spark Integration**: Enables distributed model training on Spark clusters for handling large-scale datasets.

Training and Fine-Tuning Models

DL4J enables you to both train models from scratch and fine-tune pretrained ones. You can build models using either the high-level API (`MultiLayerConfiguration`, `ComputationGraphConfiguration`) or the lower-level SameDiff API.

Here are some example use cases:

- **Train a CNN on image data**: Using Tiny ImageNet or MNIST datasets.
- **Fine-tune a pretrained Keras model**: Import it into DL4J using `KerasModelImport` and retrain with your own dataset.
- **Custom NLP models**: Use word embeddings and LSTMs for classification tasks such as patent classification.

Note For running inference in parallel (e.g., batch serving), DL4J also supports parallelized inference pipelines.

Why Use DL4J?

DL4J is a strong choice when:

- You're operating in a Java-first environment (e.g., Spring Boot, JVM microservices).
- You want to avoid switching to Python for ML tasks.
- You need to integrate with Spark or other JVM-based big data tools.
- You're building for IoT, Android, or embedded systems where Java is more prevalent.

Open Source and Community

DL4J is open-source under the Apache 2.0 license, governed by the Eclipse Foundation. Contributions are welcome, and developers can explore examples, file issues, or submit pull requests via the official GitHub repositories.

Deeplearning4j enables full-cycle machine learning in Java—from preprocessing with DataVec to training with ND4J and SameDiff, and finally deploying models using ONNX or TensorFlow runtime interop. It's a JVM-native option that combines performance, flexibility, and production readiness for modern AI applications.

Natural Language Processing Using Apache OpenNLP

Apache OpenNLP is a pure-Java library that provides a range of ready-made tools for common NLP tasks. It's lightweight, engine-agnostic, and easy to drop into any Java application. Here's how it can help you add language understanding to your projects:

- **Sentence detection:** Split raw text into individual sentences.
- **Tokenization:** Break sentences into words or tokens.
- **Part-of-speech tagging:** Label each token with its grammatical role (noun, verb, adjective, etc.).

- **Named-entity recognition (NER):** Identify proper names such as people, places, dates, and organizations.
- **Chunking and parsing:** Extract phrase structure (noun phrases, verb phrases) or full parse trees.
- **Language detection:** Guess the language of a given text.

Getting Started

Here are the steps to get started:

1. Add the dependency to your build tool (Maven example):

```
<dependency>
    <groupId>org.apache.opennlp</groupId>
    <artifactId>opennlp-tools</artifactId>
    <version>2.5.4</version>
</dependency>
```

2. Load a pretrained model (models available on the Apache website):

```
try (InputStream modelIn = new FileInputStream("en-token.bin")) {
    TokenizerModel model = new TokenizerModel(modelIn);
    TokenizerME tokenizer = new TokenizerME(model);
    String[] tokens = tokenizer.tokenize("Hello, OpenNLP makes NLP
    in Java simple!");
}
```

3. Run a task, for example, named-entity recognition:

```
try (InputStream nerModelIn = new FileInputStream("en-ner-person.
bin")) {
    TokenNameFinderModel nerModel = new TokenNameFinderModel
    (nerModelIn);
    NameFinderME nameFinder = new NameFinderME(nerModel);
    Span[] names = nameFinder.find(tokens);
```

```
    for (Span name : names) {
        System.out.println("Entity: " +
                String.join(" ", Arrays.copyOfRange(tokens, name.
                getStart(), name.getEnd())));
    }
}
```

Why Use OpenNLP?

These are the reasons to use it:

- **No external dependencies**: Everything runs on the JVM.
- **Speed**: Optimized for production workloads.
- **Flexibility**: Swap in your own custom-trained models as your use case grows.
- **Simplicity:** A consistent, intuitive API surface for all tasks.

With Apache OpenNLP, you can rapidly prototype and deploy NLP pipelines—whether you need to analyze customer feedback, extract information from documents, or build chatbots—without leaving the Java ecosystem.

Conclusion

Java's capabilities in machine learning have matured significantly, enabling developers to build intelligent applications without switching ecosystems. Java provides high-level abstraction, excellent technical representation of concepts, and low-level control of details. As we've seen, there are multiple paths to bringing AI into the Java world—from consuming APIs hosted on Hugging Face to building and deploying ONNX models with DJL. Tools like the ONNX Runtime for Java and DL4J offer flexibility for both inference and training, while JNI bridges the gap to native runtimes when performance and custom integrations matter. Meanwhile, Apache OpenNLP showcases how natural language processing tasks can be seamlessly embedded into Java applications without introducing external dependencies.

This chapter demonstrates that Java is no longer just an enterprise or backend language—it is also a viable, powerful platform for modern machine learning. Whether you're consuming, serving, or training models, the Java ecosystem now supports every major phase of the ML lifecycle. With robust libraries, growing community support, and production-grade deployment options, Java is fully equipped to support AI-driven innovation across domains.

And now for reviewing the architecture of tomorrow in the LLM ecosystem in the next chapter.

CHAPTER 20

Architectures of Tomorrow: From Monoliths to Modular Minds

The goal of this chapter is to understand common paradigms and trends in the world of generative AI (Gen AI) with a focus on the future.

Introduction

We are standing at the edge of a generational shift in software architecture—one powered not by a new language, database, or protocol, but by intelligence itself. Large language models (LLMs) have moved far beyond novelty. They now function as reasoning engines, planning agents, creative partners, and autonomous decision-makers. Yet despite their power, it's not the models alone that define the future—it's how we architect, scale, deploy, and govern them.

In this chapter, you will explore the evolving world of generative AI architectures, not through the lens of hype but through the patterns, protocols, practices, and trade-offs that software developers and system architects must understand to build responsibly and effectively in this new frontier.

You will begin by tracing the shift from monolithic models to modular, scalable systems driven by trends like mixture-of-experts, retrieval-augmented generation (RAG), and agentic orchestration. You will examine the architectural spectrum—from open-source models

S. K. Sahu, *Generative AI-Driven Application Development with Java*,
https://doi.org/10.1007/979-8-8688-1609-3_20

deployed on commodity GPUs to proprietary cloud APIs offering turnkey multimodality. You will explore the rise of LLMOps, the emergence of interoperability protocols (like MCP, ACP, A2A, ANP), and how DevOps principles are transforming to support the complexity of AI-native applications.

You will also learn how traditional ecosystems, such as Java, are evolving to support these new paradigms and why governance, ethics, and developer responsibility must be first-class design concerns in any generative AI product. Above all, the chapter speaks to the developer—the engineer caught in the whirlwind of rapid change—who wonders how to stay afloat when "too much is happening." This chapter is a reminder: if your foundations are solid and your mindset is adaptable, you are already equipped for what's next.

Architectural and Scaling Trends in Generative AI: From Monoliths to Modular Intelligence

The evolution of Gen AI is no longer defined by the race to build ever-larger models. Instead, the field is maturing toward modular, scalable, and interoperable architectures that prioritize efficiency, specialization, and coordination across systems. From mixture-of-experts (MoE) to agentic frameworks and next-generation communication protocols, the architecture of Gen AI is becoming more distributed, context-aware, and capable of functioning in real-world, multi-agent environments. This section explores the key trends shaping this transition from monolithic LLMs to intelligent, modular systems (see Figure 20-1).

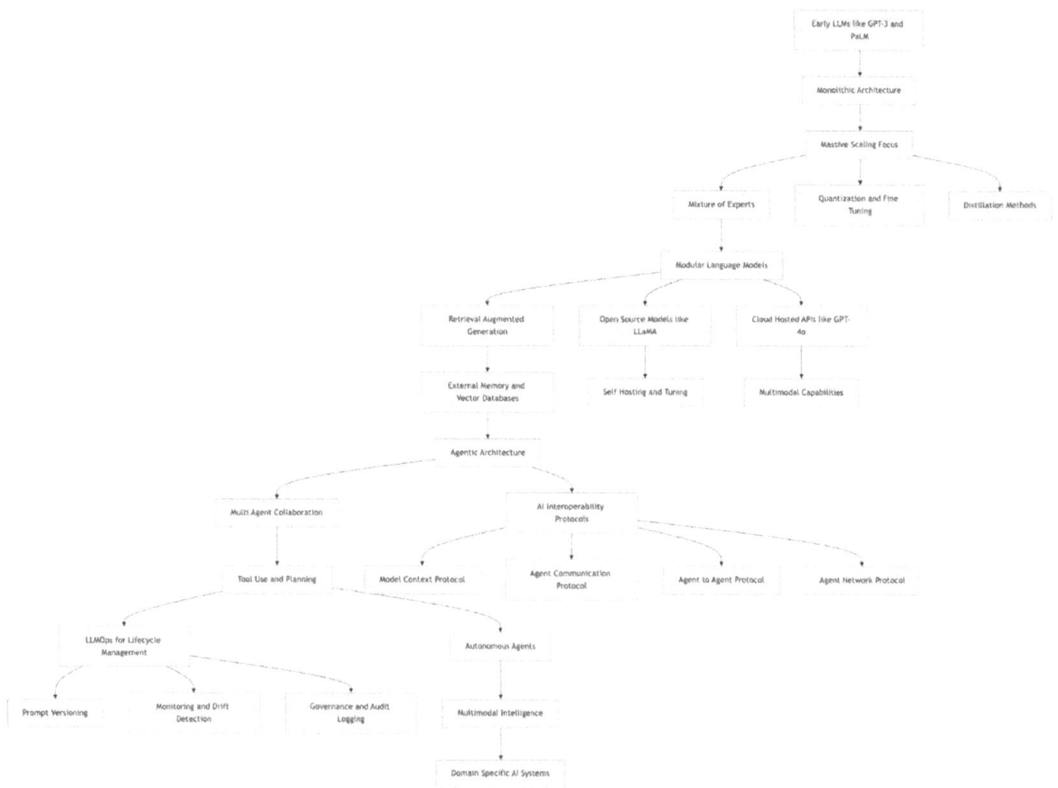

Figure 20-1. *Trends and patterns in Gen AI*

Smarter Scaling: From Large Models to Efficient Architectures

The earliest breakthroughs in generative AI were driven by scale. Models like GPT-3 and PaLM achieved powerful results through massive parameter counts. However, that era of brute-force scaling has given way to architectures optimized for performance, cost, and adaptability. Today's leading models, such as DeepSeek, Gemini 1.5, and GPT-4o, employ MoE architectures, where only a subset of model parameters—targeted expert "modules"—are activated per input. This dramatically improves efficiency, task specialization, and inference speed.

At the same time, techniques like quantization, distillation, and parameter-efficient fine-tuning (PEFT) are enabling smaller models to compete with larger counterparts on domain-specific tasks, while remaining deployable in edge and mobile environments. The scaling conversation has thus moved from "how big" to "how smart"—a shift that underpins the entire modular design philosophy.

RAG: Memory-Enhanced Systems for Real-Time Reasoning

One of the most important architectural shifts is the widespread adoption of RAG. Instead of embedding all knowledge within a model's weights, RAG systems dynamically retrieve relevant external information at inference time, giving models access to real-time data, proprietary knowledge bases, and evolving context.

RAG not only reduces the need for retraining but enables the following:

- Factually grounded generation
- Domain-specific expertise without bloated model sizes
- Lower latency through dynamic memory and caching systems

Architecturally, RAG separates the reasoning engine (LLM) from the memory system (vector DBs, structured indexes), allowing both components to scale independently and be reused across applications.

Agentic AI: Modular Orchestration Through Intelligent Agents

Generative AI systems are increasingly designed around agentic patterns—where LLMs act not as static responders but as autonomous or semi-autonomous agents capable of planning, using tools, maintaining memory, and coordinating with other agents. Agent frameworks like LangGraph, AutoGen, and Semantic Kernel offer orchestration layers for building intelligent workflows composed of multiple LLMs, tools, APIs, and user inputs.

This model of computation enables:

- Complex multistep reasoning
- Interleaving of language, code execution, and retrieval

- Division of labor across specialized agents (e.g., planner, executor, verifier)

Agentic AI is fundamentally modular—it favors loose coupling, task delegation, and tool extensibility. In effect, the LLM becomes a cognitive kernel embedded in a broader, reactive environment.

Protocol-Driven Interoperability: MCP, ACP, A2A, and ANP

As agentic systems become more prevalent, they introduce a new bottleneck: inter-agent communication. Without shared standards, agents remain siloed, unable to collaborate or scale across infrastructure and organizational boundaries.

To address this, a new class of interoperability protocols has emerged, acting as the connective tissue for distributed AI systems:

- **Model Context Protocol (MCP):** Enables agents to dynamically ingest tool definitions, usage constraints, and execution parameters via structured metadata (e.g., JSON-RPC). This eliminates hardcoded prompts and allows agents to adapt to changing capabilities without retraining—acting as the "USB-C" for AI tool integration.
- **Agent Communication Protocol (ACP):** Introduces asynchronous, multimodal messaging between agents using REST-native APIs. ACP supports streaming outputs, multipart content (text, binary, JSON), and observability hooks—crucial for debugging and reliability in complex workflows.
- **Agent-to-Agent Protocol (A2A):** Facilitates secure, peer-to-peer collaboration through standardized capability descriptions ("Agent Cards"). Agents can negotiate task delegation and access rights without exposing internal logic or relying on centralized orchestrators.
- **Agent Network Protocol (ANP):** Supports open-web discovery, identity, and trust using decentralized identifiers (DIDs) and semantic graphs (JSON-LD). ANP enables federated ecosystems where autonomous agents can authenticate, reason, and cooperate across organizational or jurisdictional boundaries.

Together, these protocols enable scalable, composable agent systems—where models and tools from different vendors and platforms can cooperate seamlessly. Just as TCP/IP and HTTP standardized the Internet, MCP, ACP, A2A, and ANP promise to standardize the AI-native software stack.

Performance-Aware Design: Beyond the Model

Today's AI architects must also contend with real-world constraints: latency, throughput, cost, and energy. Modern systems employ:

- **Speculative decoding** for faster inference
- **Async streaming APIs** for real-time UIs
- **Model routing layers** that send tasks to the right model based on complexity or domain
- **Caching and context windows** optimized for high token throughput

AI architecture is now a system-level discipline. The model is just one piece of a larger engine that includes data pipelines, agent workflows, hardware configuration, and observability infrastructure.

A New Architecture for Scalable Intelligence

The trajectory of generative AI is clear: from centralized, all-knowing monoliths to modular, specialized, interoperable systems that collaborate, adapt, and evolve. MoE architectures, RAG pipelines, agentic frameworks, and protocol-based coordination are not isolated innovations—they are interdependent building blocks of a new architectural paradigm.

LLMs are no longer endpoints. They are now intelligent components in an ecosystem of tools, retrievers, agents, and protocols. The future of AI architecture is not just about thinking better, but about thinking together—securely, efficiently, and at scale.

Ecosystem Showdown: Open-Source vs. Cloud-Hosted Models

The divide between open-source and cloud-hosted LLMs has transformed from a binary choice into a spectrum of trade-offs. Since Meta open-sourced Llama-3 in 2024, the landscape has rapidly shifted. These models, especially the 8B and 70B variants, are not only permissively licensed but also competitive with leading proprietary models like GPT-4 for a wide range of tasks including summarization, code generation, and reasoning. Downloads of open models—spanning Llama, Mistral, DeepSeek, and Falcon—have crossed hundreds of millions, powering everything from academic research to enterprise-grade applications.

Proprietary cloud-hosted models, meanwhile, continue to lead in multimodality, safety alignment, and turnkey API infrastructure. OpenAI's GPT-4o, Google's Gemini 1.5, and Anthropic's Claude 3 family offer users access to real-time speech, vision, video, and agentic memory under a single API. However, these benefits come with cost, opacity, and dependency concerns—issues that have fueled the open-source movement's push for transparency, reproducibility, and sovereignty. Visionaries such as Marc Andreessen and Yann LeCun argue that the ability to inspect, modify and self-host AI models is not just a technical preference but a strategic imperative for nations, research labs, and companies alike.

In response, cloud platforms are adapting. Amazon's Bedrock platform now lets developers invoke both proprietary models (e.g., Anthropic, Cohere) and open models (e.g., Mistral, Llama 2) within a single orchestration layer. Bedrock goes further by offering agent tools (Agents for Bedrock), security modules (Guardrails), and fine-tuning services—all pre-integrated and available via a unified API surface. Similarly, Microsoft's Azure AI and Google's Vertex AI are embedding open-source checkpoints into their model registries while enhancing them with ecosystem tools for monitoring, testing, memory, and compliance. This evolution means the "cloud" isn't limited to proprietary giants; it's becoming the execution layer for both open and closed models.

Meanwhile, the open-source ecosystem is rapidly innovating in critical areas:

- **Evaluation and benchmarking:** Tools like Open LLM Leaderboard, HELM, and Gaia Bench provide transparent, reproducible model comparisons across reasoning, bias, and instruction-following.

- **Fine-tuning and adaptation:** Libraries like LoRA, QLoRA, Axolotl, and AutoTrain allow developers to personalize open models on commodity GPUs with minimal resource overhead.
- **Agentic systems:** Projects like LangChain, Haystack, AutoGen, and CrewAI allow orchestration of multistep reasoning and tool usage over both open and closed models.
- **Inference and serving:** Open serving stacks like vLLM, TGI, Modal, and Ray Serve enable scalable deployment of local models, often rivaling or exceeding cloud API latency and throughput.

What's becoming clear is that open-source innovation is driving the broader LLM ecosystem. Research breakthroughs like flash attention, speculative decoding, RAG, and parameter-efficient fine-tuning (PEFT) have almost universally originated in or been accelerated by open communities. Proprietary models often incorporate these methods soon after, underscoring the open world's role as the R&D frontier.

In practice, most enterprises are now adopting a hybrid approach:

- For sensitive or high-risk reasoning, cloud APIs with compliance guarantees and multilayered safety systems are preferred.
- For cost-sensitive or domain-specific workloads, open models—deployed locally or via a private cloud—offer greater flexibility and long-term control.
- For experimentation and research, open models provide full transparency and customization, allowing teams to debug behavior, audit biases, or retrain with proprietary data.

As cloud providers consolidate tooling, and open-source models continue to close the performance gap, the next era of AI development will likely center around interoperability, composability, and trust. Open-source remains the compass that inspires direction and pace—defining what's possible—while cloud ecosystems serve as the industrial scaffolding to scale and standardize it.

Navigating the Challenges of Generative AI: What Developers Must Know and Do

The rise of generative AI has unlocked powerful capabilities for software developers, product teams, and digital creators—but it has also introduced a host of complex challenges that go beyond traditional engineering. As the technology matures, developers must move from merely using LLMs to understanding their risks, limits, and obligations. Doing so requires a mix of technical literacy, ethical awareness, and policy fluency. The following are key challenges developers must be aware of and the proactive habits they should adopt to stay aligned with emerging best practices.

Prompt Injection, Jailbreaks, and Model Exploits

Language models are inherently reactive and can be manipulated through clever phrasing. Attackers exploit this by crafting prompts that bypass content filters (jailbreaking) or by injecting hidden instructions (prompt injection) into seemingly benign input.

Developer actions:

- Use guardrails frameworks like OpenAI's system message enforcement, AWS Bedrock Guardrails, or Anthropic's Constitutional AI methods.
- Sanitize all user inputs, especially when they're embedded in documents, URLs, or code.
- Perform adversarial testing using red-team tools such as Rebuff, PromptInject, or Microsoft's Counterfeit simulation suite.
- Stay informed via security-focused Gen AI newsletters like AI Village, OpenPromptSecurity, and model provider updates (OpenAI, Google, Meta).

Ethical Use and Bias Mitigation

GenAI models reflect the data they're trained on, which means they inherit biases, stereotypes, and social inequities. Outputs can amplify discrimination if unchecked.

Developer actions:

- Favor models or APIs that are transparent about bias audits and mitigations, e.g., Claude or Gemini's fairness benchmarks.
- Run your own fairness evaluations using synthetic test sets that probe for gender, race, age, and socioeconomic bias.
- Implement human-in-the-loop processes for high-risk applications (e.g., hiring, legal, medical).
- Reference the OECD AI Principles and NIST AI Risk Management Framework to guide system-level decisions.

Data Privacy and Leakage

Developers often underestimate the privacy implications of sending sensitive information to external APIs. Prompts can inadvertently leak PII or trade secrets.

Developer actions:

- Use prompt inspection tools to scrub or tokenize sensitive information before it reaches the model.
- Choose models that support deployment in private environments, such as Llama 3, Mistral, or Falcon.
- Audit API usage logs and restrict GenAI access to the minimum necessary user roles and scopes.
- Ensure your implementation complies with GDPR, HIPAA, and other jurisdictional data laws.

Governance and Compliance

As regulatory frameworks solidify (e.g., the EU AI Act, AIDA in Canada, NIST's Generative AI Profile), developers will need to embed compliance into their workflows.

Developer actions:

- Track policy updates via EU AI Act trackers, U.S. AI Bill of Rights resources, and industry blogs (e.g., Stanford HAI, AI Now Institute).
- Contribute to and use open model cards, data sheets, and usage disclosures.
- Log every model version, prompt, and data source involved in production deployments.
- Treat model monitoring and documentation as part of your CI/CD pipeline, not a post-deployment task.

Energy Use and Environmental Cost

Training and running large models consumes substantial electricity. Developers working at scale must factor this into architecture decisions.

Developer actions:

- Prefer efficient model architectures (e.g., quantized, distilled, or sparse expert models).
- Offload batch workloads to low-carbon cloud regions when possible.
- Ask model providers for sustainability data (PUE, carbon intensity, compute hours).
- Stay informed via initiatives like the ML CO2 Impact Tracker or Partnership on AI's Green Software guidelines.

Model Hallucinations and Factual Integrity

LLMs can generate content that sounds confident but is factually incorrect. This poses risks in legal, medical, and scientific domains.

Developer actions:

- Use RAG to ground answers in reliable, verifiable sources.
- Flag outputs with confidence scores or provenance indicators.

- Evaluate outputs continuously using test sets designed for truthfulness (e.g., TruthfulQA, FaithDial).
- Train users to validate high-stakes outputs and treat GenAI as a **co-pilot, not an oracle**.

Staying Current: The Developer's Playbook

Generative AI is one of the fastest-evolving fields in technology. To stay effective and safe, developers must build a continuous learning mindset.

Recommended practices:

- **Follow primary sources:** AI research labs (OpenAI, Anthropic, DeepMind), benchmarks (Papers with Code, Hugging Face Leaderboards), and regulatory bodies (EU Commission, NIST, OECD).
- **Engage in community learning:** Join Discords (e.g., EleutherAI), Slack groups (e.g., ML Ops Community), and follow GitHub repos of open-source LLM projects.
- **Subscribe to focused newsletters:** "Import AI," "The Batch," "Last Week in AI," "Center for AI Safety Digest."
- **Experiment ethically:** Use sandboxes to test capabilities and edge cases, and log both successes and failures.
- **Document everything:** Prompt templates, model versions, evaluation outcomes, failure modes—treat your AI stack like a critical system.

Generative AI is not just another API or SDK—it's a dynamic, probabilistic system that can delight, deceive, and disrupt. Developers who combine technical excellence with ethical rigor will not only avoid pitfalls—they will help shape a future where powerful AI systems are transparent, accountable, and aligned with human values.

The Evolving Pathway to LLM Adoption: From Prompts to Agentic AI

The adoption of LLMs is no longer reserved for tech giants or AI research labs—it's becoming a structured, iterative journey that developers, product teams, and enterprises of all sizes are beginning to follow. This pathway—from simple experimentation to fully integrated, autonomous AI systems—mirrors the broader evolution of generative AI tooling and infrastructure. What started with basic prompt engineering has grown into a multiphase development lifecycle that increasingly resembles traditional software engineering, but with new paradigms of reasoning, control, and autonomy.

Phase 1: Prompt Engineering and Model Trials

Most teams begin their Gen AI journey by interacting with public APIs from OpenAI, Anthropic, Cohere, or Google. These early experiments focus on prompt engineering—the art of crafting inputs that reliably elicit the desired outputs. Developers typically test different models (e.g., GPT-4o, Claude 3, Gemini 1.5) and tune prompts iteratively, exploring patterns like zero-shot versus few-shot prompting, chain-of-thought reasoning, and system message scaffolding. This is a fast, low-cost entry point requiring minimal infrastructure.

At this stage, developers experiment with tools like prompt playgrounds, UI wrappers, and low-code orchestration frameworks such as LangChain, Flowise, or Semantic Kernel. The goal is to identify valuable use cases—summarization, Q&A, classification, ideation—without investing in model ownership or custom infrastructure. It is the "trial and error" phase where intuition and iteration matter more than pipelines or precision.

Phase 2: Fine-Tuning and Domain Adaptation

Once teams identify recurring tasks and consistent business value, they progress to fine-tuning, often using parameter-efficient techniques like LoRA, QLoRA, or instruction tuning. This phase involves taking a pretrained model and adapting it to a domain-specific task or voice using a small, curated dataset. Fine-tuning delivers more predictable behavior, better alignment with company-specific language, and reduced prompt complexity.

Major cloud providers like Google (Vertex AI), AWS (SageMaker JumpStart, Bedrock), and OpenAI (via fine-tuning APIs) have made this stage accessible even for teams with no ML background. With the click of a button, developers can upload datasets and generate adapted models without touching GPUs, infrastructure, or training loops. This democratization of model customization marks a major shift in LLM development—lowering the barrier while increasing the impact.

Phase 3: Model Training from Scratch (Advanced Tier)

Only a small fraction of teams ever reach the phase of training LLMs from scratch, as it requires significant compute resources, data pipelines, tokenization expertise, and safety infrastructure. This path is usually reserved for foundational model builders, governments, and large enterprises working in high-security domains or pursuing full model sovereignty.

However, tooling is catching up. New frameworks like Jlama (Java-based LLM framework from Hugging Face) and DJL (Deep Java Library) are making it possible for Java developers to train, serve, and customize LLMs without switching to Python. This indicates a broadening of the ecosystem where language-agnostic tooling empowers a wider range of engineers.

The Rise of Agentic AI

As the field matures, the next evolution is agentic AI—systems that can plan, reason, use tools, and coordinate tasks over time. Agent frameworks like LangGraph, AutoGen, CrewAI, and OpenAgents provide the scaffolding for building multi-agent systems capable of autonomous decision-making, memory recall, and collaborative workflows. This is where LLMs shift from reactive assistants to proactive systems, marking a new design frontier.

In parallel, infrastructure providers are also adapting. Amazon Bedrock's agent APIs, OpenAI's tool-use APIs, and Google's agentic toolkits aim to make agent development a plug-and-play experience. As these capabilities mature, LLMs will become not just components, but collaborators embedded within apps and business processes.

Managing the LLM Development Lifecycle

As teams move from prompt trials to fine-tuning and eventually agentic deployments, they must adopt AI engineering practices that mirror DevOps, but with new elements:

- Prompt management becomes essential, including version control, reuse, and monitoring of prompt performance over time.
- Evaluation pipelines must assess not just output quality, but truthfulness, bias, and robustness under adversarial inputs.
- Model drift detection becomes critical as user behavior or domain data shifts, requiring retraining or re-tuning.
- Testing frameworks must simulate edge cases and user intents across various tasks, ideally using synthetic data or automated agents.

Emerging platforms are beginning to offer LLMOps features—think of them as MLOps adapted for generative models—with support for prompt tracking, model A/B testing, human feedback integration, and audit logging. Companies like Weights & Biases, Arize, TruEra, and Humanloop are building the scaffolding for managing this lifecycle in production.

The pathway to LLM usage is no longer linear or reserved for elite AI teams. It is a progressive, modular journey—from exploratory prompting to scalable fine-tuning, and eventually to agent-based autonomy—made increasingly accessible by tooling, cloud platforms, and open-source innovation. Developers who understand this arc and invest early in lifecycle management will be better equipped to turn generative AI from an exciting experiment into a sustainable, trustworthy capability.

LLMOps: Operationalizing the Lifecycle of Generative AI Systems

As LLMs move from prototypes to production environments, managing them becomes more than just a data science task—it becomes a complex engineering challenge. Much like DevOps revolutionized how software is built, deployed, and maintained, large language model operations (LLMOps) has emerged as a new discipline focused on streamlining the development, deployment, monitoring, and governance of generative AI applications. It brings structure to what is otherwise an exploratory, experimental process, helping teams build scalable, reliable, and compliant LLM systems.

LLMOps is a set of tools, workflows, and best practices for managing the end-to-end lifecycle of LLM-powered systems. While traditional MLOps handles training and deployment of predictive models, LLMOps addresses these unique characteristics of generative AI:

- Prompt engineering and tracking
- Model selection, tuning, and experimentation
- Output evaluation and scoring
- Content moderation, safety, and bias mitigation
- Monitoring, versioning, and compliance logging
- Drift detection and feedback integration

LLMOps isn't just about automating model deployment; it's about creating a closed feedback loop where models continuously improve based on real-world performance, human feedback, and evolving user expectations.

Core Components of LLMOps

These are the core components:

1. **Prompt Management and Version Control**

   In LLM applications, prompts act as code. Managing them requires the same rigor as managing source files. Teams need systems to track prompt iterations, measure performance, and log which prompts were used to generate each response. Tools like PromptLayer, Helicone, and Humanloop help manage and monitor prompts at scale.

2. **Evaluation and Quality Assurance**

   LLM outputs are probabilistic, meaning they can vary—even when the input is the same. As such, static testing isn't enough. LLMOps involves setting up automated evaluation pipelines using both human-in-the-loop review and automated metrics (e.g., BLEU, ROUGE, BERTScore, or task-specific accuracy). Leaderboards and synthetic evals are often used to compare different prompt strategies, model versions, or fine-tuned checkpoints.

3. **Monitoring and Observability**

   In production, LLMs must be monitored for latency, error rates, hallucination frequency, toxicity, and bias. This requires logging not only the prompt and output but also user feedback, source grounding, and downstream actions. Tools like Arize, TruEra, and Fiddler AI are adding support for LLM observability, making it easier to flag anomalies and edge cases.

4. **Feedback Loops and Active Learning**

   LLMOps systems often integrate user corrections or feedback to improve model behavior. Whether it's thumbs-up/down, edit suggestions, or corrective rewrites, this data can be looped back into future fine-tuning rounds or prompt adjustments, forming the backbone of human-aligned learning.

5. **Drift and Behavioral Monitoring**

   As data, user intent, and context evolve, LLM outputs may become less relevant or accurate. LLMOps platforms help detect drift in performance by tracking changes in distribution, sentiment, or task success rates. This signals when to retrain, fine-tune, or update prompts and retrieval strategies.

6. **Compliance, Security, and Auditability**

   Generative AI outputs can pose serious risks if not controlled—especially in regulated sectors. LLMOps systems enforce access controls, logging, explainability, and audit trails, enabling organizations to comply with frameworks like the EU AI Act, ISO/IEC 42001, and the NIST AI Risk Management Framework. Watermarking and provenance tracking are also becoming part of the compliance toolset.

LLMOps in Practice: From Playground to Production

Consider a real-world LLM-powered application—say, an AI legal assistant. Initially built using prompt engineering and an API like GPT-4o, it may work well in controlled tests. But once in production, developers need to:

- Monitor for hallucinations in legal advice
- Update prompts and workflows as laws change
- Detect and respond to toxic or discriminatory outputs
- Log every interaction for audit and accountability
- Allow domain experts to fine-tune the model on regional case law
- Collect user feedback to refine performance

All of this requires an LLMOps layer that sits on top of the model, orchestrating feedback, compliance, quality, and governance.

The Road Ahead

LLMOps is still an emerging field, but its importance is growing rapidly as enterprises scale up generative AI initiatives. The complexity of managing multiple models, prompts, user contexts, and evolving risks calls for robust, developer-centric tooling. As models become more autonomous and embedded in core business functions, LLMOps will be essential to ensure these systems remain safe, reliable, and aligned with both user needs and regulatory expectations.

Just as DevOps and MLOps became critical to modern software and machine learning, LLMOps is set to become the operating system of generative AI deployment. Developers who invest in this layer early will not only reduce risk and increase reliability—they'll be best positioned to scale GenAI responsibly and sustainably.

Bridging the Gap: Migrating from DevOps to LLMOps Thinking

For developers and teams accustomed to the well-established principles of DevOps, the shift to LLMOps requires more than adopting new tools—it demands a fundamental change in mindset. While both disciplines aim to streamline the lifecycle of systems from development to deployment and monitoring, the nature of LLMs as probabilistic, evolving, and user-facing systems introduces unique challenges that traditional DevOps processes don't fully address.

Here's how to migrate your thinking from DevOps to LLMOps—conceptually, operationally, and culturally.

From Deterministic Code to Probabilistic Outputs

In DevOps, the goal is to ship deterministic software: given the same inputs, your code should produce the same outputs. In contrast, LLMs are stochastic systems—outputs can vary based on temperature, context, and even randomness.

Shift in mindset:

Accept that "testing" no longer means checking whether output is correct or incorrect. Instead, evaluate quality, relevance, safety, and consistency. Developers must embrace subjective, context-driven testing alongside traditional unit tests.

From CI/CD Pipelines to Continuous Evaluation

DevOps relies heavily on continuous integration/continuous delivery (CI/CD) to automate builds, tests, and deployments. LLMOps expands this to include continuous evaluation—tracking how LLMs perform over time with real-world data and evolving user behavior.

Shift in practice:

Extend your CI/CD pipelines with LLM-specific components like prompt versioning, output regression tests, bias detection, red-teaming simulations, and user feedback loops. Quality is no longer binary—it must be measured, monitored, and improved over time.

From Logs and Metrics to Semantic Observability

In DevOps, observability means monitoring metrics like latency, throughput, and error rates. In LLMOps, traditional metrics still matter, but they're not enough. You must also observe semantic metrics like hallucination frequency, sentiment shift, toxic content rates, and user trust indicators.

Shift in tools and telemetry:

Adopt LLM-aware observability tools that can understand natural language—flagging problematic outputs, surfacing abnormal responses, and tracking the effectiveness of prompts or retrieval sources over time.

From Source Code to Prompt + Model as Code

In DevOps, source code is the central artifact. In LLMOps, prompts, model weights, and data take on that role. Prompts are the new source files, models are mutable black boxes, datasets are dynamic inputs that evolve with usage.

Shift in workflow:

Version-control your prompts, datasets, model checkpoints, and evaluation benchmarks. Build infrastructure to trace which version of a prompt or fine-tuned model was used for any given output—just like you would trace bugs to code commits.

From Feature Testing to Use-Case Auditing

Feature testing in traditional apps is about ensuring functional correctness. In LLMs, it's about use-case safety and alignment. You might need to audit how the model responds to sensitive topics, how it reflects societal biases, or how its behavior changes over time.

Shift in risk posture:

Incorporate ethical audits, adversarial testing, and domain-specific evaluations into your QA process. Think like a red team and simulate real-world edge cases, misuse scenarios, and unexpected user prompts.

From Code Deployments to Model Lifecycle Management

Shipping a new version of a microservice is a routine DevOps task. In LLMOps, you're not just deploying code—you're managing the lifecycle of a language model: fine-tuning, evaluating, updating, monitoring, and sunsetting models safely.

Shift in operations:

Build repeatable, automated workflows for training, fine-tuning, retraining, and decommissioning models. Define access control, change approval, and rollback mechanisms specific to model updates, not just software patches.

From User Feedback to Human-in-the-Loop Learning

DevOps values user feedback for feature development. LLMOps treats it as a core input for system improvement. Human-in-the-loop (HITL) learning—where users rate, revise, or approve AI-generated content—feeds directly into fine-tuning and retrieval strategies.

Shift in integration:

Incorporate feedback collection natively in your application interfaces. Use that feedback to refine prompts, retrain adapters, or flag drift. Treat users not just as consumers, but as co-pilots of system learning.

Final Thought: It's Still About Culture

DevOps brought a cultural transformation around collaboration, ownership, and automation. LLMOps continues that spirit but asks teams to operate in a world of ambiguity, complexity, and nuance. Success requires developers, ML engineers, product managers, and ethicists to work together more closely than ever.

Migrating from DevOps to LLMOps doesn't mean abandoning what you know—it means extending it to handle a new class of systems. The shift is not just technical but philosophical: from building software that runs predictably to designing intelligent systems that behave responsibly.

The Evolving Culture and Practices in Java's Machine Learning Ecosystem

For years, Java has been a foundational pillar of enterprise software, powering everything from financial systems to Android apps. But when it came to machine learning and deep learning, Python stole the spotlight—dominating tooling, research, and community momentum. That's beginning to change. With the emergence of frameworks like DJL (Deep Java Library), Jlama, and Eclipse Deeplearning4j, the Java ecosystem is undergoing a cultural and technical evolution, increasingly supporting modern AI workflows within native Java environments.

Java Meets Machine Learning: A Culture Shift in the Making

The cultural shift is rooted in a broader transformation—Java is no longer seen as too static or heavyweight for machine learning. With improved support for numerical computing, GPU acceleration, and seamless Python interoperability, Java is now positioning itself not just as a consumer of AI models, but as a viable platform for model development, training, deployment, and integration.

This shift has created a new opportunity for millions of Java developers: the ability to build AI applications without switching ecosystems, rewriting codebases, or upskilling in Python. Instead, developers can use their existing Java expertise to work with ML models directly in familiar IDEs like IntelliJ or Eclipse, and integrate them into JVM-based backends, microservices, and mobile or IoT environments.

DJL: Lowering the Barrier for Java Developers

Deep Java Library, an open source initiative from Amazon, exemplifies this shift. DJL is a high-level, open-source deep learning framework that abstracts away much of the complexity of machine learning. It is engine-agnostic, meaning developers can swap between TensorFlow, PyTorch, MXNet, and ONNX runtimes without rewriting code. DJL automatically optimizes for available hardware, whether CPU or GPU, and offers easy APIs for tasks like image classification, text generation, and object detection.

What makes DJL especially appealing is its focus on developer experience. You don't need to be a machine learning expert to get started. Whether you're working on a recommendation engine, chatbot, or computer vision feature, DJL allows you to incorporate pretrained models, fine-tune them with your own data, and deploy them using standard Java infrastructure. It brings deep learning to enterprise-grade Java applications with minimal friction—effectively bridging the AI skill gap in traditional Java teams.

Eclipse Deeplearning4j: Full-Stack Deep Learning on the JVM

Complementing DJL's ease of use, Eclipse Deeplearning4j (DL4J) offers a comprehensive, full-stack deep learning toolkit for developers who want more control and lower-level access. Unlike DJL, which is optimized for ease and interoperability,

DL4J is built to support complex training pipelines, integration with big data platforms, and production-scale deployments.

DL4J's modular architecture includes:

- **SameDiff**, a lower-level API similar to PyTorch or TensorFlow, with dynamic graph execution and automatic differentiation
- **ND4J**, a NumPy-equivalent for Java that supports multidimensional arrays and vectorized operations
- **Python4J**, which enables Java applications to run Python scripts and interoperate with Python-trained models
- **Datavec**, a robust library for preprocessing and transforming raw data into model-ready tensors
- **Apache Spark integration**, allowing deep learning pipelines to scale across distributed environments

DL4J is ideal for Java developers building bespoke AI systems, working with hybrid cloud setups, or embedding AI into edge environments like IoT or mobile. It also allows you to import models trained in Python frameworks (like PyTorch or Keras), retrain or optimize them in Java, and then deploy them in production-grade JVM environments.

Jlama and the Expanding Toolchain

Adding to this momentum is the emergence of tools like Jlama, a Hugging Face initiative that brings transformer-based LLM workflows to Java. Jlama is designed to give Java developers easy access to popular transformer architectures without needing to work in Python. As LLMs and agentic AI become central to enterprise AI strategies, frameworks like Jlama will play a key role in ensuring that Java developers can participate in the next generation of AI-native applications.

Where the Culture Is Heading

The cultural shift in the Java ecosystem mirrors a larger trend: AI is becoming a generalist capability, not the domain of a select few researchers or data scientists. As frameworks like DJL and DL4J mature, Java teams can embrace AI as a first-class development concern, integrating it into microservices, web apps, enterprise workflows, and mobile apps with ease.

The convergence of Java and ML also means developers must adopt new practices:

- Managing model lifecycle in production (loading, caching, and updating models)
- Integrating LLMOps practices—like monitoring inference, tracking drift, and logging prompts
- Leveraging cross-language tooling to work seamlessly across Python and Java environments
- Incorporating agentic architectures using Java-native tooling that supports planning, memory, and tool use

A Rising Force in AI Development

With robust support for training, inference, and deployment, Java is reasserting itself as a serious contender in the machine learning space. Initiatives like DJL and DL4J signal a growing recognition that AI doesn't just belong in Python notebooks—it belongs in production systems, microservices, and business-critical applications. And that's where Java shines.

The evolution of the Java ML ecosystem is empowering a new generation of developers to move fast, build smart, and deploy at scale—without leaving the JVM. For enterprises invested in Java, this shift doesn't just unlock technical possibilities; it enables strategic alignment with the future of AI.

Emerging Frontiers: Multimodality, Agents, and Domain Specialization

Multimodality. GPT-4o fuses text, vision, and audio in real time; Google's Gemini-1.5 and Gemini-2.0 extend that to long-form video understanding. Specialized generators such as OpenAI's Sora or Google's Veo 2 create 20-second 1080p clips from plain text, while research benchmarks (Video-MME) grade cross-modal reasoning. Expect the next wave of models to incorporate 3-D, haptics, and simulation data.

Agents. Reusable "agent frameworks" (LangChain, AutoGen, Semantic Kernel) have matured to orchestrate tool use, memory, and multi-agent collaboration. Microsoft, Anthropic, and others are pushing an Agentic Web standard (Model Context Protocol) so disparate agents can reason together—much like microservices for cognition.

Domain specialization. Sector-tuned models are moving from proof-of-concept to production. Healthcare LLMs ingest EHRs and medical journals to outperform general models on clinical QA, while finance models such as BloombergGPT use proprietary filings and real-time market feeds for analytics. Regulated industries thus gain accuracy without exposing data to public clouds.

Regulations and Acts

The legal environment for Gen AI has matured from scattered guidance to a dense lattice of binding rules, voluntary frameworks, and emerging standards. Across jurisdictions the direction of travel is clear: if your model can reach or influence people, regulators will want visibility into how it is trained, how it behaves, and how you can rein it in.

Europe has taken the boldest, most prescriptive step with the EU AI Act, which entered into force on August 1, 2024. Prohibitions on manipulative or biometric uses and new "AI-literacy" duties will already apply from February 2025, while *general-purpose* (foundation) model obligations—including detailed transparency on training data and systemic-risk testing—kick in on August 2, 2025. The tougher conformity regime for high-risk applications follows in 2026–27. Developers must therefore map every new feature to the act's risk tiers and prepare evidence dossiers (data provenance logs, robustness tests, watermarking pipelines) well before the GPAI deadline. The commission's forthcoming Code of Practice is expected to become the de facto checklist for showing compliance.

Complementing the act, the Digital Services Act already obliges large online platforms to assess and mitigate systemic risks—including those posed by their generative models—and to disclose any use of copyrighted material. This dual regime means that European product launches increasingly require *both* safety dossiers and content-moderation playbooks from day one.

The United States still relies on a patchwork, yet the pieces are tightening. President Biden's 2023 Executive Order triggered NIST to publish a Gen AI Profile and a suite of red-team tools in July 2024; federal agencies are now using that profile in procurement and enforcement. Aligning your SDLC with the NIST AI Risk Management Framework—documenting model provenance, testing for adversarial robustness, tracking post-deployment drift—has shifted from "nice to have" to the price of entry for federal contracts and many venture-backed audits.

The United Kingdom is legislating more slowly, but its new AI Safety (now "Security") Institute is publishing test protocols and the *International AI Safety Report* that large labs are expected to run—and to publish results—against their frontier models. Sector regulators (FCA, CMA, ICO) then apply those results under existing consumer-protection and privacy statutes. For developers, the message is simple: assume you will be asked to release evaluation artefacts for independent replay.

China's Interim Measures for the Management of Generative AI Services have been in force since August 15, 2023. They require security assessments, sign-off by political authorities, and increasingly granular *content-labeling*. Starting September 1, 2025, all AI-generated text, images, and video must carry both visible and embedded provenance tags. If your service reaches Chinese users—even via an overseas API—these rules apply extraterritorially, with fines of up to 5% of revenue for noncompliance.

Canada is moving along a parallel track: the Artificial Intelligence and Data Act (AIDA) inside Bill C-27 passed second reading and, following new consultations launched in early 2025, is expected to impose impact assessments, audit trails, and steep monetary penalties for "high-impact" systems. Because AIDA borrows its risk language from the EU, teams that document once can reuse much of the evidence for both markets.

Across all regions, intellectual-property rules are converging toward disclosure and opt-out. Europe's *Kneschke v LAION* decision signaled that indiscriminate web scraping can infringe copyrights, and the AI Act's text-and-data-mining (TDM) clauses tighten the screws further. Developers therefore need reliable dataset inventories, license scanners, and opt-out workflows before training.

Formal standards now bridge these regimes. ISO/IEC 42001 (published in December 2023) specifies an AI management system that folds risk, quality, and supplier controls into one auditable program. Many European and Asian regulators already cite 42001 compliance as evidence of "state of the art," making certification an efficient umbrella for multijurisdiction deployments.

What This Means for Builders

This means the following:

1. Bake compliance into design. Start each project with a risk classification exercise (EU tiers, AIDA "high-impact," NIST RMF), and then align data-collection, evaluation and release gates to that class.

2. Keep a living provenance ledger. Record every dataset, license, fine-tune, and patch so you can answer future transparency or takedown requests.
3. Watermark and label by default. Visible or cryptographic signatures satisfy both EU transparency and China's forthcoming labeling mandate.
4. Run red-team and bias tests as a service. Store reproducible test suites; many regulators accept third-party attestation in lieu of in-house audits.
5. Adopt an AI-management standard early. An ISO 42001 gap-analysis today can collapse future certification cycles and reassure corporate customers.
6. Monitor worldwide updates. Extraterritorial clauses mean the strictest rule often wins; maintaining a "highest common denominator" baseline avoids fire-drills at launch.

Regulations will continue to evolve, but the direction is unmistakable: *trustworthiness is becoming a product feature.* Teams that treat compliance as engineering discipline—measured, automated, and test-driven—will iterate faster than those scrambling to retrofit legal fixes at release time.

Governance, Ethics, and Future Outlook

As Gen AI becomes a core component of modern digital products, its impact is no longer limited to backend performance or automation. It now directly shapes how users experience technology. Governance and ethics, once viewed as peripheral concerns, are now central to product development, particularly in systems that generate content, make suggestions, or influence decisions. Developers play a crucial role in operationalizing these principles—not only to comply with laws and policies but to deliver responsible, user-aligned AI experiences.

Governance in the Gen AI context refers to how models are managed, controlled, and monitored across their lifecycle. It begins at the level of code and architecture. Developers should ensure that every model used is clearly documented, version-controlled, and auditable. This includes maintaining logs of prompts, completions, and system decisions—especially for use cases involving regulated industries or sensitive outputs. Features that rely on GenAI should be designed with transparency in mind, using clear disclosure mechanisms and fallback strategies such as feature toggles or kill switches that allow teams to quickly pause or disable AI components if unexpected behavior arises. Governance also involves integrating continuous evaluation into the development workflow—red-teaming models, tracking model drift, and regularly auditing behavior to surface regressions or emergent risks.

Ethics, meanwhile, are increasingly expressed through user experience. A Gen AI system is ethical not only when it avoids harm but when it enhances user agency and trust. This means designing interfaces that are transparent about AI's involvement, such as clearly labeling generated responses or providing users with visibility into how a suggestion was derived. Ethical design also favors editability—users should be able to undo, revise, or reject AI-generated content. Developers must consider inclusivity during testing, ensuring that systems perform fairly across a range of linguistic, cultural, and demographic scenarios to prevent the amplification of social biases. In this sense, good ethics becomes good UX: a system that is honest about its capabilities, respectful of user boundaries, and clear in its communication will be trusted more than one that is opaque or misleading.

Human oversight remains essential, particularly in domains like healthcare, law, finance, or education. Generative AI should not replace domain experts—it should support them. Developers must therefore embed human-in-the-loop mechanisms into their systems. For example, AI-generated legal drafts or medical recommendations should go through a manual review phase before being finalized or delivered to users. Where possible, systems should also offer explanations for their outputs—showing sources, highlighting relevant content, or providing a rationale for decisions. Capturing user feedback, such as corrections or suggestions, is also critical. This feedback not only improves the model but strengthens trust by giving users a sense of control and involvement in the process.

Looking ahead, the future of generative AI points toward systems that are more autonomous, memory-driven, and proactive. Agents that can take initiative, recall user preferences, and orchestrate complex tasks are already emerging. But with autonomy comes responsibility. Developers must anticipate a future where governance is not just applied reactively, but built in as a core design pattern. Standards like ISO/IEC 42001 and protocols for agent alignment are beginning to offer templates for responsible development. To scale governance, developers should architect systems with modular control layers—where policies, ethical constraints, and behavioral guidelines can be updated independently of the model weights. As models operate in more jurisdictions, developers must also consider international governance norms and privacy requirements, ensuring systems are flexible enough to localize behavior while maintaining global integrity.

In the end, user experience is inseparable from governance and ethics. The most effective generative AI applications will be those that combine technical sophistication with moral clarity—tools that not only work but work in ways that are understandable, accountable, and aligned with human goals. For developers, this means looking beyond performance benchmarks and thinking deeply about how systems behave in the real world. Governance is no longer just about compliance—it is the foundation of a new kind of design practice: the architecture of trust.

There's Just Too Much Happening. What Should I Do?

If you're feeling overwhelmed by the pace of change in the world of Gen AI, you're not alone. As software developers, we've seen paradigms come and go—from monolithic servlet-based Java apps to microservices, serverless architectures, containerization, DevOps, and now AI-native systems. Each wave has brought with it new tools, patterns, terms, and responsibilities. Generative AI is no different—except it's evolving even faster and touching more parts of the software stack than any paradigm before it.

But here's the truth: we've been here before.

We adapted when REST APIs replaced SOAP. We learned new patterns when reactive programming changed how we think about latency. We embraced test-driven development, continuous integration, and infrastructure as code. Generative AI is simply the next evolution in the long lineage of software engineering. And just like previous waves, the best way forward is to evolve, adapt, and bring our foundational knowledge along with us.

Focus on Fundamentals, Not the FOMO

There will always be hype around new frameworks, protocols, and buzzwords—whether it's agentic AI, prompt chaining, or toolformer memory. Some of it will last. Much of it will evolve. But what remains constant are the core principles: understanding how LLMs function and how they can be integrated, managed, evaluated, and aligned with human and business needs.

Once you understand how models generate output, what context windows are, how retrieval works, and where risks like hallucinations or prompt injection can emerge, you're no longer lost in the noise. You're grounded. And from that grounding, you can explore new patterns and protocols without being overwhelmed.

You Already Have Transferable Knowledge

Many of the challenges we face with LLMs are not entirely new—they just have different names. Take "prompt injection," for example: it mirrors "SQL injection" or "XSS" from the security world. Guardrails and sandboxing for LLMs resemble what we've done for decades in secure web and API development. Drift monitoring? It's similar to monitoring microservice performance degradation.

If you've worked on enterprise applications, maintained distributed systems, built secure APIs, or worked through performance bottlenecks, you already have a strong foundation to build on. This is not about reinventing yourself—it's about extending what you know into a new domain.

Embrace the Culture of Learning

The Gen AI ecosystem is vast, but the community is active, passionate, and incredibly helpful. Open-source projects, Discord communities, GitHub examples, and newsletters are brimming with insights. You don't have to learn everything at once—just focus on one concept, tool, or use case at a time, and let your curiosity lead you.

What's worked for me—and what I hope works for you—is treating this not as a burden but as a passionate, continuous learning journey. Every piece you understand unlocks 10 more. And every experiment you run, every model you evaluate, brings you closer to understanding the broader picture.

Adaptation Is the Skill of the Decade

Just like we brought object-oriented thinking into RESTful APIs and brought DevOps thinking into cloud infrastructure, now we need to bring software engineering discipline into generative AI development. That means thinking about lifecycle management, testing, security, compliance, cost control, and user experience. Some responsibilities are shifting left again—prompt design, model selection, observability—all now fall partly into the developer's domain.

And that's okay. Because we're used to owning more as systems evolve. We've done this before.

It's normal to feel like there's too much happening. There is. But if your foundation is solid and your mindset is open, the wave won't drown you—it will carry you forward. You don't need to learn it all today. Just start where you are, bring your software skills with you, and trust in your ability to grow with the ecosystem.

Generative AI is not replacing developers—it's inviting us to build in new ways. And with curiosity, clarity, and community, we'll get there—one thoughtful step at a time.

Conclusion

As with every major shift in software, the emergence of Gen AI is not the end of the old—it's the beginning of something layered on top. Just as we learned to evolve from monoliths to microservices, from imperative to reactive systems, we now learn to think in terms of cognition, autonomy, and orchestration. LLMs are no longer just tools to call—they are actors in a system, participants in user journeys, and components in composable architectures.

The future of generative AI will not be built by AI researchers alone. It will be built by developers—like you—who understand systems, who care about reliability and ethics, and who are willing to learn, adapt, and push boundaries thoughtfully. Yes, the ecosystem is noisy. Yes, the pace is dizzying. But under the surface, the principles are familiar: understand the abstractions, manage the lifecycle, write clear interfaces, handle failure gracefully, and keep the user at the center.

If there's one thing we know as builders, it's that every paradigm shift feels overwhelming at first—but it always becomes manageable when we bring the right discipline and curiosity to the table. Generative AI is no different. You don't need to chase every trend. You need to master the fundamentals, stay grounded in purpose, and iterate responsibly.

What lies ahead is not just faster or smarter software—it's a new architecture of intelligence, designed, deployed, and governed by human hands. And it starts here.

Index

A

S. K. Sahu, *Generative AI-Driven Application Development with Java*,
https://doi.org/10.1007/979-8-8688-1609-3

B

C

D

E

F

G

H

I

J

K

L

M

P

Q

R

S

T, U, V, W, X, Y, Z

GPSR Compliance
The European Union's (EU) General Product Safety Regulation (GPSR) is a set of rules that requires consumer products to be safe and our obligations to ensure this.

If you have any concerns about our products, you can contact us on

ProductSafety@springernature.com

In case Publisher is established outside the EU, the EU authorized representative is:

Springer Nature Customer Service Center GmbH
Europaplatz 3
69115 Heidelberg, Germany

www.ingramcontent.com/pod-product-compliance
Lightning Source LLC
LaVergne TN
LVHW080309260326
834688LV00038B/1016

* 9 7 9 8 8 6 8 8 1 6 0 8 6 *